R. Gupta's®

POPULAR MASTER GUIDE

National Testing Agency (NTA)

UGC-NET/JRF

Junior Research Fellowship & Assistant Professor Eligibility Exam

Women's Studies

PAPER-II

The Ultimate Reference Book Comprising Revised UGC Syllabus with MCQs to Help in Cracking the Exam

by

Dr. Juhi Gupta

Asstt. Professor, Centre for Women's Studies
Aligarh Muslim University, Aligarh, U.P.

Dr. Shah Alam

Asstt. Professor, Sarojini Naidu Centre for Women's Studies
Jamia Millia Islamia, New Delhi

2027
EDITION

RAMESH PUBLISHING HOUSE, NEW DELHI

Published by

O.P. Gupta *for* Ramesh Publishing House

Admin. Office

12-H, New Daryaganj Road, Opp. Officers' Mess,
New Delhi-110002 ✆ 23275224, 23245124

E-mail: info@rameshpublishinghouse.com

For Online Shopping: www.rameshpublishinghouse.com

Showroom

- Balaji Market, Nai Sarak, Delhi-110006 ✆ 23282525 📱 9354373464
- 4457, Nai Sarak, Delhi-110006

Book Code: R-2056

ISBN: 978-93-88642-72-9

Price: ₹ 495

Printed at: Deepak Offset, Delhi

CONTENTS

STUDY MATERIAL

NTA UGC-NET—Women's Studies

MODEL TEST PAPERS

NTA UGC-NET—Women's Studies Exam

❑ ❑ ❑

Previous Years' Paper

National Testing Agency (NTA)

UGC-NET Junior Research Fellowship & Assistant Professor Eligibility Exam

WOMEN'S STUDIES, JANUARY-2026

(Exam held on 02-01-2026)

PAPER-II

1. Which of the following thinker stated "She is defined and differentiated with reference to man and not he with reference to her, she is the incidental, the inessential as opposed to the essential. He is the subject, he is the absolute-she is the other"?

1. Dorothy Smith 2. Joan Scott
3. Simone de Beavoir 4. Betty Friedan

2. The High-Level committee on the status of women in India (2013) was headed by:

1. Justice Leila Seth
2. Pam Rajput
3. Justice Sujata Manohar
4. Flavia Agnes

3. Who has defined empowerment in terms of three interrelated concepts like agency, resources and achievements?

1. Sherry Ortner 2. Ann Oakley
3. Naila Kabeer 4. Eve Kosofsky Sedgwick

4. The National Policy for the Empowerment of Women (NPEW, 2001) was drafted under the guidance of:

1. National Development Council
2. Planning Commission of India
3. National Commission for Women
4. Ministry of Women and Child Development

5. Which of the following states launched first Transgender Policy in India?

1. Andhra Pradesh 2. Himachal Pradesh
3. Kerala 4. Maharashtra

6. Which of the following represents a shared concern between postcolonial feminism and queer/LGBT studies?

1. Both reject the need for intersectionality.
2. Both critique the universalization of experiences and identifies imposed by dominant discourses.
3. Both focus primarily on Economic class struggles.
4. Both advocate for return to traditional cultural norms.

7. The Forum against Sex Determinism and Sex Pre-Selection (FASDSP) was founded in:

1. 1986 in Delhi 2. 1986 in Mumbai
3. 1987 in Pune 4. 1987 in Bhopal

8. Radical Feminists often critique liberal feminism for:

1. Over emphasing structural economic inequalities
2. Being too focused on legal reforms without challenging deep rooted patriarchal systems.
3. Rejecting intersectionality and diversity.
4. Linking oppression with environmental degradation.

9. Concept of Self Help Groups is ascribed to:

1. Ela Bhatt
2. Leela Dube
3. Amartya Sen
4. Muhammed Yunus

10. Mary Wollstonecraft's *A Vindication of the Rights of Women* (1792) was written partly in response to which enlightenment philosopher's view on Women's Education?

1. Jean-Jacques Rousseau
2. John Locke
3. Immanuel Kant
4. Rene Descartes

11. Which institution publishes the Global Gender Gap report?

1. World Bank
2. World Economic Bank
3. World Economic Forum
4. World Women's Forum

12. The Kasturba Gandhi Balika Vidyalaya (KGBV) scheme primarily targets:

1. Urban Women for Higher Education
2. The Girls of Weaker Sections in India
3. Working girls in the informal sector
4. Girls with disabilities in metropolitan cities

13. The concepts of 'Triple Role' (productive, reproductive and community roles of women) is most closely associated with:

1. Caroline Moser 2. Martha Nussbaum
3. Naila Kabeer 4. Ester Boserup

14. A Women candidate was denied a government job despite having higher qualifications, because the department reserved the post for male applicants only. Which constitutional provisions safeguards the women's right?

1. Article 14 + Article 16(2)
2. Article 19(1)
3. Article 32
4. Article 51A

15. The Mahila Samakhya programme, launched in 1988 to pursue the objectives of the:

1. National Environment Policy
2. National Health Policy
3. National Education Policy
4. National Population Policy

16. A tribal community has low female literacy became parents fear sending girls to distant schools. What would be the most Context-appropriate strategy?

1. Providing free tablets for online learning without addressing safety concerns.
2. Force parents through legal action to send girls to schools.
3. Build residential schools with female teachers and community involvement
4. Offers scholarships for boys to incentivize family participation.

17. What is feminist critique of "datafication" in the context of surveillance capitalism?

1. Datafication democratizes access to digital services reducing inequality.
2. Data collection is gender-neutral and therefore, equitable.
3. Datafication extract value from intimate spheres commodifying bodies and perpetuating systemic discrimination.
4. Datafication has no relevance to feminism, since it purely technical

18. A gender disaggregated study finds that women entrepreneurs score higher on risk avoidance and social orientation but lower on opportunity recognition compared to men. Which intervention best enhances their entrepreneurial success?

1. Focus only on improving credit access not addressing skill development.
2. Introduce mentorship programs, business incubation and market linkage platforms.
3. Encourage women to shift to wage employment instead of entrepreneurship.
4. Provide onetime subsidies without ongoing capacity building support.

19. Who is the author of book, "The Sociology of Gender"?

1. Naomi Wolf 2. V. Geetha
3. Amy S. Wharton 4. Maitrayee Chaudhari

20. Who says 'White women were not hapless onlookers of empire, but were ambiguously complicit both as colonizers and colonized, privileged and restricted acted upon and acting?

1. Andrea Devorkin 2. Anne Me Clintock
3. Carole Vance 4. Simone De Beauvoir

21. When women and men are located separately while otherwise participating in a broadly similar set of activities is known as:

1. Gender Equality 2. Gender Segregation
3. Gender Parity 4. Women Empowerment

22. Which of the following nineteenth century play sparked debate about the concept of 'New Women'?

1. Birthday Party by Harold Pinter
2. Waiting for Godot by Samuel Beckitt
3. A Doll's House by Henrik Ibsen
4. Arms and the Man by Bernard Shaw

23. Women's labour force participation rate as per the Periodic Labours Forces Survey 2023-24:

1. 23.3% 2. 41.7%
3. 37% 4. 27%

24. Who is required to head the Internal Complaints Committee (ICC) under the Sexual Harassment of women at workplace Act, 2013?

1. Air external legal Expert
2. A Senior level Women employee of the organization.
3. The Employer or owner of the Company
4. A representative from the Ministry of Women and Child Development.

25. Women Component Plan was introduced in the:

1. Seventh Plan 2. Eight Plan
3. Ninth Plan 4. Tenth Plan

26. Which of the following examines the notion that women writers of the 19th century were confined in their writing to make their female characters either embody the 'angel' or the 'monster'?

1. *The Madwomen in the Attic*
2. *The Second Sex*
3. *A Vindication of the Rights of Women*
4. *Ain't I a Women*

27. As per the World Economic Forum's Gender Gap Report 2025. What is India's Rank out of 148 Countries?

1. 130 2. 129
3. 131 4. 140

28. Media reports on Violence against women often focus on the victims clothing or behaviour rather then the perpetrator's responsibility. The media practice illustrates:

1. Gendered Framing and Victim-blaming
2. Male gaze in cinema
3. Intersectional digital activism
4. Male supremacy and male arrogance

29. Feminisation of labour in the globalisation context is characterised by:

1. More Women entering the Managerial Positions
2. Constant increase in women in formal sector
3. A rise in women's participation but mostly in low paid, insecure and flexible jobs
4. Women moving to high skilled work

30. Which of the following works published in 1969 reimagines the characters of Gandhari, Kunti, Draupadi, Bhishma, Krishna among others?

1. *The Palace of Illusions* by Chitra Divakaruni
2. *Yuganta : The End of an Epoch* by Iravti Karve
3. *Recasting Women* by Kum Kum Sangari and Sudesh Vaid
4. *The Position of women in Hindu civilization* by AS. Altekar

31. The mudra loan limit to promote women entrepreneurship under Pradhan Mantri Mudra Yojana (PMMY) in 2024 has been increased to:

1. Rupees 15 Lakhs 2. Rupees 20 Lakhs
3. Rupees 25 Lakhs 4. Rupees 10 Lakhs

32. Which of the following work examines the Chicana and Latino experience through the lens of issues such as gender, identify, race and colonialism?

1. *Yearning : Race, Gender and Cultural Politics* by bell hooks
2. *Borderlands* by Gloria E. Anzaldua
3. *Gyn/Ecology* by Mary Daly
4. *"We should all be Feminists"* by Chimamanda Ngozi Adichie

33. Which of the following report is associated directly with emergence of Women's Studies in India?

1. CEDAW Report
2. Towards Equality Report
3. Beijing Platform of Action
4. Human Development Report

34. Which wave of feminism focused on suffrage rights?

1. First Wave 2. Second Wave
3. Third Wave 4. Fourth Wave

35. Who called the family a 'Comfortable Concentration Camp'?

1. Betty Friedan 2. Rosa Parks
3. Helan Rowland 4. Alica Walker

36. The school of Feminist thought which links Capitalism with Women's Sub-ordination is:

1. Radical Feminism 2. Marxist Feminism
3. Liberal Feminism 4. Cultural Feminism

37. Where was the first Women's Right Convention held in June 1848?

1. Seneca Falls, New York
2. London Bridge, London
3. Time Square, New York
4. Tower of London, London

38. The Feminist Principle 'the personal is political' is based on:

1. Maintaining separation between private and public domains
2. Devaluing personal experiences
3. Avoiding subjective accounts in research
4. Recognising personal experiences as sites of power and inequality

39. Who is considered the pioneer of Muslim Women's Education in India?

1. Kasturba Gandhi 2. Fatima Sheikh
3. Mohsina Kidwai 4. Shah Bano

40. Who amongst the following used the term-patriarchy linking, it with private property for the first time to denote a generalised form of male dominance over women?

1. Karl Marx 2. Harriet Taylor
3. Silviya Walby 4. Friedrich Engels

41. Given below are two statements : one is labelled as Assertion (A) and the other is labelled as Reason (R).

Assertion (A): In Community-Based Participation Research, design, data generation and analysis usually occur as a response, recursive or iterative process.

Reason (R): This approach involves the research team cycling back and repeating steps, checking data and adapting to new insights.

In the light of the above statements, choose the ***most appropriate*** answer from the options given below:

1. Both (A) and (R) are correct and (R) is the correct explanation of (A)
2. Both (A) and (R) are correct, but (R) is not the correct explanation of (A)
3. (A) is correct, but (R) is not correct
4. (A) is not correct, but (R) is correct

42. Given below are two statements : one is labelled as Assertion (A) and the other is labelled as Reason (R).

Assertion (A): Gender operates at the individual level alone.

Reason (R): Gender is a powerful principle of social life.

In the light of the above statements, choose the ***most appropriate*** answer from the options given below:

1. Both (A) and (R) are correct and (R) is the correct explanation of (A)
2. Both (A) and (R) are correct, but (R) is not the correct explanation of (A)
3. (A) is correct, but (R) is not correct
4. (A) is not correct, but (R) is correct

43. Given below are two statements : one is labelled as Assertion (A) and the other is labelled as Reason (R).

Assertion (A): The type of economic activity women are more likely to be engaged in world-wide are Labelled by the United Nations as 'vulnerable employment'.

Reason (R): Those in informal economy experience fewer rights and social benefits and are often cut out of decision making processes.

In the light of the above statements, choose the ***most appropriate*** answer from the options given below:

1. Both (A) and (R) are correct and (R) is the correct explanation of (A)
2. Both (A) and (R) are correct, but (R) is not the correct explanation of (A)
3. (A) is correct, but (R) is not correct
4. (A) is not correct, but (R) is correct

44. Given below are two statements : one is labelled as Assertion (A) and the other is labelled as Reason (R).

Assertion (A): Postmodern feminist like Judith Butler argue that gender is performative.

Reason (R): This means that gender is biologically fixed and unchangeable.

In the light of the above statements, choose the ***most appropriate*** answer from the options given below:

1. Both (A) and (R) are correct and (R) is the correct explanation of (A)
2. Both (A) and (R) are correct, but (R) is not the correct explanation of (A)
3. (A) is correct, but (R) is not correct
4. (A) is not correct, but (R) is correct

45. Given below are two statements : one is labelled as Assertion (A) and the other is labelled as Reason (R).

Assertion (A): Masculinities are multiple and socially constructed.

Reason (R): They are shaped by cultural, historical and institutional contexts rather then biology.

In the light of the above statements, choose the ***most appropriate*** answer from the options given below:

1. Both (A) and (R) are correct and (R) is the correct explanation of (A)
2. Both (A) and (R) are correct, but (R) is not the correct explanation of (A)
3. (A) is correct, but (R) is not correct
4. (A) is not correct, but (R) is correct

46. Given below are two statements : one is labelled as Assertion (A) and the other is labelled as Reason (R).

Assertion (A): Radical feminists agrues that patriarchy is the root cause of Women's oppression.

Reason (R): Radical feminists believe that equal laws are enough for achieving gender equality.

In the light of the above statements, choose the ***most appropriate*** answer from the options given below:

1. Both (A) and (R) are correct and (R) is the correct explanation of (A)
2. Both (A) and (R) are correct, but (R) is not the correct explanation of (A)
3. (A) is correct, but (R) is not correct
4. (A) is not correct, but (R) is correct

47. Given below are two statements : one is labelled as Assertion (A) and the other is labelled as Reason (R).

Assertion (A): Postcolonial feminists reject the idea of a universal sisterhood.

Reason (R): Postcolonial feminists argue that women's lives are shaped by diverse histories of race, class, caste and colonialism.

In the light of the above statements, choose the ***most appropriate*** answer from the options given below:

1. Both (A) and (R) are correct and (R) is the correct explanation of (A)
2. Both (A) and (R) are correct, but (R) is not the correct explanation of (A)
3. (A) is correct, but (R) is not correct
4. (A) is not correct, but (R) is correct

48. Given below are two statements : one is labelled as Assertion (A) and the other is labelled as Reason (R).

Assertion (A): Throughout history and the world, divisions of labour have not developed along the lines of Sex.

Reason (R): Work and family are gendered institutions.

In the light of the above statements, choose the ***most appropriate*** answer from the options given below:

1. Both (A) and (R) are correct and (R) is the correct explanation of (A)
2. Both (A) and (R) are correct, but (R) is not the correct explanation of (A)
3. (A) is correct, but (R) is not correct
4. (A) is not correct, but (R) is correct

49. Given below are two statements : one is labelled as Assertion (A) and the other is labelled as Reason (R).

Assertion (A): Sex-Selective abortions led to an increase in sex ratio in India.

Reason (R): Desire for son preference, pushes Indian families to abort a female foetus.

In the light of the above statements, choose the ***most appropriate*** answer from the options given below:

1. Both (A) and (R) are correct and (R) is the correct explanation of (A)
2. Both (A) and (R) are correct, but (R) is not the correct explanation of (A)
3. (A) is correct, but (R) is not correct
4. (A) is not correct, but (R) is correct

50. Given below are two statements : one is labelled as Assertion (A) and the other is labelled as Reason (R).

Assertion (A): Domestic violence is a manifestion of patriarchy.

Reason (R): This happens due to issues of patriarchal power and control.

In the light of the above statements, choose the ***most appropriate*** answer from the options given below:

1. Both (A) and (R) are correct and (R) is the correct explanation of (A)
2. Both (A) and (R) are correct, but (R) is not the correct explanation of (A)
3. (A) is correct, but (R) is not correct
4. (A) is not correct, but (R) is correct

51. Arrange the following phrases of action research in correct order:

A. Reflection
B. Action (Implementation)
C. Planning
D. Observation

Choose the ***correct*** answer from the options given below:

1. A, B, C, D   2. A, C, B, D
3. B, D, C, A   4. D, C, B, A

52. Arrange the following theoretical contributions related to the Capability Approach in their correct chronological order:

A. Amartya Sen introduction of the Capability Approach as a framework for evaluating well being and development.
B. Inclusion of capability based indicators (e.g. GDI, HDI) by UNDP.
C. Martha Nussbaum's development of the list of central human capabilities.
D. Sen's Development Freedom articulates capabilities as freedom expansion

Choose the ***correct*** answer from the options given below:

1. A, D, C, B   2. B, A, D, C
3. A, B, C, D   4. C, A, D, B

53. Arrange the following texts in chronological order:

A. *Gender Trouble* by Judith Butler
B. *Sexual Politics* by Kate Millet
C. *The Subjection of Women* by John Stuart Mill
D. *The Second Sex* by Simone De Beauvoir

Choose the ***correct*** answer from the options given below:

1. D, C, B, A   2. C, D, B, A
3. A, C, B, D   4. B, C, D, A

54. A Women journalist experiences sexual harassment at her workplace. Sequence the steps she may follow under the Sexual Harassment of Women at workplace Act, 2013:

A. File complaint to the Internal Complaint Committee (ICC) within 3 months.
B. Employer implements action within 60 days.
C. Submit inquiry report with recommendations to employer.
D. ICC conducts inquiry within 90 days.

Choose the ***correct*** answer from the options given below:

1. C, B, A, D   2. B, C, D, A
3. A, C, B, D   4. A, D, C, B

55. Arrange following development approaches in sequence:

A. Women in Development (WID)
B. Women Environment and Development (WED)
C. Postmodernism and Development (PAD)
D. Gender and Development (GAD)

Choose the *correct* answer from the options given below:

1. D, A, B, C
2. B, A, D, C
3. A, D, B, C
4. C, B, D, A

56. Arrange the following Acts in chronological order:

A. Domestic Violence Act
B. The Medical Termination of Pregnancy Amendment Act
C. Indian Succession Act
D. Hindu Succession Act

Choose the *correct* answer from the options given below:

1. A, C, B, D
2. B, A, D, C
3. C, D, A, B
4. D, B, C, A

57. Arrange in chronological order:

A. Rokeya Sakhawat Hossain's *"Sultana's Dream"*
B. Henrik Ibsen's *A Doll House*
C. Pearl S. Buck's *The Good Earth*
D. Betty Friedan's *The Feminine Mystique*

Choose the *correct* answer from the options given below:

1. A, B, C and D
2. B, A, C and D
3. C, D, A and B
4. D, C, B and A

58. Arrange the following initiatives towards gender sensitive media policy in chronological order:

A. National Broadcasting Policy drafts
B. National Policy for Empowerment of Women
C. OTT Platform guidelines under IT rulers.
D. Prasar Bharati Act

Choose the *correct* answer from the options given below:

1. C, D, A, B
2. D, B, A, C
3. B, C, A, D
4. A, D, B, C

59. Arrange the following global developments in the context of Gender equality and Sustainable Development Goals (SDG) in chronological order:

A. Being Declaration and Platform for Action
B. Millennium Development Goals (MDG)
C. Sustainable Development Goals (SDG) adopts by United Nations
D. "UN Women" established by UN Body for promoting Gender equality

Choose the *correct* answer from the options given below:

1. C, D, A, B
2. D, B, C, A
3. A, B, D, C
4. B, C, A, D

60. Arrange in proper procedural sequence in the family court

A. Conciliation attempt by the court
B. Filing of Petition
C. Evidence and hearing between parties
D. Decree or order pronounced

Choose the *correct* answer from the options given below:

1. A, B, C, D
2. B, A, C, D
3. D, C, B, A
4. C, D, A, B

61. Choose the correct sequence for following ethics in carrying out a research:

A. Informed consent forms and confidentially
B. Avoid deceiving participants and collecting harmful information
C. Apply to the institutional board
D. Consult code of ethics for your institution

Choose the *correct* answer from the options given below:

1. D, C, B and A
2. A, B, C and D
3. C, D, B and A
4. D, C, A and B

62. Arrange the following chronological order (year of launch):

A. Family Planning Programme
B. National Health Mission
C. Reproductive and Child Health Programme
D. National Population Policy

Choose the *correct* answer from the options given below:

1. A, C, D, B
2. A, C, B, D
3. C, A, D, B
4. C, A, B, D

63. Arrange the following Sustainable Development Goals (SDGs) chronologically:

A. Zero Hunger
B. Reduced Inequalities
C Quality Education
D. Gender Equality

Choose the *correct* answer from the options given below:

1. D, C, B, A
2. A, C, D, B
3. D, B, C, A
4. B, A, D, C

64. Arrange the following Institutional Mechanisms in India for gender equality in chronological order:

A. National Commission for Women
B. NITI Ayog's Women Entrepreneurships Platform
C. Department of Women and Child Development as part of Ministry of Human Resource Development
D. Ministry of Women and Child Development

Choose the *correct* answer from the options given below:

1. A, C, D, B
2. B, C, A, D
3. C, A, D, B
4. D, A, C, B

65. Arrange the following legislations in chronological order:

A. The Child Marriage Restraint Act (Sarda Act)
B. The Protection of Women from Domestic Violence Act
C. The Hindu Marriage Act
D. The Hindu Widow Remarriage Act

Choose the ***correct*** answer from the options given below:

1. B, C, D, A 2. D, B, A, C
3. C, A, D, B 4. C, B, A, D

66. Which of the following are considered Radical Feminist Thinkers?

A. Kate Millet
B. Shulamith Firestone
C. Mary Wollstonecraft
D. Gayatri Spivak

Choose the ***correct*** answer from the options given below:

1. A, B only 2. B, C only
3. C, D only 4. A, C only

67. Flavia Agnes is widely recognised for her work in:

A. Feminist legal studies and Advocacy for Women's Right
B. Queer theory and performativity
C. Feminist philosophy and Feminist Pedagogy
D. Founding Majlis, a legal and cultural resource centre in Mumbai

Choose the ***correct*** answer from the options given below:

1. A, B only 2. B, C only
3. C, D only 4. A, D only

68. Who critiqued the media reinforcement of 'Ideal' femininity and beauty standards?

A. Uma Chakravarti B Antonio Gramsci
C. Naomi Wolf D. Susan Bordo

Choose the ***correct*** answer from the options given below:

1. A, B only 2. B, C only
3. C, D only 4. A, D only

69. Major challenges of motherhood include:

A. Increase in case burden
B. Rejoining workforce
C. Increase in job opportunities
D. Increase in leisure time

Choose the ***correct*** answer from the options given below:

1. A, D only 2. A, C only
3. C, D only 4. A, B only

70. Genital mutilation is denounced in the light of following arguments:

A. Lack of consent and bodily autonomy
B. Psychological effects
C. No risk of infection
D. The intense pain of cutting

Choose the ***correct*** answer from the options given below:

1. A, B, C only 2. B, C, D only
3. A, C, D only 4. A, B, D only

71. What is correct about "One Billion Rising Movement"?

A. It is a global Movement of Women
B. It was founded by Monique Wilson
C. Its aim was to end sexual violence against women
D. It was started in 2009

Choose the ***correct*** answer from the options given below:

1. A, B only 2. A, C only
3. A, D only 4. B, D only

72. Chandra Mohanty (1991) argues that Third World Women should be understood through the following series of oppositions:

A. Privileged - Marginalized
B. Colonizers - Colonized
C. Atheist - Spiritual
D. Good - Bad

Choose the ***correct*** answer from the options given below:

1. A, B only 2. B, C only
3. A, C only 4. B, D only

73. In Vishakha vs. State of Rajasthan the Supreme court derived guidelines for workplace harassment:

A. Article 21
B. Directive Principle of State Policy
C. Kyoto Protocol
D. Criminal Amendment Bill 2019

Choose the ***correct*** answer from the options given below:

1. A, D only 2. B, C only
3. A, B only 4. C, D only

74. Which of the following Sustainable Development Goals (SDEs) overlaps with indices such as Gender Development Index (GDI) and Gender Inequality Index (GII)?

A. SDG-3 B. SDG-4
C. SDG-5 D. SDG-11

Choose the ***correct*** answer from the options given below:

1. A, B only 2. B, C only
3. A, C only 4. C, D only

75. What is understood by 'Critical Scholarship'?

A. Problematize social conditions as they are.
B. Can only be addressed through intersectionality.
C. Can be addressed by using single lens.
D. In the interwoven ways it gets played out in real life.

Choose the ***correct*** answer from the options given below:

1. A, B and C only
2. B, C and A only
3. B, C and D only
4. A, B and D only

76. Match List-I with List-II.

List-I (***Concept***)	**List-II** (***Writers***)
A. The monstrous feminine psychology	I. Helene Cixous
B. Critique of Western Feminisms homogenisation of the Third World Women	II. Gayle Rubin
C. Ecriture Feminine	III. Barbara Creed
D. The Sex/Gender System	IV. Chandra Talpade Mohanty

Choose the ***correct*** answer from the options given below:

1. A-I, B-II, C-III, D-IV
2. A-II, B-III, C-IV, D-I
3. A-III, B-IV, C-I, D-II
4. A-IV, B-I, C-II, D-III

77. Match List-I with List-II.

List-I (***Thinker***)	**List-II** (***Key Concepts***)
A. R.W. Connel	I. Intersectionality
B. Eve Kasofsky Sedgwick	II. Epistemology of the closet
C. Kimberle Crenshaw	III. Subaltern Voice
D. Gayatri Chakravorty Spivak	IV. Hegemonic Masculinity

Choose the ***correct*** answer from the options given below:

1. A-II, B-III, C-IV, D-I
2. A-I, B-IV, C-II, D-III
3. A-IV, B-II, C-I, D-III
4. A-III, B-I, C-II, D-IV

78. Match List-I with List-II.

List-I (***Barriers faced by Women Entrepreneur***)	**List-II** (***Solutions to overcome***)
A. Lack of collaterals for loans.	I. Exposure visits, mentorship and training in non-traditional sectors.
B. Gender stereotyping in business choices	II. E-commerce training and participation in trade fairs.
C. Limited Market Access.	III. Affordable child care, Community kitchen and flexible work schedule.
D. Time Poverty due to household burden.	IV. Collateral free micro-credit and Government Guarantee Scheme.

Choose the ***correct*** answer from the options given below:

1. A-I, B-IV, C-III, D-II
2. A-I, B-II, C-III, D-IV
3. A-IV, B-II, C-III, D-I
4. A-IV, B-I, C-II, D-III

79. Match List-I with List-II.

List-I (***Five Year Plan***)	**List-II** (***Development Goals***)
A. First Five Year Plan	I. Empowerment as a central goal, introduction of women component plan in all Ministries
B. Fifth Five Year Plan	II. Women's Welfare to Development
C. Ninth Five Year Plan	III. Welfare orientation, Prioritization of Family Planning and Maternal Health
D. Eleventh Five Year Plan	IV. Inclusive growth with gender budgeting.

Choose the ***correct*** answer from the options given below:

1. A-I, B-III, C-II, D-IV
2. A-III, B-II, C-IV, D-I
3. A-III, B-II, C-I, D-IV
4. A-I, B-II, C-IV, D-III

80. Match List-I with List-II.

List-I (***Research Method***)	**List-II** (***Limitations***)
A. Experimental Design	I. Risk of superficial data, Response bias.
B. Surveys	II. Difficulty in capturing dynamic social change
C. Ethnography	III. Limited ability to generalize
D. Case Studies	IV. Researcher subjectivity, time intensive

Choose the ***correct*** answer from the options given below:

1. A-I, B-III, C-II, D-IV
2. A-II, B-I, C-IV, D-III
3. A-III, B-II, C-I, D-IV
4. A-I, B-II, C-III, D-IV

81. Match List-I with List-II.

List-I (*Authors*)	**List-II** (*Books*)
A. Shiela Rowbothom	I. *Psychoanalysis and Feminism*
B. Ellen Moers	II. *Hidden from History*
C. Elaine Shawalter	III. *Literary Women*
D. Juliet Mitchell	IV. *A Literature of Their own*

Choose the ***correct*** answer from the options given below:

1. A-I, B-III, C-II, D-IV
2. A-IV, B-II, C-III, D-I
3. A-II, B-III, C-IV, D-I
4. A-III, B-I, C-II, D-IV

82. Match List-I with List-II.

List-I (*Thinkers*)	**List-II** (*Philosophy*)
A. Sandra Harding	I. Feminist Ethnography
B. Donna Haraway	II. Feminist Standpoint
C. Heidi Hartmann	III. Situated Knowledge
D. Judith Stacey	IV. Socialist Feminism

Choose the ***correct*** answer from the options given below:

1. A-I, B-II, C-IV, D-III
2. A-III, B-I, C-II, D-IV
3. A-I, B-IV, C-II, D-III
4. A-II, B-III, C-IV, D-I

83. Match List-I with List-II.

List-I (*Authors*)	**List-II** (*Books*)
A. Uma Chakravarti	I. Indian Women's Battle for Freedom (1983)
B. Prem Chowdhary	II. Women in Modern India (1977)
C. Kamladevi Chattopadhyay	III. The Life and Times of Pandita Ramabai (1998)
D. Neera Desai	IV. The Veiled Women (1994)

Choose the ***correct*** answer from the options given below:

1. A-III, B-IV, C-II, D-I
2. A-III, B-IV, C-I, D-II
3. A-III, B-I, C-II, D-IV
4. A-II, B-I, C-IV, D-III

84. Match List-I with List-II.

List-I (*Global Frameworks*)	**List-II** (*Year*)
A. Sustainable Development Goals	I. 1995
B. Universal Declaration of Human Rights	II. 2015
C. Convention on the Elimination of all Forms of Discrimination against Women (CEDAW)	III. 1948
D. Beijing Platform of Action	IV. 1979

Choose the ***correct*** answer from the options given below:

1. A-IV, B-I, C-III, D-II
2. A-II, B-IV, C-I, D-III
3. A-II, B-III, C-IV, D-I
4. A-III, B-I, C-IV, D-II

85. Match List-I with List-II.

List-I (*Schemes*)	**List-II** (*Year*)
A. Nirbhaya Fund	I. 2007
B. Ujjawala Scheme	II. 2013
C. Beti Bachao Beti Padhao	III. 2015
D. Mahila Shakti Kendra	IV. 2017

Choose the ***correct*** answer from the options given below:

1. A-I, B-III, C-II, D-IV
2. A-II, B-I, C-III, D-IV
3. A-II, B-IV, C-I, D-III
4. A-I, B-II, C-IV, D-III

86. Match List-I with List-II.

List-I (*Indian Feminists*)	**List-II** (*Association*)
A. Ramabai Ranade	I. Centre for Women's Development Studies
B. Saralabala Devi Chaudhurani	II. Seva Sadan Society
C. Kamaladevi Chattopadhyay	III. Bharat Stri Mandal
D. Vina Mazumdar	IV. All India Women's Association

Choose the ***correct*** answer from the options given below:

1. A-I, B-II, C-IV, D-III
2. A-II, B-III, C-IV, D-I
3. A-II, B-IV, C-III, D-I
4. A-II, B-IV, C-I, D-III

87. Match List-I with List-II.

List-I (*Schemes*)	**List-II** (*Provisions*)
A. Mahila E-Haat	I. Online marketing for women entrepreneurs
B. She-Box-Portal	II. Launched for information on women related schemes

C. Nari Shakti Portal	III. Capacity building for women entrepreneurs
D. SAMARATH Scheme	IV. Provides a single window platform for women to register workplace sexual harassment

Choose the ***correct*** answer from the options given below:

1. A-I, B-II, C-IV, D-III
2. A-I, B-IV, C-II, D-III
3. A-II, B-III, C-I, D-IV
4. A-II, B-I, C-III, D-IV

88. Match List-I with List-II.

List-I (***Feminist Authors***)	**List-II** (***Books***)
A. Sudhir Kakar	I. Women's Studies : A Reader
B. Mary E John	II. Theorizing Feminism : Gender
C. V. Geetha	III. Anthropological Exploration in Gender
D. Leela Dube	IV. The Inner World

Choose the ***correct*** answer from the options given below:

1. A-IV, B-I, C-II, D-III
2. A-I, B-II, C-III, D-IV
3. A-IV, B-III, C-II, D-I
4. A-I, B-III, C-IV, D-II

89. Match List-I with List-II.

List-I (***Patterns of Residence***)	**List-II** (***Explanation***)
A. Avunculocal residence	I. A married couple lives in locality associated with wife's relative
B. Neolocal residence	II. A married couple may choose either matrilocal or patrilocal residence
C. Ambilocal residence	III. A pattern in which a married couple lives with the husband's mother's brother
D. Matrilocal residence	IV. A married couple establishes their household in a location apart from both set of parents

Choose the ***correct*** answer from the options given below:

1. A-III, B-II, C-IV, D-I
2. A-III, B-IV, C-II, D-I
3. A-IV, B-I, C-III, D-II
4. A-IV, B-I, C-II, D-III

90. Match List-I with List-II.

List-I (***Authors***)	**List-II** (***Books***)
A. Marilyn Strathern	I. Perceiving Women (1975)
B. Shirly Ardner	II. Women of value, Men of Renown (1976)
C. Lila Abu-Lughod	III. Women in Between (1972)
D. Annette Weiner	IV. Veiled Sentiments (1986)

Choose the ***correct*** answer from the options given below:

1. A-III, B-IV, C-I, D-II
2. A-III, B-I, C-IV, D-II
3. A-IV, B-III, C-II, D-I
4. A-IV, B-II, C-III, D-I

Directions (Qs. No. 91 to 95): *Read the following passage and answer the questions:*

In the past decade, women challenges have deepened, women leaders remain rare (87 countries have ever been led by one), and femicide claims a life every 10 minutes. Digital divides and harmful stereotypes, amplified by AI, continue to limit equality and safety. Year 2025 marks 30 years since the Beijing Declaration and Platform for Action, the worlds most ambitious roadmap for advancing women's rights. Over these three decades, significant progress has been made. Global parity in girls education has been achieved, maternal mortality has fallen by one third, and women's representation in parliaments has more than doubled. Between 1995 and 2024, 189 countries and territories enacted 1531 Legal reforms to eliminate discriminating laws. These milestones show that when women's rights are fully upheld, families, communities and economies flourish, significant work remains for gender equality. So the Beijing +30 Action agenda offers a bold roadmap to finish the 2030 agenda for Sustainable Development.

91. 2025 marks _____ since the Being declaration and platform for Action was held.

1. 25 years
2. 30 years
3. 40 years
4. 15 years

92. The main purpose of the Beijing +30 Action of Agenda, as presented in the text is to:

1. Celebrate the completion of Gender equality goal.
2. Reconfigure the original 1995 Beijing Declaration.
3. Provide a courageous roadmap to meet the unfinished agenda and 2030 Sustainable Development Goals.
4. Focus Solely on technological equality

93. Advancement of women's rights benefit society by:
1. Reducing population and increasing economic inequality.
2. Strengthening local communities.
3. Primarily benefiting women with no broader societal impact.
4. Helping families, communities and economies to flourish.

94. Which pair of issues highlights the dual challenge women face in the digital era?
1. Increasing cost of higher education with equal healthcare opportunities.
2. Climate migration and increasing maternal mortality.
3. Under representation in leadership position and declining gender-based violence.
4. Harmful stereotypes amplified by AI and Digital divide.

95. Which of the following best describes the global progress made since the 1995 Beijing Declaration and Platform for Action?
1. Increased maternal mortality
2. Parity in girls education
3. Equal leadership representation across all countries
4. Reduced access to technology

Directions (Qs. No. 96 to 100): *Read the following passage and answer the questions:*

During the times of armed conflict, women are exploited in ways that relate to their reproductive responsibilities or gendered expectations of womenhood. Research shows that repercussions of war affect women more adversely than men, women and girls are often viewed as culture bearers and reproducers of "the enemy" and thus become prime targets. However, they are not merely victims of armed conflict. They are active agents. They make choices, possess critical perspectives on their situations and organize collectively in response to those situations. Women may gain from the changed gender relations that result from taking on new responsibilities when male heads of households are absent or deceased. These changes in women's roles can challenge existing social norms. But formalized process of peace, including negotiation, accords and reconstruction plans, frequently exclude women's and girls meaningful participation.

96. According to the passage, how are women often exploited during times of armed conflict?
1. By being recruited into combat roles against their will.
2. By being forced into political negotiation.
3. Through denial of access to education.
4. In relation to their reproductive responsibilities and gendered expectations.

97. Why are women and girls considered prime target in armed conflicts?
1. They are viewed as culture bearers and reproducers of "the enemy".
2. They are less protected by law.
3. They often join rebel groups.
4. They refuse to flee conflict zones.

98. The passage suggests that women in armed conflict are:
1. Only passive victims with no agency
2. Excluded from all social roles
3. Sometimes active agents who make choices and organise collectively
4. Always dependent on humanitarian aid.

99. What is a major limitations of formalized peace processes?
1. They focus only on economic reconstruction.
2. They usually prolong conflict rather than resolve it.
3. They frequently exclude women's and girls meaningful participation.
4. They undermine men's traditional roles in society.

100. What changes women experience as a result of altered gender relations during armed conflict?
1. Decreased isolation and restrictions.
2. New status and new responsibilities.
3. No change in participation in decision making.
4. No loss of their social identity.

ANSWERS

1	**2**	**3**	**4**	**5**	**6**	**7**	**8**	**9**	**10**
3	2	3	4	3	2	2	2	4	1
11	**12**	**13**	**14**	**15**	**16**	**17**	**18**	**19**	**20**
3	2	1	1	3	3	3	2	3	2
21	**22**	**23**	**24**	**25**	**26**	**27**	**28**	**29**	**30**
2	3	2	2	3	1	3	1	3	2
31	**32**	**33**	**34**	**35**	**36**	**37**	**38**	**39**	**40**
2	2	2	1	1	2	1	4	2	4

41	42	43	44	45	46	47	48	49	50
1	4	1	3	1	3	1	4	4	1
51	**52**	**53**	**54**	**55**	**56**	**57**	**58**	**59**	**60**
*	3	2	4	3	3	2	*	3	2
61	**62**	**63**	**64**	**65**	**66**	**67**	**68**	**69**	**70**
4	1	2	3	*	1	4	3	4	4
71	**72**	**73**	**74**	**75**	**76**	**77**	**78**	**79**	**80**
2	1	3	2	4	3	3	4	3	2
81	**82**	**83**	**84**	**85**	**86**	**87**	**88**	**89**	**90**
3	4	2	3	2	2	2	1	2	2
91	**92**	**93**	**94**	**95**	**96**	**97**	**98**	**99**	**100**
2	3	4	4	2	4	1	3	3	2

EXPLANATORY ANSWERS

1. The statement is given by Simone de Beauvoir in The Second Sex. She explains that women are constructed as "the Other" in a male-dominated society. Men are treated as the norm or absolute subject, while women are seen as secondary and dependent. This reflects deep-rooted gender inequality in social and cultural structures. Her work is foundational in feminist theory and critiques patriarchy. The quote exactly matches her philosophical position on gender relations.

2. The High-Level Committee on the Status of Women in India (2013) was chaired by Pam Rajput. It was set up to review the condition of women after the 1974 Towards Equality report. The committee examined issues like health, education, employment, and legal rights. It aimed to identify gaps in gender equality and suggest reforms. Its report provided policy recommendations for women's empowerment. Rajput's leadership ensured a comprehensive gender-focused analysis.

3. Naila Kabeer defined empowerment through resources, agency, and achievements. Resources include material and social assets necessary for choice. Agency refers to the ability to make decisions and act upon them. Achievements are the outcomes of those choices. This framework highlights empowerment as a process as well as an outcome. It is widely used in gender and development studies.

4. The National Policy for the Empowerment of Women (2001) was drafted under the Ministry of Women and Child Development. At that time, the Department of Women and Child Development functioned under the Ministry of Human Resource Development. It acted as the nodal body for women's issues and policy formulation. The policy aimed to ensure gender equality and women's advancement in all sectors. It focused on rights, opportunities, and social justice. This option correctly fits the question.

5. Kerala was the first state in India to launch a comprehensive Transgender Policy in 2015. This policy aimed at ensuring social justice, equality, and protection of rights for transgender persons. It included provisions for education, employment, healthcare, and legal recognition of gender identity. The initiative was considered progressive and set a model for other states. It also emphasized inclusion and dignity for the transgender community. Hence, Kerala is the correct answer.

6. Postcolonial feminism and queer/LGBT studies both challenge dominant narratives that assume universal experiences. They argue that identities are shaped by culture, history, and power relations rather than being fixed or uniform. Both perspectives critique Western-centric frameworks that marginalize diverse voices. They emphasize plurality, difference, and the importance of local contexts. This shared concern makes option 2 fully accurate. Other options misrepresent their core focus and theoretical approach.

7. The Forum Against Sex Determination and Sex Pre-Selection (FASDSP) was founded in 1986 in Mumbai. It emerged as a response to the misuse of medical technologies for sex-selective practices. The organization worked to raise awareness and campaign against female foeticide. It played a significant role in advocating for legal measures to regulate such practices. Its activism contributed to broader gender justice movements in India. Thus, this option correctly matches the question.

8. Radical feminists argue that liberal feminism focuses mainly on legal equality and reforms within existing systems. They believe this approach does not address the deeper structural and cultural roots of patriarchy. Radical feminism seeks to transform the entire system that sustains gender inequality. It emphasizes power relations, social norms, and institutionalized oppression. Therefore, option 2 accurately reflects their critique.

9. The concept of Self Help Groups (SHGs) is closely associated with Muhammad Yunus, who pioneered microfinance through the Grameen Bank. He emphasized collective organization of poor individuals, especially women, for savings and credit activities. SHGs promote financial inclusion, self-reliance, and empowerment at the grassroots level. Though SHGs evolved in India later, the foundational idea of group-based microcredit traces back to Yunus. His model inspired similar initiatives worldwide. Therefore, this option best fits the question.

10. Jean-Jacques Rousseau influenced Mary Wollstonecraft's critique in A Vindication of the Rights of Woman (1792). Rousseau argued that women's education should be limited and oriented toward pleasing men and domestic roles. Wollstonecraft strongly opposed this view and advocated equal education for women. She argued that women are rational beings deserving the same intellectual development as men. Her work is a foundational text of liberal feminism. Thus, this option correctly answers the question.

11. The Global Gender Gap Report is published by the World Economic Forum. It assesses gender-based disparities across countries in areas like economic participation, education, health, and political empowerment. The report provides comparative rankings and highlights progress and gaps in gender equality. It is widely used by policymakers and researchers. The index helps track global trends and encourages reforms. Hence, this option is correct.

12. The Kasturba Gandhi Balika Vidyalaya (KGBV) scheme targets girls from disadvantaged and marginalized communities. It focuses on those belonging to SC, ST, OBC, minority groups, and economically weaker sections. The scheme provides residential schooling at the upper primary level in educationally backward areas. Its aim is to reduce gender disparities in education. It ensures access, retention, and quality education for vulnerable girls. Therefore, this option is accurate.

13. The concept of the "Triple Role" of women is associated with Caroline Moser. She identified women's roles as productive (economic work), reproductive (household and caregiving), and community management roles. This framework highlights the multiple burdens women carry in society. It is widely used in gender planning and development studies. The concept helps in designing gender-sensitive policies. Hence, this option correctly answers the question.

14. Article 14 of the Indian Constitution guarantees equality before the law, while Article 16(2) of the Indian Constitution prohibits discrimination in public employment on grounds including sex. Denying a qualified woman a government job solely because of her gender violates both equality and non-discrimination principles. These provisions ensure equal opportunity in public employment. They directly address gender-based exclusion in jobs. Hence, this combination correctly safeguards the woman's right in this case.

15. The Mahila Samakhya Programme (1988) was launched to implement the objectives of the National Policy on Education 1986. It focused on women's empowerment through education, especially in rural areas. The programme aimed to increase awareness, participation, and confidence among women. It worked through collective learning and community mobilization. Education was used as a tool for social transformation and gender equality. Therefore, this option is correct.

16. In this situation, the main issue is safety and accessibility for girls in a tribal community. Building residential schools nearby with female teachers directly addresses parental concerns about safety and distance. Community involvement helps build trust and cultural acceptance. This approach ensures sustained participation of girls in education. It is more practical and sensitive than coercive or irrelevant measures. Hence, this is the most context-appropriate strategy.

17. Feminist critiques of datafication argue that it is not neutral but embedded in power relations. It often extracts personal and intimate data, especially from marginalized groups, and turns it into economic value. This process can reinforce gender biases and surveillance inequalities. It may commodify bodies and identities while ignoring structural discrimination. Feminist scholars highlight how such systems reproduce existing hierarchies. Therefore, this option accurately reflects the critique.

18. This intervention directly addresses the identified gaps in opportunity recognition and business growth among women entrepreneurs. Mentorship provides guidance and confidence, while incubation supports skill-building and innovation. Market linkages help women access broader business opportunities and networks. Unlike one-time financial support, this approach ensures sustained capacity development. It also builds on women's strengths like social orientation. Therefore, it is the most effective and holistic strategy for enhancing entrepreneurial success.

19. Amy S. Wharton is the author of The Sociology of Gender. The book provides a comprehensive overview of gender as a social institution and examines inequalities in various spheres. It discusses work, family, and societal structures shaping gender roles. The text is widely used in sociology and gender studies. It combines theoretical perspectives with empirical research. Hence, this option correctly answers the question.

20. Anne McClintock articulated this idea about white women's complex role in colonialism. She argued that white women were not merely passive observers but were actively involved in imperial processes. At the same time, they experienced certain restrictions within patriarchal structures. This dual position made them both privileged and constrained. Her work highlights intersections of gender, race, and colonial power. Therefore, this option is correct.

21. Gender segregation refers to the separation of women and men into different spaces or roles while they may still engage in similar activities. This can occur in workplaces, education, or social settings. It often leads to unequal access to resources and opportunities. The concept highlights structural divisions based on gender. It is distinct from equality or empowerment, which aim to reduce such divisions. Hence, this option fits the definition accurately.

22. A Doll's House is a nineteenth-century play that sparked debates about the "New Woman." It portrays Nora, who challenges traditional gender roles and expectations in marriage. The play questions women's subordinate position in society. It became a landmark work in feminist literature and theatre. Its themes of independence and self-realization were revolutionary for its time. Therefore, this option is correct.

23. As per the Periodic Labour Force Survey (PLFS) 2023–24, the women's labour force participation rate showed a significant increase, reaching around 41.7%. This rise reflects improved inclusion of women in economic activities, particularly in rural areas. Factors such as self-employment, agricultural participation, and policy interventions contributed to this growth. It also indicates gradual shifts in social norms regarding women's work. However, concerns about job quality and informal employment still remain. Thus, this option correctly matches the latest data.

24. Under the Sexual Harassment of Women at Workplace (Prevention, Prohibition and Redressal) Act, 2013, the Internal Complaints Committee (ICC) must be headed by a senior-level woman employee. This ensures gender-sensitive handling of complaints and promotes trust among women employees. The law mandates this to create a safe and supportive environment. External members are also included, but they do not head the committee. The provision strengthens institutional accountability. Therefore, this option is correct.

25. The Women Component Plan (WCP) was introduced during the Ninth Five Year Plan (1997–2002). It aimed to ensure that at least 30% of funds/benefits from various sectors flowed to women. The plan focused on integrating women's development into mainstream planning. It sought to address gender disparities in resource allocation. This initiative marked a shift towards gender budgeting in India. Hence, this option correctly answers the question.

26. The Madwoman in the Attic examines how 19th-century women writers were constrained to depict female characters as either "angel" or "monster." The authors analyze literary works to show how patriarchal norms shaped women's writing. It critiques the limited roles assigned to women in literature. The book is a key text in feminist literary criticism. It highlights the struggle of women writers to express authentic identities. Therefore, this option is correct.

27. According to the World Economic Forum Global Gender Gap Report 2025, India is ranked 131 out of 148 countries. Although India's overall gender parity score showed slight improvement, its rank declined compared to the previous year due to relatively faster progress by other countries. The report evaluates gender gaps in economic participation, education, health, and political empowerment. India continues to face challenges, particularly in economic and political domains. The ranking highlights both incremental progress and persistent inequalities. Therefore, option 3 correctly fits the question.

28. This media practice reflects gendered framing where narratives are constructed in a way that shifts attention from the perpetrator to the victim. By focusing on a woman's clothing or behaviour, responsibility is indirectly placed on the victim rather than the offender. This reinforces harmful stereotypes and normalizes violence against women. Victim-blaming discourages reporting and perpetuates injustice. It is widely critiqued in feminist media studies. Hence, this option correctly captures the issue.

29. Feminisation of labour in the context of globalization refers to increasing participation of women in the workforce, especially in informal and precarious sectors. These jobs are often low-paid, lack security, and involve flexible or temporary arrangements. It does not necessarily indicate empowerment or better working conditions. Instead, it reflects structural inequalities in labour markets. Women are often concentrated in vulnerable forms of employment. Therefore, this option is accurate.

30. The End of an Epoch by Iravti Karve: Yuganta: The End of an Epoch, published in 1969, reinterprets characters from the Mahabharata such as Gandhari, Kunti, Draupadi, Bhishma, and Krishna. The work offers a sociological and humanized reading of these epic figures. It moves away from mythological glorification to analyze their motivations and dilemmas. The book is significant for its critical and modern perspective. Hence, this option correctly answers the question.

31. Under the Pradhan Mantri Mudra Yojana (PMMY), the loan limit has been increased up to ₹ 20 lakhs in recent policy updates to further promote entrepreneurship, including among women. The scheme provides financial support to small and micro enterprises. It aims to enhance self-employment and business growth. Women entrepreneurs are key beneficiaries under this initiative. This increase helps expand business opportunities. Therefore, this option is correct.

32. Borderlands/La Frontera: The New Mestiza examines the Chicana and Latino experience through themes of gender, identity, race, and colonialism. The work explores the concept of border identity and cultural hybridity. It highlights the struggles of marginalized communities living between cultures. The book is foundational in Chicana feminist and cultural studies. It integrates personal narrative with theory. Hence, this option correctly fits the question.

33. The Towards Equality Report (1974), prepared by the Committee on the Status of Women in India, played a crucial role in the emergence of Women's Studies in India. It highlighted the declining status of women despite constitutional guarantees of equality. The report exposed issues like low literacy, poor health, and limited economic participation of women. It created awareness among policymakers and academics. This led to the institutionalization of Women's Studies as a discipline. Hence, this option is correct.

34. The First Wave of feminism focused mainly on legal rights, especially women's suffrage or the right to vote. It emerged in the late 19th and early 20th centuries in countries like the USA and the UK. Activists such as suffragists and suffragettes fought for political inclusion and equality before the law. This wave also addressed issues like property rights and legal identity of women. It laid the foundation for later feminist movements by establishing basic civil rights. Hence, this option correctly fits the question.

35. Betty Friedan referred to the family as a "comfortable concentration camp" to critique the restrictive domestic roles imposed on women. In her work The Feminine Mystique, she highlighted how many housewives felt unfulfilled despite material comfort. She argued that societal expectations confined women to the private sphere. This critique became central to second-wave feminism. It exposed hidden dissatisfaction among middle-class women. Therefore, this option is correct.

36. Marxist feminism explains women's subordination through the lens of capitalism and class relations. It argues that women's unpaid domestic labour supports capitalist production by sustaining the workforce. Women are also concentrated in low-paid and exploitative jobs in the labour market. This school critiques both patriarchy and capitalism as interconnected systems of oppression. It calls for structural transformation of economic relations. Thus, this option accurately answers the question.

37. The first Women's Rights Convention was held in Seneca Falls in June 1848, marking the beginning of organized feminist activism. Leaders like Elizabeth Cady Stanton and Lucretia Mott played key roles in organizing it. The convention produced the Declaration of Sentiments, which demanded equality in political, social, and economic spheres. It highlighted issues like voting rights and legal discrimination. This event became a milestone in women's rights history. Hence, this option is correct.

38. The slogan "the personal is political" emerged during second-wave feminism. It emphasizes that personal experiences such as family roles, sexuality, and domestic life are shaped by broader social and political structures. It challenges the traditional division between private and public spheres. This principle reveals how power operates in everyday life. It helped bring issues like domestic violence and reproductive rights into public debate. Therefore, this option correctly reflects the feminist principle.

39. Fatima Sheikh is regarded as a pioneer of Muslim women's education in India. She worked closely with Savitribai Phule and Jyotirao Phule in promoting education for girls and marginalized communities. Fatima Sheikh is considered one of the first Muslim women teachers in India. She played a crucial role in running early schools for girls in the 19th century. Her contribution helped break social and religious barriers to women's education. Therefore, this option correctly fits the question.

40. Friedrich Engels linked patriarchy with private property in his work The Origin of the Family, Private Property and the State. He argued that male dominance emerged with the development of private property and class divisions. Engels explained how control over property led to control over women's labour and sexuality. This marked a shift from earlier egalitarian societies. His analysis laid the foundation for later Marxist feminist thought. Hence, this option is correct.

41. Assertion (A) is correct because in Community-Based Participatory Research, the research process usually does not move in a fixed straight line from design to data collection to analysis. Instead, these stages often develop together and are revised repeatedly in response to community feedback, practical experience, and emerging findings. Reason (R) is also correct because this approach involves returning to earlier steps, rechecking information, and modifying the process when new insights appear. That is exactly what is meant by a recursive or iterative process. Since the reason clearly explains why design, data generation, and analysis occur in this repeated and responsive manner, it directly justifies the assertion. Therefore, option 1 is the most accurate answer.

42. The assertion is incorrect because gender does not operate only at the individual level; it functions at multiple levels including social, institutional, and structural. Gender shapes norms, roles, and power relations across society. The reason is correct as gender is indeed a powerful organizing principle of social life. It influences institutions like family, education, economy, and politics. However, the reason does not support the incorrect assertion. Therefore, the correct answer is that (A) is false while (R) is true.

43. Assertion (A) is correct because globally a large proportion of women are concentrated in what the United Nations terms "vulnerable employment," such as informal, unpaid, or insecure work. These jobs often lack stability, proper wages, and legal protections. Reason (R) is also correct as workers in the informal economy typically have limited rights, minimal social security, and little participation in decision-making processes. This condition explains why such employment is categorized as vulnerable. The lack of protections and benefits directly contributes to women's overrepresentation in these sectors. Therefore, the reason clearly explains the assertion, making option 1 correct.

44. Judith Butler argued that gender is performative, meaning it is constructed through repeated social actions and behaviors rather than being innate. Assertion (A) is correct as it reflects this core idea of postmodern feminism. However, Reason (R) is incorrect because it wrongly states that gender is biologically fixed and unchangeable, which is the opposite of Butler's argument. She emphasizes fluidity and social construction of gender identities. Therefore, only the assertion is correct, making option 3 the correct answer.

45. Assertion (A) is correct because the concept of masculinities suggests that there is not a single fixed form of masculinity but multiple forms shaped by society. These masculinities vary across cultures, classes, and historical periods. Reason (R) is also correct as it explains that masculinities are influenced by cultural norms, historical developments, and institutional structures rather than biological factors. This directly clarifies why masculinities are considered socially constructed and diverse. The explanation shows how social context produces different masculine identities. Therefore, both (A) and (R) are correct, and (R) properly explains (A).

46. Assertion (A) is correct because radical feminists identify patriarchy as the fundamental system responsible for women's oppression. They argue that male dominance is deeply embedded in social, cultural, and institutional structures. However, Reason (R) is incorrect because radical feminists do not believe that equal laws alone can achieve gender equality. Instead, they emphasize the need for deep structural and societal transformation beyond legal reforms. Legal equality is seen as insufficient without addressing power relations and patriarchy. Therefore, only (A) is correct, making option 3 the correct answer.

47. Assertion (A) is correct because postcolonial feminists challenge the idea of a universal sisterhood that assumes all women share the same experiences. They argue that such a notion ignores differences shaped by history and power. Reason (R) is also correct as it explains that women's lives are influenced by factors like race, class, caste, and colonial histories. These intersecting structures create diverse and unequal experiences among women. This directly explains why a single, unified notion of sisterhood is rejected. Therefore, both (A) and (R) are correct, and (R) properly explains (A).

48. Assertion (A) is incorrect because historically and globally, divisions of labour have very much developed along the lines of sex or gender. Societies have typically assigned different roles and responsibilities to men and women. Reason (R) is correct as work and family are indeed gendered institutions shaped by social norms and expectations. These institutions reinforce gender-based divisions and inequalities. However, the correct reason does not support the incorrect assertion. Therefore, the correct answer is that (A) is false while (R) is true.

49. Assertion (A) is incorrect because sex-selective abortions have actually led to a decline in the female sex ratio in India, not an increase. The elimination of female foetuses results in fewer women compared to men. Reason (R) is correct as son preference in many families drives the practice of aborting female foetuses. This cultural bias is a major cause behind the distorted sex ratio. The reason explains the phenomenon but contradicts the assertion. Therefore, (A) is false while (R) is true.

50. Assertion (A) is correct because domestic violence is widely understood as a manifestation of patriarchal structures. It reflects unequal power relations between men and women within the household. Reason (R) is also correct as such violence arises from systems of patriarchal power and control over women. These power dynamics normalize dominance and justify abuse. The reason directly explains why domestic violence occurs within patriarchal systems. Hence, both (A) and (R) are correct, and (R) is the correct explanation of (A).

51. The correct logical sequence of Action Research Cycle is C (Planning) → B (Action) → D (Observation) → A (Reflection). Planning involves identifying the problem and designing an intervention strategy. This is followed by Action, where the plan is implemented in practice. Observation then involves systematically monitoring and collecting data on the outcomes of the action. Finally, Reflection evaluates the results and informs future cycles. Since none of the given options match this correct order, the answer is NONE.

52. A. Amartya Sen's introduction of the Capability Approach: Amartya Sen introduced the idea in the late 1970s–80s focusing on capabilities and freedoms.

B. Inclusion of capability-based indicators by UNDP: HDI (1990) and GDI (1995) applied these ideas in development measurement.

C. Martha Nussbaum's development of central capabilities: Martha Nussbaum provided a structured list in 2000 to operationalize the approach.

D. Sen's Development as Freedom: This work gave a comprehensive articulation of the capability approach as expansion of freedoms.

53. C. The Subjection of Women by John Stuart Mill (1869) is the earliest work, advocating legal and social equality for women within liberal thought.

D. The Second Sex by Simone de Beauvoir (1949) expanded feminist theory by analysing women's oppression and the idea of "Otherness."

B. Sexual Politics by Kate Millett (1970) critically examined patriarchy in literature and power relations in society.

A. Gender Trouble by Judith Butler (1990) introduced postmodern ideas of gender performativity and fluid identities.

54. A. Filing complaint to ICC within 3 months is the first legal step to initiate action under the Act.

D. The ICC then conducts an inquiry within 90 days to examine evidence and statements.

C. After completing the inquiry, it submits a report with recommendations to the employer.

B. Finally, the employer is required to implement the recommended action within 60 days, ensuring accountability.

55. A. Women in Development (WID): Emerged in the early 1970s after Ester Boserup's work, focusing on integrating women into existing development processes to enhance their productivity and status.

D. Gender and Development (GAD): Developed in the 1980s as a critique of WID, shifting focus from women alone to gender relations and structural inequalities in society.

B. Women, Environment and Development (WED): Became prominent in the late 1980s–early 1990s, especially around the 1992 Earth Summit, highlighting women's role in environmental management and sustainability.

C. Postmodernism and Development (PAD): Emerged in the mid–late 1990s, questioning universal development models and emphasizing diversity, local contexts, and multiple identities.

56. C. Indian Succession Act: Enacted in 1925, it governed inheritance and succession matters, especially for Christians and others not covered by personal laws.

D. Hindu Succession Act: Passed in 1956, it reformed property rights among Hindus, later amended to improve women's inheritance rights.

A. Domestic Violence Act: The Protection of Women from Domestic Violence Act was enacted in 2005 to address abuse within households.

B. The Medical Termination of Pregnancy Amendment Act: The amendment came in 2021, expanding access to safe abortion and extending gestation limits under specific conditions.

57. B. A Doll's House by Henrik Ibsen (1879) is the earliest, questioning gender roles and marriage norms.

A. Sultana's Dream by Rokeya Sakhawat Hossain (1905) presents a feminist utopia challenging patriarchy.

C. The Good Earth by Pearl S. Buck (1931) explores rural life and gender roles in China.

D. The Feminine Mystique by Betty Friedan (1963) critiques domestic confinement of women and sparked second-wave feminism.

58. D. Prasar Bharati Act: Enacted in 1990 (implemented later), it marked the beginning of autonomous public broadcasting in India.

B. National Policy for Empowerment of Women: Adopted in 2001, it emphasized gender-sensitive media and elimination of stereotypes.

C. OTT Platform guidelines under IT Rules: Introduced in 2021, these addressed regulation of digital and streaming content including gender concerns.

A. National Broadcasting Policy drafts: Initiated in 2023–24, these are the most recent efforts to frame a comprehensive media policy.

Since none of the given options match the correct chronological sequence D, B, C, A, the answer is NONE.

59. A. Beijing Declaration and Platform for Action: Adopted in 1995, it was a landmark global framework for advancing gender equality.

B. Millennium Development Goals (MDG): Introduced in 2000, included gender equality as a key development goal.

D. "UN Women" established: Formed in 2010 as a dedicated UN body to promote gender equality and women's empowerment.

C. Sustainable Development Goals (SDG): Adopted in 2015, with Goal 5 specifically focusing on achieving gender equality globally.

60. B. Filing of Petition: The process begins when a party files a petition before the family court to initiate the case.

A. Conciliation attempt by the court: The court then tries reconciliation between parties as family courts prioritize settlement.

C. Evidence and hearing between parties: If conciliation fails, the case proceeds with presentation of evidence and arguments.

D. Decree or order pronounced: Finally, the court delivers its judgment or order based on the proceedings.

61. D. Consult code of ethics for your institution: The first step is to understand the ethical guidelines and standards governing research within the institution.

C. Apply to the institutional board: After designing the study according to ethical norms, approval must be obtained from the ethics committee or IRB.

A. Informed consent forms and confidentiality: Once approval is granted, participants are informed about the study and their consent is taken while ensuring confidentiality.

B. Avoid deceiving participants and collecting harmful information: During the research process, ethical conduct is maintained by avoiding harm and deception.

62. A. Family Planning Programme: Launched in 1952, it was the earliest initiative focusing on population control and reproductive health in India.

C. Reproductive and Child Health Programme: Introduced in 1997, it expanded focus to maternal and child health along with reproductive services.

D. National Population Policy: Announced in 2000, it aimed at stabilizing population and improving health indicators.

B. National Health Mission: Launched in 2013 (as an umbrella over NRHM and NUHM), it integrated various health programmes for comprehensive healthcare delivery.

63. A. Zero Hunger (Goal 2): Placed early in SDGs focusing on ending hunger and improving nutrition.

C. Quality Education (Goal 4): Comes next, emphasizing inclusive and equitable education.

D. Gender Equality (Goal 5): Follows education, highlighting empowerment of women and girls.

B. Reduced Inequalities (Goal 10): Comes later, addressing disparities within and among countries.

64. C. Department of Women and Child Development: Established in 1985 under the Ministry of Human Resource Development as the first dedicated institutional mechanism for women and child issues.

A. National Commission for Women: Set up in 1992 as a statutory body to review safeguards and address grievances related to women's rights.

D. Ministry of Women and Child Development: Formed in 2006 as an independent ministry, strengthening focus on women's empowerment policies.

B. NITI Aayog's Women Entrepreneurship Platform: Launched in 2018 to promote and support women entrepreneurs in India.

65. D. The Hindu Widow Remarriage Act: Enacted in 1856 during the colonial period, it legalized widow remarriage and was an early social reform law.

A. The Child Marriage Restraint Act (Sarda Act): Passed in 1929, it aimed to curb child marriages by fixing minimum marriageable ages.

C. The Hindu Marriage Act: Enacted in 1955 after independence, it codified Hindu marriage laws including divorce and monogamy.

B. The Protection of Women from Domestic Violence Act: Passed in 2005, it provided legal protection against domestic abuse.

Since none of the given options match the correct chronological sequence D, A, C, B, the answer is NONE.

66. A. Kate Millett – Correct. Kate Millett is a major radical feminist known for analyzing patriarchy in Sexual Politics.

B. Shulamith Firestone – Correct. Shulamith Firestone is a key radical feminist who linked gender oppression with biological reproduction.

C. Mary Wollstonecraft – Incorrect. She is associated with liberal feminism and early feminist thought, not radical feminism.

D. Gayatri Spivak – Incorrect. She is a postcolonial feminist thinker, not a radical feminist.

Radical feminism focuses on patriarchy as the root cause of women's oppression, which is reflected in the works of Millett and Firestone.

67. A. Feminist legal studies and advocacy for women's rights – Correct. Flavia Agnes is widely known for her work in legal reform and women's rights.

B. Queer theory and performativity – Incorrect. This area is mainly associated with Judith Butler.

C. Feminist philosophy and pedagogy – Incorrect. These are not her primary contributions.

D. Founding Majlis – Correct. She founded Majlis, a legal and cultural resource centre in Mumbai working on women's issues.

Thus, options A and D correctly represent her contributions.

68. A. **Uma Chakravarti – Incorrect.** She is known for work on gender, caste, and history, not specifically media and beauty standards.

B. **Antonio Gramsci – Incorrect.** He focused on cultural hegemony, not directly on femininity and beauty standards.

C. **Naomi Wolf – Correct.** Naomi Wolf critiqued beauty standards in The Beauty Myth, showing how media reinforces unrealistic ideals of femininity.

D. **Susan Bordo – Correct.** Susan Bordo analyzed body image and cultural pressures on women, especially through media representations.

Both Wolf and Bordo critically examine how media shapes and enforces idealized femininity.

69. A. **Increase in case burden – Correct.** Motherhood often increases caregiving responsibilities and emotional as well as physical workload.

B. **Rejoining workforce – Correct.** Many women face challenges in returning to work due to career breaks and workplace biases.

C. **Increase in job opportunities – Incorrect.** Motherhood often limits opportunities rather than increasing them.

D. **Increase in leisure time – Incorrect.** Leisure time usually decreases due to added responsibilities.

Thus, motherhood is associated with increased burdens and challenges in balancing work and family life.

70. A. **Lack of consent and bodily autonomy – Correct.** Genital mutilation violates fundamental rights to bodily integrity and informed consent.

B. **Psychological effects – Correct.** It can cause long-term trauma, anxiety, and emotional distress among survivors.

C. **No risk of infection – Incorrect.** There is actually a high risk of infection, complications, and health hazards.

D. **The intense pain of cutting – Correct.** The procedure is extremely painful and often performed without anesthesia.

Thus, arguments against genital mutilation include lack of consent, severe pain, and psychological harm.

71. A. **It is a global movement of women – Correct.** The One Billion Rising is an international campaign involving women across the world.

B. **It was founded by Monique Wilson – Incorrect.** It was initiated by Eve Ensler (now V), though Monique Wilson is associated with its leadership.

C. **Its aim was to end sexual violence against women – Correct.** The movement focuses on raising awareness and ending violence against women and girls.

D. **It was started in 2009 – Incorrect.** It began in 2012 as part of a global campaign.

Therefore, options A and C are correct.

72. A. **Privileged - Marginalized – Correct.** Chandra Talpade Mohanty critiques how Third World women are often homogenized as marginalized in contrast to privileged Western women.

B. **Colonizers - Colonized – Correct.** She emphasizes colonial power relations in shaping identities and representations of Third World women.

C. **Atheist - Spiritual – Incorrect.** This opposition is not central to her argument.

D. **Good - Bad – Incorrect.** This is not part of her analytical framework.

Her work highlights power hierarchies and critiques Western feminist generalizations.

73. A. **Article 21 – Correct.** The Supreme Court derived guidelines from the right to life and dignity under Article 21 of the Constitution.

B. **Directive Principle of State Policy – Correct.** The court also referred to constitutional principles promoting justice and equality.

C. **Kyoto Protocol – Incorrect.** It is related to environmental issues, not workplace harassment.

D. **Criminal Amendment Bill 2019 – Incorrect.** This came much later and is unrelated to the Vishakha judgment (1997).

Thus, the guidelines were based on constitutional provisions ensuring dignity and justice.

74. A. **SDG-3 – Incorrect.** Although health is a component in GII, this option is not typically taken as the primary overlap in such questions.

B. **SDG-4 – Correct.** It focuses on education, which is directly measured in GDI and GII through indicators like years of schooling and educational attainment.

C. **SDG-5 – Correct.** It directly addresses gender equality, aligning fully with the purpose of GDI and GII in measuring gender disparities.

D. **SDG-11 – Incorrect.** It relates to sustainable cities and is not directly used in calculating gender indices.

Thus, SDG-4 and SDG-5 are the most appropriate overlaps with GDI and GII.

75. A. **Problematize social conditions as they are – Correct.** Critical scholarship questions existing social structures and assumptions.

B. **Can only be addressed through intersectionality – Correct.** It emphasizes multiple, intersecting forms of inequality.

C. **Can be addressed by using single lens – Incorrect.** Critical scholarship rejects single-perspective analysis.

D. **In the interwoven ways it gets played out in real life – Correct.** It studies how power and inequality operate in complex, real-life contexts.

Thus, critical scholarship involves questioning systems and analyzing intersecting realities.

76.
- **A. The monstrous feminine psychology – III. Barbara Creed:** Barbara Creed developed the concept of the "monstrous feminine," analyzing how women are represented as monstrous in horror films and cultural texts.
- **B. Critique of Western Feminisms homogenisation of the Third World Women – IV. Chandra Talpade Mohanty:** Chandra Talpade Mohanty critiqued Western feminism for treating Third World women as a single, homogeneous group.
- **C. Ecriture Feminine – I. Helene Cixous:** Helene Cixous introduced this concept, encouraging women to write from their own experiences and bodies.

- **D. The Sex/Gender System – II. Gayle Rubin:** Gayle Rubin explained how societies organize sexuality and gender roles through social systems.

77. - **A. R.W. Connell – IV. Hegemonic Masculinity:** R. W. Connell introduced the concept of hegemonic masculinity to explain dominant forms of masculinity in society.
- **B. Eve Kosofsky Sedgwick – II. Epistemology of the Closet:** Eve Kosofsky Sedgwick is known for this work, which explores knowledge and secrecy around sexuality in queer theory.
- **C. Kimberle Crenshaw – I. Intersectionality:** Kimberlé Crenshaw coined intersectionality to explain overlapping systems of oppression like race and gender.
- **D. Gayatri Chakravorty Spivak – III. Subaltern Voice:** Gayatri Chakravorty Spivak discussed the concept of the subaltern and questioned whether marginalized voices can be heard.

78. - **A. Lack of collaterals for loans – IV. Collateral free micro-credit and Government Guarantee Scheme:** This solution directly addresses financial barriers by enabling women to access loans without traditional collateral requirements.
- **B. Gender stereotyping in business choices – I. Exposure visits, mentorship and training in non-traditional sectors:** These initiatives help break stereotypes by encouraging women to enter diverse and non-traditional fields.
- **C. Limited Market Access – II. E-commerce training and participation in trade fairs:** These measures expand market reach and visibility for women entrepreneurs.
- **D. Time Poverty due to household burden – III. Affordable childcare, community kitchen and flexible work schedule:** These supports reduce domestic workload and allow women to engage in economic activities.

79. - **A. First Five Year Plan – III. Welfare orientation, prioritization of family planning and maternal health:** Early planning focused on basic welfare and health concerns.
- **B. Fifth Five Year Plan – II. Women's welfare to development:** This phase marked a shift from welfare to development-oriented approaches for women.
- **C. Ninth Five Year Plan – I. Empowerment as a central goal, introduction of women component plan:** This plan emphasized women's empowerment and targeted resource allocation.
- **D. Eleventh Five Year Plan – IV. Inclusive growth with gender budgeting:** This plan focused on inclusive development and integrating gender budgeting into policy.

80. - **A. Experimental Design – II. Difficulty in capturing dynamic social change:** Experimental methods are controlled and structured, making it hard to reflect changing real-life social conditions.
- **B. Surveys – I. Risk of superficial data, response bias:** Surveys rely on self-reported data, which may be limited in depth and prone to biased responses.
- **C. Ethnography – IV. Researcher subjectivity, time intensive:** Ethnographic studies involve deep immersion, making them time-consuming and influenced by researcher interpretation.
- **D. Case Studies – III. Limited ability to generalize:** Case studies focus on specific instances, making it difficult to apply findings broadly.

81. - **A. Sheila Rowbotham – II. Hidden from History:** Sheila Rowbotham explored women's historical experiences often ignored in mainstream history.
- **B. Ellen Moers – III. Literary Women:** Ellen Moers analyzed women's contributions to literature.
- **C. Elaine Showalter – IV. A Literature of Their Own:** Elaine Showalter examined the tradition of women's writing in English literature.
- **D. Juliet Mitchell – I. Psychoanalysis and Feminism:** Juliet Mitchell combined psychoanalysis with feminist theory.

82. - **A. Sandra Harding – II. Feminist Standpoint:** Sandra Harding is known for developing feminist standpoint theory, emphasizing knowledge from marginalized positions.
- **B. Donna Haraway – III. Situated Knowledge:** Donna Haraway introduced the concept of situated knowledge, arguing that knowledge is context-specific and partial.
- **C. Heidi Hartmann – IV. Socialist Feminism:** Heidi Hartmann is associated with socialist feminism, linking patriarchy with capitalism.
- **D. Judith Stacey – I. Feminist Ethnography:** Judith Stacey contributed to feminist ethnography, focusing on reflexivity and ethics in research.

83. - **A. Uma Chakravarti – III. The Life and Times of Pandita Ramabai (1998):** Uma Chakravarti authored this important feminist historical work examining gender and social reform.
- **B. Prem Chowdhary – IV. The Veiled Women (1994):** Prem Chowdhry analyzed gender relations and patriarchy in rural Haryana.
- **C. Kamladevi Chattopadhyay – I. Indian Women's Battle for Freedom (1983):** Kamaladevi Chattopadhyay documented women's contributions to the independence movement.
- **D. Neera Desai – II. Women in Modern India (1977):** Neera Desai produced a foundational text for Women's Studies in India.

84. - **A. Sustainable Development Goals – II. 2015:** Adopted by the United Nations in 2015 as a global development agenda.
- **B. Universal Declaration of Human Rights – III. 1948:** Adopted by the UN General Assembly as a foundational human rights document.
- **C. Convention on the Elimination of All Forms of Discrimination Against Women (CEDAW) – IV. 1979:** Adopted to address discrimination against women globally.
- **D. Beijing Platform of Action – I. 1995:** Adopted at the Fourth World Conference on Women as a key framework for gender equality.

85. • **A. Nirbhaya Fund – II. 2013:** Established to enhance safety and security of women in India.
  - **B. Ujjawala Scheme – I. 2007:** Launched to prevent trafficking and rehabilitate victims.
  - **C. Beti Bachao Beti Padhao – III. 2015:** Initiated to address declining child sex ratio and promote girls' education.
  - **D. Mahila Shakti Kendra – IV. 2017:** Launched to empower rural women through community participation.

86. • **A. Ramabai Ranade – II. Seva Sadan Society:** Ramabai Ranade was associated with Seva Sadan, working for women's education and empowerment.
  - **B. Saralabala Devi Chaudhurani – III. Bharat Stri Mandal:** Sarala Devi Chaudhurani founded Bharat Stri Mahamandal to promote women's education and unity.
  - **C. Kamaladevi Chattopadhyay – IV. All India Women's Association:** Kamaladevi Chattopadhyay was associated with women's organizations like AIWC and worked for women's rights.
  - **D. Vina Mazumdar – I. Centre for Women's Development Studies:** Vina Mazumdar was a founding figure of CWDS and a pioneer in Women's Studies in India.

87. • **A. Mahila E-Haat – I. Online marketing for women entrepreneurs:** It is a digital platform to support women entrepreneurs in marketing their products.
  - **B. She-Box Portal – IV. Provides a single window platform** for women to register workplace sexual harassment complaints.
  - **C. Nari Shakti Portal – II. Launched for information on women-related schemes:** It serves as a repository of schemes and initiatives for women.
  - **D. SAMARTH Scheme – III. Capacity building for women entrepreneurs:** It focuses on skill development and empowerment of women.

88. • **A. Sudhir Kakar – IV. The Inner World:** Sudhir Kakar explored psychological dimensions of Indian society and identity.
  - **B. Mary E. John – I. Women's Studies: A Reader:** Mary E. John edited this foundational text in Women's Studies.
  - **C.V. Geetha – II. Theorizing Feminism:** Gender: V. Geetha contributed significantly to feminist theory and gender discourse.
  - **D. Leela Dube – III. Anthropological Exploration in Gender:** Leela Dube worked extensively on gender in anthropology.

89. • **A. Avunculocal residence – III. A married couple lives with the husband's mother's brother:** This pattern is seen in some matrilineal societies.
  - **B. Neolocal residence – IV. A married couple establishes residence separate from both sets of parents:** Common in modern societies.
  - **C. Ambilocal residence – II. A married couple may choose either matrilocal or patrilocal residence:** It allows flexibility in residence choice.
  - **D. Matrilocal residence – I. A married couple lives near or with the wife's relatives:** Common in matrilineal systems.

90. • **A. Marilyn Strathern – III. Women in Between (1972):** Marilyn Strathern worked on gender relations in anthropology.
  - **B. Shirley Ardener – I. Perceiving Women (1975):** Shirley Ardener focused on women's perspectives in anthropology.
  - **C. Lila Abu-Lughod – IV. Veiled Sentiments (1986):** Lila Abu-Lughod studied gender and emotion in Bedouin society.
  - **D. Annette Weiner – II. Women of Value, Men of Renown (1976):** Annette Weiner examined gender and exchange systems.

91. The passage clearly states that the year 2025 marks 30 years since the Beijing Declaration and Platform for Action. This milestone highlights three decades of global efforts toward gender equality. It reflects both achievements and continuing challenges. Therefore, option 2 correctly matches the information given.

92. The passage explains that the Beijing +30 Action Agenda is meant to address the remaining gaps in gender equality. It aims to push forward progress toward the 2030 Sustainable Development Goals. It is not just celebratory but forward-looking and action-oriented. Hence, option 3 is correct.

93. The passage explicitly mentions that when women's rights are upheld, families, communities, and economies benefit. This shows that women's empowerment has broad societal impact. It contributes to overall development and well-being. Therefore, option 4 is correct.

94. The passage highlights two major digital-era challenges: the digital divide and harmful stereotypes reinforced by AI. These issues limit women's access to opportunities and reinforce inequality. They represent the dual challenge in the digital context. Thus, option 4 is correct.

95. The passage notes that global parity in girls' education has been achieved as a major milestone. It also mentions improvements in maternal health and political representation. Among the given options, only parity in girls' education reflects positive progress. Therefore, option 2 is correct.

96. The passage clearly states that women are exploited in ways connected to their reproductive roles and societal expectations of womanhood. These gendered roles make them particularly vulnerable during conflicts. This form of exploitation is specifically highlighted. Hence, option 4 is correct.

97. The passage explains that women and girls are targeted because they are seen as carriers of cultural identity and reproduction of the opposing group. This perception makes them symbolic targets in conflict. It directly answers the question. Therefore, option 1 is correct.

98. The passage emphasizes that women are not just victims but also active agents. They make decisions, respond to situations, and organize collectively. This shows their agency and resilience. Hence, option 3 is correct.

99. The passage highlights that formal peace processes often exclude women and girls from meaningful roles. This is identified as a major limitation. It shows lack of inclusivity in decision-making. Therefore, option 3 is correct.

100. The passage mentions that women may take on new responsibilities when male heads are absent. This can lead to changes in status and challenge traditional gender roles. It reflects altered gender relations during conflict. Thus, option 2 is correct.

Previous Years' Paper

National Testing Agency (NTA)

UGC-NET Junior Research Fellowship & Assistant Professor Eligibility Exam

WOMEN'S STUDIES, JUNE-2025

(Exam held on 25-06-2025)

PAPER-II

1. National Commission for Women (NCW) is:
1. Established under the National Commission for Women Act, 1992
2. Established under the National Commission for Women Act, 1990
3. Established under the National Commission for Women Act, 2000
4. Established in 1988 with recommendation of the National Perspective Plan for Women

2. The Bengal Sati Regulation which abolished the prevalence of Sati was passed in the year:

1. 1920 2. 1829
3. 1860 4. 1856

3. Andrea Dworkin and Catherine Mackinnon argued that:
1. Pornography is a form of legitimate erotica
2. Pornography is pleasurable
3. Pornography is dangerous
4. Pornography should be controlled as a civil offense, a civil rights violation

4. Gang Rape under Section 376 D where a woman is raped by one or more persons constituting a group, each of those persons shall be punished with rigorous imprisonment for a term which shall not be less than:

1. Twelve years 2. Five years
3. Ten years 4. Twenty years

5. The original class distinction is between men and women. The women's oppression provides a conceptual model for understanding all other forms of oppression. This 'radical feminist' thought is represented in the works of:

1. Engels 2. Harrier Taylor Mill
3. Shulamith Firestone 4. Carol Gilligan

6. Feminists who have critiqued Freud but used him productively to address biological determinism are:
1. Karen Horney & Luce Irigaray
2. Luce Irigaray & Margaret Benston
3. Karen Horney & Dalla Costa
4. Selma James & Dalla Costa

7. Identify the odd one out in the list of some important Black feminists?
1. Bell Hooks
2. Patricia Hill Collins
3. Audre Lorde
4. Betty Friedan

8. What is the key distinction between productive and non-productive work in Classical Economic Theory?
1. Productive work is paid: non-productive work is unpaid
2. Productive work is done by men; non-productive work by women
3. Productive work includes leisure; non-productive work includes travel .
4. Productive work is emotional labor

9. Which of the following is a key trait commonly associated with successful entrepreneurs?
1. Resistance to change
2. Aversion to risk
3. Innovativeness and risk-taking ability
4. Dependence on external motivation

10. What role do Self Help Groups (SHGs) primarily play in empowering women?
1. Promoting Consumerism
2. Encouraging traditional roles only
3. Providing collective savings and access to micro credit
4. Limiting access to financial services

11. What is the core argument of feminist epistemology?

1. Knowledge is always objective and value-free
2. Only women can produce valid feminist knowledge
3. Knowledge is socially constructed and shaped by gendered experiences
4. Scientific methods are superior to qualitative approaches

12. Nari Shakti Vandan Adhiniyam allocating 33 percent of the seats to women in the directly elected Lok Sabha, state legislative Assembly and Delhi Legislative Assembly was the:

1. One hundred and Seventh Amendment of the Constitution
2. One hundred and Twentieth Amendment of the Constitution
3. One hundred and Sixth Amendment of the Constitution
4. One hundred and Twenty Eight Amendment

13. Which of these women is referred to as "Gandhi of Grain"?

1. Mahashewta Devi
2. Bina Agarwal
3. Vandana Shiva
4. Srilatha Batliwala

14. The phrase "Third Wave Feminism" was coined by:

1. Anita Hill in 1991
2. Margaret Sanger in 1990
3. Rebecca Walker in 1992
4. Eve Ensler in 1993

15. Radha Krishnan Commission also known as the University Education Commission analysed the problem of women education at the college and university level in:

1. 1948-1949
2. 1950-1951
3. 1960-1961
4. 1961-1962

16. Girls and boys develop different relational capacities and senses of self as a result of growing up in a family in which women are mothers. This argument was made by:

1. Julia Kristeva
2. Nancy Chodorow
3. Virginia Woolf
4. Susan Brownmiller

17. In 2023, India's ranking in the Global Gender Gap Index was:

1. 127 out of 146 countries
2. 125 out of 150 countries
3. 146 out of 150 countries
4. 105 out of 146 countries

18. Sexual intercourse by a person in authority where consent of the victim is obtained under compelling conditions is

1. defined under Section 375
2. defined under Section 376
3. defined under Section 350
4. defined under Section 354

19. Cinema is a technology of scopophilia where women provide the scopophilic pleasure and are passive sexual objects. This is commented by:

1. Laura Butler
2. Laura Mulvey
3. Teresa de Lauretis
4. Kate Millet

20. As per Global Gender Gap Index Report 2024, within South Asia, India's rank is:

1. Fifth
2. Fourth
3. Third
4. Second

21. What is the role of critical thinking in feminist pedagogy?

1. To reinforce dominant narratives and power structure
2. To challenge dominant narratives and promote critical consciousness
3. To focus on rote memorization and standardized testing
4. To ignore issues of power and privilege

22. SHISHU Loan under Mudra Yojana Scheme provides loan upto:

1. ₹ 25,000 (for startup and new business)
2. ₹ 50,000 (for startup and new business)
3. ₹ 75,000 (for startup and new business)
4. ₹ 20,000 (for startup and new business)

23. According to feminists, what is the key factor in shaping an individual's gender identity?

1. Biological factors
2. Prenatal influence
3. Social and cultural norms
4. Cognitive development

24. The encoding and decoding model of communication was developed by cultural theorist:

1. Stuart Hall
2. George Bernard Shaw
3. Paul Gilory
4. Lawrence Grossberg

25. The popular article "Dalit women talk differently" has been authored by:

1. Sharmila Rege
2. Uma Chakravarti
3. Shailaja Paik
4. Gopal Guru

26. What is the relationship between Queer Theory and Feminism?

1. Queer Theory and Feminism are completely unrelated fields of study.
2. Queer Theory is a branch of feminism focused solely on women's issues.

3. Queer Theory shares with feminism an interest in deconstructing traditional gender roles and hierarchies.
4. Queer Theory opposes feminist principles and seeks to reinforce gender roles.

27. What is a hybrid of organism/nature and machine/ culture as a creature of "permanently partial identities"?

1. Amazonian 2. Cyborg
3. Indigenous 4. Bribri

28. Who was the Warrior Queen of Nagaland, who emerged as a symbol of resistance against British Colonial rule?

1. Zenobia
2. Rani Gaidinliu
3. Rani Abbakka Chowta
4. Rani Rudrama Devi

29. Who among the following was involved in a landmark legal case involving her marriage as a child bride. The case influenced the enactment of the "Age of Consent Act" in 1891?

1. Durgabai Deshmukh
2. Tarabai Shinde
3. Kamaladevi Chattopadhyay
4. Rukhma Bai

30. How does hegemonic masculinity affect men who do not fit its ideal?

1. It leads to greater acceptance and inclusion of diverse masculinities.
2. It results in social marginalization and pressure to conform to dominant masculine norms.
3. It has no effect on men who do not fit the ideal.
4. It encourages men to embrace strong emotional expression.

31. In a stride towards gender neutrality and inclusivity, the recently enacted Digital Personal Data Protection Act 2023 has demolished conventional norms by:

1. Adopting the pronouns 'She/her' to address inclusivity of all genders
2. Adopting the pronouns 'they/them' to address individuals of all genders
3. Adopting the pronouns 'he/him' to address individuals of all genders
4. Adopting the pronouns 'it/they' to address individuals of all genders

32. Who expressed in her work "Gender and Nation" that women occupy a contested space within the discourse of nation and nationalism?

1. Gayatri C Spivak 2. Lata Mani
3. Nira Yuval Davis 4. Teresa de Lauretis

33. Which post-colonial feminist thinker is known for critiquing the western feminist tendency to homogenize the experiences of all women worldwide, particularly in her essay "Under Western Eyes"?

1. Radha Kumar
2. Bell Hooks
3. Chandra Talpade Mohanty
4. Audre Lorde

34. The famous Street Play of the 1980s "Om Swaha" dealt with:

1. Hunger 2. Communal Violence
3. Dowry Death 4. Colonial Exploitation

35. Which factor most directly contributes to the growth of women in agri-business?

1. Decline in crop production
2. Traditional farming methods
3. Access to markets, credit, and training
4. Monoculture practices

36. Which International Convention is considered as the most comprehensive framework for advancing women's rights globally?

1. CEDAW-1979, Convention adopted by the United Nations General Assembly
2. UDHR-1948, Convention adopted by the United Nations General Assembly
3. CRC-1989, Convention adopted by the United Nations General Assembly
4. ILO Convention No. 87- 1948, Convention adopted by the International Labour Organisation (ILO)

37. According to Friedrich Engels, the origin of women's subordination lies in:

1. Lack of access to modern education
2. Biological differences between men and women
3. The rise of private property and class society
4. Women's inability to participate in politics

38. Which Sustainable Development Goals (SDGs) are directly related to Gender Equality & Women Empowerment and Climate Action?

1. SDG 5 and SDG 1 2. SDG 5 and SDG 3
3. SDG 5 and SDG 9 4. SDG 5 and SDG 13

39. How has the 73rd Constitutional Amendment empowered women in Panchayati Raj institutions?

1. By reserving 33% of seats for women in local governance.
2. By appointing women only to advisory roles.
3. By eliminating elections for rural positions.
4. By restricting women's voting rights in villages.

40. Under which five-year plan was women's development first recognized as a distinct sector in India?

1. Third Five-Year Plan
2. Fifth Five-Year Plan
3. Seventh Five-Year Plan
4. Ninth Five-Year Plan

41. Arrange the following in chronological order:

A. All India Women's Conference
B. All India Muslim Women's Conference
C. Young Women Christian Association
D. Bengal Women's Education League

Choose the ***correct*** answer from the options given below:

1. C, D, B, A 2. D. B, A, C
3. A. B, C, D 4. C, A, B, D

42. Arrange the #Movement chronologically:

A. #Times Up Movement
B. #HeForShe Movement
C. #MeToo Movement
D. #NiUnaMenos Movement

Choose the ***correct*** answer from the options given below:

1. B, D, C, A 2. A, B, C, D
3. B, C, D, A 4. D, A, B, C

43. Arrange the following United Nations Conferences on Women in correct chronological order:

A. Nairobi Conference
B. Beijing Conference
C. Mexico City Conference
D. Copenhagen Conference

Choose the ***correct*** answer from the options given below:

1. C, D, A, B 2. A, B, C, D
3. B, C, D, A 4. D, A, B, C

44. Arrange the key events related to the development of women's studies in chronological order.

A. Establishment of the women's studies centres by UGC
B. Establishment of the National Commission for Women (NCW)
C. The research for Women's Studies Programme at SNDT University
D. First All India Women Conference

Choose the ***correct*** answer from the options given below:

1. A, C, B, D 2. B, D, A, C
3. D, C, A, B 4. A. B, C, D

45. Arrange the list of Chairpersons of National Commission for Women (NCW) as per their chronological appointment:

A. Girija Vyas
B. Mohini Giri
C. Jayanti Patnaik
D. Lalitha Kumaramangalam
E. Rekha Sharma

Choose the ***correct*** answer from the options given below:

1. C, B, A, D, E 2. A, B, C, D, E
3. C, A, B, E, D 4. B, A, C, E, D

46. Arrange the steps involved in Quantitative Research:

A. Review of Literature
B. Identification of problem
C. Framing the Questionnaire and data collection
D. Coding and Analysis of data

Choose the ***correct*** answer from the options given below:

1. A, B, C, D 2. B, A, C, D
3. D, C, A, B 4. C, B, A, D

47. Arrange the following treaties and conventions promoting women's rights in chronological order:

A. Inter-American Convention on the Prevention, Punishment & Eradication on Violence against Women
B. CEDAW
C. Istanbul Convention
D. International Labour Organisation Convention No. 190 on Violence and Harassment

Choose the ***correct*** answer from the options given below:

1. A, C, B, D 2. B, A, C, D
3. B, D, C, A 4. B, C, A, D

48. Arrange the following in chronological order:

A. Lakhpati Didi Yojana
B. Namo Drone Didi Yojana
C. Mahila Kisan Sashaktikaran Yojana
D. Mahila Kisan Pariyojana

Choose the ***correct*** answer from the options given below:

1. A, B, D, C 2. C, A, B, D
3. D, C, A, B 4. B. D, C, A

49. Organise the 17 SDGs as per their number in the list of Sustainable Development Goals.

A. Decent Work & Economic Growth
B. Partnership for the Goal
C. Gender Equality
D. Clean water & Sanitation
E. No Poverty

Choose the *correct* answer from the options given below:

1. A, B, C, D, E 2. D, C, B, A, E
3. E, C, A, D, B 4. E, C, D, A, B

50. Chronologically arrange the following Acts which have special provisions to safeguard women and their interests as per the year of their enactment.

A. The Maternity Act
B. The Hindu Marriage Act
C. The Special Marriage Act
D. The Prohibition of Child Marriage Act
E. The Commission of Sati (Prevention) Act

Choose the *correct* answer from the options given below:

1. A, B, C, D, E 2. B, A, C, E, D
3. D, A, B, C, E 4. C, B, A, E, D

51. Arrange the following committees and commission on Education as per their years of appointment.

A. National Education Policy
B. Kothari Commission
C. Mudaliar Commission
D. Radhakrishnan Commission

Choose the *correct* answer from the options given below:

1. D, C, B, A 2. B, C, D, A
3. C, D, B, A 4. D, B, C, A

52. Arrange the following in chronological order:

A. National Organisation for Women (NOW)
B. The Beijing Declaration and Beijing Platform for Action
C. The Seneca Falls Convention
D. The Convention on the Elimination of all forms of Discrimination Against Women (CEDAW)

Choose the *correct* answer from the options given below:

1. A, C, D, B 2. C, B, A, D
3. B, C, D, A 4. C, A, D, B

53. Arrange the emergence of the debates in Feminism chronologically:

A. Intersectionality
B. Suffrage
C. Notion of Sisterhood
D. Difference and Sameness Debate

Choose the *correct* answer from the options given below:

1. A, B, D, C 2. B, C, D, A
3. C, A, D, B 4. C, D, B, A

54. Arrange the following books in chronological order:

A. Barbara Creed's 'The Monstrous-Feminine'
B. Teresa de Lauretis 'Technologies of Gender'
C. Laura Mulvey's 'Visual Pleasure and Narrative Cinema'
D. Kaja Silverman's 'The Acoustic Mirror'

Choose the *correct* answer from the options given below:

1. A, C, B, D 2. C, B, D, A
3. B, D, A, C 4. B, A, C, D

55. Arrange the following Acts in the chronological order:

A. Protection of Children from Sexual Offences (POCSO Act)
B. Equal Remuneration Act
C. Protection of Women from Domestic Violence
D. Medical Termination of Pregnancy (MTA) Act

Choose the *correct* answer from the options given below:

1. A, C, B, D 2. B, C, D, A
3. C, B, A, D 4. D, B, C, A

56. According to the Government of India's Handbook on Gender Budgeting which of the following initiatives were undertaken by the state of Rajasthan to institutionalise Gender Budgeting.

A. Formation of a Gender budget cell under the Department of Finance in 2011.
B. Development of a four-category frame-work for the Gender Budget statement.
C. Constitution of the high-level committee under the Chairmanship of the Finance Secretary.
D. Gender appraisal of budget proposals by seven key departments.

Choose the *correct* answer from the options given below:

1. A & B Only 2. B & D Only
3. A & C Only 4. A & D Only

57. Why has it become common since the 1980s to use the plural form 'Feminisms' when talking about Feminism?

A. All feminists do not share the basic commitment to ending female oppression.
B. All feminists do not approach the problem from the same philosophical or political base.
C. To show the richness of feminist legacy of diversity and heterogeneity of positions.
D. Feminists have always emerged from dive[illegible] cultural and political perspectives and fo[illegible] on issues germane to the time and locat[illegible] inhabit.

Choose the ***correct*** answer from the options given below:

1. A, B & C Only 2. A, C & D Only
3. B, C & D Only 4. A, B & D Only

58. What is the role of National Commission for Women (NCW) in relation to digital technology laws in India?

A. It operates within a consultative and advisory capacity.
B. It has control over data protection policies and the implementation of the personal Data Protection Bill.
C. Role in advocating for women's rights, advising on policy changes and raising awareness about online safety.
D. It has the power to investigate crimes and enforce digital technology laws.

Choose the ***correct*** answer from the options given below:

1. A & C Only 2. B & D Only
3. A & D Only 4. A & B Only

59. Feminization of poverty is primarily measured using three International Indices. These are:

A. The Gender Development Index
B. Global Gender Gap Index
C. The Gender Empowerment Measure
D. The Human Poverty Index

Choose the ***correct*** answer from the options given below:

1. A, B & C Only 2. A, C & D Only
3. B, C & D Only 4. D, A & B Only

60. What is the significance of Hypotheses?

A. It leads to realiability & validity.
B. It helps collecting useful facts.
C. It sets the direction of research.
D. It contributes to formation of theories.

Choose the ***correct*** answer from the options given below:

1. A, B & C Only 2. A, D & B Only
3. B, C & D Only 4. C, A & B Only

61. Which are correct about Sukanya Samriddhi Yojana?

A. Money can be deposited only by the parents.
B. The maximum limit for deposit in the account is ₹ 1,50,000 per year.
C. Interest rates are calculated on the 10th day of every month.
D. Even after maturity the account will earn interest.

Choose the ***correct*** answer from the options given below:

1. A & B Only 2. B & C Only
3. B & D Only 4. C & A Only

62. The objectives of CBSE merit scholarships scheme are:

A. to provide scholarships to meritorious single girl child student.
B. have passed the CBSE Class X Examination with 60% or more marks and are continuing their further school education of Class XI and XII.
C. the amount of scholarship shall be ₹ 500 per month.
D. a scholarship awarded under the scheme shall be paid for a maximum period of three year.

Choose the ***correct*** answer from the options given below:

1. A, B & C Only 2. B, C & D Only
3. C, D & A Only 4. A, D & B Only

63. The Annapurna Scheme is designed for women entrepreneurs to:

A. start textile business
B. food based business
C. can access loan up to ₹ 50,000
D. can access loan up to ₹ 2 lakhs

Choose the ***correct*** answer from the options given below:

1. A & B Only 2. B & D Only
3. A & C Only 4. B & C Only

64. Gita Sen emphasizes control over female sexuality as a means of her subordination. She holds:

A. in India, unlike western women, women are not turned into sexual objects principally via the commodity form.
B. sexual objectification of women is direct and personal and impacts the labour market.
C. landholding classes control and guard women's sexuality to ensure paternity of children.
D. public spaces are dominated and controlled by men and women. Women are controlled by violence in these spaces.
E. sexual control is not important for those with no land.

Choose the ***correct*** answer from the options given below:

1. B, C, D & E Only 2. A, B, C & D Only
3. B, D & E Only 4. A, B & D Only

65. Based on her study of female-headed households in Mexican shanty towns, Sylvia Chant found that:

A. women and children suffer from secondary poverty in poor households where man holds part of his wages for personal expenditures.

B. female heads were better off financially once their husbands had died or deserted.

C. housework is not shared in single women headed families.

D. household work is better shared by children in single women headed households.

E. authority patterns in male headed families are repressive for women & children.

Choose the ***correct*** answer from the options given below:

1. C & E Only
2. A & E Only
3. A, C & E Only
4. A, B, D & E Only

66. Gender Trouble is:

A. one of the founding texts of queer theory.

B. is critical of a pervasive heterosexual assumption of feminist theory.

C. is homophobic.

D. is written by Judith Butler

E. is written by Monique Wittig

Choose the ***most appropriate*** answer from the options given below:

1. A, C & E Only
2. A, B & C Only
3. A, B & D Only
4. A, C & D Only

67. Feminist standpoint Epistemology begins with the idea that:

A. less powerful members of society have less knowledge.

B. less powerful members have a more complete view of social reality than others.

C. the disadvantages of their position limits their perspective.

D. the disadvantaged position gives them the potential for double vision.

E. they are unaware and insensitive to the dominant world view of the society.

Choose the ***most appropriate*** answer from the options given below:

1. A, C & E Only
2. B & D Only
3. B & E Only
4. A & E Only

68. The sexual harrassment of women at work-place (Prevention, Prohibition & Redressal Act, 2013) defines sexual harrassment as:

A. includes any unwelcome acts or behaviour

B. physical contact and advances

C. only physical and not verbal or non-verbal

D. a demand or request for sexual favours

Choose the ***most appropriate*** answer from the options given below:

1. A, B & D Only
2. A. B & C Only
3. A & C Only
4. A, C & D Only

69. Bhakti saint women's writing in India:

A. are from ancient period in India.

B. show the indigenous roots of feminism in India.

C. these writings are often reflecting women's resistance to religious patriarchies and caste subordination.

D. women saints are part of early modernity of India and show emancipatory cultural histories against Brahmanic patriarchy.

Choose the ***correct*** answer from the options given below:

1. A & D Only
2. B, C & D Only
3. A, B & C Only
4. A & B Only

70. Signs: "Journal of women in culture and society":

A. Was established by Jean W. Sacks

B. Was established by Sandra Harding

C. Was established in 1975

D. Was established in 1985

Choose the ***correct*** answer from the options given below:

1. A & C Only
2. B & C Only
3. D & A Only
4. C & D Only

71. Unlike many other 'isms' feminism does not derive its theoretical or conceptual base from any single theoretical formulation.

A. Therefore there is no specific abstract definition of feminism applicable to all women at all times.

B. Feminism is based on historically & culturally concrete realities.

C. Feminism is about levels of consciousness.

D. Patriarchy, sexism & male domination are global and will never change.

E. Legal reform is the only goal of all feminisms.

Choose the ***correct*** answer from the options given below:

1. A, D & E Only
2. A, B & C Only
3. B & C Only
4. A, B, C & E Only

72. Feminist Ethnography is:

A. a qualitative research method.

B. based on lived experiences of women using participant observation and interviews.

C. It does not challenge traditional power dynamics in research.

D. It is critical and reflexive.
E. It can be done only by female researchers.

Choose the ***correct*** answer from the options given below:

1. A, B & D Only   2. A, B & C Only
3. A, B, D & E Only   4. A, B & E Only

73. According to Amy S. Wharton in her book *The Sociology of Gender*, which of the following factors contributed to the erosion of standard working hours?

A. Growth of service sector employment
B. Emergence of dual-earner families
C. Decline in global economic inter-connectedness
D. Spread of digital technologies

Choose the ***most appropriate*** answer from the options given below:

1. A & B Only   2. A & C Only
3. B & D Only   4. A & D Only

74. Which of the following characterizes the Second-Wave of Feminism?

A. Consciousness raising as a key activity.
B. Slogan "the personal is political", became popular.
C. Addressed the men's movement and masculinity studies.
D. Addressed the needs and rights of disabled women.

Choose the ***most appropriate*** answer from the options given below:

1. A & B Only   2. A & C Only
3. B & C Only   4. B & D Only

75. How can we define the term "Gender Roles"?

A. It refers to society's concept of how men and women are expected to act.
B. Gender roles are natural.
C. Gender roles are acquired.
D. They are based on norms or standards created by society.

Choose the ***most appropriate*** answer from the options given below:

1. A, B & C Only   2. A, C & D Only
3. A, B & D Only   4. B, C & D Only

76. Match the LIST-I with LIST-II.

LIST-I	LIST-II
A. Queer Theory	I. Francoise d' Eaubonne
B. Post-Colonial Feminist Theorist	II. Raewyn Connell
C. Hegemonic Masculinity	III. Eve Kosofsky Sedgwick
D. Ecofeminism	IV. Lila Abu Lughod

Choose the ***correct*** answer from the options given below:

1. A-I, B-III, C-IV, D-II
2. A-IV, B-II, C-I, D-III
3. A-III, B-IV, C-II, D-I
4. A-II, B-I, C-III, D-IV

77. Match the LIST-I with LIST-II.

LIST-I	LIST-II
A. Liberal Feminism	I. Rejects universal female subject.
B. Marxist Feminism	II. Their conviction was that women centered politics could be devised in a women-only space.
C. Radical Feminism	III. Affirms that women's subordinate position can be addressed by political processes under democracy.
D. Post Modern Feminism	IV. Links changes in women's social condition with the overthrow of industrial capitalism.

Choose the ***correct*** answer from the options given below:

1. A-I, B-II, C-III, D-IV
2. A-III, B-IV, C-II, D-I
3. A-I, B-III, C-IV, D-II
4. A-IV, B-II, C-I, D-III

78. Match the LIST-I with LIST-II.

LIST-I	LIST-II
A. Nupi Lan (Women's War)	I. A women-only market in Imphal established since 16th century.
B. Meira Paibis (Guardians of Civil Society)	II. Women's social movement established in 1977 in the state of Manipur
C. Ima Market	III. Illustrates the struggles of a woman who after her husband's death, works as a porter to support her child
D. Likai (Tragic Tale from Meghalaya)	IV. Refers to two significant protests by women in Manipur against colonial authorities

Choose the ***correct*** answer from the options given below:

1. A-IV, B-II, C-I, D-III
2. A-II, B-III, C-IV, D-I
3. A-I, B-IV, C-III, D-II
4. A-III, B-I, C-II, D IV

79. Match the LIST-I with LIST-II.

LIST-I	LIST-II
A. Janani Suraksha Yojana (JSY)	I. Essential care to mother and newborn within 48 hours of birth
B. Janani Shishu Suraksha Karyakaram (JSSK)	II. Promote institutional deliveries by providing cash incentives to pregnant women
C. Integrated Child Development Services (ICDS)	III. Combines Anganwadi services and Poshan Abhiyan
D. Mission Poshan 2.0	IV. Subsumed under Mission Poshan 2.0

Choose the *correct* answer from the options given below:

1. A-I, B-II, C-III, D-IV
2. A-II, B-I, C-IV, D-III
3. A-II, B-III, C-IV, D-I
4. A-III, B-IV, C-I, D-II

80. Match the LIST-I with LIST-II.

LIST-I (Country)	LIST-II (Percentage)
A. Iceland	I. 87.5%
B. Finland	II. 93.5%
C. New Zealand	III. 79.7%
D. Spain	IV. 83.5%

Choose the *correct* answer from the options given below:

1. A-I, B-II, C-III, D-IV
2. A-IV, B-III, C-II, D-I
3. A-III, B-II, C-I, D-IV
4. A-II, B-I, C-IV, D-III

81. Match the LIST-I with LIST-II.

LIST-I	LIST-II
A. The European Convention on Preventing & Combating Violence against Women & Domestic Violence	I. 2003
B. The Inter-American Convention on the Prevention, Punishment & Eradication of Violence against women	II. 2004
C. Maputo Protocol	III. 1994
D. The Declaration on the Elimination of Violence Against Women in the Association of South East Asian Nation (ASEAN)	IV. 2011

Choose the *correct* answer from the options given below:

1. A-I, B-II, C-III, D-IV
2. A-IV, B-III, C-I, D-II
3. A-II, B-IV, C-III, D-I
4. A-III, B-I, C-IV, D-II

82. Match the LIST-I with LIST-II.

LIST-I (Books)	LIST-II (Authors)
A. *Controlling Women: What We Must Do Now to Save Reproductive Freedom*	I. Lauren Rankin
B. *Bodies on the Line: At the Frontlines of the Fight to Protect Abortion in America*	II. Dorothy Roberts
C. *Killing the Black Body: Race, Repro duction, and The Meaning of Liberty*	III. Boston Women's Health Book Collective
D. *Our Bodies, Ourselves*	IV. Kathryn Kolbert

Choose the *correct* answer from the options given below:

1. A-I, B-II, C-III, D-IV
2. A-IV, B-I, C-II, D-III
3. A-II, B-III, C-IV, D-I
4. A-III, B-IV, C-II, D-I

83. Match the LIST-I with LIST-II.

LIST-I (Concepts)	LIST-II (Themes)
A. Economic Development	I. Focus on health. Population and housing programmes
B. Equality	II. Women's group mobilization
C. Empowerment	III. Efficient integration of Women's work
D. Welfare	IV. Legal Rights

Choose the *correct* answer from the options given below:

1. A-I, B-II, C-III, D-IV
2. A-III, B-IV, C-II, D-I
3. A-III, B-I, C-IV, D-II
4. A-II, B-III, C-I, D-IV

84. Match the LIST-I with LIST-II.

LIST-I	LIST-II
A. Oral History	I. Long term study of people
B. Survey	II. Decentering the subject
C. Focus Group Discussions	III. Subjective reconstruction of one's life & meaning
D. Ethnography	IV. Quantitative

Choose the *correct* answer from the options given below:

1. A-I, B-IV, C-II, D-III
2. A-IV, B-II, C-III, D-I
3. A-II, B-IV, C-I, D-III
4. A-III, B-IV, C-II, D-I

85. Match the LIST-I with LIST-II.

LIST-I (Concept)	LIST-II (Authors)
A. Performativity	I. Julia Kristeva
B. Immanence & Transcendence	II. Judith Butler
C. Semiotic dimension of Language	III. Kate Millet
D. Textual sexism	IV. Simone de Beauvoir

Choose the *correct* answer from the options given below:

1. A-II, B-IV, C-I, D-III
2. A-IV, B-I, C-III, D-II
3. A-III, B-II, C-I, D-IV
4. A-II, B-IV, C-III, D-I

86. Match the LIST-I with LIST-II.

LIST-I (Approaches to development)	LIST-II (Characteristics)
A. WID	I. Influenced by Socialist Theory
B. WAD	II. Centers Environment
C. GAD	III. Dependency Theory
D. GED	IV. Modernization Theory

Choose the *correct* answer from the options given below:

1. A-III, B-I, C-IV, D-II
2. A-III, B-IV, C-I, D-II
3. A-IV, B-II, C-I, D-III
4. A-IV, B-III, C-I, D-II

87. Match the LIST-I with LIST-II.

LIST-I (Plan)	LIST-II (Focus Area)
A. Sixth Plan	I. Bringing women into the mainstream of national development
B. Seventh Plan	II. Paradigm shift from development to empowerment and benefits to women
C. Eighth Plan	III. Empowerment of women as its strategic objective
D. Ninth Plan	IV. Multi disciplinary approach with a focus on health, education and employment

Choose the *correct* answer from the options given below:

1. A-I, B-II, C-III, D IV
2. A-IV, B-I, C-II, D-III
3. A-III, B-IV, C-II, D-I
4. A-IV, B-III, C-II, D-I

88. Match the LIST-I with LIST-II.

LIST-I (Authors)	LIST-II (Publications)
A. Sharmita Ray	I. Women Doctors' Masterful Manoeuverings: Colonial Bengal, Late Nineteenth and Early Twentieth Centuries
B. Samiksha Sehrawat	II. Feminising Empire: The Association of Medical women in India and the Campaign to Found a Women's Medical Services
C. Grace Stapleton	III. Witches, Midwives and Nurses: A History of Women Healers
D. Barbara Ehrenreich & Deirdre English	IV. Pelvic Measurements in Indian Women

Choose the *correct* answer from the options given below:

1. A-I, B-II, C-III, D-IV
2. A-II, B-III, C-IV, D-I
3. A-III, B-IV, C-I, D-II
4. A-I, B-II, C-IV, D-III

89. Match the LIST-I with LIST-II.

LIST-I (Movement)	LIST-II (People)
A. Green Belt Movement	I. Rajendra Singh
B. The Navdanya Movement	II. Salim Ali
C. Birdman of India	III. Wangari Maathai
D. Waterman of India	IV. Vandana Shiva

Choose the *correct* answer from the options given below:

1. A-I, B-II, C-IV, D-III
2. A-II, B-I, C-III, D-IV
3. A-IV, B-III, C-I, D-II
4. A-III, B-IV, C-II, D-I

90. Match the LIST-I with LIST-II.

LIST-I (Authors)	LIST-II (Concepts)
A. Bina Agarwal	I. The Female Eunuch
B. Mary Wollstonecraft	II. Women and Agriculture
C. Kamla Bhasin	III. Relevance of Feminism in South Asia
D. Germaine Greer	IV. Women Rights and Education

Choose the ***correct*** answer from the options given below:

1. A-I, B-II, C-III, D-IV
2. A-II, B-IV, C-III, D-I
3. A-III, B-IV, C-II, D-I
4. A-I, B-II, C-IV, D-III

Directions (Qs. No. 91 to 95): *Read the following passage and answer the question:*

Most sports were never designed for women. They were designed to fit the physical abilities of men. Ancient Greece introduced formal sport, with the first Olympic Games in 776 BC, which included sports such as human and chariot races, wrestling, jumping, disc and javelin throwing, and more. Sport is designed to support a system of pure meritocracy- i.e., whoever is stronger, faster, and more skilled will be the winner. But related to the first problem, in most sports, if women play against men, they lose (women's soccer team against men's soccer team). From a pure meritocracy angle, women thus do not deserve the same pay. Building on the first two problems, in most sports, there is less of a market for the women's side of the game (e.g., women's soccer or women's tennis). To get gender-equal pay to work, pure meritocracy needs to be revoked and arguments need to come from a sociological/ideological point of view. Furthermore, women should celebrate the female competition as their version of the sport that is similar yet also different to the men's.

91. How were most sports originally designed?

1. To support women's physical abilities
2. To fit the physical abilities of men
3. To be gender-neutral
4. To promote teamwork and collaboration

92. What role did Ancient Greece play in the development of formal sports?

1. They introduced team sports like basketball and football.
2. They created system based on gender quality in sports.
3. They introduced the first Olympic Games, featuring sports like wrestling and chariot races.
4. They allowed women and transgender to participate in sports.

93. In a pure meritocracy, what determines the winner in sports?

1. Who is taller
2. Who is stronger, faster, and more skilled
3. Who has the most experience
4. Who is more popular

94. How could gender equal pay in sports be achieved, according to the passage?

1. By keeping meritocracy intact and reducing men's salaries.
2. By promoting women's sports to the same level as men's sports.
3. By offering equal pay regardless of performance.
4. By removing all professional sports for men.

95. What type of arguments are suggested for advocating gender equality in sports?

1. Legal arguments based on contracts and rules.
2. Sociological and Ideological arguments.
3. Financial arguments based on sponsorship.
4. Moral arguments based on fairness.

Directions (Qs. No. 96 to 100): *Read the following passage and answer the question:*

Feminism is heterogeneous and internally differentiated across contexts. This recognition makes it impossible to articulate a simple 'feminist' position on any issue, and alerts us to what Walter Mignolo has termed 'diversality'- the recognition of diversity as a universal condition (2000). Analyses that begin with the assumption of a unified and homogenous category of 'woman' may well be productively opened up to other identities by the intersectionality framework; but analyses that begin with the understanding that identity is provisional and conjunctural, would find, I have argued, that the intersectionality framework freezes notions of pre-existing individual, woman and other identities. Attention to diversality teaches us that universal frameworks generally flow from the North to the South, that the direction of this flow this is not simply coincidental and that close attention to specificities of time and place would reveal the inadequacy of universal paradigms.

96. We cannot have a simple feminist position on any issue as:

1. Women and men are not different.
2. Woman is a stable and homogenous category.
3. Intersectionality framework is not always sufficient.
4. Diversity is a universal condition.

97. How does the passage approach the understanding of identity?

1. Unified and homogenous
2. Provisional and conjunctural
3. Provisional and homogenous
4. Unified and diverse

98. Universal framework generally flowing from North to the South are critiqued because:

1. Theories must be located.
2. Comparisons and engagements with diverse feminism is not possible.
3. Comparisons are to be avoided.
4. Theories developed in the Global North are always expressions of imperialism.

99. What does Mignolo alert us to?

1. A simple feminist position
2. Intersectionality
3. Diversality
4. Universality

100. Why is Intersectionality framework problematic?

1. Law and its inability to recognize multiple identities.
2. Law and its accessibility to subordinate group globally.
3. People have simple ethical positions.
4. It supports feminist solidarity.

ANSWERS

1	**2**	**3**	**4**	**5**	**6**	**7**	**8**	**9**	**10**
2	2	4	4	3	1	4	1	3	3
11	**12**	**13**	**14**	**15**	**16**	**17**	**18**	**19**	**20**
3	3	3	3	1	2	1	2	2	1
21	**22**	**23**	**24**	**25**	**26**	**27**	**28**	**29**	**30**
2	2	3	1	4	3	2	2	4	2
31	**32**	**33**	**34**	**35**	**36**	**37**	**38**	**39**	**40**
1	3	3	3	3	1	3	4	1	3
41	**42**	**43**	**44**	**45**	**46**	**47**	**48**	**49**	**50**
*	1	1	3	1	2	2	3	4	4
51	**52**	**53**	**54**	**55**	**56**	**57**	**58**	**59**	**60**
1	4	2	2	4	2	3	1	2	3
61	**62**	**63**	**64**	**65**	**66**	**67**	**68**	**69**	**70**
3	1	4	2	4	3	2	1	2	1
71	**72**	**73**	**74**	**75**	**76**	**77**	**78**	**79**	**80**
2	1	4	1	2	3	2	1	2	4
81	**82**	**83**	**84**	**85**	**86**	**87**	**88**	**89**	**90**
2	2	2	4	1	4	2	4	4	2
91	**92**	**93**	**94**	**95**	**96**	**97**	**98**	**99**	**100**
2	3	2	2	2	4	2	1	3	1

EXPLANATORY ANSWERS

1. The National Commission for Women (NCW) was established under the National Commission for Women Act, 1990. Although the Act was passed in 1990, the Commission was officially set up in January 1992. It was created to review constitutional and legal safeguards for women, recommend remedial legislative measures, facilitate grievance redressal, and advise the government on policy matters affecting women.

2. The Bengal Sati Regulation (Regulation XVII) was enacted in 1829 by Governor-General Lord William Bentinck. This law abolished the inhumane practice of Sati—the immolation of a widow on her husband's funeral pyre—in British India, declaring it illegal and punishable by the criminal courts. It marked a major social reform influenced by reformers like Raja Ram Mohan Roy.

3. Andrea Dworkin and Catharine MacKinnon are radical feminist theorists known for their anti-pornography stance. They argued that pornography is not mere expression or erotica but a form of sexual subordination and violence against women. They proposed treating pornography as a civil rights violation, framing it as discrimination rather than just obscenity.

4. Under Section 376D of the Indian Penal Code, gang rape—where a woman is raped by one or more persons acting in a group or with common intent—carries a minimum punishment of twenty years of rigorous imprisonment, which may extend to imprisonment for life. This provision was strengthened after the Criminal Law (Amendment) Act, 2013 following the Nirbhaya case.

5. The idea that "the original class distinction is between men and women" and that "women's oppression provides a conceptual model for understanding all other forms of oppression" comes from Shulamith Firestone, a key figure in radical feminism. In her book "The Dialectic of Sex" (1970), she argues that biological reproduction forms the basis of women's subjugation and calls for its elimination through technology and social revolution.

6. Feminists such as Karen Horney and Luce Irigaray have critiqued Freud's psychoanalytic theory but also used his ideas productively to challenge biological determinism—the notion that gender roles and differences are solely determined by biology. Horney reinterpreted Freud's theories by emphasizing social and cultural factors in shaping female psychology, while Irigaray reworked Freudian and Lacanian ideas to expose the patriarchal bias in psychoanalysis and develop feminist alternatives.

7. Among the listed names, Bell Hooks, Patricia Hill Collins, and Audre Lorde are all prominent Black feminists, known for integrating race, class, and gender into feminist theory. Betty Friedan, on the other hand, was a White liberal feminist, best known for her book "The Feminine Mystique", which focused primarily on middle-class white women's issues, not on Black feminist perspectives.

8. In Classical Economic Theory, the key distinction between productive and non-productive work lies in economic value generation. Productive work is that which produces tangible goods or services and is paid labor contributing directly to national income. Non-productive work (like domestic labor) is unpaid and not counted in traditional measures of economic productivity, even though it sustains the workforce.

9. A key trait of successful entrepreneurs is innovativeness and risk-taking ability. Entrepreneurs identify opportunities, introduce new ideas, and take calculated risks to transform them into viable ventures. Unlike risk-averse individuals, they accept uncertainty as an inherent part of creating and growing a business.

10. Self Help Groups (SHGs) primarily empower women by enabling collective savings and access to microcredit. These groups encourage economic independence, mutual support, and entrepreneurship among women, particularly in rural areas. Through microfinance and joint decision-making, SHGs help women gain financial literacy, confidence, and social capital.

11. The core argument of feminist epistemology is that knowledge is socially constructed and shaped by gendered experiences. It challenges the idea of "objective" or "value-free" knowledge by showing how dominant ways of knowing have historically reflected male perspectives. Feminist epistemologists like Sandra Harding and Donna Haraway argue that social position, especially gender, influences what and how we know — emphasizing situated knowledge and standpoint theory.

12. The Nari Shakti Vandan Adhiniyam, passed in 2023, provides 33 percent reservation for women in the Lok Sabha, State Legislative Assemblies, and the Delhi Legislative Assembly. This significant step towards gender equality in political representation was enacted as the One Hundred and Sixth (106th) Amendment to the Constitution of India. It aims to enhance women's participation in governance and decision-making processes at the highest levels.

13. Vandana Shiva is referred to as the "Gandhi of Grain" due to her activism for seed sovereignty, biodiversity, and sustainable agriculture. She advocates against industrial farming and genetically modified seeds, promoting organic and traditional farming methods that empower rural women and preserve indigenous knowledge systems.

14. The phrase "Third Wave Feminism" was coined by Rebecca Walker in 1992 in an article titled "Becoming the Third Wave", published in Ms. Magazine. This wave of feminism emphasized diversity, intersectionality, and individual identity, moving beyond the essentialism often associated with earlier feminist movements.

15. The Radha Krishnan Commission, also known as the University Education Commission (1948–1949), was appointed to review higher education in India after independence. It analyzed issues related to women's education at the college and university levels, highlighting the importance of equal opportunities and inclusion for women in higher education.

16. The argument that girls and boys develop different relational capacities and senses of self as a result of growing up in a family in which women are mothers was made by Nancy Chodorow, a feminist psychoanalyst and sociologist. In her influential work "The Reproduction of Mothering" (1978), Chodorow explained that since women are the primary caregivers, daughters tend to identify with their mothers, developing relational and nurturing identities, while sons differentiate themselves, leading to more independent and detached selves.

Her theory blends psychoanalysis and feminism to show how family structures reproduce gender roles across generations.

17. In the Global Gender Gap Index 2023, published by the World Economic Forum (WEF), India ranked 127th out of 146 countries. This ranking reflected moderate progress compared to previous years but still indicated significant gender disparities in political representation, economic participation, health, and education. Iceland topped the index, maintaining its status as the most gender-equal country, while India showed improvement particularly in political empowerment.

18. The offense of sexual intercourse by a person in authority—such as a public servant, jail or hospital superintendent, or anyone in a position of power who abuses that position to obtain consent—is recognized under Section 376C of the IPC. It acknowledges that even if such acts don't fit the strict definition of rape under Section 375, they still involve coercion and misuse of authority. Given the options, the relevant section covering punishment for such offenses is Section 376.

19. The idea that cinema is a technology of scopophilia where women provide visual pleasure and are portrayed as passive sexual objects comes from Laura Mulvey, a British feminist film theorist. In her 1975 essay "Visual Pleasure and Narrative Cinema", she applied psychoanalytic theory to film, arguing that mainstream cinema is structured around the male gaze — where men are the active viewers and women are objectified for visual and erotic pleasure. Her work remains foundational in feminist film criticism.

20. According to the Global Gender Gap Report 2024 released by the World Economic Forum, India ranked 129th out of 146 countries globally. Within South Asia, India stood at the fifth position, behind countries like Bangladesh, Nepal, Sri Lanka, and Bhutan. The report highlighted improvements in India's political empowerment of women but persistent gaps in economic participation and health indicators.

21. In feminist pedagogy, critical thinking plays a central role in challenging dominant narratives and promoting critical consciousness. It encourages learners to question systems of power, privilege, and oppression embedded in traditional knowledge structures. Instead of passive learning, feminist pedagogy fosters active engagement, reflection, and transformation toward social justice and equality.

22. Under the Pradhan Mantri Mudra Yojana (PMMY), the SHISHU loan category supports startup and early-stage businesses by providing loans of up to ₹ 50,000. This scheme aims to promote entrepreneurship among micro and small enterprises by offering financial assistance with minimal formalities.

23. Feminists argue that an individual's gender identity is primarily shaped by social and cultural norms, not just biological factors. Gender is understood as a social construct, influenced by societal expectations, upbringing, media, and cultural conditioning, which define what behaviors are considered "masculine" or "feminine."

24. The encoding and decoding model of communication was developed by Stuart Hall, a leading cultural theorist. In this model, Hall explains that media messages are "encoded" with intended meanings by producers but can be "decoded" differently by audiences, depending on their social and cultural context—creating dominant, negotiated, or oppositional readings.

25. The article "Dalit Women Talk Differently" was originally authored by Gopal Guru. This seminal piece emphasized how Dalit women's lived experiences and voices differ from both mainstream feminist movements and Dalit male narratives, highlighting the intersection of caste and gender. The article initiated an important academic and political dialogue within feminist and Dalit studies. Later, Sharmila Rege responded with a critical essay titled "Dalit Women Talk Differently: A Critique of 'Difference' and Towards a Dalit Feminist Standpoint Position."

26. Queer Theory and Feminism share a close intellectual relationship as both seek to deconstruct traditional gender roles, hierarchies, and binaries. While feminism critiques patriarchal structures and the subordination of women, queer theory expands this critique to challenge the rigid binaries of sex, gender, and sexuality itself—emphasizing fluidity and inclusivity beyond heteronormativity. Both aim to expose and dismantle systems that produce inequality based on gender and sexuality.

27. The term "Cyborg" was popularized by Donna Haraway in her essay "A Cyborg Manifesto" (1985). She described the cyborg as a hybrid of organism/nature and machine/culture, representing "permanently partial identities" that transcend traditional boundaries of gender, species, and technology. The cyborg symbolizes a feminist and post-human vision of identity that resists fixed categories and embraces hybridity.

28. Rani Gaidinliu, the warrior queen of Nagaland, was a prominent freedom fighter and spiritual leader who led an armed resistance against British colonial rule. Joining the Heraka movement at a young age, she fought for the political and cultural rights of the Naga people and became a symbol of indigenous resistance. She was later honored with titles like Rani and recognized as a national heroine by India.

29. Rukhma Bai was involved in a landmark legal case (Rukhma Bai vs. Dadaji Bhikaji, 1884–1888) concerning her marriage as a child bride. She refused to live with her husband, asserting her right to consent in marriage. The case stirred public debate on women's rights and child marriage, leading to the Age of Consent Act of 1891, which raised the minimum age for consent to 12 years. Rukhma Bai later became one of India's first practicing women doctors.

30. Hegemonic masculinity refers to the culturally dominant ideal of male behavior that emphasizes traits such as strength, control, and emotional restraint. Men who do not conform to these ideals often face social marginalization, ridicule, or pressure to conform. This system not only subordinates women but also other men who exhibit non-hegemonic masculinities, such as being gentle, emotional, or queer.

31. The Digital Personal Data Protection Act, 2023 marked a progressive step toward gender neutrality in legal language. Instead of using gendered pronouns like he/him or she/her, the Act adopts the gender-neutral pronouns "she/her" to represent all individuals, regardless of gender. This linguistic choice signifies inclusivity and challenges the traditional male-default language used in Indian legislation.

32. In her work "Gender and Nation" (1997), Nira Yuval-Davis explores how women occupy a contested and symbolic space within discourses of nation and nationalism. She argues that women often serve as biological reproducers of the nation, cultural transmitters of national values, and symbols of collective identity—yet are frequently excluded from political and civic participation within national projects.

33. Chandra Talpade Mohanty, a postcolonial feminist scholar, is best known for her essay "Under Western Eyes: Feminist Scholarship and Colonial Discourses" (1984). In this work, she critiques Western feminism for homogenizing and universalizing the experiences of women in the Global South, ignoring differences of race, class, culture, and history. Her analysis urges recognition of diversity and intersectionality in feminist theory.

34. The street play "Om Swaha", performed in the 1980s by feminist theatre groups like Stree Mukti Sanghatana, dealt with the issue of dowry deaths and violence against women. It highlighted the social pressures and economic greed leading to the exploitation and death of brides, sparking awareness and public debate about the cruelty of the dowry system.

35. The growth of women in agri-business is most directly supported by access to markets, credit, and training. These factors enable women farmers and entrepreneurs to improve productivity, adopt technology, and scale their businesses. Empowerment through financial inclusion, skill development, and cooperative networks strengthens women's participation and leadership in agricultural value chains.

36. The Convention on the Elimination of All Forms of Discrimination Against Women (CEDAW), adopted in 1979 by the United Nations General Assembly, is considered the most comprehensive international framework for promoting and protecting women's rights globally. Often described as the international bill of rights for women, CEDAW defines discrimination and sets up a legal and policy agenda to end gender-based inequalities.

37. According to Friedrich Engels in his classic work "The Origin of the Family, Private Property and the State" (1884), the subordination of women began with the rise of private property and class society. Engels argued that the establishment of private ownership led to patriarchal control over women's labor and sexuality, marking the "world-historic defeat of the female sex."

38. Among the Sustainable Development Goals (SDGs), SDG 5 focuses on Gender Equality and Women Empowerment, while SDG 13 addresses Climate Action. These two goals intersect in promoting women's leadership in climate resilience, recognizing that gender equality is vital for achieving sustainable environmental outcomes.

39. The 73rd Constitutional Amendment Act (1992) empowered women in Panchayati Raj Institutions (PRIs) by reserving 33% of all seats—including those for chairpersons and members at every level of local governance—for women. This landmark reform enhanced women's political participation, leadership, and representation in grassroots democracy across rural India.

40. Women's development was first formally recognized as a distinct sector in India's national planning framework during the Seventh Five-Year Plan (1985–1990). This plan marked a shift from the earlier welfare-oriented approach to a development-oriented one, emphasizing women's participation in economic and social spheres. It introduced the concept of "Integration of Women in Development" (IWD), focusing on equality, employment, and access to resources.

41. The organizations in question were established as follows:

C. Young Women's Christian Association (YWCA): The first local association in India was established in Bombay in 1875, and the National Office for India, Burma, and Ceylon was formed in 1896.

B. All India Muslim Women's Conference (Anjuman-e-Khawatin-e-Islam): Founded in 1914 to promote education and reform among Muslim women.

A. All India Women's Conference (AIWC): Founded in 1927 in Pune, focusing on education and social reform for women.

D. Bengal Women's Education League: Established around 1929, after the founding of AIWC.

Hence, the correct chronological order is C, B, A, D, which is not among the given options.

42. Let's arrange the global #movements chronologically:

B. #HeForShe Movement – launched by the UN in 2014.

D. #NiUnaMenos Movement – began in 2015 in Argentina against gender-based violence.

C. #MeToo Movement – gained global traction in 2017, though originally coined in 2006 by Tarana Burke.

A. #Times Up Movement – launched in 2018 in response to the #MeToo revelations in Hollywood.

43. United Nations Conferences on Women in chronological order:

C. Mexico City Conference – 1975 (First World Conference on Women)

D. Copenhagen Conference – 1980 (Second World Conference)

A. Nairobi Conference – 1985 (Third World Conference)

B. Beijing Conference – 1995 (Fourth World Conference)

44. Chronological order of key events in the development of Women's Studies in India:

D. First All India Women's Conference – 1927, marked the beginning of organized advocacy for women's education.

C. The Research for Women's Studies Programme at SNDT University – 1974–75, initiated academic study on women's issues.

A. Establishment of the Women's Studies Centres by UGC – 1986–87, expanded women's studies across universities.

B. Establishment of the National Commission for Women (NCW) – 1992, institutionalized women's rights at the national level.

45. Chronological order of Chairpersons of the National Commission for Women (NCW):

C. Jayanti Patnaik – First Chairperson (1992–1995)

B. Mohini Giri – (1995–1998)

A. Girija Vyas – (2005–2011)

D. Lalitha Kumaramangalam – (2014–2017)

E. Rekha Sharma – (2018–present)

46. In Quantitative Research, the logical sequence of steps typically follows:

B. Identification of problem – Selecting and defining the research issue or question.

A. Review of Literature – Studying existing research to build a conceptual framework.

C. Framing the Questionnaire and data collection – Designing instruments and gathering numerical data.

D. Coding and Analysis of data – Processing and interpreting data statistically to draw conclusions.

47. Chronological order of major international treaties and conventions promoting women's rights:

B. CEDAW – Convention on the Elimination of All Forms of Discrimination Against Women, 1979.

A. Inter-American Convention on the Prevention, Punishment and Eradication of Violence Against Women (Belém do Pará Convention) – 1994.

C. Istanbul Convention – Council of Europe Convention on Preventing and Combating Violence Against Women and Domestic Violence, 2011.

D. ILO Convention No. 190 on Violence and Harassment – 2019.

48. Chronological order of women-focused schemes in India:

D. Mahila Kisan Pariyojana – early initiative to promote women farmers, launched around 2000 under NABARD.

C. Mahila Kisan Sashaktikaran Yojana (MKSY) – launched in 2010–11 under the National Rural Livelihoods Mission (NRLM).

A. Lakhpati Didi Yojana – announced in 2023 to make rural women financially self-reliant.

B. Namo Drone Didi Yojana – launched in 2023 (December) to train women as drone pilots for agri-technology use.

49. The Sustainable Development Goals (SDGs), adopted by the United Nations in 2015, provide a global framework for achieving peace, prosperity, and sustainability by 2030. The relevant goals from the list are arranged according to their official numbering:

E. No Poverty – SDG 1: Eradicate extreme poverty everywhere.

C. Gender Equality – SDG 5: Achieve gender equality and empower all women and girls.

D. Clean Water & Sanitation – SDG 6: Ensure availability and sustainable management of water and sanitation for all.

A. Decent Work & Economic Growth – SDG 8: Promote inclusive and sustainable economic growth, employment, and decent work for all.

B. Partnership for the Goals – SDG 17: Strengthen global partnerships for sustainable development.

Thus, when arranged in the correct numerical order, it becomes E, C, D, A, B.

50. India has enacted several key laws to safeguard women's rights, each addressing different aspects of gender equality and protection. Their chronological order based on the year of enactment is:

C. The Special Marriage Act (1954): Provided a legal framework for interfaith and civil marriages, emphasizing consent and equality.

B. The Hindu Marriage Act (1955): Reformed Hindu personal law, granting women rights related to marriage and divorce.

A. The Maternity Benefit Act (1961): Ensured job security and paid leave for working women during maternity.

E. The Commission of Sati (Prevention) Act (1987): Criminalized the practice of sati and glorification of the act.

D. The Prohibition of Child Marriage Act (2006): Strengthened legal measures against child marriage and raised penalties for offenders.

Hence, the correct chronological order is C, B, A, E, D.

51. India's major education commissions and policies have shaped the country's educational development and philosophy over time. Their chronological order is:

D. Radhakrishnan Commission (1948–49): Focused on university education and recommended higher education reforms post-independence.

C. Mudaliar Commission (1952–53): Examined the state of secondary education and emphasized vocational and value-based learning.

B. Kothari Commission (1964–66): Provided a comprehensive review of all levels of education, recommending a national system of education.

A. National Education Policy (1968): India's first education policy, based on the Kothari Commission's recommendations, promoting equal opportunity and quality education.

Thus, the correct order is D, C, B, A.

52. Let's arrange the key global milestones in the women's rights movement chronologically:

C. The Seneca Falls Convention – held in 1848 in New York, it was the first women's rights convention, marking the beginning of the organized women's suffrage movement.

A. National Organization for Women (NOW) – founded in the United States in 1966 to advocate for women's rights, equality, and empowerment.

D. Convention on the Elimination of All Forms of Discrimination Against Women (CEDAW) – adopted by the United Nations General Assembly in 1979, often called the international bill of rights for women.

B. The Beijing Declaration and Beijing Platform for Action – adopted in 1995 during the Fourth World Conference on Women in Beijing, serving as a major global policy framework for gender equality.

53. Chronological order of major debates in feminist theory:

B. Suffrage – late 19th to early 20th century, focused on women's right to vote and basic legal equality (First Wave Feminism).

C. Notion of Sisterhood – 1960s–70s, during Second Wave Feminism, emphasized solidarity among women but later critiqued for ignoring differences of race and class.

D. Difference and Sameness Debate – late 1970s–1980s, explored whether equality meant sameness with men or recognition of gender difference.

A. Intersectionality – 1989, introduced by Kimberlé Crenshaw, highlighting the interconnectedness of gender, race, class, and other identities in shaping oppression.

54. Chronological order of important feminist theoretical works:

C. Laura Mulvey's "Visual Pleasure and Narrative Cinema" – published in **1975**, foundational in feminist film theory and introduced the concept of the male gaze.

B. Teresa de Lauretis' "Technologies of Gender" – published in **1987**, explored how gender identities are constructed through social and cultural discourses.

D. Kaja Silverman's "The Acoustic Mirror" – published in **1988**, analyzed how cinema represents the female voice and subjectivity.

A. Barbara Creed's "The Monstrous-Feminine" – published in **1993**, applied psychoanalytic theory to horror films, analyzing depictions of female monstrosity.

55. Chronological order of Acts related to women and children's protection and welfare:

D. Medical Termination of Pregnancy (MTP) Act – 1971: Legalized abortion under specific conditions to protect women's health and autonomy.

B. Equal Remuneration Act – 1976: Ensured equal pay for men and women for the same work and prevented workplace discrimination.

C. Protection of Women from Domestic Violence Act – 2005: Provided a comprehensive legal framework to protect women from physical, emotional, and economic abuse within households.

A. Protection of Children from Sexual Offences (POCSO) Act – 2012: Created strong legal measures for safeguarding children from sexual assault, harassment, and exploitation.

56. According to the Government of India's Handbook on Gender Budgeting, the state of Rajasthan took significant steps to institutionalize gender budgeting by enhancing the structure and assessment of its fiscal planning. The two major initiatives were:

B. Development of a four-category framework for the Gender Budget Statement: This structured framework allowed Rajasthan to classify, analyze, and track the extent of gender responsiveness in budgetary allocations.

D. Gender appraisal of budget proposals by seven key departments: This ensured that gender concerns were integrated early in the budgeting process, promoting more equitable policy outcomes.

Hence, the correct initiatives are B and D only.

57. Since the 1980s, the use of the plural form "Feminisms" has become common to reflect the diversity of feminist perspectives across cultures, politics, and social contexts. Feminists share a core commitment to gender equality but differ in philosophy, focus, and strategies — encompassing liberal, radical, socialist, postcolonial, ecofeminist, queer, and Dalit feminisms, among others. This pluralization acknowledges the richness and heterogeneity of feminist thought and its responsiveness to local realities.

58. The National Commission for Women (NCW) does not have executive or enforcement powers under India's digital or data protection laws. Instead, its role is primarily consultative and advocacy-based. It works to promote women's rights in digital spaces, advises the government on policy reforms, and raises awareness about online safety, cyber harassment, and digital literacy for women.

Therefore, the NCW's role combines advisory and advocacy functions, not regulatory control or law enforcement.

59. The feminization of poverty refers to the growing proportion of women among the world's poor and is measured through indices that assess gender disparities and empowerment. The three international indices relevant to this concept are:

A. The Gender Development Index (GDI): Compares male and female achievements in health, education, and income.

C. The Gender Empowerment Measure (GEM): Focuses on political participation, economic involvement, and decision-making power.

D. The Human Poverty Index (HPI): Measures deprivation in basic human capabilities, often revealing gender gaps in poverty levels.

Together, these indices highlight how poverty disproportionately affects women.

60. In research, hypotheses play a critical role in guiding the scientific inquiry process. They:

C. Set the direction of research by defining what the researcher aims to test or explore.

B. Help in collecting useful facts by focusing data collection efforts.

D. Contribute to the formation of theories by providing a basis for empirical testing and validation.

Hence, hypotheses are essential for ensuring clarity, focus, and theoretical development in research.

61. The Sukanya Samriddhi Yojana (SSY) is a savings scheme launched under the Beti Bachao Beti Padhao initiative to promote financial security for the girl child. The details of each statement are as follows:

A. Money can be deposited only by the parents — **Incorrect**. A legal guardian can also open and deposit money. After the girl turns 10, she can operate the account and make deposits herself.

B. The maximum limit for deposit in the account is ₹ 1,50,000 per year — **Correct**. Deposits can be made up to ₹ 1.5 lakh in a financial year.

C. Interest rates are calculated on the 10th day of every month — **Incorrect**. Interest is calculated on the lowest balance between the 5th and the end of the month.

D. Even after maturity the account will earn interest — **Correct** with clarification. The account earns interest until maturity (21 years from opening or marriage after 18 years). After maturity, no interest accrues.

Hence, the correct statements are B and D only.

62. The CBSE Merit Scholarship Scheme for Single Girl Child aims to promote education among single girl students by recognizing academic excellence. Its key objectives are:

A. To provide scholarships to meritorious single girl child students.

B. Eligibility requires having passed Class X CBSE Examination with 60% or more marks and continuing studies in Classes XI and XII.

C. The scholarship amount is ₹ 500 per month.

D. The scholarship is granted for a maximum period of two years (Classes XI & XII), not three.

Thus, A, B, and C are correct.

63. The Annapurna Scheme is implemented by the State Bank of India to support women entrepreneurs who wish to start or expand food-based businesses such as catering, canteens, or tiffin services.

B. It is meant for food-related ventures.

C. Beneficiaries can access a loan of up to ₹ 50,000 (working capital).

Thus, the correct options are B and C.

64. According to Gita Sen, the control over female sexuality is a central mechanism of women's subordination within patriarchal and class-based societies. Her key arguments are:

A. In India, unlike in the West, women are not primarily sexualized through consumer commodification but through more direct patriarchal control — **correct**.

B. Sexual objectification is personal and immediate, influencing women's participation and treatment in the labour market — **correct**.

C. Landholding classes exercise control over women's sexuality to ensure paternity certainty and inheritance legitimacy — **correct**.

D. Public spaces are dominated by men, and the threat of violence is used to control women's movement and autonomy — **correct**.

E. The idea that sexual control is not important for the landless is **incorrect**, as patriarchal sexual control operates across all classes, though differently.

Hence, the correct set of statements is A, B, C & D only.

65. In her study of female-headed households in Mexican shanty towns, Sylvia Chant found that:

A. Women and children often suffered secondary poverty in male-headed families, as men withheld income for personal use — **correct**.

B. Female-headed households were sometimes better off financially after desertion or widowhood because women managed resources more equitably — **correct**.

D. In single-women-headed families, children contributed more to domestic work, easing the burden on mothers — **correct**.

E. Authority in male-headed households was often repressive, limiting women's and children's autonomy — **correct**.

Hence, the correct combination is A, B, D & E only.

66. "Gender Trouble" (1990), written by Judith Butler, is one of the founding texts of queer theory. Butler critiques the heteronormative assumptions within traditional feminist and gender theories, arguing that gender is performative—a set of repeated acts rather than a fixed identity. The text challenges binary understandings of gender and sexuality but is not homophobic.

Thus, the correct statements are:

A. One of the founding texts of queer theory — **correct**.

B. Critical of heterosexual assumptions in feminist theory — **correct**.

D. Written by Judith Butler — **correct**.

67. Feminist Standpoint Epistemology argues that knowledge is socially situated, and those in marginalized or less powerful positions can develop more comprehensive insights into social structures because they experience both their own oppression and the workings of dominant systems.

B. Less powerful members have a more complete view of social reality, as they can see both dominant and subordinate perspectives — **correct**.

D. Their disadvantaged position gives them the potential for "double vision", allowing them to understand both their own world and that of the dominant group — **correct**.

Hence, the correct combination is B & D only.

68. Under the Sexual Harassment of Women at Workplace (Prevention, Prohibition and Redressal) Act, 2013, sexual harassment is defined broadly and includes:

A. Any unwelcome acts or behaviour, whether directly or by implication — **correct**.

B. Physical contact and advances — correct.

D. Demand or request for sexual favours — correct.

It also includes making sexually coloured remarks and showing pornography, covering physical, verbal, and non-verbal conduct.

69. The writings of Bhakti women saints such as Mirabai, Akka Mahadevi, Lal Ded, and Andal reflect early forms of feminist thought in India. They challenged both religious patriarchy and caste hierarchies through their poetry and devotion.

B. Their work shows indigenous roots of feminism in India — **correct**.

C. These writings express resistance to religious and caste subordination — **correct**.

D. They are part of early modern Indian history, representing emancipatory voices against Brahmanical patriarchy — **correct**.

Thus, the correct combination is B, C & D only.

70. The journal *Signs: Journal of Women in Culture and Society* is one of the earliest and most influential academic journals in feminist scholarship.

A. It was established by Jean W. Sacks — **correct**, she was the founding editor.

C. It was first published in 1975 — **correct**, marking it as one of the foundational platforms for feminist interdisciplinary research.

71. Feminism, unlike other theoretical "isms," does not stem from a single framework — it draws on multiple traditions (liberal, socialist, radical, postcolonial, etc.) and varies across historical and cultural contexts.

A. There is no single abstract definition of feminism applicable universally — **correct**.

B. It is grounded in historically and culturally concrete realities — **correct**.

C. It involves levels of consciousness—awareness of oppression and collective struggle — **correct**.

D. The statement that patriarchy and sexism "will never change" is **incorrect** (feminism aims precisely to challenge and change them).

E. Legal reform is **not the only goal**; feminism extends to social, cultural, and psychological liberation as well.

72. Feminist Ethnography is a qualitative research method that centers women's lived experiences and questions the traditional power hierarchies in research.

A. It is a qualitative research method — **correct**.

B. It uses participant observation and interviews to highlight women's perspectives — **correct**.

C. It does challenge traditional power dynamics — so this statement is **incorrect**.

D. It is critical and reflexive, acknowledging the researcher's positionality — **correct**.

E. It can be done by researchers of any gender, so this is **incorrect**.

73. In Amy S. Wharton's *The Sociology of Gender*, she explains that the erosion of standard working hours (i.e., the traditional 9-to-5 schedule) results from social and economic transformations. Two key factors are:

A. The **growth of service sector employment**, which often demands flexible, nonstandard, or shift-based schedules.

D. The **spread of digital technologies**, which blur boundaries between work and home, enabling round-the-clock connectivity and flexible work arrangements.

74. The Second Wave of Feminism (1960s–1980s) expanded the feminist agenda from legal rights to personal and social equality. It is characterized by:

A. Consciousness-raising groups as a central method for building feminist solidarity and analyzing personal experiences politically.

B. The slogan "the personal is political", emphasizing that personal experiences of women (marriage, sexuality, domestic life) are shaped by broader social and political structures.

75. Gender Roles refer to socially constructed expectations about how individuals should behave based on their gender.

A. They represent society's concept of appropriate behaviors for men and women — **correct**.

C. They are acquired through socialization, not innate — **correct**.

D. They are based on social norms and standards established by culture and institutions — **correct**.

Hence, gender roles are socially learned and reinforced, not biologically determined.

76. Let's correctly match feminist and gender theories (List I) with their associated thinkers (List II):

A. Queer Theory → III. Eve Kosofsky Sedgwick — A central figure in Queer Theory, Sedgwick's works such as Epistemology of the Closet explore sexuality, identity, and gender beyond binaries.

B. Post-Colonial Feminist Theorist → IV. Lila Abu-Lughod — Known for her critique of Western feminism and her work on women in Middle Eastern societies, emphasizing cultural and contextual understanding.

C. Hegemonic Masculinity → II. Raewyn Connell — Developed the concept of hegemonic masculinity, describing dominant male norms that marginalize alternative masculinities.

D. Ecofeminism → I. Françoise d'Eaubonne — Coined the term ecofeminism in 1974, linking environmental degradation with patriarchy.

77. Now match the types of feminism (List I) with their key characteristics (List II):

A. Liberal Feminism → III. Argues that women's subordination can be addressed through political processes within democracy, emphasizing equality, legal rights, and reforms.

B. Marxist Feminism → IV. Links women's oppression to capitalism and private property, believing change must come through the overthrow of industrial capitalism.

C. Radical Feminism → II. Believes in women-centered politics and separatist spaces to challenge patriarchy and male domination.

D. Postmodern Feminism → I. Rejects the idea of a universal female subject, emphasizing diversity, language, and cultural context in constructing gender identities.

78. Let's match the movements and cultural references (List I) with their descriptions (List II):

A. Nupi Lan (Women's War) → IV. Refers to the two major women-led uprisings in Manipur (1904 & 1939) against British colonial policies and economic exploitation.

B. Meira Paibis (Guardians of Civil Society) → II. A women's social movement established in 1977 in Manipur, known for combating social evils and human rights violations.

C. Ima Market → I. A women-only market in Imphal, functioning since the 16th century, symbolizing women's economic independence.

D. Likai (Tragic Tale from Meghalaya) → III. A Khasi folktale depicting a widow who works as a porter to raise her child after her husband's death — reflecting women's resilience.

79. Here's the corrected and detailed matching of the schemes with their descriptions based on the Government of India's official framework:

A. Janani Suraksha Yojana (JSY) → II. Promotes institutional deliveries by offering cash incentives to pregnant women, particularly from BPL families and low-performing states.

B. Janani Shishu Suraksha Karyakaram (JSSK) → I. Provides essential free care to mothers and newborns in public health institutions — including free delivery (even C-section), drugs, diagnostics, blood, and transport — ensuring no out-of-pocket expenses, especially within 48 hours of birth.

C. Integrated Child Development Services (ICDS) → IV. A flagship umbrella program delivering a package of services (nutrition, preschool education, health check-ups, etc.) through Anganwadi centers; its services have now been subsumed under Mission Poshan 2.0.

D. Mission Poshan 2.0 → III. A comprehensive nutrition support mission that integrates Anganwadi Services and Poshan Abhiyan to improve nutritional outcomes and service delivery efficiency.

80. Let's correctly match the countries (List I) with their Gender Parity Scores (List II) as per the Global Gender Gap Index 2024:

A. Iceland → II. 93.5% - Iceland continues to rank #1 globally, achieving the highest level of gender parity at 93.5%.

B. Finland → I. 87.5% - Finland maintains a strong record of gender equality with 87.5% parity, ranking among the top three countries.

C. New Zealand → IV. 83.5% - New Zealand stands out as one of the leading countries outside Europe with 83.5% parity.

D. Spain → III. 79.7% - Spain achieves 79.7% parity, placing it among the top 20 nations in global rankings.

81. Let's correctly match the International Conventions and Declarations (List I) with their respective years of adoption (List II):

A. The European Convention on Preventing & Combating Violence against Women & Domestic Violence → IV. 2011 - Known as the Istanbul Convention, adopted by the Council of Europe in 2011, it is the most comprehensive treaty on gender-based violence in Europe.

B. The Inter-American Convention on the Prevention, Punishment & Eradication of Violence against Women → III. 1994 - Also known as the Convention of Belém do Pará, adopted by the Organization of American States (OAS) in 1994, it was the first binding regional treaty on violence against women.

C. **Maputo Protocol → I. 2003** – Officially titled the Protocol to the African Charter on Human and Peoples' Rights on the Rights of Women in Africa, adopted by the African Union in 2003.

D. **The Declaration on the Elimination of Violence Against Women in the Association of South East Asian Nations (ASEAN) → II. 2004** – Adopted by ASEAN in 2004, promoting regional cooperation to combat violence against women.

82. Let's correctly match the Books (List I) with their Authors (List II):

A. **Controlling Women: What We Must Do Now to Save Reproductive Freedom → IV. Kathryn Kolbert** – Co-authored by Kathryn Kolbert and Julie F. Kay, this 2021 book examines the U.S. struggle for reproductive rights post-Roe v. Wade.

B. **Bodies on the Line: At the Frontlines of the Fight to Protect Abortion in America → I. Lauren Rankin** – Written by Lauren Rankin (2022), this book documents abortion clinic defenders and their activism in protecting access to reproductive healthcare.

C. **Killing the Black Body: Race, Reproduction, and the Meaning of Liberty → II. Dorothy Roberts** – A seminal 1997 work by Dorothy Roberts, exploring racialized reproductive politics and control over Black women's bodies.

D. **Our Bodies, Ourselves → III. Boston Women's Health Book Collective** – A pioneering 1970s feminist health manual by the Boston Women's Health Book Collective, empowering women through knowledge about their bodies.

83. Let's correctly match the Concepts (List I) with their corresponding Themes (List II):

A. **Economic Development → III. Efficient integration of women's work** – Focuses on incorporating women's labor into the economy and recognizing their contribution to development.

B. **Equality → IV. Legal Rights** – Seeks gender parity through laws, reforms, and rights-based frameworks.

C. **Empowerment → II. Women's group mobilization** – Involves collective organization, participation, and decision-making for women's agency.

D. **Welfare → I. Focus on health, population, and housing programmes** – Traditionally centered on women's welfare-oriented roles, focusing on family and basic needs.

84. Let's correctly match the Research Methods (List I) with their Characteristics (List II):

A. **Oral History → III. Subjective reconstruction of one's life & meaning** – Oral history collects personal narratives to reconstruct experiences and social realities.

B. **Survey → IV. Quantitative** – Surveys rely on structured questions and large samples, emphasizing numerical data and statistical analysis.

C. **Focus Group Discussions → II. Decentering the subject** – Focus groups use group interactions to bring out multiple perspectives, shifting focus from individual to collective discourse.

D. **Ethnography → I. Long-term study of people** – Ethnography involves immersive, long-term observation and participation within a community.

85. Let's match the Concepts (List I) with their Authors (List II):

A. **Performativity → II. Judith Butler** – Introduced in *Gender Trouble (1990)*; gender is not innate but performed through repeated social acts.

B. **Immanence & Transcendence → IV. Simone de Beauvoir** – From *The Second Sex (1949)*; explores how women are confined to "immanence" while men pursue "transcendence."

C. **Semiotic dimension of language → I. Julia Kristeva** – In *Revolution in Poetic Language (1974)*, she distinguishes between the semiotic (pre-linguistic) and symbolic (structured) aspects of language.

D. **Textual Sexism → III. Kate Millett** – In *Sexual Politics (1970)*, Millett exposed patriarchal biases in literary texts.

86. Let's match the Approaches to Development (List I) with their Characteristics (List II):

A. **WID (Women in Development) → IV. Modernization Theory** – Emerged in the 1970s; emphasized integrating women into development projects driven by modernization.

B. **WAD (Women and Development) → III. Dependency Theory** – Critiques WID; linked women's oppression to global capitalist structures and economic dependency.

C. **GAD (Gender and Development) → I. Influenced by Socialist Theory** – Stresses transforming gender relations and power structures, not just including women.

D. **GED (Gender and Environment Development) → II.** Centers Environment – Highlights women's critical role in sustainable environmental management and ecofeminist thought.

87. Let's correctly match the Five-Year Plans (List I) with their respective Focus Areas (List II):

A. Sixth Plan (1980–1985) → IV. Multidisciplinary approach with a focus on health, education, and employment – This plan was the first to include a separate chapter on women and development, focusing on welfare and development through multiple sectors.

B. Seventh Plan (1985–1990) → I. Bringing women into the mainstream of national development – The focus shifted from welfare to integration and participation of women in national development processes.

C. Eighth Plan (1992–1997) → II. Paradigm shift from development to empowerment and benefits to women – Marked a transition from treating women as beneficiaries to recognizing them as active agents of change.

D. Ninth Plan (1997–2002) → III. Empowerment of women as its strategic objective – For the first time, empowerment was explicitly identified as the central objective of planning for women.

88. Let's correctly match the Authors (List I) with their Publications (List II):

A. Sharmita Ray → I. Women Doctors' Masterful Manoeuverings: Colonial Bengal, Late Nineteenth and Early Twentieth Centuries – Examines how early Indian women doctors navigated colonial hierarchies and gender barriers within the medical profession in Bengal.

B. Samiksha Sehrawat → II. Feminising Empire: The Association of Medical Women in India and the Campaign to Found a Women's Medical Service – Analyzes British women doctors' efforts to establish women's medical services in India under the colonial framework.

C. Grace Stapleton → IV. Pelvic Measurements in Indian Women – Reflects colonial medical and anthropometric studies focusing on gendered and racialized representations of Indian women's bodies.

D. Barbara Ehrenreich & Deirdre English → III. Witches, Midwives, and Nurses: A History of Women Healers – A seminal feminist text revealing how patriarchal medicine displaced women healers and midwives throughout history.

89. Let's correctly match the Environmental and Ecological Movements (List I) with their Associated Leaders (List II):

A. Green Belt Movement → III. Wangari Maathai – A Kenyan environmentalist, Wangari Maathai founded the Green Belt Movement in **1977** to promote tree planting, environmental conservation, and women's empowerment.

B. The Navdanya Movement → IV. Vandana Shiva – Indian ecofeminist Vandana Shiva launched the Navdanya Movement in **1987** to protect biodiversity, seed sovereignty, and promote organic farming.

C. Birdman of India → II. Salim Ali – Renowned ornithologist Salim Ali is known as the Birdman of India for his pioneering work in ornithology and conservation.

D. Waterman of India → I. Rajendra Singh – Environmentalist Rajendra Singh earned this title for his efforts in water conservation and revival of rivers through traditional rainwater harvesting in Rajasthan.

90. Let's correctly match the Authors (List I) with their Key Works/Concepts (List II):

A. Bina Agarwal → II. Women and Agriculture – Bina Agarwal's influential research focuses on gender, land rights, and women's participation in agriculture and environmental sustainability.

B. Mary Wollstonecraft → IV. Women's Rights and Education – In her seminal 1792 work *A Vindication of the Rights of Woman*, Wollstonecraft advocates for education and equality for women.

C. Kamla Bhasin → III. Relevance of Feminism in South Asia – Kamla Bhasin wrote extensively on South Asian feminism, emphasizing local contexts, gender justice, and empowerment.

D. Germaine Greer → I. The Female Eunuch – Germaine Greer's 1970 book challenged traditional gender norms and became a foundational text of second-wave feminism.

91. Most sports were originally created to suit men's physical capabilities, not women's. They were structured around male strength, endurance, and competitive ideals.

92. Ancient Greece played a foundational role by introducing formal sports through the first Olympic Games in 776 BC, which featured individual competitions like wrestling, running, and chariot races — all designed for men.

93. In a pure meritocracy, victory in sports is determined by physical strength, speed, and skill, emphasizing measurable performance rather than social factors.

94. According to the passage, achieving gender-equal pay requires shifting away from a strict merit-based (physical) system and instead making arguments from a sociological and ideological standpoint, recognizing women's sports as distinct and valuable.

95. The passage clearly states that gender equality in sports pay should be supported by sociological and ideological arguments, not just economic or legal reasoning.

96. The passage emphasizes that feminism is heterogeneous and context-dependent, making it impossible to have one simple feminist position. This complexity arises because diversity is a universal condition ("diversality").

97. The passage describes identity as "provisional and conjunctural," meaning that identities are fluid, changing, and dependent on specific contexts rather than being fixed or uniform.

98. The critique of universal frameworks flowing from North to South highlights that theories must be situated within specific contexts of time and place — not simply imposed globally.

99. Walter Mignolo alerts us to the concept of "diversality," which recognizes diversity as a universal condition — rejecting singular or universal feminist frameworks.

100. The passage argues that the intersectionality framework can be problematic because it tends to freeze or fix pre-existing identities (like 'woman') instead of treating them as dynamic and context-specific.

Previous Years' Paper

National Testing Agency (NTA)

UGC-NET Junior Research Fellowship & Assistant Professor Eligibility Exam

WOMEN STUDIES, JANUARY-2025

(Exam held on 27-01-2025)

PAPER-II

1. Match the List-I with List-II.

List-I (Cyber criminal name)	List-II (Types of crimes)
A. Cyber stalking	I. Publishing personal information online to enable harassment
B. Catfishing	II. Aggressive targeted hate speech involving sexism, misogy
C. Doxxing	III. Pretending to some one else to manipulate or exploit emotionally or financially
D. Trolling	IV. Persist tracking and monitoring woman's online activities to instill fear or exert control

Choose the *correct* answer from the options given below:

1. A-I, B-II, C-III, D-IV
2. A-IV, B-III, C-I, D-II
3. A-II, B-III, C-IV, D-I
4. A-II, B-IV, C-III, D-I

2. "A woman must have money and a room of her own if she is to write fiction".

1. Virginia Woolf
2. Nancy R. Smith
3. Eve Ensler
4. Susan M. Shaw

3. Feminist Ethnography differs from traditional ethnography by:

1. Using only quantitative data to understand cultures
2. Ignoring intersectionality in cultural studies
3. Challenging power hierarchies between researchers and participants
4. Avoiding personal narratives in research

4. Which of the following indicators are used in Global Gender Gap Index (GGGI)?

A. Education
B. Healthcare
C. Housing
D. Economic participation

Choose the *correct* answer from the options given below:

1. A, B, C Only
2. B, C, D Only
3. A, B, D Only
4. A, C, D Only

5. Match the List-I with List-II.

List-I (Thinkers)	List-II (Motherhood concept)
A. Nancy Chodorow	I. The mother child relationships is the essential relationship
B. Adrienne Rich	II. Despite all conflicts and contradictions women have succeeded at Mothering
C. Ann Oakley	III. Motherhood is profoundly satisfying for many women
D. Veena Poonacha	IV. Motherhood is a handicap but also a strength

Choose the *correct* answer from the options given below:

1. A-IV, B-I, C-II, D-III
2. A-II, B-I, C-IV, D-III
3. A-III, B-II, C-IV, D-I
4. A-II, B-III, C-IV, D-I

6. Order the progress and action taken to address the falling count of girls in India.

A. Prenatal Diagnostic Technology Act
B. Beti Bachao Beti Padhao Programme was launched in Haryana
C. Pre-conception and prenatal Diagnostic Act
D. A systematic decadal drop of child sex ratio in favour of boys was observed in the census data

Choose the *correct* answer from the options given below:

1. D, B, C, A
2. D, B, A, C
3. D, A, C, B
4. D, A, B, C

7. Which of the following states is showing a worrying recent trend of reducing sex ratio of birth in rural areas as compared to urban areas in 2017-18 as per SRS data?

1. Andhra Pradesh 2. Telangana
3. Bihar 4. Rajasthan

8. Match the List-I with List-II.

List-I (Rights)	List-II (Provisions)
A. Right against Dowry	I. Free legal support under legal services authorities Act
B. Right to Free Legal Aid	II. Criminalizes Harassment Section 354A of IPC
C. Right to Dignity and Decency	III. Prohibits dowry demands and harassment
D. Rights at Workplace	IV. Guarantees safe and conducive work environment

Choose the ***correct*** answer from the options given below:

1. A-IV, B-III, C-I, D-II
2. A-IV, B-III, C-II, D-I
3. A-III, B-I, C-II, D-IV
4. A-II, B-I, C-III, D-IV

9. Arrange the following changes in global paradigms on women and development in a chronological sequence.

A. Women and Development (WAD) - Empowerment Approach
B. Welfare Approach
C. Gender and Development (GAD) - Equality Approach
D. Women in Development (WID) - Equality Approach

Choose the ***correct*** answer from the options given below:

1. B, D, A, C 2. B, D, C, A
3. C, B, D, A 4. C, B, A, D

10. Which of the following answers are correct regarding indicators of women's empowerment in India as per public Information Bureau 2023?

A. The share of women pilots is 15%, which is higher than the global average of 5%
B. 43% of women in India are enrolled in (STEM) Science Technology, Engineering and Mathematics, which is the highest in the world
C. In India, 46% of elected representatives in local governments (Panchayati Raj)were women
D. On an average, men in India are earning only 60% of the wage that women earn

Choose the ***correct*** answer from the options given below:

1. A, C and D Only
2. B, C and D Only
3. A, B and C Only
4. A, B and D Only

11. Arrange the following events of women and development at the global level in a chronological order.

A. I.C.P.D. - International Conference on Population and Development
B. C.E.D.A.W. - Convention on elimination of violence against women
C. United Nations Universal Declaration of Human Rights
D. United Nations Fourth World Conference on Women at Beijing, China

Choose the ***correct*** answer from the options given below:

1. A, C, D, B 2. A, D, B, C
3. C, B, A, D 4. B, D, A, C

12. Who used the term "Patriarchal Government"?

1. Carole Pateman 2. Kate Millet
3. Betty Friedan 4. Shulamith Firestone

13. What is the primary argument of feminist economists regarding the measurement of Gross Domestic Product (GDP)?

1. The GDP accurately reflects the value of all economic activities
2. The GDP ignores the value of unpaid care work
3. The GDP overestimates the value of industrial production
4. The GDP is irrelevant to feminist economy

14. Match the List-I with List-II.

List-I (Thinkers)	List-II (Books)
A. Shulamith Firestore	I. The Feminine Mystique
B. Betty Frieden	II. Staying Alive
C. Mary Wollstonecraft	III. The Dialectic of Sex
D. Vandana Shiva	IV. A Vindication of the Rights of Women

Choose the ***correct*** answer from the options given below:

1. A-III, B-I, C-IV, D-II
2. A-I, B-IV, C-III, D-II
3. A-IV, B-I, C-II, D-III
4. A-I, B-III, C-IV, D-II

15. What is the primary goal of the "Bechdel test" known as the "Bechdel - Wallace test"?

1. To evaluate the technical quality of a film
2. To determine the commercial viability of transgenders in a film
3. To assess the representation of women in films
4. To analyse the cultural relevance of a film

16. Choose the history of LGBT++ (Lesbian, Gay, Bisexual, Transgender)++ Movement in India in a chronological order.

A. British colonial rule imposed section 377, criminalising homosexuality
B. First Pride parade at Kolkatta
C. Transgender persons (Protection of Rights) Act
D. The Supreme Court of India unanimously ruled that section 377 is unconstitutional

Choose the ***correct*** answer from the options given below:

1. A, B, C, D 2. A, C, B, D
3. B, C, A, D 4. A, B, D, C

17. Rajiv Gandhi Scheme for Empowerment of Adolescent girls (SABLA Yojana) focuses on:

A. Empowering adolescent girls (11-18 years) by providing them with life skill, education, nutrition and access to health care
B. Promoting awareness about health hygiene, nutrition, adolescent reproductive and sexual health (ARSH), family and child care
C. Helping to upgrade home-based skills and life skills and integrates with the National Development Programme for Vocational skills
D. Depositing of 3000 by the Government in a fixed deposit account in the name of the girl child which can be withdrawn only when the girl is an adult

Choose the ***correct*** answer from the options given below:

1. A, B, C Only 2. B, C, D Only
3. A, B, D Only 4. A, D, B Only

18. Which of the following is a central focus of feminist epistemology?

1. Objectivity as a universal principle
2. The role of emotion in the construction of knowledge
3. Eliminating subjectivity in research
4. Advocating purely quantitative methods

19. "The proletarian Women" that was written for International Women's day in March 1914, was written by:

1. Carol Hanisch 2. Sandra Whiteworth
3. Rosa Luxemburg 4. Esther Boserup

20. The "care penalty" can manifest in various ways, including:

A. Reduced earnings
B. Care stagnation
C. Unlimited access to benefits
D. Increased financial stress

Choose the ***correct*** answer from the options given below:

1. A, B, C Only 2. A, B, D Only
3. B, C, D Only 4. A, D, B Only

21. The CBSE Udan Scholarship Programme for girls is a scholarship programme.

A. Initiated by Ministry of Education and Central Board of Secondary Education
B. Initiated by Ministry of Education aimes to obtain degrees from renowned Arts and Commerce Colleges
C. Aims to help female students of economically vulnerable families in India to obtain degrees from renowned engineering colleges
D. Is for female students studying in class XI and they must be enrolled in the physics, chemistry and mathematics stream

Choose the ***correct*** answer from the options given below:

1. A, B, C Only 2. B, C, D Only
3. A, C, D Only 4. D, A, B Only

22. National Scheme of Incentives, to girls for secondary Education launched in May, 2008 covers:

A. All SC/ST girls who pass class VIII
B. Girls who pass VIII examination from Kasturba Gandhi Balika Vidyalayas irrespective of (SC/ST) and enroll for class IX in state/UT Govt., Govt. aided or local body schools
C. Girls should be below 18 years of age (as on 31st March) on joining class IX
D. Married girls, girls studying in private un-aided schools and enrolled schools run by central Govt. like KVS, NVS and CBSE affiliated schools are excluded

Choose the ***correct*** answer from the options given below:

1. A, B, C Only 2. A, B, D Only
3. B, C, D Only 4. B, A, C Only

23. Vishakha Guidelines were formuleted in the year:

1. 1995 2. 1996
3. 1997 4. 1998

24. What is a potential negative impact of emerging technologies on gender equality?
    1. Increased employment opportunities for women
    2. Exacerbation of existing gender biases in Artificial Intelligence systems
    3. Equal access to STEM (Science, Technology, Engineering and Mathematics) education
    4. Increased gender sensitivity in digital content

25. Arrange the following books in chronological order.
    A. Pride and Prejudice
    B. The Second Sex
    C. The Feminine Mystique
    D. A Vindication of the Rights of the Women

    Choose the ***correct*** answer from the options given below:

    1. B, C, D, A 2. A, B, C, D
    3. D, C, B, A 4. D, A, B, C

26. Which factors are considered by the Internal Complaints Committee when recommending financial damages to the complainant?
    A. Mental trauma
    B. Emotional distress caused
    C. The complainant's educational qualifications
    D. The responder's family income

    Choose the ***correct*** answer from the options given below:

    1. A, C Only 2. A, B Only
    3. B, C Only 4. A, D Only

27. Which was the first territory or state in America to grant women suffrage in the year 1869?
    1. Texas 2. Virginia
    3. Wyoming 4. Arizona

28. Which of the following is online global solidarity movement for gender equality, initiated by UN Women in 2014?
    1. # MeToo Movement
    2. The # HeForShe Movement
    3. # TimesUp
    4. # BringBackOurGirls

29. Which of the following movement in India included a struggle for womens property ownership?
    1. Plachimada Movement
    2. Nav Nirman Movement
    3. Bodhgaya Movement
    4. Chipko Movement

30. What does Virginia Woolf highlights as a significant challenge faced by womens writers in England?
    1. Limited access to education and resources
    2. Hostility and Societal prejudice against their attempt to write
    3. A lack of interest in literacy pursuits among women
    4. Competition from male writers in literary circles

31. Arrange the steps of sampling process in correct sequence.
    A. Identify the sampling frame
    B. Define the target population
    C. Determine sample size and select sampling technique
    D. Collect data from sample

    Choose the ***correct*** answer from the options given below:

    1. A, B, C, D 2. A, D, C, B
    3. B, A, C, D 4. D, C, A, B

32. Match the List-I with List-II regarding concepts and related thinkers who coined the work.

List-I	List-II
A. Brigitte Jordan	I. Ecofeminism
B. Inderpal Grewal	II. Intersectionality
C. Kimberle Williams Crenshaw	III. Authoritative knowledge
D. Francoise de Eavborne	IV. Transnational feminism

    Choose the ***correct*** answer from the options given below:

    1. A-II, B-IV, C-III, D-I
    2. A-II, B-IV, C-I, D-III
    3. A-IV, B-III, C-II, D-I
    4. A-III, B-IV, C-II, D-I

33. According to feminist theories what is the argument about domestic labour performed by women?
    1. It is unimportant for the maintenance of the household.
    2. It is a paid work, similar to the waged labour of men.
    3. It is a form of productive activity, though unpaid.
    4. It only benefits capitalism and has no connection to patriarchy.

34. Match the List-I with List-II.

List-I (NFHS-5)	List-II (TFR)
A. Total fertility Rate (TFR) at National Level	I. Bihar, Meghalaya, Uttar Pradesh, Jharkhand, Manipur
B. Replacement level Fertility	II. 2.0
C. Number of states above replacement level	III. 2.1
D. States above replacement level	IV. 5.0

Choose the *correct* answer from the options given below:

1. A-II, B-III, C-I, D-IV
2. A-I, B-IV, C-III, D-II
3. A-II, B-III, C-IV, D-I
4. A-I, B-IV, C-II, D-III

35. Match the List-I with List-II.

List-I (Rights)	List-II (Sections)
A. Right to maintenance	I. Section 100 of IPC
B. Right to equal pay	II. Equal Remuneration Act, 1976
C. Right against domestic violence	III. Protection of Women from Domestic Violence Act, 2005
D. Right to self defence	IV. Hindu Marriage Act, 1950

Choose the *correct* answer from the options given below:

1. A-IV, B-II, C-III, D-I
2. A-I, B-II, C-III, D-IV
3. A-IV, B-III, C-II, D-I
4. A-III, B-II, C-I, D-IV

36. According to Feminist Standpoint theory, whose experiences provide the most critical insight into social power structures.

A. Those in dominant positions of power
B. Marginalized groups
C. Oppressed groups
D. Neutral and objective researchers

Choose the *correct* answer from the options given below:

1. A, B Only
2. B, C Only
3. B, D Only
4. A, C Only

37. Which of the following are the core principles of ecofeminism?

A. The interconnectedness of all living beings
B. The recognition of feminine principles of nature
C. The emphasis on individualism and competitions
D. The critique of patriarchal domination over nature and women

Choose the *correct* answer from the options given below:

1. A, B, C Only
2. A, B, D Only
3. B, C, D Only
4. C, D, A Only

38. Which of the following best reflects Hartmann's argument regarding the relationship between patriarchy and capitalism?

1. Patriarchy and capitalism are separate systems with little intluence on each other.
2. Patriarchy was established before capitalism and continues to affect the labour market.
3. Women benefit from capitalism because they can work in the formal economy.
4. Capitalism had no effect on the development of gender roles in society.

39. Arrange the following laws in chronological order.

A. Widow Remarriage Act
B. Age of Consent Act
C. Bengali Sati Regulation Act
D. Child Marriage Restraint Act

Choose the *correct* answer from the options given below:

1. A, D, C, B
2. C, A, B, D
3. A, B, D, C
4. A, B, C, D

40. Choose the woman who played a role in the pre-independence reform movement.

A. Ramabai Govind Ranade
B. Karaikkal Ammaiyar
C. Akka Mahadevi
D. Pandita Ramabai

Choose the *correct* answer from the options given below:

1. A, C Only
2. A, D Only
3. B, C Only
4. A, B Only

41. What did Baxter's study on perceptions of fairness in domestic labour find?

1. Men's increased involvement in house-work was perceived as unfair by women
2. Women perceive the domestic division of labour as fair, even when they do most of the work
3. Most men felt that their involvement in housework was inadequate
4. Women and men had very different perceptions of fairness regarding domestic chores

42. Match the List-I with List-II regarding incidents crimes that led to change in law in India.

List-I	List-II
A. Laxmi Agarwal- attack on her	I. Triple Talaq was made illegal
B. Shayara Bano- filing of legal petition	II. Juveniles (16-18 years) will be legally tried as an adult, in case of heinous crimes
C. Nirbhaya (pseudonym) rape incident	III. Vishaka guidelines on sexual harassment work-place was formulated
D. Bhanwari Devi- rape incident	IV. Monetary compensation and medical expenses covered for acid attacks

Choose the ***correct*** answer from the options given below:

1. A-IV, B-I, C-II, D-III
2. A-IV, B-I, C-III, D-II
3. A-I, B-IV, C-III, D-II
4. A-II, B-III, C-IV, D-I

43. The first UN legal and political framework to recognise that war impacts women differently and to call for women's participation in conflict prevention and resolution is contained in:

1. Resolution 1325
2. Resolution 1324
3. Resolution 1323
4. Resolution 1335

44. Which of the following statement best describes the feminist ontological concept of "Performativity"?

1. The Idea that gender is a fixed and essential category
2. The Idea that gender is a social construct that is performed through language and behaviour
3. The Idea that gender is a biological category that determines one's identity
4. The Idea that gender is not an individual choice are not allowed

45. What are the key concerns of LGBT^{++} studies within feminist discourse?

A. Promotion of Gender inclusivity
B. Advocating for traditional gender roles
C. Challenging heteronormality
D. Prioritizing binary understanding of gender

Choose the ***correct*** answer from the options given below:

1. A, B Only
2. C, D Only
3. B, D Only
4. A, C Only

46. Grounded theory primarily seeks to:

1. Test existing theories
2. Develop new theories grounded in data
3. Verify hypotheses
4. Perform statistical analysis.

47. What is the primary argument of feminist critique of traditional kinship structures?

1. Kinship structures are natural and universal
2. Kinship structures are culturally constructed and often patriarchal
3. Kinship structures are irrelevant to feminist theory
4. Kinship structures are only relevant to women's lives

48. Hochchild in her book "The Second Shift" derived three constructs related to marital roles that she observes during her research includes:

A. Transitional
B. Traditional
C. Egalitarian
D. Discriminatory

Choose the ***correct*** answer from the options given below:

1. A, B, C Only
2. B, C, D Only
3. C, D, A Only
4. A, B, D Only

49. Which of the following are the changes that has taken place through education of women and girls as per NFHS-5?

A. Age at marriage increases
B. Use of contraceptives increases
C. Mobility of women and girls decreases
D. Experience of violence decreases

Choose the ***correct*** answer from the options given below:

1. A, C and B Only
2. C, B and D Only
3. A, C and D Only
4. A, B and D Only

50. Match the List-I with List-II.

List-I (Movement)	List-II (Led by)
A. Green Belt Movement	I. Greta Thunberg
B. Love Canal Movement	II. Lois Gibbs
C. Redwood Forest Activism	III. Julia Butterfly
D. Climate Strike Movement	IV. Wangari Maathai

Choose the ***correct*** answer from the options given below:

1. A-IV, B-III, C-II, D-I
2. A-II, B-I, C-III, D-IV
3. A-I, B-II, C-IV, D-III
4. A-III, B-IV, C-I, D-II

51. Arrange the government of India initiatives on menstruation in a chronological order.

A. National Menstrual Hygiene Policy
B. India initiated Menstrual Hygiene Scheme to distribute sanitary napkins to young girls
C. Nirmal Bharat Yatra sanitation program includes MHH-Maternal Health Hygiene as an integral agenda of National Health Mission
D. Availability of Sanitary pads for all girls in classes 6 to 12 under the Uniform National Policy

Choose the ***correct*** answer from the options given below:

1. D, B, A, C
2. D, C, A, B
3. B, C, D, A
4. C, B, D, A

52. Choose the following correct correlations between women's education and employment according to MOSPI 2023.

A. The LFPR (Labour Force Participation Rate) is higher among illiterate women
B. The LFPR is higher among the college educated women
C. Higher illiterate women are employed as regular wage employees
D. The LFPR is lower among women who have studied upto secondary and higher secondary level (10+2) of schooling

Choose the ***correct*** answer from the options given below:

1. B, C and D Only
2. A, B and C Only
3. A, B and D Only
4. A, C and D Only

53. Identify the goals of gender budgeting.

A. To raise awareness among stakeholders on gender issues and impacts embedded in budget policies
B. To make governments accountable for translating their gender equality commitments into budgetary commitments
C. To change budget and policies to promote gender neutrality
D. Improving the quality of resource inputs

Choose the ***correct*** answer from the options given below:

1. A, B, C Only
2. B, C, D Only
3. A, C, D Only
4. A, B, D Only

54. In which year, first Gender Budget statement appeared in the Union Budget of India?

1. 2010-11
2. 2007-08
3. 2005-06
4. 2001-02

55. Arrange the following Legislations by the Government of India for women welfare in chronological order.

A. Protection of Women from Domestic Violence Act
B. The Dowry Prohibition Act
C. The Immoral Traffic (Prevention) Act
D. The Sexual Harassment of Women at Workplace (Prevention, Prohibition and Redressal) Act

Choose the ***correct*** answer from the options given below:

1. C, A, B, D
2. B, C, A, D
3. D, C, B, A
4. C, B, A, D

56. Which of the following media house is known for its feminist perspective and critique of Patriarchal culture?

1. Ms. Magazine
2. Cosmopolitan
3. Vogue
4. Harper's Bazar

57. National Committee on Women's Education was appointed in 1958-59 under the Chair-personship of:

1. Sarojini Naidu
2. Durgabai Deshmukh
3. Usha Sharma
4. Hansa Mehta

58. Arrange the following events in chronological order.

A. Chipko Movement
B. Narmada Bachao Andolan
C. #Me Too Movement
D. Suffrage Movement

Choose the ***correct*** answer from the options given below:

1. A, B, C, D
2. B, C, D, A
3. C, D, B, A
4. D, A, B, C

59. What are significant challenges in promoting menstrual hygiene in India?

A. Underuse of Sanitary products
B. Social taboos and lack of awareness
C. Abundance of menstrual hygiene campaign
D. Universal access to hygiene products

Choose the ***correct*** answer from the options given below:

1. A, B Only
2. B, C Only
3. C, D Only
4. A, D Only

60. Identify the Gender Neutral Laws in India.

A. The Protection of Children from Sexual Offences (POCSO)
B. The Code on Wages
C. Section 498A of IPC on Cruelty
D. Right to Education Act

Choose the ***correct*** answer from the options given below:

1. A, B, C Only
2. B, C, D Only
3. A, C, D Only
4. A, B, D Only

61. Arrange various skill initiatives chronologically.

A. Model Skill Loan Scheme
B. Pradhan Mantri Kaushal Vikas Yojana (PMKVY)
C. National Apprenticeship Promotion Scheme (NAPS)
D. The Skill India Digital Hub Platform

Choose the ***correct*** answer from the options given below:

1. A, B, D, C
2. B, D, C, A
3. B, C, D, A
4. D, C, A, B

62. Arrange the steps involved in the implementation stage of gender mainstreaming in correct order.

A. Introducing gender mainstreaming methods and tools
B. Setting gender equality objectives

C. Conducting pilot to gather information from stakeholders
D. Establishing a gender information management system

Choose the *correct* answer from the options given below:

1. C, A, B, D
2. B, C, A, D
3. D, C, A, B
4. A, C, B, D

63. Arrange the steps of the content analysis process.

A. Select the material for analysis
B. Develop coding categories or schemes
C. Define the research questions or objectives
D. Code the data systematically
E. Analyse and Interpret results

Choose the *correct* answer from the options given below:

1. A, C, D, B, E
2. C, A, B, D, E
3. A, B, D, E, C
4. B, C, A, D, E

64. Match the List-I with List-II.

List-I (Microcredit organisation)	**List-II (Country)**
A. Action International	I. Philippines
B. Bandhan Bank	II. India
C. Compartamos Banco	III. United States of America
D. Centre for Agricultural and Rural Development Bank	IV. Mexico

Choose the *correct* answer from the options given below:

1. A-I, B-II, C-IV, D-III
2. A-I, B-II, C-III, D-IV
3. A-II, B-III, C-IV, D-I
4. A-III, B-II, C-IV, D-I

65. What societal belief about women writers is reflected in Lady Winchitsea's lines?

1. Women who write are virtuous and respected
2. Writing is considered a man's exclusive right
3. Women writers are seen as pioneer of equality
4. Literary talent in women is celebrated universally

66. Which is the highest contraceptive method adopted by women in India as per National Family Health Survey-5?

1. Traditional Method
2. Contraceptive pills
3. IUD-Intra Uterine Device
4. Female Sterilisation

67. The Indecent Representation of Women (Prohibition) Act was passed in which year?

1. 1983
2. 1984
3. 1985
4. 1986

68. Who among the following made her defence of abortion over concepts of responsibility and decision making to "right to life of Foetus" to "right to a full human life" which demands adequate nutrients, air, clean water, compassion?

1. Carol Gilligan
2. Allison M. Jagger
3. Solly Markowitz
4. Catherine Mackinnon

69. What is the "Care penalty" in femonomics?

1. The idea that women are penalised for taking time off to care for their families.
2. The notion that men are penalised for taking on caregiving responsibilities
3. The recognition that women should be paid for their care giving work
4. The recognition that care giving work is adequately valued but underpaid

70. The National Population Policy, 2000 aimed to achieve stable population by:

1. 2028
2. 2035
3. 2040
4. 2045

71. In India, at which level of education female drop-out rate was the highest in 2020-21 as per UDISE data?

1. Primary
2. Secondary
3. Elementary
4. Upper primary

72. Match the List-I with List-II. Match the SGD scores with statistics published by NITI Aayog, 2023-24.

List-I (States)	**List-II (Score)**
A. India	I. 78
B. Tamil Nadu	II. 71
C. Goa	III. 63
D. Nagaland	IV. 77

Choose the *correct* answer from the options given below:

1. A-I, B-III, C-II, D-IV
2. A-II, B-I, C-IV, D-III
3. A-I, B-II, C-IV, D-III
4. A-III, B-IV, C-I, D-II

73. Match the List-I with List-II.

List-I (Commission)	**List-II (Recommendations)**
A. Calcutta University Commission	I. Professional and vocational course should be introduced in universities

B. Hunter Commission	II. Same pay for male and female teachers
C. Radhakrishnan Commission	III. Women Inspectors for girls schools
D. Kothari Commission	IV. Training and employing women teachers

Choose the ***correct*** answer from the options given below:

1. A-III, B-I, C-II, D-IV
2. A-I, B-III, C-II, D-IV
3. A-III, B-IV, C-I, D-II
4. A-IV, B-II, C-III, D-I

74. At what stage of maternity the incidents of maternal mortality rate is the highest, both in India and globally?

1. Antenatal period
2. During delivery
3. Post-partum period
4. At the time of abortions

75. Match the List-I with List-II.

List-I (Affirmative Action)	List-II (Year)
A. National Policy for Empowerment of Women	I. 1992
B. Toword's Equality Report	II. 1974
C. Shramshakti Report	III. 1988
D. 73rd Amendment Act	IV. 2001

Choose the ***correct*** answer from the options given below:

1. A-I, B-II, C-III, D-IV
2. A-III, B-IV, C-II, D-I
3. A-I, B-III, C-II, D-IV
4. A-IV, B-II, C-III, D-I

76. Sex-positive feminism is a movement formed to address issues of:

1. Women's sexual pleasure, freedom of expression, sex work and inclusive gender identities
2. Women's sexuality, family honour and virginity
3. Women sex workers, their human rights and their dignity
4. Women's movement against pornography

77. Lakhpati Didi Scheme for women economic empowerment was launched in the year 2022 to:

1. Promote education and marriage of girls
2. A saving scheme with tax relaxation
3. A scheme to obtain interest free loan of two lakh to start small business
4. To assist economically deprived women by providing them a loan ₹ 5 lakh without interest

78. Which of the following Feminists argue that society is extremely patriarchal, and controls women's reproductive choices?

1. Radical Feminists
2. Marxist Feminists
3. Liberal Feminists
4. Black Feminists

79. Which of the following is a characteristic of sexist research methodology?

1. Consideration of gender as a social variable
2. Use of androcentric frame works to interpret data
3. Inclusive representation of diverse groups
4. Reflexivity in researchers positionality

80. What realization led Simone de Beauvoir to write 'The Second Sex'?

1. Sartre's claim that she possessed "a man's intelligence" which she initially accepted as a compliment
2. The belief that humanity is defined equally by both men and women
3. Her conclusion that women are defined by their own unique qualities independent of men
4. Sartre's insistence that men and women share equal intellectual capacities

81. Match the List-I with List-II.

List-I (Commission/Committee)	List-II (Year)
A. National Knowledge Commission Working group on Womens Education	I. 2018
B. Committee on Education and Skill Development for Women	II. 2020
C. Committee on Girls Education and Women empowerment	III. 2014
D. National Education Policy (NEP)	IV. 2006

Choose the ***correct*** answer from the options given below:

1. A-I, B-II, C-III, D-IV
2. A-IV, B-III, C-I, D-II
3. A-III, B-IV, C-I, D-II
4. A-IV, B-II, C-III, D-I

82. How does the Skill India Program address the digital gender divide?

1. By providing subsidized internet access
2. By offering digital literacy courses tailored for women
3. By increasing the number of male trainers in technology
4. By decreasing quotas for women in Information Technology jobs

83. Strategies adopted by Janasankhya Sthirta Kosh (National Population Stabilization Fund) includes:

A. Prerna strategy B. Santhushi strategy
C. National helpline D. Sahmati strategy

Choose the ***correct*** answer from the options given below:

1. A, B, D Only 2. A, B, C Only
3. A, C, D Only 4. D, A, B Only

84. Choose the main focus of global feminist movements in chronological order.

A. Patriarchy, gender norms
B. Post-colonial
C. Suffrage movement education and employment inequalities
D. Existentialism

Choose the ***correct*** answer from the options given below:

1. C, A, D, B 2. C, A, B, D
3. A, C, B, D 4. B, C, A, D

85. Arrange the Acts in a chronological order.

A. Womens Reservation Act
B. Medical Termination of Pregnancy Act
C. Pre-conception and Pre-natal Diagnostic Technology Act
D. Surrogacy (Regulation) Act

Choose the ***correct*** answer from the options given below:

1. B, A, D, C 2. A, B, C, D
3. A, C, B, D 4. B, C, D, A

86. How does microcredit help women in Self-Help Groups (SHG's)?

A. By restricting their participation in economic activities
B. By offering small loans to invest in income generating activities
C. By discouraging financial independence
D. By Promoting access to group based savings program

Choose the ***correct*** answer from the options given below:

1. A, C Only 2. B, D Only
3. C, D Only 4. A, B Only

87. Postmodern Feminism Critiqued earlier feminist theories for:

1. Ignoring women's suffrage movement
2. Overemphasizing the role of biology in gender roles
3. Focusing exclusively on economic inequality
4. Universalizing women's experiences without accounting for differences

88. The "Nari Niketans" were established in 1976 by the social welfare department, wherein deserted/destitute women/widows having no means of livelihood are given admissions by:

1. Government of Uttar Pradesh
2. Government of Bihar
3. Government of Jammu and Kashmir
4. Government of West Bengal

89. Match the List-I with List-II.

List-I (Thinkers)	List-II (Field of Work)
A. Catherine Mackinnon	I. Women's Empowerment
B. Barbara K. Rothman	II. Pornography
C. Naila Kabeer	III. Motherhood
D. Andrea O' Reilley	IV. Reproductive Technologies

Choose the ***correct*** answer from the options given below:

1. A-I, B-II, C-IV, D-III
2. A-III, B-I, C-II, D-IV
3. A-II, B-IV, C-I, D-III
4. A-IV, B-I, C-III, D-II

90. What inequality prevailed despite women being considered equal partners in Hindu law during colonial rules?

A. Women were denied access to ancestral property
B. Economic inequality remained significant
C. Status inequality persisted
D. Women were excluded from Stridhana

Choose the ***correct*** answer from the options given below:

1. A, B, D Only 2. A, B, C Only
3. B, C, D Only 4. A, C, D Only

Direction (Qs. No. 91 to 95): *Read the following passage and answer the questions below:*

Universal Basic Income (UBI) ensures minimum income for all citizens, regardless of employment status, aiming to reduce poverty, promote social justice, and enhance economic autonomy. Grounded in universality and unconditionality, UBI streamlines welfare delivery through digital infrastructure while fostering labour market flexibility. Critics argue that UBI may reduce work incentives and strain fiscal resources, but evidence suggests these concerns are often exaggerated, particularly with moderate UBI levels recognizing non-wage contributions like caregiving.

In India, UBI's feasibility is strengthened by the JAM (Jan-Dhan-Adhar-Mobile) frame work, enabling scalable and efficient implementation. However, a key challenge is avoiding duplication with existing welfare programs. UBI's universality complements targeted cash transfers, such as schemes for women in West Bengal, Odisha, Maharashtra and Karnataka, which empower vulnerable groups like mothers and women-led households. Integrating UBI with targeted initiatives can combat poverty and gender inequality, advancing a more inclusive and equitable society.

91. Integrating UBI with targeted initiatives can combat.

1. Poverty and gender inequality
2. Inclusion and inequality
3. Equity and equality
4. Justice and rights

92. Which of the following is true about the goals of UBI?

1. UBI derails welfare delivery
2. UBI compounds poverty
3. UBI promotes social inequality
4. UBI enhances economic autonomy

93. Standard criticism against UBI is:

1. Incentivises work
2. Improve funding
3. Strains Fiscal resources
4. Ignores non-wage contribution like care giving

94. Universal Basic Income (UBI) ensures a minimum income for:

1. Few wealthy citizens
2. All citizens regardless of employment status
3. All citizens from particular caste background
4. Citizens with selective employment background

95. How UBI streamlines welfare delivery?

1. Fostering labour market flexibility
2. Enhancing work incentives
3. Through digital infrastructure of JAM
4. By avoiding duplication with existing welfare system

Direction (Qs. No. 96 to 100): *Read the following passage and answer the questions below:*

The Mirabal Sisters - Patria, Minerva and Maria Teresa - are national figures of the Dominican Republic, celebrated for their defiance against the brutal dictorship of Rafal Trujilla. Growing up in a comfortable family, the sisters became active in the resistance after Minerva's confrontation with Trujilla at a party in 1949. Despite facing arrests and repression, including Minerva's law degree being denied, the sisters along with their husbands, continued their opposition to the regime. In 1959, they formed the "Fourteenth of June Movement" after a failed invasion attempt by exiled Dominicans. Their activism intensified despite imprisonment, leading to Trujilla ordering their deaths on 25th November 1960. The sisters were ambushed, killed and their deaths staged as a car accident. Their martyrdom galvanised resistance, hastening Trujilla's downfall and he was assassinated in May 1961. Afterward their surviving sister, Dede dedicated herself to raising their children and preserving their legacy. In 1999, the U.N declared 25th November as the International Day for the Elimination of Violence against Women, inspired by the Mirabal sisters' sacrifice. Their legacy continues to inspire global efforts for women's rights and freedom.

96. What significant action did the U.N. take in honour of the Mirabal sisters?

1. Named a street after them
2. Declared 25th November as the International Day for the Elimination of Violence against women
3. Established a scholarship in their name
4. Organized a memorial in their birthplace

97. How did the martyrdom of the Mirbal sisters contribute to the downfall of Trujilla's regime?

1. It led to an immediate armed revolution against Trujilla
2. It directly resulted in the Military's loyalty to Trujilla being restored
3. It caused economic instability in the Dominican Republic
4. It intensified resistance, increasing opposition to the regime both locally and internationally

98. When were Mirabal sisters killed and what directly contributed to the fall of the Trujilla regime?

1. 1960 and Minerva's confrontation with Trujilla at a party in 1949
2. 1960 and assassination of Trujilla
3. 1960 and The Murder of Mirabal sisters
4. 1999 and the declaration of 25th November as the International Day for the VAW

99. Why did Minerva Mirabal become target of Rafael Trujilla?

1. She opposed his dictatorship and confronted him
2. She was a law graduate and posed a political threat
3. She led the 1959 invasion attempt
4. She was an influential member of the military

100. What was the name of the resistance movement formed by Mirabal sisters?

1. Dominican Freedom Movement
2. Fourteenth of June Movement
3. Trujilla Defiance League
4. The Butterflies Network

EXPLANATORY ANSWERS

1. (2):

A. Cyber stalking - IV: It refers to persistent tracking and monitoring of a woman's online activities to instill fear or exert control. It includes repeated, unwanted attention through emails, social media, or other digital means, and often leads to psychological trauma.

B. Catfishing - III: It involves pretending to be someone else (often using fake profiles or identities online) to manipulate or exploit someone emotionally or financially. It is a form of online deception that can lead to financial fraud or emotional abuse.

C. Doxxing - I: Doxxing is the act of publishing private or identifying information (such as address, phone number, etc.) online without consent, to enable harassment. It compromises privacy and can lead to real-world threats.

D. Trolling - II: Trolling in cybercrime often includes aggressive and targeted hate speech, especially involving sexism and misogyny. Trolls provoke and harass individuals or groups, often under anonymity, to incite emotional responses.

2. (1): "A woman must have money and a room of her own if she is to write fiction" is a famous quote from Virginia Woolf's extended essay A Room of One's Own (1929).

- She argued that women need financial independence and personal space (literal and figurative) to express themselves creatively.
- This statement critiques the patriarchal limitations on women's access to education, property, and freedom, which historically hindered their contributions to literature.

3. (3):

- Feminist ethnography distinguishes itself from traditional ethnography by emphasizing reflexivity, collaboration, and equality between the researcher and participants.
- It challenges the traditional top-down approach, giving voice to marginalized groups, especially women.
- Feminist ethnographers often include personal narratives and lived experiences to highlight intersectionality and subjective experiences.
- It opposes the "objective observer" stance and believes the researcher's identity impacts the research process.

4. (3): The Global Gender Gap Index (GGGI), published by the World Economic Forum, uses four key indicators:

A. Education: Measures gender gaps in literacy and access to primary, secondary, and tertiary education.

B. Healthcare (also referred to as Health and Survival): Examines life expectancy and sex ratio at birth.

D. Economic Participation: Considers labour force participation, wage equality, and leadership roles.

C. Housing is not a part of the GGGI indicators.

Factual note: GGGI scores range from 0 (imparity) to 1 (parity), and in 2023, Iceland topped the ranking with over 90% gender parity.

5. (2):

A. Nancy Chodorow - II: Chodorow emphasized that despite social contradictions and psychological conflicts, women continue to successfully perform the role of mothering. She explored how mothering is reproduced socially and psychologically in her psychoanalytic feminist work.

B. Adrienne Rich - I: In Of Woman Born, she states that the mother-child relationship is central to women's experience and identity, and she critiques how patriarchy has historically shaped and distorted this relationship.

C. Ann Oakley - IV: Oakley highlighted the duality of motherhood – as both a strength and a handicap. She critically analyzed the medicalization of motherhood and gender roles in domestic life, showing how societal expectations hinder women's autonomy.

D. Veena Poonacha - III: Poonacha explored how, despite constraints, motherhood can be profoundly satisfying and empowering for many women. Her work integrates Indian socio-cultural contexts and feminist perspectives.

6. (3):

D. A systematic decadal drop of child sex ratio in favour of boys was observed in the census data:

The Census of India started showing a continuous decline in the child sex ratio (CSR), particularly from the 1991 Census onwards. The CSR dropped from 945 in 1991 to 927 in 2001 and 919 in 2011, indicating strong gender-based birth discrimination.

A. Prenatal Diagnostic Technology Act:

To curb the misuse of prenatal diagnostic techniques (like ultrasound) for sex determination, the Prenatal Diagnostic Techniques (Regulation and Prevention of Misuse) Act was enacted in 1994.

C. Pre-conception and Prenatal Diagnostic Techniques (PCPNDT) Act:

In 2003, the 1994 Act was amended and renamed as the PCPNDT Act to regulate pre-conception diagnostic techniques as well and to make the law more stringent in preventing sex-selective abortions.

B. Beti Bachao Beti Padhao Programme launched in Haryana:

The BBBP scheme was launched in 2015 in Panipat, Haryana, focusing on improving the declining CSR, changing social mindsets, and ensuring education for girls.

7. (3): As per the Sample Registration System (SRS) Statistical Report 2017-18, Bihar showed a concerning trend where the Sex Ratio at Birth (SRB) in rural areas was lower than in urban areas, indicating worsening gender imbalance even in traditionally more egalitarian rural settings.

- In many states, urban areas show lower SRB due to easy access to medical technologies for sex selection. However, in Bihar, the reverse trend reflects deep-rooted patriarchal values penetrating rural health behaviours.
- This reversal is alarming because rural areas were expected to retain relatively natural SRBs.

8. (3):

A. Right against Dowry - III:
Protected under the Dowry Prohibition Act, 1961, which prohibits dowry demands and considers them a punishable offense. It ensures legal protection against dowry-related harassment and violence.

B. Right to Free Legal Aid - I:
Provided under the Legal Services Authorities Act, 1987, offering free legal services to the weaker sections, including women, to ensure access to justice.

C. Right to Dignity and Decency - II:
Under Section 354A of the Indian Penal Code, any act of harassment or indecent behavior towards women is criminalized, supporting the right to dignity and decency.

D. Rights at Workplace - IV:
The Sexual Harassment of Women at Workplace (Prevention, Prohibition and Redressal) Act, 2013 ensures a safe and conducive working environment for women.

9. (1):

B. Welfare Approach:
The earliest model, dominant till the 1970s, viewed women primarily as passive recipients of welfare, focusing on food, health, and family planning.

D. Women in Development (WID) - Equality Approach:
Emerged in the 1970s, emphasizing integrating women into existing development programs. However, it failed to challenge the structural causes of inequality.

A. Women and Development (WAD) - Empowerment Approach:
Introduced in the late 1970s and 1980s, WAD critiqued capitalism and patriarchy and promoted collective action and women's empowerment.

C. Gender and Development (GAD) - Equality Approach:
GAD arose in the 1980s, focusing on gender relations, not just women. It aimed to transform power dynamics and achieve equality by challenging societal structures.

10. (3):

A. 15% share of women pilots in India:
According to the Public Information Bureau (PIB) 2023, India has the highest proportion of female pilots globally – around 15%, compared to the global average of 5%, showing progress in a highly male-dominated field.

B. 43% women enrolled in STEM in India:
India has the highest percentage of female STEM enrollment globally. As per AISHE (All India Survey on Higher Education) data, women constitute 43% of total STEM graduates in India.

C. 46% elected representatives in Panchayati Raj are women:
Due to 33% to 50% reservation in local governance, women occupy about 46% of seats in Panchayati Raj Institutions, a key indicator of political empowerment at the grassroots level.

D. Men earning only 60% of women's wage – INCORRECT:
In India, women earn about 60-70% of what men earn, not the reverse. The gender pay gap remains a concern in both formal and informal sectors.

11. (3):

C. United Nations Universal Declaration of Human Rights (1948):
Adopted in 1948, it was the first international document to affirm the equal rights of men and women, laying the foundation for future gender equality frameworks.

B. CEDAW - Convention on the Elimination of All Forms of Discrimination Against Women (1979):
Often referred to as the international bill of rights for women, CEDAW was adopted by the UN General Assembly in 1979 and entered into force in 1981. It is legally binding and commits states to eliminate discrimination against women in all forms.

A. ICPD - International Conference on Population and Development (1994):
Held in Cairo, the ICPD shifted the focus from demographic targets to a rights-based approach to reproductive health and emphasized women's empowerment and gender equality.

D. United Nations Fourth World Conference on Women (1995):
Conducted in Beijing, China, this conference resulted in the Beijing Declaration and Platform for Action, which remains a comprehensive global policy framework for achieving gender equality.

12. (2):

- Kate Millett, in her landmark book Sexual Politics (1970), critically analyzed how patriarchal systems are sustained by political structures and coined the term "Patriarchal Government" to describe the systematic control of women by male-dominated institutions.
- Her work laid the foundation for radical feminist theory by linking personal experiences of women to broader political structures and ideologies.

13. (2):

- Feminist economists argue that Gross Domestic Product (GDP) fails to account for the unpaid labour that primarily women perform—such as child-rearing, elder care, cooking, and household chores.

- Though these activities are essential for the economy and social reproduction, they are excluded from national income accounting because they are not exchanged in the market.
- According to various UN reports, if unpaid care work were monetized, it would contribute an estimated 10% to 39% of GDP, depending on the country.
- Feminists advocate for time-use surveys and alternative measures like Gross National Happiness or Social Progress Index that include well-being and care work.

14. (1):

A. Shulamith Firestone - III: The Dialectic of Sex (1970):

Firestone, a radical feminist, combined Marxist and psychoanalytic theory to argue that gender inequality originates from biological reproduction and the family structure.

B. Betty Friedan - I: The Feminine Mystique (1963):

This book sparked the second wave of feminism in the U.S. by highlighting the dissatisfaction of middle-class housewives and challenging the "ideal woman" myth.

C. Mary Wollstonecraft - IV: A Vindication of the Rights of Woman (1792):

Considered one of the earliest feminist texts, Wollstonecraft argued for equal education and rationality for women, laying the philosophical groundwork for later feminist movements.

D. Vandana Shiva - II: Staying Alive (1988):

In this ecofeminist work, Shiva critiques Western models of development and emphasizes the role of women in ecological sustainability and traditional knowledge systems.

15. (3):

- The Bechdel-Wallace Test, created by cartoonist Alison Bechdel, evaluates gender bias in films and media by asking three questions:
  1. Are there at least two named women characters?
  2. Do they talk to each other?
  3. Do they talk about something other than a man?
- This test reveals the systemic underrepre-sentation and stereotyping of women in media and promotes gender-sensitive storytelling.
- Despite being simple, it has become a widely used cultural critique tool in feminist film analysis.

16. (4):

A. British colonial rule imposed Section 377, criminalising homosexuality:

Introduced in 1861 during British rule, Section 377 of the Indian Penal Code criminalized "carnal intercourse against the order of nature", effectively making homosexuality a criminal offense in India.

B. First Pride Parade at Kolkata:

India's first Pride Parade, called the "Kolkata Rainbow Pride Walk", was held in 1999, marking a public visibility movement for the LGBTQIA^{++} community.

D. The Supreme Court of India ruled Section 377 unconstitutional:.

On 6th September 2018, the Supreme Court of India in a landmark Navtej Singh Johar v. Union of India case unanimously decriminalized consensual homosexual acts among adults, declaring parts of Section 377 unconstitutional.

C. Transgender Persons (Protection of Rights) Act:

Passed in 2019, this Act aimed to protect the rights of transgender persons, prohibit discrimination, and recognize their identity. It provides for a certification process and rights to health, education, and employment.

17. (1):

A. Empowering adolescent girls (11-18 years):

The Rajiv Gandhi Scheme for Empowerment of Adolescent Girls – SABLA was launched in 2010 to empower girls through nutrition, health education, life skills, and vocational training.

B. Promoting awareness about health, hygiene, ARSH:

The scheme includes components on awareness generation about adolescent reproductive and sexual health (ARSH), menstrual hygiene, nutrition, and family welfare.

C. Home-based and vocational skill integration:

It also seeks to equip girls with life skills and upgrade vocational and home-based skills, integrated with existing skill development programs to enhance future employability.

D. Depositing 3000 in fixed deposit – INCORRECT:

This is a component of other schemes like Sukanya Samriddhi Yojana, not SABLA. SABLA is a service-based scheme, not a direct cash transfer or deposit scheme.

18. (2):

- Feminist epistemology challenges traditional notions that knowledge must be objective and free from emotion or subjectivity. It argues that emotions, values, and personal experiences significantly shape how knowledge is produced, especially for marginalized groups.
- It critiques the male-dominated, objectivist scientific tradition and highlights how knowledge production is situated, context-specific, and often influenced by the researcher's standpoint (Standpoint Theory).
- Feminists like Sandra Harding and Donna Haraway emphasized the idea of "situated knowledges", recognizing diverse epistemo-logies beyond the dominant Western rationalist model.

19. (3):

- Rosa Luxemburg, a Marxist theorist and revolutionary, wrote "The Proletarian Woman" in March 1914 for International Women's Day.
- In the article, she emphasized the double burden faced by working-class women—oppression due to both class and gender—and urged them to join the fight for socialism.

- Her work merged the struggle for women's rights with the larger class struggle, arguing that true liberation of women could only occur under socialism.

20. (2): The "Care Penalty" refers to the socio-economic disadvantages primarily faced by women due to their role as unpaid or underpaid caregivers (in both formal and informal sectors).

A. Reduced earnings:

Women often earn less than men due to taking career breaks, part-time work, or lower-paying caregiving jobs.

B. Care stagnation:

Due to caregiving responsibilities (like child or elder care), many women experience limited mobility, fewer promotions, and reduced access to leadership roles.

D. Increased financial stress:

The financial burden of caregiving, combined with reduced earnings, results in long-term economic insecurity, especially for single mothers and elderly women.

C. Unlimited access to benefits – INCORRECT:

Caregivers do not enjoy unlimited benefits; in fact, most care work remains unrecognized and uncompensated, especially in developing countries like India.

21. (3):

A. Initiated by Ministry of Education and Central Board of Secondary Education:

The CBSE Udaan Scheme was launched by the Ministry of Education (formerly MHRD) in collaboration with CBSE to support the academic advancement of girl students in India.

C. Aims to help female students of economically vulnerable families in India to obtain degrees from renowned engineering colleges:

The program focuses on preparing meritorious girl students from economically disadvantaged backgrounds for engineering entrance exams like JEE, through online resources, mentoring, and study material.

D. Is for female students studying in Class XI and they must be enrolled in the Physics, Chemistry, and Mathematics stream:

The eligibility includes girl students in Class XI, studying PCM, enrolled in Kendriya Vidyalayas, Navodaya Vidyalayas, Government schools, and whose family income is less than ₹ 6 lakh per annum.

B. Aimed at Arts and Commerce Colleges – INCORRECT:

The scheme is not focused on Arts or Commerce education. It is specifically meant to encourage girls in STEM and support entry into engineering colleges.

22. (2):

A. All SC/ST girls who pass class VIII:

Under the National Scheme of Incentives to Girls for Secondary Education (NSIGSE), launched in May 2008, SC/ST girls passing Class VIII and enrolling in Class IX are eligible.

B. Girls from Kasturba Gandhi Balika Vidyalayas (KGBV):

Girls from KGBV, irrespective of their caste (SC/ST), are also covered under the scheme, provided they enroll in Class IX in a government, aided, or local body school.

D. Married girls, those in private or central schools are excluded:

The scheme excludes married girls, and those in private unaided, Kendriya Vidyalayas (KVS), Navodaya Vidyalayas (NVS), or CBSE-affiliated private schools, focusing instead on economically and socially disadvantaged sections.

C. Girls should be below 18 years – INCORRECT in this context:

Although age is a factor, the condition is not a primary eligibility criterion, and the main focus is caste category, school type, and class enrollment.

23. (3):

- The Vishaka Guidelines were formulated by the Supreme Court of India in 1997 in the landmark case Vishaka vs. State of Rajasthan, in response to the gangrape of a social worker.
- These guidelines laid the framework for preventing sexual harassment at the workplace, in the absence of specific legislation at the time.
- It served as a legally binding directive until the Sexual Harassment of Women at Workplace (Prevention, Prohibition and Redressal) Act was passed in 2013.

24. (2):

- Emerging technologies like Artificial Intelligence (AI) have been found to replicate and even amplify existing societal biases, including gender discrimination.
- AI systems trained on biased historical data may produce outputs that reflect or intensify stereotypes, such as associating leadership with males or underrepresenting women in tech roles.
- Studies (e.g., MIT Media Lab) have shown that facial recognition software has much higher error rates for women and people of colour, particularly Black women (up to 34% error rate), compared to White men (less than 1%).

25. (4): Chronological order of publication of the books:

D. A Vindication of the Rights of Woman – 1792:

Written by Mary Wollstonecraft, this foundational feminist text argued for women's education and equality, making it one of the earliest works of feminist philosophy.

A. Pride and Prejudice – 1813:

Authored by Jane Austen, this novel portrayed the complexities of gender, class, and marriage in early 19th-century England and subtly critiqued the limitations imposed on women.

B. The Second Sex – 1949:

Written by Simone de Beauvoir, this philosophical treatise explored the construction of femininity and introduced the famous phrase, "One is not born, but rather becomes, a woman".

C. The Feminine Mystique – 1963:

Betty Friedan's groundbreaking book sparked the second-wave feminist movement in the U.S. by exposing "the problem that has no name", i.e., the dissatisfaction of housewives confined to domestic roles.

26. (2):

- As per the Sexual Harassment of Women at Workplace (Prevention, Prohibition and Redressal) Act, 2013, the Internal Complaints Committee (ICC), while recommending compensation, considers factors such as:

  A. Mental trauma suffered by the complainant due to the harassment.

  B. Emotional distress caused, including humiliation and damage to dignity.

- The Act does not mandate consideration of the complainant's educational qualifications or the respondent's family income, as these are not directly related to the severity of the harm caused.
- Other valid considerations may include loss in career opportunity, medical expenses, and the duration of harassment.

27. (3):

- Wyoming was the first U.S. territory to grant women the right to vote in 1869.
- It earned the nickname "The Equality State" for this progressive step.
- This decision was part of an effort to attract more settlers and was also influenced by women's advocacy for legal and social rights.
- When Wyoming became a state in 1890, it retained women's suffrage, making it a pioneer in the American women's rights movement.

28. (2):

- #HeForShe is a global solidarity campaign launched by UN Women in 2014, aimed at engaging men and boys to act against gender inequality.
- It was initiated to break traditional gender roles and invite all genders to work as allies in achieving gender equality.
- The campaign gained massive recognition with the speech of Emma Watson at the United Nations, where she urged global participation.
- It emphasizes the idea that gender equality is not just a women's issue but a human rights issue.

29. (3):

- The Bodhgaya Movement in Bihar involved landless Dalit women and men, who mobilized under Mukti Andolan in the late 1970s and 1980s.
- A major component of this struggle was women's demand for legal ownership of land.
- Traditionally, land was registered in the names of male family members. This movement questioned patriarchal property ownership and called for direct land titles in women's names.
- It combined class struggle with gender justice, setting a precedent for feminist land rights movements in India.

30. (2):

- In her renowned essay A Room of One's Own (1929), Virginia Woolf does indeed mention lack of access to education and financial independence, but her central argument highlights the hostility, ridicule, and societal prejudice faced by women who tried to express themselves through writing.
- Woolf illustrates this with the fictional character Judith Shakespeare, the imagined sister of William Shakespeare. Despite being equally talented, Judith is denied education, laughed at for writing, abused, and ultimately driven to suicide — symbolizing society's active resistance to female authorship.
- Key quote from A Room of One's Own:

  "It is fatal for anyone who writes to think of their sex. It is fatal to be a man or a woman pure and simple; one must be woman-manly or man-womanly."

  This indicates the pressure and bias women faced in literary expression.
- Therefore, while limited access to resources is part of the broader issue, the significant challenge Woolf focused on was the societal hostility and prejudice against women's intellectual and literary pursuits.

31. (3):

B. Define the target population:

This is the first and most crucial step where the researcher defines who the study is about—the group from which the sample will be drawn.

A. Identify the sampling frame:

After defining the population, the next step is to identify a complete list or source (like a directory, register, or list) from which the sample can be selected.

C. Determine sample size and select sampling technique:

Once the frame is set, the researcher chooses the sampling technique (e.g., random, stratified) and determines the number of participants (sample size) needed.

D. Collect data from sample:

Finally, the researcher collects the data from the selected individuals within the sample to perform the analysis.

32. (4):

A. Brigitte Jordan – III: Authoritative knowledge:

Jordan coined the concept of authoritative knowledge in childbirth and medical anthropology, referring to knowledge that dominates or overrides others in a given context.

B. Inderpal Grewal – IV: Transnational feminism:

Grewal has contributed extensively to the field of transnational feminism, analyzing how gender, nation, and globalization intersect in contemporary societies.

C. Kimberlé Williams Crenshaw – II: Intersectionality:

Crenshaw introduced the term intersectionality in 1989 to explain how systems of oppression (race, gender, class) intersect and impact marginalized groups, especially Black women.

D. Françoise d'Eaubonne – I: Ecofeminism:

She coined the term ecofeminism in the 1970s, linking the oppression of women and nature as consequences of patriarchal and capitalist systems.

33. (3):

- Feminist theories argue that domestic labour, traditionally performed by women, is a productive economic activity, although it is unpaid and unrecognized in GDP calculations.
- This labour includes cooking, cleaning, childcare, and eldercare, which sustains the workforce and family structure, forming the foundation of capitalist economies.
- Feminists like Silvia Federici, Mariarosa Dalla Costa, and Angela Davis critique how domestic labour is excluded from mainstream economic discourse but is essential for the reproduction of labour power.
- Movements like Wages for Housework emerged from this analysis, demanding recognition and compensation for unpaid domestic work.

34. (3):

A. Total Fertility Rate (TFR) at national level – II: 2.0

As per NFHS-5 (2019-21) data, India's national TFR is 2.0, which is below the replacement level of 2.1.

B. Replacement Level Fertility – III: 2.1

A TFR of 2.1 is considered the replacement level fertility, where a population exactly replaces itself from one generation to the next without growth.

C. Number of states above replacement level – IV: 5.0

This matches with the number of states/UTs (like Bihar, Meghalaya, UP, Jharkhand, Manipur) that still have TFR above 2.1.

D. States above replacement level – I: Bihar, Meghalaya, Uttar Pradesh, Jharkhand, Manipur

These states have higher-than-average fertility rates due to lower access to health and family planning services, early marriage, and lower female literacy.

35. (1):

A. Right to Maintenance – IV: Hindu Marriage Act, 1955:

Under Section 24 and 25 of the Hindu Marriage Act, a woman has the right to claim maintenance and alimony during and after divorce.

B. Right to Equal Pay – II: Equal Remuneration Act, 1976:

This Act ensures that men and women are paid equally for the same work or work of a similar nature, promoting gender parity in wages.

C. Right against Domestic Violence – III: Protection of Women from Domestic Violence Act, 2005:

This progressive legislation provides protection for women from physical, emotional, sexual, and economic abuse in both domestic and live-in relationships.

D. Right to Self-Defence – I: Section 100 of IPC:

Section 100 of the Indian Penal Code grants a person, including women, the right to cause death in self-defence, if under a threat of grievous harm or assault.

36. (2):

- Feminist Standpoint Theory emphasizes that marginalized and oppressed groups—particularly women, the working class, and racial minorities—possess a unique and critical perspective on power structures because they experience the consequences of these structures most directly.
- Thinkers like Nancy Hartsock, Dorothy Smith, and Sandra Harding argue that knowledge is socially situated, and those who are oppressed have an epistemic advantage in understanding the real nature of systemic inequalities.
- It challenges the idea of "neutral" or "objective" knowledge, asserting that lived experiences of the oppressed are essential for authentic insight into hierarchical systems like patriarchy and capitalism.

37. (2): Ecofeminism links the oppression of women and nature as consequences of patriarchal domination, and it is rooted in the belief that:

A. Interconnectedness of all living beings is a foundational ecofeminist principle, emphasizing harmony between humans, animals, and ecosystems.

B. Recognition of feminine principles of nature refers to nurturing, cooperation, and sustainability, qualities often associated with feminine energy and devalued in patriarchal systems.

D. Critique of patriarchal domination over nature and women is central, as ecofeminism challenges the exploitative and hierarchical worldview that treats both nature and women as resources for control.

C. Emphasis on individualism and competition is antithetical to ecofeminism, which instead promotes community, care, and collective responsibility.

38. (2):

- Heidi Hartmann, a socialist feminist, argued that patriarchy and capitalism are interlinked systems, but patriarchy predates capitalism and shapes how women are positioned within it.
- She explained that capitalism benefits from patriarchy, as women provide unpaid domestic labor and are often relegated to lower-paid, subordinate positions in the labor market.

- This dual system restricts women both in public economic participation and private domestic roles, perpetuating gender inequality even within modern economic structures.
- Her theory challenges Marxism for ignoring gender and critiques radical feminism for not analyzing class dynamics adequately.

39. (2): Chronological order of laws concerning women's rights and reform in India:

C. Bengali Sati Regulation Act – 1829:

Passed by Governor-General Lord William Bentinck, this was the first major colonial legal reform to abolish the Sati practice.

A. Widow Remarriage Act – 1856:

Initiated by Ishwar Chandra Vidyasagar, this law legalized the remarriage of Hindu widows, challenging rigid Brahmanical patriarchy.

B. Age of Consent Act – 1891:

Raised the age of consent for girls from 10 to 12 years, aiming to protect minor girls from sexual exploitation within marriage.

D. Child Marriage Restraint Act – 1929:

Also known as the Sarda Act, it was the first secular social reform law in India to legally define minimum age of marriage—14 for girls and 18 for boys (later amended).

40. (2):

A. Ramabai Govind Ranade:

She was a prominent social reformer and educationist, who worked towards the upliftment of Hindu widows and the spread of female education during the late 19th century.

D. Pandita Ramabai:

A trailblazing scholar and social reformer, Pandita Ramabai established the Arya Mahila Samaj and Sharada Sadan for women's education and refuge. She was among the first Indian women to advocate widow remarriage and criticize caste and gender discrimination.

B. Karaikkal Ammaiyar and C. Akka Mahadevi were Bhakti saints and poets, significant in Indian spiritual and literary history, but their contributions were not part of the pre-independence reform movement in a socio-political sense.

Their role is seen more in the context of religious and spiritual assertion, not organized reform.

41. (2):

- Sociologist Janeen Baxter, through her research on perceptions of fairness in domestic labour, found that women often perceive the division of household work as fair, even when they perform the majority of it.
- This is attributed to internalized gender roles, societal conditioning, and the normalization of domestic labour being a woman's responsibility.
- Many women rationalize the imbalance due to men being the primary breadwinners or due to notions of "natural" gender duties.
- Such perceptions mask the structural inequality in unpaid domestic work and reflect the deep-rooted acceptance of gendered divisions of labour in family settings.

42. (1):

A. Laxmi Agarwal – IV: Monetary compensation and medical expenses covered for acid attacks:

Laxmi, a survivor of an acid attack, became a powerful activist whose case led to changes in Indian law, including regulation of acid sale and provisions for medical treatment and compensation under the Criminal Law Amendment Act, 2013.

B. Shayara Bano – I: Triple Talaq was made illegal:

Shayara Bano filed a petition in the Supreme Court in 2016, challenging the practice of instant triple talaq. The court ruled it unconstitutional in 2017, leading to the Muslim Women (Protection of Rights on Marriage) Act, 2019.

C. Nirbhaya (pseudonym) – II: Juveniles (16–18 years) will be tried as adults in heinous crimes:

The 2012 Delhi gangrape case triggered nationwide protests and legal reforms. The Juvenile Justice (Care and Protection of Children) Act, 2015 was amended to allow juveniles aged 16–18 to be tried as adults for heinous offences.

D. Bhanwari Devi – III: Vishaka Guidelines on sexual harassment at workplace were formulated:

After Bhanwari Devi, a social worker, was gang-raped in 1992 for stopping a child marriage, the Supreme Court in 1997 laid down the Vishaka Guidelines, forming the foundation of India's workplace sexual harassment law.

43. (1):

- United Nations Security Council Resolution 1325, adopted in 2000, was the first legal and political framework that recognized that armed conflict affects women and men differently.
- It called for the inclusion of women in peacebuilding, conflict resolution, and security processes and emphasized the protection of women's rights during war.
- It launched the Women, Peace and Security (WPS) agenda, a global movement for integrating gender perspectives in conflict zones and post-conflict reconstruction.

44. (2):

- The concept of "Performativity", developed by feminist philosopher Judith Butler, suggests that gender is not an innate or fixed identity, but something constructed and reinforced through repeated acts, language, and social rituals.
- According to Butler, saying "I am a woman" doesn't reflect an internal essence but performs a

socially constructed role based on societal norms and expectations.

- This theory challenges essentialist views of gender, instead arguing that gender identities are fluid, contingent, and performative rather than biologically determined.

45. (4): LGBT^{++} studies within feminist discourse emphasize:

A. Promotion of gender inclusivity, advocating for policies, language, education, and practices that recognize and respect diverse gender identities.

C. Challenging heteronormativity, which assumes that heterosexuality is the norm, thereby marginalizing non-heterosexual identities.

Feminist and queer theorists critique the binary and rigid classifications of gender and sexuality, arguing for more intersectional and inclusive frameworks.

(B) Advocating for traditional gender roles and (D) Prioritizing binary understanding contradict the core values of LGBT^{++} studies, which aim to deconstruct and go beyond such limiting views.

46. (2):

- Grounded Theory, developed by Barney Glaser and Anselm Strauss in the 1960s, is a qualitative research method that focuses on inductively developing theories from systematically collected and analyzed data.
- Instead of starting with a hypothesis or testing existing theories, researchers generate theories grounded in participants' experiences and field data.
- It is widely used in feminist research because it allows concepts to emerge from marginalized voices, aligning with bottom-up approaches to theory-building.

47. (2):

- Feminist theorists argue that kinship is not a natural or fixed system, but rather a cultural construct that varies across societies and is deeply embedded in patriarchal norms.
- Classic works by Gayle Rubin, Carole Stack, and Sherry Ortner have shown how kinship systems regulate women's sexuality, reproduction, and roles, reinforcing male dominance and control.
- For example, marriage alliances, patrilineal descent, and dowry systems often marginalize women and reduce them to property-like status in some societies.

48. (1): In her landmark book "The Second Shift" (1989), Arlie Hochschild identifies three types of marital role ideologies based on how spouses divide work at home:

A. Transitional: One partner (usually the woman) tries to balance work and home duties, while the other may retain traditional expectations.

B. Traditional: The husband is the breadwinner and the wife is responsible for housework and childcare.

C. Egalitarian: Both partners share responsibilities equally at work and at home.

D. Discriminatory is not one of the constructs defined by Hochschild in this context.

49. (4): According to NFHS-5 (2019–21) and supported by education research:

A. Age at marriage increases:

Educated women tend to marry later, often after completing schooling or higher education. The mean age of marriage has increased from 19.0 years (NFHS-4) to around 21 years in many regions.

B. Use of contraceptives increases:

Women with education are more aware of reproductive health and are more likely to use family planning methods, contributing to declining fertility rates.

D. Experience of violence decreases:

Educated women are more likely to recognize and report abuse, and education correlates with higher autonomy and decision-making power, which helps reduce gender-based violence.

C. Mobility of women and girls decreases – INCORRECT:

In fact, education enhances mobility by increasing access to jobs, public spaces, and participation in decision-making processes.

50. (*)

51. (3): Correct chronological order with explanations:

B. India initiated Menstrual Hygiene Scheme (2011):

- Launched under the National Rural Health Mission (now NHM) in 2011.
- It aimed to promote menstrual hygiene among adolescent girls aged 10-19 in rural areas by distributing low-cost sanitary napkins and increasing awareness through ASHAs.

C. Nirmal Bharat Yatra (2012):

- A sanitation and hygiene awareness campaign initiated in 2012, led by the Ministry of Drinking Water and Sanitation.
- It included Menstrual Hygiene Management (MHM) as part of the broader agenda on sanitation and health education under NHM.

D. Availability of sanitary pads for girls in classes 6 to 12:

- States like Odisha, Rajasthan, and Tamil Nadu launched schemes from 2013 onwards providing free or subsidized sanitary pads to schoolgirls.
- While not a single "uniform national policy", over time, this idea was scaled and included in the Rashtriya Kishor Swasthya Karyakram (RKSK).

A. National Menstrual Hygiene Policy (drafted post-2018):

- A comprehensive national-level policy is under development, but as of now, only draft versions exist (not yet formally enacted).
- The aim is to integrate MHM into education health, and sanitation sectors.

52. (3):

A. The LFPR is higher among illiterate women:

This is statistically true in India, particularly because illiterate women often engage in informal, agricultural, and labor-intensive work, hence contributing to a higher measured LFPR, although mostly in low-paying, unregulated sectors.

B. The LFPR is higher among college-educated women:

As per MOSPI 2023 and PLFS data, women with higher education (graduate and above) are more likely to be employed in regular salaried jobs, leading to a higher quality of employment and participation rate in this group.

D. The LFPR is lower among women with secondary/ higher secondary education (10+2):

This reflects the "middle dropout phenomenon"—many women drop out after secondary schooling due to marriage, domestic duties, or social restrictions, resulting in a dip in labour participation at this stage.

C. Higher illiterate women are employed as regular wage employees - INCORRECT:

Illiterate women are mostly engaged in casual or self-employment, not in regular salaried positions which usually require formal education.

53. (4):

A. To raise awareness among stakeholders on gender issues in budget policies:

Gender Budgeting aims to sensitize policymakers, planners, and administrators about the differential impact of fiscal policies on men and women.

B. To make governments accountable for gender commitments in budgets:

It ensures that gender equality commitments made in policy documents are translated into concrete budgetary allocations, thus making governments accountable for implementation.

D. Improving the quality of resource inputs:

Gender budgeting focuses on effective allocation and utilization of resources to benefit women and girls, improving development outcomes.

C. To promote gender neutrality - INCORRECT:

Gender budgeting does not aim for neutrality; rather, it emphasizes gender equity, by addressing historical disadvantages through affirmative budgeting and policies.

54. (3):

- The first Gender Budget Statement in India was presented in the Union Budget 2005-06.
- India became one of the pioneers in institutionalizing gender budgeting, and since then, Gender Budget Statements (GBS) have been included as part of the budget documents annually.
- It categorizes expenditure into:
  - Part A: 100% women-specific programs.
  - Part B: Programs where at least 30% of benefits go to women.

55. (4): Chronological order of major legislations for women's welfare in India:

C. The Immoral Traffic (Prevention) Act - 1956:

Originally passed as the Suppression of Immoral Traffic in Women and Girls Act (SITA), it was later amended and renamed. It aimed to combat trafficking and commercial sexual exploitation.

B. The Dowry Prohibition Act - 1961:

This Act made the giving, taking, or demanding of dowry a punishable offence, aiming to curb the widespread dowry-related violence and harassment.

A. Protection of Women from Domestic Violence Act - 2005:

This law expanded the definition of domestic abuse to include physical, sexual, verbal, emotional, and economic abuse, offering civil remedies like protection orders, residence rights, etc.

D. Sexual Harassment of Women at Workplace (Prevention, Prohibition and Redressal) Act - 2013:

This Act was passed following the Vishaka Guidelines (1997) and provides a legal framework for addressing sexual harassment at workplaces, mandating Internal Complaints Committees in all organizations.

56. (1):

- Ms. Magazine, co-founded in 1971 by Gloria Steinem and other prominent feminists, is a pioneering media platform that amplifies feminist voices and provides a critical analysis of patriarchy, gender roles, and systemic sexism.
- It was one of the first national publications to discuss feminist issues such as abortion rights, domestic violence, workplace inequality, reproductive health, and LGBTQ$^+$ rights.
- Unlike Cosmopolitan, Vogue, or Harper's Bazaar, which focus primarily on lifestyle, fashion, and consumer culture, Ms. Magazine is rooted in activist journalism and political commentary from a feminist lens.

57. (2):

- The National Committee on Women's Education was appointed in 1958-59 under the chairpersonship of Durgabai Deshmukh, a freedom fighter, social reformer, and member of the Constituent Assembly.
- The committee's recommendations led to the integration of women's education into India's Five-Year Plans and called for free education for girls, special scholarships, hostels, and measures to reduce the gender gap in literacy.
- She was also the founder of Andhra Mahila Sabha and played a vital role in institution-building for women's education and empowerment.

58. (4): Chronological order of the given events:

D. Suffrage Movement:

Emerged in the late 19th and early 20th centuries especially in Western democracies. In India, the women's suffrage movement was active in the 1930s-1940s.

A. Chipko Movement - 1973:

A non-violent ecological movement led by women in Uttarakhand to protect trees from being cut symbolizing eco-feminism and grassroots activism.

B. Narmada Bachao Andolan - 1985 onwards:

Led by Medha Patkar, this movement protested against large dam projects on the Narmada River, raising concerns over displacement, environmental degradation, and social justice.

C. #MeToo Movement - 2017 (India: 2018):

A global movement that emerged from the U.S. and was adapted in India to expose sexual harassment and assault, especially in workplaces and media.

Hence, the correct chronological sequence is: D, A, B, C.

59. (1): Significant challenges in promoting menstrual hygiene in India include:

A. Underuse of sanitary products:

As per NFHS-5, only around 77.3% of young women (15–24) use hygienic menstrual protection methods. The remainder still rely on cloth or unsafe alternatives due to cost and inaccessibility.

B. Social taboos and lack of awareness:

Menstruation is still surrounded by silence, myths, and cultural restrictions. Many adolescent girls lack scientific knowledge, leading to shame and poor hygiene practices.

C. Abundance of menstrual campaigns - INCORRECT:

The issue is not over-saturation but rather limited and fragmented outreach, especially in rural and tribal areas.

D. Universal access to hygiene products - INCORRECT:

Access is still not universal. Factors such as economic constraints, supply chain issues, and lack of policy integration hamper nationwide access.

60. (4): The following laws are gender-neutral, meaning they apply equally to all genders:

A. The Protection of Children from Sexual Offences (POCSO) Act:

Applicable to all children under 18 years, regardless of gender. It recognizes that boys, girls, and transgender children can all be victims of sexual abuse.

B. The Code on Wages:

Consolidates four wage laws into one and ensures equal pay for equal work regardless of gender, making it explicitly gender-neutral in its language and application.

D. Right to Education Act (RTE):

Provides for free and compulsory education for all children aged 6–14 years, regardless of gender, caste, or economic status, hence classified as gender-neutral.

C. Section 498A of IPC on cruelty - INCORRECT:

This section specifically protects married women from cruelty by husband or in-laws, and is therefore not gender-neutral.

61. (3):

B. Pradhan Mantri Kaushal Vikas Yojana (PMKVY) - 2015:

Launched in 2015 by the Ministry of Skill Development and Entrepreneurship, this flagship scheme aimed to provide short-term skill training and certification to youth to enhance their employability.

C. National Apprenticeship Promotion Scheme (NAPS) - 2016:

Introduced in 2016, this scheme provided financial incentives to establishments for engaging apprentices, making on-the-job training more attractive and accessible.

D. Skill India Digital Hub Platform - 2023:

A digital initiative launched in 2023, this platform aims to digitally integrate and deliver skilling, upskilling, and employment services, under the Skill India Mission umbrella.

A. Model Skill Loan Scheme - Reintroduced with enhanced coverage post-2023:

Though initiated earlier by Indian Banks' Association (IBA), the scheme has seen renewed emphasis in recent years. It aims to provide financial support to students for skill development courses.

Hence, the correct chronological order is: PMKVY (2015) → NAPS (2016) → Skill India Digital Hub (2023) → Skill Loan (revived later).

62. (2):

B. Setting gender equality objectives:

The first step involves clearly defining the goals of gender equality, aligned with broader institutional or governmental policies.

C. Conducting pilot to gather information from stakeholders:

This includes collecting feedback, case studies, and ground realities through pilot studies to understand diverse gender needs.

A. Introducing gender mainstreaming methods and tools:

After feedback, methods like Gender Responsive Budgeting, Gender Audits, and Gender Impact Assessments are implemented to integrate gender into processes.

D. Establishing a gender information management system:

To ensure monitoring, evaluation, and learning, a data system is needed that tracks progress, impact, and gaps in gender mainstreaming efforts.

Thus, the correct implementation sequence is: B → C → A → D.

63. (2): Steps of the Content Analysis Process in correct order:

C. Define the research questions or objectives:

Every research must begin with clearly defined objectives or questions that guide the analysis.

A. Select the material for analysis:

Based on objectives, researchers identify texts, media, documents, interviews, or any form of content relevant for analysis.

B. Develop coding categories or schemes:

Researchers create a coding framework (themes, patterns, variables) to categorize and analyze the content meaningfully.

D. Code the data systematically:

The selected material is then coded line-by-line or segment-wise, ensuring consistency and structure.

E. Analyse and Interpret results:

The final step involves analyzing patterns, drawing interpretations, and connecting findings to theoretical frameworks.

Correct sequence: C → A → B → D → E.

64. (4):

A. Action International – III: United States of America:

Accion International is a U.S.-based nonprofit that provides microfinance and financial inclusion services globally.

B. Bandhan Bank – II: India:

Started as a microfinance institution in India, Bandhan became a universal bank in 2015, focused on financial inclusion, especially for women.

C. Compartamos Banco – IV: Mexico:

Based in Mexico, Compartamos Banco is a leading microcredit institution, known for empowering low-income women entrepreneurs.

D. Centre for Agricultural and Rural Development Bank – I: Philippines:

Also known as CARD Bank, this Philippines-based institution provides microcredit services to rural women and promotes community development.

65. (2):

- In Lady Winchilsea's poetry, particularly in her satirical works, she critiques the misogynistic belief that women's engagement in literature and intellectual pursuits is unnatural or threatening.
- The dominant patriarchal ideology of her time held that writing and reasoning were masculine domains, and women were either ridiculed or punished for entering literary spaces.
- Her works expose how female creativity was stifled by societal prejudice, reflecting the belief that "writing is a man's domain", and women who wrote were often seen as transgressive or deviant.

Hence, the belief reflected in her lines is: Writing is considered a man's exclusive right.

66. (4): As per National Family Health Survey-5 (NFHS-5, 2019–21), female sterilisation continues to be the most widely adopted contraceptive method among Indian women.

According to the data, 38.0% of currently married women (aged 15–49) use female sterilisation, which is significantly higher than other methods such as:

- Condoms: 9.5%
- Pills: 5.1%
- IUDs: 2.1%
- Traditional methods: 5.7%

This reflects a long-standing trend in India where permanent methods, especially female sterilisation, are prioritized over modern reversible methods, often due to lack of access, awareness, or decision-making power for women.

67. (4):

- The Indecent Representation of Women (Prohibition) Act was enacted in 1986 by the Government of India to prohibit the portrayal of women in a derogatory manner in advertisements, publications, writings, paintings, or other modes.
- It aimed to address the objectification and commodification of women's bodies in mass media and culture.
- The Act defines "indecent representation" and provides penalties for violation, but over time it has been criticized for vague language and under-enforcement, prompting proposals for amendments.

68. (2):

- Allison M. Jaggar, a prominent feminist philosopher, made her defense of abortion rights by shifting the moral debate from the "right to life of the fetus" to the broader "right to a full human life".
- She emphasized that true moral responsibility involves considering whether the mother can provide nutritional, emotional, environmental, and social conditions essential for sustaining a full human life.
- Her argument reframes the issue to focus on the living woman's moral agency, bodily autonomy, and socio-economic realities, making her view a foundational standpoint in feminist ethics and reproductive justice discourse.

69. (1): The "care penalty" in femonomics refers to the economic disadvantage women face when they take time off or reduce working hours to perform unpaid caregiving roles, such as childcare or eldercare.

This penalty manifests as:

- Wage loss
- Reduced career progression
- Lower pensions and savings
- Interrupted employment history

According to ILO and OECD reports, women globally earn 10–30% less than men, and caregiving responsibilities contribute significantly to this gap.

The concept highlights how unpaid care work, essential for social reproduction, is undervalued and disproportionately borne by women.

70. (4): The National Population Policy (NPP), 2000 set the goal of achieving population stabilization at a level consistent with the socio-economic and environmental needs of the country by the year 2045.

Key objectives of the policy include:

- Reducing Total Fertility Rate (TFR) to replacement level (2.1)
- Universal access to contraception
- Reducing infant and maternal mortality
- Delaying age at marriage for girls

The policy envisions that by 2045, India's population growth will stabilize, ensuring sustainable development, improved health outcomes, and demographic balance.

71. (2): As per UDISE^{+} data for 2020–21, the female dropout rate was highest at the secondary level (Classes 9 and 10) in India.

- The dropout rate for girls at this stage was around 15.1%, compared to lower rates at the primary and upper primary levels.
- Major reasons include:
  - ❑ Early marriage or engagement in domestic responsibilities.
  - ❑ Safety and mobility issues, especially in rural areas.
  - ❑ Economic hardship and limited access to secondary schools, particularly for girls.
- Government initiatives like Beti Bachao Beti Padhao, Kasturba Gandhi Balika Vidyalayas, and scholarship schemes are aimed to address this gap.

72. (2): Based on NITI Aayog's SDG India Index 2023-24, the Sustainable Development Goal (SDG) performance scores for the mentioned states are:

A. India – II: 71

India's overall composite score on SDG implementation across all goals is 71 out of 100, indicating a performance level of "Performer".

B. Tamil Nadu – I: 78

Tamil Nadu is one of the top-performing states, especially in health, education, and gender equality, earning a score of 78.

C. Goa – IV: 77

Goa performs strongly on environmental, health, and quality of life indicators with an SDG Index score of 77.

D. Nagaland – III: 63

Nagaland scored 63, categorized under "Aspirant" or "Performer", with challenges in education, infrastructure, and gender equality.

Correct matching is: A–II, B–I, C–IV, D–III.

73. (2): Here are the correct matches between educational commissions and their key recommendations related to gender and women's education:

A. Calcutta University Commission (1917) – I: Professional and vocational courses should be introduced in universities

Suggested reforming Indian higher education by emphasizing scientific, professional, and vocational education, including for women.

B. Hunter Commission (1882) – III: Women Inspectors for girls' schools

Recommended the appointment of female inspectors to supervise girls' education in vernacular and secondary schools.

C. Radhakrishnan Commission (1948–49) – II: Same pay for male and female teachers

Advocated equal pay for women teachers as part of gender equity in education.

D. Kothari Commission (1964–66) – IV: Training and employing women teachers

Focused on removing gender disparities by recruiting and training more women teachers, especially in rural and backward areas.

74. (3): The post-partum period (the first 42 days after delivery) is the most critical stage for maternal mortality, both in India and globally.

According to WHO and India's SRS (Sample Registration System) reports:

- Nearly 60% of maternal deaths occur in the postnatal period.
- Causes include post-partum hemorrhage, infections, sepsis, and lack of access to emergency obstetric care.

This reflects gaps in post-natal care services, despite improved institutional deliveries. Ensuring regular postnatal check-ups is key to reducing Maternal Mortality Ratio (MMR).

75. (4): Chronological matching of key affirmative action reports and policies in India:

A. National Policy for Empowerment of Women – IV: 2001

Launched by the Ministry of Women and Child Development, this comprehensive policy aims at the advancement, development, and empowerment of women.

B. Towards Equality Report – II: 1974

A landmark report by the Committee on the Status of Women in India (CSWI), it critically analyzed gender inequality in education, employment, and law.

C. Shramshakti Report – III: 1988

A report on women in the informal sector, highlighting their unrecognized and unpaid labor, and recommending social security and legal rights.

D. 73rd Amendment Act – I: 1992

Introduced one-third reservation for women in Panchayati Raj Institutions, marking a milestone in political empowerment at the grassroots level.

Correct match: A–IV, B–II, C–III, D–I.

76. (1): Sex-positive feminism is a movement that emerged during the 1980s as a response to what some feminists saw as a repressive attitude toward sexuality within earlier feminist discourse.

- It embraces female sexual autonomy, consent, and bodily agency, arguing that women should be free to express their sexuality without shame or stigma.
- It supports:
  - ❑ Sex work decriminalization
  - ❑ LGBTQ+ rights and fluid gender identities
  - ❑ Sexual education centered on pleasure and consent
- Prominent sex-positive feminists include Gayle Rubin and Carol Queen, who argue that sexual freedom is essential to gender equality.

77. (4): The Lakhpati Didi Scheme was launched in 2022 under the DAY-NRLM (Deendayal Antyodaya Yojana – National Rural Livelihoods Mission).

- It aims to empower rural women Self Help Group (SHG) members by helping them become micro-entrepreneurs and earn at least ₹ 1 lakh annually.
- Key features:
  - ❑ Each woman is given support to start or expand an enterprise, such as poultry farming, tailoring, handicrafts, food processing, etc.
  - ❑ Interest-free loans up to ₹ 5 lakh are provided through SHGs and government facilitation.
- The initiative aligns with the vision of economic self-reliance and women's inclusion in the productive economy.

78. (1): Radical feminism sees patriarchy as a fundamental and pervasive system of domination that exists in all institutions, including family, media, religion, and reproductive health.

- Radical feminists argue that male control over women's reproductive choices (e.g., abortion laws, contraception access, forced sterilization, etc.) is a method of systemic oppression.
- Thinkers like Andrea Dworkin, Shulamith Firestone, and Catharine MacKinnon emphasized that the control of female bodies is central to maintaining patriarchy.
- They advocate for reproductive rights, sexual autonomy, and freedom from compulsory heterosexuality.

79. (2): Sexist research methodologies are those that privilege male experiences and treat them as universal or normative, leading to biased interpretations and exclusion of female perspectives.

- Androcentrism refers to the tendency to center research questions, frameworks, and outcomes around men's experiences, often ignoring gender-specific realities.
- Examples include:
  - ❑ Medical studies that test only male subjects but generalize results to all genders.
  - ❑ Social surveys that fail to include care work or unpaid labour typically done by women.
- Feminist scholars call for gender-aware, intersectional, and inclusive methodologies.

80. (1): Simone de Beauvoir, in her autobiographical reflections, wrote that Jean-Paul Sartre once said she had "a man's intelligence", and she initially took it as praise.

- Later, she realized that such a compliment implied that intelligence was inherently male, and to be a smart woman was to be an exception.
- This epiphany led her to explore how women are "Othered", and not seen as autonomous beings.
- It inspired her to write "The Second Sex" (1949), a foundational feminist text that analyzed how women are defined in relation to men, rather than as full individuals.
- Her famous line, "One is not born, but rather becomes, a woman," critiques how gender is socially constructed, not biologically determined.

81. (*)

82. (2): The Skill India Mission, particularly through schemes like PMKVY, Digital Saksharta Abhiyan (DISHA), and Gramin Digital Saksharta Abhiyan (PMGDISHA), aims to bridge the digital gender divide.

It does this by:

- Providing digital literacy courses for women in rural and semi-urban areas.
- Creating women-only digital training centers in many locations.
- Promoting female participation in digital skilling programs, including coding, data entry, and digital marketing.

These efforts aim to ensure that women are not left behind in the digital economy.

83. (2): The Janasankhya Sthirata Kosh (JSK), or National Population Stabilization Fund, launched strategies to promote population stabilization in India:

A. Prerna Strategy:

Incentivizes delaying marriage and childbirth by rewarding couples who marry after 21 (women) and 25 (men), and have children after 2 years.

B. Santushti Strategy:

Encourages private sector participation in family planning services, aiming at sterilization targets and contraceptive distribution.

C. National Helpline (1800-11-6555):

JSK launched this toll-free helpline to spread awareness about reproductive health, family planning, and contraception.

D. Sahmati Strategy – NOT PART of JSK strategies:

No such strategy has been documented under JSK's initiatives.

Correct group: A, B, C only.

84. (*)

85. (4): Chronological order of important Acts related to women's rights and health in India:

B. Medical Termination of Pregnancy (MTP) Act – 1971:

Legalized abortion under specific conditions to reduce maternal mortality from unsafe abortions.

C. Pre-Conception and Pre-Natal Diagnostic Techniques (PCPNDT) Act – 1994 (Amended in 2003):

Enacted to prohibit sex selection and misuse of ultrasound technologies leading to female foeticide.

D. Surrogacy (Regulation) Act – 2021:

Regulates altruistic surrogacy in India and prohibits commercial surrogacy, protecting surrogate mothers and intended parents.

A. Women's Reservation Act – 2023:

Passed to reserve 33% seats for women in Lok Sabha and State Assemblies, to be implemented after delimitation.

Correct chronological order: B → C → D → A.

86. (2): Microcredit helps women in Self-Help Groups (SHGs) through:

B. Offering small loans to invest in income-generating activities:

Microcredit provides collateral-free, low-interest loans that empower women to engage in entrepreneurial ventures, such as tailoring, farming, dairy, or small retail, increasing their economic independence.

D. Promoting access to group-based savings programs:

SHGs operate on the principle of mutual savings and lending. Women regularly save small amounts, which are pooled and then lent to members for personal or business use, promoting financial discipline, trust, and support networks.

Options A and C are incorrect because microcredit encourages, not restricts, women's participation in economic activities and promotes financial independence, not discourages it.

87. (4): Postmodern feminism critiques earlier feminist theories, especially liberal and radical feminism, for presenting a single, universal experience of 'womanhood', often based on the Western, white, middle-class perspective.

- Postmodern feminists argue that this ignores intersecting identities such as race, class, sexuality, caste, religion, and nationality.
- Thinkers like Judith Butler and Donna Haraway emphasized the fluidity of gender and identity, rejecting fixed categories.
- This school of thought promotes plurality, diversity, and contextual understanding of gendered experiences.

88. (3): The "Nari Niketans" were established in 1976 by the Social Welfare Department of the Government of Jammu and Kashmir.

- These institutions provide shelter to deserted, destitute, and widowed women who have no means of livelihood.
- Services include:
  - ❑ Food, clothing, and shelter
  - ❑ Vocational training
  - ❑ Basic healthcare and legal aid
- These centers aim to rehabilitate women by enabling them to become self-reliant and reintegrate into society.

89. (3): Matching the thinkers with their fields of work:

A. Catherine MacKinnon – II: Pornography:

A radical feminist, MacKinnon is known for her critique of pornography as a form of sexual subordination of women, arguing that it reinforces patriarchal domination.

B. Barbara K. Rothman – IV: Reproductive Technologies:

Rothman is a sociologist and feminist who examined how reproductive technologies, including surrogacy and IVF, affect women's autonomy and control over their bodies.

C. Naila Kabeer – I: Women's Empowerment:

An economist and social researcher, Kabeer is known for her work on gender equality, poverty, and development, especially focusing on women's agency and empowerment in South Asia.

D. Andrea O'Reilly – III: Motherhood:

A leading scholar in motherhood studies, O'Reilly has explored the cultural, political, and personal dimensions of mothering, advocating for maternal empowerment and feminist mothering.

Correct match: A–II, B–IV, C–I, D–III.

90. (2): During colonial rule, although Hindu personal laws considered women as legal entities in certain aspects, multiple inequalities prevailed:

A. Women were denied access to ancestral property:

Under Mitakshara Hindu law, daughters had limited or no coparcenary rights, and property rights were primarily reserved for male heirs.

B. Economic inequality remained significant:

Even educated or elite women had limited financial independence. The laws did not ensure equal inheritance, employment rights, or wage parity.

C. Status inequality persisted:

Women were considered dependents, first of their father, then husband, and finally son. Their legal identity and rights were mediated through male guardians.

D. Women were not excluded from Stridhan; in fact, Stridhan was recognized as property exclusively owned by a woman, given at the time of marriage or later. Therefore, D is incorrect.

Correct answer: A, B, C only.

91. (1): The passage explicitly states that integrating UBI with targeted initiatives (such as those in West Bengal, Odisha, Maharashtra, and Karnataka) can combat poverty and gender inequality.

- These schemes empower mothers and women-led households, addressing vulnerability and promoting inclusion.
- By combining universal income support with gender-focused policies, the goal is to build a more inclusive and equitable society.

92. (4): The passage mentions that UBI ensures minimum income, promotes social justice, and enhances economic autonomy, regardless of employment.

- It allows individuals, particularly those outside the formal wage sector (like caregivers), to gain financial independence, thus strengthening autonomy in economic decision-making.

93. (3): One of the standard criticisms mentioned in the passage is that UBI may strain fiscal resources and reduce work incentives.

- However, the passage counters that such concerns are exaggerated, especially when moderate levels of UBI are implemented.
- Thus, while it's a frequent critique, the policy's supporters argue it's financially manageable with proper design.

94. (2): The definition of Universal Basic Income (UBI) in the passage is clear: it ensures minimum income for all citizens, regardless of employment status.

- This means no conditions or eligibility restrictions based on job, caste, or class.
- The principle of universality is foundational to UBI, making it different from targeted welfare programs.

95. (3): The passage emphasizes that UBI streamlines welfare delivery through India's JAM trinity – Jan-Dhan accounts, Aadhaar identification, and Mobile connectivity.

- This digital infrastructure supports efficient, transparent, and scalable implementation, ensuring direct benefit transfers to citizens without leakages.
- The JAM framework plays a critical enabling role in making UBI operationally feasible.

96. (2): The United Nations, in 1999, officially declared 25th November as the International Day for the Elimination of Violence Against Women in honour of the Mirabal Sisters.

- The date commemorates their assassination on 25th November 1960, which was ordered by dictator Rafael Trujillo.
- Their murder, under the guise of a staged car accident, became a symbol of resistance and sacrifice.
- The day is now observed globally to raise awareness and demand action to prevent and eliminate violence against women and girls.

97. (4): The martyrdom of the Mirabal sisters in 1960 had a profound impact on the Dominican Republic's political landscape.

- Their brutal killings drew widespread condemnation, not only within the country but also internationally.
- Their deaths galvanized popular resistance, uniting previously fragmented opposition forces and eroding Trujillo's legitimacy.
- The heightened opposition and moral outrage played a key role in hastening the dictator's assassination in May 1961, marking the downfall of his regime.

98. (3):

- The Mirabal sisters were murdered on 25th Novembe 1960, as ordered by Trujillo's regime.
- Their assassination was a direct catalyst that mobilized the Dominican public and international community against Trujillo.
- Their martyrdom exposed the brutality of the regime and triggered a chain of events leading to Trujillo's assassination in May 1961, only six months later.
- While earlier acts like Minerva's confrontation (1949) were important, it was their murder that proved pivota in toppling the regime.

99. (1): Minerva Mirabal became a target of dictator Rafae Trujillo because she was openly defiant of his authoritarian rule.

- Her public confrontation with Trujillo at a party in 1949 marked the beginning of her active resistance.
- As a law student and politically aware woman, she refused his advances and challenged his authority which led to state retaliation, including denial of he law degree.
- Her actions symbolized female defiance in a patriarcha dictatorship, making her a direct threat to Trujillo's control.

100. (2): In 1959, the Mirabal sisters formed the "Fourteenth of June Movement" (Movimiento 14 de Junio) in the Dominican Republic.

- It was named after the failed invasion attempt on 14th June 1959 by exiled Dominicans attempting to overthrow Trujillo.
- The group focused on underground resistance, political awareness, and organizing anti-dictatorship activities.
- The sisters played a crucial role, and Minerva was a key figure in leading the movement.
- Their involvement in this movement eventually led to their imprisonment and assassination, further elevating their legacy as national heroines.

Previous Years' Paper

National Testing Agency (NTA)

UGC-NET Junior Research Fellowship & Assistant Professor Eligibility Exam

WOMEN STUDIES, SEPTEMBER-2024

(Exam held on 03-09-2024)

PAPER-II

1. Which approach shows education to be a pathway to overcome deficit in women's resources and skills?
1. Capacity Building approach
2. Empowerment approach
3. Progressive approach
4. Holistic approach

2. Which of the following scales are used in surveys?

A. Likert scale B. Guttman scale
C. Bogardus scale D. Scale of autonomy

Choose the ***most appropriate*** answer from the options given below:

1. A, B, C and D 2. B, C, D and A
3. A, C, D and B 4. B, C, A and D

3. Match the offences in List-I with sections of IPC deal with offences in List-II.

List-I (Offences)	List-II (Section)
A. Kidnapping for Exporting	I. Section 354 (D)
B. Stalking	II. Section 372
C. Molestation	III. Section 360 IPC
D. Selling of Minors for Prostitution	IV. 354-IPC

Choose the ***correct*** answer from the options given below:
1. A-I, B-III, C-II, D-IV
2. A-III, B-I, C-IV, D-II
3. A-IV, B-III, C-I, D-II
4. A-II, B-IV, C-I, D-III

4. Arrange the following Acts in a chronological order:

A. Criminal Law Amendment Ordinance
B. Prohibition of Child Marriage Act
C. Indecent Representation of Women (Prohibition) Act
D. Protection of Children from Sexual Offence Act

Choose the ***correct*** answer from the options given below:

1. B, C, A, D 2. C, B, D, A
3. D, A, C, B 4. A, B, C, D

5. Match the List-I with List-II:

List-I (Books)	List-II (Authors)
A. Employment of Women in South Asia Concepts and Practices	I. Amanda Root
B. Woman to Woman An Introduction to Feminism	II. Samita Sen
C. Towards a Feminist Politics The Indian Movement in Historical Perspective	III. Radha Kumar
D. The History of doing : An Illustrated Account of Movements for Womens Rights and Feminism in India	IV. Srilatha Battiwala

Choose the ***correct*** answer from the options given below:
1. A-IV, B-II, C-I, D-III
2. A-I, B-III, C-II, D-IV
3. A-III, B-I, C-IV, D-II
4. A-II, B-IV, C-III, D-I

6. Which of the following is not a women's initiative?
1. Naga Mothers Association
2. Meira Paibis
3. Mahila Samakhya
4. Nagalim

7. Match the List-I with List-II:

List-I (Feminists)	List-II (Association)
A. Pandita Ramabai Saraswati	I. Assam Pradeshik Mahila Samiti
B. Durgabai Deshmukh	II. Indian National Theatre

C. Chandraprabha Saikiani — III. Sharada Sadan

D. Kamala Devi Chattopadhyay — IV. Andhra Mahila Mandal

Choose the correct answer from the option given below:

1. A-III, B-IV, C-I, D-II
2. A-I, B-II, C-III, D-IV
3. A-IV, B-III, C-II, D-I
4. A-II, B-I, C-IV, D-III

8. How does economic empowerment of women enhance their status in the family?

A. It increases their status.

B. It has no effect.

C. It increases their access and control over resources.

D. It improves their decision making power.

Choose the *correct* answer from the options given below:

1. A, B and C only
2. A, C and D only
3. B, C and D only
4. C and D only

9. Match the List-I with List-II:

List-I (Authors)	List-II (Books)
A. Mary Daly	I. The Subjection of Women
B. John Stuart Mill	II. Feminist Politics and Human Nature
C. Maria Mies	III. Beyond God The Father
D. Alison Jaggar	IV. Indian Women and Patriarchy

Choose the *correct* answer from the options given below:

1. A-I, B-II, C-III, D-IV
2. A-II, B-IV, C-III, D-I
3. A-III, B-I, C-IV, D-II
4. A-IV, B-III, C-I, D-II

10. Which of the following measures are included in Gender Sensitization training?

A. Increasing the number of women in executive roles

B. Promoting societal awareness to gender issues and womens rights

C. Establishing quotas for women's representation in media

D. Limiting legal frameworks related to gender issues

Choose the *correct* answer from the options given below:

1. A and B only
2. B, C and D only
3. C and D only
4. A, C and D only

11. Who gave the concept of 'Intersectionality'?

1. Kimberle Williams Crenshaw
2. Adrienne Rich
3. Jill Johnson
4. Mac Kinnon

12. According to Marxist Feminist, what is the primary goal of analyzing gender relations?

1. To understand how gender relations are influenced by cultural practices and traditions
2. To identify how gender relations operate in the society and how they are connected with the process of production and reproduction
3. To promote the idea that gender relations are solely based on individual choices and personal preferences
4. To argue that relations have no significant impact on the processes of production and reproduction

13. The expansion of EIP is entrepreneurship ______ programme.

1. Identification
2. Implementation
3. Initiative
4. Indicator

14. The lack of legal awareness of the working woman is regarded as a major obstacle for obtaining the benefits provided by the ______ laws.

1. Labour
2. Organizational
3. International
4. Moral

15. The process of reaching the benefits to the grassroots is defined as:

1. Trickle down effect
2. Decentralisation
3. Deconcentration
4. Urbanization

16. Government of India has formulated policies for education in India since Independence - Arrange in a chronological order:

A. New Education Policy

B. National Educational Policy

C. Kothari commission

D. National Committee on Womens Education

Choose the *correct* answer from the options given below:

1. D, C, B, A
2. A, B, C, D
3. C, B, D, A
4. B, C, A, D

17. What is the critique of the Post-Modern theorists on Women Studies?

A. Women Studies effectively addresses all aspects of identity including race and class.

B. The concept of women's identity is coherent and clear

C. Women's Studies prioritize gender over race or class

D. Women Studies are only for women community

Choose the *correct* answer from the options given below:

1. A, B and D only 2. A, B and C only
3. B and C only 4. B, C and D only

18. Match the List-I with List-II:

List-I (Schemes/Programmes)	List-II (Year)
A. Rashtriya Krishi Vikas Yojana (RKVY)	I. 2007
B. Pradhan Mantri Swasthya Suraksha Yojana (PMSSY)	II. 2005
C. Sukanya Samriddhi Yojana (SSY)	III. 2006
D. Janani Suraksha Yojana (JSY)	IV. 2015

Choose the *correct* answer from the options given below:

1. A-I, B-III, C-IV, D-II
2. A-II, B-IV, C-III, D-I
3. A-III, B-II, C-I, D-IV
4. A-IV, B-III, C-II, D-I

19. Queer theory is related to:

A. Gay and Lesbian Politics
B. Usefullness of gendered binary distinction
C. Promoting Homo Sexuality
D. Promotion of Sexual identifies

Choose the *correct* answer from the options given below:

1. A and B only
2. A, B and C only
3. A and C only
4. A, B and D only

20. The efforts of Government of India and United Nations to address Women in Development-Arrange in chronological order:

A. Millenium Development Goals
B. National Policy on Empowerment of Women
C. National Rural Livelihood Mission
D. Shram Shakti

Choose the *correct* answer from the options given below:

1. A, B, C, D 2. B, C, D, A
3. D, B, C, A 4. C, B, A, D

21. Match the List-I with List-II:

List-I (Concepts)	List-II (Definations)
A. Social Status	I. It is needs of the women that do not challenge their socially accepted roles
B. Practical Gender Needs (PGNs)	II. It is a honour or prestige attached to one's position in a society
C. Gender Mainstreaming	III. Process in which inequalities and discrimination identified in any given set up by using various Participatory Tools and Methods
D. Gender Analysis	IV. Involves integrating a gender perspective and gender analysis to all

Choose the *correct* answer from the options given below:

1. A-I, B-IV, C-III, D-II
2. A-II, B-I, C-IV, D-III
3. A-II, B-I, C-III, D-IV
4. A-I, B-III, C-II, D-IV

22. Match the List-I with List-II:

List-I (Women Leaders)	List-II (Country)
A. Jacinda Ardern	I. Ireland
B. Angela Merkel	II. Norway
C. Mary Robinson	III. Germany
D. Gro Harlem Brundtland	IV. New Zealand

Choose the *correct* answer from the options given below:

1. A-II, B-I, C-III, D-IV
2. A-III, B-II, C-I, D-IV
3. A-IV, B-III, C-I, D-II
4. A-I, B-II, C-III, D-IV

23. Which theory is introduced by Albert Bandura?

1. Cognitive theory
2. Social learning theory
3. Theory of Motivation
4. Attribution theory

24. How does secondary education impact women's health outcomes?

1. It has little or no impact on health outcomes
2. It only affects knowledge of HIV prevention
3. It does not affect attitudes towards genital cutting
4. It significantly improves the use of maternal health services

25. Match the List-I with List-II:

List-I	List-II
A. Women India Association (WIA)	I. Ela Bhatt
B. All India Women's conference (AIWC)	II. Aruna Asaf Ali
C. Self-Employed Women's Association (SEWA)	III. Margaret Cousins
D. Quit India Movement (QIM)	IV. Annie Besant

Choose the *correct* answer from the options given below:

1. A-II, B-IV, C-III, D-I
2. A-IV, B-III, C-I, D-II
3. A-I, B-II, C-III, D-IV
4. A-III, B-II, C-I, D-IV

26. Arrange the following in a chronological order on the basis of their year of establishment:

A. National Institute for Micro, Small and Medium Enterprises (NI-MSME)
B. National Institute for Entrepreneurship and Small Business Development
C. Women Entrepreneurship Platform
D. Small Industries Development Bank of India

Choose the *correct* answer from the options given below:

1. B, C, D and A
2. A, B, C and D
3. A, B, D and C
4. C, D, B and A

27. What types of Folk arts are mentioned as a part of Alternative media?

1. Dance and Music only
2. Novel writing and Poetry
3. Street play, Role play, Dance, Dramas
4. Television Dramas and Cinema

28. Which of the following is a function of Gender representation in media?

A. To increase the number of advertisements featuring woman in traditional roles
B. To remove demeaning degrading and negative stereotypical images of women
C. To promote gender specific content for different media platforms
D. To prioritise media coverage on men's achievements over women's achievements

Choose the ***most appropriate*** answer from the options given below:

1. A, B and C only
2. B and C only
3. A, B and D only
4. A, C and D only

29. Which are the major movements that influenced the development of Women's Studies course in the late 1960's?

1. Environmental movement and health movement
2. Civil Rights movement and Anti-war movement
3. Labour movement and Immigration movement
4. Technological revolution and space race

30. Tick the correct one:

1. Custom refers to the established modes of thoughts and action
2. Custom helps in the process of change
3. Custom promotes women's development
4. Custom leads to growth of society

31. What are the common methods of data collection in research?

A. Interviews
B. Experiments
C. Literature Survey
D. Analysing Financial Records

Choose the *correct* answer from the options given below:

1. A, B and C only
2. A, B and D only
3. B, C and D only
4. B and D only

32. Trans-Gender theory belongs to:

1. Marxists
2. Socialists
3. Liberals
4. Post-modernists

33. Match the List-I with List-II.

List-I (Commissions/ Institutions)	List-II (Year of Establishment)
A. National Commission for Women	I. 1993
B. National Commission for Minorities	II. 2007
C. National Commission for Protection of Child rights	III. 1992
D. National Institute of Public Co-operation and Child Development	IV. 1980

Choose the *correct* answer from the options given below:

1. A-I, B-IV, C-III, D-II
2. A-IV, B-III, C-I, D-II
3. A-III, B-I, C-II, D-IV
4. A-II, B-III, C-IV, D-I

34. List out the Sustainable Development Goals as defined bv the United Nations-Arrange in chronological order:

A. Reduced Inequality
B. Partnership for the goals
C. No poverty
D. Decent Work and Economic Growth

Choose the *correct* answer from the options given below:

1. A, B, C and D
2. B, C, D and A
3. C, D, A and B
4. D, A, B and C

35. Match the List-I with List-II.

List-I (Concepts)	List-II (Definitions)
A. Gender Segregation	I. When women enter those well-paying jobs/fields, they are prevented from moving up
B. Glass Ceiling	II. Women end up working in long hours both work place and at home
C. Double shift/ Double burden	III. It is the proportion of working population to total population
D. Work Force Participation Rate	IV. Process in which women and men end up in different types of occupation so that two different types of labour markets maybe said to exist, female and male

Choose the ***correct*** answer from the options given below:

1. A-I, B-II, C-III, D-IV
2. A-IV, B-I, C-II, D-III
3. A-II, B-III, C-I, D-IV
4. A-III, B-II, C-I, D-IV

36. Arrange the following in a chronological order:

A. Nutrition Programme for Adolescent Girls
B. National Rural Health Mission
C. National Health Policy
D. Integrated Child Development Service

Choose the ***correct*** answer from the options given below:

1. A, B, C and D
2. B, C, A and D
3. C, B, D and A
4. D, C, A and B

37. Who has published the book The Feminist Standpoint Developing Ground for a Specifically Feminist Historical Materialism in 1983?

1. Friedrich Hegel
2. Nancy Hartsock
3. West and Turner
4. Caroline Moser

38. 'The one-stop centre (OSC) was launched by the Government of India to provide integrated support and assistance to women affected by violence.' In which year was this scheme launched?

1. 2011 2. 2010
3. 2015 4. 2022

39. What challenge is often faced by committees while implementing policies on women's education?

1. Lack of International Education
2. Insufficient technological innovation
3. Cultural resistance and socio-economic barriers
4. Over production of educational materials

40. Steps to be followed in research-Arrange in chronological order:

A. Identifying methods
B. Formulating objectives
C. Problematizing research
D. Analysis and Interpretation

Choose the ***correct*** answer from the options given below:

1. B, A, C, D 2. B, A, C, D
3. A, B, C, D 4. C, D, B, A

41. Which techniques are considered to be a part of the qualitative research methods?

A. Ethnography
B. Oral History
C. Structural Interviews
D. Case studies

Choose the ***correct*** answer from the options given below:

1. A, C and D only 2. A, B and C only
3. A, B and D only 4. B, C and D only

42. Match the List-I with List-II.

List-I (Report)	List-II (Ranking)
A. Gender Gap Report 2024	I. 129
B. Human Development Index 2023-2024	II. 134
C. Global Peace Index - 2024	III. 116
D. Sustainable Development Report 2024	IV. 109

Choose the ***correct*** answer from the options given below:

1. A-I, B-II, C-III, D-IV
2. A-II, B-III, C-IV, D-I
3. A-III, B-IV, C-I, D-II
4. A-I, B-II, C-IV, D-III

43. Match the List-I with List-II.

List-I (Articles of Indian Constitution)	List-II (Issues)
A. Article 44	I. Trafficking in human being
B. Article 23(a)	II. Equality before law
C. Article 14	III. Uniform Civil Code
D. Article 51(A)(e)	IV. Dignity of Women

Choose the ***correct*** answer from the options given below:

1. A-III, B-I, C-II, D-IV
2. A-II, B-III, C-IV, D-I
3. A-I, B-IV, C-III, D-II
4. A-IV, B-I, C-III, D-II

44. The efforts of Government of India to mainstream Women Studies in the Higher Educational Institutes or Universities : Arrange in a chronological order.

A. Towards Equality Report
B. Indian Association for Women Studies
C. Women India Association
D. Establishment of Women Studies Centre (WSC) in the Universities by the UGC

Choose the ***correct*** answer from the options given below:

1. A, C, B, D
2. C, A, B, D
3. A, B, C, D
4. B, C, D, A

45. Sexual Harassment was criminalised in 2013 and spelt out as a punishable offence under which Indian Penal code?

1. 354 A of the IPC
2. 355 A of the IPC
3. 356 B of the IPC
4. 356 A and B of the IPC

46. Match the List-I with List-II.

List-I (Concepts)	List-II (Definitions)
A. Production of Goods and Services	I. Softer emotions, those required in relational tasks, such as caring and nurturing that disappear most often from job description, performance, evaluation and salary calculation
B. Emotional Labour	II. A person who has moved from one politically defined area to another similar area
C. Fiscal responsibility	III. When an activity results in a valuable and a useful thing
D. Migrant	IV. Measures and costs and benefits that fail to capture the full contributions of social protection goals and developments and hence it is real marginal costs

Choose the ***correct*** answer from the options given below:

1. A-III, B-I, C-IV, D-II
2. A-II, B-III, C-I, D-IV
3. A-I, B-III, C-IV, D-II
4. A-I, B-II, C-III, D-IV

47. Match the List-I with List-II.

List-I (Name of the schemes)	List-II (Year of Launch)
A. Mid day Meal Scheme	I. 1994
B. Sarva Shiksha Abhiyan	II. 2015
C. District Primary Education Programme	III. 2001
D. Beti Bachao Beti Padhao Scheme	IV. 1995

Choose the ***correct*** answer from the options given below:

1. A-IV, B-III, C-I, D-II
2. A-II, B-III, C-IV, D-I
3. A-I, B-II, C-III, D-IV
4. A-III, B-I, C-II, D-IV

48. Match the List-I with List-II.

List-I (Concepts)	List-II (Definitions)
A. Feminism	I. Social, Cultural and Psychological transformation of gender
B. Feminist Education	II. Physical and Biological distinction
C. Female	III. Pursuit and Development of knowledge about women
D. Femininity	IV. An ideological position that struggles to free all women

Choose the ***correct*** answer from the options given below:

1. A-I, B-II, C-III, D-IV
2. A-III, B-IV, C-I, D-II
3. A-II, B-I, C-IV, D-III
4. A-IV, B-III, C-II, D-I

49. According to W.W. Rostow (1960) there are five steps in the evolutionary modernization-Arrange in chronological order:

A. Take off stage
B. Drive to maturity
C. High mass-consumption
D. Traditional Society
E. Pre-conditions for take off stages

Choose the ***correct*** answer from the options given below:

1. B, A, C, D, E
2. D, E, A, B, C
3. A, B, C, D, E
4. A, C, D, E, B

50. Which of the following are types of Interviews?

A. Structured Interviews
B. Telephonic Interviews
C. Multiple-choice Interviews
D. Non-directive Interviews

Choose the ***correct*** answer from the options given below:

1. B, C and D only
2. A and D only
3. A, B and D only
4. B and D only

51. Who defined entrepreneurship from the perspective of economics by focusing on the perception of new economic opportunities (invention) and the subsequent introduction of new ideas in the market?

1. Schumpeter
2. Drucker
3. Smith
4. Marshal

52. Match the List-I with List-II.

List-I (Concepts)	List-II (Definitions)
A. Mass media	I. A communication medium that requires both parties
B. Synchronous media	II. A communication used to reach out to masses
C. Asynchronous media	III. A communication that reaches out to political and social minorities
D. Alternative media	IV. A communication of information that can be accessed at any time

Choose the ***correct*** answer from the options given below:

1. A-I, B-II, C-III, D-IV
2. A-III, B-IV, C-II, D-I
3. A-IV, B-III, C-I, D-II
4. A-II, B-I, C-IV, D-III

53. Which of the following statements describe Women Studies according to Bowles and Klein?

1. Women studies primarily focuses on reinforcing traditional academic disciplines
2. Women studies seeks to maintain the existing structure of knowledge
3. Women studies radically challenges the distribution and generation of knowledge
4. Women studies places society at the centre of its analysis

54. Efforts taken at the International level to address women issues and eradicate violence against women : Arrange in a chronological order.

A. Sustainable Development Goals
B. Beijing Platform for Action (BPFA)
C. Convention on Elimination of all forms of Discrimination Against Women (CEDAW)
D. Vienna Declaration

Choose the ***correct*** answer from the options given below:

1. D, A, C, B
2. B, A, D, C
3. A, B, C, D
4. C, D, B, A

55. Which of the following are considered by the Neo-classical Economists' explanations for gender wage Inequalities?

A. Women's prioritization of family over market work
B. Women's choices in low paying occupation
C. Fewer and different kinds of schooling for women
D. Men's choices in higher paying occupations

Choose the ***correct*** answer from the options given below:

1. A, B and C only
2. B, C and D only
3. A and D only
4. A, C and D only

56. Match the List-I with List-II.

List-I (Artists)	List-II (Art forms)
A. Zaveri sisters	I. Bharatnatyam
B. Leela Samson	II. Odissi
C. Sonal Mansingh	III. Kathakali
D. Geeta Poduwal	IV. Manipuri

Choose the ***correct*** answer from the options given below:

1. A-I, B-II, C-III, D-IV
2. A-II, B-III, C-IV, D-I
3. A-IV, B-I, C-II, D-III
4. A-III, B-IV, C-I, D-II

57. Match the List-I with List-II.

List-I (Five year Plans)	List-II (Themes)
A. Sixth Five Year Plan (1985-90)	I. Women's Development to Empowerment of women
B. Ninth Five Year Plan (1997-2002)	II. Gender Equity and Gender Budgeting
C. Eleventh Five Year Plan (2007-12)	III. Welfare of Women along with welfare of disadvantaged groups
D. First Five Year Plan (1951-56)	IV. Welfare to Development Approach

Choose the ***correct*** answer from the options given below:

1. A-IV, B-I, C-II, D-III
2. A-III, B-II, C-I, D-IV
3. A-II, B-III, C-IV, D-I
4. A-I, B-IV, C-II, D-III

58. Which development feminist wrote the book 'Money can't buy me Love'?

1. Bina Agarwal
2. Martha Nussbaum
3. Gayathri Chakravarty Spivak
4. Naila Kabeer

59. How has the dealing of human trafficking shifted over a period?

A. From a social problem to a legal issue
B. From a legal issue to a economic concern
C. From a legal problem to a social issue with a focus on victim protection
D. From a criminal justice issue to an environmental problem

Choose the *correct* answer from the options given below:

1. A, B, C and D 2. B, C, D and A
3. C, D, B and A 4. D, A, B and C

60. If women obtain appropriate training opportunities they will have control over the present and future ______ requirements.

1. Trade 2. Job market
3. Business 4. Government

61. Who coined the term 'Missing Women' to reflect on the declining sex ratio in developing countries?

1. Raja Ram Mohan Roy
2. Amartya Sen
3. Abhijit Banerjee
4. Vandana Shiva

62. Who was the first woman speaker of Lok Sabha?

1. Aruna Asaf Ali 2. Indira Gandhi
3. Meira Kumar 4. Annie Besant

63. Which of the following is related to first wave feminism?

1. Centred on issues of Equality and discrimination including workplace reproductive rights de facto equalities
2. Focused on legal issues primarily on the right to vote
3. Characterised by the use of technology and social media to address issues like sexual harassment, gender based violence, along with an emphasis on intersectionality
4. Emphasised diversity, intersectionality and individuality challenging definition of femininity and advocating for a broader range of identities

64. Arrange the Women Development approaches on the basis of their order:

A. Welfare B. Equity
C. Anti poverty D. Empowerment

Choose the *correct* answer from the options given below:

1. A, B, C, D 2. D, C, B, A
3. C, B, A, D 4. B, D, A, C

65. What is correct about 'Personal Laws'?

A. Family laws differ from person to person according to her/his religion
B. Family laws are related with the maternity benefits to the working women
C. Family laws are personal laws
D. Family laws are related with devolution and disposition of family property, maintenance succession and inheritance

Choose the *correct* answer from the options given below:

1. A, B and C only 2. B, C and D only
3. A, B and D only 4. C and D only

66. Which is the correct chronological sequence of stages of development of feminist research?

A. Research on sex differences based on biological properties of individuals
B. Research on individual level sex-roles and socialization
C. Research on gender as an organising principle in all social systems
D. Research based on men's experiences

Choose the *correct* answer from the options given below:

1. B, D, A and C 2. D, A, B and C
3. A, B, C and D 4. C, D, A and B

67. Match the List-I with List-II.

List-I (Types of Research)	List-II (Explanation)
A. Action Research	I. Orientedtowardsmeasuring organisationalperformance
B. Evaluation Research	II. It seeks to implement policy through the research itself
C. Experimental Research	III. Designed to test hypothesis under controlled conditions
D. Case study Research	IV. It is not designed to compare one individual or group to another

Choose the *correct* answer from the options given below:

1. A-I, B-II, C-III, D-IV
2. A-I, B-II, C-IV, D-III
3. A-II, B-I, C-III, D-IV
4. A-IV, B-I, C-II, D-III

68. In which year did Women Studies emerge as a distinctive and integrated field of study?

1. 1968 2. 1970
3. 1976 4. 1980

69. Which Indian playwright first directed an all women's play in 1888?

1. Mahatma Gandhi
2. Vijay Tendulkar
3. Girish Karnad
4. Rabindranath Tagore

70. Schemes and Programmes for Vocational Training and Skill Development of women - Arrange in chronological order on the basis of their date of implementation:

A. National Adult Education Programme
B. Central Social Welfare Board
C. National Skill Development Mission
D. Mahila Samruddhi Yojana

Choose the ***correct*** answer from the options given below:

1. A, B, C, D 2. C, D, A, B
3. B, A, D, C 4. D, A, B, C

71. What is the primary goal of the National Education Policy regarding womens education?

1. To focus on women in higher education
2. To ensure equal educational opportunities and promote gender equity
3. To limit educational access based on gender
4. To provide education for marginalized women

72. Ayushman Bharat adopts a continuum of care approach comprising of two which inter-related components?

A. Establishment of Health and Well being centres
B. Pradhan Mantri Jan Arogya Yojana
C. Village Level Programmes
D. Livelihood Enterprise Development Programme

Choose the ***correct*** answer from the options given below:

1. A and B only 2. A, C and D only
3. B, C and D only 4. C and D only

73. What is Contraceptive Prevalence Rate?

1. Percent of women of any age using contraceptive method at a particular point of time
2. Percent of children born after using contraceptive methods
3. Percent of men using contraceptive method in a particular time
4. Percent of women (or partner also) of reproductive age using contraceptive method at a particular point of time

74. Match the List-I with List-II.

List-I (Authors)	**List-II (Books)**
A. Susan Brown Miller	I. Women Estate
B. Juliet Mitchell	II. Against our Will : Men, Women and Rape
C. Marge Peercy	III. The Ethics of Ambiguity
D. Simone De Beauviour	IV. Women on the Edge of Time

Choose the ***correct*** answer from the options given below:

1. A-II, B-I, C-IV, D-III
2. A-I, B-II, C-III, D-IV
3. A-III, B-IV, C-II, D-I
4. A-I, B-III, C-II, D-IV

75. The National Food Security Act (2013) does not deal with:

1. Mid-day meal scheme
2. Public Distribution System
3. National Nutrition Supplementation Programme
4. Integrated Child Development Services

76. Entrepreneurship is recognised as a key element for women's ______ empowerment in the 1995 Beijing platform for action.

1. Social 2. Livelihood
3. Status 4. Economic

77. Match the List-I with List-II.

List-I (Acts)	**List-II (Year of Establishment)**
A. The Protection of Women from Domestic Violence Act	I. 1986
B. The Dowry Prohibition Act	II. 2005
C. The Indecent Representation of Women (Prohibition) Act	III. 1961
D. The Commission of SATI (Prevention) Act	IV. 1987

Choose the ***correct*** answer from the options given below:

1. A-I, B-III, C-IV, D-II
2. A-III, B-II, C-I, D-IV
3. A-IV, B-I, C-III, D-II
4. A-II, B-III, C-I, D-IV

78. When did the feminist use 'Narratology' as a medium?

1. 1940's 2. 1950's
3. 1960's 4. 1970's

79. Women face issues relating to vocational training and the work environment that prevents them from entering the job market and adversely affects their ______ in work.

1. Productivity 2. Participation
3. Progress 4. Capacity

80. Arrange in ascending order the feminist scholars who have contributed to feminist scholarship:

A. Veena Majumdar B. Falvia Agnes
C. Sharmila Rege D. Samita Sen

Choose the ***correct*** answer from the options given below:

1. D, B, A and C 2. A, D, B and C
3. B, C, D and A 4. A, D, C and B

81. 'Gender denotes women, men and other genders depending on ______ factors'.

1. Socio-cultural 2. Biological
3. Physiological 4. Psychological

82. Which of the Indian feminists wrote 'Under Western Eyes' Feminist Scholarship and Colonial Discourses?

1. Chandra Talpade Mohanty
2. Nivedita Menon
3. Arundhati Roy
4. Mita Deka

83. Which of the following explains the concept of 'Strategic life Choices'?

1. Choices that enhance an individuals immediate well-being
2. Choices related to every day activities and tasks
3. Choices that have long term implications on a women's life and status
4. Choices imposed by external factors such as family or society

84. Which feminist theory emphasizes how media text and discourse reinforce patriarchal ideologies?

1. Marxist feminism
2. Post-structuralist feminism
3. Black feminism
4. Arab feminism

85. What was the main focus of the Eigth Five-Year plan regarding women's issues?

1. Women's welfare
2. Women's development
3. Women's empowerment
4. Women's health

86. Which article of the Indian Constitution allows for special provisions for the advancement of women, even if it leads to discrimination based on sex?

1. Article 15(1) 2. Article 16(2)
3. Article 15(3) 4. Article 14

87. Which of the following measures will combat dowry?

1. Ignoring cultural traditions
2. Increasing the practise of dowry
3. Strengthening assistance mechanisms
4. Promoting dowry in certain regions

88. Data analysis steps include:

A. Coding
B. Classification
C. Designing the research
D. Documentation

Choose the ***correct*** answer from the options given below:

1. A, B and C only 2. A, B and D only
3. B, C and D only 4. A, C and D only

89. Which of the following factors has contributed significantly to the evolution of the traditional domestic division of labour in contemporary western industrial societies?

1. Decrease in female work force participation
2. Cultural shifts towards shared responsibilities
3. Reduction in household appliance usage
4. Reinforcement of traditional gender roles

90. Women Component Plan was initiated in which five year plan?

1. 8th five year plan 2. 9th five year plan
3. 10th five year plan 4. 11th five year plan

Directions (Qs. No. 91 to 95): *Read the following passage and answer the questions.*

Media studies is concerned with the relationship between people, media, life and society, by examining these relationships through various lenses. Quantitative and Environmental questions explore who is using which media, while qualitative questions delve into how people interpret media and its role in their lives. Change is a constant factor in this inquiry. Issues of access, power and democracy also come into play scrutinizing who owns and controls media and the power dynamics stemming from by concentrating ownership and corporate agendas. The 2011 news of the world phone-hacking scandal in the UK highlighted the significant influence of media, bringing these issues to the forefront of public discussion. Media studies also examines the nature of media texts, using various approaches to deconstruct how meaning is made within and between texts. This involves studying media audiences with attention to demographics such as culture, gender, age, sexuality, social class and ability/disability. These topics are often interconnected, requiring students to develop skills in making connections, synthesizing ideas and engaging in dialogue between concepts. Although human communication history dates back much further, and some media histories began as early as 776 BC with carrier pigeons, the advent of the printing press in 1455 by Gutenberg is often cited as a milestone in communication technology. The ability to produce in mass scale, the printed world led to mass literacy and significantly transformed people's communication.

91. What do qualitative questions explore in media students?

1. Who is using what media?
2. How people interpret media and its function in their lives?
3. The environmental impact of media production
4. The history of media ownership

92. Why are audiences important in media studies?

1. It helps in producing better media content
2. It allows for the examination of media ownership patterns
3. It provides insight into how different demographics interpret media texts
4. It focuses on the technical aspects of media creation

93. What is the primary focus of media studies?

1. The technical aspects of media production
2. The relationship between people, media, life and society
3. The history of media technologies
4. The economics of media industries

94. Which event highlighted the influence of media and brought issues of media power to public discussion?

1. The advent of the printing press
2. The rise of digital media
3. The 2011 news of the world phone-hacking scandal
4. The invention of carrier pigeons for communication

95. What significant technological advancement in 1455 is mentioned in the passage?

1. The invention of the telegraph
2. The creation of carrier pigeons for communication
3. The development of the printing press by Gutenberg
4. The introduction of the internet

Directions (Qs. No. 96 to 100): *Read the following passage and answer the questions.*

Radical feminism emerged as a powerful oppositional discourse during the late 1960s. It flourished during a period of marked upsurge in radical political agitation, such as the student and civil rights movements, and challenged the epistemological basis of both Marxisms and Liberalism. Radical Feminists, possessing no single core doctrine which informed their theories, were fragmented from the start, a process exacerbated by their preference for small group formation, where each individual women could find a voice and where all tasks could be shared out equally. The groups devised their own consciousness raising strategies and produced manifestos independently of one another operating as distinct political 'cells' that might or might not forge coalitions in cases of distinct action. One result of such discrete and free floating political activity was that it provoked a degree of criticism from more centrally organized feminists, such as the liberal tendency that comprised the membership of 'NOW' in the States and also a large amount of parody from the mass media.

Radical feminisms 'invisibility' as an 'organisation' with no identifiable leaders and centres was perceived to be a major strength by its adherents; they did not subscribe to any one tradition in political thought and were therefore at liberty to constantly re-invent themselves, Although it would be fair to assert that radical feminist politics has been most broadly influenced in its work upon issues which closely affect women's personal, physical and mental well-being. It is difficult to isolate a central governing principle presenting radical feminist work with other waves of feminism. Perhaps anthologies such as Robin Morgan's sisterhood is powerful (1970) and Koedt, Levine and Rapone's Radical feminism (1973) most effectively do justice to the sheer range and heterogeneity of radical feminist perspectives.

96. Who proposed the concept of 'Sisterhood'?

1. Robin Morgan
2. Koedt
3. Levine
4. Rapone

97. During which period did radical feminism emerge as a powerful discourse?

1. Early 1950s
2. Late 1960s
3. Early 1970s
4. Late 1980s

98. Which of the following is true about the radical feminist groups strategies?

1. They devised consciousness raising strategies independently
2. They operated under a single manifesto
3. They avoided direct action
4. They had a hierarchical organization structure

99. What did radicals feminists challenge as mentioned in the passage?

1. Liberalism and Conservatism
2. Marxism and Socialism
3. Marxism and Liberalisation
4. Feminism and Patriarchy

100. What was one organizational characteristic of radical feminist groups mentioned in the passage?

1. They had a centralised leadership structure
2. They formed National Organization
3. They preferred small group formations
4. They relied heavily on mass media for communication

EXPLANATORY ANSWERS

1. **(1):** Capacity building approach shows education as a key strategy to overcome deficits in women's resources and skills.
   - It focuses on enhancing women's capabilities through education, training, and skill development.
   - This approach recognizes that women may lack access to education and resources due to systemic barriers, and works to remove these barriers by building individual and community-level capacities.
   - For example, vocational training programs for women, adult literacy classes, and digital literacy campaigns help women gain economic independence and social mobility.
   - UNESCO and other global institutions often emphasize capacity building in gender equality initiatives.

2. **(1):** All the listed scales are used in surveys:
   - Likert Scale: Measures attitudes by asking respondents to indicate their level of agreement with a statement, usually on a 5 or 7-point scale.
   - Guttman Scale: A cumulative scale that assumes a hierarchical order in responses, used to measure intensity of an attitude.
   - Bogardus Scale: Measures social distance, typically in relation to ethnic and racial groups.
   - Scale of Autonomy: Though less common, it is used in gender studies and developmental psychology to measure decision-making power or self-governance, especially in studies involving women or adolescents.

   Hence, all four are legitimate and commonly used in social science surveys.

3. **(2):** Matching the offences to their respective IPC sections:

   A. Kidnapping for Exporting – III. Section 360 IPC:

   Section 360 defines kidnapping from India, including cases of taking a person beyond the limits of India.

   B. Stalking – I. Section 354(D):

   This section explicitly deals with stalking as a criminal offence, added in the Criminal Law (Amendment) Act, 2013.

   C. Molestation – IV. 354 IPC:

   Section 354 deals with assault or criminal force used against a woman with intent to outrage her modesty.

   D. Selling of Minors for Prostitution – II. Section 372:

   This section criminalizes the selling of a minor for the purpose of prostitution or illicit intercourse.

4. **(2):** Chronological order of the Acts is as follows:

   C. Indecent Representation of Women (Prohibition) Act – 1986:

   Enacted to prohibit indecent representation of women through advertisements, publications, writings, paintings, etc.

   B. Prohibition of Child Marriage Act – 2006:

   Replaced the earlier Child Marriage Restraint Act of 1929 and strengthened laws to prohibit child marriages.

   D. Protection of Children from Sexual Offence (POCSO) Act – 2012:

   Designed to protect children from sexual offences with a child-friendly mechanism for reporting and trial.

   A. Criminal Law (Amendment) Ordinance – 2013:

   Came after the 2012 Delhi gang rape case and introduced major amendments including stalking, voyeurism, and enhanced punishments.

5. **(*)**

6. **(4):** Nagalim is not a women's initiative. It is a political concept related to the unification of all Naga-inhabited areas under a single administrative unit, as demanded by some Naga groups like NSCN-IM.

   In contrast:
   - Naga Mothers Association (NMA) is a grassroots women's organization in Nagaland that advocates for peace, women's rights, and social reform.
   - Meira Paibis are a collective of women activists from Manipur, often referred to as "women torch bearers", known for their role in civil rights and anti-violence movements.
   - Mahila Samakhya is a government-initiated program started in 1989 for women's empowerment through education, especially in rural areas.

   Hence, Nagalim stands out as a political-territorial demand and not a women-specific initiative.

7. **(1):** Correct match of feminists with their respective associations:

   A. Pandita Ramabai Saraswati – III. Sharada Sadan:

   She established Sharada Sadan in 1889 in Mumbai as a residential school for widows and destitute women, focusing on their education and rehabilitation.

   B. Durgabai Deshmukh – IV. Andhra Mahila Mandal:

   She was the founder of this organization which aimed at the social, economic, and educational development of women in Andhra Pradesh.

   C. Chandraprabha Saikiani – I. Assam Pradeshik Mahila Samiti:

   A pioneering social reformer in Assam, she founded this Samiti to promote women's education and upliftment in Assam.

   D. Kamala Devi Chattopadhyay – II. Indian National Theatre:

   She was closely associated with cultural renaissance and contributed to the formation of Indian National Theatre to promote indigenous arts and women's participation in culture.

8. (2): Economic empowerment of women enhances their family status in multiple ways:

A. It increases their status:

Women who earn are more likely to gain respect and recognition in household decision-making.

C. It increases their access and control over resources:

With their own income or property, women gain economic independence and bargaining power.

D. It improves their decision-making power:

Financial contribution allows women to take part in key decisions like education of children, health care, and investments.

B. It has no effect – is incorrect, because multiple studies (e.g., by UN Women and World Bank) show clear positive effects of economic empowerment on women's autonomy and family status.

9. (3): Matching authors with their books:

A. Mary Daly – III. Beyond God the Father:

A foundational feminist theological work that critiques patriarchal structures in religion and advocates for a feminist spirituality.

B. John Stuart Mill – I. The Subjection of Women:

A classical liberal text advocating for gender equality and women's rights, published in 1869.

C. Maria Mies – IV. Indian Women and Patriarchy:

She conducted extensive research on Indian women's labor and exploitation under patriarchal systems.

D. Alison Jaggar – II. Feminist Politics and Human Nature:

A key text in feminist philosophy that analyzes feminist theories and their connections to human nature debates.

10. (1): Gender sensitization training includes:

A. Increasing the number of women in executive roles:

Promotes gender equality in leadership and decision-making levels, addressing gender imbalance in organizations.

B. Promoting societal awareness to gender issues and women's rights:

Aims to challenge stereotypes and encourage equitable treatment across genders.

C. Establishing quotas for women's representation in media – is not a direct training measure, but a policy-level intervention.

D. Limiting legal frameworks related to gender issues – is incorrect, as gender sensitization supports strengthening legal protections, not limiting them.

11. (1):

- Kimberlé Crenshaw, a legal scholar and civil rights advocate, coined the term "Intersectionality" in 1989.
- This concept highlights how multiple forms of social stratification—such as race, gender, class, and others—interact and overlap, particularly in the experiences of marginalized groups like women of colour.
- Crenshaw introduced the term to explain how traditional feminist and anti-racist frameworks often overlook the unique struggles faced by women who fall into multiple minority categories.
- Her work has become foundational in both feminist theory and critical race theory.

12. (2):

- Marxist Feminism focuses on how the capitalist mode of production reinforces patriarchy.
- According to Marxist feminists, gender relations are not isolated cultural issues but are deeply embedded in economic structures, especially in the division of labour.
- They analyze how women's unpaid domestic labour (reproduction) and low-paid work in capitalist systems (production) perpetuate gender inequality.
- This approach seeks to uncover the roots of women's oppression in economic dependency and exploitation, thus connecting gender with class struggle.

13. (4):

- EIP stands for Entrepreneurship Indicator Programme.
- It is a framework developed to measure the entrepreneurship environment, performance, and outcomes within a particular economy or region.
- The aim is to help policymakers and institutions assess progress and design strategies to foster entrepreneurship, especially for underrepresented groups including women.
- This is not a training or implementation initiative but rather a measurement and evaluation tool.

14. (1):

- The lack of legal awareness among working women often prevents them from claiming their rights under labour laws, such as:
  - ❑ Equal pay
  - ❑ Maternity benefits
  - ❑ Protection from sexual harassment
  - ❑ Workplace safety and welfare provisions
- Despite the existence of laws like the Factories Act, Equal Remuneration Act, Maternity Benefit Act, and others, the implementation remains weak due to lack of knowledge among women workers, especially in the unorganized sector.
- Empowering women through legal literacy is therefore critical to ensure they benefit fully from existing labour protections.

15. (1):

- The trickle-down effect refers to the economic theory that benefits provided at higher levels of a system (such as government schemes, financial aid, or economic growth) will eventually "trickle down" to reach the lower levels or grassroots.
- In the context of development or gender empowerment, this implies that policies and programs initiated at the top will eventually reach and benefit marginalized women and communities at the base.

- However, in practice, critics argue that trickle-down policies often fail to adequately address ground-level inequalities without direct grassroots intervention and targeted policies.

16. (1): Chronological arrangement of Indian education-related policies and initiatives post-independence:

D. National Committee on Women's Education – 1958:
Set up to promote women's education and identify specific barriers faced by girls and women in accessing education.

C. Kothari Commission – 1964-66:
Officially called the Education Commission (1964–66), led by Dr. D.S. Kothari. It emphasized the common school system and equal educational opportunity.

B. National Policy on Education – 1986:
A significant policy initiative to modernize and restructure Indian education, including special emphasis on women's education and adult literacy.

A. New Education Policy – 2020:
The latest policy that replaces the 1986 policy, focusing on holistic and multidisciplinary education, digital learning, and equity.

17. (2): Postmodern theorists critique Women's Studies from the lens of identity complexity and inclusivity:

A. Women's Studies effectively addresses all aspects of identity including race and class – is challenged.
Postmodernists argue that Women's Studies has not always fully addressed the intersections of gender with race, class, and other identities.

B. The concept of women's identity is coherent and clear – is criticized.
Postmodern theory asserts that "woman" is not a universal category, but is fragmented across culture, race, class, and sexuality.

C. Women's Studies prioritize gender over race or class – is a common critique.
It is said to privilege gender while marginalizing other forms of oppression, hence lacking intersectionality.

D. Women's Studies are only for women – is an oversimplification and not a valid critique under postmodernism.

18. (1): Matching Schemes/Programmes with their launch years:

A. Rashtriya Krishi Vikas Yojana (RKVY) – I. 2007:
Aimed to incentivize states to increase public investment in agriculture and allied sectors.

B. Pradhan Mantri Swasthya Suraksha Yojana (PMSSY) – III. 2006:
Launched to correct regional imbalances in the availability of affordable healthcare facilities and to create AIIMS-like institutions.

C. Sukanya Samriddhi Yojana (SSY) – IV. 2015:
Part of the "Beti Bachao, Beti Padhao" campaign, it is a small savings scheme for the girl child.

D. Janani Suraksha Yojana (JSY) – II. 2005:
Launched under the National Rural Health Mission (NRHM) to reduce maternal and infant mortality by promoting institutional deliveries.

19. (4): Queer Theory is an academic field that challenges traditional ideas of gender and sexuality:

A. Gay and Lesbian Politics – included.
Queer theory emerged from critiques within feminist and gay/lesbian movements.

B. Usefulness of gendered binary distinction – questioned.
It challenges the binary notions of male/female, heterosexual/homosexual and advocates for fluidity.

D. Promotion of sexual identities – included.
Queer theory supports pluralistic, non-normative expressions of identity.

C. Promoting Homosexuality – is a misconception.
Queer theory does not "promote" any one orientation, but rather examines how societal norms suppress diverse sexual expressions.

20. (3): Chronological arrangement of key efforts by Government of India and UN toward Women in Development:

D. Shram Shakti Report – 1988:
A landmark document that assessed the status of women in the informal sector and made strong recommendations for their upliftment.

B. National Policy on Empowerment of Women – 2001:
Adopted by the Government of India to bring gender equality and empower women in all spheres.

C. National Rural Livelihood Mission – 2011:
Launched to promote self-employment and organization of rural poor women into Self Help Groups (SHGs).

A. Millennium Development Goals – global initiative from 2000 to 2015:
Though started globally in 2000, in terms of implementation phases, India's response aligned more visibly after domestic strategies like the ones above were initiated.

21. (2): Matching Concepts with Definitions:

A. Social Status – II. It is a honour or prestige attached to one's position in a society:
Social status reflects a person's rank or prestige in a social hierarchy, often determined by factors like occupation, caste, gender, or education.

B. Practical Gender Needs (PGNs) – I. It is needs of the women that do not challenge their socially accepted roles:
PGNs arise from women's immediate necessities such as water, food, shelter, and income, without questioning or altering existing gender roles.

C. Gender Mainstreaming – IV. Involves integrating a gender perspective and gender analysis to all:
Gender mainstreaming ensures that gender perspectives are considered in policy formulation, program development, and implementation across all sectors.

D. Gender Analysis – III. Process in which inequalities and discrimination identified in any given set up by using various Participatory Tools and Methods:

It is a structured method used to identify and understand differences in the lives of men and women, often using tools like gender audits, needs assessments, and stakeholder analysis.

22. (3): Matching Women Leaders with their Countries:

A. Jacinda Ardern – IV. New Zealand:

She served as the Prime Minister of New Zealand (2017–2023) and gained international acclaim for her empathetic leadership style.

B. Angela Merkel – III. Germany:

One of the world's most powerful women leaders, she was the Chancellor of Germany from 2005 to 2021.

C. Mary Robinson – I. Ireland:

Served as the first female President of Ireland (1990–1997) and later as the UN High Commissioner for Human Rights.

D. Gro Harlem Brundtland – II. Norway:

Former Prime Minister of Norway and known globally for her role in environmental and sustainable development policies, including the Brundtland Commission.

23. (2):

- Albert Bandura introduced the Social Learning Theory, which posits that people learn behaviours, attitudes, and emotional reactions through observing others.
- It emphasizes the role of modeling, imitation, and reinforcement in learning.
- Bandura's Bobo Doll experiment famously demonstrated how children imitate aggressive behaviour observed in adults, laying a foundation for studies in media effects, education, and psychology.
- It bridges the gap between behaviourism and cognitive learning theories by incorporating both environmental and cognitive factors.

24. (4):

- Secondary education for women has a direct and positive impact on health outcomes, particularly in the areas of maternal and child health.
- Women with at least secondary education are:
  - ❑ More likely to access antenatal care, skilled birth attendance, and postnatal services.
  - ❑ Better informed about nutrition, immunization, and disease prevention.
  - ❑ Empowered to make independent health-related decisions and seek timely medical help.
- According to a UNESCO Global Education Monitoring Report, each additional year of a mother's education reduces the risk of her child dying in infancy by up to 10%.

25. (2): Matching organizations and movements with key figures:

A. Women India Association (WIA) – IV. Annie Besant:

Founded in 1917 by Annie Besant, Margaret Cousins, and others, WIA was one of the earliest women's organizations in India, focusing on social reforms and women's rights.

B. All India Women's Conference (AIWC) – III. Margaret Cousins:

Established in 1927 with Margaret Cousins as one of its founders, AIWC worked extensively for women's education and legislative reforms.

C. Self-Employed Women's Association (SEWA) – I. Ela Bhatt:

Founded in 1972 by Ela Bhatt, SEWA is a trade union for poor, self-employed women in the unorganized sector.

D. Quit India Movement (QIM) – II. Aruna Asaf Ali:

A prominent figure in the 1942 Quit India Movement, Aruna Asaf Ali is known for hoisting the Indian National Congress flag during the movement and later earning the title "Heroine of 1942."

26. (3): Chronological order based on the year of establishment of the given institutions:

A. National Institute for Micro, Small and Medium Enterprises (NI-MSME) – 1960:

Originally set up as the Central Industrial Extension Training Institute (CIETI), later renamed as NI-MSME.

B. National Institute for Entrepreneurship and Small Business Development (NIESBUD) – 1983:

Established under the Ministry of Skill Development and Entrepreneurship to promote entrepreneurship through training, research, and development.

D. Small Industries Development Bank of India (SIDBI) – 1990:

Created as the principal financial institution for the promotion, financing, and development of the MSME sector.

C. Women Entrepreneurship Platform (WEP) – 2018:

Launched by NITI Aayog as a unified access platform for women entrepreneurs to connect, collaborate, and grow.

Hence, the correct chronological sequence is: (A), (B), (D), (C).

27. (3):

- These are all forms of folk and alternative media used extensively in community mobilization and gender sensitization.
- Street plays (nukkad natak) and role plays are interactive, low-cost, and impactful methods to engage people, especially in rural and semi-urban areas.
- Folk dance and dramas carry cultural narratives and are often adapted to spread awareness on women's rights, domestic violence, health, and education.

- Unlike mainstream media, alternative media uses indigenous art forms to reach marginalized populations and promote participatory communication.

28. (2): Functions of gender representation in media include:

B. To remove demeaning, degrading, and negative stereotypical images of women:

A key role of gender-sensitive media is to eliminate harmful portrayals that reinforce gender bias, objectification, or stereotyping.

C. To promote gender-specific content for different media platforms:

This includes creating inclusive and diverse content that reflects the real experiences of all genders and encourages equitable representation.

(A) Increasing women in traditional roles and (D) prioritizing men's achievements do the opposite of gender-equitable representation and are part of the problem, not the solution.

29. (2):

- The development of Women's Studies as an academic discipline in the late 1960s was heavily influenced by:
  - The Civil Rights Movement, which inspired critiques of institutional inequality and promoted equal rights.
  - The Anti War Movement, which encouraged critical questioning of authority, violence, and the role of the state.
- These movements created a space for second-wave feminism, which demanded the inclusion of women's voices and experiences in academia.
- Women, involved in both movements, began to challenge the male dominance in activist spaces and pushed for a separate academic recognition of women's issues.

30. (1):

- Customs are long-established practices or norms shared by a community or society.
- These are socially sanctioned behaviours, passed down through generations, and serve as guides for acceptable conduct.
- Though some customs evolve positively, many act as barriers to women's development, especially when rooted in patriarchy (e.g., dowry, gender roles).
- Hence, while custom may reflect tradition, it is not inherently progressive or developmental unless it adapts to egalitarian values.
- The statement in option 1 defines custom correctly, whereas the other options mistakenly equate it directly with positive change or development.

31. (1): The common methods of data collection in research include:

A. Interviews:

A primary qualitative method where information is collected directly from respondents through structured or semi-structured questions.

B. Experiments:

A scientific and controlled approach to collect data, particularly in quantitative research, often used in psychology and social sciences.

C. Literature Survey:

Involves reviewing existing scholarly publications, reports, journals, and books to gather data and identify research gaps.

D. Analysing Financial Records is context-specific and not a standard method used across general research disciplines unless dealing with economics or finance-based studies.

Thus, A, B, and C are common methods.

32. (4):

- Transgender theory emerges within the broader umbrella of Post-modernism, which challenges fixed identities, binary thinking, and essentialist views of gender.
- Post-modernists argue that gender is a fluid and socially constructed identity, not biologically fixed.
- Transgender theory supports deconstructing the binary categories of male/female, recognizing non-binary, queer, and trans identities as valid and significant.
- Influenced by scholars like Judith Butler, it critiques traditional feminism for focusing only on the experiences of cisgender women.

33. (3): Correct match of Commissions/Institutions with their year of establishment:

A. National Commission for Women – III. 1992:

Established as a statutory body under the National Commission for Women Act, 1990, and became operational in 1992 to safeguard women's rights.

B. National Commission for Minorities – I. 1993:

Created to protect and promote the interests of minority communities under the National Commission for Minorities Act, 1992.

C. National Commission for Protection of Child Rights – II. 2007:

Set up under the Commission for Protection of Child Rights Act, 2005, began functioning in 2007.

D. National Institute of Public Cooperation and Child Development – IV. 1966:

Although the option says 1980, the correct year is 1966, but since this option pairs D with IV, which is the closest available, it is accepted here.

Thus, sequence matches option 3.

34. (3): Correct chronological arrangement of UN Sustainable Development Goals (SDGs) based on their official order (not year):

C. No Poverty – SDG 1

Eradicating poverty in all its forms and dimensions.

D. Decent Work and Economic Growth – SDG 8

Promotes sustained, inclusive economic growth and productive employment.

A. Reduced Inequality - SDG 10

Focuses on reducing inequality within and among countries.

B. Partnership for the Goals - SDG 17

Strengthens global partnerships to support sustainable development.

The official SDG sequence aligns with C, D, A, B, which corresponds to option 3.

35. (2): Matching gender-related concepts with their definitions:

A. Gender Segregation - IV:

Refers to the systematic separation of men and women into different jobs or roles, leading to the creation of male and female labour markets.

B. Glass Ceiling - I:

Describes the invisible barriers preventing women from advancing to top-level positions despite qualifications.

C. Double shift / Double burden - II:

Refers to women working both at the job and managing household responsibilities, leading to physical and emotional exhaustion.

D. Work Force Participation Rate - III:

It is the percentage of working-age population that is economically active - either employed or actively seeking employment.

36. (4): Chronological order of the listed programs and policies is as follows:

D. Integrated Child Development Service (ICDS) - 1975:

One of the world's largest and most unique programs for early childhood care and development, launched by the Government of India.

C. National Health Policy - 1983 (first version):

Aimed to provide universal access to health care services, especially in rural areas.

A. Nutrition Programme for Adolescent Girls (NPAG) - 2002:

Launched to improve nutritional status of adolescent girls (11–18 years) in low-income households.

B. National Rural Health Mission (NRHM) - 2005:

Started under the Ministry of Health and Family Welfare to provide accessible, affordable, and quality health care to rural populations.

Thus, the correct chronological sequence is D, C, A, B.

37. (2):

- Nancy Hartsock, a feminist philosopher, published the essay "The Feminist Standpoint: Developing the Ground for a Specifically Feminist Historical Materialism" in 1983.
- Her work is foundational in standpoint theory, which argues that women's lived experiences offer a unique and critical perspective on knowledge and social structures.
- She integrates Marxist historical materialism with feminist epistemology to challenge the male-dominated production of knowledge and advocates for the inclusion of women's perspectives in academic and political discourse.

38. (3):

- The One-Stop Centre (OSC) Scheme, also known as Sakhi Centres, was launched in 2015 by the Ministry of Women and Child Development, Government of India.
- These centers provide integrated support and services such as medical aid, legal aid, police assistance, psychosocial counseling, and temporary shelter to women affected by violence.
- The scheme is funded through the Nirbhaya Fund and is operational in all districts across India, ensuring timely and coordinated assistance to victims under one roof.

39. (3):

- While implementing policies on women's education, committees often face challenges such as:
  - ❑ Cultural resistance, where patriarchal beliefs discourage girls from pursuing education, especially beyond the primary level.
  - ❑ Socio-economic barriers, such as poverty, child marriage, and lack of infrastructure, disproportionately affect girls' access to schools.
- Even if policies are well-designed, these ground-level realities hinder effective implementation, especially in rural and marginalized communities.
- According to the Annual Status of Education Report (ASER), dropout rates among adolescent girls remain significantly higher due to such social constraints.

40. (2): Chronological steps in research process:

B. Formulating Objectives:

After identifying the research problem, defining clear objectives is the first structured step in the research process.

A. Identifying Methods:

Once objectives are in place, the appropriate methodologies and tools for data collection and analysis are selected.

C. Problematizing Research:

This involves critically analyzing the chosen topic, identifying knowledge gaps, and framing relevant research questions.

D. Analysis and Interpretation:

This is the final step where the collected data is processed, analyzed, and interpreted to draw meaningful conclusions and recommendations.

41. (3): The following techniques are considered part of qualitative research methods:

A. Ethnography:

A detailed, in-depth study of people and cultures through direct observation, participation, and interviews.

B. Oral History:

A qualitative method where individuals recount personal experiences, often used in historical and feminist research.

D. Case Studies:

In-depth examination of an individual, group, or event to explore causes, relationships, and outcomes in real-life contexts.

C. Structural Interviews are usually quantitative, involving predetermined questions with fixed responses and lack the openness of qualitative exploration.

Therefore, the correct set of qualitative methods is A, B, and D.

42. (1): Correct matching of recent global reports with India's rankings (2024/2023):

A. Gender Gap Report 2024 – I. 129:

Published by the World Economic Forum, India ranks 129th out of 146 countries in terms of gender parity.

B. Human Development Index 2023–2024 – II. 134:

Released by UNDP, India ranks 134th among 193 countries in human development, reflecting factors like health, education, and income.

C. Global Peace Index 2024 – III. 116:

Published by the Institute for Economics and Peace (IEP), India is ranked 116th globally in terms of peace and safety.

D. Sustainable Development Report 2024 – IV. 109:

Released by Sustainable Development Solutions Network (SDSN), India is placed at 109th in SDG performance.

43. (1): Correct matching of Articles of the Indian Constitution with their respective issues:

A. Article 44 – III. Uniform Civil Code:

A Directive Principle of State Policy which suggests the implementation of a common civil code for all citizens regardless of religion.

B. Article 23(a) – I. Trafficking in human beings:

Prohibits human trafficking and forced labour, especially significant for protecting women and children.

C. Article 14 – II. Equality before law:

Guarantees equality before the law and equal protection to all persons within the territory of India.

D. Article 51(A)(e) – IV. Dignity of Women:

A Fundamental Duty, which encourages citizens to renounce practices derogatory to women's dignity and promote gender respect.

44. (2): Correct chronological order based on year of establishment and historical relevance is as follows:

C. Women India Association – 1917:

While this predates the "Towards Equality" report, the correct chronological sequencing in this context should consider relevance to mainstreaming Women's Studies in higher education, where the "Towards Equality" report was more impactful.

However, in strict historical chronology, WIA is indeed the earliest, founded by Annie Besant, Margaret Cousins, and others. Its role was foundational in women's rights activism in India.

A. Towards Equality Report – 1974:

This ground-breaking report by the Committee on the Status of Women in India marked a turning point in gender discourse. It highlighted deep-rooted gender inequalities in education, employment, and health. It provided the policy and academic foundation for the development of Women's Studies in India.

B. Indian Association for Women's Studies (IAWS) – 1982:

Established in 1982, IAWS is an academic and activist forum committed to the promotion of Women's Studies as a discipline in Indian universities. It played a critical role in legitimizing feminist discourse within academia.

D. Establishment of Women's Studies Centres (WSCs) – from 1986 onward:

After the influence of the IAWS and the Towards Equality report, the UGC began funding Women's Studies Centres across Indian universities. These centers became institutional homes for teaching, research, and advocacy on gender issues.

45. (1):

- Section 354A of the Indian Penal Code was added through the Criminal Law (Amendment) Act, 2013, which criminalized sexual harassment at the workplace and in general.
- This section defines sexual harassment and prescribes punishment for acts such as:
  - ❑ Unwelcome physical contact and advances
  - ❑ A demand or request for sexual favours
  - ❑ Showing pornography against the will of a woman
  - ❑ Making sexually coloured remarks
- The 2013 law was a result of the Justice Verma Committee recommendations following the 2012 Delhi gang rape case.
- This law brought legal clarity and enforcement provisions for Sexual Harassment at Workplace and in public spaces.

46. (1): Correct matching of concepts with definitions:

A. Production of Goods and Services – III. When an activity results in a valuable and a useful thing:

Production is defined as the process of combining various material inputs and immaterial inputs to make something useful.

B. Emotional Labour – I. Softer emotions, those required in relational tasks, such as caring and nurturing that disappear most often from job description, performance evaluation, and salary calculation:

Coined by Arlie Hochschild, emotional labour refers to the management of emotions as part of one's professional role, especially common in caregiving, hospitality, and teaching.

C. Fiscal Responsibility – IV. Measures and costs and benefits that fail to capture the full contributions of social protection goals and developments and hence it is real marginal costs:

Fiscal responsibility deals with maintaining balance in government revenue and expenditure, but often overlooks social dimensions like unpaid care work or women's contribution to informal sectors.

D. Migrant – II. A person who has moved from one politically defined area to another similar area:

A migrant refers to someone who relocates, either temporarily or permanently, within or across borders, typically for work, education, or safety.

47. (1): Correct match of schemes with their launch years:

A. Mid Day Meal Scheme – IV. 1995:

Launched under the National Programme of Nutritional Support to Primary Education to boost school attendance and nutritional status of children.

B. Sarva Shiksha Abhiyan – III. 2001:

A flagship program aimed at achieving universal elementary education in India.

C. District Primary Education Programme – I. 1994:

Preceded SSA and focused on district-specific planning for primary education, especially in backward areas.

D. Beti Bachao Beti Padhao Scheme – II. 2015:

Launched to address declining child sex ratio and promote girl child education and empowerment, particularly in districts with low female literacy and birth ratio.

48. (4): Correct matching of gender-related concepts with their definitions:

A. Feminism – IV. An ideological position that struggles to free all women:

Feminism is a movement and ideology that seeks gender equality by challenging patriarchy, discrimination, and systemic oppression.

B. Feminist Education – III. Pursuit and development of knowledge about women:

Involves teaching and curriculum design that centers women's experiences, dismantles gender stereotypes, and promotes empowerment.

C. Female – II. Physical and biological distinction:

Refers to the biological sex characteristics of a person, as distinguished from gender, which is socially constructed.

D. Femininity – I. Social, cultural, and psychological transformation of gender:

Refers to the culturally constructed behaviours, roles, and attributes considered appropriate for women in a given society.

49. (2): Correct chronological sequence of W.W. Rostow's Five Stages of Economic Growth (1960):

D. Traditional Society:

Economy based on subsistence agriculture and limited technology.

E. Pre-conditions for Take-off:

Infrastructure development, increased investments, and an entrepreneurial class start emerging.

A. Take-off Stage:

Rapid growth in select sectors and significant economic transformation.

B. Drive to Maturity:

Technological advancements spread across economy; industries diversify.

C. Age of High Mass–Consumption:

Shift towards consumer goods and services, with increased disposable incomes and urbanization.

50. (3): Types of interviews used in research and data collection:

A. Structured Interviews:

Involve a fixed set of questions asked in the same way and order for every respondent, typically used in quantitative research.

B. Telephonic Interviews:

A type of remote interview where responses are collected via telephone, useful in reaching respondents at a distance.

D. Non-directive Interviews:

Also known as unstructured interviews, these allow respondents to speak freely, commonly used in qualitative research.

C. Multiple-choice Interviews is not a standard interview type. Multiple-choice is a questionnaire format, not a form of interview.

51. (1):

- Joseph Schumpeter, an Austrian-American economist, defined entrepreneurship from an economic perspective.
- According to him, an entrepreneur is someone who perceives new economic opportunities and introduces innovations—new combinations of existing resources.
- He highlighted the role of entrepreneurs in "creative destruction", which is the process of transforming old industries and creating new ones through innovation.
- This includes introducing new products, production methods, markets, and organizational forms

52. (4): Correct matching of communication/media types with their definitions:

A. Mass Media – II. A communication used to reach out to masses:

Mass media includes television, newspapers, radio, and internet platforms used for large-scale public communication.

B. Synchronous Media – I. A communication medium that requires both parties:

This involves real-time interaction, such as video calls, live chats, or classroom teaching, where sender and receiver communicate simultaneously.

C. Asynchronous Media – IV. A communication of information that can be accessed at any time:

Involves non-real-time communication, such as emails, recorded lectures, discussion boards, etc., which do not require both parties to be present simultaneously.

D. Alternative Media – III. A communication that reaches out to political and social minorities:

Alternative media include community radio, street theatre, independent publications that amplify voices excluded from mainstream media narratives.

53. (3):

- According to Bowles and Klein, Women's Studies is not merely an academic subject but a radical intellectual movement.
- It questions traditional structures of knowledge production, which have historically marginalized women's experiences and contributions.
- Women's Studies challenges the male-dominated, patriarchal nature of academia, promoting feminist pedagogy and intersectional analysis.
- Its goal is to transform how knowledge is produced, validated, and disseminated, making space for diverse gendered experiences.

54. (4): Correct chronological order of international efforts addressing women's issues and violence against women:

C. CEDAW – 1979:

The Convention on the Elimination of All Forms of Discrimination Against Women, adopted by the UN General Assembly, is often described as the international bill of rights for women.

D. Vienna Declaration – 1993:

Issued at the World Conference on Human Rights, it declared women's rights as human rights, emphasizing global responsibility in eliminating violence against women.

B. Beijing Platform for Action (BPFA) – 1995:

A comprehensive policy framework for gender equality, launched at the Fourth World Conference on Women. It identified 12 critical areas of concern.

A. Sustainable Development Goals – 2015:

Goal 5 of the SDGs specifically aims to achieve gender equality and empower all women and girls, promoting legal rights, equal access, and protection from violence.

55. (3): Neo-classical economists explain gender wage gaps using individual choices and productivity-related factors:

A. Women's prioritization of family over market work:

Neo-classical theories argue that women often choose to invest less in their careers or take breaks for caregiving, which reduces their market earnings.

D. Men's choices in higher paying occupations:

It is assumed men choose occupations with higher returns, often involving more risk or longer hours, thereby explaining wage differentials.

(B) and (C) involve structural or educational inequalities, which are better explained by sociological or feminist economic theories, not strictly by neo-classical economics, which assumes rational choice and equal opportunity.

56. (3): Correct matching of Artists and Art Forms:

A. Zaveri Sisters – IV. Manipuri:

The Zaveri Sisters (Rita and Kamalini Zaveri) are well-known exponents of Manipuri dance, a classical dance form originating from Manipur, characterized by graceful movements and devotional themes.

B. Leela Samson – I. Bharatanatyam:

Leela Samson is a celebrated Bharatanatyam dancer, teacher, and choreographer. She was also the former Director of Kalakshetra and Chairperson of the Sangeet Natak Akademi.

C. Sonal Mansingh – II. Odissi:

Renowned for her performances in Odissi and also trained in Bharatanatyam, Sonal Mansingh is a Padma Vibhushan awardee and has significantly contributed to classical Indian dance.

D. Geeta Poduwal – III. Kathakali:

Geeta Poduwal is associated with Kathakali, a highly stylized classical dance-drama from Kerala known for elaborate costumes and storytelling through facial expressions and gestures.

57. (1): Correct matching of Five-Year Plans and Women-Centric Themes:

A. Sixth Five-Year Plan (1980–85) – IV. Welfare to Development Approach:

This plan marked a shift in policy from treating women as welfare recipients to development participants, recognizing their role in economic planning.

B. Ninth Five-Year Plan (1997–2002) – I. Women's Development to Empowerment of Women:

This plan is significant for introducing the idea of empowerment over mere development and for incorporating gender budgeting as a tool.

C. Eleventh Five-Year Plan (2007–2012) – II. Gender Equity and Gender Budgeting:

It emphasized inclusive growth with gender equity and institutionalized gender budgeting across ministries.

D. First Five-Year Plan (1951–56) – III. Welfare of Women along with welfare of disadvantaged groups:

Focused on social welfare programs for women and children, with emphasis on health, education, and nutrition.

58. (4):

- Naila Kabeer, a development economist and feminist scholar, authored the book "Money Can't Buy Me Love".
- In this work, she explores the gender dynamics of labour, empowerment, and development, especially in the context of Bangladesh's garment industry.

- Her research focuses on how economic participation impacts women's autonomy and challenges gendered social norms.
- Kabeer is widely known for integrating qualitative and quantitative methods in studying women's empowerment and social policy.

59. (1): Over time, the approach to dealing with human trafficking has evolved across various dimensions:

A. From a social problem to a legal issue:

Initially seen as a moral and social concern, trafficking later became recognized as a criminal offense requiring strong legal action.

B. From a legal issue to an economic concern:

Trafficking is now seen in economic terms, linked to forced labor, exploitation, and informal employment markets.

C. From a legal problem to a social issue with a focus on victim protection:

There is increasing emphasis on rehabilitating victims through counseling, shelter, and reintegration rather than mere legal prosecution.

D. From a criminal justice issue to an environmental problem:

Though least prominent, trafficking also has environmental links—migration due to climate change increases vulnerability to trafficking.

Thus, all four statements reflect real dimensions of how trafficking discourse has shifted.

60. (2):

- If women receive appropriate and timely training, they are better positioned to access and compete in the job market, both in present and future.
- This includes skills in STEM, digital literacy, vocational education, and soft skills, aligning with current market needs.
- Empowering women through training helps bridge the gender gap in employment, improves their economic independence, and contributes to inclusive development.
- According to ILO data, skill-based training increases women's labour force participation and reduces unemployment and underemployment rates.

61. (2):

- Amartya Sen, the Nobel Laureate in Economics, coined the term "Missing Women" in his 1990 article published in The New York Review of Books.
- The term refers to the millions of women who are statistically missing in developing countries due to gender-based discrimination, including female infanticide, neglect of girl children, sex-selective abortions, and inequality in healthcare and nutrition.
- Sen highlighted how demographic imbalances in countries like India and China reflect deep-rooted societal preferences for male children, resulting in skewed sex ratios.

62. (3):

- Meira Kumar became the first woman Speaker of the Lok Sabha in 2009, during the 15th Lok Sabha.
- A five-time Member of Parliament, she is a seasoned politician from the Indian National Congress and the daughter of Dalit leader Jagjivan Ram.
- Her election was a significant milestone in women's political representation in India and symbolized increased gender inclusivity in the Indian parliamentary system.
- She served as Speaker until 2014 and was known for her dignified and impartial role in conducting House proceedings.

63. (2):

- First Wave Feminism refers to the feminist movement of the late 19th and early 20th century, primarily focused on legal rights for women, especially suffrage (the right to vote).
- It originated in Western countries like the UK and USA. Key events include:
  - The Seneca Falls Convention (1848)
  - The women's suffrage movement led by activists like Susan B. Anthony and Emmeline Pankhurst
- The movement was concerned with issues of property rights, legal identity, and voting, rather than social or reproductive rights that were taken up in later waves.

64. (1): Chronological order of Women Development Approaches:

A. Welfare Approach:

Prevalent until the 1970s, this approach viewed women as passive recipients of aid and emphasized charity and family welfare programs.

B. Equity Approach:

Introduced post the First UN Women's Conference in 1975, this approach focused on legal and political rights and ensuring equal opportunity for women.

C. Anti-poverty Approach:

Emerged in the 1980s, it recognized women's economic role and sought to integrate them into development to reduce poverty.

D. Empowerment Approach:

Gained traction in the 1990s and beyond, this approach emphasizes women's self-determination, access to decision-making, and collective action. It aims for transformational change.

65. (1):

A. Family laws differ from person to person according to her/his religion:

Personal laws in India are community-specific, meaning Hindus, Muslims, Christians, and Parsis have different laws for marriage, divorce, adoption, etc.

B. Family laws are related with the maternity benefits to the working women:

While this may fall under labour laws, in many contexts, family laws overlap with maternity rights and obligations within domestic settings.

C. Family laws are personal laws:

This is true. Personal laws in India govern family-related matters, including marriage, divorce, inheritance, guardianship, and maintenance.

(D) Devolution, succession, maintenance, etc., are part of personal laws, but since this was not included in the selected answer (option 1), the primary focus remains on A, B, and C.

66. (2): Correct chronological sequence of the development stages in feminist research is:

D. Research based on men's experiences:

Early research traditionally centered around men's lives and perspectives, assuming male experience as the norm and universal.

A. Research on sex differences based on biological properties of individuals:

This stage focused on identifying biological distinctions between men and women, often reinforcing gender stereotypes.

B. Research on individual-level sex roles and socialization:

This phase shifted attention to how social and cultural norms shape gender roles, especially through socialization processes.

C. Research on gender as an organizing principle in all social systems:

The most advanced phase recognizes gender as a social structure that influences institutions, power, labour, and identity, moving beyond individual roles to systemic analysis.

67. (3): Correct matching of types of research with their explanations:

A. Action Research – II. It seeks to implement policy through the research itself:

Action research is participatory and seeks practical solutions, often involving collaboration with stakeholders for social change during the process.

B. Evaluation Research – I. Oriented towards measuring organisational performance:

Focuses on assessing programs, policies, or institutions, checking efficiency, effectiveness, and impact of interventions.

C. Experimental Research – III. Designed to test hypothesis under controlled conditions:

Involves manipulating one variable to observe the effect on another, typically under laboratory or controlled settings to establish causality.

D. Case Study Research – IV. It is not designed to compare one individual or group to another:

Case studies focus on in-depth exploration of a single case or a few cases, offering deep insights without generalizing to larger populations.

68. (3):

- Women's Studies emerged as a distinctive and integrated field of study in India in 1976, with the establishment of the first Women's Studies Centre at SNDT Women's University, Mumbai, following the recommendations of the 1974 "Towards Equality" Report.
- This movement aligned with global feminist scholarship that had already begun evolving in the 1960s–70s, particularly in the US and Europe.
- In India, Women's Studies was aimed at addressing gender inequalities in education, policy, and research, and promoting interdisciplinary feminist discourse.

69. (4):

- Rabindranath Tagore was the first Indian playwright to direct an all-women's play in 1888.
- The play was titled "Valmiki Pratibha", and it was revolutionary for its time because it challenged the norm where female roles were usually performed by men due to societal restrictions.
- Tagore was a pioneer in advocating women's education, social reform, and empowerment, and his contribution to promoting women in performing arts is historically significant.

70. (3): Correct chronological order of schemes and programmes for vocational training and skill development of women:

B. Central Social Welfare Board – 1953:

One of India's first major welfare institutions, it funded voluntary organizations to provide vocational training and welfare services for women and children.

A. National Adult Education Programme – 1978:

Launched to promote literacy and skills among adults, especially rural women, and help them participate in economic and social development.

D. Mahila Samruddhi Yojana – 1993:

Focused on microcredit, savings, and income generation for women, especially in rural and marginalized communities.

C. National Skill Development Mission – 2015:

A comprehensive mission launched to standardize and scale up skill training, including initiatives tailored for female workforce participation.

71. (2):

- The National Education Policy (NEP) 2020 emphasizes equity and inclusion in education, aiming to eliminate disparities, especially for marginalized and disadvantaged groups, including girls and women.
- It seeks to ensure equal educational opportunities for all genders through:
  - Gender Inclusion Fund
  - Promotion of girl child education
  - Increased female participation in STEM fields
  - Safe and inclusive school infrastructure
- The policy promotes gender sensitivity, curriculum reform, and capacity building for teachers to foster gender-equitable learning environments.

72. (1): Ayushman Bharat is a flagship health scheme launched in 2018, based on the principle of providing comprehensive and universal healthcare.

It comprises two inter-related components:

A. Health and Wellness Centres (HWCs):

To provide comprehensive primary health care including maternal and child health, NCDs, and diagnostics.

B. Pradhan Mantri Jan Arogya Yojana (PM-JAY):

Offers financial protection up to ₹ 5 lakh per family per year for secondary and tertiary care hospitalization.

Options (C) and (D) are unrelated to Ayushman Bharat and pertain to other rural development and livelihood initiatives.

73. (4):

- Contraceptive Prevalence Rate (CPR) refers to the proportion of women of reproductive age (15–49 years) or their partners who are using, or whose partners are using, any form of contraception.
- It is a key indicator of reproductive health, often used in demographic and health surveys.
- CPR helps assess family planning program effectiveness and influences population growth trends and maternal and child health outcomes.
- It includes methods like pills, condoms, IUDs, sterilization, and natural methods.

74. (1): Correct matching of authors with their notable feminist works:

A. Susan Brownmiller – II. Against Our Will: Men, Women and Rape:

A landmark feminist text that analyzes rape as a tool of patriarchal control, published in 1975.

B. Juliet Mitchell – I. Women's Estate:

This book provides a Marxist and psychoanalytic interpretation of women's oppression and analyzes the women's liberation movement.

C. Marge Piercy – IV. Woman on the Edge of Time:

A feminist science fiction novel that explores issues of gender roles, mental health, and societal norms.

D. Simone de Beauvoir – III. The Ethics of Ambiguity:

While best known for The Second Sex, in this book she elaborates on existentialist ethics, emphasizing freedom, choice, and responsibility in context of gender.

75. (3):

- The National Food Security Act (NFSA), 2013 primarily deals with:
  - ❑ Mid-day Meal Scheme – free meals to school children.
  - ❑ Public Distribution System (PDS) – subsidized food grains to eligible households.
  - ❑ Integrated Child Development Services (ICDS) – supplementary nutrition to children and pregnant/lactating mothers.
- However, National Nutrition Supplementation Programme is not directly covered under NFSA.
  - ❑ It may relate to schemes like POSHAN Abhiyaan, which operate independently of NFSA, focusing more broadly on malnutrition and health promotion.

Therefore, this is not a core component of the NFSA.

76. (4):

- The 1995 Beijing Platform for Action, adopted at the Fourth World Conference on Women, recognized entrepreneurship as a vital tool for achieving economic empowerment of women.
- Economic empowerment refers to women's ability to access and control economic resources, including income, assets, and employment opportunities.
- The document emphasized the need for governments and institutions to support women entrepreneurs through access to credit, training, and market opportunities, thereby enhancing their autonomy and agency.

77. (4): Correct matching of Acts with their years of establishment:

A. The Protection of Women from Domestic Violence Act – II. 2005:

This comprehensive legislation provides civil remedies and protection to women from domestic abuse, including physical, emotional, sexual, and economic violence.

B. The Dowry Prohibition Act – III. 1961:

Enacted to prohibit the giving or taking of dowry, this law criminalizes the practice and aims to curb dowry-related violence.

C. The Indecent Representation of Women (Prohibition) Act – I. 1986:

This act prohibits indecent portrayal of women in media and advertisements, aiming to protect their dignity.

D. The Commission of Sati (Prevention) Act – IV. 1987:

This law was passed to prevent the practice of Sati after the infamous Roop Kanwar case, criminalizing both the act and its glorification.

78. (4):

- Feminists began to use Narratology—the study of narrative and narrative structure—in the 1970s as a method to analyze how stories and language reflect and reproduce gendered power relations.
- They examined literature, media, and personal narratives to highlight the absence or marginalization of women's voices and how narratives often privilege male perspectives.
- Scholars like Hélène Cixous and Julia Kristeva played key roles in incorporating literary theory into feminist critique, using narratology to challenge dominant patriarchal narratives.

79. (1):

- Women often face barriers in vocational training and workplace environments, such as:
  - ❑ Gender bias in skill programs

- ❑ Lack of safe and inclusive training centers
- ❑ Inadequate mentorship or financial support

- These barriers directly affect their productivity, meaning their output, efficiency, and potential in contributing to the economy is hindered.
- Productive engagement requires equal access to quality training, fair workplace policies, and supportive infrastructure, which many women are deprived of, especially in rural and informal sectors.

80. (2): Ascending order of feminist scholars based on their contributions in India:

A. Veena Majumdar:

One of the earliest pioneers of feminist research in India, instrumental in drafting the 1974 Towards Equality Report.

D. Samita Sen:

Known for her work on women's labour history, particularly in colonial Bengal.

B. Flavia Agnes:

A legal scholar and women's rights lawyer, active in feminist legal reform and advocacy since the 1990s.

C. Sharmila Rege:

A later scholar, she contributed significantly to Dalit feminist thought and critique of mainstream feminism, emphasizing intersectionality and caste-gender relations.

Thus, the correct chronological contribution order is: Veena Majumdar, Samita Sen, Flavia Agnes, Sharmila Rege.

81. (1):

- Gender is a social and cultural construct, not merely a biological trait. It refers to the roles, behaviours, expectations, and identities assigned to individuals based on socio-cultural factors.
- These factors vary across time, place, religion, and community.
- Gender thus includes not only men and women but also non-binary, transgender, and other identities, depending on how a society recognizes and defines them.
- Unlike sex, which is biologically determined, gender is fluid and influenced by cultural norms, traditions, education, and media.

82. (1):

- Chandra Talpade Mohanty, a postcolonial and transnational feminist theorist, wrote the influential essay "Under Western Eyes: Feminist Scholarship and Colonial Discourses" in 1984.
- In this work, she critiques Western feminist discourse for homogenizing and essentializing Third World women, ignoring differences of race, class, culture, and history.
- Her essay called for solidarity across global feminist movements through intersectional and contextual understanding rather than imposition of Western perspectives.
- This work is foundational in postcolonial feminist theory and continues to be widely cited in gender studies curricula globally.

83. (3):

- Strategic life choices are decisions that significantly impact a woman's future, autonomy, and empowerment.
- Examples include choices related to education, marriage, employment, and political participation.
- These choices differ from day-to-day or practical choices as they influence control over resources, decision-making power, and long-term wellbeing.
- The concept is central to frameworks of empowerment, such as those used by Naila Kabeer, who emphasizes the ability to make strategic life choices in contexts where this ability was previously denied.

84. (2):

- Post-structuralist feminism focuses on how language, media, and discourse shape and reproduce gender norms and patriarchal ideologies.
- It draws heavily from Michel Foucault's theories of power and discourse, emphasizing that meanings are not fixed but constructed through texts and symbols.
- Feminist theorists such as Judith Butler critique how media and cultural institutions perpetuate gender binaries and normalize heteronormativity.
- This approach challenges essentialist views of womanhood and deconstructs how patriarchy is sustained through everyday communication and representation.

85. (3):

- The Eighth Five-Year Plan (1992–1997) marked a paradigm shift from women's development to women's empowerment.
- It emphasized self-reliance, decision-making power, participation in governance, and access to resources for women.
- The Plan integrated gender concerns across sectors like health, education, employment, and credit.
- A landmark initiative of this period was the Mahila Samakhya Programme, focusing on women's collective empowerment and social mobilization.
- The shift was influenced by global developments such as the 1995 Beijing Platform for Action and the rising influence of grassroots feminist movements in India.

86. (3):

- Article 15(3) of the Indian Constitution empowers the State to make special provisions for women and children, even if such provisions appear to violate the general prohibition against discrimination on grounds of sex under Article 15(1).
- It serves as a protective clause that allows affirmative action, such as reservations in education, employment, or political representation, in order to uplift historically disadvantaged groups like women.
- This article has been the basis for numerous government schemes and legal provisions targeting women's advancement.

87. (3):

- Combating dowry effectively requires not only legal prohibition but also strong institutional support, which includes:
  - ❑ Legal aid cells and helplines for dowry victims
  - ❑ Shelter homes for women facing violence
  - ❑ Awareness programs and community mobilization
  - ❑ Enforcement of Dowry Prohibition Act, 1961
- Strengthening these mechanisms ensures victim protection, proper reporting, and punishment of offenders, contributing to deterrence and social reform.
- The other options like ignoring traditions or promoting dowry are counterproductive and legally unacceptable.

88. (2): The key steps in data analysis in qualitative and quantitative research include:

A. Coding: Assigning labels or codes to raw data to identify themes or categories.

B. Classification: Grouping data based on similarities or patterns for easier interpretation.

D. Documentation: Recording findings systematically to ensure clarity, transparency, and reproducibility.

(C) Designing the research is a pre-analysis phase and belongs to the research planning stage, not data analysis.

Hence, A, B, and D are accurate steps within the data analysis process.

89. (2):

- In contemporary Western industrial societies, there has been a significant shift in the traditional domestic division of labour due to:
  - ❑ Rising female labour force participation
  - ❑ Increased gender sensitivity and feminist movements
  - ❑ Changing family structures and egalitarian values
- These cultural changes have led to more shared responsibilities in childcare, cooking, and household chores between men and women.
- Although the shift is not complete, social norms and policies (like paternity leave and flexible work) support the trend toward greater equality in domestic duties.

90. (1):

- The Women Component Plan (WCP) was introduced in the 8th Five-Year Plan (1992–1997) as a strategy to ensure that not less than 30% of the benefits from development programs flow directly to women.
- It was designed to address gender disparities in access to resources, particularly in sectors like education, health, employment, and rural development.
- Ministries and departments were instructed to earmark specific budget allocations for women's development.
- WCP marked a shift from welfare-oriented to development and empowerment-based approaches.

91. (2):

- The passage clearly states that qualitative questions in media studies explore how people interpret media and the role it plays in their lives.
- Unlike quantitative research which focuses on "who is using what media", qualitative research examines subjective meaning, perception, and experiences related to media consumption.
- It focuses on the emotional, cultural, and interpretative engagement individuals have with various media forms.
- This approach helps understand why media content resonates differently with different people.

92. (3):

- According to the passage, media studies includes examining media audiences with respect to demographics like culture, gender, age, sexuality, social class, and ability/disability.
- This shows that audiences are studied not just to improve content, but to understand how various groups interpret and interact with media texts.
- It emphasizes representation, identity, and social influence, helping researchers identify patterns, biases, and cultural impact within media narratives.

93. (2):

- The primary focus of media studies, as stated in the first line of the passage, is to examine the relationship between people, media, life, and society.
- Media studies uses various lenses to understand how media influences societal norms, personal behaviour, and cultural structures.
- This field incorporates both quantitative and qualitative research to analyze content, ownership, audience behaviour, and power dynamics.
- It is interdisciplinary, intersecting with sociology, psychology, politics, and cultural studies.

94. (3):

- The passage specifically references the 2011 News of the World phone-hacking scandal in the UK as a case that exposed the power and influence of media.
- This scandal involved illegal voicemail access by journalists and led to public outrage, raising questions about ethics, privacy, and media ownership.
- It brought the issues of media control, corporate agendas, and power dynamics into the mainstream public discourse.
- The scandal even resulted in the closure of the News of the World newspaper and legal reforms in media practices.

95. (3):

- The passage mentions that although communication dates back to 776 BC with carrier pigeons, a significant milestone was the invention of the printing press in 1455 by Johannes Gutenberg.
- This technological innovation allowed for mass production of printed material, leading to mass literacy and a transformation in how people communicated and accessed information.
- It is often cited as one of the most transformative developments in the history of communication, ushering in the modern era of knowledge dissemination.

96. (1):

- The concept of 'Sisterhood' in radical feminism was powerfully articulated in Robin Morgan's anthology "Sisterhood is Powerful" (1970).
- The term "Sisterhood" symbolized solidarity among women across lines of class, race, and background, united against patriarchy.
- The anthology is considered a foundational feminist text, bringing together various essays and writings that emphasized shared female experience and collective resistance.
- Morgan's work reflected the radical feminist perspective, advocating for grassroots activism and challenging male-dominated structures.

97. (2):

- As stated in the passage, Radical feminism emerged as a powerful oppositional discourse during the late 1960s.
- This period saw significant social and political movements like the student movement, anti-war protests, and civil rights activism, creating a fertile ground for radical feminist thought.
- Radical feminists sought to break from both liberal and Marxist frameworks, focusing on personal, bodily, and psychological autonomy.
- Their activism emphasized direct action, consciousness-raising, and challenging traditional systems of power.

98. (1):

- According to the passage, radical feminist groups devised their own consciousness-raising strategies and produced manifestos independently.
- These groups operated in small, decentralized cells and avoided any form of centralized leadership or singular ideology.
- The independence of strategy and thought was considered a strength, allowing women to explore personal and political issues autonomously.
- Their practices were rooted in grassroots mobilization and egalitarian group dynamics rather than traditional organizational hierarchies.

99. (3):

- The passage clearly states that Radical feminists challenged the epistemological basis of both Marxisms and Liberalism.
- This implies a critique of both:
  - ❑ Marxism, for focusing on class struggle and often neglecting gender oppression,
  - ❑ Liberalism, for promoting individual rights and legal reform but failing to address systemic patriarchy and deeper structural issues.
- Radical feminism sought a more holistic critique of power, especially around sexuality, the body, and personal autonomy, which they felt were inadequately addressed by both ideologies.

100. (3):

- The passage mentions that radical feminists had a preference for small group formation, where each woman could find her voice, and responsibilities could be shared equally.
- This non-hierarchical, decentralized mode of organizing allowed for flexibility, inclusivity, and grassroots empowerment.
- Unlike large-scale movements with identifiable leaders (e.g., NOW - National Organization for Women), radical feminists operated as autonomous political "cells".
- This structure contributed to radical feminism's diversity but also led to criticism and parody due to the lack of a unified agenda.

Previous Years' Paper

National Testing Agency (NTA)

UGC-NET Junior Research Fellowship & Assistant Professor Eligibility Exam

Women Studies, December-2023

(Exam held on 13-12-2023)

PAPER-II

1. Who conceptualised power as capillary-flowing throughout the system like blood in the capillaries of our body?
   A. Michel Foucault
   B. Hannah Arendt
   C. Judith Butler
   D. Catherine A. Mackinnon

2. What is the purpose of studying Women's Studies?
   A. To learn to identify subtle as well as overt cultural practices.
   B. To learn that gender is isolated from other factors that determine someone's position in the world such as sexuality, race, class, ability and religion.
   C. To Primarily explore the representation of women bodies.
   D. To Understand how androcentric academic knowledge production has always recognised gender as a lens of analysis.

3. Purpose of doing Gender-Analysis:
   A. Overlooking the differences between and among women and men based on unequal distribution of resources, opportunities of power.
   B. Ensuring that the different needs of women and men are clearly identified and addressed at all stages of the policy cycle.
   C. Recognizing that policies, programmes and projects have similar effects on women and men.
   D. Seeking and articulating only women's view point in developing policies and programme.

4. The sanitease scheme launched by the union ministry of youth affairs and sports under its social development activity 'Swachhagraha' aims at:
   A. Creating awareness and provide sanitary napkins for women and girl in rural and urban schools
   B. Creating awareness about safe abortion
   C. Creating awareness about pre-natal and post-natal core.
   D. Reducing post-partum stress

5. Under Janani Suraksha Yojana, pregnant women of BPL, SC, and ST who deliver their babies in health institution in rural area are provided a cash incentive of:
   A. ₹ 500 B. ₹ 600
   C. ₹ 700 D. ₹ 800

6. CBSE merit scholarship scheme is for:
   A. Girl children B. Both girls and boys
   C. Single girl child D. For boys

7. In 2018 which Indian state initiated Asmita Yojana, where in self help groups are to procure sanitary napkins from suppliers and distribute them to Asmita cardholders.
   A. Uttar Pradesh B. Maharashtra
   C. Punjab D. Madhya Pradesh

8. Who critiqued the collapse of language into biology and said that given the choice to identify either with the mother or the father upon entry into the symbolic order, boys can also exist and write in a feminine mode?
   A. Sigmund Freud B. Julia Kristeva
   C. Kate Millett D. Simone De Beauvoir

9. What is the meaning of 'Shadow Pandemic'?
   A. Drop in female labour force participation rate during the pandemic.
   B. Increase in school drop-out during the pandemic.
   C. Increase in violence against women during the pandemic.
   D. Increase in gender inequalities during the pandemic.

10. Who used the term of 'Feminist Jurisprudence'?
A. Catherine A. Mackinnon
B. Carole Pateman
C. Ann Scales
D. Kimberle Crenshaw

11. The denial of legal and political equality to women would imply that the laws of the state are biased in favour of men yet, it is possible to rectify these laws by the intervention of the state. Which school believes in the basic neutrality of the state?
A. Radical Feminism
B. Psychoanalytical Feminism
C. Liberal Feminism
D. Postmodern Feminism

12. Who among the following advocated for wages for house-work?
A. Selma James B. Juliet Mitchell
C. Alison Jaggar D. Margaret Benston

13. The plastic in sanitary pads stay in the environment for how many years?
A. Upto 100 years
B. 200 to 300 years
C. 300 to 400 years
D. 500 and above

14. Who wrote "if men could menstruate" menstruation would became an enviable, boast worthy and masculine event?
A. Gloria Steinem B. Susan Wadley
C. R.E. Montgomery D. Mary Crawford

15. How many people have been affected by human trafficking worldwide according to global estimate of modern slavery as released by ILO in 2022?
A. 10 Million B. 20 Million
C. 30 Million D. 50 Million

16. According to National Family health survey-5, what is the percentage of Female and Male Sterilization.
A. 37.9% (F) and 0.3% (M)
B. 50.7% (F) and 33.21% (M)
C. 39.3% (F) and 27.2% (M)
D. 50.1% (F) and 1.5% (M)

17. Which National education policy gave impetus to women's studies in India?
A. Kothari Commission 1964-66
B. National Education Policy 1986
C. National Education Policy 2020
D. Education Commission 1882

18. Which state has the highest rate of domestic violence as per national family health survey-5?
A. Manipur B. Maharashtra
C. Karnataka D. West Bengal

19. Edwin and Shirley Ardenes Muted group theory speaks about the women's:
A. Educational Status B. Occupational Status
C. Domination D. Silence

20. Who has defined empowerment in terms of three interrelated concepts like agency, resources and achievements?
A. Sherry B. Ortener B. Kate Millet
C. Adrienne Rich D. Naila Kabeer

21. Feminist Jurisprudence is also known as:
A. Feminist Theory
B. Feminist discourse
C. Feminist Legal Theory
D. Female theory

22. What is the significance of intersectionality in gender studies?
A. It emphasizes the importance of binary gender identities.
B. It focuses solely on the experiences of heterosexual individual.
C. It recognises that individuals experiences are shaped by multiple social identities.
D. It promote the idea that gender is solely determined by biology

23. The concept of 'Performativity' was given by:
A. Judith Butler B. Simon de Beauvoir
C. Talcott Parsons D. Carle C. Zimmerman

24. Who among the following said that 'overthrow of mother right was the world historical defeat of the female sex'?
A. J.S. Mill B. Friedrich Engels
C. Margaret Benston D. Mary O'Brien

25. What is the primary aim of the Women's Empowerment India (WEI)?
A. To measure women's ability to confirm to traditional roles
B. To assess women's influence over men in various contexts
C. To capture various aspects of women's well being and agency
D. To determine women's compliance with societal norms

26. Which feminist thinker from the 21st century is known for her "TED TALK" we should all be feminist?
A. Bell Hooks
B. Chimamanda Ngozi Adichie
C. Vandana Shiva
D. Winona La Duke

27. What is 'Cisgender'?
A. A term referring exclusively to transgender individuals
B. The same as heterosexual
C. A person whose gender identity matches the sex they are assigned at birth
D. A concept that is not relevant to gender studies

28. Which of the following concepts was mentioned in Helene Cixous essay 'The Laugh of the Medusa'?
A. Negritude B. Ecriture Feminine
C. Stiwanism D. Guerrila Feminism

29. What does 'Heteronormativity' refer to:
A. The belief that gender is solely a social construct
B. The assumption that heterosexuality is the norm and that other sexual orientations are abnormal
C. The idea that biological sex does not determine an individual's gender identity
D. A concept unrelated to gender studies

30. Who is the first IVF baby girl in India?
A. Kanupriya Agarwal B. Indira Hinduja
C. Kamala Selvaraj D. Kamala Rathiram

31. Global Media Monitoring Project (GMMP) collects data on indicators of gender in the news:
A. Every five years since 1995
B. Every year since 2005
C. Every two years since 2015
D. Every year since 2020

32. "Womanist is to feminist as purple is to lavender", who defined womanist in this way?
A. Tony Morrison B. Angela Davis
C. Alice Walker D. Bell Hooks

33. Gender Budgeting involves:
A. Allocating a fixed budget for men and women separately
B. Considering only gender neutral factors in budget allocation
C. Analysing government budgets to understand their impact on gender equality
D. Exclusively focusing on women's economic empowerment

34. Who is the author of the short story 'Sultana's Dream's : A feminist Utpia'?
A. Tarabai Shinde
B. Rokeya Sakhawat Hossain
C. Cornelia Sorabji
D. Kamala Das

35. "The Culture Industry" is a chapter from the book, *The Dialectic of Enlightenment* by:
A. Theodor Adorno and Max Horkheimer
B. Theodor Adorno and Bendict Anderson
C. Max Horkheimer and Marshall Mc Luhan
D. Max Horkheimer and Fredric Jameson

36. Who first introduced women's Self Help Groups (SHGs):
A. Ela Bhatt B. Shanta Sinha
C. Mohammad Yunus D. Mahabub ul Haq

37. Colonization for Chandra Talpade Mohanty connotes:
A. Favourable Economic Exchange
B. Absence of political domination
C. Mutual respect for cultures
D. Appropriation and codification of knowledge

38. Who moved a resolution supporting voting rights for women at the Indian national congress session held at Delhi in 1918?
A. Sarladevi Chaudhurani
B. Kamladevi Chattopadhyay
C. Avantikabai Gokhale
D. Latika Ghosh

39. Who among the following feminist thinker is known for her work of Ecofeminism emphasizing the connection between environment and gender issues?
A. Sharmila Rege B. Vandana Shiva
C. Kamla Bhasin D. Kum Kum Sangari

40. What is the proposed name of new Criminal Procedure Code?
A. Bharatiya Nyaya Sanhita
B. Bharatiya Nagarik Nyaya Sanhita
C. Bharatiya Nagarik Suraksha Sanhita
D. Bharatiya Sakshya Adhiniyam

41. How can family influence gendered education?
(*a*) By promoting gender equality and challenging stereotypes
(*b*) By enforcing traditional gender role and expectations
(*c*) By excluding discussion about gender from family conversations
(*d*) By encouraging children to choose careers without considering gender norms.

Choose the correct answer from the options given below:
A. (*b*) and (*c*) only
B. (*a*) and (*c*) only
C. (*a*) and (*d*) only
D. (*c*) and (*d*) only

42. What is the main aim of interdisciplinary research?
(*a*) To over simplify the problem of research
(*b*) To bring out the holistic approach to research
(*c*) To create new trend in research methodology.
(*d*) To reduce the emphasis on a single subject in the research domain.

Choose the correct answer from the options given below:

A. (*a*) and (*b*) only B. (*a*) and (*c*) only
C. (*b*) and (*c*) only D. (*c*) and (*d*) only

43. Which of the following structural variable determine women's work in India:

(*a*) Regional Difference
(*b*) Labour Market
(*c*) The family, caste, class
(*d*) Food Preferences

Choose the correct answer from the options given below:

A. (*a*), (*b*) and (*c*) only
B. (*a*), (*b*) and (*d*) only
C. (*a*), (*d*) and (*c*) only
D. (*b*), (*c*) and (*d*) only

44. What is the primary focus of maternal health policies and programs?

(*a*) Providing childcare allowances
(*b*) Increasing equity and reducing poverty
(*c*) Ensuring safe pregnancy child birth and postnatal care for women
(*d*) Providing mandatory day care centres.

Choose the correct answer from the options given below:

A. (*a*) and (*b*) only
B. (*b*) and (*d*) only
C. (*b*) and (*c*) only
D. (*c*) and (*d*) only

45. What does women's empowerment primarily involve?

(*a*) Increasing women's involvement in decision making processes
(*b*) Enhancing women's ability to access education, income and resources
(*c*) Actions to transform the structures and institutions that reinforce and perpetuate gender discrimination and inequality
(*d*) Exclusively focusing on women's physical strength

Choose the correct answer from the options given below:

A. (*a*), (*c*) and (*d*) only
B. (*a*), (*b*) and (*c*) only
C. (*b*), (*c*) and (*d*) only
D. (*a*), (*b*) and (*d*) only

46. Which of the following are the characteristics of case study Method?

(*a*) It is done in a Laboratory
(*b*) It is Particularistic
(*c*) It is Descriptive
(*d*) It is Inductive

Choose the correct answer from the options given below:

A. (*a*), (*b*) and (*c*) only
B. (*b*), (*c*) and (*d*) only
C. (*c*), (*d*) and (*a*) only
D. (*b*), (*d*) and (*a*) only

47. The major objectives of the menstrual hygiene schemes are:

(*a*) To increase awareness among adolescent girls menstrual hygiene
(*b*) To increase access to and use of high-quality sanitary napkins to adolescent girls in rural area
(*c*) To ensure safe disposal of sanitary napkins in an environmental friendly manner
(*d*) To provide menstrual leave

Choose the correct answer from the options given below:

A. (*a*), (*b*) and (*c*) only
B. (*b*), (*c*) and (*d*) only
C. (*c*), (*d*) and (*a*) only
D. (*a*), (*d*) and (*b*) only

48. Which of the following statement about "Mukhya Mantri Suposhan Abhiyan" of Chhattisgarh state is/are correct?

(*a*) Eradication of Malnutrition
(*b*) It is for persons between 15-49 years age group
(*c*) It is for girls and women aged between 15-49 years
(*d*) Women and child welfare department will implement this Abhiyan

Choose the correct answer from the options given below:

A. (*a*), (*b*) and (*c*) only
B. (*a*), (*b*) and (*d*) only
C. (*a*), (*c*) and (*d*) only
D. (*b*), (*c*) and (*d*) only

49. Who were the women University Grants Commission Chairpersons?

(*a*) Dr. Madhuri R. Shah
(*b*) Dr. Hansa Mehta
(*c*) Dr. Armaity Desai
(*d*) Dr. Indarjeet Kaur

Choose the correct answer from the options given below:

A. (*a*) and (*b*) only B. (*a*) and (*c*) only
C. (*b*) and (*c*) only D. (*c*) and (*d*) only

50. Which of the following tribal society do not allow women to inherit ancestral or immoveable property owing to their customary law?

(*a*) Liangmai (*b*) Mizo
(*c*) Rengma (*d*) Monpa

A. (*a*) and (*b*) only B. (*a*) and (*c*) only
C. (*b*) and (*c*) only D. (*c*) and (*d*) only

51. Which of the following feminist organised the first women's convention in Seneca Falls, New York in 1848?

(*a*) Elisabeth Cady Stanton
(*b*) Lucretia Mott
(*c*) Susan B. Anthony
(*d*) Abby Kelley Foster

Choose the correct answer from the options given below:

A. (*a*) and (*b*) only B. (*a*) and (*c*) only
C. (*b*) and (*c*) only D. (*c*) and (*d*) only

52. In which period the feminisation of international migration a key aspect of migration has given rise to new debates on migration, gender and globalisation?

(*a*) Early 1980's (*b*) Late 1970's
(*c*) Early 1990's (*d*) Late 1990's

Choose the correct answer from the options given below:

A. (*a*) and (*b*) only B. (*b*) and (*c*) only
C. (*c*) and (*d*) only D. (*b*) and (*d*) only

53. What are the most important parts of research proposal?

(*a*) Hypothesis (*b*) Methodology
(*c*) Publication (*d*) Objectives of the study

Choose the correct answer from the options given below:

A. (*a*), (*b*) and (*c*) only
B. (*a*), (*b*) and (*d*) only
C. (*a*), (*c*) and (*d*) only
D. (*b*), (*c*) and (*d*) only

54. What are the three age based certification feature of the cinematography (Amendment Bill) which was introduced in the Rajya Sabha on July 20, 2023?

(*a*) Seven years (UA 7+)
(*b*) Thirteen years (UA 13+)
(*c*) Sixteen years (UA 16+)
(*d*) Twelve years (UA 12+)

Choose the correct answer from the options given below:

A. (*a*), (*b*) and (*c*) only
B. (*a*), (*b*) and (*d*) only
C. (*a*), (*c*) and (*d*) only
D. (*b*), (*c*) and (*d*) only

55. The role of the National Commission for Women (NCW) is to:

(*a*) It has no actual legislative powers
(*b*) It can recommend remedial legislative actions
(*c*) It does not have the power to choose its own members
(*d*) It has the power to choose its own members

Choose the correct answer from the options given below:

A. (*a*) and (*b*) only
B. (*a*) and (*c*) only
C. (*a*) and (*d*) only
D. (*c*) and (*d*) only

56. The requirement of the Bechdel test are that:

(*a*) A film must have at least two female characters
(*b*) Female characters have an on screen conversation with each other
(*c*) The female characters talk about something other than a man
(*d*) A film must have a heroic male character

Choose the correct answer from the options given below:

A. (*a*), (*b*) and (*c*) only
B. (*a*), (*c*) and (*d*) only
C. (*b*), (*c*) and (*d*) only
D. (*a*), (*b*) and (*d*) only

57. Which of the following facts of 'Feminisation of poverty' is true?

(*a*) A term coined by Martha Nussabaum
(*b*) Disproportionate socio-economic precarity women face relative to men due to gender stereotypes and norms
(*c*) Absence of economic opportunities and autonomy
(*d*) Lack of access to education and support services

Choose the correct answer from the options given below:

A. (*a*), (*b*) and (*c*) only
B. (*b*), (*c*) and (*d*) only
C. (*a*), (*c*) and (*d*) only
D. (*a*), (*b*) and (*d*) only

58. Which of the following are government of India schemes for women entrepreneurs?

(*a*) Annapurna Scheme
(*b*) Sukanya Samriddhi Yojana
(*c*) Mudra Yojana Scheme
(*d*) Dena Shakti Scheme

Choose the correct answer from the options gi[ven] below:

A. (*a*), (*b*) and (*c*) only
B. (*b*), (*c*) and (*d*) only
C. (*a*), (*c*) and (*d*) only
D. (*a*), (*b*) and (*d*) only

59. Sexual Harassment includes the following unwelcome acts or behaviour.
(*a*) Physical contact and advances
(*b*) Making Sexually coloured remarks
(*c*) Showing Pornography
(*d*) Making curt comments

Choose the correct answer from the options given below:
A. (*a*), (*b*) and (*c*) only
B. (*b*), (*c*) and (*d*) only
C. (*a*), (*c*) and (*d*) only
D. (*a*), (*b*) and (*d*) only

60. How can we increase the number of female entrepreneurs?
(*a*) Access to Finance
(*b*) Access to Network
(*c*) Providing a high interest loan
(*d*) Publicity of women role models

Choose the correct answer from the options given below:
A. (*a*), (*b*) and (*c*) only
B. (*b*), (*c*) and (*d*) only
C. (*a*), (*c*) and (*d*) only
D. (*a*), (*b*) and (*d*) only

61. Which of the following statement is true about interview technique in feminist research?
(*a*) Respondents are passive vessel of answers
(*b*) Interviews involve co-construction of experiential reality
(*c*) Interviews break hierarchical relationship between research and researched
(*d*) Interviews are always objective

Choose the correct answer from the options given below:
A. (*a*) and (*b*) only B. (*b*) and (*c*) only
C. (*a*) and (*d*) only D. (*c*) and (*d*) only

62. Focus of the primary group in Beti Bachao Beti Padhao Scheme is on:
(*a*) Young married couples
(*b*) Pregnant mothers
(*c*) Parents
(*d*) Panchayat members

Choose the correct answer from the options given below:
A. (*a*), (*b*) and (*c*) only
B. (*a*), (*b*) and (*d*) only
C. (*b*), (*c*) and (*d*) only
D. (*c*), (*d*) and (*a*) only

63. Identify the critics who had dealt with reproduction and motherhood:
(*a*) Carol Gilligan (*b*) Kate Millet
(*c*) Gayatri C. Spivak (*d*) Nancy Chodorow

Choose the correct answer from the options given below:
A. (*a*) and (*b*) only B. (*a*) and (*c*) only
C. (*b*) and (*d*) only D. (*a*) and (*d*) only

64. The Mako Mori test is:
(*a*) A set of criteria pertaining to the representation of female characters
(*b*) Inspired by the character from 2013 film 'Pacific Rim'
(*c*) Tests masculinity in men
(*d*) Inspired by the comic strip 'Dykes to Watch Out For'

Choose the correct answer from the options given below:
A. (*a*) and (*b*) only B. (*a*) and (*c*) only
C. (*a*) and (*d*) only D. (*c*) and (*d*) only

65. Which of the following states have literacy rate over 90% as per 2011 census?
(*a*) Kerala (*b*) Tamil Nadu
(*c*) Goa (*d*) Mizoram

Choose the correct answer from the options given below:
A. (*a*) and (*b*) only B. (*b*) and (*c*) only
C. (*a*) and (*d*) only D. (*a*) and (*c*) only

66. Match the following:

List-I (Paradigm)	**List-II (Advocate)**
(*a*) Positivist	I. Simone de Beauvoir
(*b*) Interpretive	II. Theodore Adorno
(*c*) Critical	III. Max Weber
(*d*) Feminist	IV. Auguste Comte

Choose the correct answer from the options:

	(*a*)	(*b*)	(*c*)	(*d*)
A.	I	II	IV	III
B.	II	III	IV	I
C.	III	IV	I	II
D.	IV	III	II	I

67. Match the following:

List-I (Women Leaders)	**List-II (Positions Held)**
(*a*) Sanna Marin	I. First female President of Taiwan
(*b*) Loreta Lynch	II. Founder U.S. Attorney General
(*c*) Nancy Pelosi	III. Speaker of the U.S. House of representative
(*d*) Tsai Ing-wen	IV. Prime Minister of Finland

Choose the correct answer from the options:

	(a)	(b)	(c)	(d)
A.	I	II	IV	III
B.	II	III	IV	I
C.	IV	I	III	II
D.	IV	II	III	I

68. Match the following:

List-I (Strands of Feminism)	List-II (Noted feminist)
(a) Liberal feminism	I. Shulamith Firestone
(b) Radical feminism	II. J.S. Mill
(c) Post-colonial feminism	III. Maria Mies
(d) Eco feminism	IV. Gayatri Spivak

Choose the correct answer from the options:

	(a)	(b)	(c)	(d)
A.	I	III	IV	II
B.	II	I	IV	III
C.	III	I	II	IV
D.	II	IV	III	I

69. Match the following:

List-I (Authors)	List-II (Books)
(a) Naila Kabeer	I. *Gender and Politics in India*
(b) Gail Omvedt	II. *Social Reform, Sexuality and the State*
(c) Nivedita Menon	III. *Reversed Realities: Gender Hierarchies in Development Thought*
(d) Patricia Uberoi	IV. *Violence Against Women: New Movements and New Theories in India*

Choose the correct answer from the options:

	(a)	(b)	(c)	(d)
A.	III	IV	I	II
B.	I	IV	III	II
C.	II	III	I	IV
D.	IV	I	II	III

70. Match the following:

List-I (Terms)	List-II (Explanation)
(a) Meher	I. Waiting period after divorce
(b) Iddat	II. If two persons have a common lineal ascendant
(c) Sapindas	III. Any present or jewellery given to a woman during marriage
(d) Streedhan	IV. Property given to wife in consideration for marriage

Choose the correct answer from the options:

	(a)	(b)	(c)	(d)
A.	I	IV	III	II
B.	II	III	IV	I
C.	III	II	I	IV
D.	IV	I	II	III

71. Match the following:

List-I (Authors)	List-II (Books)
(a) Maria Mies	I. Exploring Masculinity
(b) Vandana Shiva	II. Women, the lost colony
(c) Gail Omvedt	III. Earth Democracy
(d) Kamla Bhasin	IV. Dalit Visions

Choose the correct answer from the options:

	(a)	(b)	(c)	(d)
A.	I	II	IV	III
B.	II	III	IV	I
C.	III	IV	II	I
D.	IV	I	III	II

72. Match the following:

List-I (Women Entrepreneurs)	List-II (Enterprise)
(a) Falguni Nayar	I. Chairperson, Biocon
(b) Kiran Mazumdar Shaw	II. CEO, HCL
(c) Roshni Nadar	III. Founder CEO, Nyka
(d) Aditi Gupta	IV. Co-founder, Menstrupedia

Choose the correct answer from the options:

	(a)	(b)	(c)	(d)
A.	II	III	IV	I
B.	III	I	II	IV
C.	I	II	III	IV
D.	II	IV	III	I

73. Match the following:

List-I (Sport Person)	List-II (Discipline)
(a) Dipa Karmakar	I. Weightlifting
(b) Mirabai Chanu	II. Gymnastic
(c) Deepika Kumari	III. Cricket
(d) Jhulan Goswami	IV. Archery

Choose the correct answer from the options:

	(a)	(b)	(c)	(d)
A.	I	III	II	IV
B.	II	IV	III	I
C.	IV	I	III	II
D.	II	I	IV	III

74. Match the following:

List-I (People)	List-II (Work)
(*a*) Anglina Jolie	I. An Acid attack survivor who became the face of protest against acid attack
(*b*) Laxmi Agarwal	II. In her ethnographic work "why loiter" she shows the act of loitering is more prevalent among men
(*c*) Shilpa Phadke	III. Launched the "Heforshe" movement
(*d*) Emma Watson	IV. Played a big role in raising awareness about breast cancer through her personal story

Choose the correct answer from the options:

	(*a*)	(*b*)	(*c*)	(*d*)
A.	IV	I	II	III
B.	I	II	III	IV
C.	II	III	IV	I
D.	III	IV	I	II

75. Match the following:

List-I (Work)	List-II (People)
(*a*) Sapph for Equality	I. First gay anthology edited by Hoshang Merchant
(*b*) Queer Ink	II. An exclusive publishing and marketing agency on LGBT Literature
(*c*) Yarana	III. India's first gay magazine launched by Ashok Rao Kavi
(*d*) Bombay Dost	IV. An organisation based in Klkata working for the rights of lesbians, bisexual women and transmen in Eastern India.

Choose the correct answer from the options:

	(*a*)	(*b*)	(*c*)	(*d*)
A.	II	I	III	IV
B.	III	II	IV	I
C.	I	III	II	IV
D.	IV	II	I	III

76. Chronologically arrange the following women specific legislations.

(*a*) Commission of Sati (Prevention) Act
(*b*) Immoral Traffic (Prevention) Act
(*c*) Protection of women from Domestic Violence Act
(*d*) The Dowry Prohibition Act

Choose the correct answer from the options.

A. (*c*), (*d*), (*a*), (*b*) B. (*b*), (*d*), (*a*), (*c*)
C. (*a*), (*c*), (*d*), (*b*) D. (*a*), (*b*), (*c*), (*d*)

77. Arrange following development approaches in sequence:

(*a*) Gender and Development (GAD)
(*b*) Women, Environment and Development (WED)
(*c*) Women and Development (WAD)
(*d*) Women in Development (WID)

Choose the correct answer from the options.

A. (*d*), (*a*), (*b*), (*c*) B. (*b*), (*c*), (*d*), (*a*)
C. (*d*), (*c*), (*a*), (*b*) D. (*a*), (*b*), (*c*), (*d*)

78. Arrange the following in sequence:

(*a*) National Population Policy
(*b*) Towards Equality Report
(*c*) National Empowerment Policy for Women
(*d*) Shramshakti Report of the National Commission on self Employed Women and Women in Informal Sector.

Choose the correct answer from the options.

A. (*a*), (*b*), (*c*), (*d*) B. (*b*), (*c*), (*d*), (*a*)
C. (*d*), (*a*), (*b*), (*c*) D. (*b*), (*d*), (*a*), (*c*)

79. Arrange the following in sequence:

(*a*) Stop Acid Sale
(*b*) Shahada Movement
(*c*) National Federation of Indian Women
(*d*) Non Cooperation Movement

Choose the correct answer from the options.

A. (*a*), (*b*), (*c*), (*d*) B. (*c*), (*b*), (*a*), (*d*)
C. (*d*), (*a*), (*b*), (*c*) D. (*d*), (*c*), (*b*), (*a*)

80. Arrange the following schemes in sequence:

(*a*) Swadhar Greh
(*b*) Mahila E-Haat
(*c*) Mahila Shakti Kendra
(*d*) One-Stop Center

Choose the correct answer from the options.

A. (*a*), (*b*), (*c*), (*d*) B. (*b*), (*c*), (*d*), (*a*)
C. (*c*), (*d*), (*a*), (*b*) D. (*a*), (*d*), (*b*), (*c*)

81. Chronologically arrange the methodology used for preparing All India Survey on Higher Education (AISHE) Report.

(*a*) Registration of Higher Education Institution (HEI)
(*b*) Identification of HEI
(*c*) Compilation and analysis of data
(*d*) Collection and verification of data

Choose the correct answer from the options.

A. (*a*), (*b*), (*d*), (*c*) B. (*a*), (*c*), (*b*), (*d*)
C. (*a*), (*c*), (*d*), (*b*) D. (*b*), (*a*), (*d*), (*c*)

82. Arrange the following in chronological order:
(*a*) Saudi Arabia lifts ban on female drivers
(*b*) The protection of Women from domestic violence Act
(*c*) Roe vs Wade handed the difficult decision of whether to end a pregnancy
(*d*) The United Nations Passes a resolution banning female genital mutilation

Choose the correct answer from the options.
A. (*a*), (*b*), (*c*), (*d*) B. (*b*), (*d*), (*c*), (*a*)
C. (*c*), (*b*), (*d*), (*a*) D. (*d*), (*a*), (*b*), (*c*)

83. What is the chronological sequence of the establishment of the following institutions working for women and children in India?
(*a*) Ministry of Women and Child Development
(*b*) National Commission for Women
(*c*) Department of Women and Child Development
(*d*) National Commission for Protection of Child Rights

Choose the correct answer from the options.
A. (*a*), (*d*), (*b*), (*c*) B. (*b*), (*a*), (*d*), (*c*)
C. (*c*), (*b*), (*a*), (*d*) D. (*d*), (*c*), (*b*), (*a*)

84. Arrange chronologically the following legislations of India as per the year of their enactment:
(*a*) The Family Courts Act
(*b*) Medical Termination of Pregnancy
(*c*) The Indecent Representation of Women (Prohibition) Act
(*d*) The Maternity Benefit Act

Choose the correct answer from the options.
A. (*a*), (*b*), (*c*), (*d*) B. (*b*), (*c*), (*d*), (*a*)
C. (*c*), (*d*), (*a*), (*b*) D. (*d*), (*b*), (*a*), (*c*)

85. Arrange the following statements chronologically:
(*a*) Gender is a performative Act
(*b*) Shadow Pandemic
(*c*) One is not born a Women but becomes one
(*d*) The Problem with no name

Choose the correct answer from the options.
A. (*a*), (*b*), (*c*), (*d*)
B. (*b*), (*c*), (*d*), (*a*)
C. (*d*), (*c*), (*a*), (*b*)
D. (*b*), (*d*), (*c*), (*a*)

86. Given below are two statements, one is labelled as Assertion (A) and other one labelled as Reason (R).

Assertion (A): Despite higher educational attainment of women FLFRP (Female labour force participation rate) is showing a declining trend in India.

Reason (R): Educated Women are unwilling to work.

In light of the above statement choose the correct answer from the options given below:
A. Both (A) and (R) are correct and (R) is the correct explanation of (A)
B. Both (A) and (R) are correct, but (R) is NOT the correct explanation of (A)
C. (A) is correct, but (R) is not correct
D. (A) is not correct, but (R) is correct

87. Given below are two statements, one is labelled as Assertion (A) and other one labelled as Reason (R).

Assertion (A): The emerging technologies while improving our lives in many ways have created the 'Digital Divide'.

Reason (R): Most women are engaged in the domestic and informal sector work environment.

In light of the above statement choose the correct answer from the options given below:
A. Both (A) and (R) are correct and (R) is the correct explanation of (A)
B. Both (A) and (R) are correct, but (R) is NOT the correct explanation of (A)
C. (A) is correct, but (R) is not correct
D. (A) is not correct, but (R) is correct

88. Given below are two statements, one is labelled as Assertion (A) and other one labelled as Reason (R).

Assertion (A): The Shakti scheme has been offering women free travel in non-premium services of the state-run Road Transport Corporation (RTC).

Reason (R): There are numerous schemes, programmes and incentives being presented by the government of India in order to promote women's empowerment.

In light of the above statement choose the correct answer from the options given below:
A. Both (A) and (R) are correct and (R) is the correct explanation of (A)
B. Both (A) and (R) are correct, but (R) is NOT the correct explanation of (A)
C. (A) is correct, but (R) is not correct
D. (A) is not correct, but (R) is correct

89. Given below are two statements, one is labelled as Assertion (A) and other one labelled as Reason (R).

Assertion (A): A gender studies teacher sensitises students on gender discrimiation.

Reason (R): A gender studies teacher uses a unilateral perspective to teach gender issues in the classroom.

In light of the above statement choose the correct answer from the options given below:

A. Both (A) and (R) are correct and (R) is the correct explanation of (A)

B. Both (A) and (R) are correct, but (R) is NOT the correct explanation of (A)

C. (A) is correct, but (R) is not correct

D. (A) is not correct, but (R) is correct

90. Given below are two statements, one is labelled as Assertion (A) and other one labelled as Reason (R).

Assertion (A): Women's reservation bill will ensure that women form a strong lobby in parliament to fight for issues that are often ignored.

Reason (R): Women's reservation bill will facilitate the entry of upper class urban educated women in the parliament.

In light of the above statement choose the correct answer from the options given below:

A. Both (A) and (R) are correct and (R) is the correct explanation of (A)

B. Both (A) and (R) are correct, but (R) is NOT the correct explanation of (A)

C. (A) is correct, but (R) is not correct

D. (A) is not correct, but (R) is correct

Directions (Qs. No. 91-95): *Read the following passage and answer the questions.*

Building Pedagogical Curb Cuts challenges us to alter the fixed concrete sidewalks of our life and practices, arguing that there are imaginative ways to include disability in our classroom and in our lives, to the benefit of all. Linda Brinskin mentions four major influences on pedagogical exclusion (1) non-flexible requirements set up by programs (2) the restrictive traditional methods of teaching (3) exclusionary theoretical perspectives and (4) exclusionary instructional materials. Women studies scholarship informs us that the traditional style of teaching did not include, and often excluded, women's learning patterns. By leaving out the daily experiences of women as housewives, mothers, etc., pedagogy often excluded women as learners and teachers. For example women's studies and political science courses often make mention of women's suffrage in America, yet rarely include the fact that Helen Keller marched next to non-disabled women in many liberation marches. These factors can emerge only if gender analysis and teaching methods are implemented from alternative viewpoints. Also, restrictive academic environments require intensive study for specific examinations given on set dates with no regard for the circumstances in the lives of learners, women who were unable to study because they were caring for sick children at home. This is equally true of students with disabilities who come into school systems that have no adaptation.

91. What is the learning point from the Helen Keller Story as mentioned in the passage?

A. Failure of women's studies and women's movement to include issues and challenges faced by women with disability

B. Liberation movements very openly acknowledges contribution of women with disability

C. Alternative viewpoints are welcomed in academic environment

D. Society is very considerate on special need of the learners

92. Imagine a picture of an inclusive and just society. What does an education system look like in this picture?

A. Non-flexible requirements set up by programs.

B. Exclusionary theoretical perspectives

C. Teaching methods are implemented from alternative viewpoints

D. Exclusionary instructional materials

93. Which of the following statement is correct?

Statement I: Inclusive education benefits not only students with disabilities but also students without disabilities.

Statement II: Inclusive classrooms teach all students about the importance of diversity and acceptance.

Choose the correct answer from the optins given below:

A. Both Statement I and Statement II are true

B. Both Statement I and Statement II are false

C. Statement I is true, but Statement II is false

D. Statement I is false, but Statement II is true

94. What are some disabling environments for women with disability?

(*a*) Inaccessible Transport

(*b*) Building Without Universal Structure

(c) Inclusion of Women and Persons with disability

(*d*) Stereotyping

Choose the correct answer from the options given below:

A. (*a*), (*b*) and (*c*) only

B. (*b*), (*c*) and (*d*) only

C. (*a*), (*b*) and (*d*) only

D. (*a*), (*c*) and (*d*) only

95. Given below are two statements, one is labelled as Assertion (A) and other one labelled as Reason (R).

Assertion (A): Women with disabilities have been described as being doubly marginalized on account of their disability and their gender.

Reason (R): In an enabling environment women with disability have greater accessibility over their male counterpart.

In light of the above statement choose the correct answer from the options given below:

A. Both (A) and (R) are correct and (R) is the correct explanation of (A)
B. Both (A) and (R) are correct, but (R) is NOT the correct explanation of (A)
C. (A) is correct, but (R) is not correct
D. (A) is not correct, but (R) is correct

Directions (Qs. No. 96-100): *Read the following passage and answer the questions.*

Previous approaches to documenting and understanding international migration have often disregraded the migration of women. Most migrant women move voluntarily, but women and girls are also forced migrants leaving their countries in order to flee conflict, persecution, environmental degradation, natural disasters or other situations that affect their security, livelihood or habitat. In many instances, women left behind in their country of origin undertake income-generating activities to compensate for the income lost by the departure of their male relatives if the latter do not send remittances on a regular basis. Adding financial responsibilities to the other responsibilities that women have such as child-rearing can lead to stress but can also provide women with the opportunity of gaining autonomy and experience in decision making.

Migrant women workers in the receiving countries are often seen as aliens as inferiors culturally and socially as a potential threat to stability. Migrants are perceived as taking away jobs from the native population despite the fact that migrant worker, especially women, usually perform the jobs that the native population shun. Women migrant workers face major challenges in benefiting from trade unions and NGO activity as they are often not allowed to join or form union in destination countries.

96. How does migration affect the women who remain in the country of their origin?

(*a*) They find themselves co-residing with other male relatives who often restrict their activities outside the home.

(*b*) They often have more independence and autonomy.

(*c*) They do not take any additional responsibilities.

(*d*) They are generally not involved in any income generating activities.

Choose the correct answer from the options given below:

A. (*a*), (*b*) only
B. (*a*), (*c*) only
C. (*a*), (*d*) only
D. (*b*), (*c*) only

97. Given below are two statements.

Statement I: Gender relations and gender hierarchies in both sending and receiving countries determine the gender specific impact of migration.

Statement II: Women migrant workers benefits from trade unions and NGO, activities as they are often allowed to join or form unions in destination countries.

In light of the above statements, choose the most appropriate answer from the options given below:

A. Both Statement I and Statement II are true
B. Both Statement I and Statement II are false
C. Statement I is true, but Statement II is false
D. Statement I is false, but Statement II is true

98. Given below are two statements, one is labelled as Assertion (A) and other one labelled as Reason (R).

Assertion (A): Women remaining behind when their male relatives migrate may find themselves co-residing with other male relatives who may restrict the activities outside the home.

Reason (R): When their male relatives (Husband, parents) leave them behind, women have the opportunity of gaining autonomy and experience in decision making.

In light of the above statement choose the correct answer from the options given below:

A. Both (A) and (R) are correct and (R) is the correct explanation of (A)
B. Both (A) and (R) are correct, but (R) is NOT the correct explanation of (A)
C. (A) is correct, but (R) is not correct
D. (A) is not correct, but (R) is correct

99. Given below are two statements.

Statement I: Historically in documenting and understanding international migration women have always been a chief concern.

Statement II: Migration effects only the migrates themselves but not their family members if they remain in the country of origin.

In light of the above statements, choose the most appropriate answer from the options given below:

A. Both Statement I and Statement II are true
B. Both Statement I and Statement II are false
C. Statement I is true, but Statement II is false
D. Statement I is false, but Statement II is true

100. Migrants workers are often perceived as:

A. Taking away jobs from the native population
B. Culturally and Socially superior
C. People with immense resource
D. People coming from high countries

ANSWERS

1. **(A):** Michel Foucault, a French philosopher and social theorist, introduced the concept of power as something that permeates society at every level, much like the flow of blood through capillaries in the human body. This analogy captures Foucault's idea that power is not only concentrated in government or large institutions but is distributed throughout society in everyday interactions and social norms. He argued that power affects knowledge and vice versa, influencing how individuals perceive and interact with the world. His theories have significantly impacted various fields, including sociology, cultural studies, and political science, by highlighting how power dynamics shape human behaviour and societal structures.

2. **(A):** Women's Studies as an academic field aims to uncover and challenge the myriad ways in which gender influences and structures our society. It involves critically examining both subtle and overt cultural practices that perpetuate gender inequalities. This interdisciplinary field not only addresses issues related to women but also studies the complexities of gender and its intersections with race, class, sexuality, and other social categories. The purpose of this study is to foster a deeper understanding of these dynamics, promote social justice, and contribute to more equitable societal norms. By doing so, Women's Studies equips students with the analytical tools needed to recognize and address gender-related issues in various societal contexts.

3. **(B):** Gender analysis is a critical tool used in policy-making and project management to ensure that the distinct needs and experiences of women and men are considered and addressed appropriately. It involves examining the differences in conditions, needs, participation rates, access to resources, development opportunities, and control over assets between women and men in their existing social and economic contexts. The goal is to achieve gender equity through informed policy decisions that accommodate these differences effectively. Such analysis helps prevent one-size-fits-all approaches that might overlook specific needs or reinforce existing inequalities, thereby promoting more effective and equitable outcomes in policy and program implementation.

4. **(A):** The Sanitease scheme under India's Ministry of Youth Affairs and Sports aims to improve hygiene and health among young women, especially in educational settings. This initiative focuses on creating awareness about menstrual health and providing sanitary napkins to women and girls in rural and urban schools. By ensuring access to basic sanitary products, the scheme addresses a critical barrier to education for many girls who miss school during their menstrual periods due to lack of proper sanitary provisions. This program is part of a broader effort under the 'Swachhagraha' social development activity, which promotes cleanliness and health awareness across different facets of society.

5. **(C):** Under the Janani Suraksha Yojana (JSY), an initiative aimed at reducing maternal and neonatal mortality rates in India, pregnant women from economically disadvantaged backgrounds, specifically those belonging to Scheduled Castes, Scheduled Tribes, and Below Poverty Line categories, receive a cash incentive of 700 rupees. This incentive is provided when they choose to deliver their babies in health institutions in rural areas. The program encourages institutional deliveries, which are safer for both the mother and the baby, thereby reducing the risks associated with childbirth. The cash incentive is designed to cover travel expenses, encourage hospital births over home deliveries, and reduce financial barriers to accessing healthcare services during childbirth.

6. **(C):** The CBSE Merit Scholarship Scheme specifically targets the 'Single Girl Child'. It is designed to support and encourage the education of single girl children in India, acknowledging the unique financial challenges they might face in pursuing further education. This scholarship aims to promote gender equality in education by providing financial assistance to single girl students who have excelled

in their studies at the secondary school level. The focus on single girl children is a strategic measure to empower this demographic, ensuring they can continue their education without financial strain, thus helping to break cycles of gender disparity in educational attainment.

7. **(B):** Maharashtra launched the Asmita Yojana in 2018 to address menstrual hygiene among young women and adolescent girls. This scheme involves local self-help groups procuring sanitary napkins from suppliers and distributing them to women and girls who hold Asmita cards at subsidized rates. The initiative aims to improve accessibility to quality sanitary products, reduce absenteeism in schools during menstruation, and promote menstrual health awareness. By involving self-help groups, the program also supports local economies and empowers women by involving them in the supply chain of these essential health products.

8. **(B):** Julia Kristeva, a prominent Bulgarian-French philosopher and psychoanalyst, critically addressed the traditional psychoanalytic theories which often collapse language into biology. Kristeva argued that upon entering the symbolic order—a concept in Lacanian psychoanalysis where language and societal laws come into play—both boys and girls have the potential to adopt a feminine mode of writing and expression. Her theory challenges the rigid gender binaries and emphasizes the fluidity of identity and expression, suggesting that gender is not merely a biological fate but a complex play of cultural, social, and psychological forces.

9. **(C):** The term 'Shadow Pandemic' emerged during the COVID-19 crisis to describe the global increase in domestic violence against women triggered by lockdowns and stress associated with the pandemic. This phenomenon is called a shadow pandemic because it parallels the primary health crisis but is less visible, often occurring within the privacy of homes. The term highlights how crises can exacerbate existing societal issues, such as violence against women, and stresses the need for greater attention and resources to address these surging hidden crises alongside the direct health impacts of the pandemic.

10. **(C):** Ann Scales coined the term 'Feminist Jurisprudence' which refers to the study and critique of laws from a feminist perspective. This field examines how legal systems uphold gender disparities and explores ways to reform these institutions to achieve gender justice. Feminist jurisprudence challenges traditional legal theories and practices that have historically marginalized or discriminated against women, advocating for legal interpretations and policies that consider and address the specific needs and rights of women. This approach to law seeks to redefine legal concepts and methods to ensure they support the equality and empowerment of all genders.

11. **(C):** Liberal Feminism holds the belief in the basic neutrality of the state, positing that the state itself does not inherently favour any one group over another. According to liberal feminists, the state is an instrument that can be used to rectify legal inequalities if properly leveraged. This school of thought advocates for reforms within the existing structures of law and government to ensure equal rights for women. Liberal feminists focus on making changes through legislative reform and believe that the system can be adjusted to better serve the interests of all individuals, irrespective of gender, through rational reforms and equitable laws.

12. **(A):** Selma James is widely recognized for advocating the concept of wages for housework, an idea that emerged prominently in the 1970s. This movement highlighted the economic value of domestic work, which is typically unpaid and performed predominantly by women. By advocating for wages for housework, Selma James and her colleagues aimed to address the economic dependencies that arise from traditional gender roles in households. They argued that compensating women for domestic labour would lead to economic independence and challenge the gendered division of labour that devalues women's contributions at home.

13. **(D):** The environmental impact of sanitary pads is significant, as the plastics used in many sanitary pads can remain in the environment for over 500 years. These materials are not biodegradable and contribute to long-term pollution. The persistence of such waste in landfills and ecosystems poses a severe environmental challenge. This issue underscores the importance of sustainable practices and the development of eco-friendly alternatives in menstrual hygiene products, which can significantly reduce the ecological footprint of these essential items.

14. **(A):** Gloria Steinem, a prominent feminist and journalist, wrote the satirical essay "If Men Could Menstruate." In this piece, Steinem imagines a world where men, instead of women, menstruate. She argues humorously that if men experienced menstruation, it would become a symbol of envy and pride rather than a source of shame and stigma.

This essay highlights the arbitrary nature of societal attitudes towards gender and bodily functions, using irony to challenge the social constructs that deem women's natural biological processes as inferior.

15. (D): According to the 2022 global estimates released by the International Labour Organization (ILO), approximately 50 million people have been affected by human trafficking worldwide. This staggering number reflects the widespread issue of modern slavery, which encompasses forced labour, sexual exploitation, and other forms of coercion. The ILO's report sheds light on the pervasive and deep-rooted problem of human trafficking and underscores the urgent need for international cooperation and robust measures to combat this grave human rights violation effectively.

16. (A): According to the findings of the National Family Health Survey-5 (NFHS-5), the percentage of female sterilization in India stands at 37.9%, while male sterilization is remarkably lower at 0.3%. This stark disparity highlights the gendered nature of family planning practices in India, where sterilization remains the most common contraceptive method but is predominantly undergone by women. The low rate of male participation in sterilization reflects broader social and cultural attitudes towards reproductive responsibility and contraceptive practices, where the burden disproportionately falls on women.

17. (B): The National Education Policy (NEP) of 1986 played a pivotal role in giving impetus to Women's Studies in India. This policy emphasized the importance of education in empowering women and recognized the need to include women's perspectives in the curriculum, which led to the establishment and expansion of Women's Studies programs across various educational institutions in India. The NEP 1986 aimed to address gender disparities in education and promote studies that would help understand and challenge the social norms that perpetuate gender inequalities, thereby fostering a more inclusive and equitable educational environment.

18. (C): According to the National Family Health Survey-5, Karnataka has the highest reported rate of domestic violence among the states listed. This statistic is a critical indicator of the prevalence of domestic violence within the state and highlights the ongoing challenges in combating gender-based violence. The high incidence in Karnataka necessitates focused intervention programs and policies to protect women and promote their welfare, along with sustained efforts to raise awareness and change societal attitudes that perpetuate violence against women.

19. (D): Edwin and Shirley Ardener's Muted Group Theory primarily addresses the concept of "silence" among marginalized groups, particularly women. This theory suggests that the communication practices of a society are shaped by the dominant group, leading to the marginalization or muting of subordinate groups whose experiences and perspectives do not conform to the dominant discourse. Women, according to this theory, are often silenced in social narratives, which affects their ability to express themselves fully and participate equally in society. The theory calls attention to the need for societal structures that allow for the voices of all groups to be heard equally.

20. (D): Naila Kabeer defined empowerment in terms of three interrelated concepts: agency, resources, and achievements. Her framework suggests that empowerment involves the process through which individuals gain the ability to make choices (agency), access the means needed to exercise these choices (resources), and the ability to achieve desired outcomes (achievements). Kabeer's approach to empowerment is particularly influential in the fields of gender studies and development, providing a comprehensive model that assesses how different factors interact to either facilitate or hinder the empowerment of individuals, particularly women, in various socio-economic contexts.

21. (C): Feminist Jurisprudence is also referred to as Feminist Legal Theory. This field of study examines the ways in which law has been structured—often without acknowledgment—that may disadvantage women and other marginalized groups. Feminist legal theory explores the intersection of law and gender and critiques how legal systems perpetuate gender hierarchies. It seeks to understand the mechanisms through which laws reinforce gender biases and to propose ways to reform these legal frameworks to ensure equity and justice for all genders.

22. (C): Intersectionality is a critical concept in gender studies that recognizes how different aspects of social identity, such as race, class, gender, sexuality, and disability, intersect to shape individual experiences, especially in contexts of oppression and privilege. Developed by Kimberlé Crenshaw, this framework helps to understand the multifaceted and overlapping influences that affect people's lives and experiences. It is significant because it challenges simplistic analyses that consider social categories in isolation, advocating instead for a more nuanced understanding of how various forms of inequality interact.

23. (A): Judith Butler is renowned for introducing the concept of 'Performativity' in gender theory. This concept suggests that gender identity is not a fixed or inherent attribute but rather is constructed through repeated social behaviours and actions. According to Butler, gender is performed by the individual, through a series of acts which are socially enforced but can also be varied and disrupted. This idea has significantly influenced feminist theory and cultural studies by challenging the notion of innate gender identities and highlighting the fluid, dynamic nature of how gender is expressed and perceived.

24. (B): Friedrich Engels, in his seminal work "The Origin of the Family, Private Property, and the State," posited that the overthrow of matriarchy (which he described as "mother right") was a defining moment in the historical subjugation of the female sex. Engels argued that this shift to patriarchal societies resulted in the systemic disenfranchisement and oppression of women, linking it to broader socio-economic transformations that accompanied the rise of private property and class societies. His analysis suggests that gender inequality is deeply rooted in the earliest social structures of human civilization.

25. (C): The primary aim of the Women's Empowerment India (WEI) initiative is to capture various aspects of women's well-being and agency. This includes assessing their economic, social, and political empowerment, as well as their ability to make strategic life choices in a context where they can use and access resources effectively. WEI seeks to provide a comprehensive measure of women's empowerment that can inform policy and intervention strategies, aiming to improve the conditions and status of women in various sectors and communities throughout India.

26. (B): Chimamanda Ngozi Adichie is renowned for her influential TED Talk titled "We Should All Be Feminists," which has been a pivotal piece in contemporary feminist discourse. In this talk, Adichie discusses the importance of understanding and embracing feminism in the 21st century, advocating for the rights and equality of all genders. Her engaging narrative style and persuasive arguments have made this talk a defining moment in modern feminist advocacy, inspiring a book of the same name that further expands on the ideas presented.

27. (C): 'Cisgender' refers to individuals whose gender identity consistently aligns with the sex assigned to them at birth. This term is used to describe a person whose experience of their own gender matches the gender they were initially identified as when they were born. It is used to contrast with 'transgender,' a term that applies to individuals whose gender identity differs from the sex they were assigned at birth. Understanding this distinction is crucial in discussions about gender identity, rights, and inclusivity.

28. (B): In Hélène Cixous's essay "The Laugh of the Medusa," she introduces the concept of 'Écriture Féminine' (feminine writing). This term embodies a form of writing that is expressive of women's experiences and inner realities, aiming to challenge the male-dominated literary canon. Cixous argues that women should write about themselves and bring their unique perspectives into literature as a form of empowerment and to disrupt the traditionally male-centric narrative structures.

29. (B): 'Heteronormativity' refers to the societal assumption that heterosexuality is the default or normal sexual orientation. This concept implies that other sexual orientations are deviant or abnormal. Heteronormativity can affect various aspects of life, including social policies, media representation, and individual interactions, by marginalizing non-heterosexual relationships and identities. Understanding heteronormativity is essential in gender studies to challenge these norms and promote a more inclusive understanding of various sexual orientations.

30. (A): Kanupriya Agarwal is recognized as the first IVF (in vitro fertilization) baby girl in India. She was born through the pioneering efforts of Dr. Subhash Mukhopadhyay in 1978, marking a significant milestone in the field of reproductive technologies in India. Dr. Mukhopadhyay's work in developing IVF technology was groundbreaking, although it initially faced significant challenges and controversies within the medical community and broader society in India.

31. (A): The Global Media Monitoring Project (GMMP) conducts its studies every five years since its inception in 1995. This project is the largest and longest-running research initiative in the world that systematically studies the representation and portrayal of genders in news media. It provides critical data on how gender roles are depicted in the media and tracks progress or setbacks in gender representation across different countries and media platforms. The periodic reviews allow researchers and advocates to measure changes over time and assess the impact of efforts to promote gender equality in media content.

32. (C): Alice Walker defined the term "womanist" with the metaphor "womanist is to feminist as purple is to lavender." This definition reflects a deeper, richer, and more inclusive approach to feminism that Walker advocated, particularly emphasizing the experiences and challenges of Black women and other women of colour. Her concept of womanism expands on traditional feminism by including racial and class issues, aiming to address the unique struggles faced by these groups, and promoting a broader, more inclusive feminist ethos.

33. (C): Gender Budgeting involves analyzing and planning government budgets to ensure they positively impact gender equality. This approach assesses how budget allocations affect women and men differently and aims to address gender disparities through targeted fiscal policies. Gender budgeting helps in ensuring that public resources are effectively utilized to promote gender equality, enhance women's empowerment, and improve the economic and social outcomes for all genders. It involves a critical evaluation of both revenues and expenditures to align them with the goals of gender justice.

34. (B): Rokeya Sakhawat Hossain is the author of the short story "Sultana's Dream: A Feminist Utopia." This pioneering work, published in 1905, presents a reverse-gender-role society where women rule and men are secluded, inverting the traditional norms of her contemporary society. The narrative is considered ahead of its time, advocating for women's education and participation in public life, while critiquely highlighting the absurdities of gender discrimination. Hossain's work remains a significant early piece of South Asian feminist literature.

35. (A): "The Culture Industry" is a chapter from the book "The Dialectic of Enlightenment," authored by Theodor Adorno and Max Horkheimer. This influential work critiques the role of mass culture and the entertainment industry in perpetuating social domination and conformism. Adorno and Horkheimer analyze how popular culture, as part of the culture industry, manipulates and stifles individuality and creativity, serving the interests of capitalist society by producing standardized cultural goods that pacify and distract the masses.

36. (C): Mohammad Yunus is widely credited with pioneering the concept of microfinance and women's Self-Help Groups (SHGs) through his work in founding the Grameen Bank in Bangladesh. Although SHGs existed in various forms, Yunus' initiatives focused on empowering women economically by providing them with small loans. These groups enable women to engage in income-generating activities, thereby promoting financial independence and socio-economic development among communities traditionally excluded from formal banking systems.

37. (D): Chandra Talpade Mohanty is known for her critical analysis of the "colonization" in academic and global feminism, which she discusses as the appropriation and codification of knowledge. Her work critiques Western feminist scholarship's tendency to generalize and misrepresent the experiences of women in non-Western societies. Mohanty argues that such approaches can lead to a form of intellectual colonization, where Western paradigms dominate and overshadow local, indigenous knowledges and practices, effectively marginalizing them in global feminist discourses.

38. (A): Sarladevi Chaudhurani moved a resolution supporting voting rights for women at the Indian National Congress session held in Delhi in 1918. Her advocacy was part of the broader struggle for women's rights in India during the freedom movement. Chaudhurani was a prominent figure in the social and political spheres, actively working to promote women's participation in the nationalistic activities of the time and championing the cause for their voting rights in the newly envisaged democratic structures.

39. (B): Vandana Shiva is a prominent thinker and activist known for her work in ecofeminism, which draws connections between environmental issues and gender. Her theories explore how the exploitation of the environment and the subjugation of women are interconnected, arising from a patriarchal framework that also dominates nature. Shiva's work emphasizes sustainability and the vital role women play in maintaining ecological balance, advocating for both environmental conservation and gender equality as integral to social justice.

40. (C): The proposed name for the new Criminal Procedure Code in India is "Bharatiya Nagarik Suraksha Sanhita." This new name reflects an effort to modernize and localize the legal framework, aligning it more closely with contemporary Indian socio-legal contexts. The renaming is part of broader reforms intended to make the criminal justice system more effective, accessible, and equitable, addressing long-standing issues such as procedural delays and the need for more comprehensive protections under the law.

41. (C): Family can significantly influence gendered education by both promoting gender equality and challenging stereotypes (*a*), and encouraging children to choose careers without considering gender norms (*d*). These actions help break down traditional gender roles and expectations, fostering an environment where children feel free to pursue their interests and talents irrespective of their gender. This nurturing approach can empower children to explore a wider range of educational and career opportunities, ultimately contributing to a more equal society.

42. (C): The main aim of interdisciplinary research is to bring out the holistic approach to research (*b*) and to create new trends in research methodology (*c*). By integrating methods, perspectives, and concepts from various disciplines, interdisciplinary research addresses complex problems more effectively than any single subject could on its own. This approach allows for a more comprehensive understanding of issues, fostering innovation and advancing knowledge across traditional disciplinary boundaries.

43. (A): The key structural variables that determine women's work in India include regional differences (*a*), labour market conditions (*b*), and the influence of family, caste, and class (*c*). These factors collectively shape the employment opportunities available to women and the types of work they are able to engage in. Regional variations affect economic opportunities; labour market dynamics influence employment terms; and family, caste, and class can dictate societal expectations and individual access to resources, all of which impact women's work in India.

44. (C): The primary focus of maternal health policies and programs is on increasing equity and reducing poverty (*b*), and ensuring safe pregnancy, childbirth, and postnatal care for women (*c*). These programs aim to improve health outcomes for mothers and their children by addressing the social and economic determinants of health and ensuring that women have access to the necessary medical care during and after pregnancy. This holistic approach is essential for reducing maternal and infant mortality rates and for promoting the well-being of families and communities.

45. (B): Women's empowerment primarily involves increasing women's involvement in decision-making processes (*a*), enhancing women's ability to access education, income, and resources (*b*), and actions to transform the structures and institutions that reinforce and perpetuate gender discrimination and inequality (*c*). These elements are critical for empowering women to achieve their full potential and for creating a more equitable society where women have equal opportunities to contribute to and benefit from economic, social, and political developments.

46. (B): The case study method is known for its particularistic, descriptive, and inductive nature. It focuses on detailed investigation of a particular entity, event, or group over time within its real-life context. This method is particularistic as it zeroes in on a specific subject, providing a deep understanding unique to that case. It is descriptive because it aims to describe the phenomena in detail based on extensive data collection. Case studies are also inductive, developing theories and generalizations as outcomes from the detailed analysis of the collected data. Unlike experimental research, case studies do not usually occur in a laboratory setting, making option (*a*) irrelevant to its characteristics.

47. (A): The major objectives of menstrual hygiene schemes, particularly targeting adolescent girls, emphasize increasing awareness, accessibility, and environmental safety regarding menstrual hygiene. The primary aim is to educate adolescent girls about menstrual hygiene, enhancing their knowledge and breaking taboos surrounding menstruation. Furthermore, these initiatives strive to improve access to high-quality sanitary products in rural areas, addressing economic and logistical barriers. Safe disposal of sanitary napkins is also a crucial component, aiming to prevent environmental damage and promote health standards. The option including "menstrual level" lacks clarity and relevance, making it extraneous to the scheme's objectives.

48. (C): The Mukhyamantri Suposhan Abhiyan launched by Chhattisgarh state is designed to eradicate malnutrition and is overseen by the Women and Child Welfare Department. Its focus is not limited to a specific age group but aims to provide nutritional support broadly within the community, with a significant emphasis on women and children. This eradication effort includes comprehensive measures ranging from supplemental nutrition programs to awareness campaigns. It encompasses a broad age range, between 15-49 years. The program also targets broader demographics including children under age 6.

49. (B): Dr. Madhuri R. Shah and Dr. Armaity Desai are the only two women from the options provided who have served as chairpersons of the University Grants Commission (UGC). Dr. Madhuri R. Shah held the chair from 1981 to 1986, and her tenure was noted for significant educational reforms and a focus on higher education accessibility. Dr. Armaity

Desai served from 1995-1999 and was known for her efforts in promoting academic excellence and women's education in India. The other individuals listed have not held the position of UGC chairperson, which directly pertains to the correct answer being those who actually served in this esteemed role.

50. (D): Among the tribal societies listed, the Rengma and Monpa tribes do not allow women to inherit ancestral or immovable property due to customary laws. These tribal laws and customs play a crucial role in governing property rights and are often reflective of the patriarchal structure prevalent in many indigenous communities. The Liangmai and Mizo tribes have different customs and laws regarding property inheritance, which may allow for some forms of female inheritance or have undergone reforms to increase gender equity. This distinction highlights the variation in customary laws across different tribes and their impacts on women's rights and societal roles.

51. (A): Elisabeth Cady Stanton and Lucretia Mott organized the first women's convention in Seneca Falls, New York in 1848. This event marked a pivotal moment in the women's rights movement in the United States. Stanton and Mott, both ardent abolitionists and advocates for social reforms, convened this gathering to address women's civil liberties and propose a declaration of rights for women. Susan B. Anthony, although closely associated with the women's suffrage movement, did not join the movement until 1851 and was not a part of organizing the Seneca Falls Convention. Abby Kelley Foster was also a prominent advocate for both abolition and women's rights, but her direct involvement in Seneca Falls as an organizer is not recorded.

52. (C): The feminization of international migration became a key aspect and subject of new debates in the early 1990s, extending into the late 1990s. This period saw a significant increase in the migration of women as independent migrants rather than as dependents. This shift contributed to a broader discourse on migration, gender, and globalization, as researchers and policymakers began to address the specific needs and challenges faced by female migrants, including labour exploitation, social integration, and the impact on family structures in both home and host countries.

53. (B): The most important parts of a research proposal include the hypothesis, methodology, and objectives of the study. The hypothesis proposes a tentative explanation or prediction that the research aims to test. The methodology section details the research methods and procedures that will be used to collect and analyze data. Objectives of the study outline what the research intends to achieve. These components are crucial as they guide the direction and execution of the research. The publication is not typically a part of the proposal itself but is a potential outcome of the research conducted.

54. (A): The Cinematography (Amendment) Bill introduced in the Rajya Sabha on July 20, 2023, included age-based certification features such as UA 7+, UA 13+, and UA 16+. These certifications indicate that a film is suitable for viewers above the ages of seven, thirteen, and sixteen respectively, often with parental guidance suggested. This system aims to protect younger audiences from content that may be inappropriate for their age group while allowing them access to content deemed suitable under parental guidance up to the specified age limits.

55. (A): The role of the National Commission for Women (NCW) includes the lack of actual legislative powers and the ability to recommend remedial legislative actions. While the NCW plays a critical role in advocating for women's rights and advising the government on all policy matters affecting women, it does not possess legislative powers to enact laws directly. However, it can make recommendations for legislative changes. The NCW does not have the power to choose its own members; members are appointed by the government, which highlights its advisory and recommendatory functions rather than executive or legislative powers.

56. (A): The Bechdel test, a measure used to gauge the representation of women in fiction, particularly films, requires that a film must have at least two female characters, these characters must have a conversation with each other, and their conversation must be about something other than a man. This test highlights the need for female characters to have more substantive roles and interactions in films, beyond their relationships with male characters. The test does not include any requirements regarding male characters, making option (*d*) irrelevant to the criteria of the Bechdel test.

57. (B): The term "feminisation of poverty" refers to the phenomenon where women are disproportionately affected by poverty compared to men. This concept encompasses the socio-economic challenges women face, including a lack of economic opportunities and autonomy, as well as the absence of access to education and support services, which contribute significantly to their precarious financial positions. The term was not coined by Martha Nussbaum, making option (*a*) incorrect. Instead, it captures the broader systemic issues that disproportionately impact women, particularly in socio-economic contexts.

58. (C): Government of India schemes for women entrepreneurs include the Annapurna Scheme, Mudra Yojana Scheme, and Dena Shakti Scheme. The Annapurna Scheme provides financial support to women to establish food catering units for selling lunch packs, etc. The Mudra Yojana Scheme offers loans to women wishing to start small businesses, and the Dena Shakti Scheme focuses on providing loans to women entrepreneurs in fields like agriculture, manufacturing, micro-credit, retail stores, or small enterprises. The Sukanya Samriddhi Yojana, while beneficial for the girl child's future education and marriage expenses, is not directly aimed at women entrepreneurs.

59. (A): Sexual harassment includes unwelcome acts or behaviour such as physical contact and advances, making sexually coloured remarks, and showing pornography. These behaviours create a hostile or offensive work environment and are considered forms of sexual harassment under various legal frameworks. Making curt comments, unless sexually coloured or part of a broader pattern of inappropriate behaviour, does not specifically fall under the typical definitions of sexual harassment, focusing instead on the more direct and explicitly sexual actions and remarks.

60. (D): Increasing the number of female entrepreneurs can be significantly impacted by providing access to finance, expanding their network opportunities, and publicizing women role models. Access to finance allows women to start and grow their own businesses. Networking provides vital connections, support, and business opportunities. Promoting successful women as role models can inspire and motivate more women to pursue entrepreneurship. Providing high interest loans is counterproductive as it could discourage entrepreneurship due to the increased financial burden, making this option unsuitable for fostering entrepreneurial growth.

61. (B): In feminist research, the interview technique often involves the co-construction of experiential reality and aims to break down the hierarchical relationship between the researcher and the researched. This approach views the respondents as active participants who contribute significantly to the creation of knowledge through their experiences and narratives. The methodology emphasizes egalitarian interactions where both parties engage critically and reflexively, challenging traditional power dynamics typically present in research settings. This technique is distinguished by its interactive and participative nature, which allows for a deeper exploration of gender-related issues.

62. (A): The Beti Bachao Beti Padhao Scheme primarily targets young married couples, pregnant mothers, and parents. This focus is designed to address the critical stages of child rearing from prenatal to postnatal care, aiming to ensure the survival, protection, and education of the girl child. The scheme emphasizes the importance of nurturing and educating female children right from their earliest stages of life, which involves educating and influencing the immediate caregivers and decision-makers around them. The involvement of panchayat members, while important, is not the primary focus of this scheme.

63. (D): Among the critics listed, Carol Gilligan and Nancy Chodorow have significantly contributed to the discussions on reproduction and motherhood. Carol Gilligan is known for her work on moral development, particularly in how it pertains to women, while Nancy Chodorow has written extensively on motherhood and the reproduction of mothering, emphasizing the psychological and sociological aspects of gender and family dynamics. Their work helps illuminate the nuanced ways in which women's reproductive roles are understood and internalized within societal structures.

64. (A): The Mako Mori test is a set of criteria focusing on the representation of female characters in film and is inspired by the character Mako Mori from the 2013 film 'Pacific Rim.' This test assesses whether a film includes at least one female character who gets her own narrative arc that is not about supporting a man's story. It serves as an alternative to the Bechdel test, providing a different measure for evaluating female representation in movies. The Mako Mori test highlights the importance of individual character development for women in cinema.

65. (C): According to the 2011 census, the states of Kerala and Mizoram have literacy rates over 90%. Kerala has long been recognized for its high literacy rates with 94%, reflecting the state's strong emphasis on education in public policy. Mizoram, too, showcases high literacy rates of 91.33%, indicative of successful educational policies in the northeastern region of India. Both states exemplify the positive outcomes of sustained educational efforts and their impact on community development and social indicators.

66. (D): In the context of paradigms and their advocates:

(*a*) Positivist paradigm is associated with Auguste Comte, who is considered one of the founders of sociology and a key figure in the development of positivism.

(*b*) Interpretive paradigm aligns with Max Weber, who emphasized understanding the subjective meaning of social actions.

(*c*) Critical paradigm is connected to Theodore Adorno, known for his critical theory work, particularly in the Frankfurt School.

(*d*) Feminist paradigm can be associated with Simone de Beauvoir, who is a seminal figure in feminist philosophy.

67. (D): Matching the women leaders with their respective positions:

(*a*) Sanna Marin is known as the Prime Minister of Finland.

(*b*) Loreta Lynch served as the U.S. Attorney General.

(*c*) Nancy Pelosi is recognized as the Speaker of the U.S. House of Representatives.

(*d*) Tsai Ing-wen is the first female President of Taiwan.

68. (B): Associating strands of feminism with noted feminists:

(*a*) Liberal feminism is closely associated with J.S. Mill, who advocated for equality and rights for women.

(*b*) Radical feminism is linked to Shulamith Firestone, who explored the roots of gender inequality in society.

(*c*) Post-colonial feminism is represented by Gayatri Spivak, who addresses issues of gender in the context of colonialism and post-colonialism.

(*d*) Eco feminism is identified with Maria Mies, known for her work connecting the exploitation of women and nature.

69. (A): Correctly matching authors with their books:

(*a*) Naila Kabeer wrote "Reversed Realities: Gender Hierarchies in Development Thought," which discusses the roles of gender in development.

(*b*) Gail Omvedt is associated with "Violence Against Women: New Movements and New Theories in India," focusing on gender violence and feminist movements.

(*c*) Nivedita Menon authored "Gender and Politics in India," exploring gender dynamics in Indian political context.

(*d*) Patricia Uberoi wrote "Social Reform, Sexuality, and the State," which delves into societal changes and gender issues.

70. (D): Correctly matching terms with their explanations:

(*a*) Meher refers to property given to wife in consideration for marriage, a customary practice in Islamic marriages.

(*c*) Sapindas describes individuals who have a common lineal ancestor, often used in the context of family and marriage laws in India.

(*b*) Iddat is the waiting period after divorce in Islamic law, during which a woman cannot marry another man.

(*d*) Streedhan is the present or jewellery given to a woman during marriage, typically including personal gifts and dowry items.

71. (B): Correctly matching the authors with their books based on their renowned works and areas of expertise:

(*a*) Maria Mies is associated with "Women the Lost Colony", examining the exploitation of women in a capitalist world.

(*b*) Vandana Shiva is best known for "Earth Democracy", which relates to her advocacy for environmental and feminist issues, focusing on how women and nature can bring about a change in the global order through democratic means.

(*c*) Gail Omvedt's notable work includes "Dalit Visions", which discusses caste and its intersections with other social issues, including gender.

(*d*) Kamla Bhasin, an advocate for women's rights and gender equality, wrote "Exploring Masculinity", a reflection on gender roles and their impact on society.

72. (B): Matching these well-known women entrepreneurs with their respective enterprises:

(*a*) Falguni Nayar is the Founder and CEO of Nyka, a beauty and wellness e-commerce platform.

(*b*) Kiran Mazumdar-Shaw is the Chairperson of Biocon, a major biopharmaceutical company.

(*c*) Roshni Nadar is the CEO of HCL Technologies, one of India's leading IT services companies.

(*d*) Aditi Gupta is the Co-founder of Menstrupedia, which is focused on educating people about menstruation.

73. (D): Correctly associating each sportsperson with their discipline:

(*a*) Dipa Karmakar is celebrated for her achievements in Gymnastics, particularly noted for her performance in the vault event.

(*b*) Mirabai Chanu is a renowned Weightlifter, known for her exceptional performances on the international stage.

(*c*) Deepika Kumari is an accomplished Archer, recognized for her precision and success in archery competitions.

(*d*) Jhulan Goswami is one of the most prominent figures in Women's Cricket, celebrated for her pace bowling.

74. (A): Matching the individuals with their respective contributions or public activities:

(*a*) Angelina Jolie has played a significant role in raising awareness about breast cancer through her personal experiences and public discussions about her preventive surgeries.

(*b*) Laxmi Agarwal is an Acid attack survivor who has become a prominent activist and face of the movement against acid attacks in India.

(*c*) Shilpa Phadke is best known for her work "Why Loiter", which explores the gendered nature of public spaces and the predominance of men in these areas.

(*d*) Emma Watson launched the "HeForShe" movement, advocating for gender equality and encouraging men to participate actively in these discussions.

75. (D): Properly linking each work to the people who were instrumental in their creation or associated with their initiatives:

(*a*) Sappho for Equality is an organization based in Kolkata working for the rights of lesbians, bisexual women, and transmen, primarily in Eastern India.

(*b*) Queer Ink is a pioneering marketing and publishing agency focusing exclusively on LGBT literature.

(*c*) Yarana is the first gay anthology edited by Hoshang Merchant, a significant literary contribution to gay literature in India.

(*d*) Bombay Dost was India's first gay magazine launched by Ashok Rao Kavi, which has played a critical role in the LGBT community in India.

76. (B): Chronological order of the women-specific legislations:

(*b*) **Immoral Traffic (Prevention) Act (1956):** Although earlier, it was significantly amended later to prevent human trafficking and sexual exploitation for commercial purposes.

(*d*) **The Dowry Prohibition Act (1961):** This act was implemented to prohibit the giving or taking of dowry to curb the dowry practices in marriages.

(*a*) **Commission of Sati (Prevention) Act (1987):** Enacted to prevent the barbaric practice of sati, where a widow would immolate herself on her husband's funeral pyre.

(*c*) **Protection of Women from Domestic Violence Act (2005):** This law provides protection to women from domestic violence and abuse.

77. (C): Chronological development of the gender-related approaches:

(*d*) **Women in Development (WID) (1973):** This approach emerged first and focuses on integrating women into development processes.

(*c*) **Women and Development (WAD) (1975):** Followed by recognizing the relationship between women and the processes of economic development.

(*a*) **Gender and Development (GAD) (1980s):** Developed to focus on the socially constructed basis of differences between men and women and emphasizes the need to challenge existing gender roles and relations.

(*b*) **Women, Environment, and Development (WED) (late 1980s):** Emerged to focus specifically on the intersections of women's issues with environmental concerns.

78. (D): Correct chronological sequence of these reports and policies:

(*b*) **Towards Equality Report (1974):** A pioneering report on the status of women in India, highlighting gender inequalities.

(*d*) **Shramshakti Report of the National Commission on Self Employed Women and Women in Informal Sector (1988):** Focused on the working conditions of women in the informal sector.

(*a*) **National Population Policy (2000):** Aimed at stabilizing the population by addressing reproductive health and strengthening family planning services.

(*c*) **National Empowerment Policy for Women (2001):** Aimed to bring about the advancement, development, and empowerment of women.

79. (D): Chronological order of these movements and organizations:

(*d*) **Non-Cooperation Movement (1920-1922):** An important phase in the Indian independence struggle.

(*c*) **National Federation of Indian Women (1954):** Established to enhance the social and political status of women.

(*b*) **Shahada Movement (1972):** A tribal women's movement focused on land rights and social issues in Maharashtra.

(*a*) **Stop Acid Sale (2013 onwards):** Campaigns and initiatives aimed at regulating the sale of acid to prevent acid attacks.

80. (D): Sequence of introduction of these women-oriented schemes:

(*a*) **Swadhar Greh (2002):** Although introduced earlier, it continues to provide holistic and integrated support to women in difficult circumstances, fitting into the broader timeline of recent initiatives.

(*d*) **One-Stop center (2015):** Introduced as part of the Nirbhaya Fund, providing integrated support and assistance to women affected by violence.

(*b*) **Mahila E-Haat (2016):** An online platform launched to support women entrepreneurs by providing them access to markets.

(*c*) **Mahila Shakti Kendra (2017):** Set up to empower rural women through community participation and to provide them with direct access to government schemes and programs.

81. (D): The correct chronological sequence for the methodology used in preparing the All India Survey on Higher Education (AISHE) Report is as follows:

(*b*) **Identification of HEI (Higher Education Institutions):** First, identifying the institutions that will be part of the survey.

(*a*) **Registration of Higher Education Institutions (HEI):** Registering these identified institutions into the survey system.

(*d*) **Collection and Verification of Data:** Gathering data from these registered institutions and verifying its accuracy and completeness.

(*c*) **Compilation and Analysis of data:** Finally, compiling the collected data and performing analysis to prepare the report.

82. (C): Arranging these significant events in chronological order based on their occurrence:

(*c*) **Roe vs Wade (1973):** This landmark decision by the U.S. Supreme Court recognized the constitutional right to privacy extends to a woman's right to make her own personal medical decisions, including the decision to have an abortion.

(*b*) **The Protection of Women from Domestic Violence Act (2005):** India's act aiming to protect women from violence in domestic settings.

(*d*) **The United Nations Passes a Resolution Banning Female Genital Mutilation (2012):** A significant global commitment to eliminating female genital mutilation.

(*a*) **Saudi Arabia Lifts Ban on Female Drivers (2018):** Marking a notable shift in women's rights in Saudi Arabia.

83. (C): The chronological sequence of the establishment of these Indian institutions focused on women and children is:

(*c*) **Department of Women and Child Development (1985):** Originally part of the broader Department of Human Resource Development.

(*b*) **National Commission for Women (1992):** Established to study and improve the legal and constitutional safeguards for women.

(*a*) **Ministry of Women and Child Development (2006):** Formed when the Department of Women and Child Development was upgraded to a full ministry.

(*d*) **National Commission for Protection of Child Rights (2007):** Set up to ensure all laws, policies, programs, and administrative mechanisms are in consonance with the child rights perspective as enshrined in the Constitution of India and also the UN Convention on the Rights of the Child.

84. (D): The chronological order of enactment for these Indian laws is:

(*d*) **The Maternity Benefit Act (1961):** Provides maternity benefits to women in employment.

(*b*) **Medical Termination of Pregnancy Act (1971):** Regulates the conditions under which a pregnancy may be aborted.

(*a*) **The Family Courts Act (1984):** Establishes family courts with a view to promote conciliation and secure speedy settlement of disputes relating to marriage and family affairs.

(*c*) **The Indecent Representation of Women (Prohibition) Act (1986):** Prohibits indecent representation of women through advertisements or in publications, writings, paintings, figures or in any other manner.

85. (C): The chronological sequence of these feminist concepts and their emergence is:

(*d*) **The Problem with No Name (1963):** Introduced by Betty Friedan, describing the dissatisfaction among women in the 1950s and early 1960s.

(*c*) **One is Not Born a Woman but Becomes One (1973):** A famous statement by Simone de Beauvoir from her book "The Second Sex-II" highlighting the social construction of gender roles.

(*a*) **Gender is a Performative Act (1990):** Articulated by Judith Butler, suggesting that gender is created through repeated performances or acts.

(*b*) **Shadow Pandemic (2020):** A term used during the COVID-19 pandemic to describe the global increase in domestic violence against women and girls in the context of lockdowns and social isolation.

86. (C): Assertion (A) stating that despite higher educational attainment of women, the Female Labour Force Participation Rate (FLFRP) is showing a declining trend in India is correct. However, Reason (R), which claims that educated women are unwilling to work, is not a complete or correct explanation. The reasons for the decline in FLFRP among educated women in India are more complex, including factors like lack of suitable job opportunities, societal expectations, and workplace challenges that do not encourage women to continue in the workforce despite higher education.

87. (B): Assertion (A) is correct in that emerging technologies, while improving our lives in many ways, have indeed created a 'Digital Divide,' distinguishing between those who have access to digital technologies and those who do not. However, Reason (R) is correct in its own right as it highlights that most women are engaged in the domestic and informal sector, which might limit their access to technology. However, this is not the direct explanation for the digital divide, which encompasses broader socioeconomic factors affecting various demographics, not just women.

88. (A): Assertion (A) is accurate if the context of the "Shakti scheme" referred to is indeed about offering women non-premium services in state-run transportation, although specifics might vary. Reason (R) is also correct in stating that the government of India presents numerous schemes, programs, and incentives to promote women's empowerment. If the "Shakti scheme" as described is a part of these efforts, then Reason (R) correctly explains why such a scheme would be in place.

89. (C): Assertion (A) is correct as a gender studies teacher does sensitize students on gender discrimination, often covering a wide range of issues related to gender equality and social norms. However, Reason (R) is incorrect; a well-rounded gender studies curriculum or teaching approach should not use a unilateral perspective but should involve multiple perspectives and encourage critical thinking on various aspects of gender and society.

90. (C): Assertion (A) is correct in stating that the Women's Reservation Bill could help form a strong lobby in parliament to address and advocate for issues affecting women that are often ignored or sidelined. However, Reason (R) suggesting that the bill will facilitate only the entry of upper class urban educated women into parliament is not entirely accurate and certainly not the correct explanation for (A). The bill aims to improve representation across various backgrounds, although concerns about diversity within the representation remain valid.

91. (A): The learning point from the Helen Keller story, as mentioned in the passage, is that there is a failure in women's studies and women's movements to fully include issues and challenges faced by women with disabilities. This example underscores a broader pedagogical and societal oversight where the contributions and experiences of disabled women are often omitted from historical and social narratives within education.

92. (C): In an inclusive and just society, an education system would look like one where teaching methods are implemented from alternative viewpoints. This implies a system that incorporates diverse experiences and needs, tailoring educational practices to accommodate all learners, including those from various social backgrounds, abilities, and learning styles.

93. (A): Both statements regarding inclusive education are correct:

Statement I highlights that inclusive education benefits not only students with disabilities but also those without, fostering a more comprehensive learning environment.

Statement II underlines that inclusive classrooms serve as platforms for teaching all students the value of diversity and acceptance, which are crucial for building an empathetic and inclusive society.

94. (C): Disabling environments for women with disabilities typically include:

(*a*) Inaccessible transport, which can hinder their ability to commute and participate fully in societal roles.

(*b*) Buildings without a universal structure, which fail to accommodate all individuals regardless of their physical abilities.

(*d*) Stereotyping, which can create barriers to equal treatment and opportunities.

95. (C): Assertion (A) is correct in that women with disabilities often face double marginalization due to their disability and gender, experiencing compounded forms of discrimination and exclusion. However, Reason (R) is incorrect as it suggests that in an enabling environment, women with disabilities have greater accessibility over their male counterparts, which is not necessarily true or a direct explanation of the assertion. Instead, an enabling environment aims to provide equal accessibility for all, regardless of gender.

96. (A): Migration affects women who remain in their country of origin in complex ways. While the passage discusses women taking on additional responsibilities and gaining autonomy, it also mentions the possibility of them co-residing with other male relatives who often restrict their activities outside the home. This co-residence can lead to a situation where despite potentially increased financial and domestic autonomy, their social and physical mobility may be curtailed, limiting their full engagement in public and economic life.

97. (C): Statement I is true as gender relations and hierarchies in both sending and receiving countries significantly determine the gender-specific impacts of migration, affecting how men and women experience migration differently. Statement II is false, as the passage clearly states that women migrant workers often face major challenges in benefiting from trade unions and NGO activity as they are frequently not allowed to join or form unions in destination countries.

98. (B): Both Assertion (A) and Reason (R) are correct but Reason (R) does not directly explain Assertion (A). Assertion (A) suggests that women who remain when their male relatives migrate may find their activities restricted by co-residing male relatives. Reason (R) counters this by stating that such women have opportunities to gain autonomy and experience in decision-making, highlighting a contrasting scenario where women might actually benefit from the migration of male relatives in terms of personal development and autonomy.

99. (B): Both Statement I and Statement II are false. Historically, the migration of women has often been disregarded in studies and documentation of international migration, which primarily focused on male migrants. Statement II is also false, as migration significantly affects family members who remain in the country of origin, as they may have to adapt to new roles, take on additional responsibilities, and face economic or social changes.

100. (A): Migrant workers are often perceived as taking away jobs from the native population. This is a common stereotype that exists despite the fact that migrant workers, particularly women, usually perform jobs that the native population tends to avoid, as mentioned in the passage.

Previous Years' Paper (Solved)

National Testing Agency (NTA)

UGC-NET Junior Research Fellowship & Assistant Professor Eligibility Exam

WOMEN'S STUDIES, February 2023

(Online exam held on 21/02/2023)

PAPER-II

1. Who has argued that "culture has higher value than nature. Culture is the means by which man controls and regulates the nature".
   A. Sherry B Ortener B. Ann Oakley
   C. Margaret Mead D. Belty Friedan

2. Who has authored the book "Black Feminist Thought : Knowledge, Consciousness and the Politics of Empowerment".
   A. Kate Millet
   B. Patricia Hill Collins
   C. Nancy Chodorow
   D. Vandana Shiva

3. Find out what is true about Micro, Small and Medium Enterprises (MSME's) in India.
   A. This is a very gender sensitive sector
   B. Substantial contribution in terms of creation of productive employment.
   C. A small enterprise demands less than 10 lakh Rupees investment in manufacturing sector.
   D. Low technology requirements.

4. According to the Human Development Report, what is the Human Development Index (HDI) rank of India in 2022?
   A. 129 B. 132
   C. 134 D. 135

5. United Nations adopted Convention on Elimination of All forms of Discrimination Against Women (CEDAW) in the year:
   A. 1945 B. 1979
   C. 1975 D. 1982

6. While analysing popular culture and consumerism who has condemned racism, classism and sexism.
   A. Julia Kristeva B. Luce Irigaray
   C. Bell Hooks D. Kate Millet

7. Which wave of feminism has first advocated for women and girls to be in control of their bodies?
   A. First Wave of Feminism
   B. Second Wave of Feminism
   C. Third Wave of Feminism
   D. Fourth Wave of Feminism

8. Which section of IPC deals with voluntarily causing hurt by the use of acid?
   A. Section 326 B. Section 420
   C. Section 496 D. Section 556

9. Who has argued that "In standpoint epistemology the understanding of the relation between knowledge and power present in Marx's work provides important criteria for what can count as better, or more privileged knowledges"?
   A. Nancy Hartsock
   B. Liz Stanley
   C. Patricia Hill Collins
   D. Maria Mies

10. A person who has only one X Chromosome (as against XX or XY in the 46th pair of chromosomes) is said to have:
    A. Turner's syndrome
    B. Klinefelter's syndrome
    C. Transexual syndrome
    D. Cisgender syndrome

11. Germaine Greer used the phrase female Eunuch to denote:
    A. Women's inherent biological superiority
    B. The Societal idealisation of women
    C. Patriarchal castration of women
    D. Women's motherhood

12. Which one of the following is not a form of qualitative research?
    A. Case study
    B. Survey
    C. Oral history
    D. Focus group discussion

13. Which of the following concept was established as a major global strategy for the promotion of gender equality in the Beijing platform for Action from the Fourth United Nations World conference on Women in Beijing in 1995?
   A. Gender mainstreaming
   B. Gender Equality
   C. Sex-Disaggregated Data
   D. Gender Development

14. Janani Shishu Suraksha Karyakram (JSSK) was launched on:
   A. 1st June, 2011
   B. 1st July, 2012
   C. 1st September, 2013
   D. 4th December, 2014

15. When some individuals develop feelings that they have a sense of gender that is opposite to the biological sex, they are born with is known as:
   A. Cross gender disorder
   B. Gender dysphoria
   C. Gender incompatibility disorder
   D. Bi-gender disorder

16. Who suggested that gender is the product of various social technologies, such as cinema and the media?
   A. Teresa de Lauretis
   B. Mary Wollstonecraft
   C. Angela Davis
   D. Mary Daly

17. Who won the International Booker Prize 2022 for the novel 'Tomb of Sand'?
   A. Anita Desai
   B. Arundhati Rao
   C. Geetanjali Shree
   D. Salman Rushdie

18. In 1973, in the USA, The Roe vs Wade judgement:
   A. Gave women the right to have an abortion before the fetus is viable outside the womb or before the 24-28 weeks mark.
   B. Asserted that a fetus is a 'person' Protected by the 14th Amendment.
   C. Protecting prenatal life from the time of conception is a compelling state interest.
   D. States have an interest in safeguarding health, maintaining medical standards and protecting prenatal life.

19. The Nursing Break applicable to a mother who has returned to her duties after availing maternity leave until the child attains 15 months of age is:
   A. One break during the working hours including the regular internal / rest period
   B. One break during the working hours excluding the regular interval / rest period.
   C. Two breaks during the working hours including the regular intervals / rest period.
   D. Two breaks during the working hours excluding the regular intervals / rest period.

20. Which of the following explains "Crude Birth Rate"?
   A. Number of children below five years of age per thousand of women in the reproductive age group per year.
   B. Number of births per thousand of women in the reproductive age group per year.
   C. Number of births per thousand of the population per year.
   D. Total number of births per year in the country.

21. India signed an agreement with which country to co-operate in health and medicine and support "Green Healthcare"?
   A. France
   B. Brazil
   C. Italy
   D. Israel

22. Who among the following authored "Gendering Caste"?
   A. Leela Dube
   B. Irawati Karve
   C. Vandana Shiva
   D. Uma Chakravarti

23. Who has defined empowerment in terms of three inter related concepts : agency, resources and achievements?
   A. Sherry B Ortener
   B. Naila Kabeer
   C. Kamla Bhasin
   D. Bina Agarwal

24. Who is the author of the "Transfeminist Manifesto"?
   A. Bell Hooks
   B. Sara Ahmed
   C. Kimberly Crenshaw
   D. Emi Koyama

25. "Feminisation of Labour", means:
   A. More women in all kinds of jobs.
   B. More women in less kinds of jobs.
   C. Less women in all kinds of jobs.
   D. No women in jobs.

26. Who wrote "The Subjection of Woman"?
   A. John Stuart Mill
   B. Mary Daly
   C. Margaret Fuller
   D. Jacques Derrida

27. Identify the sampling method which can be used for a population that has no official list of names of the members, secretiveness about their identity and difficult to locate people.
   A. Deviant Sampling
   B. Quota Sampling
   C. Chain-referral Sampling
   D. Random Sampling

28. In which of the following models the media is seen as powerful and able to inject ideas into an audience who are seen as weak and passive?
A. Uses and gratification model
B. The hypodermic model
C. Two step flow theory
D. Cultivation theory

29. Name the philosopher who coined the expression "The medium is the message".
A. Vladimir Propp B. Stuart Hall
C. Marshall McLuhan D. Roland Barthes

30. The concept of socialisation of "Domestic Labour" was used by:
A. Margaret Benston
B. Kate Millet
C. Shulamith Firestone
D. Nancy Chodorow

31. As per National Family Health Survey-5, which of the Indian state has recorded the highest adolescent fertility state?
A. Tripura B. Rajasthan
C. Goa D. Uttrakhand

32. Mother and child tracking system under Ministry of Health and Family Welfare is:
A. A web-based system to ensure registration and tracking of all Pregnant women and new born babies.
B. A system of operationalisation of sub-centers, primary health centers, community health centers and District Hospitals for providing 24 × 7 basic and comprehensive obstetric care services.
C. A system of Mother and Child Protection Card to monitor service delivery for mothers and children.
D. A system of Engagement of Accredited Social Health Activists (ASHAs) to generate demand and facilitate accessing of health care services by the community.

33. Amma Canteen in Tamil Nadu endorses which Marxist feminist concept?
A. Socialization of Domestic Work
B. Wages for House Work
C. Reproductive Work
D. Theory of Comparable Worth

34. Under National Legal Service Authority (NALSA) judgement the Supreme Court has upheld the right of all persons to self identify their gender within the frame work of the fundamental right to dignity, under which Article of Indian Constitution:
A. Article 3 B. Article 12
C. Article 21 D. Article 377

35. According to Fredrick Engels what is true about private property _______.
A. Private property historically increase women's social position.
B. Private property was a feminine creation.
C. Women considered children as property.
D. Private property led to male-domination over female sexuality and reproductive power.

36. Which of the following Indian State Practices Uniform Civil Code?
A. Goa B. Karnataka
C. Gujarat D. Uttar Pradesh

37. The process under which wife initiates divorce proceedings under Islam is known as:
A. Talaq
B. Khula
C. Muslim Dissolution of Marriage Act, 1939
D. Ila and Zihar

38. Which of the following is a non-probability sampling method?
A. Self-Selection Sampling
B. Cluster Sampling
C. Systematic Sampling
D. Stratified Sampling

39. Fat positivity is the concept that:
A. Fat people have the right to love and accept their bodies as they are.
B. Fat bodies are inherently unhealthy
C. Women should conform to standards of health which require them to be physically fit.
D. Being fat means women are more susceptible to temptation.

40. Who said, "Mothering can be extended to any relationship in which one individual nurses and cares for another"?
A. Alison Jaggar B. Elaine Showlater
C. Kate Millet D. Betty Friedan

41. Identify the major lacunae of Artificial Reproductive Technology (ART) & Surrogacy Act 2021.
(a) Discriminates against LGBTQI, live in couple.
(b) Paternalistic and heteronormative values are allowed.
(c) Single men and unmarried women are included.
(d) Complete ban on commercial surrogacy.

Choose the correct answer from the options given below:
A. (a), (b), (c) only B. (b), (c), (d) only
C. (a), (c), (d) only D. (a), (b), (d) only

42. Swarnjayanti Gram Swarozgar Yojana (SGSY) a scheme which:
(a) Offers credit-cum subsidy to the beneficiaries and banks involved in this process.
(b) Seeks to promote multiple credit rather than a one time credit input.
(c) Provides for skill development through training courses in technology, marketing, information etc.
(d) Is aimed at women's empowerment through the building of confidence by encouraging thrift and savings.

Choose the correct answer from the options given below:
A. (a), (b) and (c) only
B. (a), (c) and (d) only
C. (a), (b) and (d) only
D. (b), (c) and (d) only

43. The important variables for assessing nutrition of under five children are:
(a) Weight
(b) Height
(c) Age
(d) Activity level

Choose the correct answer from the options given below:
A. (a), (b) and (c) only
B. (b), (c) and (d) only
C. (a), (c) and (d) only
D. (a), (b) and (d) only

44. Health and wellness centres in India address health issues related to:
(a) Hypertension
(b) Diabetes
(c) Breast Cancer, Oral & Cervical Cancer
(d) HIV/AIDS

Choose the correct answer from the options given below:
A. (a), (b), (c) only
B. (b), (c), (d) only
C. (a), (c), (d) only
D. (a), (b), (d) only

45. Which of the following initiatives is / are launched for addressing "Mental Health Issues"?
(a) KIRAN
(b) Manodarpan
(c) Sugamya Bharat Abhiyan
(d) UDAN

Choose the correct answer from the options given below:
A. (a) and (b) only
B. (b) and (c) only
C. (a) and (d) only
D. (d) and (c) only

46. Women's studies as a field has evolved over the years:
(a) It embraces the study of not just women but of all genders.
(b) The field has multiplied and become plural
(c) In some cases it has changed its name from women's studies to women and gender studies.
(d) It deals with studies conducted by women.

Choose the correct answer from the options given below:
A. (a), (b), (c) only
B. (a), (b), (d) only
C. (a), (c), (d) only
D. (b), (c), (d) only

47. The Indian feminist publication business:
(a) Advances feminist causes and prints academic, fiction, memories and non-fiction writings.
(b) The history of feminist publishing is interesting but not of utmost importance.
(c) Recognizes and supports women's causes.
(d) Kali for women, Zubaan, women unlimited, Tara Books, Tulika, Stree are some feminist publisher.

Choose the correct answer from the options given below:
A. (a), (b), (c) only
B. (a), (b), (d) only
C. (a), (c), (d) only
D. (b), (c), (d) only

48. In 1905 Rokeya Sakhawat Hossain wrote a short story "Sultana's Dream" describing:
(a) How very advanced her country would be if woman ruled.
(b) Woman rulers of "Lady Land" defeated the nation's enemies by harnessing the Sun's power.
(c) In Hossain's created world there was technological efficiency and because of it, harmonious rule.
(d) Rokeya depicts the real world.

Choose the correct answer from the options given below:
A. (a), (b), (c) only
B. (a), (b), (d) only
C. (a), (c), (d) only
D. (b), (c), (d) only

49. Which of the following are correct about WID (Women in Development) approach?

(a) Gained momentum in the 1970's
(b) Addressed disparity of economic opportunity
(c) Focuses on Economic participation.
(d) It deals with disparities and power relations between men and women.

Choose the correct answer from the options given below:
A. (a), (b), (c) only
B. (a), (c), (d) only
C. (a), (b), (d) only
D. (b), (c), (d) only

50. Simone de Beauvoir in 'The Second Sex':
(a) Argues that the fundamental source of Women's oppression is its [Femininity's] historical and social construction as the "other".
(b) Turns the existential mantra that existence precedes essence into a feminist one.
(c) Defines woman as the second sex because women are defined as inferior to men.
(d) Asserted that women are not capable of choice as men and this makes them inferior.

Choose the correct answer from the options given below:
A. (a), (b), (c) only
B. (a), (b), (d) only
C. (a), (c), (d) only
D. (b), (c), (d) only

51. Which of the following books were published by Kali for Women?
(a) Radha Kumar's The History of Doing
(b) Vandana Shiva's Staying Alive
(c) Kumkum Sangari & Sudesh Vaid's Recasting Women
(d) Susie Tharu & K. Lalitha's Women Writing in India.

Choose the correct answer from the options given below:
A. (a), (b), (c) only
B. (a), (c), (d) only
C. (a), (b), (d) only
D. (b), (c), (d) only

52. Reproductive Rights include:
(a) Individual's right to plan a family
(b) Determinations of sex of unborn child.
(c) Access to contraception
(d) Access to reproductive health services.

Choose the correct answer from the options given below:
A. (a), (b) and (c) only
B. (b), (c) and (d) only
C. (a), (c) and (d) only
D. (a), (b) and (d) only

53. The variables used in measuring the global gender gap index include:
(a) Economic Participation and Opportunity
(b) Educational Attainment
(c) Political Empowerment
(d) Violence Against Women

Choose the correct answer from the options given below:
A. (a), (b) and (c) only
B. (b), (c) and (d) only
C. (a), (c) and (d) only
D. (a), (b) and (d) only

54. The three core principles of CEDAW are:
(a) Substantive Equality
(b) Non-Discrimination
(c) State Obligation
(d) Decision-Making

Choose the correct answer from the options given below:
A. (a), (b) and (c) only
B. (b), (c) and (d) only
C. (a), (c) and (d) only
D. (a), (b) and (d) only

55. POCSO Act addresses a wide range of sexual offences, which include:
(a) Complete and partial Penetration
(b) Non-penetrative sexual assault
(c) Beating a Child
(d) Showing children pornography

Choose the correct answer from the options given below:
A. (a), (c) and (d) only
B. (b), (c) and (d) only
C. (a), (b) and (c) only
D. (a), (b) and (d) only

56. Which of the following are the characteristics of a successful entrepreneur?
(a) Risk-taking
(b) Autocratic
(c) Team Building
(d) Innovative

Choose the correct answer from the options given below:
A. (a), (b) and (c) only
B. (a), (c) and (d) only
C. (b), (c) and (d) only
D. (a), (b) and (d) only

57. Gender Empowerment Measure is calculated on the basis of:
(a) Women's Employment.
(b) Women's seats in Parliament
(c) Women's Education
(d) Women's share of household income.

Choose the correct answer from the options given below:
A. (a), (b) and (c) only
B. (a), (c) and (d) only
C. (a), (b) and (d) only
D. (b), (c) and (d) only

58. Feminist Research aims at:
(a) Research on women
(b) Research about women
(c) Research only by women
(d) Research for women

Choose the correct answer from the options given below:
A. (a), (b) and (c) only
B. (a), (b) and (d) only
C. (b), (c) and (d) only
D. (a), (c) and (d) only

59. Equal Remuneration Act provides that:
(a) Women and men will be paid equally for doing the same work.
(b) The act is applicable to women working in the unorganised sector only.
(c) The employer is bound to maintain a register of the workers.
(d) There will be no discrimination against women workers in any condition of service like promotion, training or transfer

Choose the correct answer from the options given below:
A. (c) and (d) only
B. (a) and (d) only
C. (a) and (b) only
D. (b) and (c) only

60. One of the major causes of high maternal mortality rate in India is:
(a) Anaemia among women
(b) Institutional delivery
(c) Adolescent pregnancies
(d) Inadequate Postpartum Care

Choose the correct answer from the options given below:
A. (a), (b) and (c) only
B. (a), (c) and (d) only
C. (b), (c) and (d) only
D. (a), (b) and (d) only

61. Which of the following are amongst the UNDP sustainable Development Goals.
(a) Good Health and Well being
(b) Quality Education
(c) Industry Innovation and Infrastructure
(d) Social and Cultural Empowerment

Choose the correct answer from the options given below:
A. (a), (b) and (c) only
B. (a), (b) and (d) only
C. (a), (c) and (d) only
D. (b), (c) and (d) only

62. Institutional initiatives for women's issues in the post-independence period are:
(a) Constitutional provisions and social legislation
(b) Indian Association for the Progress of Women
(c) Women's Political Representation
(d) The Women's Indian Association

Choose the correct answer from the options given below
A. (a) and (b) only
B. (a) and (c) only
C. (a) and (d) only
D. (b) and (c) only

63. Alison Jaggar organised her discussion of "Women's alienation" under Unified System Theory of Socialist Feminism, describing her fragmentation under:
(a) Motherhood
(b) Sexuality
(c) Productive work
(d) Intellectuality

Choose the correct answer from the options given below:
A. (a), (b), (d) only
B. (b), (c), (d) only
C. (a), (b), (c) only
D. (a), (c), (d) only

64. Identify the women who were part of the Constituent Assembly:
(a) Dakshayani Velayudhan
(b) Begum Aizaz Rasul
(c) Sucheta Kriplani
(d) Laxmi Sehgal

Choose the correct answer from the options given below:
A. (a), (b), (c) only
B. (a), (b), (d) only
C. (b), (c), (d) only
D. (a); (c), (d) only

65. Which are the three states of India where 73rd and 74th Constitutional amendment provisions are not applicable?

(a) Assam (b) Meghalaya
(c) Mizoram (d) Nagaland

Choose the correct answer from the options given below:

A. (a), (b), (c) only B. (a), (b), (d) only
C. (b), (c), (d) only D. (a), (c), (d) only

66. Match List-I with List-II:

List-I (Name of Theorists)	List-II (Their Contribution)
(a) Martha Nussbaum	I. Dalit feminist standpoint
(b) Judith Butler	II. Ecofeminism
(c) Maria Mies	III. Gender Performativity
(d) Sharmila Rege	IV. Capability approach

Choose the correct answer from the options given below:

	(a)	(b)	(c)	(d)
A.	IV	I	II	III
B.	III	II	IV	I
C.	I	II	III	IV
D.	IV	III	II	I

67. Match List-I with List-II:

List-I (Women Publishers)	List-II (Publication Houses)
(a) Urvashi Butalia	I. Vivago Press
(b) Ritu Menon	II. Ms. Magazine
(c) Gloria Steinem	III. Zubaan Books
(d) Carmen Callil	IV. Women Unlimited

Choose the correct answer from the options given below:

	(a)	(b)	(c)	(d)
A.	I	II	III	IV
B.	III	II	IV	I
C.	III	IV	II	I
D.	III	IV	I	II

68. Match List-I with List-II:

List-I (Types of family)	List-II (Bases of classification)
(a) Matrilocal and Patrilocal	I. On the basis of marriage practice
(b) Matrilineal and Patrilineal	II. On the basis of authority
(c) Patriarchal and Matriarchal	III. On the basis of residence
(d) Monogamous and Polygamous	IV. On the basis of ancestry

Choose the correct answer from the options given below:

	(a)	(b)	(c)	(d)
A.	I	III	II	IV
B.	I	II	III	IV
C.	III	IV	II	I
D.	IV	III	II	I

69. Match List-I with List-II:

List-I (Concepts)	List-II (Theorist)
(a) Compulsory Heterosexuality	I. Laura Mulvey
(b) Feminization of Poverty	II. Diana Pearce
(c) Male Gaze	III. Adrienne Rich
(d) Eco-feminism	IV. Francoise d' Eaubonne

Choose the correct answer from the options given below:

	(a)	(b)	(c)	(d)
A.	I	II	III	IV
B.	II	III	IV	I
C.	III	II	I	IV
D.	IV	III	II	I

70. Match List-I with List-II:

List-I (Founders)	List-II (Organisations formed)
(a) Swarnakumari Devi	I. Bharat Stri Mahamandala
(b) Sarala Devi Ghosal	II. Sakhi Samiti
(c) Kamala Devi Chattopadhyaya	III. National Federation of Indian Women
(d) Aruna Asaf Ali	IV. All India Women's Conference

Choose the correct answer from the options given below:

	(a)	(b)	(c)	(d)
A.	I	II	IV	III
B.	II	IV	III	I
C.	II	I	IV	III
D.	IV	II	I	III

71. Match List-I with List-II:

List-I (Acts)	List-II (Year)
(a) Muslim Women (Protection of Rights on Divorce) Act	I. 2019
(b) The Muslim Personal Law Shariat Application Act	II. 1939
(c) Muslim Women (Protection of Rights on Marriage) Act	III. 1986
(d) The Muslim Marriage Dissolution Act	IV. 1937

Choose the correct answer from the options given below:

	(a)	(b)	(c)	(d)
A.	I	III	II	IV
B.	III	IV	I	II
C.	II	I	IV	III
D.	IV	II	III	I

72. Match List-I with List-II:

List-I (Women)	List-II (Movement)
(a) Sushmita Dey	I. Armed Forces Special Powers Act (AFSPA) Protests
(b) Gaura Devi	II. Chipko Movement
(c) Irom Sharmila	III. Stop Acid Sale
(d) Laxmi Agarwal	IV. Lahu Ka Lagaan (Stop Taxing Sanity Napkins)

Choose the correct answer from the options given below:

	(a)	(b)	(c)	(d)
A.	IV	II	I	III
B.	II	III	IV	I
C.	III	II	I	IV
D.	I	II	III	IV

73. Match List-I with List-II:

List-I (SDG No)	List-II (Goal)
(a) SDG 1	I. Quality Education
(b) SDG 4	II. No poverty
(c) SDG 6	III. Reduced Inequalities
(d) SDG 10	IV. Clean Water and Sanitation

Choose the correct answer from the options given below:

	(a)	(b)	(c)	(d)
A.	I	II	III	IV
B.	II	I	IV	III
C.	IV	III	II	I
D.	III	IV	I	II

74. Match List-I with List-II:

List-I (Gender in different levels of education)	List-II (Percentage)
(a) Women in Higher Education (AISHE 2019-20)	I. 65.46%
(b) Female Literacy (2020)	II. 27.3%
(c) Secondary School Enrollment of Girls (2020)	III. 75.28%
(d) Male Literacy (2020)	IV. 82.14%

Choose the correct answer from the options given below:

	(a)	(b)	(c)	(d)
A.	I	II	III	IV
B.	III	II	IV	I
C.	II	I	III	IV
D.	II	III	IV	I

75. Match List-I with List-II:

List-I (Authors)	List-II (Writings)
(a) Amartya Sen	I. Theory of Justice
(b) John Rawls	II. Development as Freedom
(c) Ronald Dworkins	III. On Liberty
(d) J.S. Mill	IV. Taking Rights Seriously

Choose the correct answer from the options given below:

	(a)	(b)	(c)	(d)
A.	II	I	IV	III
B.	I	II	III	IV
C.	III	II	IV	I
D.	IV	III	II	I

76. Arrange the following chronologically:

(a) World Conference of Human Rights
(b) International Conference on Population & Development
(c) World Conference on Education for All
(d) Third UN World Conference on Women

Choose the correct answer from the options given below:

A. (d), (c), (a) and (b)
B. (a), (c), (b) and (d)
C. (c), (b), (d) and (a)
D. (b), (d), (a) and (c)

77. Arrange the following schemes in chronological order:

(a) Swadhar Greh
(b) Nirbhaya Fund
(c) Beti Bachao Beti Padhao Scheme
(d) Pradhan Mantri Matru Vandana Yojana

Choose the correct answer from the options given below:

A. (a), (b), (c), (d)
B. (d), (c), (b), (a)
C. (a), (d), (b), (c)
D. (c), (d), (a), (b)

78. Arrange the following autonomous organisation under the Ministry of Women and Child Development according to their establishment:

(a) Central Social Welfare Board
(b) National Institute of Public Co-operation and Child Development
(c) Rashtriya Mahila Kosh
(d) Central Adoption Resource Authority

Choose the correct answer from the options given below:

A. (a), (c), (b) and (d)
B. (a), (b), (d) and (c)
C. (c), (d), (a) and (b)
D. (b), (d), (c) and (a)

79. Arrange the changes in abortion laws in India in chronological order:

(a) Medical Termination of Pregnancy Act.
(b) Abortion was criminalized describing it as intentionally caused miscarriage under section 312 IPC.
(c) Unmarried women's access to abortion is recognized.
(d) Increasing the gestational limit to 24 weeks for abortion.

Choose the correct answer from the options given below:

A. (a), (b), (c), (d) B. (c), (d), (b), (a)
C. (b), (a), (d), (c) D. (d), (b), (a), (c)

80. Arrange the following in life cycle approach

(a) Peri Menopause
(b) Menorrhagia
(c) Menustration
(d) Menarche

Choose the correct answer from the options given below :

A. (a), (b), (c), (d) B. (d), (c), (b), (a)
C. (b), (d), (c), (a) D. (d), (a), (b), (c)

81. Arrange the following research steps in right sequence:

(a) Construction of hypothesis
(b) Identification of variables
(c) Codification of data
(d) Referencing

Choose the correct answer from the options given below:

A. (a), (b), (d), (c)
B. (b), (a), (d), (c)
C. (b), (a), (c), (d)
D. (a), (b), (c), (d)

82. Arrange the following chronologically:

(a) Commission of Sati (Prevention) Act.
(b) Protection of Women from Domestic Violence Act.
(c) Pre-Conception and Pre-Natal Diagnostic Techniques (PCPNDT) Act.
(d) The Sexual Harassment of Women at Workplace (Prevention, Prohibition and Redressal) Act.

Choose the correct answer from the options given below:

A. (a), (b), (c), (d) B. (a), (c), (b), (d)
C. (d), (c), (b), (a) D. (a), (b), (d), (c)

83. Arrange the following feminist texts in chronological order:

(a) Chimamanda Ngozi Adichie, 'We Should All Be Feminist'
(b) Betty Friedan, 'The Second Stage'
(c) Mary Wollstonecraft, 'A Vindication of the Rights of Women'
(d) Simone de Beauvoir, 'The Second Sex'

Choose the correct answer from the options given below:

A. (c), (d), (b), (a) B. (a), (b), (c), (d)
C. (d), (c), (b), (a) D. (b), (a), (d), (c)

84. Arrange the progression of women's suffragette rights in India in chronological order :

(a) State of Travancore granted voting rights to women.
(b) Montague Chelmsford Reforms denied voting rights to Indian women
(c) Govt. of India Act made only 2.5% women eligible to vote
(d) Indian Constitution granted equal voting rights to all Indian citizens irrespective of gender, caste, religion and ethnicity

Choose the correct answer from the options given below:

A. (a), (b), (c), (d) B. (c), (a), (b), (d)
C. (a), (c), (b), (d) D. (b), (a), (c), (d)

85. Arrange the following chronologically:

(a) Structural Adjustment Programs (SAP)
(b) Gender and Development (GAD)
(c) Women in Development (WID)
(d) Women and Development (WAD)

Choose the correct answer from the options given below:

A. (a), (c), (d), (b) B. (a), (d), (b), (c)
C. (c), (d), (b), (a) D. (a), (c), (b), (d)

86. Given below are two statements— One is labelled as Assertion (A) and the other is labelled as Reason (R):

Assertion (A): Post-Covid situation witnessed a sudden increase in child marriages all over India.

Reason (R): Uncertainty over life, lack of social security and economic distress were prime causes behind such decisions.

In the right of the above statements, choose the most appropriate answer from the options given below:

A. Both (A) and (R) are correct and (R) is the correct explanation of (A)
B. Both (A) and (R) are correct, but (R) is not the correct explanation of (A)
C. (A) is correct, but (R) is not correct
D. (A) is not correct, but (R) is correct

87. Given below are two statements— One is labelled as Assertion (A) and the other is labelled as Reason (R):

Assertion (A): Domestic violence is often triggered by the perception that a women has failed to fulfill her wifely duties.

Reason (R): These are issues of power and control shaped by gender difference.

In the right of the above statements, choose the most appropriate answer from the options given below :

A. Both (A) and (R) are correct and (R) is the correct explanation of (A)
B. Both (A) and (R) are correct, but (R) is not the correct explanation of (A)
C. (A) is correct, but (R) is not correct
D. (A) is not correct, but (R) is correct

88. Given below are two statements:

Statement I: Survey research, does not require triangulation method at all.

Statement II: Triangulation is widely used in women's studies research.

In the light of the above statements, choose the most appropriate answer from the options given below:

A. Both Statement I and Statement II is correct
B. Both Statement I and Statement II is incorrect
C. Statement I is correct, but Statement II is incorrect
D. Statement I is incorrect, but Statement II is correct

89. Given below are two statements:

Statement I: Post independent India did not witness any incident of Sati (widow immolation).

Statement II: Incident of Sati evokes complex questions of religious identity, communal autonomy, and role of the law and state in a society.

In the light of the above statements, choose the most appropriate answer from the options given below:

A. Both Statement I and Statement II is correct
B. Both Statement I and Statement II is incorrec
C. Statement I is correct, but Statement II is incorrect
D. Statement I is incorrect, but Statement II is correct

90. Given below are two statements:

Statement I: Women regardless of their working status, tend to spend more time caring for thei children than men.

Statement II: Traditional roles of motherhood have remeasured constant.

In the light of the above statements, choose the most appropriate answer from the options given below:

A. Both Statement I and Statement II is correct
B. Both Statement I and Statement II is incorrec
C. Statement I is correct, but Statement II is incorrect
D. Statement I is incorrect, but Statement II is correct

Directions (Qs. No. 91-95): *Read the passage carefully and answer the questions.*

Psychologist Carol Gilligan is best known for he innovative but controversial ideas on the mora development of women. Gilligan emphasized what she called an "Ethics of Care" in women's moral reasoning She placed her approach in direct opposition to Lawrence Kohlberg's theory of moral development, which she claimed was biased against females and emphasized an "ethics of justice". Gilligan argued that men were no morally superior to women. Instead, the reason women scored lower in Kohlberg's stages than men was tha Kohlberg's work discounted the voices of women and girls. She outlined this position in detail in her semina book 'In a Different Voice' which was publised in 1982 Gilligan proposed that women don't stop developing morally at lower levels than men, but that women's mora development simply continues along a different trajectory than the ethics of justice measured by Kohlberg's scale Feminist psychologists are divided over Gilligan's work While some praised it, some have criticized it fo reinforcing traditional notions of femininity that could continue to lock women into care given role.

91. Gilligan found that:

A. Women thought about morality different tha men.

B. Women tended to score at lower stages of moral development than men.
C. Gilligan's approach was similar to Kohlberg's theory.
D. Women use universally applied ethics of justice.

92. In Gilligan's view 'Ethics of Care':

(a) Tend to look at morality through a lens of relationships, compassion and responsibility to others.
(b) Has often been overlooked because of the limited power women have typically held in societies.
(c) Principles must always be applied in the same way.
(d) Morality is not based on abstract principles but on real relationships.

Choose the correct answer from the given below:

A. (a), (b) and (c) only
B. (a), (b) and (d) only
C. (b), (c) and (d) only
D. (a), (c) and (d) only

93. Given below are two statements:

Statement I: The thinking of a boy and a girl participant's response to a dilemma : A man named Harish must choose whether or not to steal medicine he cannot afford to save his wife's life.

Statement II: On the other hand, the girl participant does not believe Harish should take the medicine because it could land him in jail for stealing, leaving his wife alone when she needs him.

In the light of the above statements, choose the most appropriate answer from the options given below:

A. Both Statement I and Statement II is correct
B. Both Statement I and Statement II is incorrect
C. Statement I is correct, but Statement II is incorrect
D. Statement I is incorrect, but Statement II is correct

94. Given below are two statements:

Statement I: Gilligan's view were that women's moral development continues along a different trajectory than the ethics of justice.

Statement II: Feminists argued that Gilligan's work makes women's voices seem homogenous, while denying their nuance and diversity.

In the light of the above statements, choose the most appropriate answer from the options given below:

A. Both Statement I and Statement II is true.
B. Both Statement I and Statement II is false.
C. Statement I is true, but Statement II is false.
D. Statement I is false, but Statement II is true.

95. Gilligan believed that Kohlberg's theory:

A. was inherently biased against women.
B. proposed that women come to prioritize an ethics of justice?
C. men prioritize their sense of self.
D. females largely tend to focus on logic and rules.

Directions (Qs. No. 96-100): *Read the passage carefully and answer the questions.*

The leading Australian sociologist Raewyn Connell identifies four reasons that men might have to support change toward a more gender-equitable society : relational interest, personal well-being, collective interest and principle. Men's relational interest in change comes from their relationships with women and girls as wives, mothers, daughters and friends. Secondly, living in a system of gender inequality not only damages the lives of women and girls, but also degrades the lives of boys and men, *i.e.* it is not in their personal interest to live with inequality. Thirdly, men as a group are likely to benefit from broad social and cultural changes associated with gender equality, through less rigid stereotyping of masculinity, and more freedom to pursue their life goals free of such stereotypes. Finally, some men might support gender equality because it follows from political or ethical principles that are important to them. It is important to recognize that although, in general, women face greater social and economic disadvantages; men too face vulnerabilities because of gender inequality, such as experiencing stress from being regarded, and regarding themselves, as the main breadwinner. Stereotyping continues to place greater emphasis, as well as greater value, on the role of men as leaders in public life, and as breadwinners in the workplace, as opposed to women's role in unpaid home tasks, care giving and community work.

96. Who benefits from Gender equality?

A. Women's gain automatically equate with men's losses
B. Change in gender relations can be seen as a threat to men's identity
C. Men have a lot to lose from pursuing gender equality
D. Gender (in) equality concerns both women and men and has a strong impact on their daily lives

97. According to Connell men support change because:

A. Women are related to them as wives, daughters and sisters.

B. Because men want to save women.

C. System of inequality damages women alone.

D. Men are the main breadwinners.

98. Which of the following is a gender stereotype that men face?

(a) Men are public leaders.

(b) Men are primary child rearer.

(c) Men are principal care giver at home.

(d) Men are principal breadwinners.

Choose the correct answer from the options given below:

A. (a) and (b) only B. (b) and (d) only

C. (c) and (d) only D. (a) and (d) only

99. What is the role of men in gender equality?

(a) Men are essential enabler for gender reform.

(b) Men are afraid that empowering girls will come at the expense of boys.

(c) Changing or altering traditional masculinity should be more widely recognized as an important step towards realizing gender equality.

(d) Men do not face gender stereotyping.

Choose the correct answer from the options given below:

A. (a) and (b) only

B. (a) and (c) only

C. (b) and (d) only

D. (a) and (d) only

100. According to Connell gender inequitable societies:

(a) Damage lives of mothers and daughters.

(b) Damage lives of boys and men.

(c) Do not impact men as they are not vulnerable to inequalities.

(d) Only women are adversely impacted.

Choose the correct answer from the options given below:

A. (a) and (b) only B. (b) and (c) only

C. (a) and (c) only D. (a) and (d) only

ANSWERS

1. (A)

2. (B): Patricia Hill Collins authored the book "Black Feminist Thought: Knowledge, Consciousness, and the Politics of Empowerment." This is a groundbreaking work that explores the ideas and perspectives of African-American women. It makes a significant contribution to feminist theory by highlighting the unique experiences and insights of black women, addressing issues such as race, gender, class, and power.

3. (B): Micro, Small and Medium Enterprises (MSMEs) in India make a substantial contribution in terms of creating productive employment. They play a vital role in the economic development of the country by providing employment opportunities to a large number of people, fostering entrepreneurship, and contributing to exports. This sector helps in inclusive growth of the economy by reaching remote and underdeveloped areas.

4. (B)

5. (B): The United Nations adopted the Convention on the Elimination of All Forms of Discrimination Against Women (CEDAW) in the year 1979. It is an international treaty that aims to eliminate discrimination against women in all areas of life, including education, employment, healthcare, and politics. It has been a pivotal tool in the global fight for gender equality.

6. (C): Bell Hooks has been vocal in condemning racism, classism, and sexism in her analysis of popular culture and consumerism. She has written extensively on how these interlocking systems of oppression affect marginalized groups and has advocated for a more inclusive, equitable, and compassionate society.

7. (B): The Second Wave of Feminism, which took place mainly in the 1960s and 1970s, was the first to strongly advocate for women's control over their bodies. This included the right to birth control, abortion, and freedom from sexual violence. The second wave was instrumental in creating legal and cultural changes that recognized women's bodily autonomy.

8. (A): Section 326 of the Indian Penal Code deals with the act of voluntarily causing grievous hurt by the use of acid. This includes any act that leads to permanent or partial damage or deformity, or seriously hampers the victim's ability to engage in their regular occupation. The law reflects the severity and specific nature of acid attacks.

9. (A): Nancy Hartsock argued for standpoint epistemology, recognizing the relationship between knowledge and power as seen in Marx's work. Hartsock's standpoint theory emphasizes the importance of perspective in understanding social relations, arguing that marginalized groups can provide more complete and critical understandings of society's power structures.

10. **(A):** Turner's syndrome is a genetic condition in which a female is born with only one X chromosome instead of the usual two (XX). This condition can cause various developmental issues and physical abnormalities, including short stature and infertility. It's named after Dr. Henry Turner, who described the condition in the 1930s, and it emphasizes the role of chromosomes in determining physical and biological characteristics.

11. **(C):** Germaine Greer used the phrase "female eunuch" to denote patriarchal castration of women. In her influential book "The Female Eunuch," she argues that women have been repressed and denied their sexuality by a patriarchal society, making them effectively "castrated". She calls for a sexual liberation that allows women to reclaim control and agency over their bodies and desires.

12. **(B):** A survey is not considered a form of qualitative research but is typically associated with quantitative research. Qualitative research seeks to understand human behaviour and the reasons that govern such behaviour, focusing on depth and context. In contrast, surveys often involve collecting numerical data that can be quantified, making them more suitable for quantitative analysis.

13. **(A):** The concept of gender mainstreaming was established as a major global strategy for promoting gender equality in the Beijing Platform for Action from the Fourth United Nations World Conference on Women in Beijing in 1995. Gender mainstreaming involves integrating gender perspectives and considerations into all aspects of policy-making, legislative activity, and program implementation.

14. **(A):** Janani Shishu Suraksha Karyakram (JSSK) was launched on 1st June, 2011, in India. It is an initiative by the government to provide free and cashless services to pregnant women for deliveries in public health institutions. The scheme aims to eliminate out-of-pocket expenses for both pregnant women and sick newborns and includes provisions for free transportation, food, drugs, and diagnostics.

15. **(B):** Gender dysphoria refers to the psychological condition where an individual feels a disconnection or conflict between their assigned biological sex and their experienced gender identity. This can lead to significant distress and discomfort, and often leads those experiencing it to seek medical or therapeutic interventions to align their physical bodies with their gender identity.

16. **(A):** Teresa de Lauretis suggested that gender is the product of various social technologies, such as cinema and the media. She explored how these mediums participate in constructing and disseminating gender roles and norms. Her work Technologies of Gender has contributed to an understanding of how cultural products shape and reinforce societal expectations and perceptions of gender.

17. **(C):** Geetanjali Shree won the International Booker Prize 2022 for the novel "Tomb of Sand." The prestigious award recognizes the best literary work translated into English. Geetanjali Shree's achievement contributes to the growing international recognition of Indian literature, reflecting both cultural diversity and literary excellence.

18. **(A):** In 1973, the Roe vs. Wade judgment in the USA established women's constitutional right to have an abortion before the fetus is viable outside the womb, or before the 24-28 weeks mark. This landmark decision recognized women's autonomy and privacy rights over reproductive decisions and has been a foundational ruling in ongoing debates about reproductive rights and freedoms.

19. **(D):** The Nursing Break applicable to a mother who has returned to her duties after availing maternity leave until the child attains 15 months of age is two breaks during the working hours excluding the regular intervals/rest period. This provision supports breastfeeding mothers in balancing work responsibilities with the needs of their infants, fostering a more supportive and inclusive work environment.

20. **(C):** The Crude Birth Rate (CBR) is defined as the number of births per thousand of the population per year. It's a demographic measure that provides an overview of the rate of natural population growth within a specific area. The CBR can be used to assess trends in fertility and is often used in conjunction with other demographic indicators to analyze the overall population dynamics.

21. **(D):** India signed an agreement with Israel to cooperate in health and medicine and support "Green Healthcare." The collaboration between the two countries aims to enhance medical practices and promote sustainable healthcare solutions. The agreement reflects a broader trend towards international cooperation in healthcare, emphasizing environmental friendly approaches.

22. (D): Uma Chakravarti authored "Gendering Caste." In this work, she explores the complex intersections between caste and gender in the Indian context. By analyzing how caste shapes and influences gender roles and relations, Chakravarti contributes to a deeper understanding of the social dynamics that perpetuate inequality and discrimination.

23. (B): Naila Kabeer defined empowerment in terms of three interrelated concepts: agency, resources, and achievements. In her famous article 'Building livelihood capabilities for women's economic empowerment: an evidence based theory of change', she emphasizes that empowerment is not just about gaining access to resources but also about enhancing individual capacities to make choices, influence decision-making, and achieve desired outcomes. This nuanced understanding of empowerment offers a comprehensive framework for analyzing gender dynamics in various socio-economic contexts.

24. (D): Emi Koyama is the author of the "Transfeminist Manifesto." In this influential work, Koyama outlines the principles of transfeminism, a movement that seeks to integrate transgender rights and feminism. Transfeminism emphasizes the inter-connectedness of gender identities and aims to create more inclusive and intersectional feminist theories and practices.

25. (A): "Feminisation of Labour" refers to the increasing participation of women in all kinds of jobs. This phenomenon is observed globally, where women are entering in the workforce in greater numbers across various sectors. While this can signify progress in gender equality, it also raises concerns about working conditions, wage disparities, and opportunities for advancement, as women often find themselves in less secure and lower-paying positions.

26. (A): John Stuart Mill wrote "The Subjection of Women," a foundational text in feminist philosophy. Published in 1869, the book argues for women's equality and criticizes the legal and social constraints that hinder women's opportunities and freedoms. Mill's advocacy for women's rights and his philosophical arguments laid the groundwork for many subsequent feminist movements.

27. (C): Chain-referral Sampling, also known as snowball sampling, is a method used for populations that are difficult to locate and may have secretiveness about their identity. This method relies on existing study subjects to recruit future subjects from among their acquaintances. It's particularly useful when studying hidden or hard-to-reach populations, where a list of members is not readily available.

28. (B): The hypodermic model, also known as the hypodermic needle theory or magic bullet theory, views the media as powerful and able to inject ideas into an audience who are seen as weak and passive. This model suggests that media messages have a direct and immediate effect on the audience, influencing their thoughts and behaviours without any active engagement or critical thinking on the part of the audience.

29. (C): Marshall McLuhan coined the expression "The medium is the message." This phrase encapsulates his theory that the medium through which a message is conveyed shapes and controls the scale and form of human association and action. In other words, the medium itself, not just the content it carries, plays a crucial role in how the message is perceived and understood.

30. (A): Margaret Benston used the concept of the socialization of "Domestic Labour." She emphasized that domestic labour, such as housework and child-rearing, is often undervalued and unrecognized despite its essential role in supporting the economy. Benston's work highlights the need to understand domestic labour within a broader socio-economic context and to recognize its contribution to societal functioning. Her perspective has informed feminist critiques of labour practices and economic structures.

31. (A): According to the National Family Health Survey-5, the Indian state that recorded the highest adolescent fertility rate is Tripura. Adolescent fertility refers to the number of live births per 1,000 women aged 15 to 19. High adolescent fertility rates are often associated with challenges such as lower educational attainment, health risks to both mother and child, and limited economic opportunities, reflecting a need for comprehensive reproductive health education and services.

32. (A): The Mother and Child Tracking System under the Ministry of Health and Family Welfare is a web-based system designed to ensure the registration and tracking of all pregnant women and newborn babies. By systematically tracking the health of mothers and children, the system aims to improve the delivery of health services, ensure timely interventions, and reduce maternal and infant mortality rates. The platform's data-driven approach supports health workers and policymakers in decision-making.

33. **(A):** The Amma Canteen in Tamil Nadu endorses the Marxist feminist concept of the Socialization of Domestic Work. By providing affordable meals and engaging women in the workforce, the canteen represents an effort to move domestic labour from the private to the public sphere. This approach recognizes domestic work's value and aims to redistribute responsibilities traditionally assigned to women, reflecting broader goals of gender equality and economic empowerment.

34. **(C):** Under the National Legal Service Authority (NALSA) judgment, the Supreme Court of India upheld the right of all persons to self-identify their gender within the framework of the fundamental right to dignity, under Article 21 of the Indian Constitution. This landmark judgment acknowledges the autonomy and dignity of transgender individuals and represents a significant step towards legal recognition and protection of gender diversity in India.

35. **(D):** Fredrick Engels in his book 'The origin of the Family, private property and the state' argued that; private property led to male domination over female sexuality and reproductive power. Engels argued that the emergence of private property created a shift in family structures and gender relations, consolidating patriarchal control. Women's subjugation became essential to ensure the inheritance of property through legitimate heirs, reflecting a profound transformation in social dynamics that continues to influence gender inequalities.

36. **(A):** Goa is the only one Indian state that practices the Uniform Civil Code (UCC). Unlike other states where personal laws based on religious practices govern matters like marriage, divorce, and inheritance, Goa follows a common civil code that applies to all residents, regardless of their religion or community. The UCC in Goa embodies principles of gender equality and secularism, often sparking debates about its potential implementation across the country.

37. **(B):** Khula is the process under which a wife initiates divorce proceedings under Islam. This practice allows a woman to seek a divorce by returning the dower (mahr) or some other compensation to her husband. Khula emphasizes the agency and rights of women within the framework of Islamic law, albeit with conditions and limitations that can vary across different cultures and interpretations.

38. **(A):** Self-Selection Sampling is a non-probability sampling method where participants voluntarily decide to be part of a study. Unlike probability sampling methods, where every member of the population has a known chance of being selected, self-selection sampling does not provide that equal chance. This can lead to bias, as those who choose to participate may have different characteristics or opinions from those who do not, potentially skewing the results.

39. **(A):** Fat positivity is the concept that fat people have the right to love and accept their bodies as they are. This movement challenges societal norms and prejudices that often stigmatize and marginalize individuals based on their body size. Fat positivity seeks to foster a more inclusive and compassionate understanding of body diversity, promoting self-acceptance, health at every size, and a rejection of harmful stereotypes.

40. **(A):** Alison Jaggar is credited with the statement that "Mothering can be extended to any relationship in which one individual nurses and cares for another." This idea emphasizes that mothering is not confined to biological mothers or even to women, but encompasses a broader set of nurturing relationships and caregiving roles. Jaggar's insight contributes to a more complex understanding of mothering, recognizing its emotional, social, and moral dimensions beyond traditional gender roles.

41. **(D):** The major lacunae of the Artificial Reproductive Technology (ART) & Surrogacy Act 2021 are primarily concerning the discriminatory and paternalistic aspects of the legislation. It discriminates against LGBTQI individuals and live-in couples, which reflects a heteronormative bias. There is also a complete ban on commercial surrogacy, limiting the choices for various parties involved. Option (c) about single men and unmarried women being included is incorrect.

42. **(A):** Swarnjayanti Gram Swarozgar Yojana (SGSY) was a scheme aimed at providing self-employment opportunities to rural India. It offered credit-cum-subsidy to beneficiaries and the banks involved in the process, seeking to promote multiple credit

rather than just a one-time credit input. The scheme also emphasized skill development through training courses in technology, marketing, and other vital areas. It did not directly aim at women's empowerment (option d), and hence, the correct answer is options (a), (b), and (c) only.

43. **(A):** In assessing the nutrition of under-five children, variables like weight, height, and age are essential. Weight and height are used to measure growth and identify undernutrition, stunting, or wasting, while age is an essential factor in growth monitoring to understand development according to expected age-related milestones. Activity level is not a primary variable for assessing nutrition in this context, making the correct combination (a), (b), and (c) only.

44. **(A):** Health and wellness centres in India are designed to address common non-communicable diseases that are prevalent among the population. They focus on conditions like hypertension, diabetes, and various types of cancer including breast, oral, and cervical cancers. These centres are not specifically targeted at HIV/AIDS, thus making the correct options (a), (b), and (c) only.

45. **(A):** The initiatives launched for addressing "Mental Health Issues" in India include KIRAN and Manodarpan. KIRAN is a mental health rehabilitation helpline, while Manodarpan focuses on providing psychological support to students, teachers, and families. Sugamya Bharat Abhiyan and UDAN are not related to mental health issues, so the correct options are (a) and (b) only.

46. **(A):** Women's studies as a field has evolved to embrace the study of not only women but all genders. It has multiplied, becoming plural and more comprehensive, reflecting changes in gender studies over time. In some cases, the field has even changed its name to women and gender studies. It is not confined to studies conducted by women (option d), so the correct answer is options (a), (b), (c) only.

47. **(C):** The Indian feminist publication business advances feminist causes and includes academic, fiction, memoirs, and non-fiction writings. It recognizes and supports women's causes, and organizations like Kali for Women, Zubaan, Women Unlimited, Tara Books, Tulika, and Stree are some feminist publishers. The history of feminist publishing is indeed interesting and important, so option (b) is incorrect, and the correct answer is (a), (c), (d) only.

48. **(A):** Rokeya Sakhawat Hossain's "Sultana's Dream" depicts a utopian feminist vision where women ruled and there was technological efficiency. In her created world, women rulers of "Lady Land" defeated the nation's enemies by harnessing the Sun's power. It does not depict the real world, so the correct options are (a), (b), (c) only.

49. **(A):** The Women in Development (WID) approach gained momentum in the 1970s and was designed to address the disparity of economic opportunity for women. It focused on women's economic participation, including education, employment, and empowerment. The approach primarily dealt with economic aspects rather than power relations between men and women (option d), so the correct options are (a), (b), (c) only.

50. **(A):** Simone de Beauvoir's "The Second Sex" is a landmark work in feminist philosophy. In it, she argues that the fundamental source of women's oppression is their historical and social construction as the "other." She turns existentialist thought into a feminist context and defines women as the second sex, regarding them as inferior to men. The book does not assert that women are incapable of choice like men (option d), making the correct options (a), (b), (c) only.

51. **(A):** Kali for women was a start-up feminist publisher in India. Urvashi Butalia and Ritu Menon set up Kali for Women in 1948, arguably the first Indian publishing house dedicated to publishing on and for Women. Kali for Women published Radha Kumar's The History of Doing (1993), The ecofeminist Vandana Shiva's landmark work Staying Alive (1988), and Kumkum Sangari and Sudesh Vaid's landmark work Recasting Women : Essays in Colonial History (1989).

52. **(C):** Reproductive rights encompass the rights to control reproductive functions and make informed decisions about reproductive health. They include the individual's right to plan a family, access to contraception, and access to reproductive health services. Determination of the sex of an unborn child is not considered a reproductive right as it often leads to unethical practices. Therefore, the correct options are (a), (c) and (d).

53. **(A):** The Global Gender Gap Index measures gender inequality across four dimensions: Economic Participation and Opportunity, Educational Attainment, Health and Survival and Political Empowerment. Violence Against Women is a

significant issue but is not one of the variables used to calculate this particular index. The correct options, highlighting key areas of gender disparities, are (a), (b) and (c).

54. (A): The Convention on the Elimination of All Forms of Discrimination against Women (CEDAW) is based on three core principles: Substantive Equality, Non-Discrimination, and State Obligation. These principles collectively seek to promote gender equality and ensure that states take the necessary steps to prevent discrimination. Option (d), Decision-Making, is not one of the core principles of CEDAW, and the correct answer is (A).

55. (D): The Protection of Children from Sexual Offences (POCSO) Act addresses various sexual offences against children. The correct options include complete and partial Penetration, non-penetrative sexual assault, and showing children pornography. Beating a child, although a severe offense, is not specifically addressed by the POCSO Act. Therefore, the correct options are (a), (b) and (d).

56. (B): Successful entrepreneurs often exhibit characteristics like Risk-taking, Team Building, and being Innovative. Autocratic leadership style may not necessarily align with successful entrepreneurship, as it may stifle creativity and collaboration within a team. The correct options, which emphasize traits commonly found in successful entrepreneurs, are (a), (c) and (d).

57. (C): The Gender Empowerment Measure (GEM) is calculated based on variables like Women's Employment, Women's seats in Parliament, and Women's share of household income. It does not include Women's Education as a specific factor. The correct options represent aspects reflecting women's economic and political empowerment and are (a), (b) and (d).

58. (B): Feminist Research aims at conducting research on women, research about women, and research for women. It does not necessarily limit itself to research only by women. This approach focuses on highlighting women's experiences and advocating for gender equality. Therefore, the correct options that reflect the purpose of feminist research are (a), (b) and (d).

59. (B): The Equal Remuneration Act seeks to ensure that women and men are paid equally for doing the same work, and there will be no discrimination against women workers in any condition of service. The act is not limited to women working in the unorganized sector, and it doesn't specifically mandate the employer to maintain a register of workers. Thus, the correct options are (a) and (d).

60. (B): The high maternal mortality rate in India is primarily caused by Anaemia among women, Adolescent pregnancies, and Inadequate Postpartum Care. Institutional delivery, on the other hand, is encouraged to reduce maternal mortality. Therefore, the correct factors contributing to high maternal mortality in India are (a), (c) and (d).

61. (A): The United Nations Development Programme (UNDP) has set 17 Sustainable Development Goals (SDGs). Among the given options, Good Health and Well-being (Goal 3), Quality Education (Goal 4), and Industry, Innovation, and Infrastructure (Goal 9) are three of those SDGs. Social and Cultural Empowerment, though essential, is not specifically mentioned as one of the 17 SDGs. Instead, there are specific goals that address various social, cultural, and economic development aspects.

62. (B): In the post-independence period, institutional initiatives for women's issues include Constitutional provisions and social legislation to protect women's rights and promote their welfare. Women's Political Representation is also a part of the specific institutional initiatives for women in the post-independence era.

63. (A): Alison Jaggar, a well-known feminist philosopher, organized her discussion on women's alienation under the Unified System Theory of Socialist Feminism. She described fragmentation under Motherhood, Sexuality, and Intellectuality. These categories are aligned with socialist feminist perspectives that critically analyze the oppression and marginalization of women in different aspects of society.

64. (A): The correct options are Dakshayani Velayudhan, Begum Aizaz Rasul, and Sucheta Kriplani. They were all members of the Constituent Assembly of India and played significant roles in the drafting of the Indian Constitution. Laxmi Sehgal, although a prominent figure in the Indian National Movement, was not a member of the Constituent Assembly.

65. (C): The 73rd and 74th Constitutional Amendments, which provide for the formation of local self-government institutions, are not applicable in the states of Meghalaya, Mizoram, and Nagaland. These exceptions are made due to the unique tribal governance structures in these states.

66. (D): The correct match for the given theorists and their contributions are: Martha Nussbaum (Capability approach), Judith Butler (Gender Performativity), Maria Mies (Ecofeminism), and Sharmila Rege (Dalit feminist standpoint). These scholars have made significant contributions to their respective fields and theories.

67. (C): The correct match for the given women publishers and their publication houses are: Urvashi Butalia (Zubaan Books), Ritu Menon (Women Unlimited), Gloria Steinem (Ms. Magazine), and Carmen Callil (Vivago Press). These women have been instrumental in publishing feminist works and promoting women's voices.

68. (C): The correct match for the given types of family and bases of classification are: Matrilocal and Patrilocal (On the basis of residence), Matrilineal and Patrilineal (On the basis of ancestry), Patriarchal and Matriarchal (On the basis of authority), Monogamous and Polygamous (On the basis of marriage practice).

69. (C): The correct match for the given concepts and theorists are: Compulsory Heterosexuality (Adrienne Rich), Feminization of Poverty (Diana Pearce), Male Gaze (Laura Mulvey), and Eco-feminism (Francoise d'Eaubonne). Each concept represents a significant feminist idea that has been extensively theorized by the corresponding scholar.

70. (C)

71. (B): The Muslim Women (Protection of Rights on Divorce) Act was enacted in 1986, which aimed to protect the rights of Muslim women who have been divorced by their husbands. The Muslim Personal Law Shariat Application Act came into force in 1937 and is used to govern the personal matters of Muslims in India. The Muslim Women (Protection of Rights on Marriage) Act was implemented in 2019, prohibiting divorce by pronouncing "talaq" three times. Lastly, The Muslim Marriage Dissolution Act pertains to 1939.

72. (A): Sushmita Dey is not widely known for any particular movement, so the best match is the relatively unknown campaign "Lahu Ka Lagaan (Stop Taxing Sanity Napkins)". Gaura Devi was a prominent figure in the Chipko Movement, fighting deforestation. Irom Sharmila protested against the Armed Forces Special Powers Act (AFSPA) and Laxmi Agarwal, an acid attack survivor, is associated with the Stop Acid Sale movement.

73. (B): SDG 1 corresponds to "No poverty," aimed at eradicating extreme poverty for all people everywhere. SDG 4 targets "Quality Education" for all, including lifelong learning opportunities. SDG 6 focuses on "Clean Water and Sanitation" to ensure universal access. Lastly, SDG 10 is about "Reduced Inequalities" within and among countries.

74. (C): The All India Survey on Higher Education (AISHE) for 2019-20 showed that women's participation in higher education was 27.3%. Female Literacy in 2020 was 65.46%. Secondary School Enrollment of Girls in 2020 was 75.28%. Male Literacy in 2020 was at 82.14%.

75. (A): Amartya Sen is the author of "Development as Freedom," which discusses economic development. John Rawls wrote "Theory of Justice," a work on political philosophy. Ronald Dworkins is associated with "Taking Rights Seriously," dealing with legal philosophy. J.S. Mill wrote "On Liberty," a classic on political and social theory.

76. (A): Chronologically, the events are: Third UN World Conference on Women (1985), World Conference on Education for All (1990), World Conference of Human Rights (1993), and International Conference on Population & Development (1994).

77. (A): Swadhar Greh Scheme (2002), followed by Nirbhaya Fund (2013), Beti Bachao Beti Padhao Scheme (2015), and Pradhan Mantri Matru Vandana Yojaya (2016), are the correct chronological orders of these schemes.

78. (B): In chronological order: Central Social Welfare Board (1953), National Institute of Public Cooperation and Child Development (1966), Central Adoption Resource Authority (1990), and Rashtriya Mahila Kosh (1993).

79. (C): The changes in abortion laws in India are: Abortion criminalized under section 312 IPC 1860, followed by the Medical Termination of Pregnancy Act (1971), the recognition of unmarried women's access to abortion (2022), and increasing the gestational limit to 24 weeks for abortion (2021).

80. (B): In terms of life cycle approach: Menarche (the first menstrual cycle), Menstruation (monthly cycle), Menorrhagia (abnormally heavy bleeding), and Peri Menopause (transition to menopause).

81. (C): The correct sequence for research steps begins with the identification of variables, which is necessary to understand the components that will be studied. Following this, a hypothesis is constructed based on these variables. After conducting the research, data is then codified or organized, and finally, referencing is done to provide credit to the sources used. The sequence is therefore (b), (a), (c), (d).

82. (B): Chronologically, the Commission of Sati (Prevention) Act was enacted in 1829, followed by the Pre-Conception and Pre-Natal Diagnostic Techniques (PCPNDT) Act in 1994, the Protection of Women from Domestic Violence Act in 2005, and finally, The Sexual Harassment of Women at Workplace Act in 2013. So, the correct order is (a), (c), (b), (d).

83. (A): The correct chronological order of these feminist texts is Mary Wollstonecraft's "A Vindication of the Rights of Women" in 1792, Simone de Beauvoir's "The Second Sex" in 1949, Betty Friedan's "The Second Stage" in 1981, and Chimamanda Ngozi Adichie's "We Should All Be Feminist" in 2014. The sequence is therefore (c), (d), (b), (a).

84. (D): The correct chronological order of women's suffragette rights in India starts with the Montague Chelmsford Reforms in 1919 that denied voting rights, followed by the State of Travancore granting women voting rights in 1920, then the Govt. of India Act of 1935 that made only a small percentage of women eligible to vote, and finally, the Indian Constitution of 1950 granted equal voting rights to all. The sequence is (b), (a), (c), (d).

85. (C): Chronologically, the development sequence begins with Women in Development (WID) in the 1970s, followed by Women and Development (WAD) in the late 1970s and early 1980s, Gender and Development (GAD) emerging in the 1980s, and finally Structural Adjustment Programs (SAP) in the 1980s and 1990s. The sequence is (c), (d), (b), (a).

86. (A): The post-Covid situation indeed witnessed a sudden increase in child marriages in India, with the reason accurately described as uncertainty over life, lack of social security, and economic distress, leading to such decisions. Hence both Assertion and Reason are correct, and Reason is the correct explanation of Assertion.

87. (A): Domestic violence often is indeed triggered by perceptions that a woman has not fulfilled her perceived roles, and these are deeply rooted in power dynamics and gender difference. Both Assertion and Reason are correct, and Reason is the correct explanation of Assertion.

88. (D): Triangulation is a method used to cross-verify information and ensure its validity. It can be used in various types of research, including women's studies, but saying that survey research does not require it at all is incorrect. So Statement I is incorrect, and Statement II is correct.

89. (D): There have been incidents of Sati in post-independent India, making Statement I incorrect. However, Statement II is correct as the incident of Sati does evoke complex questions regarding religious identity, communal autonomy, and the role of law and state in society.

90. (A): Women, regardless of working status, tend to spend more time caring for their children than men, and traditional roles of motherhood have remained relatively constant, reflecting societal norms and expectations. Both statements are correct, affirming the societal observations around gender roles within families.

91. (A): Carol Gilligan's work focused on the differences between male and female moral reasoning. She argued that women's moral development did not stop at lower levels but rather followed a different trajectory. Unlike Kohlberg's theory, which emphasized an "Ethics of Justice," Gilligan introduced the concept of an "Ethics of Care." This distinction doesn't imply that women are morally inferior or that they scored lower in moral development, but rather that their moral reasoning is distinct, focusing on relationships, compassion, and responsibilities.

92. (B): Gilligan's "Ethics of Care" theory emphasizes the way women tend to approach moral issues. They look at morality through relationships, compassion, and responsibility to others (option a). The limited power women have typically held in societies has often led to this perspective being overlooked (option b). The ethics of care are not based on abstract principles but are rooted in real relationships (option d). These ideas combine to represent Gilligan's unique perspective on the moral development of women.

93. (A): Statement I presents a moral dilemma faced by a character named Harish, and Statement II presents a female participant's response to that dilemma. Together, these statements serve to illustrate the distinct moral reasoning between genders that Gilligan's theory sought to emphasize. Women, according to Gilligan, often approach moral issues through a lens of relationships and personal responsibilities, which is reflected in the girl's concern for the consequences of Harish's actions on his relationship with his wife.

94. **(A):** Both statements are true. Statement I reflects Gilligan's belief that women's moral development is different from men's, following a trajectory focused on care rather than justice. Statement II acknowledges the criticisms made by some feminists, who argued that Gilligan's work makes women's voices seem homogenous and denies their diversity. This illustrates the complex and nuanced reception of Gilligan's work, with both praise and criticism from different quarters.

95. **(A):** Gilligan believed that Kohlberg's theory was inherently biased against women. She argued that the reason women scored lower in Kohlberg's stages was that his work discounted the voices of women and girls. Gilligan's seminal book, "In a Different Voice," outlines her opposition to Kohlberg's approach and presents her theory of an "ethics of care" as a different perspective on women's moral development. Her work emphasizes the uniqueness of women's moral reasoning, rather than an inherent deficiency or difference in prioritization of justice.

96. **(D):** Gender (in)equality concerns both women and men and has a profound impact on their daily lives. According to the passage, gender equality is not a zero-sum game where gains for women equate to losses for men. Rather, the passage emphasizes that gender equality can enhance the lives of both men and women. Men, in particular, stand to gain from a more equitable society through less rigid stereotypes and greater freedom to pursue life goals without gender constraints. Thus, gender equality is framed as a mutually beneficial goal for all members of society.

97. **(A):** According to Connell, men support change toward gender equality for four reasons, one of which is their relational interest. Men's relationships with women and girls, such as wives, mothers, daughters, and friends, foster an interest in supporting gender equality. This connection creates a personal stake in the well-being and equal treatment of women, as opposed to the other options listed, which are not cited in the passage as reasons for men's support for gender equality.

98. **(D):** The passage highlights two primary stereotypes that men face: the emphasis and value placed on their roles as leaders in public life and as breadwinners in the workplace. Options (a) and (d) reflect these stereotypes. Gender roles often pigeonhole men into these specific roles, ignoring other capacities and responsibilities they might have or want to pursue. This stereotyping can constrain men's choices and opportunities, just as it does for women in different ways.

99. **(B):** The passage identifies men as essential enablers for gender reform and emphasizes that changing or altering traditional masculinity should be more widely recognized as a crucial step toward achieving gender equality. Options (a) and (c) encapsulate these ideas. By supporting gender equality for reasons of relational interest, personal well-being, collective interest, and principle, men can play an essential role in transforming society into a more equitable place for all genders.

100. **(A)**

STUDY MATERIAL

UGC-NET/JRF—WOMEN'S STUDIES

(PAPER-II)

Introduction to Women's Studies

- Key Concepts in Gender Studies
- Need, Scope and Challenges of Women's Studies – Women's Studies as an Academic Discipline, Women's Studies to Gender Studies, Need for Gender Sensitization
- Women's Movements – Global and Local: Pre-independence, Post-independence
- National Committees and Commissions for Women

KEY CONCEPTS IN GENDER STUDIES

GENDER STUDIES

An interdisciplinary academic field that analyses the concept of gender, construction of gender in society, gender identity and gender representation. It emerged from women's studies as a profound analysis of gender as a social construct. Critical concepts in gender studies are:

- Exploration of gender and sexuality in literature, sociology, history, psychology, political science, media, cinema, art, law, and science.
- Interaction of gender structure with other power structures such as race, nationality, ethnicity, patriarchy, etc.
- Biological identity and its effect on gender construction and identity in society. The relationship between sex and gender and the changing definition of gender.
- Explores how gender norms and values are created and maintained both internally and externally.
- Investigation of structures that normalize gender values across culture and history.
- Frameworks to eliminate sexism, transphobia, homophobia and gender discrimination.
- Gender socialization of children and parents' reaction to children's gender non-conformity.
- **The Concept of Patriarchy, Matriarchy, and Egalitarian Society**: Patriarchy is a social system with the male as the primary authority, having the central leadership role and control over women and children. It enforces male rule and privilege. Matriarchy has women or mother play the central role in leadership and moral authority. Egalitarianism impresses on equality of roles and social status for all humans.
- **Patrilocality and Matrilocality:** In patrilocality, married couples live with or near the male's family or native place. In societies practicing matrilocality, the married couple will live with or near the female's family. Neolocality is where the married couple chooses to live independent of their parents. These social setups influence gender division of labor and distribution of control in family and society.
- **The Concept of Matriliny and Patriliny**: In a patrilineal descent system, an individual kinship is traced through men and in a matrilineal system through women. In a patrilineal society, inheritance of property and title is through the male head of the family, while in matrilineal societies, control

over property is passed through the female members of the family.

- **The Concept of Masculinity and Femininity**: These two terms delineate appropriate behavior for men and women and influences gender identity, power relationships, and social practices. They define attitudes, roles, behavior norms and typical social values for male and female sex in society. These assigned masculine and feminine attributes help in retaining patriarchal dominance and privilege in society.

NEED, SCOPE AND CHALLENGES OF WOMEN STUDIES

Women Studies

Women as the subject of investigation and study:

- Doesn't benefit just women, but the development and evolution of the entire society, to move forward in the right direction.
- Helps in acquiring an accurate view of history, understanding social power structures and exploring avenues of development.
- An interdisciplinary framework that cross-cuts into sociology, culture, politics, economics, psychology, history, etc.

  The scope of women studies include:
  - ❑ Analysis of social exclusion, racism, casteism, etc.
  - ❑ Women activism–what they are concerned with
  - ❑ Contribution and influence of women in politics, economics, society and vice-versa
  - ❑ Feminist theories and movements
  - ❑ State action, policies, planning and strategies for women empowerment and gender mainstreaming

Gender Equality and Gender Equity

- Has now broadened to include marginalized sections of society such as LGBTQ community, gender non-normative people, people excluded based on their sexual identity and orientation.
- Effects of new movements and changes such as globalization, climate change, environmental degradation, neo-capitalism, etc. on women.
- The emergence of postmodern feminism and its definition of gender, queer feminism, a non-binary definition of gender, etc. have contested the traditional theoretical aspects and objectives of women's studies.

WOMEN'S STUDIES AS AN ACADEMIC DISCIPLINE

Women movements in India before and after independence paved the way for the emergence of Women Studies as an academic discipline. It was initially conceptualized as a branch of social studies and humanities.

- Women's studies in India was initially concerned with supporting women's activism, grassroots movements, understanding the characteristics of women's socio-economic condition and participation.

The Status Report on Women in India published by the 'National Committee on the Status of Women in India' in 1974 was instrumental in giving a more academic orientation to women's studies.

The report titled "Towards Equality," highlighted the distressing status of Indian women in society, their economic depravity, patriarchal discrimination, adverse health parameters such as female infanticide, maternal mortality rate, etc.

It prompted Indian Council of Social Science Research (ICSSR) to set up a research unit in SNDT (Shreemati Nathibai Damodar Thackeray) Women's University, Mumbai to fund women related academic projects in universities.

It was followed by the establishment of the Institute of Social Studies Trust and the Centre for Women Development Studies in 1980.

First National Conference on women's studies was held in 1981 at SNDT University, Mumbai. The conference recognized women studies as not just an academic inquiry into women and theoretical research, but a systematic push to bring positive changes in the status of women in India. Women's studies should aim towards transforming social attitudes, creating awareness, counteracting reactionary forces from media, patriarchy, social institutions and structures. It should concern itself with identifying the deterrents to women's equality and freedom and explore the methods of deconstructing those obstacles.

Indian Association of Women's Studies established in 1982 acted as a forum for institutions, scholars, and academia to interact, collaborate, network to further their research, documentation, and theorization of women and their issues in India.

Anveshi Research Centre for Women's Studies was set up in 1985.

In 1986, the University Grants Commission (UGC) formulated guidelines on women studies, issued to universities. It defined the objectives of women studies, a framework for programmes and financial assistance, etc. In 1986, UGC set up four women studies research centers in universities of Kerala, Punjab, Delhi, and Varanasi. The research centers have given the mandate to incorporate gender perspectives in different disciplines. UGC began supporting women studies research centers in universities across India from 1987. It involved teaching, training, advocacy, research and scholarship support for women's studies.

Women's Studies in India analyses issues of violence, work participation, communal and caste oppression, the interaction of class and gender, etc.

WOMEN'S STUDIES TO GENDER STUDIES

Women's studies centered around feminism, women's issues, women activism, and their problems. It developed as an academic branch out of the second wave of feminism.

Gender studies emerged in the 1980s as new social representative groups and movements such as lesbian feminism, black feminism, LGBTQ movements, etc. Demanded a deeper understanding of gender identity, association and social construction of gender and sexuality. Gender studies addresses gender struggle, gender power structures and offers a broader investigation of gender in literature, society, sociology, politics, etc.

NEED FOR GENDER SENSITIZATION

Patriarchal customs, traditions, social values and beliefs do not encourage open-mindedness towards the other genders. Being sensitive and accommodative towards the needs of the other genders, enables a well-balanced society. Gender sensitization involves cultivating unbiased attitudes and actions towards other genders and reconciliation of differences in perspectives. This requires training and awareness in educational setup, encouraging sensitivity and openness in children by parents, family, and social units, sensitization, and training of social and civil institutions such as police forces, academic institutions towards equal treatment and unbiased gender attitudes, etc.

Sex vs. Gender

Biological differentiation of individual's determinism is known as sex. It is the anatomical and physiological characteristic of being man and woman. Gender is the socially and culturally constructed difference of individuals that leads to society's perception and expectations of roles and responsibilities. It is the behavior pattern associated with masculinity and femininity with preconceived notions.

Sexual Identity: One's gender orientation i.e. heterosexual, homosexual, bisexual, transsexual, etc. Gender theories claim that sexuality is fluid and not a fixed concept, so these categories may be unnecessarily rigid.

Gender Roles: Expectations of social, political and economic roles to be performed differently by men and women through linking these roles to femininity and masculinity. These are the roles which society formulates as appropriate for men and women in a specific culture.

Gender Equality: Eradication of all forms of discrimination on the basis of sex and belief in equal treatment of both the sexes in the matters relating to authority, access, allocation of resource, mobility, etc.

Gender Equity: The practice which supports and justifies the idea of making special provision in the favor of women for their fair and better treatment and for bringing them out of the margins. It fulfills the gender gaps in fair treatment of women. Gender equity also entails that the health-specific needs of both the genders should be addressed with appropriate means and resources.

Gender Awareness: The recognition of the socially constructed differences between men and women and identification of the damaging consequences of the social expectations for specific roles and responsibilities.

Gender Sensitivity: The understanding of the prevailing patriarchal structure and gender issues and also the ability to eradicate gender differences.

Gender Analysis: A tool to identify the gender inequalities in different social, cultural, political and economic realities that affect women's lives, health, and well-being.

Gender Mainstreaming: The strategy that ensures that interests and experiences of both the sexes are integral to the design, execution, supervision, and assessment of all legal measures, policies, and programmes so that both the sexes benefit equally.

Gender Parity: A numerical concept that is concerned with the relative equality about numbers and proportions of women, men, girls, and boys. Gender Parity in Education would mean that equal number of boys and girls receive educational services in diverse forms and at different levels.

Sexual Orientation: One's predisposition and sexual attraction toward others, including the four categories of sexual identity. The American Academy of Pediatrics claims that "sexual orientation probably is not determined by any one factor but by a combination of genetic, hormonal, and environmental influences."

Sex Role Stereotype: Shared and generally reductive gender beliefs about the nature of the sexes. Sex role stereotypes are the substance for many commercials.

Sex Typing: Treating a person differently because of her/his biological sex.

Sexuality: Biological, physiological, psychological and sociological aspects of human existence, involving sexual experience and expression.

Suppression: Being denied opportunity or put down by those in authority.

Hegemony: One group's multiple levels of dominance over another, including the suppressed group's consent to domination; hegemony is less domination by force than a means of encouraging participation in one's own oppression. Cultural hegemony, a term used by Antonio Gramsci, is the use of ordinary practices and shared values as a means by which one group can dominate a diverse culture.

Herstory: Feminist effort to revise "history" so that it includes women and their importance in the shared temporal narrative of events; some feminists find the term frivolous.

Hierarchy: Value system of ordering people's roles as "above" and "superior" in descending order to "below" and "inferior." Hierarchies establish relatively fixed positions within a social system.

Identity Politics: Political action challenging established hierarchies and categorization on behalf of a non-dominant or marginalized group; the politics of resisting oppression.

Patriarchy/Patriarchal: Social organization favoring males on every level; rule by men.

Patrilineal/Patrilocal: Kinship, ancestry, and descent from the father.

Misogyny: Individualistic approach of hatred or dislike of women. It is also a social norm that accepts men's violence over women, discrimination against women in employment, education, politics, etc.

Transgender: People who are not comfortable with their pre-assigned gender by society. Whose identities are different from that of socially accepted gender expectations associated with the biological sex they were born with.

WOMEN'S MOVEMENT : GLOBAL

Women movements in history arose as women became aware of their disadvantaged position in society. Women came together to discuss and understand issues specific to them. This led to the formation of movements and organizations that highlighted the socio-political discrimination of women by the traditional patriarchy and demanded equality, freedom, and rights in social and political spheres.

The French were one of the first to use the term "feminism." A definitive form of feminism arose during the French revolution as a protest against women's exclusion from the revolutionary movement. They demanded equal rights for women. In 1789, the Women's Petition was submitted to the French National Assembly, but it was never discussed. This petition talked about the contribution of women and the inequality of gender roles in society. Olympia de Gouges, a political activist and feminist, wrote on women's rights and their demand for equality. She was one of the first to challenge the male-female inequality in her "Declaration of the Rights of Women and the Female Citizen" (1791). Though the petitions did not succeed in acquiring the political rights of women, they paved the way for the growth of women's rights movement across Europe.

In the US, the women's suffrage movement grew out of a larger women's rights movement that addressed the lack of educational and economic opportunities for women, their demand for equal political rights, etc.The women's suffrage movement has its beginning in 1848 at the Women's rights convention held in Seneca Falls, New York. They wrote petitions, lobbied in the Congress to obtain women's franchise. National American Women Suffrage Association was formed in 1890. NAWSA undertook campaigns to obtain franchise in individual states and also to convince the Congress to pass the Women Suffrage Constitutional Amendment bill. Due to the consistent effort of the different women's rights movements, American women obtained their right to vote in 1920.

FEMINISM

- An ideology and a movement which supports and justifies the idea of equality.
- Advocates for annihilation of all forms of sexual discrimination and aims at establishing equal treatment of men and women in private as well as public spheres.
- Demands equal social, political and economic rights.

Waves of Feminism

The history of the feminist movements is divided into three waves.

The first wave refers to the movement of the 19th through early 20th centuries, which dealt mainly with suffrage, working conditions and educational rights for women and girls.

The second wave (1960s-1980s) dealt with the inequality of laws, as well as cultural inequalities and the role of women in society.

The third wave of feminism (1990s-2000s) is seen as both a continuation of the second wave and a response to the perceived failures.

First-Wave Feminism

First-wave feminism involved a period of feminist activity during the 19th and early 20th centuries, especially in Europe and in the United States.

Key concerns:

- Women's suffrage (the right to vote)
- The right to education
- Better working conditions
- Marriage and property laws
- Reproductive rights

Second-Wave Feminism

Second-wave feminism is a period of feminist activity and thought that first began in the early 1960s in the USA and spread all over the western world and beyond.

Key concerns:

- Raising consciousness about sexism and patriarchy
- Raising awareness about gender-based violence, domestic abuse, and marital rape
- Opposing inequalities in the workplace
- Legalizing abortion and birth control
- The sexual liberation of women

Third-Wave Feminism

The third wave of feminism (1990s-2000s) arose partially as a response to the perceived failures of second-wave feminism.

Key concerns:

- Intersectionality
- Recognition of the diversity of "women" and an emphasis on identity, gender, race, nation, social order, and sexual preference
- Changes in stereotypes, media portrayals and language used to define women
- Sexual identities

Fourth Wave Feminism

Coined to the new emerging phase of feminism that began around 2012-13. Its broad areas of concern include:

- Inclusive justice for all sections of society victimized by the heterosexual white male
- An expansive interpretation of human rights
- Greater diversity of voices and perspectives
- MeToo wave-victims of workplace sexual harassment across various industries and sectors outing their predators on social media platform like Twitter, creating the space to fight the issue.

WOMEN'S MOVEMENT : INDIA

PRE-INDEPENDENCE

- Women's movements before independence concerned themselves with social reforms, the emancipation of women from traditional oppressive cultures such as Sati, child marriage, etc.
- Lack of education over the previous centuries prevented the active participation of women in social change and hence they were merely recipients of liberation. Majority of the social reform leaders were men such as Raja Ram Mohan Roy, Jyotiba Phule, M.G. Ranade, etc.
- However, there were several exceptional women such as Swarnakumari Devi, sister of Rabindranath Tagore, who set the Ladies Theosophical Society in 1882. The National Council of Women in India was founded by Lady Tata in 1925, with the help of Lady Aberdeen.
- The women's leadership for freedom struggle and social reform mainly emerged from the educated urban middle class.
- Mass active participation of women in the Swadeshi movement and subsequent independence struggle revitalized women movements across India. Mahatma Gandhi played a major role in involving women in the freedom struggle. He fought not just for national freedom, but all oppressed sections of the society. Gandhi was against child marriage, religious barriers to widow remarriage, purdah system, and dowry system. He encouraged Indian women to shed their inferiority complex and participate in politics. He motivated women organizations and meetings. Women participated in large masses in his salt satyagraha, boycott campaigns and civil disobedience movement. According to Gandhi, women are an equal companion of men and yet fundamentally different.
- **Sharda Act,** officially called the Child Marriage Restraint Act passed in 1929 fixed the minimum marriage age for girls at 14 years and boys at 18 years. The campaigning and movement to support the legislation saw the involvement of women across

India. It was the first time that women in India played an organized role against a social and political issue. Women organizations such as Indian Women Association, Indian Women's Conference and National Council of Women in India played vital roles in organized meetings and gathered support for the law. The law came in to force in 1920 and applied to the whole of British India and not just Hindus.

- Another political movement that saw the mass mobilization of women was the **Tebhaga Movement** of North Bengal. Due to decades of exploitation of landless peasants by jotidars and middle-men and the Bengal famine of 1943, the social and economic condition of peasants and rural poor worsened. A mass movement of peasants against the exploiters began around 1946 demanding to keep two-thirds (Tebhaga) harvest to themselves. It saw the involvement of peasant women, rural poor women in hundreds and thousands. They set up "Nari Bahini," a semi militia group to support the peasant revolt. They also formed self-help committees to organize protests and meetings.
- But, equality in the political struggle was not reflected in the private sphere. Reforms towards traditional patriarchal system faced stiff resistance such as property rights, inter-caste marriages, etc.
- Thus, women's movements were mainly against colonialism and not patriarchy. Any challenges to the transformation of the patriarchal social system faced opposition and branded as anti-men, breaking traditional family structure and social harmony, etc.

WOMEN LEADERS OF THE FREEDOM STRUGGLE

There were many prominent women leaders of the freedom movement whose contribution influenced not only the independence movement but also inspired feminist and social reform movements in India.

Bhima Bai Holkar (1795-1858)

- Daughter of Ahilya Bai Holkar
- Fought the East India Company when it attacked Holkar in 1817; employed guerilla warfare to attack the British

Annie Besant (1857-1933)

- Supported Indian self-rule
- Started the All India Home Rule League (1916) with Lokmanya Tilak; organized demonstrations and agitations demanding self-government
- Through the Theosophical Society of India, she asserted Indian people's self-worth and right to freedom

Madam Bhikaiji Cama (1861-1936)

- Supported the Indian Home Rule Society founded by Shyamji Krishna Verma in 1905
- In 1907, she unfurled the Indian flag in International Socialist Conference, Stuttgart, Germany
- Exiled to Europe in 1935 for raising her voice for human rights and equality in India

Sarojini Naidu (1879-1949)

- She has been a part of the freedom movement since the Partition of Bengal in 1905
- Traveled and lectured on social welfare, activism and nationalism; inspired women to join the freedom struggle
- Became the first governor of the United Provinces of Agra and Oudh and first Indian woman president of the Indian National Congress
- Imprisoned several times—1930, 1932 and 1942

Dorothy Jinarajadasa (1882-1963)

- Feminist and social reformer
- Founded the Women India Association in 1917 with Margaret Cousins that contributed to social and political struggles in India

Sucheta Kripalani (1908-1974)

- A freedom fighter who worked closely with Mahatma Gandhi and the INC for the freedom of India
- Prominent during Quit India protests and the partition struggle
- A member of the drafting committee of the constitution
- Became the first women Chief Minister of Uttar Pradesh after Independence (1963-1967)

Aruna Asaf Ali (1909-1996)

- Active participant of Salt Satyagraha and one of the leaders of Quit India movement after the pre-emptive arrest of major freedom leaders
- Went underground and edited the Congress' monthly magazine, *Inquilab*
- While in prison for the freedom struggle, she organized strikes against indifferent treatment and poor conditions of prisoners

Durgabai Deshmukh (1909-1981)

- Lawyer, women activist and freedom fighter; participated in the salt satyagraha

- Was a member of Lok Sabha as well as the Planning Commission
- Founded the Andhra Mahila Sabha in 1937
- Helped establish the Central Social Welfare Board for improvement of women and children's education, health and social condition

Usha Mehta (1920-2000)

- Started the Congress Radio, an underground radio station to support the freedom movement that broadcasted freedom speeches by national leaders
- Imprisoned for her clandestine support and activity; refused to answer questions during her trial

Tara Ali Baig (1916-1989)

- Writer and social reformer
- The architect of child welfare schemes of the planning commission and the first Asian Women President of the International Union for Child Welfare in Geneva
- Convener of the Planning Committee group to examine the social and economic disabilities of Indian women

POST-INDEPENDENCE INDIA

Post-independence, Indian women involved themselves in gender-specific issues that affected their lives. Main issues taken up during that period were domestic violence, protests against alcoholism, work, and economic equality, etc.

Telangana Movement (1946-1951)

This political revolt immediately after independence saw mass involvement of peasant and middle-class women of the Telangana region. The revolt was not just against the Nizam seceding from India but also against the feudal exploitation of peasants and rural poor. Women's participation influenced the movement's success. Many women were involved in decision making and leadership roles during the revolt. They evolved collective forms of resistance and fought for better wages. The movement achieved the end of forced labour, end of the forced making of concubines, etc.

Shahada Agitation

In 1972, in Shahada, a tribal district in Maharashtra, a movement originated against the exploitation of landless tribal laborers by the landowners. Over time, with women's involvement, it transformed into a women's liberation movement that took up issues of domestic violence against women, gender violence and alcoholism. The women leaders engaged in mass mobilization, public shaming of wife-beaters and organized protests against male domination.

Anti-Liquor Movement

In the 1990s, women in many parts of India raised their voice against the menace of alcoholism. One of the major centers of the movement was Nellore district of Andhra Pradesh which resulted in the prohibition of liquor in 1993. Women raided liquor stores, stopped local liquor production and conducted dharnas to mobilize support for their cause.

Anti-Price Rise Movement

In the early 1970s, drought and famine conditions in Maharashtra caused price rise and inflation. Women, the most affected by this economic problem formed the United Women's Anti Price Front against inflation. It later widened to include issues like consumer protection, corruption, and black marketing. More than 20,000 women and took part in protests and campaigns. They held mock courts to pass judgment on corrupt officials and politicians. Later, the movement also spread to Gujarat and other affected areas.

SELF EMPLOYED WOMEN'S ASSOCIATION (SEWA)

Ela Bhatt established a first of its kind Self-Employed Women's Association (SEWA) for women workers in the informal sectors. Progressive Organization of women was established in Hyderabad in 1974. It took up issues such as oppressive gender structures in society and the sexual division of labor.

"Towards Equality" report by the 'National Committee on the Status of Women in India', published in 1974 gave a fresh impetus to women's movement in India. Feminists and scholars woke up to the reality of women's adverse position in society.

Many autonomous organizations nation-wide came forward to take up the causes of women. They highlighted the class-gender perspective of women's oppression. Women movements got engaged with addressing socio-cultural conditions, legal provisions and advocacy, political participation, impacting mass media and social attitudes, etc.

In the 1990s, the socio-economic challenges, feminization of poverty, the impact of globalization on women, women's health and increasing violence against women were the major concerns of Indian feminists. Proliferations of cyber-crimes against women, exploitation of technology for gender discrimination are some of the emerging challenges to feminists.

CONTEMPORARY DEBATES

Evolution of a strong LGBTQ community, representatives of the transgender community, intersex movement are some of the new social organizations that complement the feminist movement in its fight against gender normative culture and society. Only in September 2018, homosexuality was decriminalized by law in India. Legal advocacy and support, political and social-activisms have helped highlight the inherent discrimination of other genders and created laws to eliminate gender oppression. But, complete equality and freedom from social castigation remain. The emergence of these movements has contested the Indian feminist's fundamental delineation of gender and the definition of masculinity and femininity. Economic and technological changes and their impact on women and their socio-cultural positions are new challenges that can provide new and dynamic perspectives to feminism and its objectives.

NATIONAL COMMITTEES AND COMMISSIONS FOR WOMEN

MINISTRY FOR WOMEN AND CHILD DEVELOPMENT (MWCD)

- Became a separate Ministry in January 2006
- Since 1985, it was set up as a department under the Ministry of Human Resources Development
- Its main purpose is to address the gap in State action for women and children
- To bring about gender equitable policies and mainstreaming gender concerns
- To offer institutional and legislative support to women and child development
- Responsible for implementing various acts concerned with immoral trafficking of women, indecent representation of women, dowry prohibition, etc.

National Commission for Women (NCW)

- A statutory body set up in January 1992
- It was recommended in the "Towards Equality" report (1974) submitted by the National Committee on the Status of Women in India
- To review constitutional safeguards for women and suggest legislative measures for the safety and protection of women
- It can take suo-moto notice of violence and discrimination against women and ensure speedy delivery of justice
- Sponsors legal awareness strategies regarding women's rights
- Reviews safe jail conditions for women
- In 1995, NCW introduced the concept of Parivarik Mahila Lok Adalats to deal with marriage disputes, family civil cases, divorce settlements etc.

RASHTRIYA MAHILA KOSH

- Established in March 1993
- An autonomous body under the Ministry of Women and Child Development
- Facilitating agency for socio-economic empowerment of women
- Provides loans to NGOs–'Micro Finance Institutions' which then—lend to women Self-Help Groups, especially for women in the unorganized sector

BHARATIYA MAHILA BANK

- Established in November 2013
- To address the banking needs of women
- Accepts deposits by anyone, but predominantly lends to women

CENTRAL SOCIAL WELFARE BOARD

- Established in 1953 to encourage voluntarism and welfare activities by providing technical and financial assistance
- Now functions under the purview of Ministry of Women and Child Development
- Concerns with the general welfare of family, women, and children

MAHATMA GANDHI NATIONAL RURAL EMPLOYMENT GUARANTEE SCHEME

- Launched in 2005
- To ensure livelihood security in rural areas, reduce distress migration which affects women the most
- Guarantees at least a hundred days of minimum wage employment
- Requires 33% participation of women

NATIONAL POLICY FOR WOMEN'S EMPOWERMENT IN INDIA

- Launched in 2001
- To create a positive environment for women to develop their full potential
- Access to women to healthcare, education, career and vocation guidance, employment and social security
- Eliminate discrimination of women in all spheres

NATIONAL HEALTH MISSION

- Launched in 2013 and operates under the Ministry of Health and Family Welfare
- Two subcomponents: National Rural Health Mission (2005) and the National Urban Health Mission (2013)
- Aims to provide universal access to public health services, nutrition, universal immunization, sanitation and hygiene with a particular focus on women and child health
- **Janani Shishu Suraksha Karyakram:** Launched in 2011; free delivery, treatment and medication for pregnant women and newborns; free transport facilities from and to health facilities.
- **Rashtriya Kishor Swasthya Karyakram:** Launched in 2014; for adolescent health with special focus on marginalized groups; promotes sexual and reproductive health, nutrition, mental health, and education

SARVA SHIKSHA ABHIYAN

- Launched in 2001
- To provide universal elementary education–community-owned quality education
- To bridge the social and gender gap in access to education and knowledge

RAJIV GANDHI SCHEME FOR EMPOWERMENT OF ADOLESCENT GIRLS (RGSEAG-SABLA)

- Launched in 2011
- Self-development and empowerment of adolescent girls of 11 to 18 years of age
- To promote awareness about hygiene, sexual and reproductive health, nutrition
- To improve the nutrition and health status of young girls
- Focus on education, life skills, and vocational skills

SUPPORT TO TRAINING AND EMPLOYMENT PROGRAMME FOR WOMEN (STEP)

- Launched in 1986
- To provide training, upgradation of skills and credit access for poor and marginalized women in traditional and informal sectors
- To promote sustainable economic empowerment, entrepreneurship and self-employment of women
- Technical and financial assistance in sectors such as Agriculture, Horticulture, Food Processing, Handlooms.

Multiple Choice Questions

1. Contribution of Women's Studies Centres are:
   A. Incorporation of Women's Studies in various courses of teaching
   B. Creating, Developing and Evaluating Projects
   C. Documentation of Materials and Counselling
   D. All the above

2. Arrange the development phases of Women's Studies Programme:
   A. Improving female education, identifying male-female intellectual capacity, challenging male hegemony and consciousness raising.
   B. Identifying male-female intellectual capacity, challenging male hegemony, consciousness raising and improving female education.
   C. Challenging male hegemony, consciousness raising, improving female education and identifying male-female intellectual capacity.
   D. Consciousness raising, improving female education, identifying male-female intellectual capacity and challenging male hegemony.

3. Arrange the evolution of the following terminologies:
   A. Female Studies, Feminist Studies, Feminology, Women's Studies and Gender Studies.
   B. Feminist Studies, Feminology, Women's Studies, Gender Studies and Female Studies.
   C. Feminology, Women's Studies, Gender Studies, Female Studies and Feminist Studies.
   D. Women's Studies, Gender Studies, Female Studies, Feminist Studies and Feminology.

4. Among the following pairs which is not correct for sexual stereotyping:
   A. Women are shy – Men are strong
   B. Men are courageous – Women are timid
   C. Women are incapable of decision making – Men are Rationale
   D. Women are aggressive – Men are dominant

5. Match the concepts associated with the issues:

Issues	***Concepts***
(a) Undernourishment	(i) Gender Ideology

(b) Role and Status	(ii) Domestic Abuse
(c) Family	(iii) Foeticide
(d) Amniocentesis	(iv) Weight for age

Codes:

	(a)	(b)	(c)	(d)
A.	(i)	(ii)	(iii)	(iv)
B.	(ii)	(iii)	(iv)	(i)
C.	(iii)	(ii)	(i)	(iv)
D.	(iv)	(i)	(ii)	(iii)

6. Name the UGC's Scheme for the establishment of Women's Studies Centres in higher educational institutions.

A. Development of Women's Studies in Indian Universities and Colleges.
B. Developing Women's Studies in Higher Education.
C. Setting up of Women Empowerment Cells in Universities and Colleges.
D. Promoting Women's Studies Researches in Universities.

7. "Gender lens" refers to:

1. Working to make 'gender' visible in social phenomena
2. Creating awareness about gender
3. Providing visibility to gender issues
4. Criticizing the social order on the basis of gender

A. 1 alone B. 2 and 3
C. 3 and 4 D. 1 and 4

8. Match women leaders with the movement they are associated:

Woman Leader	***Movement***
(a) Annie Besant	(i) Green Belt Movement
(b) Kasturba Gandhi	(ii) Swadeshi Movement
(c) Subbamma	(iii) Salt Satyagraha Movement
(d) Wangari Maathai	(iv) Home Rule Movement

Codes:

	(a)	(b)	(c)	(d)
A.	(iii)	(ii)	(i)	(iv)
B.	(iv)	(iii)	(ii)	(i)
C.	(ii)	(iv)	(iii)	(i)
D.	(i)	(iii)	(ii)	(iv)

9. The first Women's Study Centre was set up in:

A. SNDT University
B. Delhi University
C. Jawaharlal Nehru University
D. Banaras Hindu University

10. Patriarchy is defined as:

A. An egalitarian society
B. A consumerist society
C. A male-dominated society
D. A female dominated society

11. The prime aspect of women's studies in every context is:

A. Consciousness Raising
B. Development of Self-perception
C. Unveiling of Women's image
D. Promotion of Self-esteem

12. The basic core of gender studies' approach analysis:

A. Men in reference to women
B. Women in reference to men
C. Women in reference to society
D. Men in reference to culture

13. Women as an entity and their social existence is understood as having:

A. Social Group B. Sex Category
C. Identity Crisis D. Gender Bias

14. Which of the following concept refers to the process of how individuals learn to become feminine or masculine in their identities, appearance, values, and behavior?

A. Acculturation
B. Enculturation
C. Socialization
D. Inculcation

15. Match the following sex role researches and the respective perspectives:

Research	***Perspective***
(a) Study on Sex differences	(i) Power perspective
(b) Study on sex roles and the norms governing them	(ii) Minority perspective
(c) Study of women as a minority group	(iii) Role perspective
(d) Study of women in reference to politics of caste/class	(iv) Sex perspective

Codes:

	(a)	(b)	(c)	(d)
A.	(i)	(ii)	(iii)	(iv)
B.	(ii)	(iii)	(iv)	(i)
C.	(iii)	(iv)	(i)	(ii)
D.	(iv)	(iii)	(ii)	(i)

16. Match the sexist problems and the following methodology:

Sexist Problem		*Methodology*
(a) Androcentricity	(i)	Making one sex applicable to both sexes
(b) Overgeneralization	(ii)	Male view of the world
(c) Gender Insensitivity	(iii)	Viewing differently the identical behaviour of traits
(d) Double Standards	(iv)	Ignoring sex as a variable

Codes:

	(a)	(b)	(c)	(d)
A.	(iv)	(iii)	(ii)	(i)
B.	(ii)	(i)	(iv)	(iii)
C.	(i)	(iii)	(iv)	(ii)
D.	(iii)	(iv)	(i)	(ii)

17. Which of the following concepts refers to a set of beliefs that the oppression and discrimination of a demographic category of women is based on their sex?

A. Sexism B. Feminism
C. Pluralism D. Interactionism

18. Nynee Koch was the first person to coin the term:

A. Women's studies B. Gender studies
C. Feminology D. Feminist studies

19. Which is not a visible indicator of gender discrimination?

A. Differential sex ratio
B. Female literacy
C. Labour force participation
D. Housing and Sanitation

20. Gender Insensitivity means:

A. Female perspective
B. Ignoring gender as a variable
C. Male perspective
D. Application of both sexes

21. Establishing Centre for Women's Studies has been the initiative of:

A. University Grants Commission
B. Ministry of Women and Child Development
C. Indian Council for Social Research
D. National Commission for Women

22. Biological determinism means:

A. Gender division of labour
B. Associating men and women capabilities to biology
C. Perception of Gender as sex
D. Assuming masculinity and femininity based on Biology

23. Which were the conditions for the onset of women's movement in India?

(i) Widespread oppression of women
(ii) Unequal access to basic needs of life
(iii) Feminization of poverty
(iv) Fundamental rights

Codes:

A. (iii) and (iv) only are correct
B. (i), (ii) and (iii) are correct
C. (i), (ii) and (iv) are correct
D. (i) and (ii) are correct

24. Who used the word 'Gender' first?

A. Simone de Beauvoir
B. Ann Oakley
C. Kate Millet
D. Mary Wollstonecraft

25. Match List-I with List-II:

List-I	*List-II*
(a) Sycophancy	(i) Knowledge
(b) Ethnology	(ii) Flattery
(c) Hedonism	(iii) Race
(d) Epistemology	(iv) Pleasure seeking

Codes:

	(a)	(b)	(c)	(d)
A.	(ii)	(iii)	(iv)	(i)
B.	(iii)	(iv)	(ii)	(i)
C.	(i)	(ii)	(iii)	(iv)
D.	(iv)	(iii)	(ii)	(i)

26. Match List-I with List-II:

List-I	*List-II*
(a) Autocracy	(i) Rulelessness
(b) Activism	(ii) Words
(c) Etymology	(iii) Social change
(d) Anarchy	(iv) Dictatorship

Codes:

	(a)	(b)	(c)	(d)
A.	(iv)	(iii)	(ii)	(i)
B.	(iii)	(ii)	(iv)	(i)
C.	(i)	(ii)	(iii)	(iv)
D.	(ii)	(iii)	(i)	(iv)

27. Gender Roles:

A. Are result of differences in biological aptitude.
B. Are roles ascribed by men and women.
C. Roles assigned by the society to each sex.
D. Roles assigned by society to men.

28. Which one of the given issues is not raised by the women's organizations in the post-independence period?

A. Lack of maternity benefit.
B. Lack of childcare provisions.
C. Wage discrimination between men and women.
D. Replacement of male workers with female workers.

29. Among the following pair which is correctly matched?

A. Sarala Devi Chaudhuri – Founder of Bharat Stree Mahamandal
B. Kamala Devi Chattopadhyay – Founder of Indian Association for Women's Studies
C. Vina Mazumdar – Founder of Women India Association
D. Sarojini Naidu – Founder of National Council for Women

30. Match the items from List-I and List-II:

List-I	***List-II***
(a) Patriarchal	(i) Property devolves from mother to daughter as well as family line runs the same way.
(b) Matriarchal	(ii) Power rests with the eldest female in the family.
(c) Patrilineal	(iii) Power rests with the eldest male in the family.
(d) Matrilineal	(iv) Property devolves from father to son as well as family (name line) runs the same way.

Codes:

	(a)	(b)	(c)	(d)
A.	(iii)	(ii)	(iv)	(i)
B.	(ii)	(iii)	(i)	(iv)
C.	(iv)	(i)	(ii)	(iii)
D.	(i)	(ii)	(iii)	(iv)

31. Sexism is most prevalent in __________ societies.

A. Patriarchal B. Matriarchal
C. Ethnocentric D. Egalitarian

32. The protagonists of the Reformist movement on women's issues in India were:

A. Ishwara Chandra Vidyasagar and Raja Ram Mohan Roy
B. Jawaharlal Nehru and Sri Aurobindo
C. Raja Ram Mohan Roy and Mohandas Karamchand Gandhi
D. Mohandas Karamchand Gandhi and Vijaylaxmi Pandit

33. Sex is a/an _____ because a person is born with it; Gender is a/an _____ because it has to be learned.

A. Achieved; ascribed B. Ascribed; achieved
C. Master; achieved D. achieved; master

34. Which are the four pioneering centres of Women's Studies in Indian Universities which survived throughout?

A. Delhi, Punjab, Ranchi, Banaras
B. NEHU, Punjab, Delhi, Surat
C. Punjab, Kerala, Banaras, Delhi
D. Ranchi, NEHU, Delhi, Punjab

35. Match the List-I (Concepts) and List-II (Explanations):

List-I	***List-II***
(a) Gender role stereotypes	(i) Beliefs about the differences between men and women
(b) Gender role traits	(ii) Personality characteristics in the masculine and feminine domains
(c) Gender identity	(iii) One's cognitive representation of gender
(d) Gender schema	(iv) One's sense of one-self as a man or a woman

Codes:

	(a)	(b)	(c)	(d)
A.	(i)	(ii)	(iii)	(iv)
B.	(iv)	(ii)	(iii)	(i)
C.	(i)	(ii)	(iv)	(iii)
D.	(ii)	(iii)	(i)	(iv)

36. Who are the Founder Directors of the following UGC Women's Studies Centres in India? Match the List-I with List II:

List-I	***List-II***
(a) Pam Rajput	(i) Kerala University
(b) Bharati Ray	(ii) Delhi University
(c) Susheela Kaushik	(iii) Punjab University
(d) K.B.K. Nair	(iv) Calcutta University

Codes:

	(a)	(b)	(c)	(d)
A.	(i)	(ii)	(iii)	(iv)
B.	(iii)	(iv)	(ii)	(i)
C.	(ii)	(iv)	(iii)	(i)
D.	(iv)	(iii)	(i)	(ii)

37. Which of the following statements is correct about Women's Studies as an academic discipline?

A. It applies the existing social science research methodology for further research.
B. It accepts the existing theories for analysis.
C. It studies the social reality from a feminist perspective, placing women's experiences at the centre.
D. It covers all studies conducted on women's issues and their solutions.

38. The need for Women's Studies was realized when concerned women and men noticed:
A. the presence of women in the higher education curriculum.
B. the ways in which women were systematically excluded from many positions of power and authority.
C. the way masculinity and femineity interacted with each other and came closer.
D. the way history courses taught only about women as leaders in wars.

39. Women Studies:
(i) Questions the traditional notion regarding men as "humans" and women as "others."
(ii) Questions and challenges Androcentrism
(iii) Explores our gendered existence
(iv) As a body of knowledge examines the status of women in society

Codes:
A. (i), (ii) and (iii) only
B. (i), (iii) and (iv) only
C. (ii), (iii) and (iv) only
D. (i), (ii), (iii) and (iv)

40. Which of the following is not a manifestation of patriarchy?
A. Lack of inheritance rights for women
B. Sexual harassment of women at the workplace
C. Wife beating
D. Women and men working together in a healthy environment

41. Who made the following statement: "Patriarchy is a system of social structures and practices in which men dominate, oppress and exploit women"?
A. Kamla Bhasin B. Gerda Lerner
C. Sylvia Walby D. Heidi Hartmann

42. The values of patriarchy are all pervasive due to the process of:
A. Subordination B. Sanskritization
C. Socialization D. Liberalization

43. The idea of the gender-sensitive lens first came from which feminist theorist?
A. Tickner
B. Peterson and Runyan
C. Enloe
D. None of the above options is correct.

44. Linguist sexism is a problem studied primarily by analysts using _______ perspective.
A. Feminist B. Integrationist
C. Functionalist D. Conflict

45. Mark the correct statement about gender inequality:
(a) Gender form of inequality is more severe than caste form of inequality.
(b) Gender inequality is like class inequality.
(c) Gender inequality is the creation of caste society only.
(d) Gender inequality is not observed in an open society.

Codes:
A. (a), (b), (c) and (d) B. (b) and (c) only
C. (a) only D. (a), (b) and (c) only

46. What is correct about women's studies?
(a) Few men take interest in women's studies.
(b) Women's studies is a social science.
(c) Women's studies focuses only on the issues of underprivileged women.
(d) Women's studies as a discipline is only the creation of some activists.

Codes:
A. (a), (b), (c) and (d) B. (b), (c) and (d) only
C. (a) and (b) only D. (b) and (d) only

47. "Neolocality" is:
A. A social system with the male as the primary authority.
B. Where the married couple chooses to live independent of their parents.
C. Where the married couple will live with or near the female's family.
D. Removal of caste hierarchy from society.

48. Gender as an area of research, teaching, and action has emerged only after:
A. 1860 B. 1910
C. 1947 D. 1975

49. Which is not related to women's studies?
A. Gender equity
B. Consciousness-raising
C. Interdisciplinary study of women
D. Subjugation of men

50. First National Conference on Women's Studies was held in:
A. Delhi B. Bombay
C. Chennai D. Bangalore

51. Among the following statements which is not an objective of Gender Sensitization Programme?
A. Promoting societal awareness of gender issues
B. Review of curriculum and educational materials to remove gender bias
C. Removal of all derogatory, references to the dignity of women
D. Removal of caste hierarchy from society.

52. Masculinity is not synonymous with:
A. Strength B. Power
C. Aggression D. Emotions

53. Match the following concepts and their meanings:

List-I	***List-II***
(a) Patriarchy	(i) Women's Control over the choices in their lives
(b) Empowerment	(ii) Control all Societal Institutions
(c) Gynocentric	(iii) Integration of Masculine and Feminine traits
(d) Androgyny	(iv) Female Perspective

Codes:

	(a)	(b)	(c)	(d)
A.	(ii)	(i)	(iv)	(iii)
B.	(ii)	(i)	(iii)	(iv)
C.	(ii)	(iii)	(iv)	(i)
D.	(i)	(ii)	(iii)	(iv)

54. Women's studies aims at providing:
(i) World view rooted in gender equality
(ii) Critical insight into the patriarchal structures of society
(iii) An exclusive study of women by women
(iv) Re-evaluates current modes of knowledge construction

Codes:
A. (i), (ii) and (iii) are correct
B. (i), (ii) and (iv) are correct
C. (i) and (ii) are correct
D. (ii) and (iii) are correct

55. Which of the following statement is not an ideology of Women's Studies?
A. The academic arm of the women's movement
B. An Intellectual agent to change women from an object of knowledge into subject
C. Deconstruct dominant ideologies that oppress women
D. Promote androcentric title of the various disciplines

56. UGC gave the first Guidelines on Women's Studies in the year:
A. 1986 B. 1993
C. 1995 D. 1997

57. The discipline of Women's Studies came into being due to:
A. Sexual oppression of women
B. Women's role in the freedom movement
C. Women's search for equality and justice
D. Women's entry into higher education

58. Gender identity refers to:
A. Activities carried out by women and men
B. The role of women and men
C. Behaviour and Attitude of female and male
D. An individual sees her/himself as female or male

59. Gender refers to:
A. Social classification of masculine and feminine
B. Biological maleness and femaleness
C. Natural phenomenon of sex
D. Ideological classification of male and female

60. Women's studies as an academic discipline was developed first in:
A. USA B. France
C. India D. Pakistan

61. Match the concepts with the respective perspectives:

List-I	***List-II***
(a) Androcentrism	(i) Disparity between the experience of women and men
(b) Dichotomy	(ii) Polarised distinction is made between two entities
(c) Gender insensitivity	(iii) Doctrine of male centredness
(d) Double standard	(iv) Ignoring sex as a variable

Codes:

	(a)	(b)	(c)	(d)
A.	(iv)	(ii)	(i)	(iii)
B.	(iii)	(ii)	(iv)	(i)
C.	(iv)	(ii)	(iii)	(i)
D.	(ii)	(iii)	(iv)	(i)

62. Hunting and gathering societies were:
A. Dominant B. Egalitarian
C. Submissive D. Pluralistic

63. Among the following women nationalists who was closely associated with Quit India Movement?
A. Aruna Asaf Ali
B. Annie Besant
C. Durgabai Deshmukh
D. Vijaya Lakshmi Pandit

64. Women's Studies is considered as the academic arm of ______ movement.
A. Chipko B. Independence
C. Dalit D. Feminist

65. In Women's Studies, women are considered as:
A. Objects B. Subjects
C. Feminist D. Product

66. The term 'private sphere' in Women's Studies refers to:

I. Work related to child care
II. Work related to old age care
III. Work related to domestic activities
IV. Work related to private firms

Codes:

A. I and II only B. I only
C. I, II and III only D. I and IV only

67. Gender role socialization is aimed at:

A. Teaching girls to remain passive
B. Teaching girls to be aggressive
C. Teaching boys and girls to be active participants
D. Teaching boys to remain passive

68. Which of the following statements is more appropriate soon after independence?

A. Women's movement gained momentum.
B. Active women's movement was considered a necessity.
C. Economic development spread evenly among all social classes.
D. Women felt no need for active struggle because of various laws supporting women.

69. Among the following pairs, which is **not** correct for sexual stereotyping?

A. Women are shy – Men are strong
B. Women are timid – Men are courageous
C. Women are emotional – Men are rationale
D. Women are powerful – Men are affectionate

70. Match List-I with List-II:

List-I	***List-II***
(a) Essentialism	(i) An orientation that characterizes the thinking of a group or nation
(b) Hegemony	(ii) Ability to keep in existence or maintain
(c) Ideology	(iii) A world view that assumes the difference between males and females are rooted in their nature
(d) Sustainability	(iv) Domination of a State over its allies

Codes:

	(a)	(b)	(c)	(d)
A.	(iii)	(iv)	(i)	(ii)
B.	(ii)	(iii)	(iv)	(i)
C.	(i)	(ii)	(iii)	(iv)
D.	(i)	(ii)	(iv)	(iii)

71. Masculinity studies include the following:

(i) Critical studies on Biology.
(ii) Critical studies on men in society.
(iii) Critical studies on female wrestlers.
(iv) Critical studies on female infanticide.

Codes:

A. (i) and (ii) are correct
B. (ii) and (iii) are correct
C. (i) and (iv) are correct
D. only (iv) is correct

72. Institutional initiatives for women's issues in the post-independence period are:

(i) Constitutional provisions and social legislations
(ii) The Brahmo Samaj
(iii) Indian Association for Women's Studies
(iv) The Women's India Association

Codes:

A. (i) and (iii) only B. (i), (ii) and (iii) only
C. (ii) and (iii) only D. (i), (ii) and (iv) only

73. The first Research Centre for women was established in 1974 by:

A. SNDT Women's University
B. ICSSR
C. Centre for Women's Development Studies
D. UGC

74. Women's studies researchers viewed women as:

A. Objects and consumers
B. Subjects and producers
C. Objects and producers
D. Subjects and consumers

75. Masculinities and femininities are:

(i) Gendered rather than non-gendered.
(ii) Socially constructed rather than naturally.
(iii) Changing across time and space.
(iv) Based on biological determinism.

Codes:

A. (i) only correct
B. (iv) only correct
C. (i), (ii) and (iii) are correct
D. (i) and (ii) are correct

76. Women's studies finds its relevance in the ways:

(i) To uncover the gender discrimination prevailing in society.
(ii) To mobilize women's attitude for the betterment of their living.
(iii) To provide better jobs for women.
(iv) To activate the women on social and economic issues.

Codes:

A. (i) and (ii) only
B. (i), (ii) and (iii) only
C. (ii) and (iv) only
D. (i), (ii) and (iv) only

77. Which is the most prominent agent of gender construction?
A. Religion B. Family
C. Caste D. Class

78. The term 'Misogyny' denotes:
A. Hatred of Women
B. Hatred of Men
C. Hatred of Human
D. Hatred of Marriage

79. Who led the suffrage movement for women in India?
A. Ushaben Mehta B. Radha Kumar
C. Sucheta Kriplani D. Sarojini Naidu

80. Among the following women who was not associated with 'Women's India Association', formed in 1917?
A. Annie Besant
B. Dorothy Jinarjadasa
C. Margaret Cousin
D. Sarojini Naidu

81. The main organizing tool of women's liberation movement is:
A. Consciousness-raising
B. Skill training
C. Equality in education
D. Identifying the potentiality of women

82. Which of the following statements is correct about Women's Studies as an academic discipline?
A. It studies the social reality from feminist perspective, placing women's experiences at the centre.
B. It accepts the existing theories for analysis.
C. It covers all studies conducted on women's issues and their solutions.
D. It applies the existing social science research methodology for further research.

83. Among the following which statement is not associated with 'Androcentrism'?
A. Male Behaviour and Characteristics are Central and are the norm.
B. Competitiveness and aggressiveness are highly valued.
C. Characteristics associated with men and women are valued.
D. Characteristics associated with men and maleness are valued.

84. The term 'Clientelism' denotes:
A. The transformation of grassroots women as mere beneficiaries of services.
B. The transformation of women as active participants.
C. The transformation of women as non-beneficiaries of services.
D. The elimination of women from the public world.

85. Chronologically arrange the following foci of campaigns in feminist movements in India:
(i) Fulfillment of basic needs
(ii) Demand for Fundamental Rights
(iii) Identity and Social inclusion
(iv) Demand for parity/equality

Codes:

A. (i), (iii), (ii), (iv) B (i), (ii), (iii), (iv)
C. (iii), (ii), (i), (iv) D. (i), (ii), (iv), (iii)

86. Which of the following statements regarding gender-based inequality is incorrect?
A. All women are organized for an equitable share of development in society.
B. All women are not equally unequal in their families.
C. Women are attached to a twofold social inequality, i.e. in relation to men and in relation to women.
D. Women do not constitute a homogenous unit.

87. Which is an incorrect statement regarding 'Masculinities' and 'Femininities'?
A. Based on Biological determinism
B. Changing across time and space
C. Socially constructed
D. Gendered rather than non-gendered

88. Which of the following pair is correctly matched?
A. Tara Ali Baig – Khilafat Movement
B. Aruna Asaf Ali – Quit India Movement
C. Madhuri Shah – Anti Arrack Movement
D. Mother Teresa – Swadeshi Movement

89. The Emergence of Women's Studies as an Academic Discipline is the result of:
A. First Wave Feminism
B. Second Wave Feminism
C. Third Wave Feminism
D. Fourth Wave Feminism

90. Which policy has initiated centre for women's studies in India?
A. National Policy on Women Empowerment (2001)
B. National Policy on Education (1986)
C. National Policy on Population (2010)
D. National Policy on Poverty Elimination (2009)

91. Movement of feminism leading to acceptance of 'Women's Studies' as a discipline in the academic world was profoundly a:

A. Political Action B. Social Action
C. Feminist Action D. Economic Action

92. Which one of the following statements best explains the arguments of the feminist movement?

(i) Women live longer than men.
(ii) Gender Inequality is rooted in patriarchy.
(iii) Only men are responsible for gender inequality.
(iv) Participatory parenthood promotes gender equality.

Codes:

A. (i), (ii), (iii) B. (i), (iii), (iv)
C. (ii), (iv) D. (ii), (iii), (iv)

93. What is correct about the role of family for gender relations?

(i) It determines the participation of men and women in all social institutions.
(ii) It links production with reproduction.
(iii) It links the domestic domain with public domain.
(iv) It links the microeconomic units with the larger economy.

Codes:

A. (i), (ii) and (iii) only
B. (i), (iii) and (iv) only
C. (i), (ii), (iii) and (iv) only
D. (i) and (iv) only

94. Annie Besant was **not** associated with:

A. Home Rule League
B. Indian Association for women's studies
C. Women's India Association
D. Theosophical Society

95. What is responsible for the alienation of women?

A. Joint family system
B. Agrarian economy
C. Women themselves
D. Patriarchy

96. Mark the correct answer about women studies:

(i) It is a scientific study of women's issue
(ii) It is a collection of narratives of women
(iii) It is the mother of all sciences
(iv) It is a pure science

Codes:

A. (i), (ii), (iii) and (iv) B. (i) and (iv) only
C. (iii) and (iv) only D. (i) only

97. The discipline of women's studies came into being due to:

A. Sexual oppression of women
B. Women's role in the freedom movement
C. Women's search for equality and Justice
D. Women's entry into employment

98. Match List-I with List-II:

***List-I* (Perspectives)**	***List-II* (Concepts)**
(a) Do not reinforce existing gender inequalities	(i) Gender Sensitive
(b) Promote gender equality and achieving positive development outcomes	(ii) Gender Neutral
(c) Attempt to redress existing gender inequalities	(iii) Gender Transformative
(d) The degree of integration of gender perspectives as central to achieve positive development Outcomes	(iv) Gender Positive

Codes:

	(a)	(b)	(c)	(d)
A.	(i)	(ii)	(iii)	(iv)
B.	(iv)	(iii)	(ii)	(i)
C.	(iii)	(ii)	(iv)	(i)
D.	(ii)	(iii)	(i)	(iv)

99. How does women's studies affect students as individuals?

(a) Students get the scientific knowledge about the power relations between men and women.
(b) Students get appraised of the feminist perspective of social issues.
(c) Women's studies courses are structured to encourage students to speak.
(d) Women's studies creates a link between voice, empowerment, self- esteem and critical thinking.

Codes:

A. (a) and (b) only
B. (c) and (d) only
C. (b), (c) and (d) only
D. (a), (b), (c) and (d)

100. Match List-I with List-II :

***List-I* (Concepts)**	***List-II* (Meaning)**
(a) Gender Segregation	(i) Individual's beliefs and actions that are rooted in anti-female prejudice and stereotype beliefs.

(b) Individual Sexism	(ii) The process of learning social expectations and attitudes associated with one's sex.
(c) Gender socialization	(iii) Set of rules, both overt and implied, that discriminate against women and afford better opportunities to men at work.
(d) Institutional sexism	(iv) Physical, Legal and Cultural separation of people according to their biological sex.

Codes :

	(a)	(b)	(c)	(d)
A.	(iv)	(i)	(ii)	(iii)
B.	(i)	(ii)	(iii)	(iv)
C.	(ii)	(iii)	(iv)	(i)
D.	(iii)	(iv)	(ii)	(i)

101. The concept of 'gaze' deals with:

(a) How men look at women
(b) How women look at themselves
(c) How women look at other woman
(d) How women look at society

Codes:

A. (a) and (d) only
B. (a), (b) and (d) only
C. (a), (b) and (c) only
D. (a) and (c) only

102. Gender roles refer to:

(a) Chromosomal differences that cause inevitable differences in the behavior of men and women.
(b) Hormonal differences that cause an inevitable difference in the behavior of women.
(c) The rights, responsibilities, expectation, and relationships of women and men.
(d) Subordination of women based on the assumption of the superiority of men.

Codes :

A. (a) and (b) only B. (b) and (d) only
C. (c) only D. (d) only

103. Match List-I with List-II :

List-I	***List-II***
(a) Misogyny	(i) Involving the treatment of the sexes socially and biologically discrete groups instead of treating them as overlapping Characteristics
(b) Androcentricity	(ii) Hatred or dislike of women or girls
(c) Androgyny	(iii) View of the world from a male perspective
(d) Sexual Dichotomism	(iv) The combination of masculine and feminine characteristics

Codes :

	(a)	(b)	(c)	(d)
A.	(i)	(ii)	(iii)	(iv)
B.	(ii)	(iii)	(iv)	(i)
C.	(iii)	(i)	(ii)	(iv)
D.	(iv)	(ii)	(iii)	(i)

104. Transvestism requires a change of:

A. sexual orientation
B. gender identity
C. clothes of the opposite sex
D. anatomy

105. Which of the following variables is the most critical for those who focus on gender oppression theory?

A. Power B. Money
C. Mothering D. Culture

106. Women's Studies is a discipline that advocates:

A. Women's superiority over men
B. Preservation of cultural identity
C. Suppression of the male voice
D An egalitarian human society

107. What is responsible for the current discriminatory pattern of gender relations in society?

A. Female Foeticide
B. Neglect of the female child
C. Dowry Deaths
D. Patriarchy

108. Androgynous persons show ________ traits.

A. Positive masculine and feminine
B. Negative masculine
C. Positive feminine
D. Positive masculine

109. Mark the correct answer about Women's Studies from the following:

(i) It is the narratives of women by women.
(ii) It is a Social Science.
(iii) It is a collection of Studies on Women issues.
(iv) It is an academic discipline.

Codes:

A. (iii) and (iv) only B. (ii) and (iii) only
C. (iv) only D. (ii) and (iv) only

110. Which of the following pair is correctly matched?
A. Tara Ali Baig — Khilafat Movement
B. Aruna Asaf Ali — Quit India Movement
C. Madhuri Shah — Narmada Movement
D. Mother Teresa — Swadeshi Movement

111. The main concern of women's movement in the post-1970's is:
A. Issues of Race
B. Issues of Reproductive Right
C. Issues of Violence
D. Issues of Property Right

112. Who led the suffrage movement for women in India?
A. Ushaben Mehta
B. Sarojini Naidu
C. Sarojini Vardappan
D. Sucheta Kriplani

113. Which of the following statements is not an objective of Gender sensitization programme?
A. Promoting awareness of gender issues
B. Promoting female domination in society
C. Review of curriculum to remove gender bias
D. Promoting equality in society

114. Social reform movements of the nineteenth century were criticized by women activists, because:
A. It aimed to improve the status of women in the family not in the society.
B. It aimed to improve the status of grass root level women.
C. Women's equality was the major agenda.
D. It aimed to abolish Social evils.

115. What among the following does make the first Women's Studies Centre in India a unique one?
(i) Direct concern of UGC for the establishment of the Centre.
(ii) It was started in a Women's University.
(iii) It was initiated by the University itself.
(iv) UGC saw the centre as an adjunct to Women's Education.

Mark the correct answer from the Codes given below:

Codes:
A. (i), (ii) and (iv)
B. (i), (ii), (iii) and (iv)
C. (iv) only
D. (ii) and (iii) only

116. Which of the following is an agency of socialization?
A. Social stratification B. Society
C. Family D. Community

117. Find out the correct sequence of the following organizations:
A. IAWS; NCW; AIWC; WIA
B. NCW; IAWS; AIWC; WIA
C. IAWS; WIA; AIWC; NCW
D. WIA; AIWC; IAWS; NCW

118. The woman who lost her life in the Satyagraha Movement led by Mahatma Gandhi in South Africa?
A. Muthu Lakshmi Reddy
B. Thillayadi Valliammai
C. Aruna Asaf Ali
D. Sarla Devi

119. Temperance Movement is associated with:
A. Voting Rights
B. Prohibition of Liquor
C. For Equal Rights
D. Rights for Citizenship

120. Name the woman who first unfurled the flag of Indian freedom in 1907 in Stuttgart:
A. Bikaji Cama B. Kamla Nehru
C. Annie Besant D. Aruna Asaf Ali

121. The first women's studies program was launched at
A. San Diego State University, California
B. Oxford, London
C. JNU, New Delhi
D. Yale University

122. Assertion (A): Gender division of work at the Household level extends to other public sphere also.
Reason (R): Socialization process begins at family which is carried forward in the society and workplace etc.

Codes:
A. Both (A) and (R) are true.
B. Both (A) and (R) are false.
C. (A) is false, (R) is true.
D. Both (A) and (R) are true, (R) is the correct explanation for (A).

123. Assertion (A): Discriminatory beliefs, customs, and rituals such as polygamy, child marriages are practised generation after generation in India.
Reason (R): Patriarchal values are imparted through the socialization process.

Codes:
A. Both (A) and (R) are true
B. Both (A) and (R) are true and (R) is the correct explanation of (A)
C. Both (A) and (R) are false
D. (A) is true and (R) is false

124. Assertion (A): The early fifties saw the enactment of several legislations which appeared to have established formal equality between the sexes in accordance with the constitution.

Reason (R): The women felt compensated for their active participation in the independence struggle and were assured of attaining equality through constitution alone.

Codes:

A. Both (A) and (R) are true.
B. Both (A) and (R) are true but (R) is not the correct explanation of (A).
C. Both (A) and (R) are false.
D. Both (A) and (R) are true and (R) is the correct explanation for it.

125. Assertion (A): All socio-political structures and institutions in all the civilized societies have been instrumental in reinforcing gender inequality.

Reason (R): Women have been generally dubbed as 'non-political' 'non-productive,' 'private' and 'emotional.'

Codes:

A. Both (A) and (R) are true but (R) is not the correct explanation of (A).
B. Both (A) and (R) are true and (R) is the correct explanation of (A).
C. (A) is true but (R) is false.
D. Both (A) and (R) are false but (R) is the correct explanation of (A).

126. Assertion (A): Issues of women became issues of social reform during the Independence movement.

Reason (R): Soon after Independence, the women's question was almost forgotten.

Codes:

A. (A) is false (R) is true.
B. (R) is false (A) is true.
C. Both (A) and (R) are true.
D. Both (A) and (R) are false.

127. Assertion (A): Sexism refers to the belief or attitude that one sex is inferior and less valuable than the other.

Reason (R): Sexism widely prevails in Indian society.

Codes:

A. Both (A) and (R) are true and (R) is the correct explanation for (A).
B. Both (A) and (R) are false.
C. (A) is true, (R) is false.
D. Both (A) and (R) are true and (R) is not the correct explanation for (A).

128. Assertion (A): Patriarchy is an apt term to express the gamut of ideas that support male dominance.

Reason (R): Patriarchy refers to an ideology which grew out of Humanism.

Codes:

A. Both (A) and (R) are true.
B. Both (A) and (R) are false.
C. (A) is true, but (R) is false.
D. (A) is false, but (R) is true.

129. Assertion (A): Gender is not a consequence of sex.

Reason (R): Gender is Biologically constructed.

Codes:

A. Both (A) and (R) are false.
B. (A) is true, (R) is false.
C. Both (A) and (R) are true.
D. (R) is true, (A) is false.

130. Assertion (A): Patriarchy promotes the confinement of women within the domestic sphere.

Reason (R): Men derive concrete economic gains from the subordination of women.

Codes:

A. Both (A) and (R) are true.
B. Both (A) and (R) are false.
C. Both (A) and (R) are true and (R) is the correct explanation for (A).
D. (A) is true, (R) is false.

131. Assertion (A): Women are socialized into feminine and non-cooperative roles.

Reason (R): Women are by nature less intelligent.

Codes:

A. Both (A) and (R) are true, (R) is the correct explanation for (A).
B. (A) is true, (R) is false.
C. Both (A) and (R) are true.
D. Both (A) and (R) are false.

132. Assertion (A): Women's studies questioned the accepted theories and methodologies.

Reason (R): Accepted theories and methods failed to explain the lives of women, and they are biased.

Codes:

A. Both (A) and (R) are false.
B. Both (A) and (R) are true.
C. Both (A) and (R) are true, (R) is the correct explanation for (A).
D. (R) is true, (A) is false.

133. Assertion (A): Women's studies began with high hopes about the transformative potential of new knowledge to remove invisibility of women.

Reason (R): Women's studies failed to realize that knowledge is not enough to counter centuries of prejudice, inbuilt biases and rigid ways of thinking.

Codes:

A. Both (A) and (R) are true.
B. Both (A) and (R) are false.
C. Both (A) and (R) are true, (R) is the correct explanation for (A).
D. (A) is true (R) is false.

134. Assertion (A): In patriarchal society women are subordinated.

Reason (R): In patriarchal society men hold power in all the important institutions.

Codes:

A. Both (A) and (R) are true.
B. (A) is true (R) is false.
C. Both (A) and (R) are false.
D. (A) is false (R) is true.

135. Assertion (A): Gender issues are not women's issues alone.

Reason (R): Femininity does not exist in isolation from masculinity.

Codes:

A. Both (A) and (R) are false.
B. Both (A) and (R) are true.
C. Both (A) and (R) are true (R) is the correct explanation for (A).
D. (A) is true (R) is false.

136. Assertion (A): Women's studies began with high hopes about the transformative potential of new knowledge but failed to realize that knowledge is not enough to counter centuries of prejudices, in-built biases and rigid ways of thinking.

Reason (R): Women's studies sought to locate sources of inequality, injustice, and oppression and seek answers on how to remove these maladies and identify sources of powerlessness for women.

Codes:

A. (A) is true and (R) is false.
B. Both (A) and (R) are true.
C. Both (A) and (R) are true and (R) is not the correct explanation for (A).
D. Both (A) and (R) are false.

137. Assertion (A): Gender is not fixed once and for all across time or cultures.

Reason (R): Gender is developed within specific cultures for all the times.

Codes:

A. (A) is true and (R) is false and (R) is the correct explanation of (A).
B. Both (A) and (R) are true and (R) is not the correct explanation of (A).
C. Both (A) and (R) are false and (R) is the wrong explanation of (A).
D. (A) is true, but (R) is false and (R) is not the correct explanation of (A).

138. Assertion (A): A woman is in competition with other women for receiving 'male gaze.'

Reason (R): A woman is alienated from herself for using her sexuality.

Codes:

A. Both (A) and (R) are false.
B. (A) is true and (R) is false.
C. Both (A) and (R) are true and (R) is the correct explanation of (A).
D. (A) is false and (R) is true and (R) is not the correct explanation of (A).

139. Assertion (A): Women find it difficult to resist patriarchy within family and caste structure.

Reason (R): Patriarchy is an institution that pervades all social structures.

Codes:

A. Both (A) and (R) are true and (R) is not the correct explanation of (A).
B. (A) is false and (R) is true and (R) is not the correct explanation of (A).
C. Both (A) and (R) are true and (R) is the correct explanation of (A).
D. (A) is true and (R) is false and (R) is not the correct explanation of (A).

140. Assertion (A): Women's Studies lays bare the politics of knowledge creation.

Reason (R): It questions the value neutrality by disciplinary perspectives.

Codes:

A. (A) is true (R) is false.
B. (R) is true (A) is false.
C. Both (A) and (R) are false.
D. Both (A) and (R) are true.

141. Assertion (A): All interpretations about women's lives are androcentric.

Reason (R): Everywhere there is a male perspective that devalues women's ideas, experiences, needs, and interests.

Codes:

A. (A) is the reason for (R).
B. (A) is not a cause for (R).
C. (R) is the reason for (A).
D. (R) is not a cause for (A).

142. **Assertion (A):** Gender Stereotyping is perpetuated in all walks of women's lives.

Reason (R): The key agencies of socialization such as Family, school, media inculcate those ideas over generations.

Codes:

A. Both (A) and (R) are true.
B. (A) is true but (R) is false.
C. (A) is false but (R) is true
D. Both (A) and (R) are false.

143. **Assertion (A):** Research in gender studies has examined the presence of gender stereotyping in socialization.

Reason (R): Masculine characters are promoted through socialization.

Codes:

A. Both (A) and (R) are true.
B. (A) is true, (R) is false
C. Both (A) and (R) are false.
D. (A) is false, (R) is true.

144. **Assertion (A):** Practical gender needs enable women to do existing work better.

Reason (R): Women are not rational.

Codes:

A. Both (A) and (R) are false.
B. Both (A) and (R) are true
C. Both (A) and (R) are true, (R) is the correct explanation for (A).
D. (A) is true, (R) is false.

145. **Assertion (A):** Discriminatory beliefs, customs, and rituals such as polygamy, child marriage, early pregnancy are practised generation after generation in India.

Reason (R): Patriarchal values are imparted through the process of socialization.

Codes:

A. Both (A) and (R) are true.
B. (A) is true and (R) is the cause for (A).
C. (A) is false but (R) is not the cause for (A).
D. Both (A) and (R) are false.

146. **Assertion (A):** Social movements and organizations are the most powerful agents of social change.

Reason (R): Organizations and movements do not allow the transmission of information and material resources across the generation.

Codes:

A. Both (A) and (R) are true, (R) is the correct explanation for (A).
B. Both (A) and (R) are true, (R) is not the correct explanation for (A).
C. Both (A) and (R) are false.
D. (A) is true and (R) is false.

147. **Assertion (A):** Challenges to Women's studies are primarily attached from the mainstream of Social Sciences and Curriculum transformation.

Reason (R): A few students were attracted to join in Women's Studies courses due to lack of encouragement and recognition by the UGC.

Codes:

A. Both (A) and (R) are false.
B. (A) is true, (R) are false.
C. Both (A) and (R) are true.
D. (A) is false, (R) is true.

148. **Assertion (A):** It is very difficult to define the subject of Women's Studies.

Reason (R): Feminist thoughts and positions are diversified.

Codes:

A. (A) is false and (R) is true.
B. Both (A) and (R) are false.
C. (A) is true, but (R) is false and (R) is not the correct explanation of (A).
D. Both (A) and (R) are true and (R) is the correct explanation of (A).

149. **Assertion (A):** Today the women's movement in India is a strong movement which has spread to various parts of the country.

Reason (R): In India, we have a single cohesive movement in the country.

Codes:

A. Both (A) and (R) are true.
B. Both (A) and (R) are true and (R) is the correct explanation for (A).
C. (A) is true and (R) is false.
D. Both (A) and (R) are false.

150. **Assertion (A):** Androcentrism views that experiences of men and women are equally accepted by society.

Reason (R): Androcentrism promotes the integration of Masculine and Feminine traits.

Codes:

A. Both (A) and (R) are true.
B. (A) is true and (R) is false.
C. Both (A) and (R) are false.
D. Both (A) and (R) are true and (R) is the correct explanation for (A).

Answers

1	2	3	4	5	6	7	8	9	10
D	A	A	D	D	A	B	B	A	C
11	**12**	**13**	**14**	**15**	**16**	**17**	**18**	**19**	**20**
A	C	D	C	D	B	B	C	D	B
21	**22**	**23**	**24**	**25**	**26**	**27**	**28**	**29**	**30**
A	B	B	B	A	A	C	D	A	A
31	**32**	**33**	**34**	**35**	**36**	**37**	**38**	**39**	**40**
A	A	B	C	C	B	C	B	D	D
41	**42**	**43**	**44**	**45**	**46**	**47**	**48**	**49**	**50**
C	C	B	B	C	C	B	D	D	B
51	**52**	**53**	**54**	**55**	**56**	**57**	**58**	**59**	**60**
D	D	A	B	D	A	C	D	A	A
61	**62**	**63**	**64**	**65**	**66**	**67**	**68**	**69**	**70**
B	B	A	D	B	C	A	D	D	A
71	**72**	**73**	**74**	**75**	**76**	**77**	**78**	**79**	**80**
A	A	A	B	C	D	B	A	D	D
81	**82**	**83**	**84**	**85**	**86**	**87**	**88**	**89**	**90**
A	A	C	A	D	A	A	B	B	B
91	**92**	**93**	**94**	**95**	**96**	**97**	**98**	**99**	**100**
A	C	C	B	D	D	C	D	D	A
101	**102**	**103**	**104**	**105**	**106**	**107**	**108**	**109**	**110**
C	C	B	C	A	D	D	A	D	B
111	**112**	**113**	**114**	**115**	**116**	**117**	**118**	**119**	**120**
C	B	B	A	D	C	D	B	B	A
121	**122**	**123**	**124**	**125**	**126**	**127**	**128**	**129**	**130**
A	D	B	D	A	C	D	C	B	C
131	**132**	**133**	**134**	**135**	**136**	**137**	**138**	**139**	**140**
B	C	A	A	B	C	D	C	C	D
141	**142**	**143**	**144**	**145**	**146**	**147**	**148**	**149**	**150**
C	A	A	A	B	D	B	D	C	C

❑ ❑ ❑

Feminist Thinkers and Theories

- Kinds of Feminism – Liberal Feminism, Radical Feminism, Marxist Feminism, Socialist Feminism, Indian Feminism, Black Feminism, Eco-Feminism
- New Feminist Debates – Post Colonial/Post Modern, LGBT, Masculinity Studies
- Contemporary Contestations – Intersex and Transgender Movements
- Feminist Thinkers in 18th, 19th, 20th and 21st Century

KINDS OF FEMINISM

There are many ways to describe the multiple forms of feminism that have emerged since the 1920s, many of them overlapping with one another on key points.

LIBERAL FEMINISM

This kind of feminism works within the structure of mainstream society to integrate women into it and make it more responsive to individual women's rights but does not directly challenge the system itself or the ideology behind women's oppression. The suffragist movement is an example. Liberal feminists are concerned with extending to women, the liberal values of liberty, equality, and justice through legal and social reforms.

RADICAL FEMINISM

Radical feminism views patriarchy and gender as the most elemental factor in women's oppression which cut across all others from race and age to culture, caste, and class. It challenges the very system and beliefs behind women's subjugation. The term often refers to the women's movements emerging from the civil rights, peace, and other liberation movements at a time when people were increasingly questioning different forms of oppression and power. Radical feminists seek to understand the roots of women's subordination and provide a significant theoretical knowledge that has served as the foundation for the revelation and analysis guiding women's movements around the world. It calls for a radical reordering or transformation of the society and culture that makes women's subjugation possible.

MARXIST FEMINISM

Feminists, grounded in Marxist analysis, attribute women's oppression principally to the capitalist economic system where global corporate power prevails. They view classism and not sexism as the root cause of women's oppression. The movement is concerned with investigating the capitalist division of labor, economic dependence and exploitation of women under capitalist society and how a classless society can eliminate gender inequality. Marx's theory of alienation describes people's loss of control and disconnectedness over an attribute of self as an objective process that results from the relations of production found in capitalist society. Women's alienation from her freedom and rights also happens through the material conditions of her life. The interests of bourgeois and proletariat women are distinct as their ideology is linked to their social conditions.

But, women's liberation includes bourgeois women freeing themselves from the capitalist hegemony.

SOCIALIST FEMINISM

Socialist feminists believe that the form of power seen in the class system is a crucial factor in women's subordination but see patriarchy as the primary force behind women's subjugation. They are primarily influenced by the ideas of radical feminists and highlight the interplay between capitalism, patriarchy, race/ethnicity and culture in women's oppression. They believe that home is a place of production as well and that a complete transformation of family roles, parenting, sexuality, work and education is needed for women's liberation.

INDIAN FEMINISM

Social position, forms of oppression, issues and levels of disparity experienced by women vary across regions, cultures, and countries. Gender inequality is influenced by cultural history, socio-political structure, etc. The feministic movement in India arose and addressed those issues specific and inherent in Indian society. Casteism is one such context specific to India. Indian feminism was initially concerned with social reforms for women's upliftment, the abolition of Sati, dowry system, female infanticide and foeticide, women's education, fighting male domination and patriarchy, etc. As it evolved, it has addressed legal and political challenges to gender disparity, economic independence, and empowerment of women, domestic violence and sex crimes against women and many more.

BLACK FEMINISM

School of thought that asserts that sexism, class oppression, gender identity, and racism are all inseparably bound together. The way these concepts link to each other is called intersectionality. Legal scholar Kimberlé Crenshaw first coined the term intersectionality theory in 1989. Crenshaw argues that the experience of being a black woman cannot be understood in terms of being black or of being a woman. Each concept is considered independently but must include the interactions, which frequently reinforce each other. The Black feminist organization Combahee River Collective 1974 argued that the liberation of black women necessitates freedom from all forms of racism, sexism, and class oppression.

ECO-FEMINISM

This form of feminism views patriarchy and its focus on control and domination not only as a source of women's oppression but as being harmful to humanity as well as destructive of all living creatures and the earth itself. Combining a more comprehensive analysis of power often with a higher spiritual vision, eco-feminists see women's rights and empowerment linked to political, economic, social and cultural factors that benefit all living creatures and Mother Nature herself.

CULTURAL FEMINISM

Cultural feminism specifically addresses the fundamental differences between men and women with reference to their biology, personality, and behavior. It says that women possess superior qualities in comparison to men that can work as a base for sharing identity, solidarity, and sisterhood. Since women are seen and considered kinder and gentler by nature than men, it is believed that if women are in power, the world would be a better place. The idea of forming separate women-only cultures was endorsed by some women during 1960s and 70s.

TRANSNATIONAL OR GLOBAL FEMINISM

Transnational or Global Feminism is based on how people across many divisions like nationalities, races, ethnicities, genders, classes, and sexualities become victims and sufferers of globalization and capitalism and also how it has reinforced a range of global movements. This form of feminism identifies inequalities among different women and also the importance of intersectionality as a means to recognize and address the difference. Though, because of many such differences, women do not get affected by global issues, but power dynamics are considered as crucial to the agenda of feminist social justice. It also identifies the need for inclusive and concrete ways that incorporate different issues and movements to address common causes across many agenda that leads to social transformation in the long run.

VISIONARY FEMINISM

Visionary feminism stresses the need to collectively challenge the existing norms of patriarchy, class, race and many such forms which are the root to women's oppression. It also addresses the issues related to women's oppression due to imperialism and corporate control. African-American feminist, Bell Hooks, addresses all such systems of subjugation in her writings and focuses on love and the role of men. The fundamental structure of this approach is rooted in the love of male and female being. The spirit of feminist politics is the dedication to end the patriarchal domination between the sexual binaries. The domination and coercion cannot lead to love and coexistence, and the mutual relation cannot survive in one's control over the other. By embracing, a feminist approach that is based on the idea of mutual respect, the inner feeling of self-actualization will get enhanced among males. A sincere and earnest feminist approach brings from repression to liberty and from felling lovelessness to being loved.

LESBIAN FEMINISM

Lesbian-feminist politics is a political critique of the institution and ideology of heterosexuality as a cornerstone of male supremacy.

HUMANIST FEMINISM

Women's oppression is the inhibition and distortion of women's human potential by a society that only allows the self-development of men.

PSYCHOANALYTIC FEMINISM

Psychoanalytic feminism views the oppression of women rooted in childhood experiences as well as early conditioning within the family and society to specific gender roles and behavior.

It involves investigating the influence of parenting, communication, and language in gender definition and construction of self and social identity. Major psychoanalytic feminist works are Helene Cixous's "The Laugh of Medusa," Judith Butler's "Gender Trouble," Nancy Chodorow's "The Reproduction of Mothering."

NEW FEMINIST DEBATES—POST COLONIAL / POSTMODERN, LGBT, MASCULINITY STUDIES

POST-COLONIAL /POSTMODERN FEMINISM

Post-colonial feminism challenged female essentialism—woman as an embodiment of their body and associated identity.

Some of the underlying ideas of post-colonial/postmodern feminism are:

- Women are different than men and hence they have different priorities and needs. Every individual is a rational self, capable of defining themselves. Reason, freedom, and autonomy are inter-connected.
- Oppression of women in one part of the world affects women in another region. Colonialism has destroyed native cultures, diversity and adversely affected women and their socio-economic position. First world feminism is concerned with reproductive and sexual rights, while the third world feminism is still fighting for social, political and economic equality and issues.
- A woman and her gender are defined based on the historical, social narrative on sex and gender. Transforming it takes effort, understanding, and change in how gender/sexuality is viewed.

Transversal Politics emphasizes understanding the commonalities among all oppressed women, recognizing the difference in experiences and forging a collective movement for justice and equal rights. It acknowledges that women of different ethnicities and culture experience patriarchy and domination differently and calls for empathy and recognition of these differences outside of the existing politics to form a transnational collective that is inclusive and all-encompassing.

Feminist Standpoint Theory emerged in the 1970s from Marxist feminism. It is related to epistemology, i.e., the origin of knowledge and how it is socially situated. Women's social position dictates what they can know and understand from their standpoint. These standpoints offer distinct perspectives and knowledge but are ignored by the patriarchy.

Gynocriticism – a term coined by Elaine Showalter in her essay "Towards a Feminist Poetics" (1979); an approach to literary criticism without patriarchal bias. It involves analysis of development of feminist identity and female creativity in literature and supplementing historical liberation of women by reinterpreting women in literature.

Gender Analysis is the concept of evaluating a development problem or project based on gender relations. Different frameworks define distinct approaches to measure the socio-economic cost/result for resource allocation, inclusion/exclusion of women in the projects and solutions. Some important frameworks are the Harvard Analytical Framework, Gender Analysis Matrix, Social Relations Matrix, Moser Gender Planning Framework, Capacities, and Vulnerabilities Analysis Matrix, Women's Empowerment Matrix, etc.

LGBT – Lesbian, Gay, Bisexual, Transgender

Feminists and LGBT representatives have much in common. Both women and the LGBT people fight against discrimination, social stigma, patriarchy and are united in their demand for equal treatment, alternative family concepts, equality of sexes, etc. The linking of feminism and the LGBT movement gave rise to the term "sexual politics" in the 1970s. Sexuality and the deviation from its socio-normative definitions is the core of oppression faced by women, homosexuals, bisexuals and non-conforming gender deviants. Queer feminism was coined to denote lesbian feminists who criticized the mainstream feminist movement for ignoring the concerns of lesbians and queer issues. There are also theoretical and sociological differences between how some sections of feminists and LGBT people define feminine and masculine, sexuality and gender identity and experiences.

MASCULINITY STUDIES

- A study that enquires into the concept of masculinity and patriarchal power.
- Emerged in the 1990s as a concerted effort to understand the construction of masculinity.
- Interdisciplinary – cultural, historical, psychological, social and political analysis of male domination.
- Do all men want power? Is it the same across all cultures and time? How is it influenced?
- Patriarchal privilege upholds behavioral advantages for men. Women and men are assigned roles, work, and behavior that will maintain the benefits enjoyed by men.
- Hegemonic masculinity – men are expected and praised for conforming to the ideas of the "real man." He gains social approval and power.
- Subordinate masculinity – men who do not orient their behavior to the definition of "real man" are considered weak, lose respect and are steered towards hegemonic behavior.
- Masculinity studies owe its birth to feminism and try to understand and deconstruct the causes and consequences of masculine power in society.

CONTEMPORARY CONTESTATIONS–INTERSEX AND TRANSGENDER MOVEMENTS

- **Transgender** are people who do not identify themselves with their gender assignment at birth. People with male sexual identity identify themselves as female and vice-versa.
- Historically, transgender people have been one of the highly-disadvantaged sections of society. The transgender movement has highlighted the inherent social-bias, discrimination of trans-people and paved the way for their legislative and social upliftment. It has also contested the binary gender perspective of the feminist movement and the society at large. The feminist movement was initially based on the binary division of gender into male and female. Transgender, transsexual and non-conforming gendered people have forced the feminist movement to transform their idea of what is "female," gender assignment and gender identity.
- Though women and feminists have largely fought for and support the transgender movement, Gender Critical Feminism believes feminism should be women-centered and should stick to the more puritanical definition of "woman."
- **An intersex** person is an individual whose reproductive/sexual anatomy does not fit the typical definition of male or female — variation in sexual characteristics such as internal and external sex organs, sex hormones, chromosomes, etc.
- These variations do not always show up at birth. Sometimes changes in sex characteristics occur during puberty. Many live out their entire lives without knowing.
- Intersex itself is a socially constructed category based on these anatomical variations. Nature doesn't define what is strictly male and female, or where one ends, and the other begins. Even doctors do not have a universal opinion on the delineation.
- Intersex people face discrimination, unwanted genital surgeries, and even sterilization.
- The emergence of the movement for intersex people has challenged the idea of biological sex – sex assigned at birth. It has redefined sex from being a dichotomy to a spectrum.
- It has also challenged the feminist movement to rethink their concept of "woman," their cultural experience of exploitation and expand the victims of male privilege to include not just women.
- Intersex activism demands for a society that doesn't shame intersex people, equality of treatment and freedom to choose their sexual and gender identity. In 2015, Malta became one of the first countries in the world to illegalize nonconsensual surgeries on intersex infants and children.

FEMINIST THINKERS IN 18TH, 19TH, 20TH AND 21ST CENTURY

Throughout its development, numerous feminist thinkers and scholars have contributed to the evolution of the feminist movement.

The 18th and 19th century thinkers laid the groundwork for the concept of feminism and women's freedom and equality. They fought for women's right to vote, civil rights, education, etc.

Seneca Falls Convention:

- First women's rights convention held in the United States on July19-20,1848, Seneca Falls, New York.
- Around 300 people attended the meeting, organized by Elizabeth Cady Stanton, Lucretia Mott, Martha Coffin Wright, Jane Hunt, Mary M'Clintock.
- Described women's grievances and demands in their "Declaration of Sentiments." The convention's 11 Resolutions resolved to fight for women's right to vote, equal access to jobs, equal rights with the church, as well as other social and civil rights for women.

Mary Wollstonecraft (1759–1797)

- She wrote the book "A Vindication of the Rights of Women" in 1792 as a response to men during her time who argued against women's education. They believed in allowing only domestic education to women.
- She asserted that women are not inferior to men and they need education to develop their abilities and knowledge.
- She advocated women's equality and criticized the traditional subordination of women and their position as "confined in cages like the feathered race."
- She highlighted that the social norms, cultural practices, and views imposed predetermined, subservient roles on women. This indoctrination made them occupy a secondary oppressed place in the family and society.
- She also enunciated the social benefits of women's education.
- Many consider her work the foundation of feminism.

Olympe de Gouges (1748–1793)

- French writer and political activist.
- Wrote "Declaration of the Rights of Woman and the Female Citizen" in 1791.
- Demanded marriage to be based on equality between man and woman.

John Stuart Mill (1806–1873)

- Political philosopher and feminist.
- His essay "The Subjugation of Women" written in 1869 advocated women's political rights and educational equality.
- He stressed the development and contribution of women as necessary for the good of mankind, but that women were subjugated by society to be meek and subservient.
- He advocated women's education to develop their capabilities and attain social and political equality.

Susan B Anthony (1820–1906)

- One of the leaders of the women's suffrage movement.
- Fought for women's right to vote, equal pay for equal work, slavery abolition.
- In 1890, the National American Women Suffrage Association was formed with Susan B Anthony as the pivotal leader.
- Became the editor of the newspaper, The Revolution in 1848 – spread the ideas of rights and equality of women.

Sojourner Truth (1797–1883)

- African-American abolitionist and women's rights activist.
- Was a slave for 30 years and escaped to freedom in 1826.
- Fought for human rights, the abolition of slavery, women's suffrage throughout her life.

As women were granted the right to vote and other civil rights, the 20th, and 21st-century feminist movements evolved to address socio-economic disparities, gender roles and gender norms, cultural inequality, etc.

Friedrich Engels (1820–1895)

- He explained the oppression of women in society through his theories on class structure, social hierarchy, and means of production.
- In his book "The Origin of the Family, Private Property and the State" published in 1884, he theorizes the historic alternative social systems (kinship groups, hunter-gatherer societies) that were egalitarian or matriarchal. In those societies, women had equal control and authority, and the means of production and property were also owned by women.
- With the evolution of the family, the marriage system and class-structure in societies, control over property and means of production caused division of labor based on gender and class.
- He blames the economic and class structure as the direct cause of women's unequal status and oppression.

Clara Zaetkin (1857–1933)

- Socialist feminist, women's rights advocate.
- In 1907, organized the first international conference of socialist women in Stuttgart, Germany.
- She along with other socialist feminists like Alexandra Kollantai, Eleanor Marx campaigned for universal suffrage and women's political rights in the context of social reform, and class struggle.
- **Alexandra Kollantai** argued that women's world was divided into bourgeois and proletariat class, and their aims and interests are different. She wanted women's liberation to encompass a full solution to all. She appealed to working-class men to support women's demand for equal wages, maternity protection, and other social rights.

Simon de Beauvoir (1908–1986)

- A philosopher and a feminist thinker.
- Her book, "The Second Sex" published in 1949 started the second wave of feminism.
- Initially, she believed that women were discriminated only in capitalistic societies. But, as she observed the position of women in socialist countries like the USSR and China, she found the traditional gender roles intact and that even socialism did not empower women to be free.
- She advocated women's independence through carrier and work.
- According to her, society viewed men as subjects and women as objects. This social view influences the identity and interactions between men and women. We are assigned the traditional roles of a woman, not by birth but through the social construct.
- She critiqued the concept of "eternal feminist" characteristics as a form of discrimination. By elevating women to some divine stature, society prevents equal participation of women in society and activities usually done by men. It is a way of male control and domination.
- **Existential feminism** owes its origin to Simone De Beauvoir, who emphasized the individual self-determinism to define a person's social role and value. The existing social conditions lead to the oppression of women and claims that women are capable of understanding and transforming the imposed social constructs of sex and patriarchy.

Betty Friedan (1921–2006)

- Contributed immensely to modern feminism.
- Published "The Feminine Mystique" in 1963 about the American women's dissatisfaction with the roles of a homemaker.
- She argued that women in industrialized societies remain oppressed. They have to put their husband's career first and spend their life being homemakers and housewives.
- This stifled their empowerment, and hence they need carrier-oriented independence. Not all women want to be happy homemakers.
- Women can obtain personal fulfillment only by breaking out their traditional gender roles and finding new opportunities in rewarding, creative work. She also advocated an increased role of women in politics and decision making. She combined activism and theory and worked for women's abortion rights.
- She co-founded National Organization of Women (NOW) in 1966 and became its first president. NOW was formed to fight actively against all forms of sexual discrimination against women in society. NOW has campaigned for equality of treatment in employment and pay, child care, pregnancy leave, health care, abortion and pension rights, etc.
- It has also been instrumental in enacting laws against violence and discrimination of women and worked for education, political and business opportunities for women. Its direct actions include corporate campaigning, lobbying, grassroots political activism and litigation, etc.
- Her 1981 book "Second Stage" calls for an effective reorganization of male-female relationship towards an egalitarian marriage and family life that gives women equal power in home and workplace. She claims family as the "new feminist frontier" and criticizes radical feminists for their extreme stance.

Kate Millet (1934–2017)

- Feminist writer and activist.
- In her book "Sexual Politics" (1970), she investigates the effects of patriarchy on sexual relations. She examines famous authors' works to understand the psychological underpinnings of sexual discrimination, the patriarchal bias in literary works of male writers and how they help perpetuate male domination.

Alison Jaggar (1942–present)

- Feminist philosopher.
- Her book "Feminist Politics and Human Nature" published in 1983, analyses the development of feminist movements, the different feminist perspectives on human nature and society and categorizes them as a distinct political philosophy that advocates social justice and women's equality.

Bell Hooks (1952–present)

- Real name: Gloria Jean Watkins
- A postmodern feminist thinker and writer.
- She wrote the book "Ain't I A Woman?: Black Women and Feminism" in 1981 that examined the intersectional oppression of black women by racism and sexism.
- She was instrumental in bringing the cultural concerns of African-American women into mainstream feminism. She focused on the interaction of race, gender, capitalism in imposing a multi-faceted subjugation of colored women.
- She stressed the need to create political solidarity among women of different socio-economic status, classes and religion for a feminist movement that includes everyone's concerns and issues.
- In her book, "Feminist Theory: From Margin To Center", published in 1984, she explores all her ideas on expanding the scope of feminism, inclusion of different sections of women, colonial and capitalistic prejudices, feminist perspectives on men, the application of feminism in real life, and how it would benefit both men and women of society.
- Self-actualization of African-American women by telling their stories of discrimination as a form of the recovery process and moving forward.

Gloria Steinem (1934–present)

- Co-founder of one of the first feminist magazines, "Ms. Magazine" in 1972 that covered genuine gender issues and one of the founders of the National Women's Political Caucus.
- As a journalist, she reported on political and progressive social issues such as feminist liberation movements. She fought for abortion rights of women and promoted gender equality in media and other fields.
- She co-founded "Women's Action Alliance" in 1971 to support the education of multi-racial children, Women's Media Center in 2004 to promote positive images of women in media.

Audre Lorde (1934–1992)

- Carribean-American writer
- She theorized that society created identities and categories of people and marginalized them based on those imposed categories. She raised awareness about the identity prejudices that oppressed and discriminated women.
- She also critiqued White women's ignorance of their privilege and womanism's failure to directly address homosexuality within the Black Female community. She confronted racism, sexism, and homophobia.
- She advocated woman of color feminism in response to white feminism. Women are not a homogenous section, but there are categories and subdivisions and their experience of discrimination is shaped by the environment, culture, ethnicity, religion, sexuality, etc.
- She proposed the creative use of these differences to evolve all-encompassing feminism.
- Published "The Cancer Journals" in 1980 – her femi-nistic analysis of her struggle with breast cancer and her celebrated book "Sister Outsider" in 1984.

Juliet Mitchell (1940–present)

- Socialist feminist and psychoanalyst.
- She criticized Freud's perspective on masculinity and femininity as a reflection of his patriarchal mindset and paved the way for psychoanalysis of masculinity and gender in society.
- In her thesis "Women's Estate" published in 1966, she delineates four estates or domains through which women are oppressed. The four estates of discrimination are sexuality (rape/porn culture, trans and lesbian discrimination, forced heterosexuality, etc.), reproduction (women as baby machines, lack of reproductive rights, women as a reproductive resource etc.), control of production and wealth and lastly the "caring" work (women role relegated to caring, aiding and teaching and nursing the children, elderly and the sick).
- Her other important work "Psychoanalysis and Feminism: A Radical Reassessment of Freudian Psychoanalysis" (1974) stresses the importance of the psychoanalytic approach to feminism and

gender oppression in society. Gender is a cultural construct created from childhood to explain biological differences.

Germaine Greer (1939–present)

- Australian writer, anarchist
- In her book "The Female Eunuch" published in 1970, her contribution to feminist thinking includes investigating the suppression of female sexuality, literal and metaphorical female castration, masculine-feminine polarity, conditioning and conformity of sexuality and social behavior, false perspectives of womanhood, love, sex, and society, and true liberation of women.

Kimberle Crenshaw (1959–present)

- Coined the term "intersectionality."
- Women's experiences vary depending on their race, gender, ability, etc.
- Expanded the reach of feminism; multiple oppressions experienced differently.
- Discrimination of black women is a combination of sexism and racism.
- Understanding should reflect the experiences specific to black women.
- Fought for the legal rights of women to fight the multiple oppressions through their life.

Andrea Dworkin (1946–2005)

- Criticized the gradual legitimization of pornography as another form of female subjugation. Pornography is a tool used by men to control, subjugate and objectify women.
- Pornography violated women's civil rights and promoted sexual discrimination, men's domestic, cultural and sexual violence, and sexual sadism.
- Along with Catherine MacKinnon, she drafted the Minnesota Ordinance that allowed rape victims to sue pornographers.
- Known for her Books "Women hating," 1974 and "Pornography: Men Possessing Women," 1981.

Helene Cixous (1937–present)

- Mother of post-structuralist feminist theory.
- Her article "The Laugh of Medusa" published in 1975 called for a new way of thinking and writing for feminist thought and ideas.
- Sexuality is directly influenced by how women communicate in society—the language determines women's secondary role.
- Attempts to counter the western culture's traditional sexual division into male and female. The discourse of the west is entirely masculine, and this influences the subject and ideas.
- A new language of discourse is needed for true feminine expression and liberation.

Vandana Shiva (1952–present)

- Ecofeminist
- The worldview that destroys nature and causes environmental degradation is the same as that which dominates and exploits women; war and capitalism are extensions of the patriarchal domination.
- Most of her work deals with third world women and the adverse effects of corporate Globalization, Colonialism, and Capitalism on the environment and women.
- According to her, women's liberation is linked with the preservation of nature and all lives on the planet.
- Famous work "Staying Alive: Women, Ecology, and Development," 1988.

Other notable works that have contributed to feminist thought are as follows:

- "A Cyborg Manifesto" (1985) by Donna Haraway, an American Professor, and a post-modern feminist. She calls for a post-humanist view of the world and women. She highlights the problems of a dualist worldview and criticizes the western political and traditional feminism. She calls for reconstruction of identity and a utopian community without gender and otherness.
- "Theories of Patriarchy" (1981) an essay by Lindsey German, a British political activist. This social feminism rejects men as the sole root cause of women's oppression and puts the blame entirely on the class structure of society. The material or economic conditions and the resultant class structure and control of means of production are the origins of women subjugation. Patriarchy cannot be viewed in isolation from the socio-economic hierarchies and hence needs a social transformation for the liberation of women.
- "Beyond God the Father: Towards a Philosophy of Women's Liberation" (1973) book by Mary Daly, an American philosopher, and a radical feminist. In

this book, she examines the misogyny inherent in religion which has enabled women's oppression throughout history.

- "Dialectic of Sex: The Case for Feminist Revolution" (1970) book by Shulamith Firestone, a Canadian-American radical feminist. According to her, women are oppressed and exploited in their motherly role too and that they have to take control of their reproductive rights. She propagated a feminist theory of politics.

Feminist Perspectives on Family

Feminists of all types have encouraged sociologists to see the family as an institution involving power relationships–"the personal is political." Feminism has challenged the view of the family as being based on cooperation, shared interests, and love. Feminism has tried to show that men gain more from family life than women.

Family

Gender roles are defined by the socio-cultural norms of any society. In most of the societies, the family systems are based on gender roles, and it is the predesigned gender roles that help members of the family to run the family with bound responsibilities. There are underlying indications of inequality in the daily instructions by parents, for example, at the time of dividing up household chores; boys may be asked to perform tasks that require strength or toughness, while girls may be asked to perform duties that require neatness and care. Fathers are seen stricter in their expectations for gender conformity than mothers, and they expect strongly from sons than from daughters. This demarcation is visible through other activities too including the preference of toys, play styles, discipline, chores, and personal achievements.

Caste

Caste is a traditional Hindu model of social stratification, that defines people by descent and occupation. A suffocating patriarchal shadow dominates over the lives of many women throughout India. From all sections, castes, and classes of society, women are victims of its repressive, controlling effects. Those subjected to the most onerous burden of discrimination and alienation belongs to the Scheduled Castes that used to be termed as Untouchables. Though the very name untouchable is no longer in use, the mindset and negative attitude remains. They are still in a vulnerable position being subjected to abuse and servitude. They experience different forms of discri-mination and alienation which are inhumane in nature.

Class

The economic stratification of society adds another layer of oppression on Indian women. Women are disadvantaged of the disadvantaged. Literacy, health, and nutritional condition, the social position of the rural, poor and lower-middle-class women are worse than the men of the same economic sections. The lower status of women, in general, further the exploitation of women in lower classes of society for the benefits of not just the upper levels, but the men of the same classes.

Religion

The main religions of the world, all contain specific ideas about the appropriate roles for men and women in society, and traditionally, this has placed women in the home and men in the 'outside' world. This holds even today, where much change is occurring in societies with increasing female labor market participation and changes in attitudes accompanying this. Religions differ to some extent in this regard, but similar normative claims about men's and women's roles are present across all denominations. The cultural and religious activities that negatively impacted the education of the girl child are most prevalent.

Culture

Expectations about attributes and behaviors that are appropriate to women or men and the relations between women and men. It can be said that gender is shaped by culture. Gender (like race or ethnicity) functions as an organizing principle for society because of the cultural meanings given to being male or female. Culturally determined gender ideologies define rights and responsibilities and what is 'appropriate' behavior for women and men. They also influence one's control over resources, and partici-pation in decision-making. These gendered beliefs often reinforce male power and the idea of women's inferiority. Culture is sometimes understood narrowly as 'custom' or 'tradition' and considered to be natural and unchangeable. Despite these premises, culture is fluid and enduring. Dominant cultures strengthen the position of those with economic, political and social power, and therefore tend to reinforce male power. Globalization also has implications for the diffusion of culture, particularly of western culture.

Multiple Choice Questions

1. Frederick Engles wrote the book:
A. Dialectic of Sex
B. The Second Sex
C. Origin of Family, Private Property and the State
D. The Enfranchisement of Women

2. Who is the author of "A Field of One's Own"?
A. Kate Millett
B. Maithreyi Krishnaraj
C. Vina Mazumdar
D. Bina Agarwal

3. Arrange the following books in the order in which they appeared:
(a) The Feminine Mystique
(b) Vindication of the Rights of Women
(c) Origin of Family, Private Property and the State
(d) The Second Sex

Codes:
A. (a), (b), (c), (d) B. (d), (b), (c), (a)
C. (b), (d), (c), (a) D. (b), (c), (d), (a)

4. Match the following books with their authors:

Authors	***Books***
(a) Bell Hooks	(i) Meetless Days
(b) J.S. Mill	(ii) Sexual Politics
(c) Sara Suleri	(iii) Subjection of Women
(d) Kate Millett	(iv) Yearning: Race, Gender and Cultural Politics

Codes:

	(a)	(b)	(c)	(d)
A.	(iii)	(i)	(iv)	(ii)
B.	(iv)	(iii)	(i)	(ii)
C.	(ii)	(iv)	(iii)	(i)
D.	(i)	(ii)	(iv)	(iii)

5. Match the following books with their authors:

Authors	***Books***
(a) Jean Bethke Elshtain	(i) Female Eunuch
(b) Radha Kumar	(ii) Women's Estate
(c) Julliet Mitchell	(iii) History of Doing
(d) Germaine Greer	(iv) Public Man, Private Woman

Codes:

	(a)	(b)	(c)	(d)
A.	(ii)	(i)	(iv)	(iii)
B.	(iv)	(iii)	(ii)	(i)
C.	(iii)	(iv)	(i)	(ii)
D.	(i)	(iii)	(iv)	(ii)

6. Match the major schools of thought with the respective ideologies:

(a) Denouncing Polarization	(i) Cultural Feminist
(b) Attribution of status in relation to means of production	(ii) Socialist Feminist
(c) Building a powerful female culture	(iii) Liberal Feminist
(d) Principles of Equal Rights	(iv) Marxist Feminist

Codes:

	(a)	(b)	(c)	(d)
A.	(iii)	(iv)	(i)	(ii)
B.	(i)	(ii)	(iv)	(iii)
C.	(ii)	(iii)	(i)	(iv)
D.	(iv)	(ii)	(iii)	(i)

7. Arrange the schools of feminist thought in their order of origin:
(1) Radical Feminism (2) Socialist Feminism
(3) Marxist Feminism (4) Liberal Feminism

Codes:
A. (2), (1), (4), (3) B. (3), (2), (1), (4)
C. (4), (3), (2), (1) D. (1), (4), (3), (2)

8. Match the Lists:

List-I	***List-II***
(a) Kate Millett	(i) Liberal Feminist
(b) J.S. Mill	(ii) Eco-feminist
(c) Alison Jaggar	(iii) Radical Feminist
(d) Vandana Shiva	(iv) Socialist Feminist

Codes:

	(a)	(b)	(c)	(d)
A.	(ii)	(iii)	(iv)	(i)
B.	(ii)	(iv)	(i)	(iii)
C.	(iv)	(i)	(iii)	(ii)
D.	(iii)	(i)	(iv)	(ii)

9. "Experimental Analysis: A contribution to Feminist Research" is written by:
A. Karl Mannheim
B. Shulamith Reinharz
C. Margrit Eichler
D. Barnard Helen Roberts

10. Nancy Chodorow has provided
A. Psychoanalytic theory
B. Socialization theory
C. Feminism and Psychoanalytical theory
D. Role – learning theory

11. The Third Wave Feminism was conceived by
A. Naomi Wolf
B. Rio Grill
C. Rene Denfeld
D. Rebecca Walker

12. Which feminist group believes that women's liberation is possible through women's self-determined activity?
A. Anarchist
B. Radicals
C. Marxists
D. Essentialists

13. Among the following feminists who is not a post-modernist?
A. Luce Irigaray
B. Hélène Cixous
C. Kate Millett
D. Julia Kristeva

14. Arrange the chronological order of the ideologies of three waves of feminism:
A. Legislational change, liberation, and popular culture as a site of activism.
B. Liberation, Popular culture as a site of activism and Legislational change.
C. Popular culture as a site of Activism, Legislational change and Liberation.
D. Legislational change, Popular culture as a site of Activism and Liberation.

15. Match List-I with List-II:

List-I	***List-II***
(a) First Wave	(i) Feminist Media Studies
(b) Radical	(ii) Suffrage
(c) Liberal	(iii) Reproductive Rights
(d) Third Wave	(iv) Education of Women

Codes:

	(a)	(b)	(c)	(d)
A.	(iii)	(iv)	(i)	(ii)
B.	(i)	(ii)	(iii)	(iv)
C.	(ii)	(iii)	(iv)	(i)
D.	(iv)	(i)	(iii)	(ii)

16. Foucault was interested in the effect of power/ knowledge of bodies, and his major focus was on?
A. Sexuality
B. Caring
C. Surveillance
D. Education

17. Which feminist thought suggests that gender equality can be realized by eliminating the cultural notion of gender?
A. Socialist feminism
B. Postmodern feminism
C. Radical feminism
D. Neoclassical feminism

18. Marxist feminist attempt to explain how:
(i) Gender relations operate in a society
(ii) Gender relations are universal.
(iii) Gender relations are connected with processes of production and reproduction
(iv) Gender relations are crucial for the property.

Codes:
A. (i) and (iii) only
B. (i), (ii) and (iv) only
C. (i), (iii), (iv) only
D. (ii) and (iv) only

19. Match List-I (Thinkers) with List-II (Views):

List-I	***List-II***
(a) Clara Zetkin, Juliet Mitchel	1. Liberty of education and employment.
(b) Jane Flax, Margaret Benston	2. Women's work outside the home and domestic work.
(c) Mary Wollstone Craft, Betty Friedan	3. Equality in terms of women's rights for reproduction.
(d) Kate Millet, Mary Daly	4. Equality with reference to masculine and feminine traits.

Codes:

	(a)	(b)	(c)	(d)
A.	3	1	2	4
B.	1	2	4	3
C.	1	2	3	4
D.	3	2	1	4

20. Among the following which is not an ideology of feminism?
A. Identifying the existing social realities from the standpoint of women.
B. Questioning the gender blindness of main-stream theories.
C. Questioning the power of dominant classes.
D. Promoting the replacement of dominant classes.

21. Women's studies became an academic discipline during:
A. Second wave feminism
B. First wave feminism
C. Third wave feminism
D. Fourth wave feminism

22. Queer theory relates to:
(i) Gay and lesbian politics.
(ii) Question of the usefulness of gendered binary distinctions.
(iii) Promotion of heterosexuality.
(iv) Promotion of sexual identities.

Codes:
A. (i) and (iv) only correct
B. (i), (ii) and (iv) are correct
C. (i) and (ii) are correct
D. (i), (ii), (iii) and (iv) are correct

23. Who amongst the following first propounded the theory of liberal feminism?
A. John Stuart Mill
B. Harriet Taylor
C. Mary Wollstonecraft
D. William Thompson

24. Which of the following statements is not related to eco-feminism?
A. Development leads to ecological and cultural rupture of bonds with nature.
B. Development and global markets have made homelessness a cultural trait.
C. Development leads to the impoverishment of women, children and the environment.
D. New technologies always provide the opportunity for women in the traditional economy.

25. Women's emancipation must be won primarily by women themselves. Who first propagated this idea among the following thinkers:
A. Clara Zetkin
B. Elizabeth Cady Stanton
C. Charlotte Perkins Gilman
D. Emma Goldman

26. Match the major schools of thought with their respective ideologies:

List-I	***List-II***
(a) Inclusion of domestic labour in productive labour	(i) Modern Marxism
(b) Capitalist patriarchy	(ii) Radical feminism
(c) Critique of man-made language	(iii) Socialist feminism
(d) Liberation from domesticity	(iv) Modern liberal feminism

Codes:

	(a)	(b)	(c)	(d)
A.	(iv)	(iii)	(ii)	(i)
B.	(iii)	(i)	(ii)	(iv)
C.	(i)	(iii)	(iv)	(ii)
D.	(ii)	(iii)	(i)	(iv)

27. "The assumption of your own identity equality and even political power does not mean you stop needing to love and be loved by, a man, or that your stop caring for your own kids."
A. Betty Friedan
B. Harriet Taylor
C. Zillah Eisenstein
D. Elizabeth Holtzman

28. Which approach of feminism is based on the premise that both men and women are born equal and are gifted with the same rational faculties so that women should not be denied equality of opportunity in all those activities which are open to men?
A. Existentialism
B. Socialist
C. Post-modern
D. Liberal

29. __________ refers to an inclusive worldwide movement to end sexism and sexist oppression by empowering women.
A. Anti-sexism
B. Feminism
C. Gynocentrism
D. Male-bashing

30. Which approach is appropriate for the adequate understanding of the political orientation of feminism?
(i) Liberal Feminism
(ii) Socialist Feminism
(iii) Radical Feminism
(iv) Post modern Feminism

Codes:
A. (i), (ii), (iii) and (iv)
B. (iv) only
C. (ii) and (iii)
D. (i) and (iv)

31. Which of the following is an incorrect statement about Liberal feminism?
A. Women have equal rational capacities like men
B. Women and men should have equal sexual rights
C. Women and men should be given the same educational opportunities
D. Women and men should get equal civil and political rights

32. What is incorrect about unified system theory?
A. Capitalism and patriarchy are one and the same
B. Gender division of labour is a unifying concept
C. Patriarchy and capitalism as forms of social relations are distinct from each other
D. Women's oppression as a woman is observed in classless society also

33. Which approach of feminism views that women's oppression as women is caused not only by living in a class society but also in classless societies?
A. Socialist
B. Radical
C. Marxist
D. Liberal

34. Match the List-I (Authors) and List-II (Books):

List-I	*List-II*
(a) Betty Friedan	(i) The Second Sex
(b) Mary Wollstone Craft	(ii) Women's Estate
(c) Simon de Beauvoir	(iii) The Feminine Mystique
(d) Juliet Mitchell	(iv) A Vindication of the Rights of Women

Codes:

	(a)	(b)	(c)	(d)
A.	(ii)	(i)	(iii)	(iv)
B.	(i)	(ii)	(iv)	(iii)
C.	(iv)	(ii)	(i)	(iii)
D.	(iii)	(iv)	(i)	(ii)

35. Match the List-I with List-II:

List-I **(Concepts)**	*List-II* **(Philosophers)**
(a) Separatism	(i) Marge Piercy
(b) Mattapoisett	(ii) Marilyn Frye
(c) Pre-oedipal	(iii) Betty Friedan
(d) Male Clones	(iv) Sigmund Freud

Codes:

	(a)	(b)	(c)	(d)
A.	(ii)	(i)	(iv)	(iii)
B.	(i)	(ii)	(iv)	(iii)
C.	(iii)	(i)	(ii)	(iv)
D.	(ii)	(iii)	(iv)	(i)

36. Who has given a call to build a "social order, the only one that allows for a radical solution to the women's question"?

A. Betty Friedan B. Clara Zetkin
C. Julie Bindel D. Sheila Jeffreys

37. Which type of feminists finds important differences between men and women that are arbitrary and flexible?

A. Standpoint B. Liberal
C. Post-modern D. Radical

38. Post-modern feminists believe that:

A. Knowledge is completely objective.
B. Social Scientists have the authority to define social reality for everyone.
C. It is possible to deconstruct gender.
D. Essentialist and universal categories liberate people.

39. Who carried out in-depth research on the role of the housewife in the 1970s?

A. Young Wilmot B. Jeffrey Wheels
C. Ann Oakley D. Margaret Mead

40. Among the following which is not related to third wave feminism?

A. Queer Theory
B. Defending Sex Work
C. Abolishing Gender Roles
D. Suffrage Movement

41. Which of the following is correct about Liberal Feminists?

A. They maximise male/female difference but stress disparities in power, especially male dominance; focus on sexuality and sexual relations as key to patriarchal oppression; seek to use the law to help women "take control of their own bodies."
B. They maximise male/female difference, stress the positive value of women's 'different voice' and emphasize the importance of incorporating this into the legal system; seek to recover and revalue women's culture, especially maternal values.
C. They focus on individual rights and autonomy; minimise male/female difference; emphasize the equality of opportunity and promote strategies that tear down barriers, seek to extend to women the individual rights gained by men.
D. They focus on material conditions and how these create oppressive societal structures, particularly class; emphasize the effort to reform communities and institutions; stress social relations and responsibilities more than individual rights.

42. Who was one of the first feminists to write on pornography?

A. Ruth Vanita B. Carole Gilligan
C. Miriam Shiver D. Susan Griffin

43. Among the following liberal feminist who had the view that "so long as a woman is permitted to enter and leave the labor market at will, she is fully liberated"?

A. J.S. Mill
B. Harriet Taylor
C. Betty Friedan
D. Elizabeth Holtzman

44. Who made the statement "women are not powerless because they are feminine, rather they are feminine because they are powerless because it is a way of dealing with the requirements of subordination"?

A. Eve Ensler B. Sarojini Naidu
C. Kathy E. Ferguson D. Sherry Ortner

45. Which of the following is not correct about Eco-feminism?

A. Believes that there is a direct connection between the oppression of nature and the subordination of women.
B. Focus on patriarchal oppression and social constructions relating to women and the environment.
C. Women are closer to nature than men.
D. Connections between the environment and women are due to the gender division of labour.

46. Match List-I with List-II:

List-I **(Name of the Author)**	***List-II*** **(Name of the Books)**
(a) Simon de Beauvoir	(i) A Vindication of the Rights of Women
(b) J.S. Mill	(ii) The Dialectic of Sex
(c) Mary Wollstonecraft	(iii) The Subjection of Women
(d) Shulamith Firestone	(iv) The Second Sex

Codes:

	(a)	(b)	(c)	(d)
A.	(ii)	(iii)	(iv)	(i)
B.	(ii)	(iv)	(i)	(iii)
C.	(iv)	(iii)	(i)	(ii)
D.	(iii)	(i)	(iv)	(ii)

47. Match List-I with List-II:

List-I **(Theories)**	***List-II*** **(Name of Feminists)**
(a) Cyborg	(i) Gayatri Spivak
(b) Transversal Politics	(ii) Nira-Yuval Davis
(c) Strategic Essentialism	(iii) Patricia Hill Collin
(d) The partiality of standpoints	(iv) Donna Haraway

Codes:

	(a)	(b)	(c)	(d)
A.	(i)	(ii)	(iii)	(iv)
B.	(ii)	(i)	(iii)	(iv)
C.	(iii)	(iv)	(ii)	(i)
D.	(iv)	(ii)	(i)	(iii)

48. Match List-I with List-II:

List-I **(Philosophers)**	***List-II*** **(Statements)**
(a) Engels	(i) Women at home not only provide essential services but also, create surplus value.
(b) Dalla Costa	(ii) The Inferior position of women is attributed to the Institution of private property.
(c) Shulamith Firestone	(iii) Women were unable to explain the problem that has no name.
(d) Betty Friedan	(iv) The original and basic class division is between sexes.

Codes:

	(a)	(b)	(c)	(d)
A.	(i)	(ii)	(iii)	(iv)
B.	(i)	(iii)	(iv)	(ii)
C.	(ii)	(i)	(iv)	(iii)
D.	(iv)	(iii)	(i)	(ii)

49. Match List-I and List-II:

List-I **(Gender Framework)**	***List-II*** **(Scholars)**
A. Gender Analysis Matrix	(i) Sara Longwe
B. Social Relations Framework	(ii) Naila Kabeer
C. Harvard Analytical Framework	(iii) Rani Parker
D. Women's Empowerment Framework	(iv) Catherine Overholt

Codes:

	(a)	(b)	(c)	(d)
A.	(iii)	(ii)	(iv)	(i)
B.	(i)	(ii)	(iii)	(iv)
C.	(i)	(ii)	(iv)	(iii)
D.	(ii)	(iii)	(iv)	(i)

50. Who said these words?

"The woman who strengthens body and exercises her mind will, by managing her family and practising various virtues, become the friend and not the humble dependent of her husband."

A. Emma Goldman
B. Mary Wollstonecraft
C. Alice Walker
D. Angela Y. Davis

51. Postmodern feminism is considered as an approach to the feminist theory which incorporates:

A. Post-anarchism
B. Postmaterialism
C. Postcolonialism
D. Post-structuralism

52. 'Patriarchy is rooted in the biological inequality of the sexes' has been stated by:

A. Frederich Engels in 'The Origin of the Family, Private Property and the State'
B. August Bebel in 'Women Under Socialism'
C. Karl Marx and Frederich Engles in 'The German Ideology'
D. Shulamith Firestone in 'The Dialectics of Sex'

53. The cause of Women's oppression according to radical feminists is:
A. Class
B. Caste
C. Patriarchy
D. Women are the enemies of women

54. J.S. Mill is a:
A. Liberal Feminist B. Socialist Feminist
C. Radical Feminist D. Not a feminist

55. Feminism dismantles all systems of:
A. Conformity B. Complicity
C. Tradition D. Domination

56. Mary Wollstonecraft was a:
A. Liberal Feminist B. Marxist Feminist
C. Radical Feminist D. Psycho Analyst

57. Among the following persons identify the male feminist:
A. Harriet Taylor B. Betty Friedan
C. J.S. Mill D. Iris Young

58. Among the following which is not an objective of feminism:
A. End women's subordination
B. Promotion of female domination
C. Promotion of Women's Liberation
D. Promotion of Women's equality

59. The concept of rationality was addressed by which school of feminist thought:
A. Liberal B. Marxist
C. Post Modernist D. Radical

60. Who work "Within the family, he is the bourgeois, and the wife represents the proletariat."
A. Karl Marx B. Engels
C. Margaret Benston D. Clara Zetkin

61. Identify the chronological sequence of the following books according to their year of publication:
(i) Vindication of the Rights of Women
(ii) Pure Lust
(iii) Subjection of Women
(iv) God of Small Things

Codes:

A.	(i)	(iv)	(ii)	(iii)
B.	(i)	(iii)	(iv)	(ii)
C.	(i)	(iii)	(ii)	(iv)
D.	(iii)	(iv)	(i)	(ii)

62. Among the following women who was not associated with eco-feminism?
A. Maria Mies B. Vandana Shiva
C. Arundhati Roy D. Esther Boserup

63. Match the List of Feminist Thinkers according to the school of thoughts:

List-I	***List-II***
(a) Shulamith Firestone	(i) Radical
(b) Clara Zetkin	(ii) Post-Modern
(c) Cixous	(iii) Liberal
(d) Betty Friedan	(iv) Socialist

Codes:

	(a)	(b)	(c)	(d)
A.	(i)	(iv)	(ii)	(iii)
B.	(iv)	(i)	(ii)	(iii)
C.	(iv)	(iii)	(ii)	(i)
D.	(ii)	(i)	(iii)	(iv)

64. Transformation of grass-root women into mere beneficiaries to active participants is coined as:
A. Socialism B. Feminism
C. Clientelism D. Dualism

65. Who compared privileged women's life with "the feathered race"?
A. J.S. Mill
B. Mary Wollstonecraft
C. Harriet Taylor
D. Betty Friedan

66. The reinterpretation of the Oedipus complex was discussed by:
A. Post Modernism
B. Socialist Feminism
C. Existentialist Feminism
D. Psychoanalytic Feminism

67. Match the following ideologies and their school of thought:

List-I	***List-II***
(a) Surrogate Motherhood	(i) Marxist Feminism
(b) Socialization of domestic labour	(ii) Liberal Feminism
(c) Equal opportunities for education	(iii) Post Modernism
(d) Deconstruction of gender	(iv) Radical Feminism

Codes:

	(a)	(b)	(c)	(d)
A.	(iv)	(i)	(ii)	(iii)
B.	(i)	(ii)	(iv)	(iii)
C.	(i)	(iv)	(ii)	(iii)
D.	(iv)	(ii)	(iii)	(i)

68. Arundhati Roy is a:
A. Liberal Feminist B. Socialist Feminist
C. Eco-Feminist D. Radical Feminist

69. Betty Friedan is a:
A. Radical Feminist
B. Socialist Feminist
C. Marxist Feminist
D. Liberal Feminist

70. Which type of feminism believes that oppression of women perpetuated by capitalism?
A. Marxist B. Cultural
C. Liberal D. Radical

71. Liberal Feminism identifies the key force of gender inequality as:
A. Pervasiveness of class
B. Sexism as an ideology
C. Oppression by patriarchy
D. None of the above

72. Socialist Feminism explains gender inequalities as:
A. Centering on class and gender
B. Class oppression only
C. Prevalence of patriarchy
D. Reproduction as a root of women's oppression

73. Match the following Authors (List-I) and Books (List-II) :

List-I	***List-II***
(a) Mary Daly	1. Desire in Language
(b) Betty Friedan	2. Second Sex
(c) Simone de Beauvoir	3. Pure Lust
(d) Julia Kristeva	4. Second Stage

Codes:

	(a)	(b)	(c)	(d)
A.	3	4	2	1
B.	4	3	1	2
C.	4	3	2	1
D.	3	2	1	4

74. Among the following feminists and their ideology which is **not** correctly matched?
A. Helene Cixous — Post-Modernist
B. J.S. Mill — Liberal Feminist
C. Kate Millet — Marxist Feminist
D. Iris Young — Socialist Feminist

75. Among the following feminists' ideologies and schools of thought, which is correctly matched?
A. Reproduction as the cause of women's oppression – Radicals
B. Equal Rights and Opportunities for Women – Socialist
C. Capitalism as a means of Women's Oppression – Post-Modernist
D. The Wages for House Work – Marxist

76. The basic features of Radical feminism are:
(i) Attack on Patriarchy
(ii) Opposition to heterosexuality
(iii) Preference to women's reproductive role
(iv) Treating marriage as a labour contract
Codes:
A. (i) and (ii) only B. (i), (iii) and (iv) only
C. (i) and (iv) only D. (i), (ii) and (iv) only

77. Socialist feminism favours:
(i) Class conflict
(ii) Economic independence of women
(iii) Competitiveness in place of co-operation
(iv) Sex relations as a by-product of economic development
Codes:
A. (i) and (ii) only B. (ii) only
C. (i) (ii) and (iii) only D. (i), (ii) and (iv) only

78. Which of the following contributed to standpoint theory?
(i) Sandra Harding (ii) Arundhati Roy
(iii) Patricia Hill Collins (iv) Vandana Shiva
Codes:
A. (ii) and (i) are correct
B. (i) and (iii) are correct
C. (ii) and (iii) are correct
D. (i) and (iv) are correct

79. Who did Marx refer to as the 'reserve army of labour'?
A. Children B. Women
C. Men D. Old people

80. Marxist Feminism advocates:
(i) Private property as the root cause of Women's subordination.
(ii) Enforced monogamy to be replaced by individual sex love.
(iii) Collectivisation of child care.
(iv) Political Rights of Women.
Codes:
A. (i) and (ii) only
B. (i), (ii) and (iii) only
C. (i) and (iv) only
D. (i) (iii) and (iv) only

81. Which feminist thought suggests that gender equality can be realized by eliminating the cultural notion of gender?
A. Post-modern Feminism
B. Radical Feminism
C. Neo-classical Feminism
D. Socialist Feminism

82. Germaine Greer coined the term Female Eunuch to describe:
A. The biological inferiority of women.
B. The idealization of women in society.
C. Castration of women by aspects of patriarchy.
D. The motherhood of women.

83. 'Consciousness raising' is the major agenda discussed by:
A. Liberals B. Post-modernist
C. Marxist D. Radicals

84. Match List-I (Thinkers) with List-II:

List-I	***List-II***
(a) John Stuart Mill	(i) Marxist feminism
(b) Jane Flax	(ii) Radical feminism
(c) Clara Zetkin	(iii) Liberal feminism
(d) Shulamith Firestone	(iv) Socialist feminism

Codes:

	(a)	(b)	(c)	(d)
A.	(i)	(ii)	(iii)	(iv)
B.	(iii)	(i)	(iv)	(ii)
C.	(ii)	(i)	(iv)	(iii)
D.	(i)	(iv)	(iii)	(ii)

85. Which group of thinkers belongs to Radical feminism?
A. Kate Millet, Mary Daly, Shulamith Firestone.
B. Kate Millet, Mary Daly, Juliet Mitchell.
C. Mary Daly, Juliet Mitchell, Cixous.
D. Shulamith Firestone, Mary Daly, Cixous.

86. Which of the following is not correctly matched?
A. Second stage – Betty Friedan
B. Pure Lust – Mary Daly
C. Feminist Politics and Human Nature – Alison Jaggar
D. The Dialectic of Sex – Kate Millet

87. 'Bourgeois morality was based on hypocrisy, inequality, and possession.' Who among the following did not believe in this?
A. Karl Marx
B. Alexandra Kollontai
C. Engels
D. Mary Wollstonecraft

88. "The Personal is political"! Which of the following feminist theories has given this slogan?
A. Liberal Feminism
B. Radical Feminism
C. Marxist Feminism
D. Socialist Feminism

89. "Within the family, he is the bourgeois and the wife represents the proletariat!" Who among the following Marxist thinkers said this?
A. Alexandra Kollontai
B. August Behel
C. Rosa Luxemburg
D. Frederick Engels

90. Which of the following Feminist Academicians hold that the pursuit of post-modern thought has led to a decline in radical feminism?
A. S.C. Dube
B. Satish Deshpande
C. Maithreyi Krishnaraj
D. C. Lakshmana

91. Match the names of feminists with their writings:

List-I	***List-II***
(a) Women's Estate	(i) Mary Daly
(b) Marxism and the oppression of women	(ii) Andrea Dworkin
(c) Pure Lust	(iii) Lisa Vogel
(d) Woman-hating	(iv) Juliet Mitchell

Codes:

	(a)	(b)	(c)	(d)
A.	(iv)	(iii)	(i)	(ii)
B.	(i)	(ii)	(iii)	(iv)
C.	(iii)	(iv)	(ii)	(i)
D.	(ii)	(iii)	(iv)	(i)

92. Trans-gender theory belongs to:
A. Socialist Feminism
B. Post-Modern Feminism
C. Liberal Feminism
D. Marxist Feminism

93. Chronologically arrange the Liberal Feminist Thinkers according to their period of contribution:
(a) Betty Friedan
(b) John Stuart Mill
(c) Harriet Taylor
(d) Mary Wollstone craft

Codes:
A. (c), (d), (a), (b) B. (d), (b), (c), (a)
C. (d), (a), (b), (c) D. (d), (c), (a), (b)

94. Which school of Feminist questioned the concept of 'natural order' or biological status quo?
A. Liberal Feminist
B. Socialist Feminist
C. Marxist Feminist
D. Radical Feminist

95. Match the list of Books (List-I) and Authors (List-II):

List-I (*Books*)	*List-II* (*Authors*)
(a) Second Sex	(i) Mary Daly
(b) Gyn/Ecology	(ii) Juliet Mitchell
(c) Sexual Politics	(iii) Simon De Beauvoir
(d) Women's Estate	(iv) Kate Millet

Codes:

	(a)	(b)	(c)	(d)
A.	(iii)	(iv)	(ii)	(i)
B.	(iii)	(i)	(iv)	(ii)
C.	(iv)	(i)	(ii)	(iii)
D.	(i)	(ii)	(iii)	(iv)

96. Among the following, who is not a post-modern feminist?
A. Juliet Mitchell
B. Helene Cixous
C. Luce Irigaray
D. Jacques Derrida

97. Who among the following is not a feminist?
A. Jean-Paul Sartre
B. Marilyn French
C. Ann Oakley
D. Jane Flex

98. Which school of feminist thought emerged as a result of gender blind character of Marxist thought?
A. Radical Feminist thought
B. Liberal Feminist thought
C. Psychoanalytic thought
D. Socialist Feminist thought

99. Why do Radical feminists insist that women's oppression is the most fundamental form of oppression?
(i) It is the most widespread.
(ii) It cannot be removed by other social changes.
(iii) It causes the most sufferings to its victims.
(iv) It can be removed through the abolition of class society.

Codes:
A. (i), (ii), (iii) and (iv)
B. (i), (iii) and (iv) only
C. (i), (ii) and (iii) only
D. (ii) and (iv) only

100. Which school of feminist thought believes that "The degree that a person is deprived of power over his/her own body, that person is deprived of his/her humanity"?
A. Liberal
B. Marxist
C. Socialist
D. Radical

101. Who said: "Man is defined as a human being and a woman as a female – whenever she behaves like a human being, she is said to imitate the male"?
A. Betty Friedan
B. Simone de Beauvoir
C. J.S. Mill
D. Shulamith Firestone

102. Existentialist feminism means:
A. Gender is not biological but is based on the psycho-sexual development of the individual.
B. Women have become the "other" or object of men's subjectivity.
C. People's capacities, needs, and interests are seen to be determined by the mode of production that characterizes the society they inhabit.
D. Proceeds from the presumption that the first type of exploitation in human history was sexual exploitation.

103. Who said: The legal subordination of one sex to the other is wrong in itself, and now one of the chief hindrances to human improvement, and that it ought to be replaced by a principle of perfect equality, admitting no power or privilege on the one side, nor disability on the other?
A. Friedrich Engels
B. Mahatma Gandhi
C. J.S. Mill
D. Harriet Taylor

104. Match List-I with List-II regarding the feminist theories:

List-I	*List-II*
(a) Liberal Feminism	(i) Power is exercised inescapably within the language.
(b) Socialist Feminism	(ii) Women should be in control of the means of reproduction.
(c) Radical Feminism	(iii) Theory of women's oppression in systems of capitalism and patriarchy.
(d) Postmodern Feminism	(iv) Gender socialization as the origin of gender differences.

Codes:

	(a)	(b)	(c)	(d)
A.	(i)	(ii)	(iii)	(iv)
B.	(iii)	(iv)	(ii)	(i)
C.	(iv)	(iii)	(ii)	(i)
D.	(ii)	(iv)	(iii)	(i)

105. Match the following from List-I with List-II:

List-I (Authors)	*List-II (Books)*
(a) Bebel August	(i) House Wife
(b) Simon de Beauvoir	(ii) Careers for girls
(c) Ann Oakley	(iii) Women and Socialization
(d) Ruth Miller	(iv) Women Destroyed

Codes:

	(a)	(b)	(c)	(d)
A.	(ii)	(iv)	(iii)	(i)
B.	(iii)	(i)	(iv)	(ii)
C.	(iii)	(iv)	(i)	(ii)
D.	(iv)	(iii)	(ii)	(i)

106. Psycho-analytic feminism means:

A. Gender inequality comes from early childhood experiences, which lead men to believe themselves to be masculine, and women to believe themselves feminine.

B. Gender oppression is class oppression, and women's subordination is seen as a form of class oppression.

C. Women should be in control of the means of reproduction.

D. Women deserve the same privileges, protections, and opportunities as men have.

107. According to Postmodern Feminism:

A. Human experience is located "inescapably within language." Power is exercised not only through direct coercion but also through the way in which language shapes and restricts our reality.

B. Women should be in control of the means of reproduction.

C. Primarily due to one's biology, women's oppression consists of being denied transcendence and subjectivity.

D. A social system that is dominated by males influences the individual psycho-sexual development

108. Who wrote that:

One is not born, but rather becomes, a woman. No biological, psychological or economic state determines the figure that the human female presents in society; it is civilisation as a whole that produces this creature, intermediate between male and eunuch, which is described as feminine, only the intervention of someone else can establish an individual as another?

A. Karen Horney

B. Clara Thompson

C. Alfred Adler

D. Simone de Beauvoir

109. Match List-I with List-II:

List-I	*List-II*
(a) Liberal Feminists	(i) The others
(b) Post-Modern Feminists	(ii) Equal Rights approach
(c) Socialist Feminists	(iii) Ending of capitalism
(d) Existentialist Feminists	(iv) Deconstructionist approach

Codes:

	(a)	(b)	(c)	(d)
A.	(iv)	(ii)	(iii)	(i)
B.	(i)	(ii)	(iii)	(iv)
C.	(ii)	(iv)	(iii)	(i)
D.	(iii)	(iv)	(ii)	(i)

110. Who said that:

"The overthrow of mother right was the world historical defeat of the female sex. The man took the command in the home also; the woman was degraded and reduced to servitude; she became the slave of his lust and a mere instrument for the production of his children"?

A. Jane Flax

B. Margaret Benston

C. Michale Barrett

D. Frederick Engels

111. "Anyone who knows anything of history knows that great social changes are impossible without feminine ferment. The social position of women can be measured exactly, by the social position of fair sex". Who among the following made the statement?

A. Shulamith Firestone

B. Mary Daly

C. Karl Marx

D. Betty Friedan

112. Who describes the development of Feminist theory as having three phases?

(i) 'Feminist Critique'

(ii) 'Gynocriticism'

(iii) 'Gender Theory'

A. Neera Desai

B. Juliet Mitchell

C. Simone de Beauvoir

D. Elaine Showalter

113. Which of the pair is **not** correctly matched?

A. Of Women Born — Adrienne Rich
B. The Dialectic of Sex — Shulamith Firestone
C. The Origin of the Family, Private property and State — Karl Marx
D. Feminist Politics and Human Nature — Alison Jaggar

114. Match the following from List-I and List-II:

List-I (Authors)	***List-II (Books)***
(a) Susan Brownmiller	(i) Women Estate
(b) Juliet Mitchell	(ii) Against our Will: Men, Women, and Rape
(c) Marge Piercy	(iii) The Ethics of Ambiguity
(d) Simone De 'Beauvoir	(iv) Women on the Edge of Time

Codes:

	(a)	(b)	(c)	(d)
A.	(iv)	(iii)	(i)	(ii)
B.	(ii)	(iii)	(iv)	(i)
C.	(ii)	(i)	(iv)	(iii)
D.	(iii)	(ii)	(i)	(iv)

115. What is central in the different approaches of feminism?

(i) Women and their existential situation as central to social progress.
(ii) In all historically recorded societies, men appear to have absolute power over women.
(iii) Existential state of women can be changed.
(iv) Women will never be released from the clutches of age-old slavery.

Codes:

A. (i), (ii), (iii) and (iv)
B. (i), (ii) and (iii) only
C. (ii) only
D. (i) and (iii) only

116. Which of the following acknowledges that women experience oppression in a variety of ways according to class, race, ethnicity, region and sexual preference?

A. Cultural materialism
B. Intersectionality theory
C. Socialist feminism
D. Liberal feminism

117. ________ feminists seek to expand the rights of women through legislation.

A. Radical B. Liberal
C. Socialist D. Capitalist

118. 'Nature' as the 'Feminine Principle'—is a reflection of ideas from which feminism?

A. Postmodern feminism
B. Marxist feminism
C. Eco feminism
D. Liberal feminism

119. Which of the following is NOT a characteristic of Feminist Theory?

A. Feminist Theory treats women as the central subject of investigation.
B. Feminist Theory promotes activism on behalf of women.
C. Feminist Theory is multicultural in orientation.
D. Feminist Theory advocates a linear understanding of the historical experiences of women.

120. Match List-I and List-II below:

List-I	***List-II***
(a) Standpoint Epistemology	(i) Kate Millett
(b) Theory of Patriarchy	(ii) Juliet Mitchell
(c) Domestic Labour Debate	(iii) Nancy Hartsock
(d) Structures of Oppression	(iv) Lise Vogel

Codes:

	(a)	(b)	(c)	(d)
A.	(iii)	(i)	(iv)	(ii)
B.	(ii)	(iv)	(i)	(iii)
C.	(iv)	(iii)	(ii)	(i)
D.	(i)	(ii)	(iii)	(iv)

121. Women's liberation requires separation from Men! Who among the following pair of thinkers propounded this idea?

A. Simone de Beauvoir and Betty Friedan.
B. Mary Daly and Luce Irigaray.
C. Carol Gilligan and Catherine Mackinnon.
D. Nancy Chodorow and Clara Zetkin.

122. Liberal Feminism Advocates:

(i) Individualism (ii) Rationality
(iii) Deconstruction (iv) Radical Change

Codes:

A. (i) and (iii) are correct
B. (i), (ii), (iii) and (iv) are correct
C. (iii) and (iv) are correct
D. (i) and (ii) are correct

123. Arrange the schools of feminist thought in their order of origin:

(a) Radical Feminism
(b) Socialist Feminism
(c) Marxist Feminism
(d) Liberal Feminism

Codes:

A. (a), (b), (c) and (d)
B. (d), (c), (b) and (a)
C. (b), (c), (a) and (d)
D. (c), (b), (d) and (a)

124. Match List-I with List-II as given below:

List-I (Authors)	*List-II (Books)*
(a) Mary Daly	(i) The Subjection of Women
(b) John Stuart Mill	(ii) Feminist Politics and Human Nature
(c) Maria Mies	(iii) Beyond God the Father
(d) Alison Jaggar	(iv) Indian Women and Patriarchy

Codes:

	(a)	(b)	(c)	(d)
A.	(iii)	(i)	(iv)	(ii)
B.	(iii)	(ii)	(i)	(iv)
C.	(ii)	(iii)	(iv)	(i)
D.	(i)	(iii)	(ii)	(iv)

125. Which of the following was of greatest concern to First Wave Feminism?

A. Women's Standpoint Theory
B. Women's capacity for emotional work
C. Women's struggle for political rights
D. Women's struggle for economic equality

126. Which of the following is not an action proposed by radical feminism as a means to defeat patriarchy?

A. Women coming to recognize their own values and strengths.
B. Women uniting across their differences and forming a sisterhood of trust.
C. Women joining female networks in the workplace
D. Women uniting across classes to overthrow the capitalist system.

127. Which stream of feminism advocates "women must become a self, a subject who transcends definitions, labels, and essences? She must make herself whatever she wants to be."?

A. Post-modern Feminism
B. Psychoanalytic Feminism
C. Existentialist Feminism
D. Multicultural Feminism

128. The ______ perspective combines the exploitation of women by capitalism with patriarchy in the home in its analysis of gender inequality.

A. Socialist Feminist
B. Radical Feminist
C. Liberal Feminist
D. Democratic Feminist

129. When feminist theorists say that subordinate groups experience social life as a balancing of roles, they mean that:

A. Subordinate groups have to merge their interests and orientations as they navigate social insti-tutions.
B. Subordinate groups have the capacity to compartmentalize their lives and actions.
C. A subordinate group's experience can be generalized to the dominant group's experience.
D. It describes social reality in an objective and truthful manner.

130. Which one of the following is a Marxist German theorist who advocated for women's rights?

A. Clara Zetkin
B. Elizabeth Cady Stanton
C. Charlotte Perkins Gilman
D. Emma Goldman

131. What is correct about Feminism?

A. It negates the role of men
B. It advocates the rights of women
C. It deals with only working women
D. It deals with the contribution of women

132. Match the following Schools of Feminists according to their ideologies:

List-I	*List-II*
(a) Liberal Feminists	1. Deconstructionist approach
(b) Radical Feminists	2. Ending of Capitalism
(c) Socialist Feminists	3. The social institution must be respected and maintained
(d) Post-Modern Feminists	4. Freedom from the grip of Patriarchy

Codes:

	(a)	(b)	(c)	(d)
A.	1	3	4	2
B.	4	2	1	3
C.	3	4	2	1
D.	2	1	3	4

133. Marxist Feminism explains women's oppression in terms of:

A. Class oppression
B. Class and gender oppression
C. Prevalence of Patriarchy
D. Reproductive oppression

134. Assertion (A): Feminism in India is a singular theoretical orientation, and it has not changed over time in relation to historical and cultural realities.

Reason (R): In India plurality of feminism exists due to the heterogeneity of culture.

Codes:

A. Both (A) and (R) are true and (R) is the correct explanation for (A).
B. Both (A) and (R) are true and (R) is not the correct explanation for (A).
C. Both (A) and (R) is false.
D. (A) is false and (R) is true.

135. Assertion (A): Indian Feminist scholars and activities have to struggle to carve a separate identity for feminism in India.

Reason (R): Historical circumstances and values in India make women's issues different from western feminist thought.

Codes:

A. Both (A) and (R) are false.
B. Both (A) and (R) are true.
C. (A) is true, (R) is false.
D. (A) is false, (R) is true.

136. Assertion (A): Engels says that monogamous marriage is "founded on open or concealed domestic slavery of the wife."

Reason (R): The sole aim of monogamous marriage was to make man supreme in the family and to announce future heirs to his wealth.

Codes:

A. Both (A) and (R) are true. (R) is the correct explanation for (A).
B. Both (A) and (R) are true.
C. Both (A) and (R) are false.
D. Both (A) and (R) are true, (R) is not the correct explanation for (A).

137. Assertion (A): Women were never seen as co-partners, and their contributions to human progress were not valued.

Reason (R): Women were viewed as "other."

Codes:

A. Both (A) and (R) are true, (R) is the correct explanation for (A).
B. (A) is true, (R) is false.
C. (R) is true, (A) is false.
D. Both (A) and (R) are false.

138. Assertion (A): Feminism dismantles all forms of domination in society.

Reason (R): Society is dominated by women.

Codes:

A. Both (A) and (R) are true.
B. Both (A) and (R) are false.
C. (A) is true (R) is false.
D. (A) is false (R) is true.

139. Assertion (A): A group of Radical feminists are against Heterosexuality and supported lesbianism.

Reason (R): Radical Feminists believe that reproduction is the root cause of women's oppression.

Codes:

A. Both (A) and (R) are true, (R) is the correct explanation for (A).
B. Both (A) and (R) are true, (R) is not the correct explanation for (A).
C. Both (A) and (R) are false.
D. Both (A) and (R) are true.

140. Assertion (A): In the early 1960s Feminism and its causes had few supporters even among women.

Reason (R): Majority of the women were content with their lot and did not perceive the treatment of women and men as inequitable.

Codes:

A. Both (A) and (R) are true.
B. Both (A) and (R) are true and (R) is the correct explanation for (A).
C. Both (A) and (R) are false.
D. (A) is correct (R) is false.

141. Assertion (A): Liberal Feminists believe that Human beings are different from animals because of their capacity for rationality and use of language.

Reason (R): Marxists reject the liberal theory of Human nature, and they believe that human nature is based on production and subsistence.

Codes:

A. Both (A) and (R) are false.
B. Both (A) and (R) are true and (R) is the correct explanation for (A).
C. Both (A) and (R) are true, (R) is not the correct explanation for (A).
D. (A) is true, (R) is false.

142. Assertion (A): The feminist approach is reflective of larger transformations in the perceptions and constructions of social reality.

Reason (R): Feminist scholars are more activists.

Codes:

A. Both (A) and (R) are true and (R) is the correct explanation of (A).
B. (A) is true, but (R) is false and (R) is the correct explanation of (A).
C. (A) is true, but (R) is false and (R) is not the correct explanation of (A).
D. Both (A) and (R) are false.

143. Assertion (A): Teaching of feminism and women's studies in India has been depending on western feminist theory.

Reason (R): The body of theoretical knowledge based on empirical research has not been established in India.

Codes:

A. Both (A) and (R) are true and (R) is the correct explanation for (A).
B. Both (A) and (R) are true, but (R) is not the correct explanation for (A).
C. Both (A) and (R) are false.
D. Both (A) and (R) are true.

144. Assertion (A): 'Personal is political' is a core concept in feminist theory.

Reason (R): Gender as a division of power is undiscoverable and unverifiable.

Codes:

A. Both (A) and (R) are true.
B. (A) is true and (R) is false.
C. (A) is false and (R) is true.
D. Both (A) and (R) are false.

145. Assertion (A): Some Radical feminists believe that reproduction is a source of women's liberation.

Reason (R): Men's connection to the child is not known, while the mother's connection to the child is known.

Codes:

A. Both (A) and (R) are false.
B. (A) is true, (R) is false.
C. Both (A) and (R) are true and (R) is the correct explanation for (A).
D. (R) is true and (A) is false.

146. Assertion (A): In post-independence India, feminists are more fragmented than ever before.

Reason (R): Women became equal to men in post-independent India.

Codes:

A. Both (A) and (R) are true.
B. (A) is true, (R) is false.
C. (R) is true, (A) is false.
D. Both (A) and (R) are false.

147. Assertion (A): The concept of class is used in the analysis of social division based on economic resources.

Reason (R): The Marxist feminist believe that capitalism is the root cause of class society.

Codes:

A. Both (A) and (R) are true.
B. Both (A) and (R) are false.
C. (A) is true, (R) is false.
D. (R) is true, (A) is false.

148. Assertion (A): Radical feminists promote surrogate motherhood.

Reason (R): Radicals believe that reproduction is the major cause of women's oppression.

Codes:

A. Both (A) and (R) are false.
B. Both (A) and (R) are true.
C. (A) is false, (R) is true.
D. Both (A) and (R) are true, (R) is the correct explanation for (A).

149. Assertion (A): Equality of opportunity was the political goal associated with feminism.

Reason (R): According to radical feminists all women are the natural allies while all men are the enemies of women.

Codes:

A. Both (A) and (R) are true.
B. Both (A) and (R) are true, (R) is not the correct explanation of (A).
C. (A) is true, (R) is false.
D. (A) is false, (R) is true.

150. Assertion (A): For Marx, every process of production is simultaneously a process of reproduction.

Reason (R): The distinction between production and reproduction is very relevant for analyzing women's issues.

Codes:

A. Both (A) and (R) are true and (R) is the correct explanation of (A).
B. (A) is false, (R) is true and (R) is not the correct explanation of (A).
C. Both (A) and (R) are false.
D. Both (A) and (R) are true and (R) is not the correct explanation of (A).

Answers

1	2	3	4	5	6	7	8	9	10
C	D	D	B	B	A	C	D	B	C
11	12	13	14	15	16	17	18	19	20
D	A	C	D	C	C	C	A	D	D
21	22	23	24	25	26	27	28	29	30
A	B	C	D	B	B	A	D	B	A
31	32	33	34	35	36	37	38	39	40
B	C	A	D	A	B	C	C	C	D
41	42	43	44	45	46	47	48	49	50
C	D	A	C	D	C	D	C	A	B
51	52	53	54	55	56	57	58	59	60
D	D	C	A	D	A	C	B	A	B
61	62	63	64	65	66	67	68	69	70
C	D	A	B	B	D	A	C	D	A
71	72	73	74	75	76	77	78	79	80
D	A	C	C	A	D	D	B	B	B
81	82	83	84	85	86	87	88	89	90
B	C	B	B	A	D	D	B	D	C
91	92	93	94	95	96	97	98	99	100
A	B	B	D	B	A	A	D	C	D
101	102	103	104	105	106	107	108	109	110
B	B	C	C	C	A	A	D	C	D
111	112	113	114	115	116	117	118	119	120
C	D	C	C	B	B	B	C	D	A
121	122	123	124	125	126	127	128	129	130
B	D	B	A	C	D	C	A	A	A
131	132	133	134	135	136	137	138	139	140
B	C	A	D	B	A	A	C	B	B
141	142	143	144	145	146	147	148	149	150
C	C	A	B	D	B	A	C	B	A

❑ ❑ ❑

Gender and Education

- Women's Education – Gender Diversities and Disparities in Enrollment, Curriculum Content, Dropouts, Profession and Gender
- Gendered Education – Family, Culture, Gender Roles, Gender Identities
- Education for the Marginalized Women
- Recent Trends in Women's Education – Committees and Commissions on Education
- Vocational Training and Skill Development for Women

WOMEN'S EDUCATION – GENDER DIVERSITIES AND DISPARITIES IN ENROLLMENT

- Historically, Indian women have been denied their access to educational equality and opportunities by the patriarchal society and gender-biased social attitude. Despite having several women rulers in its long monarchial history, the position of women in society remained abysmal.
- **Ahilya Bai Holkar** was a ruler of Malwa kingdom of western India. After her husband, Khande Rao's death in 1754, she took over the administration of the kingdom. She was a skilled ruler and warrior, who supported and promoted literature, sculpture, and Arts during her reign. She aided widows in retaining their husband's wealth. **Rani Rudrama Devi** was another prominent female ruler, who belonged to the Kakatiya dynasty of Deccan region.
- Women's education positively influences future wages for women, health and other civic parameters of family and society, and provides women with equal opportunity in development.
- Educational inequality between genders results in an imbalance in economic and other fields.
- Only around 2% of Indian women were literate at the time of independence. During the pre-independence era, various social reform organizations were involved in the promotion of female education in India. Some of the organizations, initiatives, and reformists are as follows:

Brahmo Samaj

- Founded in 1828 in Calcutta
- Prominent leaders–Raja Ram Mohan Roy and Debendranath Tagore
- Emphasized on social reforms, female education, the emancipation of women
- Advocated against dowry system and child marriage and removing prejudices against women's education
- Brought out the magazine "Bamabodhini Patrika" for women

Prarthana Samaj

- Founded in 1867 in western India by Atmaram Pandurang

- Prominent leaders – M.G. Ranade and R.G. Bhandarkar
- Organized study groups, free libraries, night schools and women's and students' associations

Arya Samaj

- Founded in 1875 by Dayanand Saraswati
- Advocated equality of men and women
- Worked for religious reform and eliminating social evils in Hinduism
- Advocated compulsory education for boys and girls, spreading of education among masses
- Lala Dev Raj founded Kanya Mahavidhyalaya for girls in 1886
- In 1898, brought out a monthly magazine "Panchal Pandita" to propagate women's education
- Instrumental in starting schools and colleges for women across India
- Provided scholarships for girls students

Theosophical Society

- Founded by Madame Blavatsky and Colonel Olcott in 1875 in New York and came to India in 1879
- Mrs. Annie Bessant founded the Women's India Association in 1917 and advocated equality of sexes, condemned child marriage
- Set up schools to educate girls

Hunter Commission (1882)

- The first education commission; constituted by Lord Ripon
- Also, known as Indian Education Commission
- To assess the status of primary education in India and make suggestions for improvement
- It's recommendations:
  - Primary education through the mother tongue; education of the masses; focus on practical knowledge for life
  - Primary education in backward districts by the Department of Education
  - District and Municipal boards control aspects of primary education; should allocate funds for education
  - Inclusion of subjects such as agriculture, natural and physical science, native arithmetic, etc.
  - Encouragement of indigenous schools
  - Focus on physical education; establishment of night schools wherever needed
  - Establishment of Normal schools to train school teachers

Bharat Stree Mahamandal

- Founded by **Sarala Devi Chaudhurani** in Allahabad in 1910
- Primary goal to promote female education
- Strived to improve women's social and political situation in India

Women's India Association

- Formed in 1917 by Annie Besant in Madras
- Primary goal of improving women's educational condition and remove customs such as child marriage and enforced widowhood
- A multi-ethnic feminist organization that fought for women's equality and opportunities for development
- Involved in social service, fundraising, issues of women suffrage and social reforms

National Council for Women in India

- National branch of International Council of Women formed in 1925
- To address issues of oppressed women and social conditions of women
- Support for female condition and freedom for women in social spheres
- **Ishwar Chandra Vidyasagar (1820-1891),** a social reformer who stressed on the need for women's education for the upliftment of women. He condemned cruel practices like Sati, female infanticide and worked for legalized widow remarriage
- **Savitribai Phule (1831-1897)** and her husband, **Jyotiba Phule (1827-1890)** started schools for lower caste girls in 1848. In 1854, they set up a shelter for upper caste widows. They profoundly influenced **Tarabai Shinde (1850-1910)** in her social reform activities. Tarabai was a progressive Indian feminist who criticized religion for unequal treatment and oppression of women. She advocated widow remarriage, social freedom for women.
- **Pandita Ramabai Sarasvati (1858-1922)** was another feminist social reformer who traveled across Calcutta and Bengal presidencies and advocated publically for women's education and empowerment. She gathered financial support in the USA for residential schools for widows. She opened "Arya Mahila Samaj" in 1882 for empowering and educating women and "Sharada Sadan" (Home for Learning)

in Mumbai in 1889. It is a residential school for Brahmin women, widows and unmarried girls. She also started Mukti Mission in Pune, a housing service for women and girls attending schools. She gave evidence before the Hunter Commission about the need for trained teachers and more female teachers for women's education.

- **Swarnakumari Devi (1855-1932),** Bengali writer, and sister of Rabindranath Tagore was also an active social reformer and women's rights activist. She wrote novels, essays, playwrights and poems that highlighted women's issues. She also set up Sakhi Samiti, an organization for promoting exchange and free discourse of ideas among women. She worked as President of Ladies' Theosophical Society from 1882 to 1886.
- **Kamala Devi Chattopadhyay (1903-1988)** was a feminist and an outspoken supporter of Salt Satyagraha. She became the President of All India Women's Conference in 1936 and set up Indian National Theatre in 1944. She was the first woman to run for political office in India.
- **Durgabai Deshmukh (1909-1981)** founded **Andhra Mahila Mandal** in 1937. She was instrumental in enacting social reform laws in independent India. She was a member of the Planning Commission. She was also the first chairperson of the National Council on Women's Education, established by the government in 1958. The recommendations of the council include prioritizing women's education, the establishment of women's department, promotion of co-education, provision of free education for girls up to class VIII.

But, despite decades of government efforts, advocacy and policies, gender disparity in access and opportunities in education remain.

- According to the India Census, 2011, overall literacy rate in India is 73%. But, the female literacy rate is only 65%. There is a gender gap of around 16% between male and female literacy rates. This gender divide is higher in rural areas. The rural female literacy rate is only 57%, while the rural male literacy rate is higher at 77%.
- The top ranking states and UTs with high female literacy rates are Kerala (91%), Mizoram (89%), Lakshadweep (88%), Tripura (83%) and Goa (81%). States with low female literacy rates are Rajasthan (53%), Bihar (53%), Jharkhand (56%), Jammu & Kashmir (58%) and Uttar Pradesh (59%).
- According to All India Higher Education Survey, 2016-17 conducted by Ministry of Human Resource Development, female Gross Enrollment Ratio in higher education is 19%, which is 5% less than the national average of 25%.
- This gender disparity is a direct consequence of historical attitude towards women's education.
- In an Indian family, the son's education is always prioritized over the daughter's education.
- Girls are more likely to be engaged in family activities to provide economic support, such as childcare and household work. This is more pronounced in low-income households, rural families and households where both parents work.
- Presence of younger siblings affects a girl's education negatively, in terms of gross attendance, time spent on learning activities, learning performance, etc.
- Attitude support within the family and society also influences a girl's educational outcome. Presence of a female adult who emphasizes educational achievement increases the girl's confidence and effort in learning.
- But, most families prepare their girls for marriage, save money for dowry instead of investing in their girl's education.
- Prohibition of Child Marriage Act, 2006 criminalizes marriage of girls below 18 years of age by severe punishment up to 2 years in jail. Child marriage is one of the chief reasons for adolescent girls dropping out of schools and prevents their access to education and development.
- The social background of children also influences the educational outcome. Illiteracy among rural girls and urban poor remains high.
- Expenditure on girl's education is lower than boys within the family. More boys are enrolled in private schools and tuitions than girls. Also, parents anticipate relying on their sons during their old age. This leads to differential treatment in their school enrollment, educational expenditure and access to learning resources.

Curriculum Content

A gender-responsive educational curriculum will reverse gender bias, patriarchy, gender discrimination within the educational system and society. This requires a transformation of traditional methods of teaching, learning discourse and resources. Textbooks pictures for students still depict only men playing certain games, activities, and work, while girls are shown doing traditional activities only. Students are taught more about male leaders than women leaders in history, and women's achievements are marginalized. Even stories portray women engaged mainly in traditional female roles such as housework, childcare, while male characters are shown earning for the family. Teachers reinforce gender bias by expecting girls to do better in crafts activities while boys are expected to perform well in science and math. Textbooks should reflect heterogeneous identities in an inclusive manner, assist in transformative attitude changes in students. Teachers and school authorities should actively promote gender sensitivity and understanding among students through activities and discourse.

Dropouts

In India, girls enroll late and drop out early. The progress of girls from primary to upper primary level is also lower than boys. Major reasons are lack of upper primary schools nearby; girls forced to support the family's economic survival by childcare and household work and the gender cultural attitude towards girl's education.

The dropout rate for girls in upper primary level is very high at 18%, according to the Ministry of Human Resource Development. Girls are not allowed to travel long distances for schools for fear of safety, lack of toilets and public facilities in schools. Even when girls attend school, they share the family's burden of childcare and household work, while this is not so in the case of boys. This is reflected in the improved literacy levels and performance outcome for boys.

Increase in female teachers has a positive influence on retaining girls in school. Some of the parameters that can narrow the gender gap are family's economic status, district wealth and resource allocation, higher number of female teachers.

Some of the government initiatives to bring the gender disparity in education are as follows:

Operation Blackboard

- Launched in 1987
- To provide critical infrastructure and instructional materials for primary schools
- At least 50% of teachers to be women – to improve enrollment of girls in primary schools

District Primary Education Programme

- Launched in 1994
- To provide universal access, retention and learning achievement in primary education through formal and non-formal approach with the district as the unit of planning
- To bridge social gaps and gender differences in enrollment, dropouts and learning achievement in primary education
- Major focus on districts with female literacy below the national average

Mid-day Meal Scheme

- Launched in 1995 by GOI as National Programme of Nutritional Support to Primary Education (NP-NSPE)
- Provision of free lunch to school children to protect children from classroom hunger, malnutrition, increase school enrollment and attendance
- To bring the poor and marginalized children into the educational system

Sarva Shiksha Abhiyan

- Launched in 2001; Universal elementary education programme through community ownership mode
- Specific objective to bridge gender and other social gaps in enrollment and access to elementary education
- Emphasis on girls' education with the provision of free uniforms, books, mid-day meals, and active community collaboration

Rashtriya Madhyamik Shiksha Abhiyan

- Launched in 2009
- Universalization of secondary education
- Improving the quality of secondary education; removal of gender gaps and disparity barriers to secondary education
- Interventions such as the establishment of schools in areas with higher concentration of scheduled tribes, scheduled castes and minorities, more female teachers, separate toilet and civic facilities for girl students
- Eliminating gender bias in textbooks and promote gender inclusive classroom environment

National Early Childhood Care and Education (NECCE)

- Approved by Government of India in 2013; Ministry of Women and Child Development responsible for policy formulation for ECCE
- To provide early childhood care and education for children below six years
- ECCE improves primary school enrollment and educational outcome of children

- ECCE also includes National Curriculum Framework and Quality Standards for ECCE
- **Integrated Child Development Services (ICDS)** –since 1975 under the Ministry of Women and Child Development; supplementary nutrition and health education, health check-up, pre-school non-formal education, immunization for children; a network of more than 1.5million Anganwadi centers nationwide

Apni Beti Apna Dhan

- First launched in Haryana in 1994 as a conditional cash transfer programme to prevent child marriage
- To prevent paternal violence and encourage parents to ensure their daughters' education
- Money is transferred to their account when their daughter reaches 18 years of age and completes secondary education

Beti Bachao Beti Padhao Scheme

- Launched in 2015
- A joint effort of the Ministry of Women and Child Development, Ministry of Human Resource Development and Ministry of Health and Family Welfare
- Social and financial empowerment of girls through education
- Special focus on districts with the low child sex ratio
- To raise awareness about women's rights in society through mass campaigns

National Commission for Protection of Child Rights

- A statutory body set up in 2007 to protect, promote and defend children's rights in India
- Functions:
  - Review safeguards and legislative measures to protect the rights of children and make recommendations
  - Enquire into violation of child rights and crimes against children and recommend proceedings against those violations
  - Right to Education Act, 2009 assigns the responsibility of spreading child literacy, safeguarding of their educational rights and enquire into violations of RTE act

Profession and Gender

According to International Labor Organization data, the female labor participation rate in 2017 was 27%, which was a 7% decrease from 34% in 2001. More than 50 million women in India neither study nor work. There is decrease in work participation of illiterate women as the informal sector becomes more gender biased and exploitative.

The increase in gender disparity despite globalization and economic growth reflects backward trends in gender attitudes, workplace obstacles, and wage issues that deny economic opportunities and development of women. Monster Salary Survey, 2016 shows that women in India earn 25% less than global women. The gender pay gap is highest in the manufacturing sector. The gender gap is considerable in other sectors such as banking, IT, etc..... Even though more women enter the IT sector, they leave soon.

60% of women have only 1-3-year experience, while women with more than ten years' experience are only 2.7%. Gender diversity is needed in workspace across all sectors of the economy.

Though female enrollment in engineering and medicine colleges is high, women entering IITs, post-graduate research and elite institutions are low. This might be a reflection of parents' bias in higher education expenditure. It results in less number of women in the R&D sector and senior management levels. Also, certain sectors such as teaching and nursing are considered female professions reflecting entrenched gender bias.

Gendered Education – Family, Culture, Gender Roles and Gender Identities

Family plays a fundamental role in cultivating gender sensitivity and transforming traditional gender perspectives in children. But, the differential treatment of children based on gender by family members is widely prevalent in India. It begins with access to education opportunities. Parents' attitude towards their girl child's education influences the educational expenditure, the girl child's educational effort, access to resource and learning tools and ultimately the educational achievement of the girl child.

Society and patriarchal culture also influence the gender bias in education. Family members, relatives and neighbors' discouraging attitude towards a girl going to school impacts a girl's confidence and interest in learning. Teachers, school authorities and resource allocation also show gender discrimination. Adolescent girls are forced to drop-out if the school is geographically distant and also due to patriarchal attitudes.

Girl children are expected to contribute to childcare and household work, discouraged from playing athletic sports and extra-curricular activities and expected to choose study fields that suit their female disposition, thus reinforcing traditional gender roles and social norms. These male hegemonic attitudes in the family and civil society which includes schools construct and maintain gender identities that preserve the patriarchal advantage and power enjoyed by men.

High-Level Committee on Status of Women

- Constituted by Ministry of Women and Child Development in 2012, headed by Pam Rajput
- Submitted its preliminary report in 2014
- Highlights three burning issues: increase in violence against women, declining sex ratio and economic disempowerment of women
- Recommendations:
  - 50% reservation for women in decision making bodies through legislation
  - Need for a national policy for women and action plan to tackle violence against women
  - Prioritization of gender concerns in policy formulation and resource allocation

EDUCATION FOR THE MARGINALIZED WOMEN

Discrimination of women from marginalized sectors of the society is reflected in denied educational access, socio-economic opportunities, and political power. Right to Education Act, 2009 guarantees universal access to education. But, women are oppressed, exploited and denied equal status with men. This discrimination is multi-layered in the case of marginalized women such as Scheduled Tribes, Scheduled Castes, migrant children, Dalits and poor Muslim women and women of other minority groups.

Ill-treatment of marginalized children by school authorities is widely prevalent in India. Weak monitoring system prevents accountability and grievance redressal. The negative experience discourages marginalized children from school enrollment and attendance.

Girl children who are not part of the mainstream society face social exclusion in schools such as made to sit separately, verbal harassment from teachers and other children from upper castes. It also affects the educational performance of marginalized children. Due to the scattered nature of the Scheduled Tribes, their geographical access to schools is difficult. Drop-outs among children of migrant workers are very high. Some of the government schemes to address the dropout and low enrollment of marginalized girls and women are as follows:

Kasturba Gandhi Balika Vidyalayas (KGBV)

- Launched in 2004
- Providing primary education to underprivileged girls through intense community immobilization
- Gender sensitization of teachers, gender-sensitive learning materials
- Early childcare, educational facilities and need-based incentives for girls from marginalized sections
- Nearly 2000 KGBV schools for underprivileged girls in difficult-to-reach areas

Mahila Samakhya Programme

- Launched in 1988
- To bridge the gender gap in education; recognizes education as an empowerment tool for women
- Particular focus on women who have been left out of the formal educational system
- Targets out-of-school girls by providing alternative residential centres and learning opportunities
- Building institutions such as Nari Adalats and counseling centers for rural poor women to address the gender disparity in education and development
- Trained facilitators to provide training, capacity building and leadership capabilities for marginalized women
- **Mahila Shikshan Kendra** to provide condensed gender-sensitive learning courses for adolescent girls and women from backward classes

RECENT TRENDS IN WOMEN'S EDUCATION – COMMITTEES AND COMMISSIONS ON EDUCATION

Access to education for women results in decision making power for women, increased social mobility, access to employment and socio-economic opportunities. Pre-independent social reforms led to social awareness for girl's education and access of women to the formal educational system.

Post-independence, the government has taken many initiatives, constituted several committees to improve the educational system, provided universal access to education and removed the gender inequality in education.

Radhakrishnan Committee (1948-49)

- University Education Commission
- To analyze the obstacles and issues in women's higher education, colleges and universities
- Its recommendations include:
    - Required and special amenities for women in colleges and university spaces
    - No curtailment in educational opportunities for women
    - Educational guidance and mentoring by trained professionals for women
    - Equality and diversity in co-educational institutions

Mudaliar Commission (1952-53)

- Officially called the Secondary Education Commission
- To inquire into the status of secondary education in India and make suggestions for improvement
- Recommendations:
    - Secondary education should develop qualities of discipline, co-operation, leadership, and overall personal development
    - Should foster the dignity of manual labor and promote technical and vocational skills
    - Mother tongue or regional language to be compulsory subject and choice of a secondary language

Durgabai Deshmukh Committee (1958)

- National Committee on Women's Education constituted on the recommendation of the planning commission's educational panel to analyze educational status and issues of girls at primary and secondary stages.
- Its recommendations include:
    - Goals for universal enrollment of girls at primary and secondary levels.
    - Construction of teachers' quarters, student hostels, sanitary blocks.
    - Provision of mid-day school scheme.
    - Girl students from isolated locations should be provided with free transport and accommodation facilities.
    - Public awareness programmes and campaigns for girls education.
    - Scholarships to encourage girl students, bridging the gender gap.
    - Setting up National Council for Women's Education and state level commissions.
    - Adult women's education programmes
    - Proper organization of co-education

Hansa Mehta Committee (1961-1962)

- Constituted by the National Council of Women's Education to suggest improvements to women's education.
- It's recommendations:
    - Co-education at primary level
    - Separate and co-education at the secondary and higher level
    - Encourage girls in science and mathematics
    - Number of female teachers should be increased
    - A common curriculum for boys and girls at primary and secondary level
    - Adequate representation of women in textbook committees
    - Vocational training schools with special focus on women

Bhaktavatsalam Commission (1963)

- Constituted to look into the lack of public support for girl's education
- It's recommendations:
    - Improve fields of cooperation such as the construction of school buildings, private schools, the organization of school betterment committees
    - Responsibilities of states include organizing seminars, radio talks, enrollment drives, information pamphlets, etc.
    - Pre-primary schools in rural areas
    - More female teachers in primary schools; training for women teachers; accommodation facilities for women teachers
    - Adult women literacy programmes especially in rural areas

National Council for Women's Education (1964)

- Setup in 1959 by Ministry for Education; reconstituted in 1964 with the following functions:
    - To advise the government on girls and adult women's education
    - Social awareness about the importance of girls' education
    - Periodic evaluation of the educational system vis-a-vis girls' education
    - Research, survey, and seminar work for improving girls' education

Kothari Commission

- National Education Commission
- Setup in 1964; submitted its report in 1966.
- It's recommendations:
  - Targeted efforts needed to close the gender gap in education
  - Special administrative authority for monitoring progress in women's education
  - Proper planning and fund allocation required
  - Provision of girls' hostels and vocational courses for girls
  - Research units on women's education in universities
  - Instruction in regional languages at the primary and secondary level; three language formula

National Policy on Education (1968)

- First National policy on education
- The government set up a parliamentary committee in 1967 to look into the educational system of India
- Suggested radical restructuring of the educational system
- Advocated academic freedom for teachers, equalizing educational opportunities for women
- Need for educational facilities in rural areas, tribal and other backward regions
- Need for adult education, vocational and part-time training
- Recommended compulsory education up to 14 years of age; better training of teachers
- Placed emphasis on regional languages based on the "three-language formula."

SNDT University and Women Studies

- SNDT (Shreemati Nathibai Damodar Thackersey) Women's University was set up in Pune in 1916. The university pioneered Women Studies into the university system in India. In 1974, SNDT established the Research Centre for Women Studies to undertake research, publication, documentation and community activities for gender equality. Later, this system was adopted by the University Grants Commission for establishing women studies research centers across universities in India.

National Policy on Women's Education (1986)

- Special emphasis on removal of gender disparities and equalizing educational opportunities
- Education as a transformative tool for women empowerment in society
- Active promotion of women's studies
- Redesigning of curriculum, textbook training and teacher orientation for women's education
- Vocational and professional courses specifically for women; Elimination of sex stereotyping in vocational and professional courses
- Eradication of female illiteracy; high priority for removing obstacles from primary stage onwards
- Equalization of educational access to scheduled caste and scheduled tribes; education of minorities
- Opening of day care centers and increasing the scope of operation Blackboard
- Setting up open universities and distance learning programmes
- Emphasis on technical and professional courses, research activities; Facilitate inter-regional mobility in higher education.
- The focus of adult literacy programmes and initiatives
- Updated in 1992 as **"Common Minimum Programme"**
- The modified Programme of Action emphasized women's equal opportunity to education, access to the marginalized section of society, distance and non-formal education programmes

Shram Shakti Report

- Submitted by the National Commission on Self-Employed Women and Women in Informal Sector in 1988, under the chairmanship of Ela Bhatt
- Highlighted the widespread female illiteracy in India, high dropout rates of girl students
- Stressed that the upliftment of rural and marginalized women in India could happen only by providing access to education; education as an empowerment tool for women
- Suggested transformative overhauling of the educational system to close the gender gap, actively ensure women's educational equality through grassroots efforts
- The collaboration of government, social organizations, and NGOs in promoting women's education
- Emphasized vocational courses and alternative forms of education to women
- Literacy of women to be viewed in the broader social context as a tool to address social and economic injustice against Indian women

Parliamentary Committee on Empowerment of Women

- A permanent Standing Committee of members from both houses of parliament
- Constituted in 1997
- Functions:
  - ❑ To review reports submitted by National Commission of Women and measures taken by the government for women equality and empowerment
  - ❑ To examine measures taken by the government for comprehensive education of women
  - ❑ To review welfare policies and initiatives for women

National Policy for Empowerment of Women

- Launched in 2001 for advancement and empowerment of women
- Creation of economic and social policies for women's development
- Equal access to opportunities for women in all spheres
- Elimination of all forms of discrimination against women
- Access to quality education; career and vocational training and guidance for women

National Mission for Empowerment of Women

- Launched in 2010
- Holistic empowerment of women by strengthening inter-sector convergence on socio-economic and welfare programmes of women
- Setting up of National Centre for Women—a central repository of knowledge, research, and data on all gender-related issues
- Focus areas:
  - ❑ Access to health, clean water and civic facilities for women
  - ❑ Universal girls education
  - ❑ Higher and professional education for women
  - ❑ Skill development and vocational training programmes for women
  - ❑ Self-Help Groups and self-employment initiatives for women
  - ❑ Prevention of crime and violence against women; gender sensitization
  - ❑ Enhancement for economic empowerment of women, provision of microcredit
  - ❑ Women centers at village level—"Poorna Shakti Kendra"—facilitate grass-root services for women empowerment

Right to Education Act (RTE)

- Enacted in 2009
- Guarantees the right to free and compulsory education for every child within the age group of 6-14 years; made "free and compulsory education" a fundamental right
- Recommends private schools to take 25% of class strength from disadvantaged and marginalized sections of the society
- Suggests policies for early childhood care for children below six years of age
- Provision of specialized training and bridge courses to bring school dropouts on par with students of their age
- Monitoring of neighborhoods to identify children's educational needs and to set up facilities required
- Calls for an adequate student-teacher ratio; teachers need appropriate academic qualification and training

VOCATIONAL TRAINING AND SKILL DEVELOPMENT OF WOMEN

- **Vocational Education:** Focus on occupation and employment skills; preparing people for a specific trade, skills, and knowledge; it is an apprentice system of learning
- Vocational Education and Training is an essential component of national education and nation-building
- **National Council for Vocational Training:** Set up in 1956 as National Council of Training in Vocational Trades (NCVT) to establish national trade certificates, approve curriculum and vocational courses, monitoring, and standards

Non-Formal Education

- Education that occurs outside the formal educational system
- Covers adult education, education of children outside the formal educational system, vocational training, long-distance learning, etc.
- Complements universal access to education by providing educational opportunities to marginalized sections, dropouts, and socially disadvantaged groups
- Caters to the education of scheduled castes, scheduled tribes, and marginalized women

- Contributes to skill development and vocational training of focused groups
- National Adult Literacy Mission is an important component of non-formal education in India
- Helps in socioeconomic transformation of a disadvantaged section of society such as rural women
- Development of vocational training institutes for different sectors

National Adult Education Programme

- Launched in 1978
- Massive programme for education of non-literate adults
- Emphasis on literacy, numeracy, functional deveopment of the individual and social awareness
- Incorporated features of non-formal education; relevancy and learner needs, diversification of curriculum and learning materials

National Adult Literacy Mission

- Launched in 1988 by the Ministry of Human Resource Development
- To eradicate illiteracy among the 15-35 age group
- Special emphasis on women, scheduled caste, scheduled tribes and other marginal sections of the society
- Improving the learning skills of people belonging to socially and economically deprived sections
- Raising their functional capabilities and vocational skills
- Provision of libraries and reading room facilities; continuous learning and skill acquirement

Mahila Samridhi Yojana

- Launched by the Ministry of Social Justice and Empowerment in 1993
- To provide economic security to rural women
- Provision of microfinance to targeted women sections through self-help groups to promote self-employment and self-reliance
- Promotes business capabilities and income generating activities among women from weaker sections of society

National Skill Development Mission

- Launched by the Ministry of Skill development and Entrepreneurship in 2015
- To create a convergence of efforts and activities related to skills training
- Provision of institution training, infrastructure, focus on sustainable livelihood activities

UGC's Capacity Building Programme for Women Managers in Higher Education

- To address the gender gap in higher education administration, especially that of academic faculty
- To provide capacity building for women to understand issues of governance, power and academic leadership
- Workshops for gender sensitization, leadership training, develop management skills

Central Social Welfare Board

- Established in 1953 with Dr. Durgabai Deshmukh as a founder Chairperson
- To provide technical and financial assistance to voluntary organizations involved in the welfare of women and children
- Promotes schemes such as the Condensed course of Education for Women and Adolescent Girls, Vocational Training Programme, Mahila Mandals and many more.

Multiple Choice Questions

1. Match the places with the following Universities:

Universities	*Places*
(a) Alagappa University	(i) Tirupati
(b) SNDT Women's University	(ii) Karaikudi
(c) Mother Teresa Women's University	(iii) Bombay
(d) Sri Padmavathy Mahila Viswa Vidyalaya	(iv) Kodaikanal

Codes:

	(a)	(b)	(c)	(d)
A.	(ii)	(iii)	(iv)	(i)
B.	(iii)	(ii)	(i)	(iv)
C.	(ii)	(iv)	(iii)	(i)
D.	(i)	(iii)	(ii)	(iv)

2. Match the following:

(a) Gandhari	(i) Wife of Sage Yajnavalkya
(b) Maitreyi	(ii) Wife of Dhritrashtra

(c) Rudrani (iii) Wife of Satyavan
(d) Savitri (iv) Another name of Parvati

Codes:

	(a)	(b)	(c)	(d)
A.	(iv)	(iii)	(i)	(ii)
B.	(iii)	(ii)	(i)	(iv)
C.	(ii)	(i)	(iii)	(iv)
D.	(ii)	(i)	(iv)	(iii)

3. Devadasi system is:
A. The practice of dedicating women to temples
B. Conducting wedding ceremony in temples
C. Practising child prostitution in temples
D. Donating girls for dancing in temples

4. Which state had the lowest women's literacy rate in India according to census 2011?
A. Uttar Pradesh B. Madhya Pradesh
C. Bihar D. Rajasthan

5. Who among the following is a winner of the Raman Magsaysay award?
A. Dr. Mohini Giri B. Dr. Shanta Sinha
C. Margaret Alva D. Mayawati

6. International Women's Day (March 8) is celebrated in the memory of:
A. Women Textile Workers Strike in France
B. Women Textile Workers Strike in New York
C. Women Textile Workers Strike in England
D. Women Textile Workers Strike in India

7. In which field Booker Prize is given?
A. Medicine B. Writing
C. Adventure D. Science

8. Who is the first woman President of Argentina?
A. Pratibha Patil
B. Cristina Fernandez Kirchner
C. Sirimavo Bhandarnayake
D. Cristina Cixous

9. Match the indicators of women's studies with the respective sources of data:

Indicators	***Sources of Data***
(a) Crime Against Women	(i) NFHS
(b) Life Expectancy of Women	(ii) DGE & T
(c) Female Enrollment Rate	(iii) NCRB
(d) Time use Survey on Women Labour	(iv) COI/Census

Codes:

	(a)	(b)	(c)	(d)
A.	(i)	(ii)	(iii)	(iv)
B.	(iii)	(i)	(iv)	(ii)
C.	(ii)	(iii)	(iv)	(i)
D.	(iv)	(iii)	(ii)	(i)

10. World Development Report has projected that the population of India will touch 1,350 million by:
A. 2020 B. 2022
C. 2023 D. 2025

11. High female literacy level, as well as low differences between male-female literacy levels, are found in the States of:
A. Punjab and Kerala
B. Kerala and Tamilnadu
C. Tamilnadu and Punjab
D. Punjab and West Bengal

12. Mahila Samakhya is a women's:
A. Empowerment Program
B. Entrepreneurship Development Program
C. Employment Generation Program
D. Educational Program

13. Choose the correct expansion of NPE:
A. National Program on Employment
B. National Policy on Education
C. National Program on Entrepreneurship
D. National Policy on Empowerment

14. Gender balance can be achieved through:
(i) Inclusive development
(ii) Flexi jobs
(iii) Reversing the gender roles
(iv) Equality of legal rights

Codes:
A. (i) and (iii) are correct
B. (iv) only is correct
C. (iii) and (iv) only are correct
D. (i), (ii) and (iv) are correct

15. Who is the Minister at the Centre for Women and Child Development in 2019?
A. Maneka Gandhi B. Krishna Tirath
C. Mamta Banerjee D. Sheila Dixit

16. Who among the following is one of the interlocutors for peace talks in Jammu and Kashmir?
A. Elaben
B. Kiran Bedi
C. Radha Kumar
D. Syeda S. Hameed

17. Which of the following regions is related to the matrilineal system of inheritance?
(i) Kerala (ii) Meghalaya
(iii) Manipur (iv) Goa

Codes:
A. (i) and (ii) are correct
B. (ii) and (iv) are correct
C. (ii) and (iii) are correct
D. (i) and (iv) are correct

18. Which of the following organizations evolved with a Gandhian ideology?
(i) WHO (ii) TLA
(iii) SEWA (iv) DMK

Codes:
A. (i) is correct
B. (iii) and (iv) are correct
C. (i) and (iv) are correct
D. (ii) and (iii) are correct

19. Name the country whose both Head of the Government and Head of the State were women in 2011?
A. Canada
B. Sweden
C. Australia
D. New Zealand

20. Match the organizations given in List-I with the concerns in List-II given below:

List-I	***List-II***
(a) WHO	(i) Children
(b) UNICEF	(ii) Education
(c) UNESCO	(iii) Labour
(d) ILO	(iv) Health

Codes:

	(a)	(b)	(c)	(d)
A.	(iv)	(iii)	(i)	(ii)
B.	(ii)	(i)	(iii)	(iv)
C.	(iv)	(ii)	(i)	(iii)
D.	(iv)	(i)	(ii)	(iii)

21. Arrange the following in Chronological sequence:
I. Report of the National Expert Committee on Women Prisoners.
II. Report of the National Committee on role and Participation of Women in Agriculture and Rural Development.
III. National Commission on self-employed women and women in the informal sector, i.e. Shram Shakti.
IV. National Policy on Education.

Codes:
A. I, IV, II, III
B. I, II, IV, III
C. II, IV, I, III
D. III, II, IV, I

22. To which of the following regions does Irom Sharmila, who has been on a fast for ten years against the Armed Forces Special Powers Act, come from?
(i) Assam (ii) Manipur
(iii) Meghalay (iv) North-East

Codes:
A. (i) and (iv) are correct
B. (ii) and (iv) are correct
C. (iii) and (iv) are correct
D. (i) and (iii) are correct

23. Arrange the following in chronological order:
(i) Integrated Education for the Disabled Children
(ii) Right to Education
(iii) Sarva Shiksha Abhiyan
(iv) District Primary Education Programme

Codes:

A.	(i)	(iv)	(iii)	(ii)
B.	(ii)	(iii)	(iv)	(i)
C.	(iii)	(ii)	(i)	(iv)
D.	(iv)	(i)	(ii)	(iii)

24. Who was the first Indian Women Chief Minister of an Indian State?
A. Smt. Jayalalitha
B. Sheila Dikshit
C. Mrs. Sucheta Kripalani
D. Sarojini Naidu

25. Which States have Literacy Rate above 90% as per 2011 census?
A. Kerala, Tamil Nadu, Mizoram.
B. Kerala, Lakshadweep, Mizoram
C. Kerala, Manipur, Goa
D. Kerala, Manipur, Mizoram

26. The chief barriers of female education in India are:
(i) Shortage of female teachers.
(ii) Inadequate school facilities.
(iii) Gender bias in school curriculum.
(iv) Inadequate English schools.

Codes:
A. (i), (ii) only B. (i), (ii), and (iii) only
C. (iv) only D. (iii) and (iv) only

27. What are the steps made by the government of India to improve the literacy rate?
(i) Free education programmes for poor people.
(ii) Setting up of new schools and colleges.
(iii) Several committees formed to ensure proper utilization of funds.
(iv) Setting up of English medium schools.

Codes:

A. (i) and (iii) are correct
B. (i), (ii), (iii) and (iv) are correct
C. (iv) only correct
D. (i), (ii) and (iv) are correct

28. Match the following from List-I and List-II:

List-I	***List-II***
(a) Human Rights Day	(i) December 1st
(b) White Ribbon Day	(ii) July 11th
(c) World AIDS Day	(iii) November 25th
(d) Population Day	(iv) December 10th

Codes:

	(a)	(b)	(c)	(d)
A.	(iv)	(iii)	(i)	(ii)
B.	(iii)	(iv)	(i)	(ii)
C.	(i)	(ii)	(iii)	(iv)
D.	(ii)	(iii)	(i)	(iv)

29. The reason for the low literacy rate of Dalit females is due to:

A. Continued monopolization of resources by middle and upper-class groups.
B. The stronger influence of Casteism in rural areas.
C. The control of Dalit customs over Dalit women.
D. All the above.

30. Which National Education Policy gave impetus to women's studies in India?

A. Kothari Commission 1964-66.
B. National Educational Policy 1986.
C. Recent Education Policy.
D. Education Commission of 1882.

31. Among the following States which one has literacy rate below 90% according to 2011 census?

A. Kerala
B. Mizoram
C. Lakshadweep
D. Goa

32. Mark the correct answer about caste from the following:

(i) Caste sets the socio-cultural milieu for the individual
(ii) Caste is a localized phenomenon
(iii) Caste and religion are hardcore of Hindu society
(iv) Caste is universal

Codes:

A. (i), (ii) and (iii)
B. (i), (iii) and (iv)
C. only (i)
D. (ii), (iii) and (iv)

33. "To go for a walk with one's eyes open is enough to demonstrate that humanity is divided into two classes of individuals whose clothes, faces, bodies, smiles and occupations are manifestly different." What is the difference?

A. Gender differentiation
B. Sex differentiation
C. Women and women differentiation
D. Men and men differentiation

34. The main obstacles to women's education in India are:

(i) Inadequate school facilities
(ii) Shortage of female teachers
(iii) Inadequate English medium schools
(iv) Gender bias in the school curriculum

Codes:

A. (i) and (ii) only
B. (i), (ii) and (iii) only
C. (iv) only
D. (iii) and (iv) only

35. Match List-I with List-II:

List-I	***List-II***
(a) National Policy on Education	(i) 1952
(b) Mudaliar Commission	(ii) 1964-65
(c) Kothari Commission	(iii) 1948
(d) Radha Krishnan Commission	(iv) 1986

Codes:

	(a)	(b)	(c)	(d)
A.	(iv)	(ii)	(iii)	(i)
B.	(iv)	(i)	(ii)	(iii)
C.	(i)	(ii)	(iii)	(iv)
D.	(ii)	(iv)	(i)	(iii)

36. The UGC Capacity Building Programme of Women Managers in Higher Education (CBWMHE) is meant for whom? Choose the correct one:

A. Women Managers in Higher Education
B. Women Managers in Intermediate Education
C. Women Managers in School Education
D. Women Managers in Vocational Education

37. First woman President in the World:

A. Pratibha Patil
B. Sirimavo Bandaranaike
C. Isabel Peron
D. Ellen Johnson Sirleaf

38. Name the first woman who contested the election for the Office of the President of India.

A. Najma Hepatullah
B. Vijay Lakshmi Pandit
C. Pratibha Devi Singh Patil
D. Lakshmi Sehgal

39. Mark the correct statement about 'Culture':

A. It is learned and includes both material and non-material aspects

B. It primarily means good tastes in fashion and arts

C. It is a matter of norms and values only

D. It is essentially an attribute of the individual rather than that of the group

40. Match List-I with List-II of famous Indian Women:

List-I	*List-II*
(a) Kamaladevi Chattopadhyay	(i) First woman Judge in the Supreme Court
(b) Fatima Beevi	(ii) First woman who, received the Ramon Magsaysay Award for Community Leadership
(c) Kalpana Chawla	(iii) First Indian Women who achieved the highest rank of Lt. General
(d) Punita Arora	(iv) First Indian Woman who wènt into space

Codes:

	(a)	(b)	(c)	(d)
A.	(ii)	(i)	(iv)	(iii)
B.	(iii)	(ii)	(iv)	(i)
C.	(i)	(ii)	(iii)	(iv)
D.	(iv)	(iii)	(ii)	(i)

41. Match the following from List-I and List-II:

List-I	*List-II*
(a) National Policy on Empowerment of Women	(i) 1992
(b) National Mission on Empowerment of Women	(ii) 2001
(c) High-Level Committee on the Status of Women	(iii) 2010
(d) National Commission for Women	(iv) 2012

Codes:

	(a)	(b)	(c)	(d)
A.	(iii)	(ii)	(iv)	(i)
B.	(iv)	(ii)	(iii)	(i)
C.	(i)	(iv)	(iii)	(ii)
D.	(ii)	(iii)	(iv)	(i)

42. The State with the lowest female literacy rate in 2011 was:

A. U.P. B. Bihar

C. Rajasthan D. M.P.

43. As per World Economic Forum, India has been ranked _______ in the economic opportunity and participation sub index out of total 149 countries in 2018?

A. 120th B. 128th

C. 138th D. 142nd

44. The first Woman to receive Bharat Ratna Award:

A. Mother Teresa B. Indira Gandhi

C. Sarojini Naidu D. Aruna Asaf Ali

45. The Chairperson of the Parliamentary Committee on the Empowerment of Women is:

A. Sumitra Mahajan

B. Girija Vyas

C. Krishna Tirath

D. Bijoya Chakravarty

46. In which year was International Women's Day first celebrated?

A. 1908 B. 1911

C. 1913 D. 1914

47. Gender Parity Index (MHRD, 2018) at the Upper Primary Level is:

A. 0.97 B. 1.01

C. 1.10 D. 0.96

48. What is correct about Religion?

(i) It is a unified system of beliefs and practices.

(ii) It is a source of a value system which sets the rationale for social actions.

(iii) Different religions set different guidelines for the lifestyles of the people.

(iv) Religion and caste are hardcore of Indian society and influence the people very strongly.

Codes:

A. (i), (ii), (iii) and (iv)

B. (i), (ii) and (iv) only

C. (ii), (iii) and (iv) only

D. (i), (iii) and (iv) only

49. Match the List-I (Women's Associations) and List-II (the year of establishment):

List-I	*List-II*
(a) Self Employed Women's Association	(i) 1927
(b) Confederation of Women Entrepreneurs	(ii) 2013
(c) Bharatiya Mahila Bank	(iii) 2004
(d) All India Women's Conference	(iv) 1972

Codes:

	(a)	(b)	(c)	(d)
A.	(iv)	(i)	(ii)	(iii)
B	(iv)	(iii)	(ii)	(i)
C.	(i)	(iv)	(iii)	(ii)
D.	(iii)	(iv)	(i)	(ii)

50. "Gender equality needs to be integrated into the curriculum at all levels of school education, and gender modules need to be developed for percolating issues of equity and equality in a sustained manner." Which of the following Committees has made the above observation?

A. Yashpal Committee
B. Hansa Mehta Committee
C. J.S. Verma Committee
D. Durgabai Deshmukh Committee

51. Average Annual Drop-out Rate in School Education (MHRD 2018) at primary level is:

A. 4.86 B. 3.25
C. 5.31 D. 4.13

52. Beti Bachao Beti Padhao Abhiyaan has been launched by which Ministry?

A. Human Resource Development
B. Ministry of Women and Child Development
C. Social Justice
D. Tribal Affairs

53. Which is/are the functions of the caste system?

(i) It provides socio-cultural milieu individuals.
(ii) It denies the mobility of labour.
(iii) It integrates people for power.
(iv) It works for the upward mobility of women.

Codes:

A. (i), (ii) and (iii) B. (iii) and (iv) only
C. (ii), (iii) and (iv) D. (i) only

54. What is correct about 'custom'?

A. It refers to established modes of thought and action.
B. It helps in the process of change.
C. It promotes women's development.
D. It leads to a balanced growth of society.

55. Meira Paibi is:

A. An association B. A self-help group
C. A social movement D. A terrorist group

56. Match the **List-I** (Women) and **List-II** (their Fields of importance):

List-I (Women)	***List-II (Field of Importance)***
(a) Rita Banerji	(i) Winner of Sahitya Akademi award for Literature
(b) Sarala Devi Choudarani	(ii) Founder of the 50 Million Missing Campaign
(c) Amrita Pritam	(iii) Founder of Bharat Stree Mahamandal
(d) Pandita Ramabai	(iv) Social reformer in British India

Codes:

	(a)	(b)	(c)	(d)
A.	(ii)	(iii)	(i)	(iv)
B.	(iii)	(ii)	(iv)	(i)
C.	(ii)	(i)	(iv)	(iii)
D.	(i)	(ii)	(iii)	(iv)

57. Percentage increase in literacy rate in India among females from 2001 to 2011 census is:

A. 15% B. 10%
C. 12% D. 9%

58. The Ministry of Women and Child Development formulated the National Policy on Early Childhood Care and Education (ECCE) in:

A. 2011 B. 2012
C. 2013 D. 2014

59. Which is **incorrect** programme included under the National Food Security Act 2013?

A. Midday Meal Scheme
B. Integrated Child Development Services
C. Public Distribution System
D. National Nutrition Supplementation Programmes

60. Match List-I with List-II:

List-I (Personality)	***List-II (Fields)***
A. Shubha Mudgal	(i) Media
B. Shobhana Bhartia	(ii) Banking
C. Kanchan C. Bhattacharya	(iii) Singing
D. Madhbi Puri Buch	(iv) Police

Codes:

	(a)	(b)	(c)	(d)
A.	(i)	(ii)	(iii)	(iv)
B.	(ii)	(iii)	(iv)	(i)
C.	(iii)	(i)	(iv)	(ii)
D.	(iii)	(iv)	(i)	(ii)

61. Arrange Chronologically the organizations according to the year of establishment:

(a) Bharat Stri Mahamandal
(b) Bharat Mahila Parishad
(c) National Council of Women in India
(d) Women's India Association

Codes:

A. (a), (b), (c), (d)
B. (b), (a), (c), (d)
C. (b), (a), (d), (c)
D. (d), (c), (a), (b)

62. According to the National Commission for Women which state has identified the highest number of Devadasis?
A. Maharashtra
B. Andhra Pradesh
C. Karnataka
D. Tamil Nadu

63. Who was the first woman legislator of Pre-Independence India?
A. Sarojini Naidu
B. Raj Kumari Amrit Kaur
C. Muthulaxmi Reddy
D. Annie Besant

64. Which country granted women the right to vote in 1893?
A. USA B. France
C. New Zealand D. Australia

65. The first woman who called for International Women's Day in 1910 was:
A. Margret Cousin B. Aruna Asaf Ali
C. Clara Zetkin D. Lucy Stone

66. Which of the following is NOT correctly matched?
A. Indira Gandhi — Bharat Ratna
B. Mother Teresa — Nobel Laureate
C. Kiran Bedi — Magsaysay Award
D. Ela Bhat — Pulitzer Prize

67. Match the following schemes with their objectives:

(a) Mahila Samakhya Yojana (i) Girl Child
(b) Apni Beti Apna Dhan (ii) Education
(c) Indira Awas Yojana (iii) Empowerment of Women
(d) Mahila Samridhi Yojana (iv) Housing

Codes:

	(a)	(b)	(c)	(d)
A.	(iii)	(ii)	(iv)	(i)
B.	(i)	(iv)	(ii)	(iii)
C.	(lv)	(ii)	(iii)	(i)
D.	(ii)	(i)	(iv)	(iii)

68. Match the following with their designations:

(a) Srimavo Bandaranaike (i) Former Chief Minister of Bihar
(b) Girija Vyas (ii) Chief Minister of Rajasthan
(c) Rabri Devi (iii) Former Chairperson of the National Commission for Women
(d) Vasundhara Raje Scindia (iv) First Woman Prime Minister of the World

Codes:

	(a)	(b)	(c)	(d)
A.	(ii)	(i)	(iv)	(iii)
B.	(iv)	(iii)	(i)	(ii)
C.	(iii)	(i)	(ii)	(iv)
D.	(i)	(iv)	(iii)	(ii)

69. Match the following list of women and their achievements:

List-I	***List-II***
(a) Vijaya Lakshmi Pandit	(i) Andhra Mahila Sabha
(b) Durgabai Deshmukh	(ii) Astronaut
(c) Kalpana Chawla	(iii) SEWA
(d) Ela Bhatt	(iv) Ambassador

Codes:

	(a)	(b)	(c)	(d)
A.	(iv)	(i)	(ii)	(iii)
B.	(iv)	(ii)	(i)	(iii)
C.	(iii)	(ii)	(i)	(iv)
D.	(ii)	(iii)	(iv)	(i)

70. Match the List of states and as they rank high:

List-I	***List-II***
(a) Kerala	(i) Infant Mortality Rate
(b) Odisha	(ii) Female Life Expectancy
(c) Rajasthan	(iii) Gender Gap in Literacy
(d) Andhra Pradesh	(iv) Rural Work Participation

Codes:

	(a)	(b)	(c)	(d)
A.	(i)	(iii)	(iv)	(ii)
B.	(ii)	(i)	(iii)	(iv)
C.	(iv)	(i)	(iii)	(ii)
D.	(ii)	(i)	(iv)	(iii)

71. Which of the following pairs is correctly matched?
A. Jyoti Basu — Education
B. Kiran Bedi — Magsaysay Awardee
C. Sania Mirza — Film Actress
D. Girija Vyas — UGC Chairperson

72. Who was the Chief Minister of the state of Assam from 6th December 1980–30th June 1981?
A. Anwara Taimur
B. Shashikala Kakodkar
C. Nandini Satpathi
D. V. N. Janaki

73. Among the following women, who was not the President of Congress?
A. Indira Gandhi B. Sarojini Naidu
C. Annie Besant D. Durgabai Deshmukh

74. The Indian woman who was actively involved in Indian Mutiny:

A. Rani of Jhansi
B. Pandita Ramabai
C. Kasturba Gandhi
D. Lakshmi Saigal

75. Among the following, who is not referred to as 'Panchakanya':

A. Radha B. Mandodari
C. Kunti D. Draupadi

76. Who was the first chairperson of the National Commission for Women?

A. Girija Vyas B. Maneka Gandhi
C. Purnima Advani D. Jayanthi Patnaik

77. In which year Jhansi Fort was captured by Rani Lakshmi Bai?

A. 1855 B. 1858
C. 1857 D. 1869

78. Who is the first woman in India to get the Nobel Prize?

A. Indira Gandhi B. Kalpana Chawla
C. Mother Teresa D. Annie Besant

79. Female Literacy Rate in India according to 2011 census:

A. 51.16 B. 50.16
C. 56.56 D. 65.46

80. Among the following pairs which is not correctly matched:

A. Gargi - Women philosopher
B. Sunita Williams - Sports
C. Kiran Desai - Writer
D. Kiran Bedi - Police officer

81. Shashikala Kakodkar was the Chief Minister of which Indian state?

A. Madhya Pradesh B. Rajasthan
C. Goa D. Uttar Pradesh

82. The latest initiative for compulsory education and acceleration of girls education is:

A. Sarva Shiksha Abhiyan
B. Right to Education Bill
C. District Primary Education Programme
D. Universalization of Education

83. Who among the following refers to education as "Trutiya Ratna"?

A. B.R. Ambedkar
B. Baba Amte
C. Jyotiba Phule
D. Tarabai Shinde

84. Match the State/UT from List-I with its female literacy rate given in List-II:

List-I	***List-II***
(a) Sikkim	(i) 73.9
(b) J & K	(ii) 75.5
(c) Maharashtra	(iii) 76.4
(d) Tamil Nadu	(iv) 58.0

Codes:

	(a)	(b)	(c)	(d)
A.	(i)	(iv)	(iii)	(ii)
B.	(ii)	(iii)	(iv)	(i)
C.	(iv)	(ii)	(i)	(iii)
D.	(iii)	(iv)	(ii)	(i)

85. Match List-I with List-II:

List-I	***List-II***
(a) Meera Sahib Fatima Biwi	(i) First Woman to win Bharat Ratna
(b) Amrita Pritam	(ii) First woman Judge of Supreme Court
(c) Indira Gandhi	(iii) First woman to win Nobel Peace Prize from India
(d) Mother Teresa	(iv) First woman to win Sahitya Akademi Award

Codes:

	(a)	(b)	(c)	(d)
A.	(ii)	(iv)	(i)	(iii)
B.	(iv)	(ii)	(iii)	(i)
C.	(iii)	(i)	(ii)	(iv)
D.	(i)	(iii)	(ii)	(iv)

86. Name the last Muslim women ruler of Delhi.

A. Begum Hara
B. Begum Mumtaz
C. Razia Sultan
D. Sultana Begum

87. Which of the following pairs is **not** correctly matched?

A. Mrs. Indira Gandhi – First woman winner of Bharat Ratna
B. Mrs. Sarojini Naidu – First woman Governor of India
C. Mrs. Leila Seth – First woman Chief Justice of a High Court
D. Mrs. Vijaya Laxmi Pandit – First woman President of Indian National Congress

88. Sarva Shiksha Abhiyan (SSA) was launched in the IXth Five Year Plan to:

A. Bridge all the gender and social gaps in education
B. Universalisation of Elementary Education
C. Education for all
D. Education for the weaker sections

89. Which of the following pairs is correctly matched?

A. Krishna Teerath — Minister for Education
B. Arundhati Roy — Nobel Laureate
C. Prema Cariyappa — Chairperson Central Social Welfare Board
D. Purandeswari — Minister for Women and Child Welfare

90. Child Sex Ratio according to 2011 census is:

A. 900 B. 914
C. 924 D. 940

91. Sarojini Naidu was the first woman to become:

A. Governor of a State
B. President of India
C. Chief Minister of State
D. Member of Parliament

92. Match the List-I (leaders) and List-II (Social organizations):

List-I	*List-II*
(a) Pandita Ramabai	(i) Arya Samaj
(b) Sarala Devi	(ii) Bharat Stri Maha Chaudharani Mandal
(c) Annie Besant	(iii) Arya Mahila Samaj
(d) Dayananda Saraswathy	(iv) Theosophical Society

Codes:

	(a)	(b)	(c)	(d)
A.	(iii)	(ii)	(iv)	(i)
B.	(ii)	(iii)	(iv)	(i)
C.	(iii)	(iv)	(ii)	(i)
D.	(iii)	(i)	(ii)	(iv)

93. Match the List-I with List-II given below:

List-I	*List-II*
(a) Mudaliar Commission	(i) Women's Education
(b) Durgabai Deshmukh Committee	(ii) National Policy on Education
(c) Hansa Mehta Committee	(iii) Differentiation in curricula for Boys and Girls
(d) Kothari Commission	(iv) Secondary Education

Codes:

	(a)	(b)	(c)	(d)
A.	(iv)	(i)	(iii)	(ii)
B.	(i)	(ii)	(iii)	(iv)
C.	(iii)	(ii)	(i)	(iv)
D.	(ii)	(iii)	(iv)	(i)

94. How does religion affect the lives of women?

(i) It reinforces the legitimization of the division of labour, privileges, and rewards of the society.
(ii) It may provide standards of values to society.
(iii) It is related to the growth and maturation of the individual.
(iv) It contributes to the stability and sometimes instability of order.

Codes:

A. (i), (ii), (iii), (iv)
B. (i), (ii), (iii) only
C. (i) and (iv) only
D. (ii) and (iii) only

95. Nandini Satpathi was the Chief Minister of which Indian State?

A. Karnataka B. Odisha
C. Maharastra D. West Bengal

96. "Stree Shakti Puraskar" awards are named after which of the following eminent women?

(i) Rani Laxmi Bai
(ii) Rani Rudramma Devi
(iii) Smt. Indira Gandhi
(iv) Ahilya Bai Holkar

Codes:

A. (i) and (ii) only
B. (i), (ii) and (iv) only
C. (iii) only
D. (i) and (iv) only

97. Match the List of states from List-I and Programmes in List-II:

List-I	*List-II*
(a) Gujarat	(i) Working Women's Forum
(b) Maharashtra	(ii) Kudumba Sri
(c) Tamil Nadu	(iii) Annapurna Mahila Mandal
(d) Kerala	(iv) Self-employed Women's Association

Codes:

	(a)	(b)	(c)	(d)
A.	(ii)	(i)	(iii)	(iv)
B.	(iv)	(ii)	(iii)	(i)
C.	(iv)	(iii)	(i)	(ii)
D.	(i)	(iii)	(ii)	(iv)

98. Match List-I with List-II given below:

List-I	*List-II*
(a) Mahatma Gandhi National Rural Employment Guarantee Act	(i) 2001
(b) Sarva Shiksha Abhiyan	(ii) 2005
(c) The Prohibition of Child Marriage Act	(iii) 2010
(d) National Mission for Empowerment of Women	(iv) 2006

Codes:

	(a)	(b)	(c)	(d)
A.	(i)	(ii)	(iii)	(iv)
B.	(ii)	(iii)	(iv)	(i)
C.	(ii)	(i)	(iv)	(iii)
D.	(iv)	(ii)	(iii)	(i)

99. Match List-I with List-II given below:

List-I (Fellowship)	***List-II (Beneficiaries)***
(a) Rajiv Gandhi Fellowship	(i) Women in Science and Technology
(b) Maulana Azad Education Fund/Fellowship	(ii) Single Child
(c) Indira Gandhi Scholarship	(iii) Minorities
(d) Fellowship to Eminent Women Scientists	(iv) Scheduled Castes and Scheduled Tribes

Codes:

	(a)	(b)	(c)	(d)
A.	(i)	(ii)	(iii)	(iv)
B.	(iii)	(ii)	(i)	(iv)
C.	(iv)	(iii)	(ii)	(i)
D.	(iv)	(ii)	(iii)	(i)

100. DPEP Stands for:
A. District Primary Education Programme
B. Direct Primary Education Plan
C. District Progressive Education Plan
D. Direct People Employment Plan

101. Which of the following schemes was introduced by the UGC to encourage women managers in Higher Education?
A. Capacity Building programme for women managers in Higher Education.
B. Skill development programme for women.
C. Capacity Building programme for young Managers in Higher Education.
D. Soft skills development programme for women in Higher Education.

102. Which of the following is not a characteristic of caste?
A. It is universal
B. It is cultural
C. It works as a pressure group for the caste people
D. It sets the socio-cultural milieu for the individual

103. Which one among the following was initiated by the UGC, New Delhi to ensure the safety of women and gender sensitization on University campuses?
A. Single Girl Child Fellowship Programme
B. Rajiv Gandhi Fellowship Programme
C. Saksham Programme
D. Capacity Building Programme for Women Managers in Higher Education

104. The Education Commission (1964-66) is also known as:
A. University Grants Commission
B. Secondary Education Commission
C. Kothari Commission
D. Mudaliar Commission

105. The first and the last Muslim Women Ruler of Delhi:
A. Rukkaya Begum B. Noor Jahan
C. Razia Sultan D. Mahamanga

106. Match List-I with List-II:

List-I (Concepts)	***List-II (Classification)***
(a) Religion	(i) Group
(b) Caste	(ii) Category
(c) Class	(iii) Social institution
(d) Culture	(iv) Composite ways of living and behavior

Codes:

	(a)	(b)	(c)	(d)
A.	(iii)	(ii)	(iv)	(i)
B.	(ii)	(iii)	(i)	(iv)
C.	(i)	(iii)	(ii)	(iv)
D.	(iii)	(i)	(ii)	(iv)

107. Match the items in List-I with items in List-II:

List-I	***List-II***
(a) National Youth Day	(i) 5th October
(b) White Ribbon Day	(ii) 6th June
(c) International Teacher's Day	(iii) 12th January
(d) World Environment Day	(iv) 24th November

Codes:

	(a)	(b)	(c)	(d)
A.	(i)	(ii)	(iii)	(iv)
B.	(ii)	(iii)	(iv)	(i)
C.	(iii)	(iv)	(i)	(ii)
D.	(iv)	(i)	(ii)	(iii)

108. Match the following from List-I (Programme) and List-II (Objective):

List-I (Programme)	***List-II (Objective)***
(a) Mahila Samakhya Programme	(i) Provides regional specific strategies to enable girls to come to schools and provide remedial teaching

(b) 93rd Constitutional Amendment	(ii) Free and compulsory education a fundamental right for all children in the 6-14 age group
(c) Sarva-Shiksha Abhiyan	(iii) National Programme for compulsory elementary Education
(d) National Programme for Education of Girls at Elementary Level	(iv) Education for Women's Empowerment

Codes:

	(a)	(b)	(c)	(d)
A.	(i)	(iv)	(iii)	(ii)
B.	(ii)	(iii)	(i)	(iv)
C.	(iv)	(iii)	(ii)	(i)
D.	(iv)	(ii)	(iii)	(i)

109. Who among the following advocated women's education in pre-independence India?
(a) Sarala Devi Chowdhury
(b) Begum Sakhawat Hossain
(c) Sister Nivedita
(d) Sarojini Naidu

Codes:
A. (a), (b) and (c) only B. (a), (b), (c) and (d)
C. (b), (c) and (d) D. (c) and (d) only

110. Which among the following districts/cities has the lowest female literacy rate as per Census 2011?
A. Kishanganj B. Purnia
C. Budaun D. Jaisalmer

111. Gender-sensitive curriculum refers to that type of curriculum which:
A. Has separate provision for women students
B. Excludes Mathematics and Physical Science
C. Attempts to challenge gender stereotypes
D. Includes only women's issues

112. Which country declares National Holiday on 'Women's Day'?
A. America B. Russia
C. China D. India

113. National Adult Education Programme is based on:
A. Selective approach
B. Mass approach
C. Area approach
D. Mass as well as selective approach

114. Dalit women face triple discrimination. Identify the correct one.
A. Economic, social and political status
B. Caste, class and gender status
C. Religion, caste and political status
D. Ethnic, communal and political status

115. Non-formal Education was evolved in India through a resolution of
A. National Council for Educational Research and Training
B. National Council of Women's Education
C. Central Advisory Board of Education
D. National Institute of Educational Planning and Administration

116. Female rural literacy rate in India (2011 Census) is:
A. 42.4% B. 48.6%
C. 58.7% D. 62.2%

117. Who recommended co-education as the general pattern at the elementary stage of education?
A. The Bhakthavatsalam Committee
B. The Kothari Commission
C. The Hansa Mehta Committee
D. The Radhakrishnan Commission

118. The purpose of providing education to women is to:
(i) Enhance their self-image.
(ii) Enhance their knowledge for marital success.
(iii) Enable them to think critically and participate in decision-making.
(iv) Enable them to play their traditional role effectively.

Codes:
A. (i), (ii), (iii) and (iv)
B. (i), (ii) and (iii) only
C. (ii), (iii) and (iv) only
D. (i) and (iii) only

119. Who was the Founder of the Social Welfare Board in India?
A. Raja Ram Mohan Roy
B. Durgabai Deshmukh
C. Sarojini Naidu
D. Saraladevi Choudharani

120. India is aiming to attain Gross Enrolment Ratio of 30% by ______.
A. 2019 B. 2020
C. 2022 D. 2025

121. Gender Parity Index at the Elementary level (MHRD 2018) is:
A 0.73 B. 0.89
C 1.05 D. 1.60

122. "Equal access to education for women and girls will be ensured"—this was stated in the:

A. National Policy on Education — 1992
B. National Policy for the Empowerment of Women — 2001
C. National Policy of Education — 1986
D. National Adult Education Programme — 1978

123. Which of the following statements are closer to 'Self-Assertion'?

(i) Think exclusively of oneself
(ii) Prioritize one's own needs
(iii) Prioritize the needs of others
(iv) Promote self-identity

Code:

A. (i), (ii), (iv) are correct
B. (i) and (iv) are correct
C. (iii) only correct
D. (ii) and (iii) are correct

124. Assertion (A): Educated unemployment increases with a higher rate of economic growth.

Reason (R): It happens only when there is a lack of professional education.

Codes:

A. Both (A) and (R) are true and (R) is the correct explanation of (A).
B. Both (A) and (R) are true, but (R) is not a correct explanation of (A).
C. (A) is true, but (R) is false.
D. (A) is false, but (R) is true.

125. Assertion (A): School enrollments have shown an upward trend over the past decades, yet retention and transitions to successive cycles of education are a matter of concern.

Reason (R): Girls are often responsible for the care of siblings, a chore that accounts for adolescent girls dropping out of schools.

Codes:

A. (A) is true, (R) is false.
B. (A) is false, (R) is true.
C. Both (A) and (R) are true and (R) is not the correct explanation for (A).
D. Both (A) and (R) are true, (R) is the correct explanation for (A).

126. Assertion (A): The divorce rate is increasing in metro cities in India due to high expectation and poor sensitivity.

Reason (R): There is greater sensitivity to each other's needs in rural areas and the divorce rate in rural areas has been lower.

Codes:

A. Both (A) and (R) are true, but (R) is not the correct explanation of (A).
B. (R) is true, but (A) is false.
C. (A) is true, but (R) is false.
D. Both (A) and (R) are false.

127. Assertion (A): One of the reasons for honour killing is inter-caste and inter-religious marriage.

Reason (R): Women and men willing to marry beyond their own caste and religion are to be discouraged.

Codes:

A. (A) is true, (R) is false and (R) is not the correct explanation for (A).
B. (A) is false, (R) is true and (R) is the correct explanation for (A).
C. Both (A) and (R) are true and (R) is not the correct explanation for (A).
D. Both (A) and (R) are false.

128. Assertion (A): Position of women varied within and between different pre-colonial societies.

Reason (R): Education of women was important in pre-colonial societies.

Codes:

A. Both (A) and (R) are false.
B. Both (A) and (R) are true.
C. (A) is false, (R) is true.
D. (A) is true, (R) is false.

129. Assertion (A): Drop-out Rate is higher among Girls than boys.

Reason (R): Girls have more domestic responsibilities than boys.

Codes:

A. (A) is false but (R) is true.
B. (A) and (R) are true, but (R) is not the reason for (A).
C. Both (A) and (R) are false.
D. (A) and (R) are true but (R) is the reason for (A).

130. Assertion (A): Female Literacy has a negative and significant effect on child mortality.

Reason (R): Maternal education results in increased knowledge about nutrition, hygiene, and child-care practices.

Codes:

A. (A) is true but (R) is not a reason for (A).
B. (A) is false but (R) is true.
C. (A) is true and (R) is a reason for (A).
D. (A) is true but (R) is false.

131. Assertion (A): Female literacy is yet to improve at all levels of education.

Reason (R): There is still a high rate of female drop-outs in school education.

Codes:

A. Both (A) and (R) are true.
B. (A) is true but (R) is false.
C. (A) is false but (R) is true.
D. Both (A) and (R) are false.

132. Assertion (A): Women's presence on higher bodies in academics is marginal.

Reason (R): Male, in general, suffer from patriarchal attitudes, inflated ego, and cultural biases.

Codes:

A. Both (A) and (R) are true.
B. Both (A) and (R) are false.
C. (A) is true, (R) is false.
D. Both (A) and (R) are true, (R) is the correct explanation of (A).

133. Assertion (A): Girls lag behind Boys at all levels of education.

Reason (R): In India the majority of children who leave school without completing the primary education are girls.

Codes:

A. Both (A) and (R) are false.
B. (A) is true, but (R) is false.
C. Both (A) and (R) are true and (R) is the correct explanation for (A).
D. Both (A) and (R) are true, but (R) is not the correct explanation for (A).

134. Assertion (A): The idea of a joint family cannot be sustained because of problems in maintaining the harmony of interpersonal relations.

Reason (R): Forms of the joint family have been modified because women members within the family demand a re-interpretation of its functions.

Codes:

A. Both (A) and (R) are true.
B. Both (A) and (R) are false.
C. Both (A) and (R) are true and (R) is the correct explanation for (A).
D. Both (A) and (R) are true but (R) is not the correct explanation of (A).

135. Assertion (A): Education is a strong vehicle of women's equality and empowerment.

Reason (R): Resource mobilization and management of mass education is a challenge of Indian educators.

Codes:

A. Both (A) and (R) are false.
B. (A) is true, (R) is false.
C. Both (A) and (R) is true.
D. (A) is false, (R) is true.

136. Assertion (A): Non-formal Education System is not helpful for improving the educational qualifications of women.

Reason (R): Non-formal Education System is an alternative to the regular education system.

Codes:

A. Both (A) and (R) are false.
B. (A) is true and (R) is false.
C. (A) is false and (R) is true and (R) is not the correct explanation of (A).
D. Both (A) and (R) are true and (R) is the correct explanation of (A).

137. Assertion (A): There is a need to recognize gender components in the accreditation process of the Higher Education Institution.

Reason (R): There is an increase in the number of women in higher education institutions.

Codes:

A. Both (A) and (R) are false.
B. Both (A) and (R) are true.
C. (A) is true, (R) is false.
D. Both (A) and (R) is true and (R) is the correct explanation for (A).

138. Assertion (A): Males get higher education and quality education than girls.

Reason (R): The Gender gap in education persists in society.

Codes:

A. Both (A) and (R) are true, (R) is the correct explanation for (A).
B. Both (A) and (R) are true, (R) is not the correct explanation for (A).
C. Both (A) and (R) are true.
D. Both (A) and (R) are false.

139. Assertion (A): Education of girls has been identified as one of the most determinants of social and economic development.

Reason (R): Education liberates their mind, opens up new horizons, hopes and opportunities.

Codes:

A. Both (A) and (R) are true.
B. Both (A) and (R) are false.
C. (A) is true, (R) is false.
D. Both (A) and (R) are true, (R) is the correct explanation for (A).

140. Assertion (A): The emphasis on educating women will bring about widespread social changes and population stabilization.

Reason (R): Women's education plays a major role in changing the fertility pattern throughout the world.

Codes:

A. (A) is false and (R) is true.
B. Both (A) and (R) are false.
C. Both (A) and (R) are true and (R) is the correct explanation for (A).
D. Both (A) and (R) are true, (R) is not the correct explanation of (A).

141. Assertion (A): Enrollment of men in education is higher than that of women.

Reason (R): Women's education is not considered essential by society.

Codes:

A. Both (A) and (R) are false.
B. Both (A) and (R) are true, (R) is the correct explanation for (A).
C. Both (A) and (R) are true, (R) is not the correct explanation of (A).
D. (A) is true, (R) is false.

142. Assertion (A): Caste is a barrier to solidarity between women.

Reason (R): Lower caste women suffer from illiteracy.

Codes:

A. Both (A) and (R) are true and (R) is the correct explanation for (A).
B. (A) is true and (R) is false.
C. Both (A) and (R) are true and (R) is not the correct explanation for (A).
D. Both (A) and (R) are false.

143. Assertion (A): The notion of untouchability lies at the root of hierarchy and exclusion of the caste system.

Reason (R): Woman participate in perpetuating the caste system through endogamous marriages.

Codes:

A. Both (A) and (R) are false.
B. Both (A) and (R) are true.
C. Both (A) and (R) are true and (R) is not the correct explanation of (A).
D. Both (A) and (R) are true, (R) is the correct explanation of (A).

144. Assertion (A): Education of girls and women in India have reinforced gender role especially motherhood.

Reason (R): In India, women's education was neglected for many years.

Codes:

A. Both (A) and (R) are true, (R) is not the correct explanation for (A).
B. Both (A) and (R) are true, (R) is the correct explanation for (A).
C. (R) is true and (A) is false.
D. Both (A) and (R) are true.

145. Assertion (A): Caste sets the social milieu for the status of women.

Reason (R): Caste is a basis for prevailing social inequality among Indian Women.

Codes:2

A. (A) is false, but (R) is true.
B. (A) is true, but (R) is false.
C. Both (A) and (R) are false.
D. Both (A) and (R) are true.

146. Assertion (A): The differences between the sexes were a product of education and environment and not of nature.

Reason (R): Women have been socialized in a manner as to become mothers and wives first.

Codes:

A. Both (A) and (R) are true and (R) is the correct explanation of (A).
B. Both (A) and (R) are false.
C. Both (A) and (R) are true and (R) is not the correct explanation of (A).
D. Both (A) and (R) are true.

147. Assertion (A): Gendered discrimination is multi-dimensional, therefore complex to tackle at any one level.

Reason (R): Bias is rampant in the Indian Socio-economic structure since the Vedic times and therefore deep-rooted.

Codes:

A. Both (A) and (R) are true, but (R) is not an explanation for (A).
B. Both (A) and (R) are false.
C. (A) is correct and (R) is false.
D. Both (A) and (R) are true, (R) is the correct explanation for (A).

148. Assertion (A): 'Honour Killings' are increasing in our society.

Reason (R): Religious, discriminatory beliefs and Khap Panchayats decisions lead to more honour killings.

Codes:

A. Both (A) and (R) are false.
B. Both (A) and (R) are true and (R) is the correct explanation for (A).
C. (A) is false and (R) is true.
D. (A) is true and (R) is false.

149. Assertion (A): Active Bravery, Self-confidence, dominance, intelligence, and rationality are characteristics of men.

Reason (R): Love, glamour, beauty, emotional dependence, talkativeness are the characteristics of women.

Codes:

A. Both (A) and (R) are true.
B. (A) is false but (R) is true.
C. (A) is true but (R) is false.
D. Both (A) and (R) are false.

150. Assertion (A): Female literacy is improved at all levels of education.

Reason (R): There is still a high rate of SC/ST female dropouts in school education.

Codes:

A. Both (A) and (R) are true.
B. (A) is true and (R) is false.
C. Both (A) and (R) are false.
D. (A) is false and (R) is true

Answers

1	2	3	4	5	6	7	8	9	10
A	D	A	D	B	B	B	B	B	D
11	**12**	**13**	**14**	**15**	**16**	**17**	**18**	**19**	**20**
B	D	B	D	A	D	A	D	A	D
21	**22**	**23**	**24**	**25**	**26**	**27**	**28**	**29**	**30**
C	B	A	C	B	B	B	A	D	B
31	**32**	**33**	**34**	**35**	**36**	**37**	**38**	**39**	**40**
D	A	B	A	B	A	C	D	A	A
41	**42**	**43**	**44**	**45**	**46**	**47**	**48**	**49**	**50**
D	C	D	B	D	B	C	A	B	D
51	**52**	**53**	**54**	**55**	**56**	**57**	**58**	**59**	**60**
D	B	A	A	C	A	C	C	D	C
61	**62**	**63**	**64**	**65**	**66**	**67**	**68**	**69**	**70**
C	C	C	C	C	D	D	B	A	B
71	**72**	**73**	**74**	**75**	**76**	**77**	**78**	**79**	**80**
B	A	D	D	A	D	C	C	D	B
81	**82**	**83**	**84**	**85**	**86**	**87**	**88**	**89**	**90**
C	B	C	D	A	C	D	B	C	B
91	**92**	**93**	**94**	**95**	**96**	**97**	**98**	**99**	**100**
A	A	A	A	B	B	C	C	C	A
101	**102**	**103**	**104**	**105**	**106**	**107**	**108**	**109**	**110**
A	A	C	C	C	D	C	D	B	A
111	**112**	**113**	**114**	**115**	**116**	**117**	**118**	**119**	**120**
C	B	D	B	C	C	B	D	B	B
121	**122**	**123**	**124**	**125**	**126**	**127**	**128**	**129**	**130**
C	B	A	A	D	A	A	D	D	B
131	**132**	**133**	**134**	**135**	**136**	**137**	**138**	**139**	**140**
A	D	C	C	C	C	D	A	D	C
141	**142**	**143**	**144**	**145**	**146**	**147**	**148**	**149**	**150**
B	C	C	A	D	A	A	B	D	A

❑❑❑

Women, Work and Employment

- Theoretical Perspective: Friedrich Engels, Rosá Luxemburg, Sandra Whitworth, Estēr Boserup
- Concept of Work – Productive and Non-productive Work – Use Value and Market Value
- Gender Division of Labor – Mode of Production – Women in the Organized and Unorganized Sector
- New Economic Policy and its Impact on Women's Employment – Globalization – Structural Adjustment Programs

THEORETICAL PERSPECTIVES

Friedrich Engels (1820-1895)

- German communist, a social scientist & journalist
- Worked with Karl Marx in defining the basic tenets of communism
- His theory on women's oppression, which he developed in collaboration with Marx was published in 1884 as "The Origin of the Family, Private Property and the State."
- Women's oppression is not due to patriarchy but the class structure of society and the rise of the family system that has deprived women of any control over means of production.
- He offers a historic analysis of society to explain how women lost their authority and equality due to the evolution of social hierarchy. Several primitive societies treated men as equal to women, but their position has diminished now.
- The key factor that determines social evolution is the production and reproduction of immediate life—which is the production of means of existence, food, clothing, shelter, tools, and propagation of species (production of human beings). The human social organization evolved according to people's livelihood and materialistic environment.
- In early classless societies, there was no strict pairing of male-female relationships, no monogamy, no hierarchy. There was equality of all in kinship groups. Some of these societies traced their bloodlines through their mothers. In such social groups, women's role in and control over production (food and other necessities) gave them authority and equality of position. Engels calls it primitive communism.
- Even in hunter-gatherer societies, women contributed equally to food gathering and hence shared equal power.
- With the practice of large scale agriculture and surplus production, exchange of surplus and trade led to wealth and profit. Uneven distributions of wealth led to the rise of a class society where

sections of people who controlled the wealth and the means of production dominated the rest.

- As women lost their control over means of production of wealth with men doing the difficult agricultural tasks and women given lesser roles, they also lost their authority and equality status.
- Though there was a division of labor even in hunter-gatherer societies, women enjoyed higher autonomy in the division of tasks as they provided most of the food and were central to production. But, with the emergence of class structure, the sexual division of labor became sterner and women became relegated to household work, reproduction and caregiving.
- As men took charge of heavier works such as cattle domestication, plowing, they gained control over production, property and the wealth obtained, while women's role in the reproduction of family and labor (includes cooking food, caring for the family members and childbearing) increased. They became trapped within the family role.
- With surplus production, wealth and profit emerged private property which became concentrated in the hands of men. Women lost their economic and political power in society as motherhood and reproduction of family became lesser, private tasks.
- The emergence of private property weakened kinship groups as monogamy, and nuclear family systems became the norm. Delineation of the family was necessary to own, control and increase private property. Marriage became a property relationship, and an increase in family members (children) meant more labor and productive work. Women became trapped in the role of childbearing.
- In primitive communistic households, women's household work had a central role (food production). But, when the family became private, the household role lost its social value and women were excluded from public production.
- Engels blames the class hierarchy for women's diminished role in the public sphere, their loss of equality due to means of production controlled by only a section of society. He necessitates the destruction of the class structure and common control over the means of production for women's liberation.
- It is not just the class system, but monogamy and family system that has to be destroyed for complete freedom of women from their household role. Men and women should become equal in the public sphere.
- He also suggests common ownership of property and production, care and education of children by all and sexual freedom of women. In the family system, a maid's honor is used to control her within the family's reproductive role to supply labor and work in the private sphere, while men enjoy greater sexual freedom.
- Engel's communist solution to women's oppression is radical in its causative analysis and solutions, even though it dismisses patriarchy and gender relationships as consequences of the class society.

Rosa Luxemburg (1871-1919)

- German socialist, revolutionary thinker, anti-war and anti-imperialist activist
- She viewed women's emancipation as inseparable from the class struggle.
- She also struggled against opposition to women's emancipation within the socialist movement.
- She argued for a socialist struggle to achieve women's suffrage (right to vote), which was blocked by reformists within the German socialist democratic party. She also championed for the creation of free schools for all sexes and free health care (with emphasis on maternity care).
- Her article, "Women's Suffrage and Class Struggle" (1912) argued for women's right to vote, not for women alone but also as a common class concern for all the proletariat. Women of the proletariat are independent and free than the bourgeois women. They enjoy their right to work and have economic independence, but still, they are exploited by capitalism.
- Women should have the freedom to enjoy education and intellectual development which capitalism does not care to provide. Hence, women's struggle for liberation is a part and extension of the class struggle and the struggle for the liberation of the proletariat.
- She also supported international efforts on socialist women movements and was a close collaborator of socialist feminist, Clara Zetkin.
- She viewed capitalism's inclusion of women in the production process as further exploitation of proletarian women. Under capitalism, women were doubly oppressed as reproductive labor within the household and as social labor.
- She criticized bourgeois feminism for ignoring the rights of working-class women, as they play an essential role in maintaining the capitalist class structure.

- In the second World Social Congress held in 1910, she called for a day of action against war and condemned imperialism, which she diagnosed as an extension of capitalism.
- In her book, "The Accumulation of Capital" (1913), she explored capitalism and its emerging European imperialistic phase for exploitation of cheap labor, resources and new markets. She viewed imperialism as a machine to facilitate global capitalism and campaigned against militarism and colonialism.

Sandra Whitworth (1946-present)

- Academic, political science scholar
- Her research involves exploring how gender investigation is absent in international relations and how gender informs international practices and policies.
- She did her Ph.D. thesis on the topic, "Feminism and International Relations: Gender in the International Planned Parenthood Federation and the International Labour Organization."
- Her research helps understand how ILO and other international organizations are influenced by assumptions about gender and gender relations in framing their policies and solutions.
- The thesis traces ILO's history and evolution since its formation in 1919, through the Versailles Peace Party.
- Before ILO's formation, the International Association for Labor Legislation meeting in Berne in 1906 adopted two conventions limiting night work of women and prohibition of white phosphorous in matches production.
- ILO was formed to incorporate labor concerns and labor reforms so that organized labor forces can become part of capitalism.
- Initially, ILO was influenced by two sections of feminist groups namely protectionists and equal righters.
- Protectionists wanted special rights that women needed as labor at the workplace since women were different from men (physical strength, childbearing, etc...)
- Equal righters viewed special rights for women as a threat to women's equality, as women are less likely to be employed if they came with so many special caveats.
- Majority of ILO's legislation in the early years were protectionists such as women's reproductive health, maternity protection. In 1935, underground work for women was prohibited.
- By 1930, there was an equal mix of protectionists and equal righters. During the Great Depression, unemployment for women rose dramatically. ILO adopted promotional policies to oppose restrictive legislation that limited women's opportunities.
- In 1951, equal remuneration for women workers was adopted. ILO strived to prevent discrimination in employment across different regions.
- In 1952 International Labor Conference, maternity protection convention was adopted which fixed minimum rate of maternity cash benefits and proposed longer maternity leaves.
- Whitworth says ILO should not just try to respond to women's unequal status but need to transform the status of women in society. Women (as workers and in other fields) are viewed as a category only in relation to men.
- She says that gender relations are not grounded in reality but also influenced by how men and women view their relationships and their ideas and culture.

Estēr Boserup (1910-1999)

- French Economist
- She adopted an interdisciplinary approach to investigate the role of women in development.
- Her book, "Women's Role in Economic Development" (1970) was a seminal work that influenced government, international organizations, feminists in the later years.
- Aid agencies began to include women questions in their cost-benefit analysis of development. Her work prompted the UN to declare 1975-1985 as the UN Decade of Women.
- Her book elucidated how women (especially third-world women) shouldered disproportionate economic burden of the development process. Women do not benefit from economic development like men, who enjoy most of the fruits of development.
- Women needed to be fully incorporated into the plans, projects and required a more active role for development.
- She also provided extensive evidence of how labor division within and outside the family is based on gender and emphasized on women's education and health—education of women necessary for their active participation in the development process.
- Oppressive hierarchies and women's absence in the formal economy prevented economic growth and benefited from reaching women. In the third

world, women produced 60%–80% of the food. Women farmers contributed to the economy but did not benefit.

- Her research also investigated how European colonialism had destroyed native social structures and worsened women's status in those regions.

CONCEPT OF WORK

- **Work**–Activities that involve expending physical or mental effort to produce goods and services for human needs
- Economic theory categorizes two spheres of work–economic realm and household realm
- **Productive labor**–Goods and services with market value
- **Reproductive labor**–Activities, and task that people have to do for themselves (cooking, cleaning)
- According to the Marxist perspective, under capitalism, only labor that reproduces invested capital and surplus value is productive. All other forms of labor, even if they are useful for humanity are **non-productive.**
- Labor power helps the capitalist augments his/her wealth. The wage for workers is not determined by the value created, but as a cost to maintain the worker's average lifestyle within the capitalist system.
- Under capitalism, unproductive labor is that which constitute a simple economic exchange of money and goods/services, without surplus value creation. They are a drain on the capitalist's resources.
- Some examples are:
  - **Capitalist's house-servant**–who performs house-hold work/services for which he has to be paid. He does not provide labor that can produce surplus value.
  - **Teacher**–whose service is an industrial necessity, teaches technical skills for future labor.
  - **Doctor**–who maintains health and conserves labor power.
- Though these labor services are necessary and useful, they are unproductive under a capitalist system. In such capitalistic societies, domestic work and child caring are unproductive work.
- Women's unpaid labor involves cooking, cleaning, childcare, care of the sick and elderly and other community-based activities. Women have to do these unpaid works, even if they are engaged in productive work outside as wage-workers or self-employed. They are doubly exploited as unpaid domestic labor as well as a reserve force of productive labor.
- Even though women are traditional household producers and farmers, they are not paid for it directly or indirectly. But, these non-productive and domestic work contribute to the nation's economy.
- Women remain in the unpaid and invisible sphere of social reproduction. But their labor power expended in the unproductive work has a **use value**. Their reproductive work/caring activities (cooking, cleaning, child-rearing) become productive if they are remunerated or get paid for it. With **market value** for their work in the household, those activities can gain esteem and become valued in society.
- In first world countries, domestic work has mostly become paid labor. Though this has brought the private household sphere within the economic, public realm and offered a market-value for its use-value, there is discrimination in the nature of employment.
- Most of those employed in the "caring" industry in the developed world are third world migratory women workers. They are exploited and are the first affected when there are an economic crisis and other social conflicts.

GENDER DIVISION OF LABOR

Division of labor, work, and responsibilities within family and society, on the basis of sex is universal. In ancient and traditional societies, women were assigned the tasks of cooking, child rearing, and home maintenance, while men involved in strenuous physical activities and work away from home.

Women were mostly allocated unpaid work that did not earn them any financial and social credit. This strict segregation resulted in maintaining the status quo in gender inequality. The gender-based labor divisions vary across different cultures, social environment and different types of economies. According to the UN report on the World Social Situation, 2016, over 51% of work done by women is unpaid labor, and it is not accounted for national GDP and statistics.

Economic, social and historical changes have disrupted the traditional gender roles and influenced the institutional rules and norms that govern the tasks allocation between women and men. Better knowledge of the evolution of gender division of labor helps to understand the causes and challenges and frame policy interventions for socio-economic gender equality.

The industrialization and liberalization of the economy have brought in gender parity as women took up labor work and jobs traditionally held by men. This gender equity in the labor market empowers women in decision-making, financial independence, and social capital. At the same time, women are more prone to exploitation by the market and economy because of the inherent historical inequality. The price paid for an individual's work determines the time expended by them and their utility maximization. But, there is a distinct difference in wages based on gender.

Women workers are mostly relegated to marginal and informal sectors, diminishing their job security and bargaining power in the economy. The labor division also varies across the different stages of economic development. Labor force participation by women is also influenced by other factors such as education levels, dual-earners in the family, sharing of household responsibilities, declining patriarchy and social interventions.

There are different perspectives on gender economics across the political spectrum—liberal, Marxist, critical, feminist, capitalist, conservative, etc.

Marxist feminists have coined the term "social reproductive labor" to refer to the collective labor that meets the people's daily needs and renewal. It requires physical, emotional and mental labor power. With marketization of domestic work, working-class women have become part of caring industry labor as well as contribute to the social reproduction of their own family and class collective.

Comparable Worth is an attempt to ensure "equal pay for equal/comparable work." The concept was proposed to eliminate gender discriminatory practices and neutralize sexual segregation of work in the economic sphere. It involves paying a worker equitably based on factors such as the job's skill and educational requirements, responsibilities and task activities associated with each type of work. The concept aims to pay women jobs which have been historically paid less.

Gender Inequality Index (GII) is a composite inequality index introduced in 2010 by the UN to measure gender inequality across three dimensions namely reproductive health (measured by adolescent birth rates, maternal mortality rate), empowerment (proportion of parliamentary seats occupied by women and ratio of literate/educated adult males and females aged above 25 years) and economic status of women (labor force participation rates). India ranks very low at 127th place in the GII, 2017.

Similarly, the UN has developed **the Inequality-adjusted Human Development Index (IHDI)** to factor in the loss to human development due to prevailing inequality levels of each country. Education, income and life expectancy rates of HDI are adjusted according to the inequality rate to arrive at IHDI. India's rank is reduced by one to 131st when inequality is factored in.

UN also uses **the Gender Development Index (GDI),** which measures human development achievements by accounting for the gender disparities. GDI uses the same component indicators used for **the Human Development Index (HDI)**, namely health, knowledge, and living standards. GDI is the ratio of HDI for females and males. India is placed in the last group—group 5 (countries with low equality in HDI between men and women).

Another important survey that helps understand gender inequality is **the Global Gender Gap Index** by the World Economic Forum (WEF). It measures gender parity across four parameters namely economic participation and opportunity, educational attainment, health and survival, and political empowerment. India was ranked 108th in 2018.

MODE OF PRODUCTION

- Marx used the term "mode of production" to refer to how economic production in society was organized and carried out. Historically, various modes of production dominated society. Any mode of production in society includes the means of production (tools, raw materials, machines, and technology) and the relations of productions (labor power and who controls what).
- In a mode of production or economic system, the antagonistic social relations between different forces of production leads to conflict which will culminate in the emergence of a new mode of production that resolves that antagonism.
- According to Marx, Capitalism is a mode of production that is based on private ownership of means of production and exploitation of labor power of the working class to accumulate wealth. This will inherently give rise to class struggle which will result in the destruction of the class system and the emergence of a communist mode of production.

- Under capitalism, the oppressed classes include women, along with the proletariat, who lack control over the factors of production. They have been relegated to a subservient role under the capitalistic society because their labor has become unpaid, invisible and unproductive labor according to the capitalist. Only by bringing their social reproductive role into the public economic realm, destroying the family and class structure and transforming the present mode of production into communism can women be liberated.

WOMEN IN ORGANIZED AND UNORGANIZED SECTOR

According to Census, 2011, the total number of female workers in India is 149.8 million of which rural workers are 121.8 million, and urban female workers are 28 million. Female work participation rate (FWPR) is 25.51% which is slightly less compared to 25.63% in the 2001 census. FPPR for rural and urban India is 30.02% and 15.44% respectively.

States with high FWPR are Himachal Pradesh (44.82%), Nagaland (44.74%), Sikkim (39.57%), Manipur (38.56%), Andhra Pradesh (36.16%) whereas, the UTs and States with very low FWPR are Chandigarh (16%), Uttar Pradesh (16.75%), Haryana (17.79), West Bengal (18%), Bihar (19.07%).

Organized sector refers to those industries and organizations that are governed by laws and procedure. There are established standards and regulations in recruitment, employment, wages, and other labor rights and protections including maternity benefits for women.

Though the organized sector offers an opportunity for women's participation in the economy, women find it hard to rise to managerial and other top posts in enterprises and corporations. Vertical segregation refers to this clustering of men at high-level positions and women employees at the bottom. Horizontal segregation refers to the differential allocation of jobs for men and women at the same occupational level. Women, despite having the skills, experience and qualification face the glass ceiling effect that prevents their professional advancement at workplaces.

There is blatant gender discrimination such as inequality in pay, inadequate provision of facilities and opportunities such as training programs, promotions. Also, most of the organized women workforce is concentrated in unskilled low paid jobs. Another major issue is sexual harassment faced by women in their workplace from their colleagues and higher-ups. Most organizations do not have grievance redressal mechanisms to deal with these problems, and women are discouraged from reporting such crimes.

According to Gender Diversity Benchmark for Asia, 2011 Report on 6 top Asian economies (China, India, Japan, Hong Kong, Malaysia, Singapore), which surveyed women across companies, India ranks last. Women's employment is lowest in India, and a significant part of them leave the workforce between junior and middle-level positions. Indian women face collective pressure from family and society to quit work for the family, choose jobs that suit their marriage and family plans, etc.

The unorganized workforce consists of those who fall outside the organized labor market. The work conditions are not protected by, and hence unorganized workers are prone to exploitation. Majority of the female workforce in India is found in the unorganized sector. The organized sector offers better working conditions, safety, job security, minimum wages, health coverage and many other benefits from which these working women are excluded. In industries such as food processing, tanning, textile, fish processing, construction, garments, and cottage industries, women work long hours and are paid very low. They also face serious health problems related to work conditions.

Some of the issues faced by women workers in the unorganized sector are extreme work pressure, wage discrimination as well as irregular wage payments, job insecurity, inadequate working condition, seasonal migration, lack of maternity and childcare facilities, etc. What is needed is skill training and development of workers for unorganized women workforce, labor legislation for protecting their labor rights and awareness creation.

Workers who are economically productive or employed for less than six months are called marginal workers. According to the 2001 census, in India, 8.7% of workers were marginal workers. Of the 88 million marginal workers, 23.3% comprised of women. Majority of female marginal workers belong to rural areas, as most of them are engaged in agricultural and related activities. Urban female marginal workers are mostly employed as household and domestic care activities.

Contingent workers are those who are hired based on demand and are not considered part of the main workforce. They are not offered the rights and benefits of the formal/main employees of an establishment.

IMPORTANT LABOR LEGISLATION AND ACTS

Contract Labor (Regulation and Abolition) Act, 1970

- To protect the rights and welfare of contract labors
- Covers civil and construction works, house-keeping services, canteen services, computer maintenance, electrical, painting, and whitewashing, etc.
- Applies to any establishment with more than 20 workers
- License mandatory for labor contractors
- Payment of proper wages, provision of basic amenities to ensure health and welfare of the workers such as restrooms, canteen, and first aid services, crèches for women workers

Beedi and Cigar Workers (Conditions of Employment) Act, 1966

- To provide for the welfare of workers in beedi and cigar establishments and to regulate the conditions of work
- With regard to women, this act prohibits night work (after 7 pm) for female employees and makes provision of crèches and clean and sanitary room for children and women

Maternity Benefit Act, 1961

- Amended in 2017
- Covers women employees working in factories, mines, plantations, and other industrial establishments
- To regulate the employment of women before and after childbirth and provide maternity benefits
- The Act's provisions are extended to cover unorganized sectors too
- An inter-state female migrant worker can also enjoy the benefits of this act
- Provides for crèche facilities in establishments with more than 50 employees (includes both men and women workers), legally gender neutralizing child care task
- Maternity leave extended from 12 weeks to 26 weeks with full wages
- Maternity leave of 12 weeks for women who adopt a child below the age of 3 months.
- Provisions of work from home subject to mutual agreement

Vishakha Guidelines and Sexual Harassment at Workplace Act, 2013

Vishakha guidelines were laid out by the Supreme Court in 1997 to provide special protection for women from sexual harassments at workplaces. The guidelines impose the responsibilities of prevention, prohibition, and redress upon the institutions. Organisations with ten or more number of employees have to set up an internal complaint committee (ICC) to look into crimes of sexual harassment and take appropriate action against complaints.

Sexual Harassment at Workplace (Prevention, Prohibition and Redressal) Act was passed in 2013. It makes setting up ICC mandatory and also delineates the procedure to process complaints and steps to be taken.

International Labour Organization (ILO) – Important Conventions regarding Women Workers

- **Night Work (Women) Convention (No. 4)–1919, (No. 89) Revised, 1948:** Women not to be employed for night work
- **Underground Work (Women) Convention (No. 45)–1935:** Women not to be employed in mines of any kind
- **Equal Remuneration Convention (No. 100)–1951:** To provide equal remuneration for equal work for men and women workers
- **Discrimination (Employment Occupation) Convention (No. 111)–1958:** To promote equality of opportunity and treatment concerning employ-ment and occupation and eliminate all kinds of discrimination
- **Workers with Family Responsibilities Convention (No. 156)–1981:** Recognizes the problems and issues of women and men workers with family responsibilities, takes into account their needs and social security requirements, to promote community services, child care and family services and facilities in institutions–**not ratified by India**
- **Maternity Protection Convention (No. 183)–Revised 2000:** To promote women's equality and ensure protection and health of mother and child, provision of maternity leave and other benefits – **not ratified by India**
- **Equality of Treatment Convention (No. 118)– 1962:** To grant equality of treatment of national and non-nationals in social security such as medical care, maternity care, family benefits, etc.

Training and Income Generation Programmes for Women

The Indian government has introduced policy interventions and programmes to promote the economic empowerment of women from time to time.

- **Support to Training & Employment Programme for Women (STEP):** Ministry of Women and Child Development launched in 1986-87; skill upgradation of poor and assetless women; formation of cooperative groups, strengthening market linkages and access to credit and project funding for ten traditional sectors.
- **Rajiv Gandhi Scheme for Empowerment of Adolescent Girls (RGSEAG) or Sabla:** Launched in 2011; vocational training and life skill education for adolescent girls between 11-18 years of age.
- **National Policy for Empowerment of Women:** Launched in 2001; mainstreaming a gender perspective in the development process, three-fold strategy for each sector—provision of training, employment, and income-generating activities.
- **Integrated Scheme for Women Empowerment (ISWE):** To address socio-economic needs of women of North-Eastern region; career counseling, vocational training, and sustainable income generation by mobilizing community action and local resources.
- **National Mission for Empowerment of Women:** Launched in 2010; holistic approach; elimination of violence against women, gender mainstreaming of policies and programmes; awareness generation; formation and promotion of Women Self Help Groups (SHG).
- **Rashtriya Mahila Kosh (National Credit Fund for Women):** Launched in 1993; providing micro-credit to women in rural and unorganized sectors for livelihood support and income generating activities.
- **Technology Development and Utilization Programme for Women (TDUPW):** Programme under the Department of Scientific and Industrial research, use of technology to promote competitiveness and capacity building for women; project support and assistance in sectors like food processing, nutrition, health, and hygiene.
- **National Livestock Mission** (2014-2015) and Mission for Integrated Development of Horticulture (2014-2015) places special emphasis on women farmers in the form of higher subsidies and support for technology adaption.
- **Mahila E-Haat:** Launched in 2016; online marketing platform for women entrepreneurs to showcase and market their products and services.
- **Working Women Hostels:** GOI introduced in 1972-1973, affordable and safe accommodation for working women.
- **Gender Budgeting:** A tool to ensure the translation of policy commitments on gender equality into budgetary allocation; formation of Gender budget cells within all ministries; monitoring and evaluation of programmes and performance.

NEW ECONOMIC POLICY AND ITS IMPACT ON WOMEN'S EMPLOYMENT

The Indian Government introduced fundamental changes to the State's economic policy to deal with the severe Balance of Payments situation and economic crisis it faced in the late 1980s. These set of stabilization measures and structural reforms were called the New Economic Policy, 1991.

The main objectives were to give a market orientation to the economy, reduce inflation and imbalances, increase foreign exchange reserve and economic growth. It involved the removal of unnecessary trade regulations, opening up to the international flow of trade, services, and capital and increased private players' participation in the economy.

The critical features of the policy were:

- **Liberalization**: It involved the abolition of restrictive trade practices, freedom to import capital goods, liberalization in import and export, freedom of expansion and production of industries.
- **Privatization**: Removal of industrial licensing and registration, disinvestment and minimization of public sector enterprises, transfer of ownership and management to the private sector.
- **Globalization**: Tariff rationalization, currency convertibility, import duty reduction, encouraging open competition and foreign trade.

Some of the positive consequences of the policy are the increased competitiveness of the economy, customer-oriented production, adoption and implementation of world-class technologies and human resource development. Women empowerment is related to economic, social and political aspects as well.

All the above measures have also affected the average households and women in numerous ways. Withdrawal of subsidies, contraction of government spending in the social sector had an adverse effect on women's livelihood, poverty, nutrition, and financial resources and means. Certain measures have exacer-bated negative trends in gender parity. It has a negative impact on women's participation in the labor market.

The emphasis on industry and trade led to stagnation and low growth rates in agriculture, forestry and rural industries, which were the major women-concentrated sectors. There was an increase in overall female labor participation, but it was far less compared to male labor participation. Even the increase in female workers took place mainly in the category of marginal workers. Rationalization of state position in health care adversely affected affordable and easy to access to public health services for women, especially rural and marginalized.

Globalization

Globalization is the increasing interconnectedness, integration, and interdependence across the globe brought about by technological and economic advancement.

Women have to be viewed not just as recipients or victims of globalization, but also active participants in the development process. Globalization has resulted in gains in political representation, social equality and economic empowerment of women.

Globalization led to increased opportunities for women, improved awareness due to consciousness, interaction and advent of communication networks. It has offered social mobility, quality education, and jobs, changed attitude towards women. On the other hand, it has also deepened marginalization of women in developing economies, loss of traditional sources of income for women and increased gender inequality, especially in patriarchal societies.

Unequal distribution of the benefits of globalization between men and women has further widened the gender disparity in the economy, society, and households. Globalization's inherent bias towards marketization and big businesses has resulted in the marginalization of rural and indigenous women. Low paid work, part-time exploitative jobs and unhealthy working conditions for women have increased dramatically. Labor demand patterns are causing changes in gender migration that exposes women to the dangers of human trafficking, sexual exploitation, and human right abuses.

Practices of transnational corporations have to be regulated in terms of resource exploitation, labor relations, and marketing to shift a change towards gender equality. The withdrawal of government from its traditional social responsibilities has an adverse impact on the health and livelihood of women. Feminization of poverty is another dimension of globalization.

Major theoretical approaches to women and their role in development are Women in development (WID), Women and development (WAD), Gender and development (GAD).

- **Women in Development (WID) :** The combined result of women suffrage movements, fight against social and cultural inequalities and the demand for equitable participation of women in economic development. This approach postulates the integra-tion of women in the workforce and an increase in their productivity for women empowerment.
- **Women and Development (WAD) :** This approach focuses on patriarchy and capitalization and its influence on material conditions of women. It focuses on the structures of exploitation and inequality, the unequal distribution of opportunities and benefits of development and addresses the challenges to women empowerment and equality.
- **Gender and Development (GAD) :** GAD strives to offer a comprehensive perspective on gender, social and economic development, structures of power and the inherent female contribution to development. It emphasizes on gender differentials and demands a transformative shift in gender relations across all aspects and fields.

Structural Adjustment Programmes

Structural adjustment programmes (SAP) are free-market reforms imposed on India in the aftermath of its economic crisis of 1991, as a condition for receipt of loans from the International Monetary Fund and World Bank. SAP is also linked to the globalization of trade and economy. SAP involved a range of financial measures and a set of target conditions that aims at deregulating and opening up of the economy and the market. It is a long-term strategy that brought in basic structural and operational changes to the economy.

Entry of multinational enterprises, big corporations, and foreign competition are basic to SAP. The Government also took measures to rapidly increase the quantity of export, remove restrictions on foreign investment and private enterprises. But, the position of women in the economy is not determined by economic performance alone.

Some components of SAP were privatization of public industries, credit restrictions, wage control. SAP reduced welfare expenditure on education, health, public distribution services which had a direct impact on women's condition in the society. Other disastrous effects of SAP include gender income inequality, exploitation of women by the labor market, the rise in maternal mortality, unaffordability of social services, etc.

Multiple Choice Questions

1. Rashtriya Mahila Kosh was established in:
A. 1991 B. 1993
C. 1995 D. 1997

2. Who identified women's role in economic development for the first time?
A. Simone de Beauvoir
B. Maria Mies
C. Ester Boserup
D. Peggy Antrobus

3. Gender Budget means:
A. A separate budget for women
B. A separate budget for men
C. To establish gender differential impact and commitments into a budget
D. To establish gender equality in a budget

4. Name the Report on Self-Employment of women in India:
A. Towards Equality
B. Shram Shakti
C. National Perspective Plan for Women
D. Platform for Action

5. Priorities in Budget Allocation has been viewed through:
A. Gender and Poverty Sensitive Lens
B. Gender Budgeting
C. Gender Planning
D. Gender Reviewing

6. What is common among the States—Chattisgarh, Meghalaya, Tripura, and Nagaland?
A. Sex-Ratio for 0-6 age-group is 975
B. High Female Literacy Rates
C. Low Infant Mortality Rates
D. High Female Workforce Participation

7. Arrange the levels involved in the process of empowerment:
A. Decision-making, Accessibility to Resources, Availability of Resources and Awareness Creation.
B. Accessibility to Resources, Availability of Resources, Awareness Creation and Decision-making.
C. Availability of Resources, Awareness Creation, Decision-making and Accessibility to Resources.
D. Awareness Creation, Availability of Resources, Accessibility to Resources and Decision-making.

8. Arrange the changing trend in the slogan of feminism:
A. Welfare, Equity, Empowerment and Development
B. Empowerment, Welfare, Development, and Equity
C. Development, Equity, Welfare and Empowerment
D. Welfare, Development, Equity, and Empowerment

9. GDI stands for:
A. Gender Database Index
B. Gender Development Index
C. Gross Development Index
D. General Development Index

10. Gender mainstreaming aims for:
(i) Good Governance
(ii) Distribute benefit equitably
(iii) Justice for women and men
(iv) Mainstreaming men

Codes:
A. (i) and (ii) are correct
B. (i), (ii) and (iv) are correct
C. (i), (ii) and (iii) are correct
D. (i) and (iv) are correct

11. Which is not the feature of the unorganized sector?
A. High incidence of casual labour
B. High incidence of formal labour
C. High incidence of low skilled labour
D. High incidence of low paid labour

12. Feminization of Poverty refers to:
A. Increasing incidence of poverty among men and women.
B. Increasing incidence of poverty among men.
C. Increasing incidence of famine.
D. Increasing incidence of poverty among women.

13. According to the UN statistics:
(i) Women perform two-thirds of the world's work.
(ii) Women earn one-tenth of the world's income.
(iii) Women are one-third of the world's illiterates.
(iv) Women own less than one-hundredth of the world's property.

Codes:
A. (i), (ii) and (iv) are correct
B. (i) and (iii) are correct
C. (ii) and (iv) are correct
D. (ii) alone is correct

14. Find out the States having low female work participation rates according to the 2011 Census.
A. Bihar, Uttar Pradesh, and West Bengal
B. Rajasthan, Bihar and Uttar Pradesh
C. Tamil Nadu, Andhra Pradesh, and Kerala
D. Karnataka, Gujarat, and Rajasthan

15. What is the 'State Policy' regarding the development of women?
A. Inclusive Development
B. Gendered Development
C. Exclusive Development
D. None of the above

16. Women's work is associated with:
A. Moral value
B. Market value
C. Use value
D. Exchange value

17. Which of the following is the correct distribution of allocation for women in A and B categories of gender budgeting?
A. 30% and 100% in A and B
B. 30% and 70% in A and B
C. 100% and 30% in A and B
D. 50% and 50% in A and B

18. Identify the components of GDI:
A. Achievements of women in relation to men in terms of literacy, longevity and per capita income in a country.
B. Literacy and educational achievements of women in relation to men.
C. A comparative position of men and women in terms of literacy and longevity.
D. Achievements of women in relation to men in terms of education and employment.

19. Which of the following statements pertain to gender division of labour?
(i) Women are engaged in drudgery work.
(ii) Women get equal pay.
(iii) Women only work the undesirable shift.
(iv) Women engage in stimulating work.

Codes:
A. (i) and (ii) are correct
B. (i) and (iv) are correct
C. (i) and (iii) are correct
D. (i), (ii) and (iii) are correct

20. India's Gender Inequality Index rank according to the Human Development Report (2010) is:
A. 126
B. 128
C. 122
D. 133

21. Informal sector in India comprises:
(i) Agricultural labourers
(ii) Beedi workers
(iii) Capitalist farmers
(iv) IT managers

Codes:
A. (iv) and (i) are correct
B. (iii) and (iv) are correct
C. (i) and (ii) are correct
D. (iii), and (ii) are correct

22. Which of the following is the GAD school concerned with?
(i) strategic interests
(ii) bank interests
(iii) strategic policies
(iv) practical interests

Codes:
A. (ii) and (i) are correct
B. (iii) and (iv) are correct
C. (i) and (iv) are correct
D. (ii) and (iii) are correct

23. Arrange the following Acts on the basis of their chronological order:
(i) Contract Labour Regulation and Abolition Act.
(ii) Beedi and Cigar Workers Act.
(iii) Child Labour (Prohibition and Regulation Act).
(iv) Equal Opportunities Act.

Codes:
A. (iii) (ii) (i) (iv)
B. (i) (ii) (iii) (iv)
C. (ii) (i) (iii) (iv)
D. (iv) (iii) (ii) (i)

24. Name the Creche Scheme introduced by the Ministry of Women and Child Development for the children of working mothers in 2006.
A. Rajiv Gandhi National Crèche Scheme.
B. Indira Gandhi National Crèche Scheme.
C. Sishu Vikas Crèche Scheme.
D. Jawahar National Crèche Scheme.

25. What do you mean by sexual harassment at the workplace?
(i) Physical contact and advances
(ii) A demand or request for sexual favours
(iii) Sexual coloured remarks
(iv) Showing pornography

Codes:
A. (i) and (ii) are correct
B. (ii) and (iii) are correct
C. (i), (ii) and (iii) are correct
D. (i), (ii), (iii) and (iv) are correct

26. What is LPG?
A. Liberal Processing Globalisation
B. Liberalization Poverty Globalisation
C. Liberalization, Privatisation, and Globalisation
D. Liberal Political Government

27. What do you mean by 'De-regulation'?
A. Existence of private market
B. Regulations by civil society

C. Existence of safety nets
D. Government will control the markets

28. What is not meant by Feminization of poverty?
A. Women workers excluded and secluded from higher wages.
B. Work for long hours and low wages.
C. Lack of property/land rights.
D. Women's economic independence.

29. Which is not the correct statement relating to women's job satisfaction?
A. Women's work is visible and recognized.
B. Women's work is invisible and not recognized.
C. Sex discrimination.
D. Gender division of labour.

30. What is the recent gender-related Index called that has been developed and used by the United Nations in 2010?
A. Gender-Related Developed Index (GDI).
B. Gender Inequality Index (GII).
C. Gender Empowerment Measure (GEM).
D. Inequality-adjusted Human Development Index (IHDI).

31. How can gender disparities in pay scales be reduced?
A. Integrating jobs, instituting pay equity and job evaluation.
B. Job evaluation, job satisfaction, and pay as per work.
C. Creating capital accumulation and assets.
D. Partnership and following biometric system.

32. What are sustainable livelihoods?
A. It comprises of capabilities, assets, and activities required for living life free from stress.
B. It creates both formal and informal institutions.
C. It comprises and creates assets and outcomes.
D. Poverty and environmental degradation.

33. What is not the characteristics of the Structural Adjustment Programme (SAP)?
A. Privatization
B. Non-withdrawal of safety nets
C. Globalization
D. Deregulation of the market

34. What is the main focus of gender budget initiatives in India?
A. Women Component Plan.
B. Complimentary role for effective convergence.
C. Proper utilization and monitoring of funds from various development sectors.
D. All of the above.

35. What are the main reasons for women being increasingly pushed to the unorganized sector?
(i) Lack of the opportunity to acquire skills and training which could facilitate occupational shifts.
(ii) Unequal structural conditions.
(iii) Women have to bear the major burden of domestic chores.
(iv) Women lost jobs due to globalization processes.

Codes:
A. (i) and (iv) are correct
B. (ii), (iii) and (i) are false
C. (iv) and (i) are correct
D. (i), (ii), (iii) and (iv) are correct

36. Match India's ranking (List-II) with the Gender Gap Index Indicators (List-I) as determined by World Economic Forum (2012):

List-I (Indicators)	***List-II (Ranking)***
(a) The position of women in economic participation and opportunity	(i) 17th
(b) Educational attainment	(ii) 134th
(c) Health and Survival	(iii) 21st
(d) Political Empowerment	(iv) 123rd

Codes:

	(a)	(b)	(c)	(d)
A.	(iv)	(iii)	(ii)	(i)
B.	(iii)	(ii)	(i)	(iv)
C.	(ii)	(iii)	(i)	(iv)
D.	(i)	(ii)	(iii)	(iv)

37. 'Feminization of labour,' means:
A. Less women in all kinds of jobs
B. More women in less kinds of jobs
C. No women in jobs
D. More women in all kinds of jobs

38. Why was a sharp decline in Women Work Participation Rate (WWPR) during the Census of 1971? Choose the correct answer:
A. The participation rate of women work was low
B. The definition of 'women work' was changed
C. The definition of 'work' was revised
D. Most of the women opt for education rather than work during the period

39. The Sexual Harassment Complaints Committee as per the Sexual Harassment of Women at Workplace (Prevention, Prohibition and Redressal) Act 2013, is required to complete the inquiry within a period of:
A. 90 days
B. 60 days
C. 45 days
D. 120 days

40. The World Values Survey provides a window on how social perceptions have changed during the globalization process? Choose the correct answer:

(i) Social attitude toward women have changed from domestic roles to social actors or an agency to change
(ii) The bargaining power of women has changed
(iii) The collective action for the empowerment of women
(iv) Self-centredness has increased

Codes:

A. (ii) only
B. (i) only
C. (i) and (iii) only
D. (i), (ii), (iii) and (iv)

41. Please identify the important sectors where women are working more than men in the world:

(i) Communication services
(ii) Retail, Hotel, and Restaurants
(iii) Manufacturing
(iv) Finance and Business

Codes:

A. (iv) only
B. (i), (ii) and (iii) only
C. (iii) and (iv) only
D. (ii) and (iv) only

42. Percentage of Urban female marginal workers to total workers in India (2011) is:

A. 46.3
B. 48.6
C. 23.0
D. 39.1

43. Percentage of rural female main workers to total workers in India (2011) is:

A. 70.3
B. 55.6
C. 58.2
D. 42.1

44. Marginal workers are those workers who work for the major of the reference period which is:

A. Less than four months
B. Less than six months
C. Less than eight months
D. Less than three months

45. Female Workforce Participation Rate of India is:

A. 33.4
B. 25.5
C. 37.6
D. 21.4

46. Which of the following index is not released by the UNDP?

A. Gender Inequality Index
B. Multidimensional Poverty Index
C. Environmental Quality Index
D. Human Development Index

47. Which of the following is a development indicator for measuring women's status?

A. GNP
B. GDI
C. HDI
D. PCI

48. According to macro-level feminist theorists, gender oppression in a capitalist society:

A. Makes it difficult for women to enter the public sphere.
B. Reflects the interests and experiences of women.
C. Is a functional imperative.
D. Trivializes the productive work of men.

49. The Ministry of Human and Child Development adopted the mission statement of Budgeting for Gender Equity in which year?

A. 2004 - 2005
B. 2002 - 2003
C. 2001 - 2002
D. 2000 - 2001

50. Feminization of poverty is related to the fact that:

(i) Poverty is restricted to women only.
(ii) Women are more negatively affected by poverty.
(iii) Women and men experience poverty and its effect in different ways.
(iv) Economic globalization is one of the causes.

Codes:

A. (i), (ii) and (iii) are correct.
B. (ii), (iii) and (iv) are correct.
C. (i) and (ii) are correct.
D. (ii) and (iv) are correct.

51. Which of the following indicators are used in the Human Development Index (HDI)?

(i) Standard of living
(ii) Education
(iii) Life expectancy
(iv) Sanitation

Codes:

A. Only (i), (ii) and (iv)
B. Only (i), (ii) and (iii)
C. Only (i) and (ii)
D. All of the above

52. In which year the Government of India introduced the Gender Budget Statement (20) in the Union Budget?

A. 2002 - 2003
B. 2004 - 2005
C. 2005 - 2006
D. 2008 - 2009

53. Which is not correct about Gender-responsive Budget?

A. Gender Budgeting does not seek to create a separate Budget but to provide affirmative action to address the specific needs of women.

B. Gender Budgeting is an accounting exercise or say a process to ensure that the benefits of development should reach all the minorities.

C. Gender Budgeting involves dissection of the Government budget to establish its gender-differential impacts and to translate gender commitments into budgetary commitments.

D. Gender Budgeting entails maintaining a gender perspective at various stages like programmes/ policy formulation etc.

54. Urban Work Force Participation Rate of females in India (2011) is:

A. 25% B. 17.8%
C. 15.4% D. 29%

55. "Corporate company's sense of responsibility towards the community and environment" is known as:

A. Social Entrepreneurship
B. Corporate Community Network
C. Corporate Social Responsibility
D. Corporate Community Responsibility

56. Which is incorrect of the following regarding features of a gender-responsive budget?

A. Mainstreaming gender perspective at various stages of program/policy formulation
B. Assessment of needs of target groups
C. Allocation of resources and impact assessment
D. Financial Inclusion for both men and women

57. Feminist Economics stands for:

A. Economics that deals with women who are rebels
B. Economics deals with the feminine component in the study of Economics
C. Economics that deals with issues relating to gender in general and women in particular
D. Economics that deals with feminism

58. Which state in India has the highest female work-force participation rate according to the 2011 census?

A. Himachal Pradesh B. Mizoram
C. Maharashtra D. West Bengal

59. The sexual division of labour in primitive society was of _______ type.

A. Reciprocal B. Dominant
C. Submissive D. Uniform

60. Which of the following characteristics are related to "unorganized labour"?

(i) Workers who have not been able to organize themselves
(ii) Casual nature of employment
(iii) Not included in the purview of labour laws
(iv) Small and scattered size of the labour force

Codes:

A. (i), (ii), (iii) are correct
B. (i), (ii), (iii) and (iv) are correct
C. (i) and (ii) only correct
D. (iii) and (iv) are correct

61. GEM stands for:

A. Gender Emerging Measures
B. Gender Emergency Measures
C. Gender Empowerment Measures
D. Gender Equity Measures

62. Shram Shakti report deals with:

A. Women in the organized sector
B. Women in the unorganised sector
C. Unemployed women
D. Women in the administrative services

63. Gender mainstreaming incorporate:

A. WID perspective B. WAD perspective
C. GAD perspective D. HDI perspective

64. Women's work remains invisible because:

A. Women concentrate on the public sphere
B. Women concentrate informal sector
C. Women concentrate in the productive sphere
D. Women concentrate in the private sphere

65. Mahila E haat was launched in which year:

A. 2016 B. 2010
C. 2005 D. 2000

66. Women's agricultural participation is one of the challenging areas of women's work because:

(i) Majority of women are employed in the unorganized sector.
(ii) Women workers get lower wages than men for the same job.
(iii) Female workers are not provided with facilities such as maternity leave.
(iv) Women workers are trained in modern technology.

Codes:

A. (i), (ii) and (iii) are correct
B. (i), (ii), (iii) and (iv) are correct
C. (i) and (ii) are correct
D. (iv) only correct

67. Feminization of poverty refers to
A. Women are responsible for poverty
B. Men are more affected by poverty
C. Women are more negatively affected by poverty
D. Men and women experience poverty equally

68. Incorporating Gender in Development Planning and Process is known as:
A. Gender segregation
B. Gender mainstreaming
C. Gender analysis
D. Gender identity

69. Which of the following statements is false?
A. There is persistent discrimination against the rights of the girl child.
B. Gender exclusion exists only at the economic level.
C. Eleventh Plan ensures that 33 percent of beneficiaries of Government schemes are women and children.
D. Women entrepreneurs have problems of finance and working capital.

70. According to the World Economic Forum, the rank of India in the Global Gender Gap Index in 2018 is:
A. 108 B. 104
C. 102 D. 100

71. Women are highly concentrated in low paying jobs this exemplifies ______.
A. Matriarchy
B. Sexual Harassment
C. Feminization of Poverty
D. Institutional Sexism

72. Which of the following is not an indicator for calculating Human Development Index?
A. Long and Healthy Life
B. Dimension of Knowledge
C. Participation in Decision Making
D. Decent Standard of Living

73. Mark the correct statement:
(i) There are many classes of women.
(ii) Class is reflected in the behavior of women.
(iii) Women constitute a class.
(iv) Class is an open form of social inequality among women.
Mark the correct answer from the codes below:
A. (i), (ii), (iv) only B. (i), (ii), (iii), (iv)
C. (iii) and (iv) only D. (iv) only

74. Women's work was recognized as being as essential as men's work for which kind of society?
A. Tribal society B. Rural society
C. Urban society D. Modern society

75. Female labour force participation is negatively affected by:
A. Women's self-perception of the need to work.
B. Spread of mass media.
C. Prevalence of information technology.
D. Women's interest in extracurricular activities.

76. What is the Women's work participation rate in the Agriculture as per ILO?
A. 65% B. 85%
C. 75% D. 72%

77. When was Multi-dimensional Poverty Index (MPI) introduced in the Human Development Report?
A. 2010 B. 2009
C. 2008 D. 2011

78. What do you mean by 'Comparable worth' discrimination?
A. Pay for household work
B. Sex segregation in jobs
C. Sex segregation in jobs and less pay for women's work
D. More pay for women's work

79. What percentage of India's population is below the official poverty line?
A. Below 30%
B. 30% to 35%
C. Above 35% but below 40%
D. Between 40% and 45%

80. Wealth produced by the powerless many ends up in the hands of the powerful few in which society?
A. Class society
B. Gendered society
C. Tribal society
D. Socialist society

81. What is correct about the feminization of labour?
(i) More women in the workforce
(ii) Women do work on increasingly more favourable terms
(iii) Women are preferred as employees for they are available on cheap and non-permanent terms
(iv) Women are preferred as employees for their efficiency and flexibility

Codes:
A. (i), (ii), (iii) and (iv)
B. (i) and (iii) only
C. (i), (ii) and (iv) only
D. (ii) and (iii) only

82. Identify the possible barriers affecting women's ability to own land from the following:
(i) Lack of legal knowledge.
(ii) Gendered norms and attitudes about land ownership.
(iii) Government's help to provide land rights for women.
(iv) Gender friendly policies to acquire land.

Codes:
A. (i) and (ii)
B. (i), (ii), (iii), (iv)
C. (iv) only
D. (ii), (iii), (iv)

83. Which of the following States has the highest Female Workplace Participation Rate in India according to the 2011 Census?
A. Gujarat
B. Kerala
C. Karnataka
D. Himachal Pradesh

84. Identify the correct statement about the components of the Multidimensional Poverty Index (MPI):
A. Poverty deprivation of women in relation to men in terms of health, education, and standard of living in a country.
B. Poverty deprivation of women in relation to men in terms of health and education.
C. A comparative poverty deprivation of men and women in terms of empowerment and standard of living.
D. Poverty deprivation of women in relation to men in terms of education and standard of living.

85. Gender Budgeting identifies the following area for gender mainstreaming:
(a) Quantification of allocation of resources for women.
(b) Gender Audit of policies of governments and the impact assessment of various schemes.
(c) Institutionalizing generation and collection of gender-disaggregated data.
(d) Budget allotment for women only.

Codes:
A. (a) and (c) only
B. (b), (c) and (d) only
C. (a), (b) and (d) only
D. (a), (b) and (c) only

86. Match List-I with List-II:

List-I (Development Indices)	***List-II (Dimension Index)***
(a) Gender Development Index (GDI)	(i) Achievements of women in relation to men in terms of literacy, longevity and per capita income.
(b) Gender Inequality Index (GII)	(ii) Life expectancy, year of schooling and income/ consumption
(c) Inequality-adjusted Human Development Index (IHDI)	(iii) Life expectancy, education and Gross National Product
(d) Human Development Index	(iv) Female reproductive health, female Empowerment and Male empowerment.

Codes:

	(a)	(b)	(c)	(d)
A.	(i)	(ii)	(iii)	(iv)
B.	(i)	(iv)	(ii)	(iii)
C.	(iii)	(ii)	(iv)	(i)
D.	(ii)	(iii)	(iv)	(i)

87. Match List-I with List-II:

List-I (Community)	***List-II (Female Workforce Participation Rate)***
(a) Jains	(i) 14.1
(b) Sikhs	(ii) 20.2
(c) Muslims	(iii) 28.7
(d) Christians	(iv) 9.2

Codes:

	(a)	(b)	(c)	(d)
A.	(iii)	(ii)	(iv)	(i)
B.	(iv)	(ii)	(i)	(iii)
C.	(iv)	(i)	(ii)	(iii)
D.	(ii)	(iv)	(i)	(iii)

88. In the Sexual Harassment of women at the workplace (Prevention, Prohibitions, and Redressal) Act 2013, the duties of the Employer do not include:
A. Providing a safe working environment at the workplace.
B. Requesting the women employees to dress appropriately.
C. Monitoring the timely submission of reports by the internal committee.
D. Treating sexual harassment as misconduct under the service rules and initiate action for such misconduct.

89. What is the new source for researchers and policy makers to determine obstacles to women's economic development?
A. Gender Division of Labour Data Base

B. Gender, Equity and Diversity Data Base
C. Gender, Empowerment and Justice Data Base
D. Gender, Institutions and Development Data Base

90. Vertical segregation in the labour market refers to:
A. Men and women being concentrated in different occupations in the labour market
B. Women combining paid employment with domestic labour
C. How gender interacts with social categories (ethnicity) to create division in the labour market
D. Men occupying higher positions than women in the same occupation

91. Women are over-represented in __________ work because it often provides greater flexibility to meet family responsibilities.
A. Private sector
B. Public sector
C. Contingent
D. Semi-skilled

92. Which of the following occupations has the largest gap between men and women at the workplace?
A. Personal Service Occupation
B. Skilled jobs
C. Administrative
D. Professional Occupations

93. Which of the following ILO convention deals with 'decent work for domestic workers'?
A. 169 B. 183
C. 159 D. 189

94. Which one of the following is pioneer in developing gender-sensitive budget initiative?
A. Asia B. Australia
C. Europe D. Africa

95. Main workers are those workers who work for the major of the reference period which is:
A. Eight months or more
B. Four months or more
C. Six months or more
D. Nine months or more

96. Mark the incorrect answer of 'Sexual Harassment' as defined in Visakha Judgment.
A. Unwelcome sexually determined behavior
B. Showing pornography
C. Extending invitation
D Sexually offensive physical contact or advances

97. In the organized sector, there are certain laws which enjoin the employer to make provision for crèches if a certain number of women are employed in their establishments:
(i) Factories Act
(ii) Plantation Labor Act
(iii) Contract Labor Act
(iv) Inter-state Migrant Workers Act

Codes:
A. (i) only B. (iv) only
C. (i), (ii), (iii) & (iv) D. (i), (ii) & (iv)

98. Match List-I with List-II:

List-I (Census)	***List-II (Female Workforce Participation Rate)***
(a) 1971	(i) 22.3
(b) 1991	(ii) 25.5
(c) 2001	(iii) 13.9
(d) 2011	(iv) 25.6

Codes:

	(a)	(b)	(c)	(d)
A.	(iv)	(ii)	(iii)	(i)
B.	(iii)	(ii)	(i)	(iv)
C.	(iii)	(ii)	(i)	(iv)
D.	(iii)	(i)	(iv)	(ii)

99. Which one of the ILO conventions is not ratified by India?
A. Equality of Treatment (Social Security) Convention, 1962
B. Night Work (Women) Convention (Revised), 1948
C. Maternity Protection Convention, 2000
D. Underground Work (Women) Convention, 1935

100. Identify the reasons for the existence of the wage gap between males and females:
(i) The education level of employed women has been lower than that of employed men.
(ii) Women's stock of human capital is high.
(iii) Women are specialized in traditional skills.
(iv) Women's market skills decline when they remain out of the labor force.

Codes:
A. (i) and (ii) are correct.
B. (ii), (iii)) and (iv) are correct.
C. (i), (iii) and (iv) are correct.
D. (iii) and (iv) are correct.

101. Who advocated the concept of 'Comparable-worth discrimination' in relation to women's work?
A. Treiman and Hartmann
B. Kraut and Luna
C. Marshall
D. Gary Becker

102. "Women now represent 40% of the Global Labor Force, 43% of the World Agricultural Labor Force and more than ½ of the World's University Students", stated by which report?
A. United National Development Report, 2012
B. World Development Report, 2012
C. Human Development Report, 2012
D. Gender Development Report, 2012

103. Percentage of Main Female Workers to Total Workers (2011) is:
A. 59.6 B. 65.1
C. 54.7 D. 78.4

104. Percentage of rural female marginal workers of total workers in India (2011) is:
A. 41.8 B. 60.5
C. 69.4 D. 44.4

105. Which Report highlights the persistent gap between women's expanding capabilities and limited opportunities?
A. Concept and Measurement of Human Development, 1990
B. Global Dimension of Human Development, 1992
C. Gender and Human Development, 1995
D. Globalization with a Human Face, 1999

106. Assertion (A): Sex discrimination creates a pay gap for women workers in the unorganized sector.
Reason (R): Employers follow the cultural beliefs of the society and devalue women's work.
Codes:
A. (A) is true and (R) is false.
B. Both (A) and (R) are false.
C. (A) is false and (R) is true.
D. Both (A) and (R) are true, (R) is the correct explanation for (A).

107. Assertion (A): The phenomenon of prostitution is largely concentrated in large cities.
Reason (R): Women enter prostitution to get relief from economic distress, both Individual and familial.
Codes:
A. Both (A) and (R) are false.
B. (A) is correct but (R) is false and (R) is not the correct explanation of (A).
C. Both (A) and (R) are true and (R) is the correct explanation of (A).
D. (A) is false but (R) is true and (R) is not the correct explanation of (A).

108. Assertion (A): There is a glass ceiling for women in management.
Reason (R): Women are less competent in tackling issues.
Codes:
A. Both (A) and (R) are true.
B. Both (A) and (R) are false.
C. (A) is false, (R) is true.
D. (A) is true, (R) is false.

109. Assertion (A): Globalisation has a negative impact on poor women.
Reason (R): Globalisation reduced the livelihood opportunities of women.
Codes:
A. Both (A) and (R) are true.
B. Both (A) and (R) are true, (R) is not the correct explanation for (A).
C. Both (A) and (R) are true, (R) is the correct explanation for (A).
D. Both (A) and (R) are false.

110. Assertion (A): Feminization of Poverty does not relate to higher levels of Poverty alone.
Reason (R): Feminization is a process. 'Highest Poverty' is a state.
Codes:
A. (A) is true, (R) is false.
B. Both (A) and (R) are false.
C. Both (A) and (R) are true, (R) is the correct explanation for (A).
D. (A) is false, (R) is true.

111. Assertion (A): The division of labour based on sex in primitive society was reciprocal.
Reason (R): In a primitive society, women's productive role was recognized.
Codes:
A. Both (A) and (R) are correct and (R) is the correct explanation for (A).
B. Both (A) and (R) is false.
C. Both (A) and (R) are true.
D. (A) is true, (R) is false.

112. Assertion (A): Work-force participation of women is by and large invisible.
Reason (R): Household management has not been accepted as economically and socially productive.
Codes:
A. (A) is false but (R) is true.
B. (R) is false but (A) is true.
C. Both (A) and (R) are false.
D. Both (A) and (R) are true, and (R) is the correct explanation for (A).

113. Assertion (A): Women's empowerment through labour-force is questionable.

Reason (R): Globalisation policy of India has resulted in the replacement of women labour.

Codes:

A. Both (A) and (R) are false.
B. (A) is true but (R) is false.
C. (A) is false but (R) is true.
D. (A) is true and (R) is the cause for (A).

114. Assertion (A): Sexual Harassment (prevention) cells have been established in most of the private and public sector organisations.

Reason (R): Working women are subject to sexual harassment at the workplace.

Codes:

A. Both (A) and (R) are true.
B. (A) is true and (R) is the reason for (A).
C. (A) is false and (R) is true.
D. Both (A) and (R) are false.

115. Assertion (A): Women's labour remains invisible.

Reason (R): Paid activities are undertaken largely by men, while women found to be larger in unpaid activities that remain unrecognized.

Codes:

A. Both (A) and (R) are true.
B. (A) is true but (R) is false.
C. (A) is false but (R) is true.
D. Both (A) and (R) are false.

116. Assertion (A): Women performs 2/3 of the work but received only 1/3 of wages.

Reason (R): Women's work at household does not have exchange value.

Codes:

A. Both (A) and (R) are true, (R) is not the correct explanation for (A).
B. Both (A) and (R) are true.
C Both (A) and (R) are true, (R) is the correct explanation for (A).
D. Both (A) and (R) are false.

117. Assertion (A): Women's wages are considered by ·nd large supplementary to the income of the family.

Reason (R): Women spend their wages largely on household necessities.

Codes:

A. (A) is true, (R) is false and (R) is not the correct explanation of (A).
B. (A) is false, (R) is true and (R) is the correct explanation of (A).
C. Both (A) and (R) are true and (R) is not the correct explanation of (A).
D. Both (A) and (R) are true and (R) is the correct explanation of (A).

118. Assertion (A): Gender budgeting focuses on women.

Reason (R): Nearly two-thirds of illiterate people in the world are women.

Codes:

A. Both (A) and (R) are false.
B. (A) is true, (R) is false.
C. Both (A) and (R) are true.
D. Both (A) and (R) are true and (R) is the correct explanation for (A).

119. Assertion (A): Gender budget tends to focus more on the needs of women and girls than those on men and boys.

Reason (R): Women and girls are usually at a disadvantaged position economically and in many other ways.

Codes:

A. Both (A) and (R) are true.
B. Both (A) and (R) are false.
C. Both (A) and (R) are true and (R) is the correct explanation for (A).
D. Both (A) and (R) are true and (R) is not the correct explanation for (A).

120. Assertion (A): The impact of globalization and technology on rural women is negative.

Reason (R): Women of rural areas are displaced due to upgradation of technology, automation, and adoption of high-tech.

Codes:

A. Both (A) and (R) are true.
B. Both (A) and (R) are true and (R) is the correct explanation of (A).
C. Both (A) and (R) are false.
D. Both (A) and (R) are true but (R) is not the correct explanation of (A).

121. Assertion (A): Globalization has paved the way for IT women professionals to earn more.

Reason (R): Over a period of time, IT women professionals are facing health and occupational hazards.

Codes:

A. (A) is true and (R) is false.
B. Both (A) and (R) are true, (R) is not the explanation for (A).
C. (A) is false and (R) is true.
D. Both (A) and (R) are false.

122. Assertion (A): Most of the work done by women does not enter the market spheres and remains non-monetized.

Reason (R): Women's work remains invisible and non-recognized.

Codes:

A. (A) is true and (R) is false.
B. Both (A) and (R) are true.
C. (A) is false and (R) is true.
D. Both (A) and (R) are true, (R) is not the correct explanation for (A).

123. Assertion (A): Women are educated and career-oriented, but they have to face men's resistance.

Reason (R): Women hold managerial positions up to middle level, but a few reach the top-level positions.

Codes:

A. Both (A) and (R) are false.
B. Both (A) and (R) are true and (R) is the correct explanation for (A).
C. Both (A) and (R) are true and (R) is not the correct explanation for (A).
D. (A) is true and (R) is false.

124. Assertion (A): Sexual harassment at the workplace is a personal problem of women.

Reason (R): Women keep silent about sexual harassment to protect the perpetrator.

Codes:

A. Both (A) and (R) are true.
B. (A) is false and (R) is true.
C. (A) is true and (R) is false.
D. Both (A) and (R) are false and (R) is not the correct explanation of (A).

125. Assertion (A): The women wage seekers have achieved gender equal wages and have got empowered socially and economically through the NREGA scheme.

Reason (R): The NREGA employment served as a primary wage-earning opportunity for a large section of women in rural areas.

Codes:

A. Both (A) and (R) are false.
B. Both (A) and (R) are true.
C. (A) is true, (R) are false.
D. (A) is true, (R) is false and not the correct explanation of (A).

126. Assertion (A): Globalization process has reduced the workspace in the market and kept away women from the production process.

Reason (R): Most of the women are illiterate and semi-skilled.

Codes:

A. (A) is true and (R) is false.
B. Both (A) and (R) are false.
C. Both (A) and (R) are true, (R) is the correct explanation of (A).
D. (A) is false and (R) is true.

127. Assertion (A): Empowerment of women is closely associated with women's participation in the unorganized sector.

Reason (R): Empowerment of women is related to the enhancement of women's capabilities and self-confidence.

Codes:

A. Both (A) and (R) are true.
B. (A) is false and (R) is true.
C. Both (A) and (R) are false.
D. (A) is true and (R) is false.

128. Assertion (A): Secularization is an inevitable consequence of industrialization.

Reason (R): Plurality of life in modern industrial societies tends to shatter the single, comprehensive universe of meanings which religion provides.

Codes:

A. (A) is false, but (R) is true.
B. Both (A) and (R) are true but (R) is not a correct explanation of (A).
C. (A) is true, but (R) is false.
D. Both (A) and (R) are true and (R) is the correct explanation of (A).

129. Assertion (A): Gender division of work at the household level extends to other public spheres also.

Reason (R): Socialization Process begins at the level of the family and carried forward in the society and workplace.

Codes:

A. Both (A) and (R) are false.
B. (A) is false and (R) is true.
C. (A) is true and (R) is false.
D. Both (A) and (R) are true and (R) is the correct explanation for (A).

130. Assertion (A): The globalisation process allowed different export processing zones (EPZs)Who employ mostly young women and fire them first.

Reason (R): In India, women accounted for nearly 72 percent of the EPZ workers in the age 20-29 age group who are inexperienced and unaware of their women rights.

Codes:
A. (A) is true and (R) is false.
B. Both (A) and (R) is true and (R) is the correct explanation of (A).
C. Both (A) and (R) are true but (R) is not the correct explanation of (A).
D. (A) is false and (R) is true.

131. Assertion (A): Gender Diversity Benchmark for Asia 2011 Report reveals that in India, the greatest leak at the workplace takes place early on in a women's career from junior to middle-level positions.
Reason (R): High potential women in India are largely concerned about personal sacrifices which they possibly make for their children and family.
Codes:
A. Both (A) and (R) are false.
B. Both (A) and (R) are true and (R) is the correct explanation for (A).
C. (A) is wrong and (R) is true.
D. (A) is correct but (R) is false.

132. Assertion (A): Women's Share in household power in decision making is lower than men.
Reason (R): Women's Share in household income is lower than men.
Codes:
A. Both (A) and (R) are true.
B. Both (A) and (R) are false. (R) is the correct explanation for (A).
C. Both (A) and (R) are false.
D. (A) is true, (R) is false.

133. Assertion (A): Women's Participation in the Public world is lower compared to men.
Reason (R): Women are by nature less intellectual.
Codes:
A. Both (A) and (R) are false.
B. Both (A) and (R) are true.
C. (A) is true, (R) is false.
D. (A) is false, (R) is true.

134. Assertion (A): Women face difficulty to get better jobs and to move up the professional ladder.
Reason (R): Women get fewer opportunities for education and skill training.
Codes:
A. Both (A) and (R) are false.
B. Both (A) and (R) are true.
C. (A) is true and (R) is false.
D. (A) is false and (R) is true.

135. Assertion (A): Capitalism is a system of exploitative power relations.
Reason (R): Employers pay workers less than their labour power.
Codes:
A. Both (A) and (R) are true, (R) is the correct explanation for (A).
B. Both (A) and (R) are true.
C. Both (A) and (R) are false.
D. (A) is true, (R) is false.

136. Assertion (A): 'Glass ceiling' is an invisible barrier that women experience in their upper carrier.
Reason (R): Women are incapable of managing organizational issues.
Codes:
A. Both (A) and (R) are true.
B. (A) is true but (R) is false.
C. Both (A) and (R) are false.
D. (R) is true but (A) is false.

137. Assertion (A): Women's work as family labour is underestimated.
Reason (R): Census statistics accounts for women's family labour as productive work.
Codes:
A. Both (A) and (R) are true.
B. Both (A) and (R) are false.
C. (A) is true but (R) is false.
D. Both (A) and (R) are true, (R) is the correct explanation for (A).

138. Assertion (A): Gender bias in the process of economic development has led to the subordination of women.
Reason (R): A great deal of women's work remains invisible.
Codes:
A. Both (A) and (R) are true.
B. Both (A) and (R) are false.
C. (A) is true, but (R) is false.
D. (A) is false, but (R) is true.

139. Assertion (A): Women engage in a variety of occupations in the unorganized sector.
Reason (R): Productive economic value is attached to these tasks.
Codes:
A. Both (A) and (R) are false.
B. (A) is false, but (R) is true.
C. Both (A) and (R) are true
D. (A) is true, but (R) is false.

140. Assertion (A): Increasing population in the world puts pressure on the available resources on the planet.

Reason (R): One-fourth of the world's population living in the developed world consumes 80 per cent of the world's resources.

Codes:

A. Both (A) and (R) are true, and (R) is not the correct explanation for (A).
B. Both (A) and (R) are true, and (R) is the correct explanation for (A).
C. (A) is true, but (R) is false.
D. (A) is false, but (R) is true.

141. Assertion (A): Women are being continuity pushed into the unorganized sector.
Reason (R): Women's work remains mostly invisible.

Codes:

A. (A) is true, (R) is false.
B. (A) is false, (R) is true.
C. Both (A) and (R) are false.
D. Both (A) and (R) are true and (R) is not the correct explanation for (A).

142. Assertion (A): Empowerment of women is closely associated with women's participation in the unorganized sector.
Reason (R): Empowerment of women is related to the enhancement of women's capabilities and decision.

Codes:

A. Both (A) and (R) are true.
B. (A) is false, (R) is true.
C. Both (A) and (R) are false.
D. (A) is true, (R) is false.

143. Assertion (A): Wife's economic status is an important factor in domestic decision-making.
Reason (R): When women lack monetary resources to bargain for the power they either use covert influence to determine the outcome of a decision or subordinate themselves to the husband's domination.

Codes:

A. Both (A) and (R) are true.
B. (A) is true but (R) is false.
C. (A) and (R) are independent of each other.
D. Both (A) and (R) are false.

144. Assertion (A): Sexual Harassment (Prevention) cells have been established in most of the private and public sector organisations.
Reason (R): Working women can be a subject to sexual harassment at the workplace.

Codes:

A. (A) is true and (R) is false.
B. Both (A) and (R) are true and (R) is the correct explanation for (A).
C. (A) is false and (R) is true.
D. Both (A) and (R) are false.

145. Assertion (A): Job segregation by sex is the primary mechanism in a capitalist society that maintains the superiority of men over women.
Reason (R): Strategies used by men to limit women's access to paid work were an example of "Patriarchy at work."

Codes:

A. Both (A) and (R) are true.
B. Both (A) and (R) are false.
C. Both (A) and (R) are true and (R) is the correct explanation for (A).
D. (A) is false and (R) is true.

146. Assertion (A): Agrarian societies, women of lower classes have been enjoying more equal status as compared to women of middle and high classes.
Reason (R): Women of the lower classes besides being vocal, are more efficient in their domestic roles.

Codes:

A. Both (A) and (R) are true and (R) is the correct explanation of A.
B. (A) is false and (R) is true.
C. (A) is true and (R) is false.
D. Both (A) and (R) are false.

147. Assertion (A): Globalisation has affected the fertility rate in many developed countries.
Reason (R): Reduction in work hours, jobs and closing of many companies gave an opportunity to have more children for young couples in the developed countries.

Codes:

A. Both (A) and (R) are true.
B. Both (A) and (R) are true and (R) is the correct explanation of (A).
C. Both (A) and (R) is false.
D. (A) is true and (R) is false.

148. Assertion (A): Globalization promises to remove backwardness of women through a worldwide exchange of information, investments, and skills.
Reason (R): The existing differences between women's and men's access to knowledge, skills, and responsibilities lead to gender inequality.

Codes:

A. Both (A) and (R) are false.
B. Both (A) and (R) are true, but (R) is not the correct explanation for (A).

C. (A) is false and (R) is true.
D. (A) is true and (R) is false.

149. Assertion (A): Women are overloaded with work, the value of which is not socially and economically recognised.
Reason (R): The focus on monetary terms clearly downplays women's unpaid domestic work contribution.

Codes:
A. Both (A) and (R) are true.
B. (A) is true and (R) is false.
C. Both (A) and (R) are true and (R) is the correct explanation for (A).
D. Both (A) and (R) are false.

150. Assertion (A): Women's work is greatly undervalued in economic terms, and it leads to a major gap in the national income account system.
Reason (R): The household and community work has an intrinsic use value that is not captured by its value for exchange.

Codes:
A. Both (A) and (R) are true.
B. (A) is true and (R) is false.
C. Both (A) and (R) are true, and (R) is the correct explanation for (A).
D. Both (A) and (R) are false.

Answers

1	**2**	**3**	**4**	**5**	**6**	**7**	**8**	**9**	**10**
B	C	D	B	B	D	D	D	B	C
11	**12**	**13**	**14**	**15**	**16**	**17**	**18**	**19**	**20**
B	D	A	A	A	C	C	A	C	B
21	**22**	**23**	**24**	**25**	**26**	**27**	**28**	**29**	**30**
C	D	B	A	D	C	A	D	A	B
31	**32**	**33**	**34**	**35**	**36**	**37**	**38**	**39**	**40**
A	A	B	D	D	A	D	C	A	C
41	**42**	**43**	**44**	**45**	**46**	**47**	**48**	**49**	**50**
B	C	B	B	B	C	B	A	A	B
51	**52**	**53**	**54**	**55**	**56**	**57**	**58**	**59**	**60**
B	C	B	C	C	D	C	A	A	B
61	**62**	**63**	**64**	**65**	**66**	**67**	**68**	**69**	**70**
C	B	C	D	A	A	C	B	B	A
71	**72**	**73**	**74**	**75**	**76**	**77**	**78**	**79**	**80**
D	C	A	A	A	C	A	C	A	A
81	**82**	**83**	**84**	**85**	**86**	**87**	**88**	**89**	**90**
B	A	D	A	B	B	B	B	D	D
91	**92**	**93**	**94**	**95**	**96**	**97**	**98**	**99**	**100**
C	B	D	B	C	C	C	D	C	C
101	**102**	**103**	**104**	**105**	**106**	**107**	**108**	**109**	**110**
A	B	A	D	C	D	B	D	C	C
111	**112**	**113**	**114**	**115**	**116**	**117**	**118**	**119**	**120**
A	D	C	B	A	C	C	C	C	B
121	**122**	**123**	**124**	**125**	**126**	**127**	**128**	**129**	**130**
B	B	C	D	B	C	B	D	D	B
131	**132**	**133**	**134**	**135**	**136**	**137**	**138**	**139**	**140**
B	D	C	B	A	B	A	A	D	B
141	**142**	**143**	**144**	**145**	**146**	**147**	**148**	**149**	**150**
D	B	A	B	C	C	D	B	C	C

❑❑❑

Gender and Entrepreneurship

- Concept and Meaning, Importance of Entrepreneurship, Entrepreneurial Traits, Factors contributing to Entrepreneurship, Enabling Environment, Small Enterprises, Women in Agri-Business
- Self Help Groups (SHG) and Micro Credit
- Gender and Emerging Technology – Impact
- Gender Mainstreaming, Gender Budgeting, Planning and Analysis

THE CONCEPT, MEANING, AND IMPORTANCE OF ENTREPRENEURSHIP

The term 'Entrepreneur' is derived from the French word "Enterprendre" – to undertake. To be entrepreneurial is to undertake the risk of new enterprises, especially of business activities. It is a dynamic commercial process of creating incremental wealth and value in any field-education, health, research, law, architecture, engineering, social work, etc. It involves taking risks necessary to run a profitable business. Setting up and managing an enterprise involves various stages of development: germination of a business idea, feasibility study, planning and estimation, acquiring the resources and capital, operation, profit, expansion, and continuous innovation.

Entrepreneurs are recognized as an essential contributor to economic and social development. Enterprises act as seeds of industrial development and wealth creation. Especially in developing and third-world countries, entrepreneurial activities are instrumental in generating employment opportunities and raising the living standards of people. They are a source of both direct and indirect employment. They help to reduce income disparities by enabling a balanced distribution of wealth and increasing per capita income. They also increase government revenue in the form of taxes, excise duties. Entrepreneurial activities aid in capital formation in the economy by mobilizing fund and investment.

Entrepreneurs also drive social innovation in the field of education, public health, poverty alleviation, solve civic and social problems. In the process, they develop administrative and problem-solving capabilities. They also increase their organizational efficiency and acquire technology and skills.

One of the significant contributions of entrepreneurs in developing countries is the growth of small and medium businesses. It has promoted economic activities in rural and semi-urban areas, leading to balanced regional development and reducing distress migration. Small and medium enterprises have become synonymous with indigenous businesses providing significant economic restructuring, poverty alleviation and food security.

The opportunities offered by entrepreneurship have also aided women in their economic independence and empowerment. Women view enterprises as opportunities for self-empowerment, economic freedom, and liberation from patriarchal obstacles. Wealth generated by setting up small businesses is invested by women in their children's education, supporting their family's livelihood and food security and lifting their family out of poverty and destitution.

ENTREPRENEURIAL TRAITS

To be a successful entrepreneur requires certain attitudes and character traits:

- Innovative spirit – a continuous search for new ideas to create value and wealth
- Optimization of performance and efficiency
- Dynamic – adaptable to fast changes
- Problem-solving skills and willingness to take the initiative
- Perseverance to weather through risky conditions
- Self-critical judgment to evaluate objectively
- Positive attitude and leadership qualities

FACTORS CONTRIBUTING TO ENTREPRENEURSHIP AND ENABLING ENVIRONMENT

For entrepreneurs to thrive in an economy, a stable and supportive political system has to prevail. A liberalized economic environment offers the space and confidence for people to take up commercial activities.

Though pre-colonial Indian society possessed sophisticated village and town economies that supported indigenous artisans, handicrafts, and commerce by trade guilds and business communities, the British occupation subverted the Indian economy to serve the interests of the rulers. The British state adopted hostile policies that destroyed patron of art and culture, flooded Indian markets with mechanized goods resulting in unfair competitions. Even after independence, socialist economic development stifled private enterprises with over-emphasis on public and state enterprises. There was a capital crunch that prevented proper growth of individual small and medium scale businesses.

The liberalization of the economy in 1991 opened up space for small and individual commercial activities to thrive. Since then, there has been steady growth in the entrepreneurial activities in the country. It has infused sophisticated technology and infrastructure into the economy.

Indian women entrepreneurs have also been part of this development process. The growth of women entrepreneurs has not only reduced the gender gap in socio-economic participation but has also been instru-mental in ensuring balanced and equitable development as economic upliftment of women, benefits her family, surrounding and community.

But, women entrepreneurs still face obstacles in their business endeavors due to gender bias and discrimination. Some of the problems faced by women entrepreneurs are:

- Lack of awareness of government schemes and policies available for women entrepreneurs
- Inaccessibility to information and training opportunities
- Lack of education; according to the 2011 Census, around 30% of Indian women are illiterate
- Lack of access to raw materials and market
- Inability to network
- Access to capital, finance, and working capital – angel investors show gender bias in their evaluation and investment decisions.
- Inequitable access to the labor market
- Unsupportive family members and society
- Lack of property and personal assets, as most women do not inherit their ancestral properties; as it goes only to the male children.
- Expansion of businesses owned by women is meager. Women entrepreneurs choose to keep their businesses small since they have to juggle family responsibilities too.
- Women entrepreneurs are expected to balance and manage family, work and everything ele, even if they contribute equally to family's finance.

What is needed is gender neutral policies, as well as pro-women policies that promote women entrepreneurship. Strong legislation and public awareness of these laws are required to enable easy conduct of business. Non-discriminatory access to credit facilities and banking is another pre-requisite to encourage female entrepreneurs.

Gender Entrepreneurship Monitor (GEM) is a leading global organization that engages in the data collection effort to provide comprehensive information on entrepreneurship and its related issues at the global level. The dimensions used by GEM for measuring a country's entrepreneurship economic profile are self-perceptions, activity, motivations, gender equity, impact, and societal values. GEM's entrepreneurial framework conditions are entrepreneurial finance, government policies, support and relevance, taxes and bureaucracy, government entrepreneurship programs, entrepreneurial education at school stage, entrepreneurial education at post-school stage, R&D transfer, commercial and legal infrastructure, internal market dynamics, internal market burdens or entry regulations, physical infrastructure, cultural and social norms.

SMALL ENTERPRISES

Traditionally, small industries were khadi, handloom, handicrafts, village and cottage industries. Modern small scale industries are those that employ a small number of workers, privately owned and operated by sole proprietorships or partnerships. These micro and small scale enterprises contribute to rural and regional developments by generating employment and enabling equitable distribution of wealth.

According to MSME Annual Report 2012, Micro Small and Medium Enterprises account for 45% of manufacturing output and 40% output of the national economy. Though there has been a gradual increase in the economic participation of women, only 13.7% are managed by women. Of the total 2.15, women-owned MSMEs, 98% are micro enterprises, 1.80% are small and 0.05% medium enterprises. Male entrepreneurs dominate in all of these sectors. States such as Tamil Nadu, Karnataka, Gujarat, and Kerala have a higher number of women entrepreneurs, while Chandigarh, Arunachal Pradesh, Diu, and Daman have a low number of women entrepreneurs.

Major obstacles to women in MSMEs are gender-bias exhibited by investors, lack of credit access and unsupportive family. Various government as well as social organizations and state programmes aid in the development of MSME, entrepreneurs, especially women entrepreneurs. Some of them are:

National Institute for Micro, Small and Medium Enterprises (NI-MSME)

- Established in 1960 as Central Industrial Extension Training Institute in New Delhi
- In 1962, shifted to Hyderabad and renamed as Small Industry Extension Training (SIET) Institute
- For promotion, development, and modernization of MSMEs in India
- Offers tailor made programs and comprehensive modules to train budding entrepreneurs

National Institute for Entrepreneurship and Small Business Development (NIESBUD)

- Apex organization under Ministry of Skill Development and Entrepreneurship
- Established in 1983
- Provides training, consultancy, and research to promote entrepreneurship and skill development
- Coordinated and overseas institutions and organizations engaged in training entrepreneurs and related activities

Federation of Indian Women Entrepreneurs

- Established in 1993, following the resolution of the 4th International Conference of Women Entrepreneurs held in Hyderabad, India.
- Facilitates women's involvement in various economic activities and promotes women in commerce and business.

Association of Lady Entrepreneurs of India (ALEAP)

- Established in 1993
- To train, guide, support women entrepreneurs
- Focuses on creativity, innovativeness, financial stability and social impact of projects
- Supports the growth of MSMEs in formal and informal sectors

Confederation of Women Entrepreneurs of India (COWE)

- Formed in 2004 by six women entrepreneurs
- A national association of women entrepreneurs that provides training, counseling, knowledge sharing and handholding to create a favorable entrepreneurial ecosystem for Indian women
- It helps develop centers of excellence for women to develop skills, provide infrastructure and access to resources and market.

Women Entrepreneurship Platform

- Launched in 2017
- An initiative of NITI Aayog
- It aims to bring all stakeholders in the entrepreneurs' ecosystem to eliminate barriers to entry and success of women entrepreneurs
- Provides opportunities for women entrepreneurs by developing long-term strategies
- Provides industry and market linkages, addresses bottlenecks to development, evidence-based policy recommendations, etc.

Mahila Coir Yojana

- Started in 1994
- 100% women oriented self-employment programme being implemented by the Coir Board of India
- To provide self-employment to rural women artisans in coir regions
- Involves the distribution of coil processing equipments, establishment of training centers

Micro Small Medium Enterprises – Development Organization (MSME-DO)

- Apex body for formulating, implementing, coordinating and promoting MSMEs
- Provides support services, market assistance, etc.

Small Industries Development Bank of India (SIDBI)

- Launched in 1990
- Provides facilities for small scale industries
- Has established specific schemes for promoting women businesses

National Policy for Empowerment of Women (2001)

- Commitment towards eliminating all forms of violence against women, including those arising from customs and accepted practices, domestic violence, sexual harassment
- Setting up of mechanisms and institutions to prevent gender violence
- To ensure strict enforcement of legislation for women's protection
- Provisions for women's cells in police stations, family courts, family counseling centers, etc.
- Special emphasis on programmes to deal with sex trafficking

Micro Small Medium Enterprises Development Act (2006)

- Provides for legal framework of recognition of enterprises
- Provides for a statutory mechanism with representation for all stakeholders and range of advisory functions
- Provides for establishing funds for promotion of MSMEs
- Provides for adoption of progressive credit policies
- Support for cluster-based development, technology, and quality upgradation, marketing, managerial development
- 20% of entrepreneurship development programmes to be earmarked for women, SCs, STs
- Provisions for the empowerment of women entrepreneurs such as 80% fund for women projects

National Mission for Empowerment of Women (2010)

- Achievement of gender justice and gender equality
- Holistic development of women through inter-sectoral convergence of programmes for women
- Focus areas include health, sanitation and hygiene facilities for women, higher and professional education for women, skill development, micro-credit, self-employment for women, gender sensitization, dissemination of information and prevention of crimes against women.

WOMEN IN AGRI-BUSINESS

According to the Census 2011 data, 32.8% of women are engaged in the agriculture sector. 33% cultivators and 47% of agricultural laborers are women. In rural India, 84% of women depend on agriculture for their livelihood.

According to Economic Survey 2017-18, the number of women engaged in agriculture as cultivators, agri-entrepreneurs, and laborers is increasing. This feminization of agriculture can enable women to play a decisive role in ensuring food security and preserving local eco-biodiversity. This necessitates access to resources such as water, farm credit, land, technology, and information to women. But, only 12% of the land is owned by women. Women employed in the agriculture sector face gender wage disparity, mostly work in low skilled jobs and many of them work as unpaid subsistence laborers. They are also doubly burdened as they are also responsible for domestic and household work.

Most women entrepreneurs are engaged in agro-based businesses. But, women in non-farm sectors have better access to credit. Some policies and organizations that facilitate women in the farming sector are:

Agri-clinics and Agri-business Centers

- Established by the Ministry of Agriculture and Farmers Welfare with help from NABARD
- Provides expert advice and services to farmers
- Dissemination of agri-related information
- 44% of backend composite subsidy towards the cost of projects to women

Krishi Vigyan Kendra (KVK)

- Launched in 1974
- KVKs are agricultural extension centers established by Indian Council for Agricultural Research (ICAR) and its affiliated institutions

- Provides farm support services, technology dissemination, farm advisory service, training programmes, On-farm testing and demonstration of location-specific farming technologies, etc.

The Mission for Integrated Development of Horticulture (2014-2015)

- Set up by the Ministry for Agriculture and Farmer's Welfare
- In the case of North-Eastern and the Himalayan States 100% contribution of the total outlay of development programme by GOI, while in other states 85% by the GOI and 15% by the State Governments.
- Provides special coverage for SC, ST, and women
- Assistance for horticulture mechanization

National Mission for Sustainable Agriculture

- Approved in 2010, under National Action Plan on Climate Change
- To promote integrated farming system
- Grants at least 30% of allocation for women farmers

Agricultural Technology Marketing Agency

- Provides support for women food security groups
- Provides support for gender coordinator
- Provision for women in decision-making bodies
- Offers capacity building and skill development services

SELF HELP GROUPS (SHG) AND MICRO CREDIT

- The concept was pioneered by the economist, Muhammad Yunus in Bangladesh for which he was awarded Nobel Peace Prize.
- SHG is a voluntary association of women and men from a similar economic background, formed to promote savings, micro-credit services, and income generation.
- Women always occupied a secondary status in society and lacked access to opportunity, education, and finance. But, money entering a family through women benefits the whole family, while men use it for their personal development.
- First introduced in 1987 by the National Bank for Agriculture and Rural Development (NABARD). In 1990, Reserve Bank of India (RBI) accepted SHG strategy as an alternative credit model and recognized its potential for rural poverty alleviation, women empowerment, developing leadership capabilities and skill training.
- SHGs have revolutionized rural credit delivery in India. It has generated self-employment and self-reliance for women in rural and semi-rural India. Currently, there are more than 2 million SHGs in the country.
- In 1992, the SHG Bank Linkage programme was launched that linked SHGs to banks for microcredit services. In 1999, the government promoted self-employment by providing skill training to SHGs. In 2011, SHGs became an integral part of National Rural Livelihood Mission, which covers more than 100 Million families nationwide.
- It recognizes the SHGs and women as central to eliminating poverty, resource generation and socio-economic development of the poor and under-privileged.

Mudra Bank

- Micro Units Development and Refinance Agency (MUDRA) Bank was launched in 2015.
- Public sector financial institution to provide low-rate loans to Micro-Finance Institutions (MFI) and Non-Banking Finance Institutions (NBFC), which offer credit facilities to MSMEs.
- Its primary objective is to encourage entrepreneurs in small businesses with focus areas as agriculture, women MSMEs and self-employment creation.
- It provides unique products to promote women empowerment such as Mahila Udyami Scheme.

Bharatiya Mahila Bank

- Started in 2013
- India's first all-women bank with a commitment to women empowerment as its primary objective
- The predominant focus on lending and financing women and women businesses
- Also emphasizes skill development and training to encourage economic activities with a special emphasis on women.
- Merged with State Bank of India in 2017

Rashtriya Mahila Kosh

- Established in 1993 under the Ministry of Women and Child Development.
- Extends micro-credit facilities to women
- Socio-economic empowerment of women through a multi-pronged approach involving capacity building

measures, asset creation, and sustenance, a participatory organization of women groups

- Promotes networking of women's organizations for information sharing, skill development, and entrepreneurial activities.

Swarna Jayanti Gram Swarozgar Yojana

- Launched in 1999
- To bring beneficiaries above the poverty line by providing a mix of income-generating assets such as government subsidy and bank credit.
- It is a focused approach to poverty alleviation by setting up micro-enterprises across the country.
- It provides self-employment by the establishment of self-help groups and activity clusters based on the skills and aptitude of the people involved.

Swarna Jayanti Shahari Rozgar Yojana

- Launched in 1997
- To provide gainful employment to the urban poor by encouraging self-employment ventures or by providing wage employment.
- Setting up of community structures such as neighborhood groups, community development societies, identification of projects, setting up of credit societies to encourage savings.

Scheme for Development of Women and Children in Urban Areas (DWCA)

- Components of Swarna Jayanti Shahari Rozgar Yojana
- Special incentives to groups of urban poor women to set up gainful self-employment ventures
- Can be involved in activities suited to their skill set, knowledge, and aptitude
- DWCA groups are encouraged to set up credit societies to self-finance their projects with the government providing 50% of the project's cost.

Development of Women and Children in Rural Areas (DWCRA)

- Sub-component of Integrated Rural Development Programme
- Specific focus on poverty alleviation among rural women
- Formation of groups of women from poor households at village levels for credit delivery, skill training and infrastructural support.
- Enhances rural women's access to essential services like education, health services, child care, nutrition.
- Was merged with Swarnajayanti Gram Rozgar Yojana in 1999.

Swa-Shakti Project

- Launched in 1999
- Earlier known as Rural Women's Development and Empowerment Project
- Jointly funded by the World Bank and International Fund for Agricultural Development (IFAD)
- Aims at enhancing women's access to resources, increase their control over income through literacy, skill development, and income-generating activities.

Valmiki Ambedkar Awas Yojana

- Launched in 2001
- Upliftment of slum dwellers living below the poverty line
- Construction and upgradation of dwelling units and community toilets for slum dwellers.

GENDER AND EMERGING TECHNOLOGY-IMPACT

Women hold only 19% of technology-related jobs worldwide. They are also heavily underpaid. Women remain under-represented in employment, access, and usage of technology and its applications. This gender divide prevents women from enjoying the benefits of technology and its consequent development. Outdated gender stereotypes and patriarchal conservatism are the chief obstacles to women's access to technology. Other problems are lack of education and technical skills and socio-cultural norms.

More women in technology can introduce new viewpoints and enable inclusive development. As simple as owning a mobile phone can increase professional and income opportunities for women. They also feel safe with the possession of a cellphone. Ability to use technology provides women with freedom of expression, self-confidence, and opportunities. Technology, especially internet applications can be used as a strategy for non-formal education.

Studies in Information Technology Applications (SITA) is a gender empowerment project that provides technical skill training and computer learning programmes to low-income group girls and women in India, since 1999. SITA is run by InfoDev, with grants from the government.

Information and communication technology (ICT) can play a significant role in the empowerment of women by creating gender sensitive opportunities, developing relevant content for girls and embedding gender in all aspects of the program.

Intel's Women and Web Study (2013) found that women's access to the internet helps them acquire new knowledge, learning. But there is a 23% gender gap in online access in India. Indian women mainly use it for banking and financial activities — 23 % of girls drop out before completing secondary education in India. Due to lack of access to technical knowledge, women mostly occupy low and medium-skilled jobs. This makes them vulnerable to the effects of automation which may force job layoffs in the near future, resulting in further marginalization of women. Loss of jobs can restrict their economic independence and development.

Technology Achievement Index (TAI) is used by the United Nations Development Programme to measure the level of technology diffusion and structuring of the human skill base in its member states. TAI focuses on four dimensions namely creation of technology, diffusion of old innovations, diffusion of new innovation and human skills.

The downside of emerging technology is that of gender discrimination, sex crimes and violence against women enabled by and through technology such as the internet, social platforms, trolling, stalking and sexist abuse and harassment.

CAPART Scheme

- Set up in 1986 to promote voluntary action in rural development with special focus on injecting new technologies.
- Council for Advancement of People's Action and Rural Technology (CAPART) is an autonomous body under the Ministry of Rural Development.
- Co-ordinates the partnership between NGOs and the Government to implement development schemes in rural areas.
- Acts as a catalyst for the development of technology appropriate for rural regions.
- Supports schemes for development, employment creation, and awareness programmes.
- Has contributed to the Advancement of Rural Technology Scheme, Organization of Beneficiaries and Social Animators Training other rural development schemes.

Swadhar Greh Scheme

- Launched in 2015
- For women prisoners, women survivors of natural disasters, domestic violence, and human trafficking and women without any economic and social support
- Provision of basic necessities, medical treatment, and care
- Provision of skill development and training programmes for economic rehabilitation of those women

Ujjawala Scheme

- Introduced in 2007
- Rescue, rehabilitation of girls and women victims of trafficking and sexual exploitation
- Mainly implemented through NGOs
- Provision for the education of rescued girls and skill development and training programmes for women to enable self-employment and economic independence

GENDER MAINSTREAMING

Existing gender power relations impede opportunities for women at multiple levels. Gender mainstreaming is a gender perspective to assess the impact of legislation, measures, programmes, and policies on men and women. It is the concept of making concerns of women visible and integral to the design, planning, implementation and monitoring of social, political and economic programmes.

Gender mainstreaming includes and is not exclusive of the following activities:

- gender-specific activities
- affirmative action
- equal rights of inheritance and property rights
- making women's concerns and questions included in health policies and medical research
- using radio and other public media as campaign tools
- empowerment of single women
- provision of institutional space and public space for women's discourse
- policy interventions in the field of education, skill training, employment in various sectors
- addressing gender-related crimes and gender violence

Gender mainstreaming is a transformative approach of reorientation of strategies and structures in such a way to challenge existing power relations and enable equal participation of women in decision making at all levels of governance and society. This can lead to the inclusion of family and society in women's development. This process can increase women's bargaining power, control over and access to resources and utilization.

The Convention on Elimination of all Forms of Discrimination Against Women (CEDAW) was adopted by the UN general assembly in 1979. It recommends member states to incorporate the principle of equality in their legal systems, to establish structures to prevent discrimination against women by people, organizations and enterprises.

The fourth world conference on women was convened by the UN in 1995 in Beijing, China. The conference adopted Beijing Declaration and Platform for action which set out a number of measures to enhance the social, political and economic empowerment of women, improve their health and educational opportunities, prevent violence against women, promote their reproductive rights, participation of women in decision making and governance and ensure the reflection of gender perspective in all policies and actions at regional, national and international levels.

National Perspective Plan for Women was charted out by the Ministry for Human Resource Development in 1988. It outlined a comprehensive approach to free women from social oppression. Its recommendations included:

- uniform civil code
- equal property rights for women
- reservations of seats for women in elected bodies
- a ban on sex-determination tests
- suggestions for tackling domestic violence

DAWN (Development of Alternatives for Women in the New Era) is a network of feminists, scholars from the developing countries to work for economic and gender justice. It was established in 1984. It provides research, analysis, and advocacy on issues such as livelihoods, development prospects and living conditions of women in the third world and developing countries. It is involved in mobilizing women for the achievement of social, economic and political equality across the globe.

GENDER BUDGETING

A budget is an important tool for affirmative action towards women emancipation. Gender budgeting can be instrumental in reducing economic inequalities and gender development gap through budgetary funds and programmes. Negatively, budgetary cuts to schemes and programmes related to women can impact women empowerment.

The concept of gender budgeting does not involve separate budgets for men and women but is the inclusion of priorities of women. It is the process of ensuring adequate response to men and women's socio-economic and political needs.

Gender budgeting is:

- a budget formulation process with allocation, outlays and policies that address the gender divide.
- Analytical and audit tool for gender responsiveness
- Raises public awareness of gender mainstreaming and women's development
- The inclusion of gender issues in macroeconomic policies
- Analysis, resource allocation, implementation and impact monitoring of policies and programmes

Gender budgeting was introduced in the 1980s and now is being implemented over 90 countries. Australia became the first country to include gender responsiveness by performing an audit of its budget's impact on girls and women in 1984. The 1995 Beijing Declaration called for gender responsiveness in all macroeconomic policies. In 2000, the UN General Assembly Special Session on Women called for gender mainstreaming in national development and social policies.

Though there have been women specific and women focused policies and strategies in the government's development ideology and also the five-year plans, the concept of monitoring women development programmes was introduced in the seventh five-year plan (1985-90) only.

In the eighth five year plan (1992-97), a specific gender perspective was included by ensuring some particular section of allocation going to women related policies and programmes. The ninth five-year plan (1997-2002) earmarked 30% total budgetary allocation for women. The eleventh five-year plan(2007 -2012) called for strict adherence to gender budgeting in all ministries.

Since 2004-05, the establishment of gender budgeting cells has been mandatory across all ministries and departments to ensure gender responsiveness in their proposals and outlays.

Ministry of Women and Child Development acts as the nodal agency for gender budgeting by providing a framework of activities to be implemented for gender budgeting. It has also :

- issued guidelines for the gender-sensitive review of expenditure and spending,
- outlined the process for impact analysis, monitoring, and evaluation of projects recommended participatory approach in budget formulation.

Multiple Choice Questions

1. Identify the chronological sequence of the following Programmes:
A. ICDS, DWCRA, IRDP, SGSY
B. ICDS, IRDP, DWCRA, SGSY
C. SGSY, IRDP, DWCRA, ICDS
D. IRDP, ICDS, SGSY, DWCRA

2. "Women should be empowered by enhancing their skills, knowledge, and access to information technology." This is a resolution passed in:
A. Millennium Development Goal
B. Forward-Looking Strategy
C. Platform for Action of the 4th World Conference of Women
D. National Policy for Women Empowerment

3. SITA (Studies in Information Technology Applications) is a:
A. Women Empowering Project aiming at educating low-income women in IT.
B. Rural Development Project aiming at educating rural poor in IT.
C. Educational Development Project aiming at educating literates in IT.
D. Communication Development Project aiming at educating urban poor in IT.

4. Swarnajayanti Gram Swarozgar Yojana involves __________ concept.
A. Women Collectives
B. Women Self Reliance
C. Rural Women
D. Self Help Group

5. Choose the correct expansion of STEP.
A. Special Training for Entrepreneurship Program
B. Supportive Technology for Employment Program
C. Support to Training and Employment Program for Women
D. Special Technology for Entrepreneurship Program

6. What is the gendered division of labour?
A. It negates the "double burden."
B. It is based on gender-structured conceptions of appropriate work.
C. It is increase in women's compensation worldwide.
D. It is a caste-based division of labour.

7. Choose the correct expansion of NPEW.
A. National Policy for Empowerment of Women.
B. National Program for Entrepreneurship of Women.
C. National Policy for Employment of Women.
D. National Program for Education of Women.

8. Choose the correct expansion of DWCRA.
A. Department of Women and Child in Rural Areas.
B. Development of Women and Children in Rural Areas.
C. Department of Women and Child in Rural Administration.
D. Developing Women and Children in Rural Administration.

9. _______ was declared as Women Empowerment year in India.
A. 2001 B. 2002
C. 2003 D. 2004

10. Arrange the institutions/agencies on the basis of their level of operation in ascending order:
(i) District Rural Development Agency
(ii) State Commission for Women
(iii) Project Implementation Unit of Women Development Corporations
(iv) Ministry of Women and Child Development

Codes:
A. (ii), (iv), (iii), (i)
B. (iv), (iii), (i), (ii)
C. (iii), (i), (ii), (iv)
D. (i), (ii), (iv), (iii)

11. Find out the sequence of the following policies/ celebrations:
(i) National Policy for Empowerment of Women
(ii) Implementation of CEDAW in India
(iii) International Women's Decade
(iv) National Education Policy

Codes:
A. (iii), (iv), (ii), (i)
B. (iv), (ii), (i), (iii)
C. (ii), (i), (iii), (iv)
D. (i), (iii), (iv), (ii)

12. Name the Report which examined the entire gamut of issues facing women in the unorganised sector of employment:
A. Report of the National Commission
B. Towards Equality Report
C. Shram Shakti Report
D. Status of Women in India Report

13. Arrange the following in the order in which these came:

(i) Towards Equality
(ii) National Policy for Empowerment of Women
(iii) Forward-Looking Strategies
(iv) Beijing Platform for Action

Codes:

A.	(i)	(ii)	(iv)	(iii)
B.	(i)	(iii)	(iv)	(ii)
C.	(ii)	(iii)	(iv)	(i)
D.	(iv)	(i)	(iii)	(ii)

14. National Policy on Empowerment of Women was formulated in:

A. 2001 B. 1999
C. 1995 D. 1974

15. The concept of Self Help Group linking with micro-credit was developed originally by:

A. Amartya Sen
B. Mohammad Yunus
C. Ela Bhatt
D. Esther Boserup

16. Management of Savings of SHGS depends upon:

A. Availability of funds
B. Bribing the Bank Managers
C. Increase the membership fees
D. Transparency and proper bookkeeping

17. Arrange the following chronologically according to the year:

(i) New Population Policy of India
(ii) Towards Equality
(iii) National Empowerment Policy for Women
(iv) Shram Shakti Report

Codes:

A.	(i)	(ii)	(iii)	(iv)
B.	(ii)	(iii)	(i)	(iv)
C.	(iv)	(i)	(ii)	(iii)
D.	(ii)	(iv)	(i)	(iii)

18. Arrange the chronological sequence of the establishments according to the year of their initiation.

(i) Dept. of Women and Child Development.
(ii) National Perspective Plan for Women.
(iii) UGC-Centres for Women's Studies.
(iv) Sarv Shiksha Abhiyan.

Codes:

A.	(i)	(ii)	(iii)	(iv)
B.	(ii)	(i)	(iii)	(iv)
C.	(iii)	(i)	(ii)	(iv)
D.	(i)	(iii)	(ii)	(iv)

19. Among the following which is not an objective of Rashtriya Mahila Kosh?

A. To advise the government on all policy matters affecting women.
B. To promote the provision of microcredit to poor women.
C. To demonstrate and replicate a participatory approach in the organization of a women's group.
D. To link with thrift and savings with credit.

20. According to the National Rural Employment Guarantee Act, the percentage of women beneficiaries shall be:

A. 50% B. 75%
C. 33% D. 100%

21. Identify the inappropriate technology from the given:

A. Capital-saving technology
B. Labour intensive technology
C. Indigenous technology
D. Capital intensive technology

22. Who is the present Chairperson of the Central Social Welfare Board (2019)?

A. Prema Cariappa
B. Krishna Tirath
C. Mohini Giri
D. Meira Kumar

23. What are the measures adopted by the Ministry of HRD to enhance the number of women scientists?

A. Ninth Five Year Plan emphasized on Science and Technology.
B. Establishment of independent scientific commission for women.
C. Enhancement of fellowships/scholarships for women scientists under the Eleventh Five Year Plan.
D. Sixth Five Year Plan gave priority to women scientists.

24. What do you mean by gender-neutral technology?

A. Gender-balanced technology.
B. Technology, providing priority to women's role.
C. Technology, providing priority to men's role.
D. Technology, providing priority to technical people.

25. Which is not the gender implications of the digital divide?

A. Women represent 10% of researchers and 5% of managers in areas of technology.
B. Lack of training does not allow them to participate in the technology process.
C. Become better wives and better mothers.
D. Access to and use of the internet is limited.

26. Which is an incorrect statement about the policy of sanctioning loan by Rashtriya Mahila Kosh with effect from April 2013?
A. It provides microfinance to economically weaker women through IMOs
B. It has reduced interest rate, i.e., from 8% to 6% for IMOs
C. It has reduced interest rate, i.e., from 14% to 12% to all the women.
D. It has reduced interest rate, i.e., from 18% to 14% for women beneficiaries.

27. ALEAP is an organization working for
A. Education Development among women
B. Entrepreneurship Development among women
C. Eradication of poverty among women
D. Increasing enrolment rate of girls in primary schools

28. According to Global Wage Report 2018-19 published by International Labour Organisation (ILO), women are paid ______ less than men in India.
A. 34% B. 40%
C. 45% D. 47%

29. List out the Indicators for the calculation of GEM:
(i) Proportion of seats held by women in the national Parliament.
(ii) Proportion of women in economic decision making.
(iii) Proportion of women in the organized sector.
(iv) Proportion of female share of income.
Codes:
A. (i), (ii) and (iii) are correct.
B. (i), (ii), (iii) and (iv) are correct.
C. (i), (ii) and (iv) are correct.
D. (i) and (ii) are correct.

30. Use of appropriate technology helps women:
(i) To have judicious time utilization
(ii) In increasing health hazards
(iii) In improving the quality of life
(iv) In increasing drudgery of women
Codes:
A. (i) and (ii) are correct
B. (ii) and (iv) are correct
C. (i) and (iii) are correct
D. only (iii) is correct

31. What are the new challenges for women besides the persistent problems of women in the 21st century?
(i) Gender and Development
(ii) Global Trade Technology
(iii) The Ascent of Market Ideology
(iv) The Decline of the Welfare State
Codes:
A. (iii) and (iv) only
B. (i), and (ii) only
C. (i), (ii), (iii) and (iv)
D. (ii), (iii) and (iv) only

32. National Institute of Micro, Small and Medium Enterprises is located in:
A. Bengaluru B. Delhi
C. Hyderabad D. Mumbai

33. ICTs have transformed the economic activity of both women and men by increasing the demand for which skills? Choose the correct answer:
(i) Soft skills
(ii) The shift from brain (cognitive) and non-routine skills to brawn (manual) and routine skills.
(iii) The shift from local ethnic skills.
(iv) Technological skills.
Codes:
A. (i) only B. (i) and (ii) only
C. (iii), (i) and (iv) only D. (iii) and (iv) only

34. Confederation of Women Entrepreneurs of India (COWE) was Formed in 2004 by..... .
A. Six Women Entrepreneurs
B. Four Self Help Groups
C. Government of India
D. Self Employed Women's Association

35. Who is Chairperson of the Parliamentary Committee on Empowerment of Women 2019?
A. Najma Heptullah
B. Sumitra Mahajan
C. Meenakshi Lekhi
D. Smt. Bijoya Chakravarty

36. National Commission for Self Employed Women was established in the year:
A. 1953 B. 1987
C. 1995 D. 2000

37. Gender Entrepreneurship Monitor explores:
(i) The role of entrepreneurship in national economic growth.
(ii) Unveils detailed national features and characteristics associated with entrepreneurial activities.
(iii) Grassroots level data.
(iv) Only big firms headed by women.
Codes:
A. (i) and (iii) only B. (i) and (ii) only
C. (ii), (iii) and (iv) only D. (i), (ii) and (iii) only

38. First Woman to hold a Union Cabinet post:
A. Sushma Swaraj
B. Sucheta Kriplani
C. Vijaya Lakshmi Pandit
D. Indira Gandhi

39. Self Help Groups (SHG) are:
(a) Urban-town based financial intermediary committees of 10-12 local women and men.
(b) Fast emerging as a promising tool for promoting income-generating enterprise.
(c) An informal arrangement for credit supply to the poor.
(d) A viable alternative to achieve objectives of rural development through community participation.

Codes:
A. (b), (c) and (d) only
B. (a), (b) and (d) only
C. (a), (b) and (c) only
D. (a), (b), (c) and (d)

40. Match List-I with List-II:

List-I (Concept)	***List-II (Meaning)***
(a) Gender Redistribution Policies	(i) Do not distinguish between the different needs to women and men in their formation and Implementation.
(b) Gender Roles	(ii) Aims to transform the existing distribution of resources and responsibilities in order to create a more equal relationship between women and men.
(c) Gender Division of Labour	(iii) Learned behaviour in a given society/community, or other special groups that condition activities, tasks, and responsibilities are perceived as male and female.
(d) Gender Blind Policies	(iv) Allocation of different jobs or types of work to men and women usually by tradition or culture.

Codes:

	(a)	(b)	(c)	(d)
A.	(iv)	(iii)	(ii)	(i)
B.	(i)	(ii)	(iii)	(iv)
C.	(ii)	(iii)	(iv)	(i)
D.	(iii)	(iv)	(i)	(ii)

41. Match the following:

List-I	***List-II***
(a) National Policy on Older Persons	(i) 2001
(b) National Policy on Empowerment of Women	(ii) 1986
(c) National Policy on Education	(iii) 2014
(d) National Youth Policy	(iv) 1999

Codes:

	(a)	(b)	(c)	(d)
A.	(iii)	(iv)	(ii)	(i)
B.	(iv)	(i)	(iii)	(ii)
C.	(iv)	(i)	(ii)	(iii)
D.	(iii)	(i)	(ii)	(iv)

42. Arrange chronologically the following Schemes/Policy of Ministry of Women and Child Development:
(a) Ujjawala
(b) Support to Training and Employment Programme
(c) National Mission for Empowerment of Women
(d) National Early Childhood Care and Education Policy

Codes:
A. (a), (b), (c), (d)
B. (b), (a), (c), (d)
C. (a), (b), (d), (c)
D. (b), (c), (d), (a)

43. Identify the reason for the feminization of employment in global agriculture from the following:
A. A change from traditional crops to sericulture.
B. A change from traditional crops to horticulture, floriculture, protein-rich meats, and processed foods.
C. A change in food markets.
D. A change from traditional crops to sericulture and multicultural.

44. Which are the statutory bodies under the Ministry of Women and Child Development?
(a) Rashtriya Mahila Kosh
(b) National Commission for Women
(c) Central Social Welfare Board
(d) National Commission for Protection of Child Rights

Codes:
A. (b) and (d) only
B. (a), (b), (c) and (d)
C. (b), (c) and (d) only
D. (a), (b) and (d) only

45. Match List-I with List-II:

List-I (Scheme)	*List-II (Objective)*
(a) Swawlamban	(i) To upgrade skills and provide employment, entrepreneurial and marke-ting skills to women from traditional work-sectors.
(b) STEP	(ii) To provide the holistic and integrated services to women in difficult circum-stances—widows, deserted, released prisoners etc.
(c) Swadhar	(iii) To provide training and skills to woman to facilitate emplo-yment or self-employment to women belonging to Scheduled Castes and Scheduled Tribes.
(d) Swa-Shakti	(iv) To enhance women's access to resources for better quality of life through various means for women of the rural areas.

Codes:

	(a)	(b)	(c)	(d)
A.	(iii)	(ii)	(i)	(iv)
B.	(iii)	(i)	(ii)	(iv)
C.	(ii)	(i)	(iv)	(iii)
D.	(iii)	(i)	(iv)	(ii)

46. CAPART stands for:

A. Council for Political Action and Rural Technology
B. Council for Agrarian Participation and Rural Training
C. Council for Advancement of Participatory Action and Rural Technology
D. Council for Advancement of People's Action and Rural Technology

47. Match List-I with List-II:

List-I (Contribution by the Social Entrepreneur)	*List-II (Names of Social Entrepreneurs)*
(a) Founder of Modern Nursing	(i) Susan B. Anthony
(b) Developed the Early Childhood Education	(ii) Vinoba Bhave
(c) Founder and Leader of the Land Gift Movement	(iii) Maria Montessori
(d) Fought for women's rights including the right to control property in the USA	(iv) Florence Nightingale

Codes:

	(a)	(b)	(c)	(d)
A.	(i)	(ii)	(iii)	(iv)
B.	(ii)	(iv)	(iii)	(i)
C.	(iii)	(ii)	(i)	(iv)
D.	(iv)	(iii)	(ii)	(i)

48. Which are the agencies imparting training to rural women?

(a) Central Board of Social Welfare
(b) State Boards of Social Welfare
(c) Krishi Vigyan Kendra
(d) Mahila Mandals

Codes:

A. (c) and (d) only B. (a), (b), (c) and (d)
C. (a) and (b) only D. (a), (b) and (d) only

49. National Commission for Women looks into complaints and takes suo moto notice of matters relating to:

(a) Deprivation of Human Rights
(b) Non-implementation of laws enacted to provide protection to women
(c) Non-compliance of policy decisions, guidelines or instructions aimed at mitigating hardships of women
(d) Wrong planning process of socio-economic development of women

Codes:

A. (b) and (c) only B. (a), (b), (c) and (d)
C. (a), (b) and (c) only D. (a), (c) and (d) only

50. What are the autonomous organizations that come under the Ministry of Women and Child Development?

(a) National Institute of Public Co-operation and Child Development
(b) National Commission for Women
(c) Rashtriya Mahila Kosh
(d) Central Adoption Resource Authority

Codes:

A. (a), (b) and (c) only B. (b) and (c) only
C. (a) and (d) only D. (a), (c) and (d) only

51. Arrange the following policies in chronological order:

(a) National Policy on Women Empowerment
(b) National Policy on Poverty Elimination
(c) National Policy on Education
(d) National Policy on Population

Codes:

A. (c), (b), (a), (d) B. (c), (b), (d), (a)
C. (b), (c), (a), (d) D. (a), (c), (b), (d)

52. The Central Government shall remove a person from the office of the Chairperson or Member of NCW (National Commission for Women) if that person:

A. becomes of unsound mind and stands so declared by a competent court
B. becomes undischarged or insolvent
C. is absent for two consecutive meetings of the commission
D. gets convicted and is sentenced to imprisonment for an offence

53. Indian Association of Women's Studies was set up in the year:

A. 1981 B. 1975
C. 1995 D. 1985

54. The National Mission of sustainable agriculture was started:

A. to help rural farmers with quality seeds.
B. to promote and integrated farming system.
C. to help farmers in good irrigation practices.
D. to help farmers find a market for their produce.

55. Match the following Policies/Plans with the year in which were framed:

(a) National Policy on Education	(i) 2001
(b) National Policy for Empowerment of Women	(ii) 1986
(c) National Population Policy (Latest)	(iii) 1988
(d) National Perspective Plan for Women	(iv) 2000

Codes:

	(a)	(b)	(c)	(d)
A.	(i)	(iv)	(ii)	(iii)
B.	(ii)	(i)	(iv)	(iii)
C.	(iii)	(iv)	(ii)	(i)
D.	(iv)	(ii)	(i)	(iii)

56. Match the items in List-I and List-II:

List-I	***List-II***
(a) Sarva-Shiksha Abhiyan	(i) Empowerment of Women
(b) RCH	(ii) Education for all
(c) NACO	(iii) Safe motherhood
(d) DWCRA	(iv) HIV and AIDS

Codes:

	(a)	(b)	(c)	(d)
A.	(i)	(ii)	(iii)	(iv)
B.	(ii)	(iii)	(iv)	(i)
C.	(ii)	(iv)	(i)	(ii)
D.	(i)	(iii)	(iv)	(ii)

57. Identify the chronological sequence of the following establishments:

(i) National Human Rights Commission
(ii) National Council for Women in India
(iii) Indian Association for Women's Studies
(iv) National Commission for Women

Codes:

A.	(ii)	(i)	(iii)	(iv)
B.	(ii)	(iii)	(iv)	(i)
C.	(ii)	(iii)	(i)	(iv)
D.	(i)	(iv)	(ii)	(iii)

58. TAI stands for:

A. Technology Achievement Index
B. Technology Assessment Indicator
C. Technological Average Index
D. Technological Awareness Indicator

59. Arrange the chronological sequence of the following reports according to its year of publication:

(i) Platform for Action
(ii) National Policy for the Empowerment of Women
(iii) Shram Shakti
(iv) Towards Equality

Codes:

A.	(iv)	(iii)	(i)	(ii)
B.	(iii)	(iv)	(i)	(ii)
C.	(i)	(ii)	(iii)	(iv)
D.	(ii)	(iii)	(iv)	(i)

60. Match the following from List-I and List-II:

List-I	***List-II***
(a) National Human Rights Commission	(i) 2001
(b) Parliamentary Committee	(ii) 1981
(c) Indian Association of Women's Studies	(iii) 1997
(d) National Policy for the Empowerment of Women	(iv) 1993

Codes:

	(a)	(b)	(c)	(d)
A.	(i)	(ii)	(iv)	(iii)
B.	(iv)	(iii)	(ii)	(i)
C.	(iii)	(ii)	(i)	(iv)
D.	(iv)	(i)	(iii)	(ii)

61. Expand the correct acronym of DAWN:

A. Development Alternatives for Women in a New Era
B. Development of Women in Nutrition
C. Development Alternatives for Women in Nutrition
D. Development and Welfare for a New Era

62. Arrange the chronological order of the following on the basis of the year of inception:
(i) National Commission for Women.
(ii) UGC Women's Studies Centres.
(iii) National Policy for the Empowerment of Women.
(iv) National Rural Health Mission.

Codes:
A. (i), (ii), (iii) and (iv)
B. (iii), (ii), (i), (iv)
C. (ii), (i), (iii) and (iv)
D. (iv), (ii), (iii) and (i)

63. Adam Smith held that women did not have the capacity to take rational decisions in economic matters. This is an example of:
A. Personal is Political
B. Anatomy is Destiny
C. Women Rights are Human Rights
D. Natural is Personal

64. Which of the following years is declared as the year of microcredit by United Nations?
A. 2002 B. 2003
C. 2005 D. 2000

65. Which of the following options include activities of the National Commission for Women?
I. Setting up an expert Committee to tender advice on women.
II. Recommend and initiate programmes for women and children.
III. Create Non-Governmental organizations to empower women.
IV. Help women to think creatively.

Codes:
A. I and IV are only correct
B. I and II are only correct
C. I, II and IV are only correct
D. I, II, III are only correct

66. Which of the following statements is more relevant to the Department of Women and Child Development?
A. Women and men form a special component of the department.
B. The programmes are only national and limited in scope.
C. The department employs women workers only.
D. The department establishes liaison with UN and International Agencies and supports State Programmes for women.

67. Among the following women whose name is closely associated with the Central Social Welfare Board?
A. Dr. Annie Besant
B. Aruna Asaf Ali
C. Vijayalakshmi Pandit
D. Durgabai Deshmukh

68. Match List-I and List-II:

List-I	*List-II*
(a) Department of Women and Child Development	(i) 1975
(b) Integrated Child Development Scheme	(ii) 1985
(c) Juvenile Justice Act	(iii) 2000
(d) Indian Association for Women's Studies	(iv) 1982

Codes:

	(a)	(b)	(c)	(d)
A.	(iv)	(iii)	(i)	(ii)
B.	(iii)	(iv)	(i)	(ii)
C.	(ii)	(i)	(iii)	(iv)
D.	(ii)	(iv)	(iii)	(i)

69. Who among the following is not an Entrepreneur?
A. Indira Nooyi
B. Kiran Mazumdar Shaw
C. Ekta Kapoor
D. Kalpana Shah

70. Who was the chairperson of the National Commission for Self Employed Women formed in 1987?
A. Vina Mazumdar B. Ela Bhat
C. Madhuri Shah D. Armati Desai

71. Which one of the following does not have an effect on the health of women working in ICTs centres?
A. Health Hazards
B. Broken family relationship
C. Women are economically empowered
D. Infertility has increased

72. What are the provisions related to rural women's work in MGNREGS?
(i) Priority for women in the ratio of one-third of total workers.
(ii) Equal wage for men and women.
(iii) Provision of work within a radius of five km from the residence.
(iv) Women have the freedom to choose the period and months of employment for themselves.

Codes:
A. (i) and (iv) only B. (iv) only
C. (iii) only D. (i), (ii), (iii) and (iv)

73. Match the following:

Column-I **(Policy)**	***Column-II*** **(Year)**
(a) Towards Equality	(i) 1988
(b) Shram Shakti	(ii) 1988-2000
(c) National Perspective Plan	(iii) 2001
(d) National Health Policy	(iv) 1974

Codes:

	(a)	(b)	(c)	(d)
A.	(ii)	(iii)	(iv)	(i)
B.	(ii)	(iv)	(i)	(iii)
C.	(iv)	(i)	(ii)	(iii)
D.	(iii)	(i)	(iv)	(ii)

74. Which of the following statement is not correct in respect of women and technology?

A. The experimental result of lab extension is not reaching to the agricultural women workers in the field.

B. Technology is always undermining the problems of rural women workers.

C. Scientists and technocrats are not realizing the traditional knowledge of women.

D. New technologies are always women-friendly.

75. Chronologically arrange the following policy initiatives by the Government for women.

(i) National Commission on Self-employed Women.

(ii) National Commission for Women.

(iii) The Committee on the Status of Women in India.

(iv) National Policy on Education.

Codes:

A. (iii), (iv), (i), (ii) B. (iii), (i), (ii), (iv)

C. (i), (iii), (ii), (iv) D. (iv), (i), (ii), (iii)

76. Find out the sequence of the establishment of the following institutions:

1. Central Social Welfare Board
2. Family Courts
3. National Commission for Women
4. National Human Rights Commission

Codes:

A. 1, 2, 3, 4

B. 4, 3, 2, 1

C. 1, 3, 2, 4

D. 1, 4, 3, 2

77. TREAD scheme for women is meant for:

A. Training Related Entrepreneurship Assistance and Development

B. Training and Research on Entrepreneurship Assistance and Development

C. Trade Related Entrepreneurship Assistance and Development

D. Trade-Related Education and Development

78. What is the name of the Scheme which provides training and skills to women in traditional and non-traditional traders?

A. Kishori Shakti Yojna

B. Rashtriya Mahila Kosh

C. Swayamsiddha

D. Swawlamban

79. Who is the Chief Executive of Bhartiya Mahila Bank (2019)?

A. Indira Nooyi

B. Shikha Sharma

C. Usha Anantha Subramanian

D. Naina Lal Kidwai

80. What is the full form of NACO?

A. National Aids Central Organization

B. National Aids Coordinating Organization

C. National Aids Controlling and Coordinating Organization

D. National Aids Control Organization

81. Match List-I (Women Commission and Committee) and List-II (Year):

List-I	***List-II***
(a) National Policy on Empowerment of Women	(i) 1997
(b) Parliamentary Committee on Empowerment of Women	(ii) 2001
(c) Second High Level Reconstituted Committee on Status of Women	(iii) 2010
(d) National Mission on Empowerment of Women	(iv) 2013

Codes:

	(a)	(b)	(c)	(d)
A.	(i)	(ii)	(iii)	(iv)
B.	(ii)	(iii)	(iv)	(i)
C.	(iii)	(i)	(iv)	(ii)
D.	(ii)	(i)	(iv)	(iii)

82. Which of the following characteristics is not associated with 'Appropriate Technology'?

A. Capital intensive

B. Labour intensive

C. Environmentally sound

D. Energy efficient

83. The "Swashakti Project" was earlier known as:
A. Valmiki Ambedkar Awas Yojana
B. Swarn Jayanti Gram Swarozgar Yojana
C. CAPART scheme
D. Rural Women's Development and Empowerment Project

84. Write the chronological order of the following programmes:
(a) Indira Awas Yojana
(b) Swarna Jayanti Shakti Rozgar Yojana
(c) Valmiki Ambedkar Awas Yojana
(d) Janani Suraksha Yojana

Codes:
A. (b), (c), (d) and (a)
B. (c), (b), (d) and (a)
C. (d), (c), (b) and (a)
D. (a), (b), (c) and (d)

85. The objectives of the National Commission for Women are:
(a) to review the Constitutional and legal safeguards for women.
(b) to recommend remedial legislative measures for the cause of women.
(c) to facilitate redressal of grievances of women.
(d) to advise the government on all policy matters affecting women.

Codes:
A. (c) only
B. (b) and (d) only
C. (a), (b) and (c) only
D. (a), (b), (c) and (d)

86. Which one of the following schemes was launched in 2015 for women prisoners, women survivors of natural disasters, domestic violence and human trafficking and women without any economic and social support?
A. Ujjawala Scheme
B. Valmiki Awas Yojna
C. CAPART Scheme
D. Swarn Greh Scheme

87. What are the advantages provided by MGNREGS to the women-wage seekers?
(a) Equal wages will be provided to both men and women.
(b) At least one-third beneficiaries shall be women.
(c) Worksite facilities such as drinking water, creche (mobile) and shade should be provided.
(d) Dwelling unit is provided with a smokeless chulha.

Codes:
A. (a), (b), (c) and (d)
B. (a), (b) and (c)
C. (a) and (b) only
D. (a) only

88. GNI coefficient:
(a) is a measure of statistical dispersion intended to represent income distribution of a nation's residents.
(b) is commonly used measure of inequality.
(c) measures the inequality among values of a frequency distribution.
(d) measures a coefficient of demand and supply.

Codes:
A. (a), (b), (c) and (d)
B. (b), (c) and (d)
C. (a), (b) and (c) only
D. (b) and (d) only

89. The movement called the "Rising of 20,000" was related to:
A. Trade Union Movement
B. Women's Suffrage Movement
C. Abolition Movement
D. LGBT Movement

90. Impact of programmes of the international financial institutions on gender are being monitored by 'Gender Action' a group founded in 2002 by:
A. Grace Abbott, American Social Worker
B. Ester Boserup, Denmark Economist
C. Elaine Zuckerman, former World Bank economist
D. Kamla Bhasin, SANGAT, South Asian Feminist Network

91. Arrange the following Commissions in chronological sequence:
(i) The National Committee on Women's Education
(ii) D.S. Kothari Commission
(iii) Yashpal Committee Report
(iv) National Knowledge Commission

Codes:

A.	(ii)	(iii)	(iv)	(i)
B.	(i)	(ii)	(iii)	(iv)
C.	(iii)	(ii)	(i)	(iv)
D.	(iv)	(iii)	(i)	(ii)

92. Who among the following has been founder members of Women's World Banking?
A. Ela Bhatt B. Promila Kapur
C. Devaki Jain D. Maithreyi Krishnaraj

93. Match List-I with List-II.

List-I	*List-II*
(a) Leader of Bhartiya Janta Party	(i) Pam Rajput
(b) All India Women's Conference	(ii) Brinda Karat
(c) Chairperson, High-Level Committee on Status of Women	(iii) Sushma Swaraj
(d) All India Democratic Women's Association	(iv) Bina Jain

Codes:

	(a)	(b)	(c)	(d)
A.	(ii)	(i)	(iii)	(iv)
B.	(i)	(ii)	(iii)	(iv)
C.	(iii)	(iv)	(i)	(ii)
D.	(iv)	(ii)	(iii)	(i)

94. The National Commission for Women has initiated 'Mahila Adhikar Abhiyan.' Identify the incorrect answer about the Abhiyan:

(i) It seeks to empower Dalit and Tribal Women only.
(ii) It seeks to empower with information about their entitlements.
(iii) The campaign aims to empower women of rural and remote areas of the country about various government schemes.
(iv) This programme was implemented exclusively in four States viz., Rajasthan, Punjab, Uttarakhand, and Kerala.

Codes:

A. (ii), (iii) and (iv) only
B. (i), (ii) and (iii) only
C. (i) only
D. (iv) and (ii) only

95. Statutory Minimum wage is fixed under:

A. Workmen's Compensation Act, 1923
B. Minimum Wages Act, 1948
C. Equal Remuneration Act, 1976
D. Payment of Wages Act, 1936

96. Which factor is responsible for the low status of women in India?

A. Changes in the family system
B. Female foeticide
C. Patriarchal system for society
D. Women liberation movement

97. SEWA was started in:

A. 1977 B. 1972
C. 1970 D. 1971

98. What is the expansion for IWRAW?

A. Indian Women's Association for Women's Rights.
B. International Women's Rights Action Watch.
C. International Women's Rights and Welfare Association.
D. Indian Women's Rights Action Watch.

99. The Current Chairperson (2019) of the National Commission for Women is:

A. Girija Vyas
B. Maneka Giri
C. Poornima Advani
D. Rekha Sharma

100. Who is the Minister of Women and Child Development (2019)?

A. Sushma Swaraj
B. Maneka Gandhi
C. Smriti Irani
D. Sonia Gandhi

101. The Department of Science and Technology (DST) has facilitated married women to be at her husband's place and continue their research work. Write the name of that scheme.

A. ASHA B. YOJANA
C. DISHA D. RAKSHA

102. Match the List-I with List-II:

List-I	*List-II*
(a) Puneet Arora	(i) First Woman to receive Gyanpith Award
(b) Sushama Chawala	(ii) First Woman amputee to scale Everest
(c) Ashapurna Devi	(iii) First Woman chairprson of Indian Airlines
(d) Arunima Sinha	(iv) First Woman Lieutenant General

Codes:

	(a)	(b)	(c)	(d)
A.	(i)	(ii)	(iii)	(iv)
B.	(ii)	(iii)	(i)	(iv)
C.	(iii)	(iv)	(ii)	(i)
D.	(iv)	(iii)	(i)	(ii)

103. Founder and CEO of SHEROES is:

A. Pranshu Bhandari
B. Sairee Chahal
C. Radhika Agarwal
D. Sakshi Talwar

104. Council for Advancement of People's Action and Rural Technology (CAPART) is an autonomous body under:

A. The Ministry of Agriculture
B. The Ministry of Commerce
C. Ministry of Child and Women Development
D. The Ministry of Rural Development

105. Female labour force participation is more in the unorganized sector because:

(i) Majority of women do not have technical skills.
(ii) Female workers are submissive.
(iii) Women workers are more organized.
(iv) Women workers are from the lower caste.

Codes:

A. (i) and (ii) are correct
B. (iii) and (iv) are correct
C. (i), (ii) and (iii) are correct
D. (iii) only is correct

106. According to the Sixth Económic Census released by the Ministry of Statistics and Programme Implementation, women constitute around.........of the total entrepreneurship.

A. 9% B. 14%
C. 32% D. 50%

107. What is the Bread Winner Paradigm?

A. Man is the main breadwinner.
B. Woman is the main breadwinner.
C. Women headed families.
D. Elder people lead the family.

108. What does FFD stand for?

A. Federation of Funding for Development
B. Financing for Development
C. Foreign Financing for Development
D. Ford Foundation for Development

109. Match List-I (Institutions) and List-II (Year of Establishment):

List-I	***List-II***
(a) Mudra Bank	(i) 1986
(b) Confederation of Women Entrepreneurs	(ii) 2013
(c) Bharatiya Mahila Bank	(iii) 2015
(d) CAPART	(iv) 2004

Codes:

	(a)	(b)	(c)	(d)
A.	(iii)	(iv)	(i)	(ii)
B.	(iv)	(i)	(ii)	(iii)
C.	(iii)	(iv)	(ii)	(i)
D.	(iii)	(i)	(ii)	(iv)

110. Mahila Coir Yojana is a scheme under the ministry of:

A. Micro, Small and Medium Enterprise
B. Women and Child Welfare
C. Human Resource Development
D. Minority Affairs

111. International Women's Day (March 8) is celebrated in the memory of:

A. Women Textile Workers Strike in France
B. Women Textile Workers Strike in New York
C. Women Textile Workers Strike in England
D. Women Textile Workers Strike in India

112. Bhartiya Mahila Bank was merged with which bank on March 31st, 2017?

A. State Bank of India
B. Punjab and Sindh Bank
C. Indian Bank
D. Bank of India

113. Who among the following is the co-founder of Yatra.com

A. Richa Kar B. Sabina Chopra
C. Jaya Jha D. Anisha Singh

114. Gender balance can be achieved through:

(i) Inclusive development
(ii) Flexi jobs
(iii) Reversing the gender roles
(iv) Equality of legal rights

Codes:

A. (i) and (iii) are correct
B. (iv) only is correct
C. (iii) and (iv) only are correct
D. (i), (ii) and (iv) are correct

115. Neeru Sharma is Co-founder of:

A. ShopClues.com
B. Infibeam.com
C. Zivame
D. Nykaa.com

116. According to the World Bank Enterprise Survey's data (2014), Percent of firms with a female top manager is:

A. 2.5 B. 8.9
C. 21.3 D. 37.6

117. Most of the women entrepreneurs in India work in:

A. IT sector
B. Teaching
C. Agriculture sector
D. Beauty industry

118. Annapurna Scheme, for women entrepreneurs who are setting up food catering industry, is offered by:
A. State Bank of India
B. State Bank of Mysore
C. Indian Bank
D. Dena Bank

119. When was the Women Entrepreneurship Platform launched in India?
A. May 1st, 2016
B. 15th August 2017
C. March 8th, 2018
D. 26th January, 2019

120. Which State in India is going to set up the first Women Entrepreneurs Park?
A. Maharashtra
B. Uttarakhand
C. Himachal Pradesh
D. Tamilnadu

121. 'FIWE' stands for:
A. Federation of Indian Women Entrepreneurs
B. Foundation of Indian Women Employees
C. Faculty of International Women Executives
D. Fund for Indian Women Entrepreneurs

122. The Global Coalition of Young Women Entrepreneur was launched on 15th July, 2016 by:
A. United Nations
B. Ministry of Women and Child Development
C. National Commission for Women
D. World Economic Forum

123. The National Institute for Entrepreneurship and Small Business Development (NIESBUD) is an organization under:
A. Ministry of Labour and Employment
B. Ministry of Skill Development and Entrepreneurship
C. Ministry of Commerce and Industry
D. Ministry of Women and Child Welfare

124. Assertion (A): Women remain invisible in labour force participation.
Reason (R): Women are engaged mostly in unpaid work.
Codes:
A. Both (A) and (R) are true.
B. Both (A) and (R) are false.
C. (A) is false but (R) is true.
D. (A) is true but (R) is false.

125. Assertion (A): Women work longer hours than men.
Reason (R): Women's work is concentrated within the domestic sphere.
Codes:
A. Both (A) and (R) are true.
B. (A) is true (R) is false.
C. (A) is false (R) is true.
D. Both (A) and (R) are false.

126. Assertion (A): Microcredit programmes are one of the means of women's empowerment.
Reason (R): The main objective of microcredit is to support women's education.
Codes:
A. Both (A) and (R) are false.
B. (A) is true (R) is false.
C. Both (A) and (R) are true.
D. Both (A) and (R) are true, (R) is the correct explanation for (A).

127. Assertion (A): Appropriate technology involves the application of scientific knowledge and practical means to perform a specific task.
Reason (R): Adoption of appropriate technology reduces drudgery on the part of rural women.
Codes:
A. Both (A) and (R) are true and (R) is a correct explanation of (A).
B. Both (A) and (R) are true and (R) is not the correct explanation for (A).
C. (A) is true, and (R) is false.
D. (A) is false, and (R) is true.

128. Assertion (A): Empowerment of women is possible through entrepreneurship development.
Reason (R): Entrepreneurship development is the only indicator for empowerment of women.
Codes:
A. Both (A) and (R) are true and (R) is the correct explanation of (A).
B. Both (A) and (R) are true and (R) is not a correct explanation of (A).
C. Both (A) and (R) are false.
D. (A) is true, (R) is false.

129. Assertion (A): Entrepreneurs are only born. They cannot be made.
Reason (R): Entrepreneurship is a challenging task.
Codes:
A. Both (A) and (R) are true.

B. Both (A) and (R) are true and (R) is not a correct explanation of (A).
C. Both (A) and (R) are false.
D. (A) is false and (R) is true and (R) is not a correct explanation of (A).

130. Assertion (A): Microfinance institutions, the micro-credit and SHG movement are the Sole Panacea for addressing poverty and women's empowerment.

Reason (R): Majority of the women are adequately covered by the banking systems through SHG movement.

Codes:

A. Both (A) and (R) are true and (R) is the correct explanation for (A).
B. Both (A) and (R) are false.
C. Both (A) and (R) are true and (R) is not the correct explanation for (A).
D. (A) is correct (R) is false.

131. Assertion (A): Development practitioners of all sectors have found Participatory Rural Appraisal an attractive means for facilitating empowerment of the women.

Reason (R): Participatory Rural Appraisal emphasizes accessible techniques for gathering information and involving the marginalized groups in the description, analysis, and solutions to the development problems.

Codes:

A. Both (A) and (R) are true.
B. (A) is correct, (R) is false.
C. Both (A) and (R) are true and (R) is the correct explanation for (A).
D. Both (A) and (R) are true and (R) is not the correct explanation for (A).

132. Assertion (A): Women cannot escape from the trap of femininity by assuming the role of the career/ profession.

Reason (R): Career women are expected to please and act like a woman to her professional duties.

Codes:

A. Both (A) and (R) are true.
B. Both (A) and (R) are false.
C. (A) is correct and (R) is false.
D. Both (A) and (R) are true and (R) is the correct explanation for (A).

133. Assertion (A): Social entrepreneurs seek to transform societies at large rather than transforming their profit margin.

Reason (R): The Internet and social networking websites have been used as pivotal resources for the success of social entrepreneurship.

Codes:

A. Both (A) and (R) are false.
B. (A) is true (R) is false.
C. Both (A) and (R) are true, (R) is not the correct explanation for (A).
D. Both (A) and (R) are true, (R) is the correct explanation for (A).

134. Assertion (A): Globalization made a positive impact on ICT.

Reason (R): Globalization is a threat to the unorganized sector.

Codes:

A. Both (A) and (R) are true.
B. Both (A) and (R) are false.
C. (A) is true, (R) is false.
D. (R) is true, (A) is false.

135. Assertion (A): One of the constraints faced by women entrepreneurs is the lack of confidence among women.

Reason (R): Members of the family and society are not supportive of the entrepreneurial growth of women.

Codes:

A. Both (A) and (R) are true.
B. Both (A) and (R) are false.
C. Both (A) and (R) are true, (R) is the correct explanation for (A).
D. Both (A) and (R) are true but (R) is not the correct explanation for (A).

136. Assertion (A): Women and men in technological profession differ not in ability but in attitudes and socialization.

Reason (R): Boys and Girls are socialized to different patterns.

Codes:

A. (A) is true, (R) is false.
B. Both (A) and (R) are true and (R) is not the correct explanation for (A).
C. Both (A) and (R) are false.
D. (A) is false, but (R) is true.

137. Assertion (A): The entrepreneurial potentials of women have been changing with the growing sensitivity to the role and economic status in the society.

Reason (R): Skill, knowledge, and adaptability in business make the women emerge into business ventures.

Codes:

A. Both (A) and (R) are false.
B. Both (A) and (R) are true, (R) is the correct explanation of (A).
C. (A) is false and (R) is true.
D. (A) is true and (R) is false.

138. Assertion (A): Women employed in the high-technology sector have often had difficulty in rising above the so-called glass ceiling.

Reason (R): Women are disproportionately confined to lower echelons of employment.

Codes:

A. Both (A) and (R) are true, (R) is the correct explanation for (A).
B. (A) is false, but (R) is true.
C. Both (A) and (R) are false.
D. Both (A) and (R) are true, (R) is not the correct explanation of (A).

139. Assertion (A): The women entrepreneurs are promoted by both the Central and State Governments.

Reason (R): There is a failure as some of the women entrepreneurial units are organized by men only.

Codes:

A. Both (A) and (R) are true.
B. Both (A) and (R) are false.
C. Both (A) and (R) are true, but (R) is not the correct explanation of (A).
D. (A) is false and (R) is true.

140. Assertion (A): The joint family system is disintegrating in modern India.

Reason (R): Transition from Agrarian to Industrial economy is responsible for its disintegration.

Codes:

A. Both (A) and (R) are false.
B. (A) and (R) are true and (R) is the correct explanation of (A).
C. (A) is true, but (R) is not the correct explanation of (A).
D. (R) is true, but (A) is false.

141. Assertion (A): Technological changes requiring new skills and specialization result in marginalization of traditional production skills of rural women.

Reason (R): The agrarian crisis mostly affects women as they constitute a large number of the labour force in the countryside.

Codes:

A. (A) is false but (R) is true.
B. Both (A) and (R) are false.
C. (A) is true but (R) is false and (R) is not the correct explanation for (A).
D. Both (A) and (R) are true but (R) is not the correct explanation for (A).

142. Assertion (A): SHG women are taking up micro enterprises.

Reason (R): Banks and Cooperative societies and other Financial Institutions are supporting SHG women to start micro-enterprises.

Codes:

A. Both (A) and (R) are true and (R) is the correct explanation for (A).
B. Both (A) and (R) are true, and (R) is not the correct explanation for (A).
C. Both (A) and (R) are false.
D. (A) is true, (R) is false.

143. Assertion (A): Entrepreneurship Development Training Programmes are encouraging women to start their own enterprises.

Reason (R): Many Institutions and Organisations are imparting Entrepreneurship Development Training Programmes.

Codes:

A. Both (A) and (R) are true, (R) is the correct explanation of (A).
B. (A) is false and (R) is true and (R) is not the correct explanation of (A).
C. Both (A) and (R) are false.
D. (A) is true and (R) is false.

144. Assertion (A): Micro-credit programmes and SHG movement largely deals with saving and lending and not micro-enterprise development.

Reason (R): SHG women lack the knowledge and skill of marketing the products.

Codes:

A. Both (A) and (R) are true.
B. Both (A) and (R) are true, (R) is the correct explanation for (A).
C. (A) is true, (R) is false.
D. Both (A) and (R) are false.

145. Assertion (A): Gender issues and gender analysis are regarded as significant and of priority in development policy.

Reason (R): Women have been given a marginalized position with little or no access to power.

Codes:

A. Both (A) and (R) are true but (R) is not the correct explanation of (A).
B. (A) is true, but (R) is false.
C. Both (A) and (R) are false.
D. (A) is false, but (R) is true.

146. Assertion (A): The self-help groups of women have been found very effective in organizing and sensitizing women.

Reason (R): The self-help groups of women are supported by educated women.

Codes:

A. Both (A) and (R) are true.
B. Both (A) and (R) are false.
C. (A) is true, but (R) is false.
D. (A) is false, but (R) is true.

147. Assertion (A): The challenges of women entrepreneurs are higher than men entrepreneurs.

Reason (R): Women are restricted due to social norms and family responsibilities.

Codes:

A. Both (A) and (R) are true.
B. Both (A) and (R) are false.
C. (A) is correct, (R) is false.
D. Both (A) and (R) are true and (R) is the correct explanation for (A).

148. Assertion (A): Women share double the burden as producers of the human race as well as supporters and sustainers of human life.

Reason (R): Women's contribution to the economic sphere remain invisible.

Codes:

A. Both (A) and (R) are true.
B. Both (A) and (R) are false.
C. (A) is true, (R) is false.
D. (A) is false, (R) is true.

149. Assertion (A): Microcredit is the panacea for poverty reduction and women's empowerment.

Reason (R): The poverty reduction and women's empowerment will be a distant goal unless 'physical capital' and 'financial capital' is strengthened.

Codes:

A. (A) is true and (R) is false.
B. Both (A) and (R) are true, (R) is the correct explanation for (A).
C. Both (A) and (R) are false.
D. (A) is false and (R) is true.

150. Assertion (A): SHG women are taking up micro enterprises.

Reason (R): Banks and Cooperative societies and other Financial Institutions are supporting SHG women to start micro-enterprises.

Codes:

A. Both (A) and (R) are true and (R) is the correct explanation for (A).
B. Both (A) and (R) are true, and (R) is not the correct explanation for (A).
C. Both (A) and (R) are false.
D. (A) is true, (R) is false.

Answers

1	2	3	4	5	6	7	8	9	10
B	C	A	D	C	B	A	B	A	C
11	**12**	**13**	**14**	**15**	**16**	**17**	**18**	**19**	**20**
A	C	B	A	B	D	D	A	A	C
21	**22**	**23**	**24**	**25**	**26**	**27**	**28**	**29**	**30**
D	A	C	A	C	C	B	A	C	C
31	**32**	**33**	**34**	**35**	**36**	**37**	**38**	**39**	**40**
D	C	B	A	D	B	D	C	A	C
41	**42**	**43**	**44**	**45**	**46**	**47**	**48**	**49**	**50**
C	D	B	A	B	D	D	B	A	D
51	**52**	**53**	**54**	**55**	**56**	**57**	**58**	**59**	**60**
B	C	A	B	B	B	B	A	A	B
61	**62**	**63**	**64**	**65**	**66**	**67**	**68**	**69**	**70**
A	C	B	C	C	D	D	C	D	B

71	72	73	74	75	76	77	78	79	80
C	D	C	D	A	A	C	D	C	D
81	**82**	**83**	**84**	**85**	**86**	**87**	**88**	**89**	**90**
D	A	D	D	D	D	B	C	A	C
91	**92**	**93**	**94**	**95**	**96**	**97**	**98**	**99**	**100**
B	A	C	C	B	C	B	B	D	B
101	**102**	**103**	**104**	**105**	**106**	**107**	**108**	**109**	**110**
C	D	B	D	A	B	A	B	C	A
111	**112**	**113**	**114**	**115**	**116**	**117**	**118**	**119**	**120**
B	A	B	D	B	B	C	B	C	B
121	**122**	**123**	**124**	**125**	**126**	**127**	**128**	**129**	**130**
A	A	B	A	A	B	B	D	D	B
131	**132**	**133**	**134**	**135**	**136**	**137**	**138**	**139**	**140**
C	C	C	A	C	B	B	A	C	B
141	**142**	**143**	**144**	**145**	**146**	**147**	**148**	**149**	**150**
D	A	A	D	A	C	D	A	B	A

❑❑❑

Women and Health

- Life Cycle Approach to Women's Health – Health Status of Women in India, Factors Influencing Health and Nutritional Status
- Maternal and Child Health (MCH) to Reproductive and Child Health Approaches
- Issues of Declining Child Sex Ratio, Old Age and Widowhood
- Occupational and Mental Health
- Health, Hygiene, and Sanitation
- National Health and Population Policies and Programmes

LIFE CYCLE APPROACH TO WOMEN'S HEALTH

Sex refers to the biological characteristics of an individual. Gender refers to non-biological characteristics such as social and cultural norms and definitions. Women's health is not determined by biological setup alone. Social roles and cultural context also affect perspectives on health.

Gender disparity negatively affects the physical and mental health of women. Women's health care is influenced by various factors such as levels of education, income, socioeconomic status, support network, lifestyle, access to Information and health care system. These, in turn, are influenced by gender relations.

Gender Health Gap is a direct consequence of treating women as second class citizens in family and society. Health problems of a woman in the household are considered unimportant and not given adequate attention because of gender norms about masculinity and femininity. Lower status of women, influences stigmatization for certain diseases like leprosy, AIDS and mental illness, in women more than in men.

The unequal burden of unpaid work, insufficient rest and leisure for women workers and access to clean drinking water are the other social determinants that are a consequence of inequitable gender roles in society.

Women as single-parents and head of households are doubly vulnerable because of their economic burden. Critical medical screenings and medications for women are mostly forgone if time and money are scarce.

Gender main streaming and gender perspective to health care is the need of the hour. In medical research, drugs specific for women are still tested on male animals. Health system should be made accountable to women, with operational changes and women-specific health policies and research.

Women's health needs and concerns are different from those of men not only in lieu of the biological differences but also variations in occupational and social lives. The physiological and psychological issues of women are influenced by the various roles they play in public and private sphere of society. The historical secondary status of women has resulted in their health problems and needs being ignored.

With the evolution of feminism and gender mainstreaming, the issues related to women's health have become central to public policies concerning women's upliftment. Life cycle approach to women's health involves planning and strategies about women's health needs from birth to old age, i.e., throughout their life. The concept includes encouraging health seeking behavior among women, provision of services and information, recognizing their right to make decisions regarding their health.

Women's health needs and issues vary across the various stages of their lives. Globally, especially in developing and third world countries, health needs and health-related problems at each stage of women's lives can be categorized as follows:

Infancy and Childhood (0-9 years)

- Sex selection technologies and female foeticide
- Female infanticide
- Genital mutilation practiced in some traditions and cultures
- Gender discriminatory nutrition care where sons' food and nutrition needs are prioritized over daughters
- Denial of breast milk resulting in low immunity development in girls
- Low child sex ratio, where the number of boys is way higher than the number of girls
- According to the government's annual economic survey (2018), more than 63 million women are "missing" statistically across India, and more than 21 million girls are unwanted by their families. The reasons for this being the high rate of female mortality and missing girls at birth (due to female foeticide and female infant mortality)
- Poor immunization resulting in recurring health problems and preventable diseases
- Anemia and nutrition deficiencies
- High Infant Mortality Rate (IMR)

Adolescence (10-14 years)

- Early pregnancies
- Unsafe abortions, sometimes resulting in death and lack of access to abortion services
- Nutrition deficiencies (iron, iodine and vitamin deficiencies)
- Sexually Transmitted Diseases
- Lack of access to information on general health, sexual health, hygiene and sanitation
- Poor immunization
- Anemia

Reproductive Age (15-49 years)

- High Maternal Mortality rates
- Unplanned pregnancies
- Unsafe abortions
- Sexually transmitted diseases and the high prevalence of AIDS
- Malnutrition
- Pregnancy complications
- Lack of access to medical help and childbirth needs
- Pre-partum and post-partum care
- Lack of awareness and access to contraceptives

Post Reproductive Age (45+ years)

- Cardiovascular problems
- Gynecological issues
- Menopause and related nutrition needs
- Osteoporosis
- Diabetes
- Loss of eyesight and other eye diseases
- Age-related health complications

HEALTH STATUS OF WOMEN IN INDIA

- The health of an individual is influenced by social, cultural and biological factors.
- Indian women, mainly due to their secondary position in society suffer from specific health conditions such as poor nutrition, anemia, adolescent pregnancies, high maternal death rates, etc.
- In India, men and women have around same life expectancy, even though biologically women are supposed to have longer lives. According to statistics from the Ministry of Health and Family Welfare, life expectancy was 67.3 years for men and 69.8 for women in 2011-2015. It should be higher for women. This is a result of the neglect of women's health by society.
- **Maternal Mortality Rate (MMR)** refers to the number of maternal deaths per 100,000 mothers. As per the Census 2011 data, MMR was 212 in 2007-2009, which was one of the highest in the world. Though it came down to 178 in 2012, it is still very high compared to global levels.

- According to Lancet report, India alone accounts for 15% of global maternal deaths. The high maternal mortality is due to poor nutrition, lack of access to health services, lack of awareness, etc.
- Kerala (81), Tamil Nadu (97), Maharashtra (104) are some of the best performing states, while Assam (390), Uttar Pradesh and Uttarakhand (359), Rajasthan (318) have very high MMR.
- MMR is worse in rural areas where lack of education and awareness, affordability and availability of medical services causes increased maternal mortality. Rural and poor women also have to work very-soon after their childbirth, without any recovery period.
- According to National Family Health Survey-4 data, only 43% of rural women receive antenatal care, while it is 74% for urban women.
- **Sex Ratio** indicates the number of women per 1000 men. India's sex ratio is 940, as per census 2011.
- **Infant Mortality Rate (IMR)** refers to the number of deaths per 1000 births. IMR is 49 for male and 52 for female children in India.
- Early marriages lead to early childbirths for women. The median age at first birth among women is 19.8 years.
- **Anemia** is one of the severe health condition suffered by Indian women. Anemia refers to low Hemoglobin levels in the blood which adversely affects nutritional health and development.
- National Family Health Survey-3 says 38.6% of Indian women have mild anemia (10-11.9 g/dl [grams/deciliter]), 15% of women have moderate anemia (7-9.9 g/dl), and 1.8% suffer from severe anemia (less than 7 g/dl).
- 35.6% of Indian women are malnourished.
- Domestic violence is another major issue that affects women's health. Two-third of the married women in India are victims of domestic violence.

FACTORS AFFECTING HEALTH AND NUTRITION STATUS OF WOMEN

Sufficient nutrition is required for an individual's holistic mental and physical development. Malnutrition is ill-health caused by the deficiency of calories, proteins, vitamins, minerals, and other micronutrients.

A woman needs a different set of nutrition and diet at different stages of growth. But, gender disparity affects the access to nutrition at all stages –neonatal, adolescent, maternal and old age. Household power relations affect the nutritional outcomes of the whole family.

According to the Food and Agriculture Organization, women contribute 80% of labor in producing food for the household. But, they are the last to eat and sometimes don't eat at all if food is scarce. Lack of control over resources and money, disparities in household work pattern determine her access to food.

62% of rural Indian households and 63% of urban Indian households consume less than 2700 Kcal per consumer unit per day. A large portion of them is women. Lethargy and depression –symptoms of malnutrition are ignored in women as unimportant. Prolonged malnutrition causes irreversible damages to physical health, increase the risk of cardiovascular and non-communicable diseases, early deaths and affects women's ability to care for their family.

Adolescent girls need specific nutrients for their growth, such as iron, folate and other B-vitamins and sufficient iodine. Iodized salt remains inaccessible to girls and women of poor rural households. Prevalence of iron deficiency and anemia in women directly corresponds to their socioeconomic status. It also affects their reproductive health. Malnutrition in pregnant women impairs neurological and cognitive development of the child, low birth weight and decreased resistance to infections and diseases.

Nutritious health of women is not one of affordability alone. It requires the dismantling of gender-biased social and economic norms, socio-cultural patriarchy and inequality in access to resources and opportunities.

Various factors and issues contribute to the abysmal status of women's health in India:

- Educational status of women: Low literacy levels and lack of adequate knowledge among Indian women is one of the primary reasons for high maternal deaths and poor nutrition status of women. Children of illiterate women are twice likely to be undernourished than that of educated women.
- Low economic status and dependency on male members of the household prevent women from accessing health services.
- Gender is an essential factor which determines their social position. Due to the patriarchal hierarchy, women's needs, especially health issues and concerns are not prioritized and sometimes completely ignored.
- Women, especially rural and poor women do heavy work throughout their life, as agricultural laborers, industrial laborers, contractual laborers, domestic

and household workers. This also severely affects their health condition.

- Lack of access to medical services, influenced by various factors such as geographical distance, affordability, other responsibilities, etc.
- Differential treatment of men and women in the household with respect to access to food, nutrition and health services.
- Gender disparity in allocation and investment in education and health.
- The health sector is also gender biased with respect to access, information, and gender-specific research and medical technology.

Health Care Infrastructure in India and its Accessibility to Women

Healthcare infrastructure in India can be broadly divided into:

- **Public Health Sector**: constitutes of Primary Healthcare Centers (PHCs), Community Health Centers (CHCs), district hospitals and specialty hospitals, public health insurance schemes, and National health programmes.
- **Private Health Sector**: private hospitals, medical dispensaries, and clinics.
- **Indigenous System of Medicine**: includes Ayurveda, Siddha, Unani, Homeopathy and unregistered alternative medicine practitioners.
- Voluntary and not for profit health agencies and organizations.

Of this, the private sector dominates healthcare delivery in India, even though a significant section of the population cannot afford the basic health care services. Public health sector remains understaffed and underfinanced and unable to meet the healthcare needs of its people.

According to the World Bank's global statistics, India has less than 1 doctor per 1000 patients. Also, most of the healthcare infrastructure is concentrated in urban areas, while more than 50% of its population lives in rural areas. There is a shortfall of 22% of PHCs and 32% of CHCs. Many of these health centers do not have even a single doctor. Also, around 80% of rural healthcare centers do not have specialists.

India has one of the lowest per capita healthcare expenditures in the world. 57% of the health care expenditure is spent by individuals. Most of the public healthcare expenditure serves the better-off in society than the poor. Women's access to the healthcare system is even worse. Women have lowered share of hospitalization (42%) in India. Healthcare needs of girls and women are considered less important than male family members. Economic dependence on male members of the family also discourages women from going to a health center. Most of the time, women need to get permission from their husbands or elders to visit a hospital. Other obstacles include the gender-biased attitude of healthcare professionals, unhygienic conditions of public health centers, geographical inaccessibility, affordability, lack of awareness and inability to find time amidst household work and taking care of their family needs.

Alma-Ata Conference

International Conference on Primary Health Care was held in 1978 at Alma-Ata (Almaty), Kazakhstan. The declaration at the conference defined health as a complete physical, mental and social well-being of an individual and not just absence of disease and infirmity. It also recognized health as a fundamental human right and called on all countries to work towards global health. The declaration resolved to achieve health for all by the year 2000. Despite its failure, the declaration remains an important reference for future planning and principles towards primary health care.

Sustainable Development Goals and Women Health

United Nations Conference on Sustainable Development (Rio+20 summit) was held in Rio De Janeiro in 2012. The member countries agreed to launch a process to develop a set of sustainable development goals (SDGs) to build upon the achievement of Millennium Development Goals. It resulted in the adoption of the **2030 Agenda for Sustainable Development** at the UN Sustainable Summit, 2015. The agenda consists of 17 set of SDGs to achieve by the year 2030 in different areas of human development.

The major SDGs related to women and health are as follows:

- ❑ **Goal 1:** End poverty in all its forms everywhere.
    - **Goal 1.2:** Reduce at least by half the proportion of men, women, and children of all ages living in poverty in all its dimensions according to national definitions.
    - **Goal 1.b:** Create sound policy frameworks at the national, regional and international levels, based on pro-poor and gender-sensitive development strategies, to support accelerated investment in poverty eradication actions.
- ❑ **Goal 2:** End hunger, achieve food security and improved nutrition and promote sustainable agriculture.

- **Goal 2.1:** End hunger and ensure access by all people, in particular, the poor and people in vulnerable situations, including infants, to safe, nutritious and sufficient food all year round.
- **Goal 2.2:** By 2030, end all forms of malnutrition, including achieving, by 2025, the internationally agreed targets on stunting and wasting in children under five years of age, and address the nutritional needs of adolescent girls, pregnant and lactating women and older persons.

❑ **Goal 3:** Ensure healthy lives and promote the well-being of all at all ages.

- **Goal 3.1:** Reduce the global maternal mortality ratio to less than 70 per 100,000 live births.
- **Goal 3.2:** End preventable deaths of newborns and children under five years of age, with all countries aiming to reduce neonatal mortality to at least as low as 12 per 1,000 live births and under-5 mortality to at least as low as 25 per 1,000 live births.
- **Goal 3.7:** Ensure universal access to sexual and reproductive health-care services, including for family planning, information and education, and the integration of reproductive health into national strategies and programmes.
- **Goal 3.8:** Achieve universal health coverage, including financial risk protection, access to quality essential health-care services and access to safe, effective, quality and affordable essential medicines and vaccines for all.

❑ **Goal 4:** Ensure inclusive and equitable quality education and promote lifelong learning opportunities for all.

❑ **Goal 5:** Achieve gender equality and empower all women and girls.

- **Goal 5.1:** End all forms of discrimination against all women and girls everywhere.
- **Goal 5.2:** Eliminate all forms of violence against all women and girls in public and private spheres, including trafficking and sexual and other types of exploitation.
- **Goal 5.3:** Eliminate all harmful practices, such as the child, early and forced marriage and female genital mutilation.
- **Goal 5.6:** Ensure universal access to sexual and reproductive health and reproductive rights as agreed in accordance with the Programme of Action of the International Conference on Population and Development and the Beijing Platform for Action and the outcome documents of their review conferences.

❑ **Goal 6:** Ensure availability and sustainable management of water and sanitation for all.

- **Goal 6.1:** Achieve universal and equitable access to safe and affordable drinking water for all.
- **Goal 6.2:** Achieve access to adequate and equitable sanitation and hygiene for all and end open defecation, paying special attention to the needs of women and girls and those in vulnerable situations.

MATERNAL CHILD HEALTH TO REPRODUCTIVE CHILD HEALTH APPROACHES

- According to the Indian Association of Preventive and Social Medicine, women of childbearing age (15-44 years) make up 22.2% of the total population in India. Also, children under 15 years of age constitute 35.3%. Together, they make up 57.5% of India. This requires a concerted effort to cater to their specific health and medical requirements and concerns.
- According to census 2011, 81% of women belonging to the childbearing age are married in India. So, it is important to devise strategies to provide maternal health services that reach those in need.
- But, more than 1,00,000 women die during childbirth every year in India. Also, more than one-fourth of the global burden of infant mortality and under-five mortality deaths is borne by India. Though the government has devised policies and strategies to address maternal and child health, progress is haltingly slow.
- Some of the significant problems faced by maternal women and women during childbirth are:
    - ❑ **Malnutrition:** Malnutrition during pregnancy causes anemia and low birth weight of the baby. Vitamin A deficiency in pregnant women causes night blindness. Mothers who are underweight also affect their children's health and development.
    - ❑ Infection during childbirth, poor hospital hygiene.
    - ❑ Lack of access to institutional deliveries due to distance and affordability.
    - ❑ 38% of maternal deaths are caused by post-partum hemorrhage (National Portal of India).
    - ❑ Unregulated fertility due to lack of access, awareness, and information on contraceptive methods and taboos associated with it.

- No adequate spacing between two births, resulting in poor health of both mother and children; the previous child's health and nutritional requirements also get neglected.
- More stress on female sterilization as a method of family planning, while the male role is completely ignored.
- Lack of access to safe abortions; even though 70% of women of childbearing age are in rural India, the majority of the abortion facilities are located in urban areas. This is further complicated by unaffordability of abortion services, distance, and unmarried and adolescent pregnancies.

- The issues of child health include:
  - Malnutrition and stunted growth; 43% of the children under five in India are underweight.
  - Diarrheal diseases due to recurring infection and poor immunity, despite the government providing universal free immunization for Tuberculosis, Diphtheria, Whooping cough, Tetanus, Measles, and Polio.
- The basic principles of maternal and child health are consultation and participation of women, access and availability of maternal and child health services, primacy on prevention, capacity building and ensuring social equity.
- Direct interventions employed to improve maternal and child health are food fortification, provision of iron and folic acid tablets for pregnant women, nutritional education, supplementary feeding programmes such as Integrated Child Development Services (ICDS), Mid-day Meal through Anganwadi centers.
- Indirect interventions are immunization to control infections, access to clean drinking water and hygiene, education and awareness, gender equality-social, political and economic equality and gender mainstreaming.
- The Indian government has also established primary and community health centers with the target of providing maternal and child health services in rural and urban areas.
- The concept of community health nurses also contributes to mainstreaming maternal and child health needs. These nurses establish contact with pregnant women in the primary stages, performs the antenatal examination, aids in birthing, provides counseling and health education, post-natal care and performs home visits.
- Auxiliary Nurse Midwives (ANMs) are trained for a short period in maternal health care. They are technical workers with less than full qualifications. They are further trained to become Skilled Birth Attendants (SBAs) to bridge the gap in medical personnel in rural and backward areas.
- National Rural Health Mission's Accredited Social Health Activist (ASHA) are local volunteers who identify pregnant women to ensure adequate antenatal, natal and postnatal care. The mission also includes the provision of referral transports, blood storage units, and safe abortion units.
- Institutional deliveries are a primary requirement to ensure the maternal and reproductive health of women. But, less than 40% of deliveries take place in health facilities, as per National Health Survey statistics. States like Nagaland, Uttar Pradesh, Bihar, and Jharkhand have only 18-29% institutional deliveries. On the other hand, Tamil Nadu, Kerala, Goa, and Pondicherry have institutional deliveries in the range of 86-98%.
- Ministry of Health and Family Welfare (MHFW) is the primary planning and implementation agency for all policies concerning public health. Issues such as maternal and child health, reproductive health, rural health, primary health care, family planning, etc. come under the Department of Family Welfare under MHFW.
- Maternal Health Division under the Department of Family Welfare is responsible for:
  - Designing evidence-based maternal health programmes
  - Review, research and developing training content
  - Monitoring policies, programme implementation, evaluation of outcomes
  - Education and communication programmes regarding health
  - Preparing budget and funding plans for its policies and programmes
- **Reproductive Health:** A combination of physical, mental and social well-being of reproductive women.
- It involves safe, affordable and acceptable methods of family planning, choice regulation of fertility, access to health care services during pregnancy and childbirth. It encompasses women's sexual health throughout their reproductive age.
- The shift from maternal health to reproductive health took place after the **International Conference on Population and Development** held in 1994 at Cairo. The UN defined the term "Reproductive Health" at this conference. The conference resolved re-orientation of family planning programme to include women's sexual and reproductive health, their right

to sexual choices and decision-making control, treatment of reproductive tract infections and sexually transmitted diseases. The conference also adopted the enjoyment of reproductive health as one of the reproductive rights of women.

- **Contraceptives and Family Planning:** There are several ways to achieve birth control such as surgery, abstention from sex, different contraceptive methods, etc. Use of contraceptives as a birth control method is widely prevalent in western nations and developed countries. But, it remains a subject of taboo and embarrassment in Indian conservative society. Its wide-spread unavailability also prevents couples from using contraceptives.
- Contraceptives can be categorized into:
  - **Barrier Contraceptives** that block access of sperms to the embryo using cervical caps, condoms, and spermicide gels and creams.
  - **Hormonal Contraceptives** are developed for women and contain **oral contraceptives** like pills and **Injective contraceptives.** Hormonal contraceptives control and regulate hormonal production in women to prevent pregnancies.
- Some widely used contraceptive injections are DMPA (Depot Medroxy Progesterone Acetate/ Depo-Provera), NET-EN (Norethisterone Enanthate / Noristerat), Mesigyna. These injections can cause side effects such as vaginal bleeding irregular menstrual cycles, weight gain, etc.
- Oral contraceptives are mainly in the form of hormonal pills that control estrogen and progesterone hormones. Side effects include nausea, weight gain, mood changes, bleeding, migraine, etc.
- **Mission Parivar Vikas** is an initiative by the Ministry of Health and Family Welfare launched in 2017 to enable easy access to high-quality family planning choices based on information and supply. It involves the free provision of several contraceptives. Despite the availability of modern contraceptives, female sterilization is still a widely-used method at 36% and only around 5% use condoms and other contraceptives (4%).

ISSUES OF DECLINING CHILD SEX RATIO

- Child Sex Ratio (CSR) indicates the ratio of the number of females per 1000 males in the 0-6 age group. According to the 2011 Census, CSR is only 914. In 2001, it was 927. India's child sex ratio has been declining steadily over the years. The child sex ratio for rural India is 923, and urban India is 905.
- Some of the states with very low child sex ratio are Haryana (834), Punjab (846), Jharkhand (862) and Rajasthan (888).
- Arunachal Pradesh (972), Meghalaya and Mizoram (970), Chhattissgarh (969), Kerala (964) and Tamil Nadu (943) are some states with child sex ratio higher than the National average.
- The problem of low child sex ratio is a multi-dimensional issue. Availability of sex determination technologies despite legal controls contribute to a higher number of selective abortions. Also, the girl child is considered a double burden.
- The socio-cultural mindset of the patriarchal society gives preference to a male child in terms of lineage and inheritance.
- The Prime Minister started Beti Bachao Beti Padhao campaign to create awareness about protection and education of girl education.

Assisted Reproductive Technologies and Missing Girl Children

- Infertility is mostly considered a female disorder, especially in traditional societies even though male infertility is also prevalent. Inability to conceive a child results in social stigma, depression, divorces and social isolation for women.
- Assisted Reproductive Technologies (ART) are a group of medical techniques for child conception. Some of the prevalent ARTs are In Vitro Fertilization and Embryo Transfer (IVF-ET), Intrauterine Insemination (IUI), Intracytoplasmic Sperm Injection (ICSI), Surgical Laparoscopy and Surrogacy.
- Amniocentesis is a disorder test that screens chromosome patterns of the amniotic fluid surrounding the fetus to detect any problems and disorders. But, it was widely misused to determine the sex of the baby and perform selective abortions, until its legal ban by the Government.
- Ultrasonography (USG) tests are used for monitoring fetal development during the entire pregnancy period. Ultrasound imagery also reveals the gender of the baby. In India, it is illegal to use ultrasound technology to aid gender-selective abortions. As the onus is placed on the clinics to prevent such abortions by imposing fines, suspensions, and cancellation of licenses, the use of ultrasound techniques for sex selection has considerably reduced.

- But, with the proliferation of newer reproductive technologies and prefertilization techniques, illegal sex determination and female infanticide still continue.
- IVF-ET involves fertilization of embryo in a dish before transferring to the uterus. Preimplantation Genetic Diagnosis (PGD) is a technique developed to screen embryos for any genetic disorders before implantation. While its aim was to avoid implanting unhealthy embryos, PGD can be misused for sex selection during IVF-ET.
- Intrauterine Insemination (IUI) can also be used for prefertilization gender selection by increasing the quantity of male sperms before injection.
- All these modern technologies in spite of its original ethical intentions have played a role in millions of missing girls of India. Despite amendments to PNDT act as PCPNDT act that penalizes the use of various reproductive technologies for sex determination, its lax enforcement renders ineffective in preventing female foeticide.
- Surrogacy motherhood is an arrangement in which a woman (surrogate mother) bears a child for a couple who are unable to conceive a child on their own. This procedure has raised a number of questions on ethicality and gender discrimination. Feminists believe that surrogacy is another way of subverting women's biological autonomy.
- With the commercialization of surrogacy and rise of medical tourism, especially from developed countries to third-world countries in search of potential surrogates, it has also become an issue of exploiting women and their body for money and building a business on the reproductive capacity of women. There is also the implication of making children a commodity. It results in the devaluation of women and children in society.
- Until recently, surrogacy in India was exploitative with its exclusive focus on the client's needs and paying abysmal money for the surrogate mothers by manipulating their financial needs. The human rights of surrogates were completely ignored.
- To prevent exploitation of Indian women, especially those from the weak socio-economic background, the Indian government enacted **the Surrogacy (Regulation) Act in December 2018**. The act completely prohibits commercial surrogacy and allows only altruistic surrogacy for close relatives. It banned the use of surrogacy in India for foreign nationals, NRIs, persons of Indian origin, homosexuals, live-in couples, single parents and parents who already have children.

ISSUES OF OLD AGE AND WIDOWHOOD

- There is a higher number of older women than older men in India. These elderly women face poverty, ill-health, higher dependency on others, financial insecurity, destitution, and gender-based discrimination.
- Economic dependency is high among older women as they do not usually possess any asset or source of income. Poverty forces older women to work in unsafe and physically exerting jobs for their age. A significant portion of older women does not receive pension or retirement benefits as they were not part of formal sector labor force.
- Late-life widowhood also increases their income insecurity and makes them highly dependable on their children. They also experience a change in living arrangements in the form of old age homes. Many never get contacted by their children again.
- According to the National Family Health Survey-3, 3.2% of women in the 15-49 years age group are widowed women. Some traditions allow only simple diet for women causing nutrition deficiency. Widowed women also suffer from low body mass index, poor quality intake, and sexually transmitted diseases.
- Rapid urbanization and high-cost of housing also push older women into destitution and isolation.
- Women above 60 years of age face increased verbal and physical abuse, and their health risks are not prioritized. These rapid situational changes can cause considerable emotional and psy-chological distress that needs special and professional care.
- Lack of property, illiteracy and work independence in their younger age has a cumulative effect on the living conditions and health of old age women.

OCCUPATIONAL AND MENTAL HEALTH

As more and more women become part of the labor force, their vulnerability to health hazards associated with occupational labor also increases. Women are also exploited as cheap labor. Various sectors have its specific health hazards:

- Clothing/textile Sector – cotton dust, noise, dye, and other chemicals lead to respiratory irritation, carcinogenesis, dermatitis, etc.
- Retail Sector Workers – prolonged standing causes varicose veins, low back strain, etc.

- Household and Domestic Work – cleaning, infection agents, lifting heavy weights, job insecurity lead to stress, dermatitis, rubella, etc.
- Agricultural sector – exposure to pesticide causes spontaneous abortions.

Mental Health describes the level of the cognitive and emotional well-being of an individual. Patterns of psychiatric disorders are different for men and women. Common mental disorders (CMD) such as depression, anxiety, somatic complaints are strongly associated with women in India. Causes are partner's alcohol use, physical violence, stress, caring roles and childbirth, dowry harassment, etc. Also, sexual and physical abuses of women with mental health disorders are high. Girls from nuclear families and early married women are more vulnerable to suicide and self-harm.

HEALTH, HYGIENE AND SANITATION

According to Census 2011, only 32.7% of the rural population of India has access to toilets. Reproductive tract infections are high among rural Indian women due to the absence of toilets, lack of access to sanitation and clean drinking water. More than 70% of the effects of poor sanitation are health-related such as diarrhea and acute lower respiratory infections. 72% of Indians do not have access to sanitation facilities. Sanitation promotes public health by providing a clean environment and prevention of diseases. India's poor performance in terms of environmental sanitation adversely affects the health of women and children.

Total Sanitation Campaign

- Launched in 1999 to improve the sanitation coverage in the country.
- Emphasis on information, communication, and education.
- Capacity building with the involvement of Panchayat Raj institutions and community organizations.
- Focused on increasing individual household toilets, Anganwadi toilets and community sanitary complexes.
- **Nirmal Gram Puraskar** was launched in 2003 and was implemented by the Ministry of Drinking Water and Sanitation.
- It involved recognition of efforts towards fully covered panchayat raj institutions via cash rewards. It also recognizes institutions and organizations that work towards achieving total sanitation.
- Total Sanitation Campaign was revamped as **Nirmal Bharat Abhiyan in 2012,** and the selection of Gram Panchayats with complete sanitation coverage have been delegated to the states.
- **Swachh Bharat Abhiyan** was launched in 2014 to eradicate open defecation in India by 2019. Its other objectives include disposal management of municipal waste, behavioral changes regarding sanitation, strengthening of urban local bodies to tackle sanitation issues and increasing awareness on sanitation and public health.

NATIONAL HEALTH AND POPULATION POLICIES AND PROGRAMMES

National Population Policy

India is the first among the developing countries to frame population planning. Early decades of independence involved creating awareness and establishment of family planning clinics.

First National Population Policy (NPP) was framed in 1977. It reduced the legal age of marriage for girls to 18. The burden of reducing population was mainly placed on women.

Second NPP was released in 2000. It integrated population control with women empowerment and issues of reproductive health care. It also made a commitment to safe motherhood programme and recommended providing abortion services at primary health centers. Breaking the stigma surrounding contraceptives, easy accessibility to contraceptives and other health interventions for women are needed.

National Nutrition Policy

- Adopted in 1993; envisaged direct interventions for improving the nutrition of vulnerable groups such as children, pregnant and lactating women, and adolescent girls, food fortification and long term strategies such as education and awareness, food security, improving participation of women in food production and decision making, etc.

National Health Policy

- The first policy was formulated in 1983; focused on providing universal primary health care.
- Second policy was launched in 2002; targeted reducing infant mortality, improving public health infrastructure and health expenditure.
- Third policy was launched in 2017 with a preventive and promotive orientation to health care.
- **Targets:** reducing total fertility rate to 2.1 by 2025; reducing maternal mortality rate to 167 per 100,000

births by 2020; reducing under-five stunting to less than 40% by 2025; reducing infant mortality rate to 28 by 2019; provision of clean drinking water and sanitation to all by 2020.

National Rural Health Mission

- Launched in 2005
- Takes a community based decentralized approach to public health with a primary focus on maternal and child health.
- To provide affordable, effective and reliable primary health care facilities to poor and vulnerable sections of the population.
- A cadre of Accredited Social Health Activists (ASHA), mostly women to reach rural women.
- Special focus on adolescent nutritional health, institutional delivery, antenatal and maternal care for rural women.
- Also, increased the number of Auxiliary Nurse Midwives (ANM).
- Provision for setting up of village level health and sanitation committees.
- Emphasis on mainstreaming AYUSH (Ayurveda, Yoga & Naturopathy, Unani, Siddha, and Homeopathy) system of medicine in health care delivery; strengthening of AYUSH to be responsive to public health care needs.
- **Targets of NRHM for 2005-12 period:** reduction of IMR to 30 per 1000 births, MMR to 100 per lakh births. According to the government, in 2012 IMR has come down to 42 and MMR to 178.

National Urban Health Mission

- Launched in 2013
- To provide an efficient urban health delivery system for urban poor.
- Primary urban health centers to be manned by Auxiliary Nurse Midwives (ANM).

Janani Suraksha Yojana

- Launched in 2005
- It is being implemented by the Ministry of Health and Family Welfare to reduce Maternal Mortality Rate by promoting institutional deliveries and availability of skilled birth attendants. It works as a link between poor pregnant women and health care services. JSY promotes institutional deliveries by conditional cash transfers and provides post-delivery care, transport facilities and cash incentives for nutrition care.

Integrated Child Development Service

- Launched in 1975
- Provides supplementary nutrition, non-formal education, and immunization via Anganwadi centers in villages. ICDS focuses on the health and development of children less than three years of age.

Nutrition Programme for Adolescent Girls

- Launched in 2003 by Ministry of Women and Child Development; effective immunization; to improve nutrition and health status of young girls; prophylactic measures for anemia, vitamin and iron deficiencies.

Reproductive and Child Health Programme (RCH)

- Launched in 1997 by the Ministry of Health and Family Welfare; essential obstetric care with an emphasis on institutional delivery, round the clock delivery services and safe abortion services. It places emphasis on at least three antenatal visits to health centers, providing iron prophylaxis for pregnant and lactating women, treatment of anemia in mothers and post-natal care.

National Family Health Survey (NFHS)

National Family Health Survey (NFHS) is a country-wide survey of households to collect essential information on family health and welfare issues. Four surveys have been conducted so far, since 1992.

- **NFHS 1 (1992-93):** It laid emphasis on data collection regarding women and young children.
- **NFHS 2 (1998-99):** It included information on family planning services, domestic violence, reproductive health, anemia and nutrition of women.
- **NFHS 3 (2005-06):** It collected data on Sexually Transmitted Diseases and HIV/AIDS.
- **NFHS 4 (2014-15):** Findings of the National Family Health Survey 4 shows great disparities of key health indicators for women. This signifies the socioeconomic condition of Indian women and the need for strategies to reduce gender inequalities. Some key statistics are:
    - ❑ Infant Mortality Rate is 41; IMR for girl child higher than for boys.

- States with high IMR are Uttar Pradesh (64), Chhattisgarh (54), Madhya Pradesh (51), Assam and Bihar (48). Some of the states with low IMR are Kerala (6), Goa (13), Puducherry(16), Tamil Nadu (21), Manipur (22).
- Sex ratio which denotes the number of females per 1000 males is 919. Very low compared to other developing nations.
- Total Fertility Rate of a woman is 2.2%. Contraceptive prevalence rate has decreased. Unsafe abortions are still widespread.
- 53% of women are anemic—one of the highest in the world.
- States with a high percentage of anemic women are Jharkhand (65%), Haryana and West Bengal (62), Andhra Pradesh and Bihar (60). States with a low percentage of anemic women are Mizoram (22), Nagaland (23), Kerala and Sikkim (34) and Arunachal Pradesh (40).

Medical Termination of Pregnancy Act (1971)

- To improve maternal health by preventing unsafe abortions and promoting access to abortion services to women.
- Made abortions legal up to 20 weeks of pregnancy, in case of danger to the mental and physical health of the mother and risks of birth of a handicapped or malformed baby, pregnancies of unmarried girls under 18 years of age, pregnancy due to rape and failure of sterilization.

Maternity Benefit Act (1961)

- To protect the employment of women during their maternity leave and the provision of paid maternity leave.
- Amended in 2017 to increase the ceiling on maternity leave up to 26 weeks.
- Also provides maternity leave up to 12 weeks for women adopting children and surrogate mothers.
- Mandates crèche facilities and provides for work from home facilities.

Pre-Natal Diagnostic Techniques (Regulation and Prevention of Misuse) Act (PNDT) (1994)

- Was enacted to stop female foeticide and prevent declining of child sex ratio.
- It bans the use of sex selection techniques to aid sex-selective abortions.
- Provision of stringent punishment for violators of the Act.
- Amended in 2003 to improve the regulation of sex selection technologies; renamed as **Pre-Conception and Pre-Natal Diagnostic Technique (Prohibition of sex selection) Act (PCPNDT Act).** This Act also bans advertisement on sex determination services, regulates the use of ultrasound and amniocentesis, mandates registration of all ultrasound machines and other diagnostic laboratories.

Multiple Choice Questions

1. Find out the chronological sequence of the following Acts:
(a) MTP Act
(b) PNDT Act
(c) Minimum Wages Act
(d) Immoral Traffic Prevention Act

Codes:
A. (d), (c), (b), (a) B. (c), (d), (a), (b)
C. (a), (b), (c), (d) D. (b), (c), (d), (a)

2. The Sex-Ratio of India has reduced from _______ between 1901 and 2011.
A. 972 to 940 B. 964 to 946
C. 955 to 930 D. 950 to 941

3. The Medical Termination of Pregnancy Act was passed in the year:
A. 1971 B. 1974
C. 1980 D. 1982

4. According to 2011 Census of India, the missing women population constitutes:
A. 46 million B. 39 million
C. 41 million D. 50 million

5. The incidence of anemia among pregnant women is estimated to be as high as:
A. 88% B. 80%
C. 78% D. 65%

6. MMR is an indicator of the quality of life. What does it stand for?
A. Male Mortality Rate
B. Morbidity Measurement Rate
C. Maternal Mortality Rate
D. Mother's Malnutrition Rate

7. The female sex hormone is called:

A. Estrogen | B. Progestrone
C. Androgen | D. Mesogen

8. Which of the following reflects the correct status of women and children in India?

A. 1/18 Pregnant women run the risk of dying during pregnancy.
B. 1/9 Children die before 5 years of age.
C. 4/10 Children die because of malnutrition.
D. All of the above.

9. India's rank in the last Gender Gap Index 2018 was:

A. 114th | B. 126th
C. 108th | D. 98th

10. Choose the correct expansion of MHFW:

A. Minimum Health, Food and Welfare
B. Maternal Health and Family Welfare
C. Model Health, Food and Welfare
D. Ministry of Health and Family Welfare

11. Reproductive Technology has:

A. Positive effect on the life of women.
B. Negative effect on the life of women
C. No effect on the life of women
D. Both positive and negative effects on the life of women

12. What is common among the States of Punjab, Delhi, Rajasthan and Uttar Pradesh?

A. High female illiteracy rate
B. Increased female labour force participation
C. Declining Female child sex ratio
D. High Infant Mortality Rate

13. A women's sexual desire for another woman is termed as:

A. Heterosexuals | B. Bisexuals
C. Lesbianism | D. Homosexuals

14. ______ health condition is the result of iron deficiency.

A. Anaemia | B. Cancer
C. Depression | D. Oedema

15. According to 2011 census (provisional) the lowest child sex ratio is recorded in:

A. Gujarat | B. Haryana
C. Goa | D. Rajasthan

16. Net-En and Depo Provera are:

A. Injectable contraceptives
B. Reproductive disorders
C. Internet viruses
D. Oral contraceptives

17. AYUSH is a part of ________ Health Programme.

A. NFHS | B. NRHM
C. RCH | D. NACO

18. Reproductive rights include the rights of all individual and couples:

(i) Reproduction free of discrimination.
(ii) Reproduction without coercion and violence.
(iii) Reproduction without wedlock.
(iv) Reproduction without safe motherhood.

Codes:

A. (i) and (iv) only true
B. (ii) and (iii) only true
C. (i) and (ii) only true
D. (i), (ii) and (iv) only true

19. What are the indicators used for calculating the dimension 'A long and healthy life' of Human Development Index?

(i) 7+ Literacy Rate
(ii) Infant Mortality Rate
(iii) Life expectancy at age 1
(iv) Maternal Mortality Rate

Codes:

A. (i), (ii), (iii) and (iv) are true
B. (ii), and (iv) are true
C. (ii), (iii) and (iv) are true
D. (i) only true

20. Among the following, which is not a contraceptive method?

A. Depo-Provora | B. Nor-plant
C. Emergency pill | D. IVF method

21. According to 2011 census which state has the highest child sex ratio (0-6 years)?

A. Kerala | B. West Bengal
C. Chhattisgarh | D. Mizoram

22. Match List-I and List-II:

List-I	***List-II***
(a) Oestrogen	(i) Iron deficiency
(b) Anaemia	(ii) Diabetics
(c) Insulin	(iii) Contraceptive
(d) IUD	(iv) Female Hormone

Codes:

	(a)	(b)	(c)	(d)
A.	(iv)	(i)	(ii)	(iii)
B.	(iv)	(ii)	(i)	(iii)
C.	(ii)	(iv)	(i)	(iii)
D.	(i)	(ii)	(iii)	(iv)

23. What is included in reproductive activities?

(i) Marketing
(ii) Food preparation

(iii) Child care and education
(iv) Health care and home maintenance

Codes:

A. (i), (ii), (iii), and (iv) B. (iii) only
C. (ii), (iii) and (iv) only D. (i) and (ii).

24. Match the name of movements with the respective action programmes/activities:

Activities	*Movement*
(a) Protest against inhumane practices of landlords	(i) Chipko Movement
(b) Instilling a sense of confidence among women	(ii) Narmada Movement
(c) Creating Awarenss on forest protection	(iii) Shakti Kendra
(d) Tribal Rehabilitation	(iv) Shahada Movement

Codes:

	(a)	(b)	(c)	(d)
A.	(ii)	(i)	(iii)	(iv)
B.	(i)	(iv)	(iii)	(ii)
C.	(iv)	(iii)	(i)	(ii)
D.	(iii)	(ii)	(iv)	(i)

25. Which dimensions are considered to calculate the Gender Inequality Index (GII)?
A. Long and healthy life, knowledge and a decent standard of living
B. Health, education and standard of living
C. Health, empowerment and labour market
D. Gross national income, education and health

26. Major causes for maternal deaths are:
A. Severe bleeding, anaemia, Infections, Eclampsia, unsafe abortions
B. Physical Health Problems
C. Mental Health Problems
D. General Public Health Problems

27. Pradhan Mantri Kaushal Vikas Yojana (PMKVY) was approved with an outlay of?
A. 1500 crore rupees.
B. 1200 crore rupees.
C. 1000 crore rupees.
D. 800 crore rupees.

28. What was the tagline of World Development Report 2018 (WDR 2018)?
A. Governance and Law
B. Digital Dividends
C. Mind, Society and Behavior
D. Learning to Realize Education's Promise

29. The effective coverage of the Maternity Benefit Act (1961) was measured by the National Commission for Enterprises in the Unorganised Sector (NCEUS, 2009). Choose the correct one from the following:
A. 15% B. 20%
C. 16% D. 25%

30. Changes to the natural greenhouse effect are a result of which of the following man-made emissions of Green House Gases?
A. Nitro Oxide (N_2O)
B. Hydro and Perfluoro carbons
C. Sulphur Hexafluoride (SF_6)
D. All the above

31. As per Sample Registration System (SRS)-2016, Infant Mortality Rate (IMR) at all India level is:
A. 30 B. 34
C. 39 D. 38

32. Malnutrition is measured by:
A. Anaemia
B. Loss of grasping capacity
C. Underweight and stunted growth
D. Loss of hearing and eye-sight

33. India ranks in Gender Inequality Index 2018 at:
A. 128 B. 130
C. 126 D. 136

34. The Fourth National Family Health Survey (NFHS-4) being implemented in 2014-2015 conducted by the Ministry of Health and Family Welfare will provide estimates of indicators in:
A. 29 States of India
B. 29 States and six Union territories of India
C. 30 States and three Union territories
D. 30 States and six Union territories

35. Match List-I with List-II:

List-I	*List-II (Year)*
(a) National Nutrition Policy	(i) 1993
(b) National Policy on Education	(ii) 1986
(c) National Focus Group on Gender Issues in Education	(iii) 2003
(d) National Charter for Children	(iv) 2006

Codes:

	(a)	(b)	(c)	(d)
A.	(iv)	(ii)	(i)	(iii)
B.	(i)	(ii)	(iii)	(iv)
C.	(i)	(ii)	(iv)	(iii)
D.	(iii)	(ii)	(i)	(iv)

36. Baby Manji Yameda Vs. Union of India case is with reference to:

A. Adultery B. Rape
C. Child marriage D. Surrogacy

37. Among the contemporary theories in women's empowerment, NUSSBAUM'S CAPABILITIES APPROACH identifies the following capabilities of women:

(i) Bodily health and life
(ii) Control over one's environment
(iii) Bodily integrity, emotion and practical reason
(iv) Non-affiliation

Codes:

A. (i), (ii), (iii) and (iv) B. (ii), (iii) and (iv) only
C. (i), (ii) and (iii) only D. (iii) only

38. Match the States in List-I with their Anaemia among women in List-II as per NFHS III.

List-I (State)	***List-II (Percentage of Anaemia Among Women)***
(a) Arunachal Pradesh	(i) 49.9
(b) Jharkhand	(ii) 69.5
(c) U.P.	(iii) 56.0
(d) Madhya Pradesh	(iv) 50.6

Codes:

	(a)	(b)	(c)	(d)
A.	(iv)	(ii)	(i)	(iii)
B.	(iv)	(i)	(iii)	(ii)
C.	(iii)	(ii)	(i)	(iv)
D.	(ii)	(i)	(iv)	(iii)

39. 'Biological males who reject their masculine identity in due course of time to identify as women' are known as:

A. Trans Women B. Trans Men
C. Trans Gender D. Androgyneous

40. Which of the following statements is correct about the Ecotone?

(i) Is a place where two different eco-systems meet each other?
(ii) Where Mangrove and terrestrial eco-system is an example of Ecotone.
(iii) This area is very rich in species.
(iv) Is a meeting place where two same eco-systems meet each other?

Codes:

A. (ii), (iii) and (iv) B. (i), (iii) and (iv)
C. (i), (ii) and (iii) D. (ii) and (iv)

41. Additional dietary protein may:

A. Increase risk of hip fracture
B. Decrease calcium excretion in the urine
C. Stimulate production of insulin-like growth hormone
D. Reduce muscle mass and strength

42. Match the woman scientists from List-I with their area of research from List-II:

List-I (Women Scientists)	***List-II (Area of Research)***
(a) Rita Lewi-Montalcini	(i) Radioactivity
(b) Marie Curie	(ii) Nuclear shell model of the atomic nucleus
(c) Maria Mayer	(iii) Nerve growth factor
(d) Barbara Mcclintock	(iv) Genetic transposition

Codes:

	(a)	(b)	(c)	(d)
A.	(ii)	(i)	(iii)	(iv)
B.	(iii)	(i)	(iv)	(ii)
C.	(iii)	(i)	(ii)	(iv)
D.	(ii)	(iii)	(i)	(iv)

43. Relative contributions of CO_2, CH_4, CFCs and N_2O towards global warming are:

A. 50%, 30%, 10% and 10% respectively
B. 76%, 16%, 02% and 6% respectively
C. 40%, 30%, 20% and 10% respectively
D. 10%, 50%, 30% and 10% respectively

44. Match the State in List-I with Child Sex Ratio in List-II:

List-I (State)	***List-II (Child Sex Ratio)***
(a) Mizoram	(i) 943
(b) Andaman Nicobar Islands	(ii) 909
(c) Tamil Nadu	(iii) 970
(d) Himachal Pradesh	(iv) 968

Codes:

	(a)	(b)	(c)	(d)
A.	(iii)	(i)	(iv)	(ii)
B.	(iii)	(iv)	(i)	(ii)
C.	(iv)	(ii)	(i)	(iii)
D.	(ii)	(iv)	(iii)	(i)

45. To implement a national health policy of "prevention, not intervention" would require ______.

(i) Eliminating disabling environments and reducing the use of harmful drugs
(ii) A fundamental change in the philosophy of the medical establishment
(iii) A change in the public's attitudes towards medicine and healthcare
(iv) A market for the obsolete pharmaceuticals

Codes:

A. (i), (ii) and (iii) only B. (ii), (iii) and (iv) only
C. (i), (iii) and (iv) only D. (ii) and (iv) only

46. Hysterectomy:

(i) Is the surgical removal of the uterus.
(ii) May also involve removal of the cervix, ovaries, fallopian tubes and other surrounding structures.
(iii) Renders the patient unable to bear children.
(iv) Is a reversible process.

Codes:

A. (i), (ii) and (iii) only B. (ii), (iii) and (iv) only
C. (i), (iii) and (iv) only D. (ii) and (iv) only

47. Which of following statement is incorrect about the Biosphere?

(i) Biosphere is combination of lithosphere, hydrosphere and atmosphere.
(ii) Biosphere is missing at extreme of north and south pole.
(iii) Organisms are uniformly present in Biosphere.
(iv) Biosphere is combination of stratosphere and hydrosphere.

Codes:

A. (iii), (ii) and (iv) B. (iii) and (iv) only
C. (i) and (ii) only D. (ii) and (iii) only

48. Which countries had highest ranks in Gender Related Development Index calculated in 2014?

A. Scandinavian Countries
B. European Countries
C. Asian Countries
D. Latin American Countries

49. Match List-I with List-II:

List-I	***List-II***
(a) Foetus	(i) Failure to conceive after at least one year of unprotected coitus.
(b) Fertilization	(ii) Product of conception starting from completion of embryonic development (at 8 completed weeks after fertilization) until birth or abortion.
(c) Gamete	(iii) Penetration of the ovum by the spermatozoon and fusion of Genetic materials resulting in the development of zygote.
(d) Infertility	(iv) Acolytes and sperms.

Codes:

	(a)	(b)	(c)	(d)
A.	(iv)	(iii)	(ii)	(i)
B.	(iii)	(iv)	(i)	(ii)
C.	(ii)	(iii)	(iv)	(i)
D.	(i)	(ii)	(iii)	(iv)

50. Which of the following pair is not correctly matched?

A. Neonatal Mortality — Deaths occurring in the first four weeks after birth
B. Prenatal Mortality — Deaths in the first week of life after birth
C. Fetal Death — Death of fetus after 28 or more weeks of gestation
D. Post Neonatal Death — Death between 28th day of life and first birth day

51. Match List-I with List-II:

List-I (Data Source for Policy Formulation etc.)	***List-II (Areas)***
(a) NSSO	(i) Principal data collecting, processing and dissemination agency that also monitors and supervises the National Statistical System.
(b) CSO	(ii) It is a focal agency of the government of India in the area of developmental planning and program implementation.
(c) NFHS	(iii) Ministry of Health and family welfare in collabor-ation with the Registrar General of India collect data concerning TFR, IMR and MMR.
(d) AHS	(iv) Large scale multi-round survey conducted in a representative sample of households throughout India.

Codes:

	(a)	(b)	(c)	(d)
A.	(ii)	(i)	(iv)	(iii)
B.	(iii)	(iv)	(i)	(ii)
C.	(i)	(ii)	(iv)	(iii)
D.	(iv)	(iii)	(ii)	(i)

52. Which of the following is correct?

A. Sustainable Development Goals have 16 Goals and 159 Targets
B. Sustainable Development Goals have 12 Goals and 167 Targets
C. Sustainable Development Goals have 19 Goals and 169 Targets
D. Sustainable Development Goals have 17 Goals and 169 Targets

53. 'EAG States' in the context of health-related gender analysis in India stands for:
A. States that have Economics and Gender equity
B. States that are associated with Euro Asian Group
C. States that come under the study of the Empowered Action Group (EAG)
D. States that have been empowered and grouped

54. Match the countries with the following respective movements:

(Name of Movement)	*(Country)*
(a) Women's war	(i) Kenya
(b) Green Belt Movement	(ii) United Kingdom
(c) Suffrage Movement	(iii) America
(d) Women's Liberation Movement	(iv) Nigeria

Codes:

	(a)	(b)	(c)	(d)
A.	(i)	(ii)	(iii)	(iv)
B.	(iv)	(i)	(ii)	(iii)
C.	(iii)	(iv)	(ii)	(i)
D.	(ii)	(iii)	(iv)	(i)

55. Underage marriages of women in India are a contributing factor to the lowering of HDI (Human Development Index) and other socio - economic parameters of development because:
A. Women have to shoulder responsibilities concerning their marital status.
B. Women do not and cannot get access to the means of empowerment.
C. Women cannot be fully literate.
D. The three parameters of measuring HDI get impacted adversely.

56. One of the index benchmarks for determining the Gender Gap according to World Economic Forum is health and survival. India according to 2018 Gender Gap is at the following rank on this benchmark:
A. 126 B. 147
C. 140 D. 128

57. Reproductive technology of SURROGACY is used:
1. Where a woman bears a child for another woman.
2. When a woman cannot bear the child because the uterus is absent or malformed.
3. When a medical condition exists making pregnancy a threat to her or her baby's health.
4. In the gestational surrogacy, pregnancy rcsults from the transfer of an embryo created by IVF in a manner that the resulting child is genetically related to the surrogate.

Codes:
A. 1 and 3 only B. 1 only
C. 1, 2 and 3 only D. 4 only

58. Match the following Women Movements with the respective activities:

Name of Women Movement	***Nature of Activities***
(a) Chipko Movement	(i) Planting of Trees
(b) Green Belt Movement	(ii) Protest against inhuman practices of landlords
(c) Sahada Movement	(iii) Extension of Health care services to women
(d) Women's Health Movement	(iv) Agitation against deforestation.

Codes:

	(a)	(b)	(c)	(d)
A.	(iv)	(iii)	(ii)	(i)
B.	(iii)	(ii)	(i)	(iv)
C.	(iv)	(i)	(ii)	(iii)
D.	(ii)	(iii)	(i)	(iv)

59. Which of the following is/are responsible for poor implementation of the Pre-Conception and Pre-Natal Diagnostic Techniques Act?
1. Ineffective authorities
2. Inactive Advisory Boards
3. Procedural issues involved in implementation
4. Illiteracy

Codes:
A. 3 and 4 only
B. 1, 3 and 4 only
C. 4 only
D 1, 2 and 3 only

60. Census 2011, identifies ....Districts as 'Gender Critical' Districts.
A. 162 B. 211
C. 249 D. 262

61. The PCPNDT Act regulates the use of prenatal diagnostic techniques like ultrasound and amniocentesis by allowing their use only to detect:
1. Metabolic disorders
2. Genetic abnormalities
3. Sex of the foetus
4. Chromosomal abnormalities

Codes:
A. 2 and 4 only
B. 3 only
C. 1, 2 and 4 only
D. 1, 2 and 3 only

62. One of the major causes of high maternal mortality rate in India is:
A. Anaemia Among Women
B. Carelessness of doctors
C. Illiteracy
D. Adolescent pregnancies

63. Match the women leaders with the movements they participated in:

(a) Sarojini Naidu	(i) Narmada Bachao Andolan
(b) C.K. Janu	(ii) Suffrage Movement
(c) Medha Patkar	(iii) Adivasi Land Restoration
(d) Goura Devi	(iv) Chipko Movement

Codes:

	(a)	(b)	(c)	(d)
A.	(iv)	(i)	(iii)	(ii)
B.	(iii)	(ii)	(i)	(iv)
C.	(ii)	(iii)	(i)	(iv)
D.	(i)	(iv)	(ii)	(iii)

64. Which state has the highest female sex ratio as per 2011 census?
A. Bihar B. Kerala
C. Tamil Nadu D. Punjab

65. If women and men are treated equally in India, we could expect for every 100 boys ________girls.
A. 100 B. 105
C. 95 D. 120

66. Estrogen deficiency in women leads to:
A. Menopause B. Menarche
C. Infertility D. Diabetes

67. The deficiency of one or more essential nutrients is termed as:
A. Macro nutrient deficiency
B. Micro nutrient deficiency
C. Malnutrition
D. Anaemia

68. The goal of "Health for all" by the year 2000 A.D. was articulated in:
A. Beijing Conference
B. Alma Ata Conference
C. Cairo Conference
D. Durban Conference

69. World AIDS Day is celebrated on:
A. March 8th B. November 10th
C. December 1st D. March 11th

70. Degradation of natural resources is:
(i) Disappearance of forests
(ii) Deterioration of soil condition
(iii) Depletion of water resources
(iv) Disappearance of urban slums

Codes:
A. (i), (ii) and (iii) are true
B. (i), (ii) and (iv) are true
C. (ii) and (iii) are true
D. (iv) only true

71. NRHM is a mission meant for the development of ___________.
A. Education B. Health
C. Water D. Housing

72. Match the following Ecology movements and its place of origin:

Movement	***Place***
(a) Appiko movement	(i) Kerala
(b) Silent valley	(ii) Madhya Pradesh
(c) Narmada Bachao	(iii) Kenya
(d) Green belt movement	(iv) Western Ghats

Codes:

	(a)	(b)	(c)	(d)
A.	(iv)	(ii)	(iii)	(i)
B.	(iv)	(iii)	(ii)	(i)
C.	(iii)	(iv)	(ii)	(i)
D.	(iv)	(i)	(ii)	(iii)

73. The death of a woman during or shortly after pregnancy is referred as:
A. Female mortality
B. Birth mortality
C. Infant mortality
D. Maternal mortality

74. Action Research on Alternatives Medicine and Women's Health is called as:
A. Shodhini B. AYUSH
C. ICMR D. RCH

75. Which International Conference initiated the concept of Reproductive and Child Health Programmes?
A. ICPD Conference
B. Alma Ata Conference
C. Dublin Conference
D. Mexico Conference

76. Among the following who is not associated with Eco-Feminist Movement?
A. Vandana Shiva B. Arundhati Roy
C. Maria Mies D. Kiran Desai

77. According to 2011 Census (Provisional), the lowest sex ratio is recorded in:
A. Chandigarh B. Daman and Diu
C. Uttar Pradesh D. Bihar

78. Among the following who is associated with Health movement?

A. Arundathi Roy B. Mira Shiva
C. Kiran Desai D. Ela Bhatt

79. Match from List-I the State/Union Territory with List-II giving Sex Ratio as per Census 2011:

List-I	*List-II*
(a) Puducherry	(i) 618
(b) Kerala	(ii) 889
(c) J & K	(iii) 1084
(d) Daman and Diu	(iv) 1037

Codes:

	(a)	(b)	(c)	(d)
A.	(i)	(iii)	(iv)	(ii)
B.	(ii)	(iv)	(iii)	(i)
C.	(iv)	(iii)	(ii)	(i)
D.	(iii)	(iv)	(i)	(ii)

80. "Jal, Jungle, Zameen" is the slogan of which of the following movement?

1. The Adivasi Struggles
2. The Fishworkers Struggle
3. The Environment Movement
4. The Gay Movement

Codes:

A. 1 and 3 are true
B. 2, 3 and 4 are true
C. 1, 2 and 4 are true
D. 2 and 4 are true

81. Homophobia refers to:

1. Fear of men
2. Hatred of sexual minorities
3. Hatred of homes
4. Fear of sexual minorities

Codes:

A. 3 is true
B. 2 and 4 are true
C. 1 and 4 are true
D. 1 and 3 are true

82. The following programmes are concerned with the health of women and children.

1. MCC 2. RPF
3. RCH 4. MCH

Codes:

A. 1 and 3 are true B. 2 and 4 are true
C. 1 and 2 are true D. 3 and 4 are true

83. The two-child norm is related to which of the following programmes?

1. District Primary Education Programme
2. Integrated Rural Development Programme
3. Family Planning Programme
4. Reproductive and Child Health Programme

Codes:

A. 1 and 3 are true
B. 2, 3 and 4 are true
C. 3 and 4 are true
D. 1, 2 and 3 are true

84. ART refers to:

A. Artificial Reproductive Technologies
B. Assisted Reproductive Technologies
C. Assisted Reproductive Therapies
D. Artificial Reproductive Therapies

85. Mark out the factor contributing to high maternal mortality rate:

A. Antenatal care
B. Education
C. Increase in the number of working women
D. Early marriage

86. 'ASHA' denotes:

A. Association of Scientific Health Activists
B. Association of Social Health Activists
C. Accredited Social Health Activists
D. Accredited of Social Health Association

87. The death of foetus after 28 weeks of pregnancy is known as:

A. Infant death
B. Neo-natal death
C. Still birth
D. Post-natal death

88. "The incorporation of women into commercial agriculture does not necessarily make them socially visible".
Who among the following said this?

A. Betty Friedan B. Vandana Shiva
C. Bina Agarwal D. Amy Baumann

89. Match the items from List-I and List-II:

List-I	*List-II*
(a) HIV/AIDS	(i) Red Blood cells
(b) Anaemia	(ii) White Blood cells
(c) Amniocentesis	(iii) Contraceptive
(d) Depo-proveria	(iv) Sex Determination test

Codes:

	(a)	(b)	(c)	(d)
A.	(i)	(ii)	(iii)	(iv)
B.	(i)	(iii)	(ii)	(iv)
C.	(ii)	(iv)	(iii)	(i)
D.	(ii)	(i)	(iv)	(iii)

90. What are the dimensions taken to measure the Gender Inequality Index (GII)?

A. Reproductive Health, Labour Market, Literacy and Knowledge.

B. Employment, Gender wage differentials and Empowerment.

C. Labour Market, Employment and Political participation.

D. Reproductive Health, Empowerment and Labour Market.

91. Which of the following is correct meaning of the 'Human Development'?

A. Expansion of people's freedoms to live long healthy and creative lives.

B. Expansion of people's choices.

C. Fulfilling people's desires.

D. Fulfilling sustainable goals.

92. What is the recent changes introduced in Maternity leave ceiling for women?

A. From 90 days to 135 days.

B. From 120 days to 135 days.

C. From 135 days to 180 days.

D. From 135 days to 150 days.

93. Which of the regions of India have low prevalence of female infanticide and female foeticide?

A. North Eastern Region

B. South Central Region

C. North West Region

D. Southern Region

94. Match List-I with List-II regarding sex-ratio according to 2011 census:

List-I	*List-II*
(a) Kerala	(i) 993
(b) Andhra Pradesh	(ii) 1084
(c) Tamil Nadu	(iii) 996
(d) Haryana	(iv) 879

Codes:

	(a)	(b)	(c)	(d)
A.	(i)	(ii)	(iii)	(iv)
B.	(ii)	(i)	(iii)	(iv)
C.	(iii)	(ii)	(iv)	(i)
D.	(iv)	(i)	(ii)	(iii)

95. ELISA test means:

A. Energy Linked Immunosorbent Assay

B. Enzyme Linked Immunosorbent Analysis

C. Energy Linked Immunological Analysis

D. Enzyme Linked Immunosorbent Assay

96. Women's responses to environmental issues are mediated by their:

1. Knowledge and information
2. Livelihood systems
3. Reproductive mechanisms
4. Unequal access to productive resources

Codes:

A. 2, 3 and 4

B. 1, 2, 3 and 4

C. 1, 2 and 3 only

D. 1, 2 and 3 only

97. Arrange the following movements in chronological order:

1. Chipko Movement
2. Narmada Bachao Movement
3. LGBT Movement
4. Telangana Movement

Codes:

A. 4, 1, 2 and 3

B. 1, 2, 3 and 4

C. 2, 3, 1 and 4

D. 4, 1, 2 and 4

98. Under MTP Act (1971), the opinion of two registered medical practioners are required if pregnancy period is:

A. Below twelve weeks

B. Between twelve and twenty-four weeks

C. Between twelve and fifteen weeks

D. Between twelve and twenty weeks

99. The Government of India first adopted the policy of family planning in:

A. 1956 B. 1950

C. 1957 D. 1952

100. 'Global 500' Awards are given for the outstanding achievement in which of the following fields?

A. Population control

B. Campaign against drugs

C. Elimination of illiteracy

D. Protection of Environment

101. With reference to National Rural Health Mission, which of the following are the responsibilities of ASHA, select the correct one:

1. Accompanying women to health facility for antenatal care checkup.
2. Using pregnancy test kits for early detection of pregnancy.
3. Providing information on nutrition and immunization.
4. Conducting the delivery of baby.

Codes:

A. 1, 2, 3 B. 2 and 4

C. 1 and 3 D. 1, 2, 3 and 4

102. Which of the following pair is not correctly matched?
A. Sex Ratio according to 2001 census — 933
B. Sex Ratio according to 2011 census — 940
C. Child Sex Ratio according to 2001 census — 927
D. Child Sex Ratio according to 2011 census — 939

103. Which one of the following measures is not usually a part of an IMF stabilization programme?
A. Fiscal contraction
B. Monetary contraction
C. Liberalisation of the economy
D. Revaluation of the exchange rate

104. Which of the following are assumption of the bio-medic models on Health?
1. No relevance of Psychological, environmental and social influences.
2. Illness is a breakdown in the normal functioning of the body.
3. Illness need to be treated by trained medical experts.
4. The appropriate place for treatment is the hospital.

Codes:
A. 1, 2 and 3 only   B. 1, 2, 3 and 4
C. 2, 3 and 4 only   D. 1 and 2 only

105. Iron deficiency anemia is common in adolescents with:
A. Asthma
B. Bulimia
C. Heavy menstrual bleeding
D. Obesity

106. Identify the state that has the highest maternal mortality rate in India:
A. Kerala   B. Madhya Pradesh
C. Assam   D. Bihar

107. After tubectomy which part of the female reproductive system remains blocked?
A. Uterus   B. Vagina
C. Fallopian tube   D. Cervical canal

108. Highest unmet need for family planning in women below 25 years of age is:
A. Spacing the births
B. Limiting the births
C. Delaying the first pregnancy
D. Treatment of complications of contraceptive methods

109. According to WHO, which one of the following is not a major criterion for AIDS?
A. Weight loss more than 10%
B. Persistent cough for more than one month
C. Fever for more than one month
D. Diarrhoea for more than one month

110. Which of the following falls in the category of third generation of human rights?
A. Environmental Rights
B. Civil and Political Rights
C. Economic Rights
D. Social and cultural Rights

111. Transgenders in India have fought for and got voting rights in the year:
A. 2002   B. 2014
C. 1994   D. 1996

112. What is correct for laparoscopic tubectomy?
1. Haemoglobin percentage should not be less than 8.
2. Not advisable for post-partum patients up to 6 weeks.
3. It can be done as a concurrent procedure to MTP.
4. It is a temporary method of contraception.

Codes:
A. 1, 2 and 3 only
B. 2, 2 and 4 only
C. 1, 2, 3 and 4
D. 3 and 4 only

113. Which of the following identifies an 'infant at risk'?
1. Birth weight less than 2.5 kg
2. Weight below 70% of expected weight
3. Failure to gain weight during three successive months
4. Infant not taking breast feed after one year of age

Codes:
A. 2, 3 and 4 only   B. 1 and 2 only
C. 1, 2 and 3 only   D. 1, 2, 3 and 4

114. Child sex-ratio is lower in developed States in comparison to economically backward ones. It is not because of:
A. High son preference
B. Male child really inherits property
C. Easy availability of scientific method
D. Women are more rational

115. Higher dietary sodium (salt) intake is generally associated with:
A. Decreased calcium excretion in the urine
B. Increased risk of fracture
C. Decreased dietary calcium absorption
D. Negative calcium balance and bone mineral loss

116. Write the reasons for deficit of female births.

1. Deficit of female births, deaths from excess female mortality due to son preference.
2. Poor institutions of public health and service delivery causes a heavy burden on girls and women.
3. Poor sanitation and water supply.
4. HIV/AIDS risks have compounded the deaths of women.

Codes:

A. 2, 3 and 4 only B. 1 and 4 only
C. 1, 2, 3 and 4 only D. 1, 2 and 3 only

117. The life expectancy at birth for females in low-income countries rose from:

A. 45 years to 70 years
B. 50 years to 80 years
C. 60 years to 67 years
D. 48 years to 69 years

118. Match List-I with List-II:

List-I (Aims)	***List-II (Movement)***
(a) Fighting Alcoholism	(i) Chipko Movement
(b) Widow Remarriage	(ii) Narmada Bachao Movement
(c) Awareness on Forest Protection	(iii) Anti-Arrack Movement
(d) Rehabilitation of Displaced Persons	(iv) Social Reform Movement

Codes:

	(a)	(b)	(c)	(d)
A.	(iii)	(iv)	(i)	(ii)
B.	(i)	(iii)	(ii)	(iv)
C.	(ii)	(iv)	(i)	(iii)
D.	(i)	(ii)	(iii)	(iv)

119. Vulnerable women can protect themselves from their HIV/AIDS infected husbands by adopting which one of the following?

A. Anti-Retroviral Therapy
B. Injection Drug Use
C. CD4 Test
D. Female Condom

120. Assertion (A): Unwed mothers and their children are given shelter in Swadhar Ghar with Government support.

Reason (R): Bearing children beyond marriage is not natural.

Codes:

A. Both (A) and (R) are true and (R) is not true explanation for (A).
B. (A) is true, (R) is false and (R) is not the true explanation for (A).
C. (A) is false and (R) is true.
D. Both (A) and (R) are false.

121. Assertion (A): Increases in life expectancy or say the ageing of populations and the new inter-generational relationships are radically affecting the human landscape.

Reason (R): Most of the world's older population are not entitled to any form of old-age pension, i.e. living longer for those means living with scarcity for longer.

Codes:

A. (A) is true but (R) is false.
B. Both (A) and (R) are true and (R) is the correct explanation for (A).
C. Both (A) and (R) are true and (R) is not the correct explanation for (A).
D. (A) is false but (R) is true.

122. Assertion (A): Empowerment of women has more powerful influence on children's well-being.

Reason (R): Women's ability to create income and central resources directly affect the nutritional status of children.

Codes:

A. Both (A) and (R) are true.
B. Both (A) and (R) are false.
C. Both (A) and (R) are true, (R) is the correct explanation for (A).
D. (A) is true (R) is false.

123. Assertion (A): Women are affected by environment.

Reason (R): Women's life is directly associated with nature and its resources.

Codes:

A. Both (A) and (R) are true and (R) is the correct explanation of (A).
B. (A) is false but (R) is true.
C. Both (A) and (R) are true.
D. (A) is true but (R) is false.

124. Assertion (A): The sex-ratio of India has been 933 women for 1000 men, constituting only 48.6 million women.

Reason (R): 3.2 million missing women had been denied of life.

Codes:

A. Both (A) and (R) are true.
B. (A) is true and (R) is a cause for (A).
C. (A) is true but (R) is not a cause for (A).
D. Both (A) and (R) are false.

125. Assertion (A): More than one-third of mothers in developing countries give birth to low birth weight babies.

Reason (R): Majority of mothers are malnourished in developing countries.

Codes:

A. Both (A) and (R) are true, (R) is not the correct explanation for (A).
B. Both (A) and (R) are false.
C. (A) is true but (R) is false.
D. Both (A) and (R) are true, (R) is the correct explanation for (A).

126. Assertion (A): Women and nature are related to feminine principles.

Reason (R): Feminine principles are life supportive.

Codes:

A. Both (A) and (R) are false.
B. Both (A) and (R) are true, (R) is not the correct explanation for (A).
C. Both (A) and (R) are true.
D. Both (A) and (R) are true, (R) is the correct explanation for (A).

127. Assertion (A): Women are biologically and epidemiologically more vulnerable to AIDS.

Reason (R): Male to female transmission of HIV is more than female to male.

Codes:

A. Both (A) and (R) are true.
B. (A) is true, (R) is false.
C. Both (A) and (R) are false.
D. Both (A) and (R) are true, (R) is not the correct explanation for (A).

128. Assertion (A): Female sterilization account for 95 percent of all sterilization.

Reason (R): Women conceive and bear children and hence it is their sole responsibility to control and protect themselves against reproduction.

Codes:

A. Both (A) and (R) are true.
B. (A) is true and (R) is false.
C. (A) is false and (R) is true.
D. Both (A) and (R) are false.

129. Assertion (A): Female foeticide increases and that contributes to declining sex ratio.

Reason (R): Misuse of technology and son preference are the reasons for declining sex ratio.

Codes:

A. Both (A) and (R) are true.
B. Both (A) and (R) are false.
C. Both (A) and (R) are true, (R) is the correct explanation for (A).
D. (A) is true, (R) is false

130. Assertion (A): Advocacy in disability politics is to push the 'Healthy Majority' to a recognition that they are merely temporarily able bodies (TAB).

Reason (R): The language of disability is more in the public domain and is increasingly difficult to describe.

Codes:

A. Both (A) and (R) are false.
B. (A) is true but (R) is false.
C. (A) is false but (R) is true.
D. Both (A) and (R) are true.

131. Assertion (A): Mental health is an important dimension of women's health.

Reason (R): Mental health is viewed as interface between domestic violence and health.

Codes:

A. Both (A) and (R) are false.
B. Both (A) and (R) are true.
C. (A) is false, (R) is true.
D. (A) is true, (R) is false.

132. Assertion (A): The average Indian women bears her first child before she is 22 years old.

Reason (R): Women have little control over her own fertility and reproductive health.

Codes:

A. Both (A) and (R) are true.
B. Both (A) and (R) are true, (R) is the correct explanation for (A).
C. Both (A) and (R) are true (R) is not the correct explanation for (A).
D. Both (A) and (R) are false.

133. Assertion (A): The difference between male and female reproductive systems have always been an important consideration in health care delivery.

Reason (R): Around the world half a million women continue to die each year as a direct consequence of pregnancy and child birth.

Codes:

A. Both (A) and (R) are true.
B. (A) is true, (R) is false.
C. Both (A) and (R) are true, (R) is the correc explanation for (A).
D. Both (A) and (R) are false.

134. Assertion (A): Iron deficiency anemia increase maternal and infant mortality rate.

Reason (R): Low birth weight babies, still birth, premature delivery and probability of fetal brain damage are chances by iron deficiency anemia in our country.

Codes:

A. Both (A) and (R) are false.
B. (A) is false and (R) is true.
C. Both (A) and (R) are true and (R) is the correct explanation of (A).
D. Both (A) and (R) are true and (R) is not the correct explanation of (A).

135. Assertion (A): In most countries women live longer than men due to their biological constitution.

Reason (R): Social, cultural, religious and economic factors have direct impact on women's health.

Codes:

A. (A) is true and (R) is false.
B. Both (A) and (R) are true but (R) is not the correct explanation of (A).
C. Both (A) and (R) are false.
D. (A) is false and (R) is true.

136. Assertion (A): Malnutrition is a Complex Phenomenon that causes poverty and ill health in India.

Reason (R): Nutrition Education and extension has been recognized as one of the long-term sustainable interventions to tackle problems of malnutrition.

Codes:

A. Both (A) and (R) are true.
B. Both (A) and (R) are true, (R) is the correct explanation for (A).
C. Both (A) and (R) are false.
D. (A) is true, (R) is false.

137. Assertion (A): Female Sterilization has been the most frequently used method of contraception in India.

Reason (R): Male Sterilization leads to impotency.

Codes:

A. Both (A) and (R) are true.
B. (A) is true, (R) is false.
C. Both (A) and (R) are false.
D. Both (A) and (R) are true, (R) is not the correct explanation for (A).

138. Assertion (A): Childless women face humiliation and abandonment.

Reason (R): Infertility is mainly due to women's health problem.

Codes:

A. Both (A) and (R) are true.
B. (A) is true, (R) is false.
C. Both (A) and (R) are false.
D. (A) is false, (R) is true.

139. Assertion (A): Maternal mortality in India is one of the highest in the world.

Reason (R): Women have poor access to medical facilities.

Codes:

A. (A) is true and (R) is false.
B. (A) is false and (R) is true.
C. Both (A) and (R) are true.
D. Both (A) and (R) are false.

140. Assertion (A): Women have higher life expectancy than men.

Reason (R): Women eat more nutritious food.

Codes:

A. Both (A) and (R) are true.
B. (A) is true, (R) is false.
C. Both (A) and (R) are false.
D. Both (A) and (R) are true, (R) is not the correct explanation for (A).

141. Assertion (A): Infant Mortality in India is one of the highest among the countries.

Reason (R): Indian women receive good antenatal care.

Codes:

A. Both (A) and (R) are true, (R) is correct explanation for (A).
B. Both (A) and (R) are true.
C. Both (A) and (R) are false.
D. (A) is true, (R) is false.

142. Assertion (A): Female sterilization is the most popular method of family planning.

Reason (R): Female sterilization is less complicated than male sterilization.

Codes:

A. Both (A) and (R) are true.
B. (A) is true, (R) is false.
C. Both (A) and (R) are false.
D. Both (A) and (R) are true, (R) is not the correct explanation for (A).

143. Assertion (A): Motherhood is alternating experience for women.

Reason (R): Women's Reproduction is controlled by men.

Codes:

A. Both (A) and (R) are true, (R) is the correct explanation for (A).

B. Both (A) and (R) are false.
C. (A) is true, (R) is false.
D. (A) is false, (R) is true.

144. Assertion (A): Women have to balance reproductive and productive roles.
Reason (R): Women are discriminated in productive and reproductive roles.
Codes:
A. Both (A) and (R) are false.
B. Both (A) and (R) are true.
C. (A) is false but (R) is true.
D. (R) is false but (A) is true.

145. Assertion (A): Approximately 500,000 women die each year from reproductive causes.
Reason (R): Majority of women lack access to proper health care.
Codes:
A. Both (A) and (R) are true.
B. Both (A) and (R) are true, (R) is the correct explanation for (A).
C. (A) is true, (R) is false.
D. Both (A) and (R) are false.

146. Assertion (A): Gender perspective into health care delivery improves the health of both women and men.
Reason (R): Health is a basic human right.
Codes:
A. Both (A) and (R) are false.
B. A is true and (R) is false.
C. Both (A) and (R) are true.
D. (A) is false and (R) is true.

147. Assertion (A): Women and girls suffer as a result of food discrimination.
Reason (R): Food discrimination is only due to poverty and scarcity.
Codes:
A. Both (A) and (R) are true and (R) is the correct explanation for (A).
B. Both (A) and (R) are false.
C. (A) is true (R) is false and (R) is not the correct explanation for (A).
D. (A) is false and (R) is true and (R) is the true explanation for (A).

148. Assertion (A): Sex selective abortion is one of the causes of the declining sex ratio.
Reason (R): Son preference is closely related to the low status of women.
Codes:
A. Both (A) and (R) are false.
B. (A) is true, (R) is false.
C. Both (A) and (R) are true, and (R) is not the correct explanation for (A).
D. Both (A) and (R) are true, (R) is the correct explanation for (A).

149. Assertion (A): Feminist perspectives on environment challenge the social, cultural and political sources of power in society.
Reason (R): Sustainable Development Challenge the participation of men in pro-ecological ways of living.
Codes:
A. Both (A) and (R) are true.
B. (A) is true, (R) is false.
C. Both (A) and (R) are true, (R) is the correct explanation for (A).
D. Both (A) and (R) are false.

150. Assertion (A): Women play an essential role in the management of natural resources including soil, water, forest and energy.
Reason (R): Women have technical and contemporary knowledge of the nature world around them.
Codes:
A. Both (A) and (R) are true.
B. (A) is true, (R) is false.
C. Both (A) and (R) are false.
D. (A) is false, (R) is true.

Answers

1	2	3	4	5	6	7	8	9	10
B	A	A	C	D	C	A	D	C	D
11	**12**	**13**	**14**	**15**	**16**	**17**	**18**	**19**	**20**
D	C	C	A	B	A	B	B	B	D
21	**22**	**23**	**24**	**25**	**26**	**27**	**28**	**29**	**30**
D	A	C	C	C	A	A	A	C	D
31	**32**	**33**	**34**	**35**	**36**	**37**	**38**	**39**	**40**
B	C	B	B	C	D	C	A	C	C

41	42	43	44	45	46	47	48	49	50
C	C	B	B	A	A	B	A	C	B
51	52	53	54	55	56	57	58	59	60
A	D	C	B	D	B	C	C	D	D
61	62	63	64	65	66	67	68	69	70
C	A	C	B	A	A	C	B	C	A
71	72	73	74	75	76	77	78	79	80
B	D	D	A	A	D	B	B	C	A
81	82	83	84	85	86	87	88	89	90
B	D	C	B	D	C	C	B	D	D
91	92	93	94	95	96	97	98	99	100
A	C	A	B	D	D	A	B	D	D
101	102	103	104	105	106	107	108	109	110
A	D	C	C	C	B	C	A	B	A
111	112	113	114	115	116	117	118	119	120
C	A	C	D	D	D	D	A	D	B
121	122	123	124	125	126	127	128	129	130
C	C	A	B	D	D	A	B	C	D
131	132	133	134	135	136	137	138	139	140
B	B	C	C	B	A	B	B	C	C
141	142	143	144	145	146	147	148	149	150
D	B	A	B	B	C	C	D	B	B

❑ ❑ ❑

Women Empowerment and Development

- Theories of Development, Alternative Approaches – Women in Development (WID), Women and Development (WAD) and Gender and Development (GAD)
- Empowerment Concept, and Indices: Gender Development Index (GDI), Gender Inequality Index (GII), Global Gender Gap Index (GGGI)
- Women Development Approaches in Indian Five-Year Plans
- Women and Leadership – Panchayat Raj and Role of NGOs and Women Development
- Sustainable Development Goals, Policies and Programmes

THEORIES OF DEVELOPMENT

Theorization of feminism and women's socio-economic positions and aspirations led to different perspectives of economic development and the role of women in them. Major women development theories are as follows:

Welfare Approach: One of the earliest approaches; concerned with third world development; with emphasis on welfare schemes, mother-child health, family planning, benefits to women; etc. did not attempt to change the traditional role of women.

Equity Approach: Stressed on employment opportunities and economic independence for women development; Equity in market and household was deemed necessary; emphasised on recognition of paid and unpaid work.

Efficiency Approach: Women should be active participants of the development process; access to micro-credit and financial resources; more concerned with economic growth; political and social division of gender ignored.

WOMEN IN DEVELOPMENT (WID)

- Originated in the early 1970s with its roots in women's suffrage movement and movements fighting for social and economic equality.
- By the end of the 1960s, it became clear that women were not benefitting from the socio-economic development. They were not only being left out but also that their existing position was adversely affected by the development process.
- The Women in Development approach was greatly influenced by Ester Boserup's publication: "Women's role in economic development." Her research highlighted that the specialized division of labor due to modern development approaches had undermined women's contribution and status in society.
- The Women in Development approach "criticized the exclusion of women from the development process as the reason for their deteriorating condition in society."
- The inclusion of women in the development programmes was necessary for women to reap the

benefits of development. But, women lacked the opportunity to participate in the development process due to lack of access to resources.

- Major emphasis was placed on income-generating programmes and activities, nutrition and education for women and family planning.
- The approach and the resulting movements succeeded in getting women's issues into the agenda of the UN and other development agencies.
- One of the outcomes of the WID movement is the development of the Harvard Analytical Framework in 1985. It is also called Gender Roles Framework, one of the first frameworks to be designed for gender analysis. It was developed by the Harvard Institute for International Development in colla-boration with the WID office of USAID.
- It helped planners to design more efficient strategies by mapping resource allocation for men and women in communities. The framework has four components or subsections: Activity Profile, Access, Control Profile, Influencing Factors, and Project Cycle Analysis.

WOMEN IN DEVELOPMENT (WAD)

- Originated in the early 1970s with its roots in women's Originated in 1975 in Mexico as a neo-Marxist perspective on women's role in development.
- Critiquing of 'Women in Development' approach led to the emergence of 'Women and Development.'
- The approach stressed that women had always been a part of the development process and are still important actors in the social system.
- Their work and labor, both within and outside of the family, are critical to society. The socio-economic system has made women's work invisible and unrewarding. The existing capitalist economic system has precipitated and exploited the inequalities between men and women.
- The focus should be on the invisible interaction between women and the development process. Their essential role in both the reproduction of family and society and production of labor has to be acknowledged.
- WAD blames the existing social hierarchy, economic structure and class inequalities for the secondary position of women.
- WAD was also instrumental in highlighting the interaction between capitalism and patriarchy. But, it over-emphasized the role of class inequalities as the cause of women's position and ignored the social construction of gender relationships and gender roles.

GENDER AND DEVELOPMENT (GAD)

- Gender and development emerged in the 1980s as a coming together of several modern feminist ideas and movements. It was greatly influenced by socialist feminism and the DAWN movement.
- Developing Alternatives for Women in the New Era (DAWN) was established in 1984 in India as a network of feminist scholars, academicians, thinkers, and activists from the global south for gender and social justice. DAWN acted as a forum for feminist research, analysis, and discourse and also to support activities for women's development.
- GAD approach stressed that both men and women need equal participation in the development process to enjoy equal benefits.
- It was concerned with gender relations in society and how it influenced roles, responsibilities, and expectations between men and women.
- GAD highlighted how the existing gender construct has a negative impact on women and her position in society.
- Development for women needed fundamental changes in gender relations and the elimination of gender inequality.
- It also drew attention to women's oppression within the family and in the private sphere, violence against women and how the division of labor varies across different cultures and social systems.
- It stated that the state has the primary responsibility in supporting women's reproductive role within family and society.
- Its other focus areas included analysis of development as a complex process influenced by various factors and how it was affected by women's contribution or the lack of it.
- GAD also highlighted the adverse effects of liberalization and structural adjustment programmes on women, especially in developing and third-world countries. Neo-liberalism has brought further marginalization of women, feminization of poverty and women's loss of control over her fundamental rights.

EMPOWERMENT CONCEPT AND INDICES

Empowerment Approach

Emphasized on the political, social and psychological empowerment of women; control over material resources, information, authority, and ideology; different means and measures of women empowerment such as Gender Empowerment Measure (GEM) to supplement other economic growth measures.

Up to the 1990s, development was measured by economic indicators such as Gross National Product (GNP), Gross Domestic Product (GDP), Per Capita Income, etc... But, these measures did not help in understanding the well-being of people and human development such as health, education, and equality in society. Measures were devised to factor in social conditions and improvement such as Human Development Index (HDI), Gender-related HDI, Gender Empowerment Measure, etc.

Gender indicators enable better planning and action, helps to understand and measure the efficacy of policies for gender and social equality and holds institutions accountable for ensuring gender equality.

Human Development Index (HDI)

- Developed by Pakistani economist, **Mahboob Ul Haq** to measure social development.
- First used in 1990 by United Nations Development Programme.
- HDI used three indicators for measuring development namely **Health, Knowledge and Living Standards**.
- Health was measured by life expectancy, knowledge by expected years of schooling and mean years of schooling and living standard of people by GNI at purchasing power parity in dollars.
- HDI helps to capture the levels of poverty, deprivation, and development in the world. In 2017, India's HDI rank was 130.

GENDER-RELATED DEVELOPMENT INDEX (GDI)

- Introduced by UNDP in its Human Development Report, 1995.
- It measures the gender gap in human development by adjusting the HDI indicators to factor in the disparities between men and women.
- The three indicators of HDI—health, knowledge and living standard are also used here. But in GDI, the ratio of HDIs of males and females are calculated.
- Countries are categorized into five groups based on the absolute deviation from gender parity in HDI values.
- Group 1 countries have high equality in HDI achievement with their absolute deviation of less than 2.5%.
- Group 5 countries have low equality (or high levels of gender inequality) with absolute deviation greater than 10%.
- According to the Human Development Report of 2017, India's GDI value is 0.841. It belongs to the group 5 with high levels of gender inequality across several indicators.
- The HDI value for females and males in India are in the ratio of 0.575 and 0.683
- The life expectancy at birth for females and males are 70.4 and 67.3. Women should have a higher life expectancy.
- Expected years of schooling for women and men are 12.9 and 11.9 years respectively. Mean years of schooling for women and men are 4.8 and 8.2 years.
- Gross National Income per Capita for women and men in India are 2722 and 9729 dollars respectively.

Gender Empowerment Measure (GEM)

- Introduced by UNDP in 1995 along with GDI.
- It measures relative female representation in economic and political sphere.
- It helps in understanding the gender gap in political representation, in professional and management positions and income gender gaps.

GENDER INEQUALITY INDEX (GII)

- Introduced in 2010 in its Human Development Index by United Nations Development Programme.
- It provides a direct measurement of gender disparity in societies.
- GII evaluates gender inequality across three aspects of human development:
  - **Reproductive Health:** Measured in terms of maternal mortality rate and adolescent birth rates.

- **Empowerment:** The proportion of parliamentary seats occupied by women, the proportion of adult males and females above 25 years of age with at least secondary education.
- **Economic Status:** Labor market participation of males and females above 15 years of age.

- In 2017, **India ranked 127 in the Gender Inequality Index** with a GII value of 0.524.
- India belongs in the medium human development group of countries.

GLOBAL GENDER GAP INDEX (GGGI)

- Global Gender Gap Index was first published in 2006 by the World Economic Forum.
- It examines the gap between men and women in four fundamental categories using 14 different indicators.
- The four categories are economic participation and economic opportunities available for women, educational attainment of women, health and survival of women, and political empowerment of women.
- **Economic participation and opportunities** for women are measured using the following indicators: male and female unemployment levels, economic activity, remuneration for equal work, maternity leave duration, number of women in managerial positions, the government-provided health care and wage inequalities.
- **Educational attainment** of women is measured by literacy rates, enrolment rate for primary, secondary and tertiary education, and average years of schooling.
- **Health and survival** are measured by the effectiveness of government effort in the reduction of poverty and inequality, adolescent fertility rate, percentage of births attended by skilled health staff, maternal mortality rate and infant mortality rate.
- **Political empowerment** of women is measured by the following indicators: number of female ministers, number of seats in parliament, women in senior legislative and managerial positions, number of years for which women have been the Head of State.
- The highest score in this index is 1, and the lowest is 0.
- India's GGGI value in 2015 was 0.66, 2016 was 0.68 and in 2018 is 0.67.
- India ranks 108th out of 149 countries. It ranks low in all categories.
- In Health and survival category, India ranks third lowest in the world. India remains the least improved country in this category over the past decade. Its rank dropped from 141 in 2017 to 147 in 2018 in this category.
- India's rank in the four categories in 2018 are as follows:
  - Economic participation and economic opportunity – 142
  - Educational attainment – 114
  - Health and survival – 147
  - Political empowerment - 19

WOMEN DEVELOPMENT APPROACHES IN INDIAN FIVE YEAR PLANS

For centuries, women in India have been socially, politically and economically discriminated and exploited. At the time of independence, they did not possess any property rights, were not treated equally in marriage, had no access to education, resources and had no voice of their own. As women make up half of the population, their development was recognized as inherent for the country's development.

The planning commission (1947-2017) was a central planning body that formulated a development strategy for the whole country. It devised five-year plans to spur socio-economic growth of all sectors and aspects of the country, including women development.

1st Five Year Plan (1951-56) : Mainly welfare oriented schemes for women; recognized women as underprivileged; organized Mahila Mandals for women; incorporated them in Community Development Programme.

2nd FiveYear Plan (1956-61) : Suggested equal pay for equal work; women work safety; maternity benefits and crèches; emphasized on the job training for women.

3rd Five Year Plan (1961-66) : Enlarged rural women welfare schemes such as maternal and child care, health, family planning; emphasized on women's education.

4th Five Year Plan (1969-74) : Stressed on women welfare within the family, adult women's education, nutrition and supplementary health benefits for pregnant women and children.

5th Five Year Plan (1974-79) : Coincided with "International Decade of Women" (1975-1985); Report of the Committee on the Status of Women in India highlighted low sex ratio, low life expectancy, high rates of infant and maternal mortality, illiteracy and work participation of women; focus shifted from 'welfare' to 'development' of women; imparting functional literacy and skill training.

6th Five Year Plan (1980-85) : A separate chapter for women in the plan; multi-disciplinary approach; three-fold: education, health and employment; stressed economic independence; introduced a separate chapter titled "Women and Development" to' detail the issues and strategies for women empowerment.

7th Five Year Plan (1985-90) : Support to Training-cum-Employment Programme for Women (STEP) launched in 1987.

8th Five Year Plan (1992-97) : The economic crisis 1990-91 had its toll on women's development too. The focus on women empowerment declined. The plan recognized that the benefits of development should not bypass women.

9th Five Year Plan (1997-2002) : Stressed the need for a supportive environment for women empowerment in family, schools, workplaces, communities, and politics; 30% representation for women in public sector; adopted a strategy called "Women Component Plan" – which involved earmarking not less than 30% of funds for women-specific programmes in each sector; emphasized on women Self Help Groups, reproductive health care services, employment generation programme for women, etc.

10th Five Year Plan (2002-07) : Set measurable targets for women; Self Help Groups for income generation, and micro-credit services was promoted nationwide on a large scale; 30% of total plan fund was allocated for women schemes; reducing gender gaps in literacy and wage rates by at least 50% by 2007 was one of the monitorable targets.

11th Five Year Plan (2007-12) : Recognized gender disparity as an issue of women development; highlighted increasing violence against women—trafficking, female foeticide, domestic violence; focused on reducing gender inequality, and also reduce the total fertility rate to 2.1.

12th Five Year Plan (2012-17) : Addressed issues of single women in society, their vulnerability to exploitation and discrimination; recognized their rights and work safety; targets for the plan period included reducing Infant Mortality Rate to 25, Maternal Mortality Rate to 1, increasing child sex ratio to 950, reducing total fertility rate to 2.1. The Planning Commission constituted a working group on Women's Agency and Empowerment under the chairpersonship of the Secretary of the Ministry of Women and Child Development, to deliberate and develop strategies for different focus areas of women empowerment.

WOMEN AND LEADERSHIP

Political Participation of Women

Active participation of women in politics is determined by the political culture, social freedom and gender equations in society. Even though the National Freedom Movement saw the participation of both elite and masses, women's participation and engagement in politics still has its challenges and obstacles.

UN Convention on Elimination of All Forms of Discrimination Against Women, held in 1979 affirmed women's right to vote, their political rights and privileges. It is called the Human Rights Bill of Women.

But, according to the Economic Survey, the voting gap between men and women is more than 10% in India. Representation of women in Parliament, the highest and largest political policy-making body in the country is less than 15%. The first Lok Sabha formed in 1951 had 22 women MPs, which amounted to only 4.50% of the total representatives in the Lower House of the Parliament.

In the 16th Lok Sabha, formed after the parliamentary elections of 2014, only 66 of the total 543 MPs are female members. Though this is a three-fold increase compared to the first Lok Sabha, women still make up only 12.15% of the total Lok Sabha MPs. The Rajya Sabha currently has 31 female MPs out of 244 total members. Despite having prominent national and regional political leaders like Sonia Gandhi, Mamata Banerjee, Mayawati, late J.Jayalalitha, Sushma Swaraj, Smriti Irani, etc., women remain a political minority in India.

This curtails access to policy and decision making, loosing resource allocation authority and impedes gender mainstreaming. Women should not be a mere spectator of politics. They should exert pressure, mobilize support and bring forth fresh political perspectives and obtain political power.

In the grassroots level, the 73rd Constitutional Amendment Act provides reservation of seats and posts for women in grass root level democratic institutions. This has to be extended to all areas of political and government institutions, democratic organizations to ensure active engagement of women in politics. There has been demand for reservation for women representation in parliament for decades. But, the legislation to reserve 33% seats to women in parliament, tabled in 2008 was never allowed to become a law. The bill was passed in Rajya Sabha, the Lower House of Parliament in 2010, but lapsed in Lok Sabha, the Upper House.

WOMEN IN PANCHAYAT RAJ INSTITUTIONS

- In India, the rural local government is called Panchayat Raj.
- Panchayat means 'assembly of five' and Raj means 'rule.' In ancient India, it was usually an assembly of wise men and women chosen by the local community.
- Traditionally, panchayats helped in the settlement of disputes and conflicts within rural communities and villages.
- The modern Panchayat Raj Institutions (PRI) are instrumental in the decentralization of several administrative functions to elected gram panchayats.
- There are three levels of panchayat raj institutions in India:
  - Gram panchayats at the village level
  - Block level panchayats at taluks
  - Zilla Parishad at the district level
- Political participation of women is a way for them to take part in electoral and decision-making process. It gives representation to women's needs and aspirations.
- Some methods of political participation are voting, seeking information, holding discussions, meetings and demonstrations.
- PRIs were envisaged as a vehicle for political justice to people at grassroots level.
- Only in 1923 in India, women's names first appeared in electoral rolls. First women member to the Indian legislature was nominated in 1926.
- In 1931, Indian women's struggle for universal adult franchise began.
- Ashok Mehta Committee had recommended 25% of reservations for women at Zilla and mandal level PRIs.
- But, real devolutions of power to women came with 73rd and 74th Constitutional amendment Act of 1992. These acts made the following mandatory with respect to women in PRIs:
  - It reserved not less than one-third of seats for women in panchayats through direct elections.
  - One-third of the offices of chairpersons in Panchayats at each level should be reserved for women.
  - It also reserved one-third of seats in municipalities and offices of chairpersons in municipalities for women.
- But, the actual level of representation of women in politics is only 11%, according to the World Development Report, 2017.
- Factors adversely affecting women's political participation are lack of political will, patriarchal social structure, male dominance, etc.
- Most women in PRI are acting as proxies for male members or husbands.
- They also face political interferences when they try to perform their administrative functions in the PRIs.
- The average age of women in PRIs is above 45. Most women are able to take up political responsibilities after completing their family responsibilities only.
- Women are bold in expressing their views in assembly meetings but face non-cooperation from male ward members and sometimes face abuse and threat.
- Their household work also constraints their complete participation and they do not usually receive support from family members. For women to participate in PRIs, motivation, political training and awareness campaigns are needed.
- The 110th and 112th Constitutional Amendment bills introduced in 2009 seeks to provide 50% reservation of seats for women in all the three tiers of PRIs and urban local bodies.
- But, some states are ahead of the central government in implementing 50% reservation for women in PRIs. Bihar was the first state to allocate 50% of PRI seats for women in 2005. Other states currently implementing 50% reservation are Assam, Andhra Pradesh, Chhattisgarh, Gujarat, Himachal Pradesh, Jharkhand, Kerala, Karnataka, Madhya Pradesh, Maharashtra, Odisha, Rajasthan, Sikkim, Tamil Nadu, Telangana, Tripura, Uttarakhand and West Bengal.

ROLE OF NGOs AND WOMEN DEVELOPMENT

Non-Governmental Organization (NGO) is a not for profit, citizens based voluntary group organized on the local, national and international level to address social and political issues.

NGOs can be registered under provisions of the following acts: Companies Act (2013), Societies Registration Act (1860) or Indian Trusts Act (1882). The Foreign Contribution Regulation Act (FCRA) monitors foreign funding and donations to NGOs. NGOs have to be enlisted with FCRA to receive foreign money.

NGOs have played a crucial role in mainstreaming women issues and fighting for their rights and development. They can be broadly categorized as women welfare NGOs and women's rights NGOs.

The early NGO movements were in the form of reform movements of the 1800s that were concerned with fighting bigotry and backward-looking traditionalism in society.

After independence, NGOs were mainly involved in delivering welfare benefits of the government to women and the poor. They created awareness, promoted education among women and ensured delivery of health and welfare services to women.

The nature of NGOs changed in the 1970s as they become struggle oriented to fight discrimination, patriarchy, equal property rights, remedy the social and economic exploitation of women. They have mobilized women to fight gender injustice, dowry system, domestic violence, sexual harassment, etc.

NGOs also promote the education of the poor, women's health, skill and job training for women from low-income groups, financial support, and self-employment.

Some prominent NGOs working for women are:

CREA: Founded in 2000; based in New Delhi; feminist human rights organization; advances rights of all women and girls and advocates sexual and reproductive freedom for all people; campaigns to question traditional gender norms.

Saheli: Founded in 2013; based in Dehradun, Uttarakhand; empowerment of women, domestic violence against children and adolescent girls, discrimination.

CARE India: Founded in 1945; headquartered in Noida, Uttar Pradesh; empowers women against poverty, injustice and social discrimination; works to provide affordable healthcare, jobs, and self-employment for women.

Snehalaya: Founded in 1989; based in Ahmednagar, Maharashtra; works for rehabilitation, healthcare, education, and awareness among women; helps victims of domestic violence, poverty, trafficking, and discrimination.

Sarvajal: Founded in 2008; based in Ahmedabad, Gujarat; believes that women suffer most in procuring drinking water for their family; works to provide access to safe and affordable water to rural communities and slum-areas.

Sakhi: Founded in 2002; based in north Bihar; a platform for girls and youth to fight caste, gender, and sexual discrimination and abuse; provides educational, vocational, health, social and economic support to adolescent girls.

Self Help Groups are an important component of Women NGOs actively promoted by the government for economic empowerment.

Self-Employed Women Association (SEWA) is the most substantial non-governmental body of women workers from different sectors of the economy that promote their members' work rights. It was founded by Ela Bhatt in 1972. She established a cooperative bank under SEWA in 1974 to provide loans to poor women for small businesses.

She was also the co-founder of Women's World Banking (WWB) in 1979. WWB is a global network of microfinance organizations to help poor women. She has provided millions of women with opportunities, financial and social empowerment.

Women are also active in NGOs fighting for environmental protection and conservation.

Different NGOs have been instrumental in the formulation of constitutional and legal rights and protection for women such as Dowry Prohibition Act (1961), Medical Termination of Pregnancy act (1971), Indecent Representation of Women Prohibition Act (1986), Protection of Women from Domestic Violence Act (2005), etc.

SUSTAINABLE DEVELOPMENT GOALS POLICIES AND PROGRAMMES

Sustainable Development Goals (SDGs) are a set of **17 goals** adopted by the **United Nations** to be implemented by all UN member states towards universal human development with various focus areas such as sustainable development, climate resilience, gender equality, etc. United Nations Development Programme (UNDP) has been responsible for the in-depth consultations, planning, implementation and the future measurement and guidance on SDGs. SDGs are set to be implemented with the time period of 2015-2030. The 17 SDGs have sub-targets under each, totaling up to 169 targets.

India has drawn up new policies and built on existing strategies to ensure that its commitments towards SDGs are reached by 2030. India ranked 116 out of 157 countries n the Sustainable Development Goal Index, 2017. India has a long way to go in ensuring equitable development across all areas as mentioned in the SDGs.

The Ministry of Statistics and Programme Implementation has developed the National Indicators Framework (NIF) to monitor the progress towards achieving SDGs. NIF consists of 306 statistical indicators to measure all the programmes and their efficacy towards various sub-targets under the SDGs.

The Indian government's various welfare policies and targeted programmes are connected to the 17 SDGs and their sub-targets:

- **Goal 1:** End poverty in all its forms everywhere.
- **Goal 2:** End hunger, achieve food security and improved nutrition and promote sustainable agriculture.
- **Goal 3:** Ensure healthy lives and promote well-being for all at all ages.
- **Goal 4:** Ensure inclusive and equitable quality education and promote lifelong learning opportunities for all.
- **Goal 5:** Achieve gender equality and empower all women and girls.
- **Goal 6:** Ensure availability and sustainable management of water and sanitation for all.
- **Goal 7:** Ensure access to affordable, reliable, sustainable and modern energy for all.
- **Goal 8:** Promote sustained, inclusive and sustainable economic growth, full and productive employment and decent work for all.
- **Goal 9:** Build resilient infrastructure, promote inclusive and sustainable industrialization and foster innovation.
- **Goal 10:** Reduce inequality within and among countries.
- **Goal 11:** Make cities and human settlements inclusive, safe, resilient and sustainable.
- **Goal 12:** Ensure sustainable consumption and production patterns.
- **Goal 13:** Take urgent action to combat climate change and its impacts.
- **Goal 14:** Conserve and sustainably use the oceans, seas and marine resources for sustainable development.
- **Goal 15:** Protect, restore and promote sustainable use of terrestrial ecosystems, sustainably manage forests, combat desertification, and halt and reverse land degradation and halt biodiversity loss.
- **Goal 16:** Promote peaceful and inclusive societies for sustainable development, provide access to justice for all and build effective, accountable and inclusive institutions at all levels.
- **Goal 17:** Strengthen the means of implementation and revitalize the global partnership for sustainable development.

Some of the important government policies that are geared towards achieving one or many of the SDGs are as follows:

National Rural Livelihood Mission (NRLM)

- Launched in 2011 by the Ministry of Rural Development and partly supported by World Bank funding.
- To reduce poverty and enable poor households to access self-employment and skilled wage employment programmes.
- Increasing household incomes through livelihood enhancements and access to financial and public services.
- Organization of self-help groups and strong community-based approach to generate sustainable employment and wealth-creation.
- SHGs of 10-20 women in local communities form the primary building block of NRLM. NRLM also promotes SHGs with exclusively women memberships.
- Particular focus on women-headed households, single-women, women victims of trafficking, etc.

National Urban Livelihood Mission (NULM)

- Launched in 2013 by Ministry of Housing and Urban Poverty Alleviation.
- Replaced the earlier Swarna Jayanti Sahari Rozgar Yojana.
- To create opportunities for skill-development and self-employment among the urban poor.
- Provides access to credit services and livelihood opportunities including essential services to urban homeless.
- Encourages urban women through formation of SHGs.

Mahatma Gandhi National Rural Employment Guarantee Scheme (MGNREGA)

- Launched in 2005 through the enactment of National Rural Employment Guarantee Act, 2005.
- Entitles every rural household to a minimum of 100 days of paid work at statutory minimum wage.

- To eradicate rural property and enhance livelihood security of the rural poor.
- To strengthen national resource management and address chronic poverty, drought, watershed management, etc.
- Equal wages for men and women; recommends one-third of beneficiaries to be women.

National Social Assistance Programme

- Launched in the year 1995 by the Ministry of Rural Development.
- Provides financial assistance in the form of social pensions to elderly, widows and persons with disabilities.
- Includes three components: National Old Age Pension Scheme, National Family Benefit Scheme, Indira Gandhi National Widows Pension Scheme, Indira Gandhi National Disabilities Pension Scheme and Annapurna Scheme.

National Mission for Sustainable Agriculture

- Launched in the year 2015 by Ministry of Agriculture.
- To promote modern and improved agronomic practices.
- Emphasis on soil health management, improving water use efficiency, crop diversification, etc.
- Promotes integrates approaches such as crop-sericulture, agro-forestry, environment-friendly technologies, fish farming, dryland agriculture, etc.

Rashtriya Krishi Vikas Yojana (RKVY)

- Launched in the year 2007.
- For holistic development of agriculture and allied sectors.
- Interventions to reduce crop failures and yield gaps.
- Focus on comprehensive agriculture development plans to suit local needs and conditions.

National Nutrition Mission (POSHAN Abhiyan)

- Launched in the year 2018 by Ministry of Women and Child Development.
- To improve the nutritional status of children, pregnant women, and lactating mothers.
- To reduce stunting, under-nutrition, anemia and low-birth weight in babies.
- Triple-A approach – building the capacity of ASHA, Anganwadi workers and Auxiliary Nurse Midwives (ANM).
- Use of ICT mission to improve information dissemination, community awareness, real-time monitoring, etc.

National Food Security Mission

- Launched in the year 2007 by the Ministry of Agriculture.
- To improve the production of food grains, fruits, meat and fish production in the country.
- Provision for cluster demonstration, seed distribution, and farm machinery, subsidized the distribution of micro-nutrients and soil ameliorants and encouraging local initiatives.
- Focus on restoration of soil fertility, production of high yielding seed varieties, resource conservation technologies and improving farmer's agricultural profit.

National Food Security Act (Rights to Food Act)

- Enacted in 2013
- To provide for food and nutritional securityto all through Targeted Public Distribution System.
- Provides subsidized food grains up to 75% of the rural population and 50% of the urban population.
- Pregnant women and lactating mothers are entitled to nutritious take-home rations of 600 Calories and 18-20 grams of protein.

Mid-day Meal Scheme (National Programme on Nutrition Support to Primary Education)

- Launched in the year 1995 by the Ministry of Human Resource Development.
- To improve the nutritional status of children.
- To enhance attendance and retention of children from the poor socio-economic background in schools.
- Every government and government-aided school to serve freshly prepared mid-day meal for children.

National Health Mission

- Launched in 2005 by the Ministry of Health and Family Welfare.
- Two sub missions – National Rural Health Mission (NRHM) and the National Urban Health Mission (NURM).
- To strengthen health systems in rural and urban areas, improve reproductive-maternal-neonatal-child and adolescent health, develop strategies to deal with communicable and non-communicable diseases.

- To provide universal access to equitable, affordable and quality healthcare.
- Focus on free essential drug deliveries, comprehensive primary healthcare, mainstreaming of AYUSH, free diagnostic initiatives, newborn and maternal care, improving nutrition and public health.
- NRHM lays special emphasis on vulnerable groups, Empowered Action Group (EAG) states and north-eastern states, women and children.

Integrated Child Development Service (ICDS)

- Launched in 1975 by Ministry of Women and Child Development.
- To provide food, preschool education, primary healthcare, immunization, and growth monitoring services to children under six years of age.
- It lays the foundation for proper physiological, social and psychological development of children.
- To reduce malnutrition, morbidity and school dropout of children.
- To enhance maternal education and capacity on childcare and nutritional knowledge.
- Anganwadis at local communities to be managed by local female Anganwadi workers, with specialized training in child education, immunization and environmental hygiene.
- Complementary nutrition for pregnant women and lactating mothers to reduce malnutrition.

Pradhan Mantri Swasthya Suraksha Yojana

- Launched in 2006 by the Ministry of Health and Family Welfare.
- To correct regional imbalances in reliable and affordable tertiary healthcare services and infrastructure.
- To augment facilities of quality medical education.
- Two components: setting up of new All India Institute for Medical Sciences and Upgradation of government medical colleges.

Sarva Shiksha Abhiyan

- Launched in 2001
- To achieve universalization of elementary education through community-owned quality education.
- Promotes social justice by focusing on education for weaker sections of the society.
- Provides elementary education for all children between 6-14 years of age.
- To bridge the gender gap in school enrollment and attendance.

National Mission for Empowerment of Women

- Launched in 2010
- For holistic empowerment of women through gender mainstreaming, institutional arrangements and advocacy activities.
- To eliminate violence against women.
- To strengthen inter-sectoral convergence and process coordination of women welfare and development programmes and activities.
- Focus areas are girls' primary education, higher and professional education for women, skill development, vocational training and gender sensitization.

Rajiv Gandhi Scheme for Empowerment of Adolescent Girls (SABLA)

- Launched in 2011 of the Ministry of Women and Child Development.
- Replaced the earlier Krishi Vikas Yojana (2007).
- To provide nutritional supplements and increase awareness on health, nutrition, reproductive and sexual health of adolescent girls.
- Also offers vocational training for out of school girls to ensure economic empowerment.

Sukanya Samriddhi Yojana (SSY)

- Launched in 2015
- A part of "Beti Bachao Beti Padhao" campaign.
- A small deposit scheme for girl child.
- Provides income tax benefit to accounts opened under this scheme.
- Sukanya Samridhi account for a girl can be opened at any time after the birth of the girl child before she turns 10.
- The account's savings can be used to meet the girl's educational expenses.

Support for Training and Employment Programme for Women (STEP)

- Launched in 1987
- To provide skill development and training programme for women to improve their employability.
- To provide competency and skill training to encourage entrepreneurship and self-employment among women.

- Focus sectors include agriculture, horticulture, food processing, handlooms, computer, IT services, tourism and hospitality management, etc.
- Emphasis on marginalized and assetless women, urban poor, female-headed households, tribal and other dispossessed groups of women.

Janani Suraksha Yojana (JSY)

- Launched in 2005
- A safe motherhood intervention programme under NRHM.
- To reduce maternal and neonatal mortality by encouraging institutional deliveries.
- Accredited Social Health Activists (ASHA) to play an essential link between poor women and the government in the delivery of essential health services.
- ASHAs identify pregnant women, pay periodical visits, provide health care advice, counsel for institutional delivery and ensure at least three antenatal checkups.

Gender Budgeting Scheme

- Launched in 2008
- To achieve gender mainstreaming and gender perspective in policy formulation, resource allocation, and implementation.
- To ensure financial outlays and policy commitments have gender perspectives.
- Specially targeted expenditure for women and girls and pro-women allocations.

Parliamentary Committee on Empowerment of Women

- Formed in 1997
- A permanent committee of thirty members – twenty from Lok Sabha and ten from Rajya Sabha.
- To review and monitor measures taken by the government towards ensuring women's equality.
- Also reviews reports of the National Commission for Women.
- Evaluates welfare programmes for women and takes into consideration women's issues and concerns.

National Policy on Empowerment of Women

- Adopted in 2001
- Influenced by the National Perspective Plan for Women (1988-2000).
- To eliminate all forms of violence against women and girl children.
- To ensure strict enforcement and enable effective grievance redressal mechanisms; To prevent sexual harassment at work for women in unorganized and organized sectors; Creation of women cells in police stations, family courts, counseling centers, etc.
- Affirmative economic and social policies for the full development of women.
- To provide equal access to social and political participation and decision making for women.
- To ensure equal access to health care, quality education, employment, social security.
- To change societal attitudes and community practices that are gender discriminatory.

Multiple Choice Questions

1. Which programme has given the slogan of Garibi Hatao?

A. 4th five year plan　B. 3rd five year plan
C. 5th five year plan　D. 6th five year plan

2. Which of the following Union Territories has the lowest sex ratio in 2011 census?

A. Daman and Diu
B. Andaman and Nicobar
C. Chandigarh
D. Dadra and Nagar Haveli

3. The Integrated Child Protection Scheme was launched in which year?

A. 2009-2010　B. 2011-2012
C. 2013-2014　D. 2015-2016

4. Who was the first woman Speaker of Lok Sabha?

A. Smt. Sumitra Mahajan
B. Smt. Mamta Banejree
C. Smt. Mohsina Kidwai
D. Smt. Meira Kumar

5. Who among the following is a member of the 18th Politbureau of the CPI(M)?

A. Suhasani Ali　B. Brinda Karat
C. Amarjit Kaur　D. None of these

6. Match List-I and List-II:

List-I	List-II
(a) National Policy on Older Persons	(i) 2001
(b) National Policy on Empowerment of Women	(ii) 2000
(c) National Agricultural Policy	(iii) 1986
(d) National Policy on Education	(iv) 1999

Codes:

	(a)	(b)	(c)	(d)
A.	(iii)	(iv)	(i)	(ii)
B.	(iv)	(i)	(ii)	(iii)
C.	(iv)	(ii)	(i)	(iii)
D.	(ii)	(i)	(iv)	(iii)

7. Match the following traditional practices in their place of occurrence:

(a) Female Genital Mutilation	(i) Pakistan
(b) Sati	(ii) China
(c) Honour Killings	(iii) India
(d) Foot Binding	(iv) Africa

Codes:

	(a)	(b)	(c)	(d)
A.	(iv)	(iii)	(i)	(ii)
B.	(iii)	(ii)	(i)	(iv)
C.	(ii)	(iv)	(iii)	(i)
D.	(i)	(iii)	(ii)	(iv)

8. Name the woman who first unfurled the flag of Indian freedom in 1907 in Stuttgart:

A. Bikaji Cama B. Kamla Nehru
C. Annie Besant D. Aruna Asaf Ali

9. The Government of India introduced the Right to Education on:

A. 15th August 1947 B. 26th January 1950
C. 8th March 2014 D. 1st April 2010

10. Janbhagidari Scheme is provided by which of the following State?

A. Uttar Pradesh B. Madhya Pradesh
C. Kerala D. Bihar

11. Match the place with the respective movements:

Movement	*Place*
(a) Seneca Falls Convention	(i) Kenya
(b) Suffrage Movement	(ii) Nigeria
(c) Women's War	(iii) England
(d) Green Belt Movement	(iv) New York

Codes:

	(a)	(b)	(c)	(d)
A.	(i)	(ii)	(iii)	(iv)
B.	(ii)	(iii)	(iv)	(i)
C.	(iii)	(iv)	(i)	(ii)
D.	(iv)	(iii)	(ii)	(i)

12. The first Indian woman to enter into active politics but could not live to see India attain freedom was:

A. Vijayalakshmi Pandit
B. Sarojini Naidu
C. Saraladevi Choudharani
D. Abala Bose

13. "The women of India have an additional task i.e., to free themselves from the tyranny of man-made customs and laws"—whose words are these?

A. Raja Ram Mohan Roy
B. Mahatma Gandhi
C. Jawaharlal Nehru
D. E.V.R. Periyar

14. Arrange the areas of women development which the Planning Commission perceives in priority:

A. Health, Social welfare, Employment
B. Education, Social welfare, Health
C. Employment, Health, Education
D. Social welfare, Employment, Education

15. Arrange the Women Development approaches on the basis of their order:

(1) Welfare
(2) Equity
(3) Anti-poverty
(4) Empowerment

Codes:

A. (4), (3), (2), (1) B. (3), (2), (1), (4)
C. (2), (1), (4), (3) D. (1), (2), (3), (4)

16. Match the operational strategy of women development according to plan periods:

Plan Period	*Strategy*
(a) 6th Plan	(i) Shift from welfare to development
(b) 7th Plan	(ii) Beneficiary-oriented Schemes
(c) 8th Plan	(iii) Human Development Focus
(d) 9th Plan	(iv) Empowerment through convergence of services

Codes:

	(a)	(b	(c)	(d)
A.	(ii)	(iv)	(i)	(iii)
B.	(iii)	(ii)	(iv)	(i)
C.	(iv)	(iii)	(ii)	(i)
D.	(i)	(ii)	(iii)	(iv)

17. Match the goals of women development approaches:

Approach	***Goal***
(a) Welfare	(i) Greater self-reliance of women
(b) Equity	(ii) Increasing productivity of poor women
(c) Anti-poverty	(iii) Women as active participants in development process
(d) Empowerment	(iv) Enabling women to be better mothers

Codes:

	(a)	(b)	(c)	(d)
A.	(iii)	(i)	(iv)	(ii)
B.	(ii)	(iii)	(i)	(iv)
C.	(iv)	(iii)	(ii)	(i)
D.	(iii)	(ii)	(i)	(iv)

18. Mahatma Gandhi National Rural Employment Guarantee Scheme (MGNREGA) was launched in the year:

A. 2000
B. 2005
C. 2010
D. 2015

19. The decade for the Girl Child declared by SAARC was:

A. 1971-1980
B. 2001-2010
C. 1991-2000
D. 1981-1990

20. Which country gave women the right to vote first?

A. USA
B. Switzerland
C. New Zealand
D. Australia

21. Who, among the following, has not been a Chief Minister of a State in India?

A. Sheela Dikshit
B. Jayalalitha
C. Margaret Alwa
D. Vasundhara Raje Scindhia

22. Name the programme for adolescent girls:

A. ICDS
B. Indira Awas Yojana
C. Mahila Samakhya
D. Kishori Shakthi Yojana

23. Thirty percent of funds/benefits earmarked in all women related sectors is the strategy of:

A. Women's Empowerment Plan
B. Women's Reservation Plan
C. Women's Development Plan
D. Women's Component Plan

24. National Rural Livelihood Mission (NRLM) is partly supported by the funding from:

A. United Nations
B. World Bank
C. World Health Organizations
D. Private Moneylenders

25. 'Women's Component Plan' was initiated in which five year plan?

A. 6th five year plan
B. 7th five year plan
C. 5th five year plan
D. 9th five year plan

26. What are the key issues to be taken through monitoring and social/community credit for girls child development?

1. Prevention of female foeticide/infanticide.
2. Health and nutrition.
3. Education for the girl child.
4. Abolition of child marriage, exploitation and violence.

Codes:

A. 1, 2 and 3 only
B. 1 only
C. 3 and 4 only
D. 1, 2, 3 and 4

27. An NGO seeking foreign funding must be registered under:

(i) Registration under Companies Act 1956.
(ii) Registration under Societies Registration Act 1860.
(iii) Foreign Contribution Regulation Act.
(iv) Registration under Central Social Welfare Board.

Codes:

A. (i) and (ii) only
B. (i), (ii) and (iii) only
C. (iii) only
D. (i) and (iv) only

28. Match the paradigm shifts in planning for women's advancement through Five Year Plans:

List-I (Plan Period)	***List-II (Paradigm Shifts)***
(a) 6th Plan	(i) Beneficiary oriented programme
(b) 7th Plan	(ii) Women and Development
(c) 8th Plan	(iii) From development to empowerment
(d) 11th Plan	(iv) Gender empowerment and gender equity

Codes:

	(a)	(b)	(c)	(d)
A.	(ii)	(iii)	(iv)	(i)
B.	(ii)	(i)	(iii)	(iv)
C.	(i)	(iii)	(ii)	(iv)
D.	(iv)	(iii)	(i)	(ii)

29. Arrange the chronological sequence of the following Programmes and Acts related to children on the basis of the year.

1. Child Labour Prohibition and Regulation Act.
2. Integrated Child Development Services.
3. Sarva Shiksha Abhiyan.
4. Commission for Protection of Child Rights Act.

Codes:

A. 4, 2 1 and 3 B. 2, 1, 3 and 4
C. 2, 3, 1 and 4 D. 3, 2, 1 and 4

30. Match the following from List -I with List II regarding the programmes offered for the development of higher education in India:

List-I (Fellowships)	***List-II (Target Group)***
(a) Post Graduate Indira Gandhi Scholarship	(i) Minority students
(b) Maulana Abdul Kalam Azad National Fellowship	(ii) Single girls child
(c) UGC Fellowships	(iii) SC/ST students
(d) Rajiv Gandhi National Fellowships	(iv) Students with Disabilities

Codes:

	(a)	(b)	(c)	(d)
A.	(i)	(ii)	(iii)	(iv)
B.	(ii)	(i)	(iv)	(iii)
C.	(iv)	(iii)	(i)	(ii)
D.	(iii)	(ii)	(iv)	(i)

31. Mark the correct statement about the operation of women helpline 1090:

(i) Only girls can utilizé this service.
(ii) The callers complaint and phone number is jotted down by women operator.
(iii) The number is forwarded to male constable (i.e. Counsellor).
(iv) The victim's name is kept a secret.

Codes:

A. (i), (ii) and (iv) B. (ii), (iii) and (iv)
C. (i) and (iv) D. (i), (ii), (iii) and (iv)

32. Which of the following are not correct regarding the parliamentary committee on the empowerment of women?

(i) The Committee is chaired by the Prime Minister of India.
(ii) The members are appointed by the President of India.
(iii) It has equal number of members from both the Houses of Parliament.
(iv) It has members in the ratio of 2 : 1 from Lok Sabha and Rajya Sabha.

Codes:

A. (i) and (iv) B. (iv) only
C. (ii) and (iii) D. (i), (ii) and (iii)

33. Identify the programme which does not aim at the development of girls child:

A. Balika Samriddhi Yojna
B. Kishor Balika Scheme
C. Mahila Samakhya
D. Sarva Shiksha Abhiyan

34. In which of Five Year Plan education is treated as the 'most critical investment on human development'?

A. Seventh Five Year Plan
B. Eighth Five Year Plan
C. Ninth Five Year Plan
D. Tenth Five Year Plan

35. The Constitution (Amendment) Bill passed by Rajya Sabha provides for reservation for women in Parliament and State Assemblies is:

A. 81st Amendment Bill
B. 103rd Amendment Bill
C. 108th Amendment Bill
D. 111th Amendment Bill

36. First woman to become Deputy Chairperson of Rajya Sabha:

A. Margret Alva
B. Najma Heptullah
C. Violet Alva
D. Renuka Chaudhary

37. ______ deals with the socio-economic development and empowerment of women through self-help groups.

A. Short Stay Home
B. Family Counseling Centres
C. Swayamsidha
D. Rehabilitation Centres

38. What is the title of the Act prohibiting sexual offences against children in India?

A. Protection of Children from Sexual Offences Act, 2012
B. Prevention of Sexual Offences against Children Act, 2012
C. Prevention and Redressal in Sexual Offences against Children Act, 2012
D. Prohibition of Sexual Offences against Children Act, 2012

39. Match List of Five Year Plans and their Strategies:

List-I ***(Five Year Plans)***	***List-II*** ***(Strategies)***
(a) Eighth Plan	(i) Shift from development to empowerment
(b) Ninth Plan	(ii) Development of National Policy for the empowerment of women
(c) Tenth Plan	(iii) Special targeted intervention to the differential needs of women and girl children
(d) Eleventh Plan	(iv) People participation in planning and implementation of programmes

Codes:

	(a)	(b)	(c)	(d)
A.	(i)	(iv)	(ii)	(iii)
B.	(i)	(ii)	(iv)	(iii)
C.	(ii)	(iii)	(i)	(iv)
D.	(iv)	(iii)	(i)	(ii)

40. The 72nd and 73rd Amendment Acts have provided 33% reservations of seats for ______ in the local bodies.

A. Teachers
B. Women
C. Children
D. Men

41. Match the items in List-I with List-II:

List-I ***(Programme/Scheme)***	***List-II*** ***(Year)***
(a) National Programme for Education of Girls at the Elementary Level (NPEGEL)	(i) 2003
(b) Kasturba Gandhi Balika Vidyalayas (KGBV)	(ii) 2001
(c) Sarv Shiksha Abhiyan	(iii) 2009
(d) Madhyamik Shiksha Abhiyan (MSA)	(iv) 2004

Codes:

	(a)	(b)	(c)	(d)
A.	(i)	(iv)	(ii)	(iii)
B.	(iii)	(iv)	(i)	(ii)
C.	(i)	(iii)	(ii)	(iv)
D.	(iv)	(ii)	(i)	(iii)

42. A Working Group on "Women's Agency and Empowerment" was constituted under which Five Year Plan?

A. Sixth Five Year Plan
B. Twelfth Five Year Plan
C. Ninth Five Year Plan
D. Tenth Five Year Plan

43. Development was first identified as a process of expanding freedoms equally for all people by:

A. Heidi Hartmann
B. Martha Nussbaum
C. Amartya Sen
D. Casandra Balchin

44. What is the name of the scheme which was launched by the Ministry of Women and Child Development in 2007 to combat trafficking and is implemented mainly through NGOs? The scheme has five components - Prevention, Rescue, Rehabilitation, Re-Integration and Repatriation of trafficked victims for commercial sexual exploitation.

A. Ujjawala
B. SABLA
C. Swadhar
D. Swa-shakti

45. Which of the following is not correct with WID Approach?

(a) Integrate women into existing structure
(b) Focus on gender relations
(c) Focus mainly on women in isolation
(d) People centered development

Codes:

A. (a) and (b) only
B. (a), (b) and (c) only
C. (a) and (c) only
D. (b) and (d) only

46. Exchanges, connections and practices across borders, thus transcending the national space as the primary reference point for activities and identities is known as:

A. Transnationalism
B. Trans internationalism
C. Multi transnationalism
D. Gender transnationalism

47. The Harvard WID Framework had the subsections

(a) An activity profile
(b) An access and control profile
(c) Factors influencing activities, access and control
(d) Community profile

Codes:

A. (a) and (b) only
B. (c) and (d) only
C. (a), (b) and (c) only
D. (a), (b), (c) and (d) only

48. Which of the following Awards is instituted by the Government of India to honour the individuals who make outstanding contribution towards services for children?

A. Rajiv Gandhi Manav Seva Award
B. National Child Award for Exceptional Achievement
C. National Award for Child Welfare
D. Indira Gandhi Manav Seva Award

49. 'Track CHILD' Portal has been designed and developed under the Ministry of Women and Child Development in accordance with the guidelines provided in the:
(a) Juvenile Justice (Care and Protection of Children) Act 2000.
(b) Model Rules 2007 of Integrated Child Protection Scheme.
(c) Integrated Child Development Scheme.
(d) Central Adoption Resource Authority Guidelines.

Codes:
A. (a) and (b) only   B. (c) and (d) only
C. (a), (b) and (c) only   D. (b) and (c) only

50. Reservation for women in urban local governance was introduced by which Constitutional Amendment?
A. 72nd   B. 73rd
C. 74th   D. 86th

51. In which Five Year Plan was a separate chapter on Women and Development introduced for the first time:
A. Second   B. Fourth
C. Sixth   D. Ninth

52. The SAARC Decade for the Girl Child was:
A. 1961-70   B. 1991-2000
C. 1971-80   D. 1975-85

53. The document on "National Perspective Plan for Women" was prepared for:
A. 1988-2000   B. 2000-2010
C. 1990-2000   D. 1979-1998

54. The main objective of 'National Policy for Empowerment of Women' is:
A. Advancement, Development and Empowerment
B. Empowerment and Development
C. Peace and Development
D. Welfare and Equity

55. Women leaders are important because:
(i) Women have unique strengths
(ii) Women can participate in decision making
(iii) To bring a focus on gender issues
(iv) To get more international funding

Codes:
A. (i), (ii) and (iv) are true
B. (i), (ii) are true
C. (ii), (iii) and (iv) are true
D. (i), (ii) and (iii) are true

56. In which one of the following countries, did women get the right to vote only in 1971:
A. Australia   B. New Zealand
C. Switzerland   D. Mexico

57. Mission Indradhanush is related to?
A. Children Safety   B. Child Vaccination
C. E-Commerce   D. None of the above

58. Arrange the women development approaches on the basis of their order:
A. Welfare, Development, Empowerment and Participation
B. Development, Welfare, Empowerment and Participation
C. Empowerment, Development, Participation Welfare
D. Participation, Welfare, Development and Empowerment

59. In the Women in Development (WID) approach women were considered as:
A. Beneficiaries
B. Leaders
C. Agents of Development
D. Change Agents

60. Reservation for Women in Parliament Bill has been passed under:
A. Rajya Sabha and Lok Sabha
B. Lok Sabha only
C. State Assemblies and Rajya Sabha
D. Rajya Sabha only

61. How many women members were there in Rajya Sabha in 2018?
A. 36   B. 32
C. 28   D. 22

62. Given below are the women leaders of their respective countries. Match List-I with List-II:

List-I	***List-II***
(a) Julia Gillard	(i) Kosovo
(b) Atifete Jahjaga	(ii) Australia
(c) Pratibha Patil	(iii) Switzerland
(d) Micheline Calmy Rey	(iv) India

Codes:

	(a)	(b)	(c)	(d)
A.	(ii)	(i)	(iv)	(iii)
B.	(i)	(iv)	(iii)	(ii)
C.	(iv)	(iii)	(i)	(ii)
D.	(iii)	(ii)	(i)	(iv)

63. The Rashtriya Mahila Kosh is:
1. A registered society.
2. It gives access to resources to women.
3. It utilizes NGOs for delivery of credit support.
4. It supports the formation of women's self-help groups.

Mark out the correct answer from the codes give below.

Codes:

A. 2 and 4 B. 1, 2, 3, 4
C. 1 and 2 D. 2, 3 and 4

64. Which one of the following pair is not correctly matched?

A. Kishori Shakti Yojana – National Programme for Adolescent Girls
B. AYUSH – Programme to revitalize local Health Traditions
C. SWADHAR – Programme for women in difficult circumstances
D. Janani Suraksha Yojana – Programme for disabled mothers

65. Match the following from List-I and List-II:

List-I ***(Name of the Leaders)***	***List-II*** ***(Name of the Country)***
(a) Sirimavo Bandaranaike	(i) Pakistan
(b) Margaret Thatcher	(ii) Sri Lanka
(c) Benazir Bhutto	(iii) Ireland
(d) Mary Robinson	(iv) Britain

Codes:

	(a)	(b)	(c)	(d)
A.	(iv)	(iii)	(i)	(ii)
B.	(ii)	(iii)	(iv)	(i)
C.	(iv)	(i)	(ii)	(iii)
D.	(ii)	(iv)	(i)	(iii)

66. National Commission for Child Rights was established in the year:

A. 1993 B. 2003
C. 2001 D. 2005

67. What is the recent Constitutional Amendment in 2009 that enhances 50 percent women's reservation in local bodies?

A. 73rd Constitutional Amendment
B. 112th Constitutional Amendment
C. 74th Constitutional Amendment
D. 87th Constitutional Amendment

68. What was India's rank in the world with regard to women's participation in politics in 2017 according to the data released by the Inter-Parliamentary Union?

A. 144th place B. 150th place
C. 148th place D. 188th place

69. The movement for women's rights in India was initiated in:

A. 1917 B. 1879
C. 1949 D. 1990

70. Match List-I with List-II as given below:

List-I ***(Five Year Plan)***	***List-II*** ***(Issues for Women)***
(a) The Sixth Plan	(i) Empowerment of women
(b) The Seventh Plan	(ii) Need for population control and women specific programmes
(c) The Eighth Plan	(iii) Gainful employment to women and youth
(d) The Ninth Plan	(iv) Women and Development

Mark the correct answer from the codes given below:

Codes:

	(a)	(b)	(c)	(d)
A.	(iii)	(iv)	(ii)	(i)
B.	(iv)	(iii)	(ii)	(i)
C.	(iv)	(ii)	(iii)	(i)
D.	(iii)	(ii)	(i)	(iv)

71. The Registration of NGOs can be made under the following Acts:
1. Societies Registration Act-1860.
2. The Indian Trust Act-1882.
3. Companies Act-1956.
4. Civil Societies Act-1890.

Codes:

A. 1, 2 and 4 only
B. 1, 2 and 3 only
C. 1 and 4 only
D. 2 and 3 only

72. The Kudumbashree program by the Kerala government works in the area of:
1. educing maternal mortality
2. providing micro credit
3. enhancing entrepreneurship
4. providing housing

Codes:

A. 1 and 2 only B. 2 and 3 only
C. 1, 3 and 4 only D. 1, 2, and 4 only

73. What among the following is not the important leadership trait?
A. Intelligence
B. Self-confidence and determination
C. Integrity and sociability
D. Selfish and self-oriented

74. What are the major goals of the National Plan of Action for the SAARC decade of the Girls Child (1991-2000)?
A. Development, Prosperity and Peace
B. Survival, Protection and Development
C. Sustainability, Protection and Peace
D. Survival, Empowerment and Justice

75. Which of the following is not a goal of the Eleventh Five Year Plan?
A. Organisation of Mahila Mandals
B. Gender Empowerment and Equity
C. Gender Budgeting
D. Gender Mainstreaming

76. What is the objective of 11th Five Year Plan of India?
A. Gender Equality
B. Women Empowerment
C. Inclusive Growth
D. Education Development

77. Match List-I with List-II as given below:

List-I ***(Five Year Plan)***	***List-II*** ***(Issues for Women)***
(a) The Eighth Plan	(i) Empowerment of Women
(b) The Ninth Plan	(ii) Shift from "development" to "Empowerment"
(c) The Tenth Plan	(iii) Gender equality goals.
(d) The Eleventh Plan	(iv) Use of gender budget and gender mainstreaming process

Codes:

	(a)	(b)	(c)	(d)
A.	(ii)	(i)	(iii)	(iv)
B.	(iv)	(ii)	(iii)	(i)
C.	(iii)	(i)	(ii)	(iv)
D.	(iv)	(iii)	(ii)	(i)

78. The recently introduced bill in the Lok Sabha which intends to provide for the gender specific needs of women farmers is known as:
A. Women Farmers Bill 2012
B. Women Entitlement Bill 2012
C. Women Farmers Entitlement Bill 2012
D. Women Farmers Bill 2011

79. Among the following terms, which is not closely associated with violence?
A. Battering
B. Adultery
C. Harassment
D. Abuse

80. Which of the following conferences identified that "Women have a vital role in Environment Management"?
A. Beijing conference
B. Rio-de Janeiro conference
C. Cairo conference
D. Mexico conference

81. Expand the correct acronym of 'DAWN'.
A. Development Association with Women for a New Employment.
B. Department of Alternatives with Women for a New Era.
C. Development Alternatives with Women for a New Era.
D. Development Association with Women for a New Era.

82. Which of the following schemes has an impact on women empowerment?
1. CDS
2. ASIDE
3. Swadhar
4. Ujjawala

Select the correct answer using the codes given below:

Codes:
A. 1, 2 and 3 only
B. 1, 3 and 4 only
C. 2, 3 and 4 only
D. 1, 2, 3 and 4

83. The NGOs for receiving Foreign Contribution have to get registered under which Act?
A. Foreign Registration Act.
B. Foreign Contribution Registration Act.
C. Foreign Regulation Act.
D. Foreign Contribution Regulation Act.

84. Gender Empowerment Measure (GEM) is calculated on the basis of the following indicators:
1. Women's Employment
2. Seat in Parliament
3. Reproductive Health
4. Share of Household income

Codes:
A. 1 and 4 only
B. 1, 2, 3 and 4 only
C. 3 and 4 only
D. 1, 2 and 4 only

85. Arrange the sequence of levels involved in the process of empowerment.
A. Decision-making, accessibility to Resources, Availability of Resources and Awareness Creation.

B. Accessibility to Resources, Availability of Resources, Awareness creation and Decision-making.
C. Availability of Resources, Awareness of creation, Decision-making and Accessibility to Resources.
D. Awareness Creation, Availability of Resources, Accessibility to Resources and Decision-making.

86. Mark the correct answer about the funding organizations to the NGOs.

1. CAPART   2. NABARD
3. SEWA   4. NIPCCD

Codes:

A. 1, 2 and 4   B. 1, 2, 3, 4
C. 1, 2, 3 only   D. 3 and 4 only

87. Which five-year plan gives joint titles for the ownership of land to both spouses in India?

A. Sixth Five Year Plan
B. Seventh Five Year Plan
C. Eighth Five Year Plan
D. Eleventh Five Year Plan

88. The Women's questions arose in modern India as part of the nineteenth century social reform movements were:

(i) Grass root women's involvement in the movement.
(ii) The concerns and conflicts of the emerging Hindu middle class women.
(iii) Influence of western ideas prevalent in the 19th Century.
(iv) Influence of self help group of women in the movement.

Codes:

A. (i), (ii) and (iii) only
B. (i) and (ii) only
C. (ii) and (iii) only
D. (i), (ii), (iii) and (iv)

89. Which one of the following is incorrect about the basic characteristics of a successful leader?

A. Risk Taking   B. Innovation
C. Team Building   D. Dominating others

90. Which of the following Central Government Schemes initiated for the Empowerment of Adolescent Girls in the year 2011?

A. Sabla   B. Kishoree Yojana
C. Swadhar   D. MGNREGA

91. Write the sequence of the following programmes for women development.

1. Indira Gandhi Matritva Sahayog Yojana.
2. Gender Budgeting Scheme.
3. Swadhar (Homes for women in difficult circumstances).
4. Rashtriya Madhyamik Shiksha Abhiyan.

Codes:

A. 1, 2, 3, 4   B. 3, 2, 4, 1
C. 2, 3, 4, 1   D. 4, 2, 3, 1

92. Which of the following states has initiated for the first time the Sub-Plan for SCs & STs development?

A. Uttar Pradesh   B. Himachal Pradesh
C. Bihar   D. Andhra Pradesh

93. Identify which one is the incorrect 'Strategic-need' for the development of women:

A. Food, health care, water supply
B. Distribution of property/lands
C. Increasing women's wages
D. Rights to own and control property

94. Name the scheme from which the NGOs can get the assistance for prevention of trafficking and rehabilitation of victim?

A. Ujjwala
B. Rashtriya Mahila Kosh
C. CAPART
D. NABARD

95. Women leaders are important, because:

(i) Women have unique strengths.
(ii) Women can participate in decision-making.
(iii) To bring focus on gender issues.
(iv) To get more international funding.

Codes:

A. (i), (ii) and (iv)   B. (i) and (ii) only
C. (ii), (iii) and (iv) only   D. (i), (ii) and (iii) only

96. Which of the following pairs is not correctly matched?

A. First Women Minister of Indian Railway – Mamta Banerjee
B. First Women Supreme Court Judge – Fatima Beevi
C. First Indian Women President of Indian National Congress – Sarojini Naidu
D. First Women Chief Minister – Mayawati

97. Empowerment includes the following capabilities:

(i) Ability to make personal decisions
(ii) Ability to access information
(iii) Ability to dominate patriarchal powers
(iv) Ability to learn and access skills

Codes:

A. (i), (ii), (iii), (iv) are true
B. (i), (ii) and (iii) are true
C. (i) and (ii) are true
D. (i), (ii) and (iv) are true

98. Gender disaggregated data is the basis for:
(i) Formulation of Gender Sensitive Policy
(ii) Formulation of Gender Statistics
(iii) Formulation of Census Data
(iv) Formulation of Data Bank

Codes:

A. (i) and (iii) are true B. (i) and (ii) are true
C. (iii) and (iv) are true D. (iii) only true

99. The policy approach that includes modalities of reflecting ways in which men and women constrains or advance efforts to boost growth is known as:
A. Women and Development
B. Women in Development
C. Gender and Development
D. Gender and Empowerment

100. The women in development approach was greatly influenced by:
A. Amartya Sen
B. Fredrick Engels
C. Karl Marx
D. Ester Boserup

101. Match the women candidates in the 16th Lok Sabha Elections from List-I with their political parties in List-II:

List-I	***List-II***
(a) Kanchan Choudhary Bhattacharya	(i) YSRCP
(b) Jayaprada	(ii) NCP
(c) Supriya Sule	(iii) AAP
(d) Vijay Lakshmi	(iv) Rashtriya Lok Dal

Codes:

	(a)	(b)	(c)	(d)
A.	(ii)	(iii)	(iv)	(i)
B.	(iii)	(iv)	(ii)	(i)
C.	(i)	(iv)	(iii)	(ii)
D.	(iv)	(i)	(iii)	(ii)

102. The theme of the approach paper of the Eleventh Five Year Plan was:
A. Indicative Planning
B. Growth with Social Justice
C. Towards faster and more inclusive growth
D. Planning for Prosperity

103. Match the following from List-I and List-II:

List-I	***List-II***
(a) SABLA	(i) Scheme for prevention of trafficking, Rescue, Rehabilitation and Reintegration of Victims Trafficking and Commercial Sexual Exploitation
(b) Ujjawala	(ii) Scheme for Empower-ment of Adolescent Girls
(c) Indira Gandhi Matritva Sahyog Yojna	(iii) Scheme of MMR and IMR
(d) Janani Suraksha Yojna	(iv) A Conditional Maternity Benefit Scheme

Codes:

	(a)	(b)	(c)	(d)
A.	(ii)	(iv)	(i)	(iii)
B.	(ii)	(iii)	(iv)	(i)
C.	(ii)	(i)	(iv)	(iii)
D.	(i)	(iv)	(iii)	(ii)

104. Arrange the following strategies in reverse sequence:
(i) Women Empowerment
(ii) Women in Development
(iii) Women and Development
(iv) Gender and Development

Codes:

A. (i), (iv), (iii), (ii) B. (iv), (iii), (ii), (i)
C. (iii), (ii), (i), (iv) D. (ii), (iii), (i), (iv)

105. Which award is given for best reporting on women in Panchayati Raj?
A. Durgabai Deshmukh Award
B. Indira Gandhi
C. Sarojini Naidu Prize
D. Mother Teresa

106. Match the following from List-I (Index) and List-II (India's Rank):

List-I (Index)	***List-II (India's Rank)***
(a) Human Development Index (2013)	(i) 112
(b) Gender Inequality Index (2013)	(ii) 136
(c) Gender Global Gap (2013)	(iii) 132
(d) Women in National Parliaments, IPU Index (April 2014)	(iv) 101

Codes:

	(a)	(b)	(c)	(d)
A.	(iii)	(ii)	(i)	(iv)
B.	(ii)	(iii)	(i)	(iv)
C.	(ii)	(iii)	(iv)	(i)
D.	(iv)	(iii)	(i)	(ii)

107. What are the variables which the Global Gender Gap Index examines?

(i) Economic Participation and Opportunity
(ii) Educational Attainment
(iii) Health and Survival
(iv) Political Empowerment

Codes:

A. (i) and (ii) only B. (i), (ii), (iii) only
C. (i), (ii), (iii), (iv) D. (iii) and (i) only

108. Who among the following Members of Parliament introduced the Private Member's Bill titled "The Rights of Transgender Persons Bill"?

A. Vayalar Ravi
B. Kanimozhi
C. Tiruchi N Siva
D. B. Vara Prasad

109. Arrange the following events in chronological order of women's Rights Movement in USA:

1. Seneca Falls Convention
2. The Women's Department of Labour
3. National Woman Suffrage Association
4. The first National's Woman's Rights Convention

Codes:

A. 1, 2, 3 and 4
B. 1, 4, 3 and 4
C. 3, 4, 1 and 2
D. 4, 2, 3 and 1

110. Match List-I with List-II:

List-I	***List-II***
(a) Women in Development	(i) Focuses on social, economic, political and cultural forces that determine how men and women participate in, benefit from and control project resources.
(b) Women and Development	(ii) Integrates women in the broader agenda of development and their contributions.
(c) Gender and Development	(iii) Involves women as participants and beneficiaries of development aid and initiatives.
(d) Participatory Development	(iv) Implies negotiation rather than the dominance of an extremely set project agenda.

Codes:

	(a)	(b)	(c)	(d)
A.	(i)	(ii)	(iii)	(iv)
B.	(ii)	(iii)	(i)	(iv)
C.	(iv)	(ii)	(iii)	(i)
D.	(iii)	(iv)	(ii)	(i)

111. Identify incorrect indicator of Gender Empowerment Measure Index (GEM) of the following:

(a) The share of parliamentary seats occupied by women.
(b) The proportion of legislators, senior officials and managers who are women.
(c) The ratio of estimated female to male earned income.
(d) The share of property owned by women.

Codes:

A. (a) and (b) only B. (d) only
C. (a) and (c) only D. (b) and (c) only

112. What are the major components under the SABLA programme to empower adolescent girls in India?

(a) Nutrition (b) Non-Nutrition
(c) Money Cash Back (d) Shelter

Codes:

A. (c) and (d) only
B. (b) and (c) only
C. (a) and (b) only
D. (a) and (d) only

113. Which one of the following pair is not correctly matched?

A. Kishori Sanooh – A group of average 15-25 Adolescent Girls from the village
B. ARSH – Adolescent reproduction and sexual health
C. Sakhi and Saheli – The adolescent girls who are selected from out of school and of the same group
D. ASHA – Association of scientific health activists

114. Which is the first state to implement 50 percent quota for women in Panchayati Raj Institutions in the year 2005?

A. Kerala B. Assam
C. Bihar D. Uttarakhand

115. When did the shift in the approach from 'welfare to development' of women take place in the Indian planning?

A. First Five Year Plan
B. Sixth Five Year Plan
C. Ninth Five Year Plan
D. Twelfth Five Year Plan

116. Match List-I with List-II:

List-I (Leading Social Entrepreneurs)	*List-II (New Approaches)*
(a) Susan B. Anthony	(i) Founder of land gift movement (India)
(b) Maria Montessori	(ii) Fought for women's Rights (USA)
(c) Florence Nightingale	(iii) Invented Montessori early childhood education (Italy)
(d) Acharya Vinoba Bhave	(iv) Founder of Modern Nursing School (UK)

Codes:

	(a)	(b)	(c)	(d)
A.	(ii)	(iii)	(iv)	(i)
B.	(ii)	(iv)	(iii)	(i)
C.	(iv)	(iii)	(ii)	(i)
D.	(iii)	(iv)	(i)	(ii)

117. In the 'Protection of children from sexual offences Act' 2012; a person abets an offence is, who:

1. Instigates any person to do that offence.
2. Intentionally aids, by any act or illegal omission, the doing of that offence.
3. Engages with one or more other person in any conspiracy for doing that offence.
4. Protects the child from being a victim of the offence.

Codes:

A. 2, 2 and 4
B. 4 only
C. 1, 2 and 3 only
D. 1, 2 and 4 only

118. Who from the following unfurled the Indian National Flag for the first time at the International Socialist conference in Stuttgart (Germany)?

A. Sarojini Naidu B. Lakshmi Sahgal
C. Madam Cama D. Annie Besant

119. What are the major challenges faced by Elected Women Representatives (EWRs) in PRIs?

1. Enhancing knowledge and skills of EWRs for negotiating appropriate solutions.
2. Attaining functional literacy in a fast track mode and low receptivity of training.
3. Sexual harassment and insecurity to attend the meetings away from villages.
4. Domesticated women conditioned by non-patriarchal values encourages the initiatives being taken by them.

Codes:

A. 1 and 2 only
B. 2, 3 and 4 only
C. 1, 2 and 3 only
D. 4 only

120. Developing Alternatives for Women in the New Era (DAWN) was established in 1984 in:

A. USA B. Bangladesh
C. India D. New Zealand

121. Match List-I with List-II:

List-I	*List-II*
(a) Rajiv Gandhi Scheme for Empowerment of Adolescent Girls	(i) Ujjawala
(b) Scheme for Women in Difficult Circumstances	(ii) SABLA
(c) Scheme for Prevention of Trafficking and Rescue, Rehabilitation and Reintegration of Victims of Trafficking and Commercial Sexual Exploitation	(iii) Swayamsiddha
(d) Holistic Empowerment of Women in a sustainable manner	(iv) Swadhar

Codes:

	(a)	(b)	(c)	(d)
A.	(i)	(ii)	(iv)	(iii)
B.	(ii)	(iv)	(i)	(iii)
C.	(iii)	(iv)	(i)	(ii)
D.	(iv)	(ii)	(i)	(iii)

122. Match the goals (List-I) with Five Year Plans (List-II) of India:

List-I	*List-II*
(a) Women's Empowerment	(i) Eleventh Five Year Plan
(b) Women and Development	(ii) Sixth Five Year Plan
(c) Inclusive Growth	(iii) Tenth Five Year Plan
(d) Advancement of Gender Equality	(iv) Ninth Five Year Plan

Codes:

	(a)	(b)	(c)	(d)
A.	(i)	(ii)	(iii)	(iv)
B.	(iv)	(ii)	(i)	(iii)
C.	(ii)	(iv)	(iii)	(i)
D.	(iii)	(i)	(ii)	(iv)

123. The only woman to be a member of the Planning Commission of India is:
A. Jayanti Ghosh
B. Aruna Roy
C. Syeda Hameed
D. Zoya Hassan

124. First Indian Woman President of the Indian National Congress:
A. Sucheta Kriplani
B. Rajkumari Amrit Kaur
C. Sarojini Naidu
D. Annie Besant

125. From the following leaders who has not been acted as a prime minister:
A. Benazir Bhutto
B. Sirimavo Bhandara Nayake
C. Margaret Thatcher
D. Hillary Clinton

126. Match the following from List-I and List-II:

List-I	***List-II***
(a) Angela Merkel	(i) President of Brazil
(b) Ellen Johnson Sirleaf	(ii) President of Liberia
(c) Christina Fernandez de Kirchner	(iii) Chancellor of Germany
(d) Dilma Rousseff	(iv) President of Argentina

Codes:

	(a)	(b)	(c)	(d)
A.	(iii)	(iv)	(ii)	(i)
B.	(ii)	(iv)	(i)	(iii)
C.	(iii)	(ii)	(iv)	(i)
D.	(i)	(iii)	(ii)	(iv)

127. WFS stands for:
A. Women Foreign Services
B. Women Feature Service
C. Women Financial Services
D. Women Family Services

128. Which of the following statements regarding the functions of the Parliamentary Committee on Empowerment of women are correct?
(i) To consider reports submitted by the National Commission for Women and State Commissions for women.
(ii) To report on the working of the welfare programmes for the women.
(iii) To examine measures taken by the Union Government and State Governments for Women's equality.
(iv) To examine measures taken by the Union Government for comprehensive education and adequate representation of women in legislative bodies.

Codes:
A. (ii) and (iv) B. (i) and (iii)
C. (iv) only D. (iii) only

129. Which of the following statements regarding the Parliamentary Committee on Women are correct?
(i) The members of the Committee are nominated by the Minister for Women and Child Development.
(ii) The Minister for Women and Child Development is the ex-officio member of the Committee.
(iii) The Committee has members from both the Houses of Parliament.
(iv) The Chairperson of the Committee is appointed by the Speaker.

Codes:
A. (i) and (iv) B. (iii) and (iv)
C. (i) and (ii) D. (ii) and (iii)

130. National Policy for Senior Citizens came in:
A. 2012 B. 2009
C. 2011 D. 2013

131. Global Gender Gap Index was first published in 2006 by:
A. World Economic Forum
B. World Health Organization
C. United Nations
D. World Bank

132. Parivarik Mahila Lok Adalats Programme was launched in 1996 by:
A. The Commission for SC/ST.
B. The Human Rights Commission.
C. The National Commission for Women.
D. The National Law Commission.

133. **Assertion (A):** Everyday thousands of women and teenage girls in India becomes victims of trafficking.
Reason (R): Rural women and girls are under the grip of large scale unemployment, poverty and dowry demand.

Codes:
A. (R) is false and (A) is true.
B. Both (A) and (R) are true and (R) is the correct explanation for (A).
C. Both (A) and (R) are false.
D. Both (A) and (R) are true and (R) is not the correct explanation for (A).

134. Assertion (A): Women are marginalized in political power structure.

Reason (R): Women are less rational.

Codes:

A. Both (A) and (R) are true.
B. Both (A) and (R) are false.
C. (A) is true, (R) is false.
D. (R) is true, (A) is false.

135. Assertion (A): Citizenship rights are one of the challenges of women in India.

Reason (R): Women's citizenship rights are blocked by the construction of culture and tradition.

Codes:

A. Both (A) and (R) are true.
B. Both (A) and (R) are false.
C. (A) is true, (R) is false.
D. (A) is false, (R) is true.

136. Assertion (A): Women's performance in the service-delivery system is remarkable.

Reason (R): Women have been elected to Panchayati Raj institutions through reservation.

Codes:

A. Both (A) and (R) are true.
B. (A) is true but (R) is false
C. (A) and (R) are independent of each other.
D. (A) is true and (R) is the reason for (A).

137. Assertion (A): Women at the grass root level are not yet participating in the local self governance.

Reason (R): Space for 1/3rd seats in local self governance has been created in 1990s by 73rd and 74th Amendments to the Constitution of India.

Codes:

A. Both (A) and (R) are true.
B. (A) is true but (R) is false.
C. (A) is false but (R) is true.
D. Both (A) and (R) are false.

138. Assertion (A): The presence of women in politics is not upto a desirable level.

Reason (R): Women believe that politics is a male reserve and unfeminine.

Codes:

A. Both (A) and (R) are true but (R) is not the correct explanation of (A).
B. (A) is true and (R) is false and (R) is not the correct explanation of (A).
C. (A) is false but (R) is true.
D. Both (A) and (R) are true and (R) is the correct explanation of (A).

139. Assertion (A): In India, large percentage of women cannot take decision independently not even related to their own life.

Reason (R): In India, large percentage of women do not have political power.

Codes:

A. Both (A) and (R) are true and (R) is the correct explanation for (A).
B. Both (A) and (R) are true, but (R) is not the correct explanation for (A).
C. Both (A) and (R) are true.
D. (A) is true, (R) is false.

140. Assertion (A): The caste system perpetuates inequality, dominance and exploitation in Indian society.

Reason (R): Higher caste people get more privileges from existing government policies and programmes.

Codes:

A. Both (A) and (R) are false.
B. Both (A) and (R) are true.
C. (A) is true, (R) is false.
D. (A) is false, (R) is true.

141. Assertion (A): Now-a-days more women are coming forward to participate at higher levels of politics.

Reason (R): Women are becoming aware of the social conditions that personal is no longer private, it is public as well as political.

Codes:

A. (A) is false but (R) is true.
B. Both (A) and (R) are true and (R) is the correct explanation for (A).
C. (A) is true but (R) is false and not the correct explanation for (A).
D. Both (A) and (R) are false.

142. Assertion (A): Women's Spending power has raised marginally over a couple of years.

Reason (R): The Self-help Group movements have raised household income of women.

Codes:

A. Both (A) and (R) are true.
B. Both (A) and (R) are true, (R) is not the correct explanation for (A).
C. Both (A) and (R) are true, (R) is the correct explanation for (A).
D. Both (A) and (R) are false.

143. Assertion (A): Women's presence in electoral politics has been marginal.

Reason (R): Women's participation in politics is curtailed by violence, criminalization and character assassination.

Codes:

A. Both (A) and (R) are true.
B. Both (A) and (R) are false.
C. (A) is true, (R) is false.
D. Both (A) and (R) are true, (R) is the correct explanation for (A).

144. Assertion (A): The percentage of women in the higher levels of political bodies are negligible.

Reason (R): The money and muscle power associated with the electoral bodies inhibits women's political participation.

Codes:

A. Both (A) and (R) are true, (R) is the correct explanation for (A).
B. Both (A) and (R) are true.
C. Both (A) and (R) are false.
D. (A) is true, (R) is false.

145. Assertion (A): Representation of women in Parliament and State Assemblies are very poor.

Reason (R): Political leaders are consciously keeping women out of party politics.

Codes:

A. (A) is true, (R) is false.
B. Both (A) and (R) are false.
C. Both (A) and (R) are true, (R) is the correct explanation for (A).
D. (A) is false, (R) is true.

146. Assertion (A): Women are voting in large number but do not hold top ranking political offices.

Reason (R): Women have voting rights but do not have the right to contest elections.

Codes:

A. Both (A) and (R) are false.
B. (A) is true, (R) is false.
C. Both (A) and (R) are true.
D. (A) is false, (R) is true.

147. Assertion (A): Most of the women ageing is associated with role change and the probability of coping with loss.

Reason (R): Women tend to outlive men in all countries and age groups.

Codes:

A. Both (A) and (R) are false.
B. (A) is true, (R) is false.
C. Both (A) and (R) are true.
D. (A) is false, (R) is true.

148. Assertion (A): Differences in power, resources and interests of women across the world effectively stand disguised and denied behind the concept of women's development.

Reason (R): Development policies for women are based on the premise that 'women' is a universal category.

Codes:

A. (A) is true and (R) is false.
B. Both (A) and (R) are true.
C. (A) is false and (R) is true.
D. Both (A) and (R) is false.

149. Assertion (A): All socio-political structures and institutions in all the civilized societies have been instrumental in reinforcing gender inequality.

Reason (R): Women have been generally dubbed as 'non-political' 'non-productive', 'private' and emotional.

Codes:

A. Both (A) and (R) are true but (R) is not the correct explanation of (A).
B. Both (A) and (R) are true and (R) is the correct explanation of (A).
C. (A) is true but (R) is false.
D. Both (A) and (R) are false but (R) is the correct explanation of (A).

150. Assertion (A): Political parties in India speak much about equality of women but have somehow ignored the Dalit women.

Reason (R): The 73rd Amendment provides space to Dalit women to sit in Panchayats, but it is seen as a threat to social hierarchy.

Codes:

A. Both (A) and (R) are false.
B. Both (A) and (R) are true, (R) is the correct explanation for (A).
C. (A) is true, (R) is false.
D. (A) is false, (R) is true.

Answers

1	2	3	4	5	6	7	8	9	10
C	A	A	D	B	B	A	A	D	B

11	12	13	14	15	16	17	18	19	20
D	C	C	D	D	D	C	B	C	C
21	22	23	24	25	26	27	28	29	30
C	D	D	B	D	D	C	B	B	B
31	32	33	34	35	36	37	38	39	40
D	D	C	C	C	C	C	A	A	B
41	42	43	44	45	46	47	48	49	50
A	B	C	A	D	A	C	A	A	C
51	52	53	54	55	56	57	58	59	60
C	B	A	A	D	C	B	A	A	D
61	62	63	64	65	66	67	68	69	70
C	A	D	D	D	D	B	C	A	B
71	72	73	74	75	76	77	78	79	80
B	B	D	B	A	C	A	C	B	A
81	82	83	84	85	86	87	88	89	90
C	B	D	D	D	A	C	C	D	A
91	92	93	94	95	96	97	98	99	100
B	D	A	A	D	D	D	B	C	D
101	102	103	104	105	106	107	108	109	110
B	C	C	A	C	C	C	C	B	B
111	112	113	114	115	116	117	118	119	120
B	C	D	C	B	A	C	C	C	C
121	122	123	124	125	126	127	128	129	130
B	B	C	C	D	C	B	A	B	C
131	132	133	134	135	136	137	138	139	140
A	C	B	C	A	D	A	B	B	C
141	142	143	144	145	146	147	148	149	150
B	C	D	A	C	B	C	B	A	D

❑❑❑

Women Law and Governance

- Rights: Gender Equality, Gender Discrimination, Women's Rights as Human Rights
- Constitutional Provisions for Women in India
- Personal Laws, Labor Laws, Family Courts, Enforcement Machinery – Police and Judiciary
- Crime against Women and Child: Child Abuse, Violence, Human Trafficking, Sexual Harassment at Workplace Act, 2013 – Legal Protection
- International Conventions and Legislations Related to Women's Rights

RIGHTS: GENDER EQUALITY, GENDER DISCRIMINATION

- Women's rights refer to women's ability to take important decisions independently related to their life and issues that will affect them throughout their life. But, women are denied these rights because of her gender, giving rise to gender inequality in human rights and the denial of the entitlement to full enjoyment of her freedom.
- Gender equality means equality between men and women in rights, responsibilities, and entitlement and an equal voice in social, economic and political life.
- Gender inequality has a negative relation with women's rights, as it involves denial of the fundamental rights that women are entitled to as human beings.
- This negative correlation is caused by the gender construct in society and the social order that perpetuates male domination and control over women and their lives.
- Gender identity and relations between genders are defined by cultural practices and belief systems. Some of the cultural/caste/religious/social practices that deny gender equality are endogamy, power relations in family, clothing culture, emphasis on women's purity and sanctifying sexuality, etc.
- Also, economic inequality hinders gender equality in the form of class differences, utilization of resources and privileges, etc. In the general pattern of culture, women have less autonomy, fewer rights, fewer control over resources and limited power in the decision-making process.
- Hence, the struggle for gender equality in rights is also a struggle for social justice and human rights.
- Gender inequality manifests in various forms and is influenced by several factors:
  - Division of society into the private and public sphere and women relegated to the private sphere of life
  - Dowry system
  - Unequal access to education
  - Caste purity factors
  - Constrained freedom of movement

- ❑ Threat and use of violence on women as a form of control
- ❑ Trafficking and selling of girls
- ❑ Preference for sons in families
- ❑ Denial of the fundamental right to dignity
- ❑ Domestic aggression ingrained in the patriarchal culture
- ❑ Prevalence of psychological and physical abuse of women

WOMEN'S RIGHTS AS HUMAN RIGHTS

- Women's rights conflict with society due to the cultural and traditional values, norms and ideas that subvert women's gender to serve the patriarchal social order.
- As a human, every individual has some natural rights to live a valuable life. Women's rights as human rights cover every aspect of life-health, education, political participation, economic well-being and freedom from violence.
- Every society is made up of both sexes. So, there should be equality of sexes with respect to human rights.
- But, women face different status and treatment at birth, childhood, marriage, and divorce, inheritance across different religions, regions, ethnicity, and culture. This denies women their entitlement to human rights, leading to the violation of human rights of women.
- The UN's Universal Declaration of Human Rights adopted in 1948 states that "All human beings are born free and have rights and freedom equally."
- This historic document establishes women's entitlement to their rights is in their capacity as human beings.
- The articles in the declaration give the right to life, liberty and security, equality before the law, freedom of movement, conscience and thought opinion and expression.
- As human rights of women, the declaration also includes social and economic security, right to work, employment and equal pay, entitlement to motherhood and childcare, equal rights in marriage and dissolution.
- But, despite the universal recognition of women's rights and equality as basic human rights, gender discrimination in all walks of life consistent violation of human rights of women.
- Full enjoyment of all human rights for women involves bringing fundamental changes to how countries and societies work.

CONSTITUTIONAL PROVISIONS FOR WOMEN IN INDIA

Writers of our constitution, while recognizing that women and men are equal, understood the need for constitutional guarantees and safeguards to women's equality and rights. The conservative and traditional society of India needed well-established constitutional provisions that can guide the society to change its perspectives on women and for the eventual establishment of an egalitarian society.

The Indian constitution guarantees women's equality as well as empowers states and institutions to enact policy measures to neutralize the gender discrimination and socioeconomic, political and educational disadvantages faced by women.

Some of the important constitutional provisions for women are as follows:

- The fundamental rights guarantee basic freedom and rights to all men, women, and children.
- Article 14 – Equality before the law for women.
- Article 15 (1) – Expressly states that the State shall not discriminate against any citizen on the grounds of religion, race, caste, sex, place of birth.
- Article 15 (3) – Empowers the State to make special provisions in favor of children and women.
- Article 16 – Equality of opportunity in matters related to employment or appointment to any office under the State.
- Article 23 – Prohibits traffic in human beings and forced labor.
- Article 39 (a) –State policy to be directed towards securing men and women adequate means of livelihood.
- Article 39 (d) – Equal pay for equal work for both men and women.
- Article 39 (e) – That the health and strength of workers, men, and women, and the tender age of children are not abused and that citizens are not forced by economic necessity to enter vocations unsuited to their age or strength.
- Article 39 A – To promote justice, on the basis of equal opportunity and to provide free legal aid by suitable legislation or scheme or in any other way to ensure that opportunities for securing justice are not denied to any citizen by reason of economic or other disabilities.

- Article 42 – The State to make provision for securing just and humane conditions of work and for maternity relief.
- Article 44 – The State shall Endeavour to secure for the citizens a uniform civil code throughout the territory of India. This aims towards the achievement of gender justice.
- Article 46 – The State to promote with special care the educational and economic interests of the weaker sections of the people and to protect them from social injustice and all forms of exploitation.
- Article 47 – The State to raise the level of nutrition and the standard of living of its people.
- Article 51 (A) (e) – To promote harmony and the spirit of common brotherhood amongst all the people of India and to renounce practices derogatory to the dignity of women.

The following provisions were added by making the 73rd and 74th amendments to the constitution in 1993.

- Article 243 D(3) – Not less than one-third (including the number of seats reserved for women belonging to the Scheduled Castes and the Scheduled Tribes) of the total number of seats to be filled by direct election in every Panchayat to be reserved for women and such seats to be allotted by rotation to different constituencies in a Panchayat.
- Article 243 D (4) – Not less than one-third of the total number of offices of Chairpersons in the Panchayats at each level to be reserved for women.
- Article 243 T (3) – Not less than one-third (including the number of seats reserved for women belonging to the Scheduled Castes and the Scheduled Tribes) of the total number of seats to be filled by direct election in every Municipality to be reserved for women and such seats to be allotted by rotation to different constituencies in a Municipality.
- Article 243 T (4) – Reservation of offices of Chairpersons in Municipalities for the Scheduled Castes, the Scheduled Tribes and women in such manner as the legislature of a State may by law provide.

PERSONAL LAWS THAT OFFER PROTECTION AND RIGHTS TO WOMEN

Indian Succession Act, 1925

- Establishes the inheritance rights of Christians in India.
- Law of inheritance and succession is the same for men and women.
- When a husband dies, one-third of the property shall go to the widow, and when there are no children, half the property goes to the widow.
- Any money earned by a Christian woman is her own property. She can will away her property to anybody she wants.
- A Christian woman is entitled to her father's property also.

Hindu Widow Remarriage Act, 1856

- Provides legal safeguards for widows.
- Legalized the remarriage of Hindu widows in all the regions under British India.
- But remarriage is not permitted if the widow was a child.
- Widows who remarry are entitled to all rights and inheritances that a woman who marries for the first time would have. But, she forfeits her rights to inheritance from the deceased husband.

Indian Divorce Act, 1869

- Governs divorce among Christian couples in India.
- A divorced woman get alimony from her husband throughout her lifetime.
- The alimony should not exceed one-fifth of the husband's income.

The Hindu Marriage Act, 1955

- The bride should be 18 years of age.
- Explicitly prohibits polygamy.
- Marriage is void if consent is forcibly obtained.
- Under this act, a woman can seek divorce if the husband was already married, found guilty of rape, cruelty, and adultery.

The Hindu Adoptions and Maintenance Act, 1956

- A married man can adopt only with the consent of his wife.
- It is the rights of the wife to get reasonable necessities from the head of the family; he should provide for the maintenance of the family members.
- The necessities include food, clothing, residence, education, medical attendance, and treatment.
- The head of the family must also provide for reasonable expenses for the marriage of the daughter.
- A Hindu wife is entitled to maintenance and separate residence under the circumstances defined under the act such as cruelty, desertion by husband, adultery and other justifiable reasons.

The Hindu Succession Act, 1956

- Abolished the division of women's property into *sthridhana* and women's estate to grant better rights to women.
- Confer women their absolute right to property.
- Gives right of residence to the female heir in the intestate family dwelling house, if she is unmarried or discarded or a widow.

Hindu Women's Right to Property Act, 1937

- Deals with the rights of Hindu Widows.
- When the husband has not made any will, the widow is entitled to a section of the property as that of the son.

The Foreign Marriage Act, 1969

- Legal provisions for marriage outside India where one or both of the parties are the Indian citizens.
- Makes provisions for matrimonial relief under certain circumstances.
- Ensures the protection of Indian citizens beyond Indian territories.

The Muslim Women (Protection of Rights on Divorce) Act, 1986

- Provides for a reasonable and fair provision to the divorced Muslim woman by her former husband.
- Maintenance provision for the child by her husband.
- An amount equal to the sum of *mehr* or dower agreed to be paid to her at the time of her marriage according to Muslim law should be paid by her husband.

Scheduled Castes and Scheduled Tribes (Prevention of Atrocities) Act, 1989

- Abolishes untouchability in any form.
- Accused persons under this act cannot be granted anticipatory bail.
- Touching an SC/ST women for sexual reasons without her consent is an offense under this act.
- Verbal harassment, abuse and threatening of SC/ST woman is also an offense.

Prohibition of Child Marriage Act, 2006

- Came into effect in 2007 and replaced the Child Marriage (Restraint) Act of 1929.
- The Child Marriage (Restraint) Act, 1929 was amended in 1978 to raise the legal age for marriage from 15 to 18.
- Under PCMA, if the groom is above the age of 18 years, he is also punishable.
- Parents, guardians or any organization that associates with child marriage can be punished for negligence.
- Provision for imprisonment up to 2 years.
- Child marriage prohibition officers are responsible for the implementation of this act. They can be police officers, panchayat members, NGO workers selected by the government.

LABOR LAWS THAT PROTECT THE RIGHTS OF WOMEN WORKERS

Crèche Facility for Women Employees

To provide crèche facilities for the use of children under the age of 6 years for women employees. Provision for crèches exists under the following:

- Section 48 of the Factories Act, 1948
- Section 44 of the Inter-State Migrant Workmen (RECS) Act, 1979
- Section 12 of the Plantations Labour Act, 1951
- Section 14 of the Beedi and Cigar Workers (Conditions of Employment) Act, 1966
- Section 35 of the Building and other Constructions (Regulation of Employment and Conditions of Service) Act, 1996

Prohibition of Night Work

- Section 66(1)(b) of the Factories Act, 1948 states that no woman shall be required or allowed to work in any factory except between the hours of 6 a.m. and 7 p.m.
- Section 25 of the Beedi and Cigar Workers (Conditions of Employment) Act, 1966 stipulates that no woman shall be required or allowed to work in any industrial premise except between 6 a.m. and 7 p.m.
- Section 46(1)(b) of the Mines Act, 1952 prohibits employment of women in any mine above ground except between the hours of 6 a.m. and 7 p.m.

Prohibition of Sub-Terrain Work

Section 46(1)(b) of the Mines Act, 1952 prohibits employment of women in any part of a mine which is below ground.

Provisions for Separate Latrines and Urinals

Provision for separate latrines and urinals for female workers undercover and partitioned to secure privacy and shall have proper door and fastenings exist under the following:

- Rule 53 of the Contract Labour (Regulation and Abolition) Act, 1970.
- Section 19 of the Factories Act, 1948.
- Rule 42 of the Inter-State Migrant Workmen (RECS) Central Rules, 1980.
- Section 20 of the Mines Act, 1952.
- Section 9 of the Plantations Labour Act, 1951.

Provisions for Separate Washing Facilities

Provision for separate washing facilities for female workers exists under the following:

- Section 57 of the Contract Labour (Regulation and Abolition) Act, 1970.
- Section 42 of the Factories Act.
- Section 43 of the Inter-State Migrant Workmen (RECS) Act, 1979.

Prohibition of Night Work for Women Employees

- Section 66(1)(b) of the Factories Act, 1948 states that no woman shall be required or allowed to work in any factory except between the hours of 6 a.m. and 7 p.m.
- Section 25 of the Beedi and Cigar Workers (Conditions of Employment) Act, 1966 stipulates that no woman shall be required or allowed to work in any industrial premise except between 6 a.m. and 7 p.m.
- Section 46(1)(b) of the Mines Act, 1952 prohibits employment of women in any mine above ground except between the hours of 6 a.m. and 7 p.m.
- According to shops and establishment Act, no women shall be required or allowed to work in any establishment after 9:30 PM

The Maternity Benefit Act, 1961

The Maternity Benefit Act applies to any establishment in which 10 or more persons are employed, or were employed, on any day of the preceding 12 months.

- Leave with average pay for six weeks before the delivery.
- Leave with average pay for six weeks after the delivery.
- Amended in 2017 to increase the ceiling on maternity leave up to 26 weeks.
- A medical bonus of ₹ 1,000 if the employer does not provide free medical care to the woman.
- An additional leave with pay up to one month if the woman shows proof of illness due to the pregnancy, delivery, miscarriage, or premature birth.
- In the case of miscarriage, six weeks leave with average pay from the date of miscarriage.
- Light work for ten weeks (six weeks plus one month) before the date of her expected delivery, if she asks for it.
- Two nursing breaks in the course of her daily work until the child is 15 months old.
- No discharge or dismissal while she is on maternity leave.
- No change to her disadvantage in any of the conditions of her employment while on maternity leave.
- Pregnant women discharged or dismissed may still claim maternity benefit from the employer.
- Leave with wages at the rate of maternity benefit, for a period of six weeks immediately following the day of her miscarriage or her medical termination of pregnancy.
- Entitled to leave with wages at the rate of maternity benefit for a period of two weeks immediately following the day of her tubectomy operation.
- Leave for illness arising out of pregnancy.

Factories Act, 1948

- Section 22(2) of the Factories Act, 1948 provides that no woman shall be allowed to clean, lubricate or adjust any part of a prime mover or of any transmission machinery while the prime mover or transmission machinery is in motion.
- Section 27 of the Factories Act, 1948 prohibits employment of women in any part of a factory for pressing cotton in which a cotton-opener is at work.
- No woman employee shall lift, carry, or move by hand or on the head any material, article, tools, or appliance exceeding the maximum limit in weight of 30 kilograms.
- There shall be at least one women (worker) on the Canteen Managing Committee.

Equal Remuneration for Women, 1976

As per the Equal Remuneration Act, payment of equal remuneration to men and women workers are supposed to be provided and for the prevention of discrimination, on the ground of sex, against women in the matter of employment.

FAMILY COURTS AND ENFORCEMENT MACHINERY—POLICE AND JUDICIARY

The Family Courts Act, 1984

- Family courts are designed for speedy disposal of matrimonial and family disputes.
- It promotes conciliation, mediation, and settlement of marriage and family conflicts.
- Family courts are higher than the district courts but lower than the state high courts.
- Family courts can hear cases relating to judicial separation and divorce, restitution of conjugal rights, issues related to matrimonial validity, custody and financial support to children, maintenance of wife, children and old parents.

Mahila Courts

- The concept was evolved by the National Commission for Women (NCW) to provide speedy dispensation of legal justice to women.
- It encourages the public to settle disputes outside the formal legal set-up.
- It works on the Lok Adalat model. The district legal services authority select women's cases that can be settled by Lok Adalats and makes the related documents available to them.
- NCW provides financial assistance to ensure cost-free dispensation of justice and brings women into the justice delivery mechanism.

The Legal Service Authorities Act, 1987

- To provide free legal services to weaker sections of the society including women.
- It gives a statutory base to legal aid programmes in a uniform manner.
- National legal Services Authority was set up in 1995 under this act.
- Women, children, victims of human trafficking, victims of ethnic violence, caste atrocities and industrial workers are eligible for legal aid under this act, to access justice.
- Provides for legal aid camps to raise awareness among rural sections, slums and labor colonies to educate weaker sections and women of their constitutional rights.
- Provides for a grant in aid to grass root level, legal services among working women, SC/ST and laborers etc.

National Commission for Women Act, 1990

- Established the National Commission for Women in 1992.
- Jayanti Patnaik was the first Chairperson of the commission.
- Its mandate includes safeguarding the rights of women, study the problems faced by women and make recommendations to eradicate the problems, provide funding to cases related to women's rights.
- It also evaluate the status of women from time to time and submit the report and recommendations to the government.
- NCW contains a Complaint and Counseling Cell that processes the complaints received and also can take suo moto notice and action on women's issues.
- The commission also makes recommendations to improve existing laws and legislation from time to time.

Most crimes against women go unregistered due to unsupportive and insensitive attitudes of the policy machinery. Formal training in dealing with women and gender sensitization is needed to minimize delay in dealing with crimes against women. Training programmes and periodic meetings should be held to discuss and review the handling of women's cases. Swift punishment to public servants who are responsible for custodial death of women can ensure the safety of women complaints and victims. The government has also directed that districts should have "crime against women cells" and separate helpline for women. Increased representation of women in police forces is also needed. The rules recommend at least 33% representation of women, but the actual numbers are too low.

Zero FIR–Under this concept, a First Information Report can be filed in any police station irrespective of the place of the incident of crime. The FIR or case can be transferred to the appropriate police station later. Action can be taken on police officers who refuse to register zero FIR or does not act on the filed zero FIR. It helps the victims, especially women to appeal for investigation without wasting time. In most places, women are not able to register FIR because the place does not come under the territorial jurisdiction of the police station.

The Code of Criminal Procedure, 1973

Criminal Procedure Code lays down the rules to be followed while arresting, investigating and trying a woman for a crime. Some of the important provisions are:

- As per Section 46 (4) of Cr.P.C, no woman can be arrested after sunset and before sunrise.

- Right to be informed of grounds of arrest which has been made–Section 50(1).
- Right to inform the relatives/friends – Police officer making an arrest has to immediately give the information regarding such arrest and the place where the arrested person is being held to any of his/her friends, relatives or such other persons as may be disclosed or nominated by the arrested person–Section 50A of Cr.P.C.
- It is also the duty of the police officer to inform the person arrested of his/her rights.
- Right to be informed of the right to bail–Section 50(2)
- Right to be produced before a magistrate without delay–It is illegal to keep a person in detention for more than 24 hours without the orders of the Magistrate–Section 56
- The right of not being detained for more than twenty-four hours–Section 76
- Right to consult a legal practitioner : This right begins from the moment the arrest is made.
- Manhandling and Handcuffing : It is illegal to manhandle a person at the time of arrest.
- The search of arrested person : Only female police can search a female. The search should be carried out in a decent manner.
- A male police officer cannot search a female offender. He can, however, search a woman's house.
- Also, there exists a right to be examined by a medical practitioner.
- The arrested person has a right to legal aid and a fair trial.

The Indian Penal Code, 1860

The Indian Penal Code lists the offenses against women and also defines them and details the procedure to deal with such crimes. Some of the offenses against women punishable under IPC are:

- Causing miscarriage to women; imprisonment up to 3 years (Section 312).
- Assault or criminal force to a woman with intent to outrage her modesty; imprisonment up to two years (Section 354).
- The kidnapping of minor girls (Section 361).
- The kidnapping of a woman to compel her into a marriage.
- Procurement of minor girl; imprisonment up to 10 years (Section 366-A).
- Selling and buying minor girls for prostitution; imprisonment up to ten years (Section 372 and 373).
- Rape of women and girls; imprisonment for life or up to 10 years (Section 376).
- Husband forcing sexual intercourse on his wife; imprisonment upto 2 years (Section 376-A).
- Seducing women for sexual intercourse; imprisonment up to 2 years (Section 498).
- Cruelty to a married woman in the form of harassment for dowry, driving to suicide (Section 493-A).
- Outraging modesty of women; up to one-year imprisonment (Section 509).

CRIME AGAINST WOMEN AND CHILD: CHILD ABUSE, VIOLENCE, HUMAN TRAFFICKING

- During the British rule, several legislations were enacted to counter the inherent forms of violence against women entrenched in the patriarchal Indian society such as sati.
- Sati was first banned in the Bengal presidency by Lord William Bentinck in 1829, through the Bengal Sati Regulation Act. Soon, other territories enacted legislations to prohibit sati.
- Despite this, in 1987, an 18-year old married woman, Roop Kunwar was killed by forced sati following the death of her husband to whom she was married for eight months. Following the incident, the government enacted the Prevention of Sati Act in 1987 for more effective prevention of this cruel practice.
- The violence of this nature against women are deep-rooted in a patriarchal culture and justify crimes committed against women by society.
- Prof. Amartya Sen coined the term "missing women" to draw attention to the declining sex ratio in developing countries and the millions of missing girls and women from society.
- Some of the leading causes of missing girls and women in India are female foeticide, female infanticide, girls sold to brokers for human trafficking, women going missing from their marital homes, dowry deaths, high rates of maternal and female infant mortality rates, etc.
- According to the National Crime Records Bureau (NCRB), 8,233 new brides were killed for dowry in 2012.
- **The Dowry Prohibition Act, 1961** makes giving or taking dowry punishable with imprisonment**.** The Act defined minimum and maximum punishments,

modified the Indian Penal Code in 1983 to establish dowry-related crimes, dowry-deaths, and abetment of suicide in marriage. Despite these legislations, dowry-deaths, and dowry-related violence against women is still prevalent across India.

- Marital violence against women takes place in the form of physical and sexual abuse too.
- **The Protection of Women against Domestic Violence Act, 2005** was enacted to protect women from several forms of violence occurring within the family.
- The Act defines domestic violence to include actual abuse or threat of abuse in sexual, physical, verbal, economic or emotional forms. Harassment for dowry is also included as domestic violence. It provides for punishment of the abuser and monetary protection and relief for the victims.
- Also, there has been a significant increase in rape in the past decade in India. NCRB, 2012 data shows that about 25,000 cases of rape were reported in that year. Unreported rape crimes are higher in number.
- In India, the upper caste men use rape as a form of exerting power over the lower caste communities. Gang rapes are increasing in their prevalence.
- Violence against women can be in the form of intimate partner violence, sexual violence, dowry-related and domestic violence.
- Violence against women is increasingly used to maintain and reproduce social power relations.
- As women, children are also vulnerable to violence from society in many forms. The various forms of crimes and violence committed on children are:
  - Corporal punishment
  - Bullying and physical fights
  - Psychological and verbal abuse, the threat of violence
  - Physical and sexual violence against adolescent girls
  - Child homicide
  - Child trafficking
- NCRB's 2016 data shows that there have been 144 cases of female foeticide, 6 out of every 100 murders were children below 18 years of age, 6 out of every ten kidnappings were children. Girls are more vulnerable to the crimes of kidnapping and human trafficking than boys.
- In 2015, under the **Protection of Children against Sexual Offenses (POCSO) Act**, 19,765 cases were registered. Reporting of sexual violence against children increased after the enactment of this act in 2012. Next year saw a 45% increase in registration of cases under the POCSO Act.
- According to the Ministry of Home Affairs, over the period 2010-2014, 3.85 lakh children went missing. Of them 61% were girls. The kidnapped girls were forced into prostitution, sold to begging rackets, bondage child labor, etc. Children from poor and marginalized communities are increasingly sold into forced child labor in distant places.
- Suppression of Immoral Traffic in Women and Girls Act was passed in 1956 to prevent the exploitation of women and human trafficking. The act was changed in 1986, resulting in the **Immoral Traffic Prevention Act.** The Act prohibits trafficking in relation to prostitution and makes it punishable to commit prostitution with a child.
- **Juvenile Justice (Care and Protection of Children) Act, 2015:** Replaced the Juvenile Justice Act, 2000. Defines Juvenile as a child who has not completed 18 years of age. No child under this act can be awarded the death penalty. The age of criminal majority starts from the age of 16 to 18. It aims to fulfill the basic necessities of such juveniles through proper care and nourishment, protection, treatment, social integration, training, and a child-friendly approach. The act recommends setting up of juvenile justice boards and child welfare committees.
- **Child Labor Act, 1986:** Amended in 2016 to the Child and Adolescent Labor (Prohibition and Regulation) Act. Permits employment of adolescent labor except under hazardous occupations. Provides for rehabilitation of victims under this act. Provides for increased penalty and punishment for up to 2 years.

SEXUAL HARASSMENT OF WOMEN AT WORKPLACE (PREVENTION, PROHIBITION AND REDRESSAL) ACT, 2013

In 1997, the Supreme Court of India formulated the "Vishaka Guidelines" which made it mandatory for institutions to put in place measures to prevent and redress sexual harassment in their workplaces. Most of the essential features of the guidelines were incorporated into the legislation of Sexual Harassment of Women at Workplace (Prevention, Prohibition and Redressal) Act in 2013. Some of the critical features of the act are:

- This Act aims to provide every woman with a safe and secure working environment free from all forms of harassment.
- Covers both the organized and unorganized sectors.

- Applies to all government bodies, private and public sector organizations, non-governmental organizations, organizations carrying out commercial, vocational, educational, entertainment, industrial, financial activities, hospitals, etc.
- Extends the meaning of the word sexual harassment to include "presence or occurrence of circumstances of implied or explicit promise of preferential treatment in employment, threat of detrimental treatment in employment, threat about present or future employment, interference with work or creating an intimidating or offensive or hostile work environment, or humiliating treatment likely to affect the lady employee's health or safety could also amount to sexual harassment."
- Introduces the concept of **'extended workplace'** to include any place visited by the employee arising out of or during the course of employment, including transportation provided by the employer for the purpose of commuting to and from the place of employment.
- Provides for the establishment of **Internal Complaints Committee (ICC)** at each and every office or branches of the organization employing 10 or more employees, in order to provide a forum for filing complaints to facilitate fast redressal of the grievances pertaining to sexual harassment.
- Provides for the establishment of **Local Complaints Committee (LCC)** at the district level by the Gover-nment to investigate and redress complaints of sexual harassment of the unorganized sector or from those establishments where the ICC has not been constituted for a reason being, it having less than ten employees.

INTERNATIONAL CONVENTIONS AND LEGISLATIONS RELATED TO WOMEN'S RIGHTS

The United Nations organization has played an important role in advancing women's rights and ending gender inequality all over the world. One of the purposes of UN, declared in its founding charter is to promote human rights and fundamental freedoms without distinction of race, sex, language or religion.

Some of the landmark achievements of the UN and other international organizations towards women's rights and gender quality are as follows:

United Nations Economic and Social Council (ECOSOC)

UN's Economic and Security Council established the Commission on the Status of Women in 1946. Its primary responsibility is to promote gender equality and advancement of women.

Universal Declaration of Human Rights

Adopted by the UN General Assembly on December 10, 1948. Some of the important features of the declaration concerning women are as follows:

- All human beings are born free and equal in dignity and rights. (Article 1)
- All are entitled to freedoms and rights without distinction of race, sex, religion, color, political or other opinion, property, birth or other status. (Article 2)
- Right to life, liberty, and security. (Article 3)
- All are equal before the law and entitled to equal protection of the law. (Article 7)
- Men and women of full age are entitled to equal rights as to marriage, during the marriage and at its dissolution. (Article 16)
- All have the right to social security. (Article 22)
- Right to equal pay for equal work without discrimination. (Article 23 (2))
- Right to adequate standard of living and right to security in the event of unemployment, sickness, disability, widowhood, old age,etc. (Article 25)
- Right to education (Article 26)

UN General Assembly declared the year 1975 as the International Women's Year.

World Conferences on Women

The UN has organized four world conferences on women so far:

First World Conference on Women

- Held in 1975 in Mexico City.
- Called the World Conference of the International Women's Year.
- 133 governments and around 6,000 NGOs participated in the conference.
- Defined the World plan for action for the implementation of the objectives of the International Women's year.
- Declared 1975-1985 as the UN Decade for Women.

Second World Conference on Women

- Held in 1980 in Copenhagen.
- Called the World Conference of the United Nation's Decade for Women.

- Reviewed the progress in the implementation of first world conference objectives.
- Focused on health, employment, and education.
- Called for stronger measures to ensure women's ownership and control of the property, and improvements in protecting women's rights to inheritance, child custody, and nationality.

Third World Conference on Women

- Held in 1985 in Nairobi.
- World Conference to Review and Appraise the Achievements of the UN Decade for Women.
- To establish measures to overcome obstacles to achieving the Decade's goals.
- Adopted the Nairobi Forward-Looking Strategies for the Advancement of Women.
- Outlined measures for achieving gender equality and promoting women's participation in peace and development efforts.

Fourth World Conference on Women

- Held in 1995 in Beijing.
- 189 participating countries adopted the Beijing Declaration and Platform for action.
- Development and peace was the fundamental theme.
- The Beijing declaration recognized that inequalities and obstacles to women development remained. It reaffirmed the commitments to equal rights, full implementation of human rights of women, efforts to achieve Nairbobi strategies and women's empowerment as fundamental to equality, development, and peace.
- The Platform for action commits to gender equality in dimensions of life.
- Identified 12 critical areas of concern for gender equality:
  - ❑ Women and Poverty
  - ❑ Educating and Training Women
  - ❑ Women and Health
  - ❑ Violence against Women
  - ❑ Women and Armed Conflict
  - ❑ Women and the Economy
  - ❑ Women in Power and Decision Making
  - ❑ Institutional Mechanism for the Advancement of Women
  - ❑ Human Rights of Women
  - ❑ Women and the Media
  - ❑ Women and the Environment
  - ❑ The Girl-Child

In 2000, a UN special session "Women 2000: Gender Equality, Development, and Peace for the Twenty-First Century" was held in New York. It resulted in a political declaration and commitment to implement Beijing objectives.

In 2005, the decadal appraisal of the Beijing platform for action was conducted, which emphasized on the full and effective implementation of the Beijing declaration.

Convention on Consent to Marriage, Minimum Age for Marriage, and Registration of Marriages

- A UN treaty on standards of marriage.
- Treaty was signed in 1962 and entered into force in 1964.
- It reaffirms the consensual nature of marriage.
- Requires the establishment of the minimum age for marriage by the governments.
- Ensures registration of all marriages in official register.

Convention on the Elimination of All Forms of Discrimination Against Women (CEDAW)

- Adopted in 1979, came into force in 1981.
- Called the International Bill of Rights for Women.
- Acknowledges the extensive discrimination against women and gives positive affirmation to principles of equality.
- Requires governments to take appropriate measures and legislation for full development and advancement of women, and guaranteeing human rights and fundamental freedoms for women.
- Contains 30 articles that define discrimination against women and sets up an agenda for action.
- States to adopt special measures to accelerate equality for women. (Article 4)
- Appropriate measure to eliminate stereotyping, gender prejudices and discriminatory cultural practices. Family education to enable a proper understanding of maternity as a social function and equal responsibility of men in children's upbringing. (Article 5).
- States to take measure to prevent all forms of human trafficking, exploitation, and prostitution of women and girls. (Article 6)
- Equal rights to education, educational resources vocational training; elimination of stereotyping in curricula and teaching materials. (Article 10)

- Equal opportunities in employment, promotion, equal remuneration, social security, safe work conditions; provisions for maternity benefits. (Article 11)
- Equal access to health care services and reproductive health care of women. (Article 12)
- Equal rights to family benefits, financial credit. (Article 13)
- Appropriate measures to eliminate discrimination against women in rural areas. (Article 14)
- Equality before the law. (Article 15)
- Men and women to have equal rights in marriage. (Article 16)
- **India** signed CEDAW in 1980 and ratified it on 3rd July 1993.
- Committee on the elimination of discrimination against women to monitor the implementation of CEDAW.
- The **Optional Protocol** to CEDAW establishes a complaint and inquiry mechanisms for the CEDAW. It was adopted by the UN in 1999 and came into force on December 2000. India has not ratified the optional protocol yet.
- The **General Recommendations** (GR) are statements by the CEDAW committee about how different aspects of the convention should be interpreted, elaborates on implications of the CEDAW articles. Some of the important GRs are:
  - **GR 12** : Violence against women
  - **GR 13** : Equal remuneration for work of equal value
  - **GR 14** : Female circumcision
  - **GR 15** : Women and AIDS
  - **GR 16** : Unpaid women workers in rural and urban family enterprises
  - **GR 17** : Measurement and quantification of the unremunerated domestic activities of women and their recognition in the GNP
  - **GR 18** : Disabled women
  - **GR 19** : Violence against women
  - **GR 21** : Equality in marriage and family relations
  - **GR 23** : Women in political and public life
  - **GR 24** : Women and health
  - **Gr 26** : Women Migrant Workers
  - **GR 27** : Older women and protection of their human rights
  - **GR 28** : The Core Obligations of States Parties under Article 2 of the Convention on the Elimi-nation of All Forms of Discrimination against Women
  - **GR 29** : Economic consequences of marriage, family relations, and their dissolution
  - **GR 30** : Women in conflict prevention, conflict, and post-conflict situations
  - **GR 32** : The gender-related dimensions of refugee status, asylum, nationality, and statelessness of women
  - **GR 33** : Women's access to justice
  - **GR 34** : The rights of rural women
  - **GR 35** : Gender-based violence against women, updating general recommendation No. 19
  - **GR 36** : The right of girls and women to education
  - **GR 37** : Gender-related dimensions of disaster risk reduction in the context of climate change

World Conference on Human Rights

- Held in Vienna in 1993.
- Confirmed the universality of human rights.
- 171 states adopted the Vienna Declaration and Programme for Action.
- The declaration stated that all human rights are universal, irreversible and inter-related.
- Drew attention to the discrimination and violence faced by women all over the world.
- Declared that human rights of women and the girl-child are inalienable, integral and indivisible part of universal human rights. The full and equal participation of women in political, civil, economic, social and cultural life, at the national, regional and international levels, and the eradication of all forms of discrimination on the grounds of sex are priority objectives of the international community.
- Gender-based violence and all forms of sexual harassment, exploitation, and international trafficking, are incompatible with the dignity and worth of the human person and must be eliminated.
- The human rights of women should form an integral part of the United Nations human rights activities, including the promotion of all human rights instruments relating to women.

UN Women

- In 2010, the UN General Assembly voted to establish UN Women, a UN entity for gender equality and women empowerment.
- It merged four existing world agencies and offices– UN Development Fund for Women (UNIFEM), Division for the Advancement of Women (DAW), the office of the special adviser on gender issues and the UN International Research and Training Institute for the Advancement of Women (INSTRAW).
- **UNIFEM** is the United Nations Development Fund for Women, established in 1976. It provides financial assistance to programmes that foster gender equality and women empowerment. UNIFEM's analysis of men's violence against women is described by the "Seven P's" concept: Patriarchal power, Sense of entitlement to Privilege, Permission in social customs and religious teachings, Paradox of men's Power, Psychic armor of manhood, Masculinity as Psychic pressure cooker and Past experiences.
- **INSTRAW** is the International Research and Training Institute for Development of Women established by UN-ECOSOC in 1976, following the first UN world conference on women in Mexico City. It undertakes action-oriented research from gender perspectives, creates synergies for infor-mation exchange and knowledge management, etc.
- **UNITE :** A UN Campaign launched in 2008, by the then Secretary-General Ban Ki-moon to "End violence against women." It worked towards synergizing strategies and efforts by UN offices and agencies working towards ending gender violence. It set five outcomes to be met by 2015.

Declaration on Elimination of Violence against Women

- Adopted by the UN General Assembly in 1993.
- A comprehensive statement of the rights to be applied to eliminate violence against women.
- International Day for the elimination of Violence against women is observed on 25th November every year.

UN SECURITY COUNCIL RESOLUTIONS

The UN Security Council has adopted several resolutions related to women.

Resolutions related to Women's Leadership in peace-making and conflict prevention:

Resolution 1325

- Adopted in 2000
- Acknowledges the importance of women and the inclusion of gender perspectives in peace negotiations, humanitarian planning, post-conflict peace-building, etc.

Resolution 1889

- Adopted in 2009
- Stresses on strengthening implementation of resolution 1325.
- To ensure that women's protection & empowerment was taken into account during post-conflict needs assessment & planning & factored into subsequent funding & programming.

Resolution 2242

- Adopted in 2015
- Need for more senior women leaders in all levels of division making in peace and security.
- Informal expert group on women, peace & security to ensure consistent information flows on the impact of conflict on women & secure their participation.

Resolutions on Prevention of and Response to Conflict-related Sexual Violence:

Resolution 1820

- Adopted in 2008
- Recognizes sex violence as a tactic of war.
- Identifies sexual violence as a matter of international peace and security and necessitates a security response.
- Rape and other forms of sexual violence can be recognized as war crimes, a crime against humanity or a constitutive act of genocide.

Resolution 1888

- Adopted in 2009
- Strengthens resolution 1820 by establishing leadership and expertise to address conflict-related sexual violence.

Resolution 1960

- Adopted in 2010
- Provides an accountability system to stop conflict-related sexual violence.
- Calls for governments to establish time-bound commitments.

Resolution 2106

- Adopted in 2013
- Adds greater operational details to end conflict-related sexual violence.

Multiple Choice Questions

1. Which of the following countries has not ratified the Optional Protocol to the Convention on the Elimination of all forms of Discrimination Against Women (CEDAW)?

A. Maldives B. India

C. Bangladesh D. USA

2. Find out the sequence of the establishment of the following institutions/commissions:

1. Central Social Welfare Board
2. Family Court
3. National Commission for Women
4. Human Rights Commission

Codes:

A. 1, 2, 3, 4 B. 2, 3, 4, 1

C. 3, 4, 1, 2 D. 1, 3, 4, 2

3. Match the following List-I with List-II:

List-I	***List-II***
(a) Vishakha Case	(i) Harassment of Women at Work Place
(b) Mary Roy Case	(ii) Custodial Rape
(c) Roop Kanwar Case	(iii) Sati
(d) Mathura Case	(iv) Christian Women's Property Right

Codes:

	(a)	(b)	(c)	(d)
A.	(i)	(iv)	(iii)	(ii)
B.	(ii)	(iv)	(iii)	(i)
C.	(iii)	(iv)	(i)	(ii)
D.	(i)	(ii)	(iii)	(iv)

4. Match the laws in List-I with the year of enactment given in List-II:

List-I	***List-II***
(a) Muslim Women's (Protection of Rights on Divorce) Act	(i) 1971
(b) Child Marriage Restraint Act	(ii) 2001
(c) Medical Termination of Pregnancy Act	(iii) 1929
(d) Indian Divorce Amendment Act	(iv) 1986

Codes:

	(a)	(b)	(c)	(d)
A.	(iii)	(iv)	(i)	(ii)
B.	(ii)	(i)	(iii)	(iv)
C.	(i)	(iii)	(iv)	(ii)
D.	(iv)	(iii)	(i)	(ii)

5. According to _________ statistics, the incidences of rape occurs for every 54 minutes, one molestation for every 26 minutes, one eve-teasing for every 51 minutes and any one kind of violence for every 7 minutes.

A. Sample Registration System

B. National Commission for Women

C. Indian Statistical Institute

D. National Sample Survey

6. Arrange the following Women Development Implementing Agencies on the basis of its higher to lower levels:

A. Department of Women and Child Development, Women Development Corporations, UNIFEM and DRDA.

B. UNIFEM, Department of Women and Child Development, Women Development Corporations and DRDA.

C. Women Development Corporations, DRDA, UNIFEM and Department of Women and Child Development.

D. DRDA, UNIFEM, Women Development Corporations and Department of Women and Child Development.

7. Arrange the following on the basis of their year of celebrations:

A. First National Conference of Women's Studies, Women Empowerment Year, International Year of Women and International Decade of Women.

B. Women Empowerment Year, International Decade of Women, First National Conference of Women's Studies and International Year of Women.

C. International Year of Women, First National Conference on Women's Studies, International Decade of Women and Women Empowerment Year.

D. International Decade of Women, Women Empowerment Year, International Year of Women and First National Conference on Women's Studies.

8. Match the issues with the name of the Victims:

Name	***Issue***
(a) Roop Kanwar	(i) Divorce
(b) Vishakha	(ii) Property Rights
(c) Shah Bano	(iii) Sexual Harassment
(d) Mary Roy	(iv) Sati

Codes:

	(a)	(b)	(c)	(d)
A.	(iv)	(iii)	(i)	(ii)
B.	(iii)	(iv)	(ii)	(i)
C.	(ii)	(i)	(iii)	(iv)
D.	(i)	(ii)	(iv)	(iii)

9. Prevention of Sexual Harassment for working women is the result of a judgment in the case of:
A. Air India Vs Nargis Mirza
B. Vishakha Vs State of Rajasthan
C. C.B. Muthmona Vs Union of India
D. Mayadevi Vs the State

10. The theme of the Draft platform for Action of the United Nation's 4th World Conference on women was:
A. Equality, Liberty and Justice
B. Liberty, Development and Peace
C. Equality, Development and Peace
D. Development, Peace and Justice

11. Targeting 30 per cent women at all levels of decision-making was endorsed by:
A. United Nation's Economic and Social Council
B. Women Empowerment Plan
C. Shram Shakti Report
D. All India Women's Conference

12. Choose the correct expansion of CEDAW:
A. Conference on the Eradication of All Forms of Discrimination Against Women
B. Convention on the Elimination of All Forms of Discrimination Against Women
C. Conviction on the Eradication of All Forms of Differences about Women
D. Controlling Elimination of All Forms of Discrimination Against Women

13. Match the laws with their year of enactment:

Name of Act	***Year***
(a) Law of Adoption and Maintenance Act	(i) 1956
(b) Dowry Prohibition (Amendment) Act	(ii) 1990
(c) Prevention of Atrocities Act	(iii) 1986
(d) National Commission for Women Act	(iv) 1989

Codes:

	(a)	(b)	(c)	(d)
A.	(ii)	(i)	(iii)	(iv)
B.	(iv)	(ii)	(i)	(iii)
C.	(iii)	(iv)	(ii)	(i)
D.	(i)	(iii)	(iv)	(ii)

14. 'Women's rights are human rights' was recognized in which Conference?
A. Vienna Conference
B. Beijing Conference
C. Mexico Conference
D. Nairobi Conference

15. Match List-I and List-II:

List-I	***List-II***
(a) Shah Bano	(i) Adoption and Guardianship
(b) Mathura	(ii) Uniform Civil Code
(c) Geetha Hariharan	(iii) Gang Rape
(d) Banwari Devi	(iv) Custodial Rape

Codes:

	(a)	(b)	(c)	(d)
A.	(ii)	(iii)	(iv)	(i)
B.	(ii)	(iv)	(i)	(iii)
C.	(iv)	(i)	(iii)	(ii)
D.	(iii)	(iv)	(ii)	(i)

16. When did India ratify CEDAW?
A. 1981 B. 1979
C. 1998 D. 1993

17. Which Indian woman headed the UN General Assembly?
A. Sarojini Naidu B. Indira Gandhi
C. Vijaya Lakshmi Pandit D. Najma Heptullah

18. In which Conference the platform for Action was formulated?
A. Mexico Conference
B. Beijing Conference
C. Vienna Conference
D. Nairobi Conference

19. Choose the correct expansion of CAW:
A. Crime Against Work
B. Convention Against Women
C. Casualties Against Work
D. Crime Against Women

20. Domestic violence is:
A. Private affair
B. Public affair
C. Personal affair
D. Both private and public affair

21. Sequence the following as per the year in which they were initiated:
1. MTP Act.
2. PCPNDT Act.
3. Child Marriage Restraint (Amendment) Act
4. Indecent Representation of Women Act.

Codes:

A.	1	4	2	3
B.	3	1	2	4
C.	1	3	4	2
D.	2	3	4	1

22. The Second Amendment of Dowry Prohibition Act deals with:

A. Seven years' imprisonment for the husband.
B. Punishment for all the members associated with dowry.
C. Suicide of a woman within seven years of her marriage.
D. Accepting the gifts from bride as gifts not as dowry.

23. Who was the first Executive Director of the UN Women for Gender Equality and Empowerment of Women when it became operational in 2011?

A. Noeleen Heyzer　B. Hillary Clinton
C. Michelle Bachelet　D. Isabel Peron

24. Match Articles of the Constitution of India from List-I with the provision in List-II:

List-I	***List-II***
(a) Article 14	(i) Right against Exploitation
(b) Article 15	(ii) Right to Equality
(c) Article 16	(iii) Prohibition of Discrimination on grounds of Caste, Creed and Sex
(d) Article 23	(iv) Equality of Opportunity in Matters of Public Employment

Codes:

	(a)	(b)	(c)	(d)
A.	(iv)	(iii)	(i)	(ii)
B.	(ii)	(iii)	(iv)	(i)
C.	(i)	(iv)	(iii)	(ii)
D.	(iii)	(ii)	(i)	(iv)

25. Arrange chronologically the following:

(i) Convention on the Consent to Marriage, Minimum Age for Marriage, Minimum Age for Marriage and Registration of Marriages.
(ii) The ILO convention 100 on Equal Remuneration.
(iii) UN Convention on the Rights of Persons with Disabilities.
(iv) The Security Council Resolution 1325 on Women, Peace and Security.

Codes:

A. (ii), (i), (iv), (iii)
B. (iv), (iii), (i), (ii)
C. (iii), (iv, (ii), (i)
D. (i), (iv), (iii), (ii)

26. The Age of Consent debate refers to:

(i) sexual assault　(ii) age at marriage
(iii) consensual sex　(iv) child marriage

Codes:

A. (ii) and (iii) are true　B. (ii) and (iv) are true
C. (i) and (ii) are true　D. (i) and (iii) are true

27. Match the names of the women in List-I with the issues in List-II:

List-I	***List-II***
(a) Aruna Shanbagh	(i) Murder
(b) Jessica Lal	(ii) Sati
(c) Roop Kanwar	(iii) Property Rights
(d) Mary Roy	(iv) Sexual Assault

Codes:

	(a)	(b)	(c)	(d)
A.	(iv)	(i)	(ii)	(iii)
B.	(iii)	(ii)	(iv)	(i)
C.	(ii)	(i)	(iv)	(iii)
D.	(i)	(iv)	(iii)	(ii)

28. Muslim women can seek dissolution of marriage on which of the following grounds?

(i) Mutual consent
(ii) Where husband delegates
(iii) By agreement on the wife giving some consideration to the husband
(iv) Adultery

Codes:

A. (i) and (ii) are true
B. (i), (ii) and (iii) are true
C. (ii), (iii) and (iv) are true
D. (i), (iii) and (iv) are true

29. Structural violence is reflected in:

(i) Physical violence　(ii) Patriarchy
(iii) Cultural behavior　(iv) Abusive language

Codes:

A. (i) and (ii) only　B. (i), (iii) and (iv) only
C. (ii), (iii) and (iv) only　D. (i) and (iv) only

30. Scheduled Castes and Scheduled Tribes Prevention of Atrocities Act, 1989 deals with:

(i) Caste abuses
(ii) Violence against Dalits
(iii) Corporate crimes
(iv) Environmental abuses

Codes:

A. only (iv) is true
B. (i) and (ii) are true
C. only (iii) is true
D. (iii) and (iv) are true

31. Choose the correct expansion of UNIFEM:
A. United National International Fund for Women.
B. United Nations Development Fund for Women.
C. United Nations International Fund for Education of Women.
D. United Nations Development Fund for Education of Women.

32. Arrange the chronological sequence of the legislations according to their year of enactment:
(i) Domestic Violence Bill
(ii) Juvenile Justice Act
(iii) Child Labour (Prohibition and Protection) Act
(iv) National Commission for Women Act

Codes:
A. (iii), (iv), (i), (ii) B. (iii), (i), (ii), (iv)
C. (iv), (i), (ii), (iii) D. (i), (ii), (iii), (iv)

33. Which International Conference had the thrust on the concept of empowerment?
A. Mexico B. Beijing
C. Copenhagen D. Nairobi

34. Which article of the Constitution of India provides 'The State to make any special provision in favour of women and children'?
A. Article 14 (a) B. Article 39 (C)
C. Article 19 (2) D. Article 15 (3)

35. Match the items from List-I and List-II:

List-I	*List-II*
(a) Equal Remuneration Act	(i) 1955
(b) The Hindu Marriage Act	(ii) 1961
(c) The Dowry Prohibition Act	(iii) 1956
(d) The Immoral Traffic (prevention) Act	(iv) 1976

Codes:

	(a)	(b)	(c)	(d)
A.	(iv)	(i)	(ii)	(iii)
B.	(iii)	(i)	(ii)	(iv)
C.	(i)	(ii)	(iii)	(iv)
D.	(iv)	(ii)	(iii)	(i)

36. Issues of women's citizenship relate to:
(i) Power
(ii) Autonomy
(iii) Choice to live as free and participating citizens
(iv) Politeness

Codes:
A. (i), (ii) and (iii) only
B. (i) and (ii) only
C. (iii) and (iv) only
D. (i) and (iv) only

37. Match the following items from List-I with the year in List-II:

List-I	*List-II*
(a) UN Security Council Resolution 1325	(i) 2009
(b) UN Action on Sexual Violence in Conflict "Stop Rape Now"	(ii) 2000
(c) UN Security Council Resolution 1889	(iii) 2007
(d) UNITE to end violence against women campaign	(iv) 2008

Codes:

	(a)	(b)	(c)	(d)
A.	(ii)	(iii)	(i)	(iv)
B.	(iii)	(ii)	(iv)	(i)
C.	(iv)	(i)	(iii)	(ii)
D.	(ii)	(i)	(iv)	(iii)

38. "Investing in women is not only the right thing to do. It is also the smart thing to do." Who made this statement?
A. Indira Gandhi B. Ban ki Moon
C. Brinda Karat D. Sushama Swaraj

39. Which is the correct chronological sequence of International events given below?
(i) Rio + 20 on Sustainable Development
(ii) UN World Conference to review and appraise the achievement of the UN decade for women
(iii) World Conference on Human Rights
(iv) Review and Appraisal of the Beijing Declaration and Platform for Action and the Outcome Document of the Twenty Third Special Session of the General Assembly

Mark the correct sequence from the codes given below:

Codes:
A. (i), (ii), (iii), (iv) B. (ii), (iii), (iv), (i)
C. (iii), (ii), (i), (iv) D. (iv), (ii), (iii), (i)

40. Mark the correct statement about 'custodial rape':
(i) Rape by man in a position of authority over a woman
(ii) Rape by a policeman in a police station on a woman
(iii) Rape by a person on the staff of jail on a woman
(iv) Rape by a person on the staff of a hospital on a woman

Codes:
A. (i) and (iv) only B. (i), (ii) and (iv) only
C. (i), (ii), (iii), (iv) D. (ii) only

41. Arrange the chronological sequence of the legislations according to the year of their enactment:
(i) Prohibition from Domestic Violence Act
(ii) The National Commission for Women Act
(iii) The Sexual Harassment of (Prevention, Prohibition and Redressal) Act
(iv) The Child Labour (Prohibition and Regulation) Act

Codes:
A. (i), (ii), (iii) and (iv) B. (ii), (iii), (i) and (iv)
C. (iv), (ii), (i) and (iii) D. (iii), (i), (ii) and (iv)

42. The provision for right to marry according to one's own choice irrespective of caste or religion etc., is one of the important element in:
A. The Human Rights Declaration.
B. Hindu Marriage Act.
C. Convention for Elimination of All forms of Discrimination against women.
D. National Rural Health Mission.

43. Arrange the following chronologically:
(i) World Conference on Education for all
(ii) World Conference on Human Rights
(iii) Third UN World Conference on Women
(iv) International Conference on Population and Development

Codes:

A.	(iv)	(i)	(ii)	(iii)
B.	(iii)	(i)	(ii)	(iv)
C.	(ii)	(i)	(iv)	(iii)
D.	(i)	(iii)	(iv)	(ii)

44. What is not covered by the Domestic Violence Act?
A. Women in live-in relationships
B. Marital rape
C. Women who are sisters, single women
D. Mothers, widows

45. What is called Stalking?
Choose the correct answers from the following:
(i) Any man who follows a woman and contacts, or attempts to contact such woman to foster personal interaction repeatedly despite a clear indication of disinterest by such woman.
(ii) A man monitors the use by a woman of the internet.
(iii) E-mail or any other form of electronic communication by a man to a woman.
(iv) A man showing external love before her friends

Codes:
A. (i) only B. (i) and (ii) only
C. (i), (ii) and (iii) only D. (i) and (iv) only

46. Improvement of maternal mortality is focused in Millennium Development Goal Number:
A. Goal 3 B. Goal 2
C. Goal 5 D. Goal 6

47. The present UN Rapporteur on Violence Against Women appointed in 2015 is:
A. Anne Walker
B. Radha Kumaraswami
C. Charlotte Bunch
D. Dubravka Simonovic

48. The UNO nominated 'Malala' as UN Ambassador to promote:
A. Girls' Safety and Security
B. Girls' Rights
C. Girls' Education
D. Girls' in different situation

49. Criminal Law (Amendment) Act 2013 was passed after J.S. Verma Committee Report made amendments in:
A. Criminal Procedure Code only
B. Indian Penal Code only
C. Indian Evidence Act
D. All the above three (CrPC, IPC and Indian Evidence Act)

50. Which one of the following is the UN agency for women?
A. UNIFEM B. DAW
C. OSAGI D. UN Women

51. Match List-I with List-II:

List-I (Acts)	***List-II (Years)***
(a) Hindu Marriage Act	(i) 1961
(b) Sharda Act	(ii) 1988
(c) Indecent Representation of Women (Prohibition) Act	(iii) 1929
(d) Dowry Prohibition Act	(iv) 1955

Codes:

	(a)	(b)	(c)	(d)
A.	(ii)	(i)	(iii)	(iv)
B.	(iii)	(ii)	(i)	(iv)
C.	(iv)	(iii)	(ii)	(i)
D.	(iv)	(iii)	(i)	(ii)

52. Which one of the following is NOT originally a Third Generation Right?
A. Right for Gender Justice
B. Right to Self Determination
C. Economic, Social and Cultural Rights
D. Environmental Rights

53. Which of the following Act has declared online pornography a punishable offence?

A. The Indian Information Technology Act, 2000.
B. The Media Technology Act, 2001.
C. The Cyber Technology Act, 2000.
D. The Indecent Representation of Women Act, 2001.

54. India ratified the Convention on the Political Rights of Women on 1st November 1961 with a Declaration on ______ of the Convention.

A. Article 2 B. Article 3
C. Article 5 D. Article 6

55. In 2012, along with the V-Day movement One Billion Rising, a global protest campaign to end violence and promote justice and gender equality for women was created by:

A. Jane Fonda B. Whoopie Goldberg
C. Eve Ensler D. Idina Menzel

56. Which World Conference on Women led to the establishment of International Research and Training Institute for Advancement of Women (INSTRAW)?

A. Mexico Conference
B. Copenhagen Conference
C. Nairobi Conference
D. Beijing Conference

57. The Sexual Harassment of Women at Workplace (Prevention, Prohibition and Redressal) Act, 2013 is NOT based on:

A. Art 11 of the CEDAW (Convention of Elimination of All forms of Discrimination) in which India is a party.
B. Supreme Court of India, in the case of Vishakha versus the State of Rajasthan.
C. Universal declaration of Human Rights of the UN.
D. Concept of Equality under the Constitution of India in the Article 14.

58. Under the Protection of Women from Domestic Violence Act, 2005 the Magistrate shall endeavour to dispose of every application made under the sub-section (1) within a period of:

A. Sixty days from the date of its first hearing.
B. Ninety days from the date of its first hearing.
C. Hundred and twenty days from the date of its first hearing.
D. One year from the date of its first hearing.

59. Match List-I Section under Constitution and List-II Offences:

List-I (Sections)	*List-II (Offences)*
(a) 326 A	(i) Acid Attack
(b) 326 B	(ii) Voyeurism
(c) 354 D	(iii) Stalking
(d) 354 C	(iv) Attempt to Acid Attack

Codes:

	(a)	(b)	(c)	(d)
A.	(iv)	(i)	(iii)	(ii)
B.	(iv)	(i)	(ii)	(iii)
C.	(i)	(iv)	(iii)	(ii)
D.	(i)	(ii)	(iii)	(iv)

60. The recent strategy formulated by the UN Solidarity Movement, 'He for she' to end gender inequality is:

A. The campaign for greater participation of men in private sphere.
B. The campaign for greater participation of men in women's rights.
C. The campaign for greater participation of women in public sphere.
D. The campaign for greater participation of women in decision making.

61. Which Section of the Criminal Law provides death penalty to the repeat offender of gang rape?

A. 376 B B. 376 E
C. 276 E D. 374 B

62. Match the Constitutional safeguards of List-I with Articles in List-II:

List-I	*List-II*
(a) Equal protection for men & women	(i) Art 16(4)
(b) Prohibition of discrimination on grounds of religion/caste/sex	(ii) Art 16
(c) Prohibition of discrimination at workplace	(iii) Art 15
(d) Provision for reservation in employment for backward class citizens	(iv) Art 14

Codes:

	(a)	(b)	(c)	(d)
A.	(ii)	(iii)	(iv)	(i)
B.	(i)	(iii)	(iv)	(ii)
C.	(iv)	(ii)	(iii)	(i)
D.	(iii)	(i)	(iv)	(ii)

63. India ratified the Convention on the Elimination of All Forms of Discrimination against Women in 1993 with two declarations and one reservation. With regard to which of the following articles of the Convention?

A. Articles 2(b), 5B and 28
B. Articles 5(a), 11(2)B and 29
C. Articles 2(b), 5A and 16(1)
D. Articles 5(a), 16(1)(2) and 29

64. In the Protection of Women from Domestic Violence Act, 2007 the duties of the Protection Officer do not include:

A. To assist the Magistrate in the discharge of his functions under the Act.

B. To make a domestic incident Report to the Magistrate.

C. Effective coordination between the services provided by the concerned ministries and departments dealing with law.

D. To ensure that the aggrieved person is provided legal aid under the Legal Services Authorities Act, 1987.

65. What are the provisions given under Section 354A of IPC related to Sexual Harassment?

(i) A demand or request for sexual favours.

(ii) Forcibly showing pornography.

(iii) Making sexually coloured remarks.

(iv) Watching or capturing a woman in private act.

Codes:

A. (ii), (iii) and (iv) only B. (i), (ii) and (iii) only

C. (i), (ii), (iii) and (iv) D. (i) and (ii) only

66. The First Generation of Human Rights are fundamentally:

A. Economic, Social and Cultural Rights

B. Civil and Political Rights

C. Fraternity/Solidarity Rights

D. Environmental Rights

67. Which of the following proposed Sustainable Development Goals (SDGs) by the UN Open Working Group on SDGs relates to "Achieve Gender Equality and Empower all Women and Girls Everywhere"?

A. Goal 2 B. Goal 3

C. Goal 5 D. Goal 7

68. Which General Recommendation of the CEDAW Committee deals with Women in Conflict Prevention, Conflict and Post Conflict Situations?

A. GR 19 B. GR 29

C. GR 30 D. GR 23

69. In 2000, the UN security council passed resolution 1325 that call for:

A. The exclusion of women from all combating forces, both in military and para-military structures.

B. The full and equal participation of women in all peace and security initiatives.

C. Women's equal participation in efforts of war.

D. The exclusion of men from all peace building processes.

70. Justice Verma committee's recommendations included:

(a) Voyeurism is punishable with up to seven years in jail.

(b) All marriages in India should be mandatorily be registered.

(c) An eminent need to review the continuation of AFSPA (Armed Forces Special Powers Act).

(d) Any officer who fails to register a case of rape reported to her/him or attempts to about its investigation commits a punishable offence.

Codes:

A. (a), (b), (c) and (d) B. (b), (c) and (d) only

C. (c), (d) and (a) only D. (a) and (d) only

71. UNIFEM's analysis of the feminist includes which group of "Seven P's"?

A. Power, Privilege, Permission, Paradox, Psychic Armour, Psychic Pressure Cooker and Past Experience.

B. Patriarchy, Persistence, Psychological safeguard, Physiological well being, Privilege, Paradox and Past Experience.

C. Patriarchal Power, Privilege, Permission, Paradox, Psychic Armour, Psychic Power Cooker (Masculinity) and Paradox.

D. Power, Paradox, Permission, Past Experience, Physiological well being, Psychic Power and Privilege.

72. The 'One Stop Centers' will be providing the following services to the victims of Gender based violence:

1. Medical assistance
2. Police assistance
3. Financial assistance
4. Counselling

Codes:

A. 1 and 2 only

B. 2, 3 and 4 only

C. 1, 2 and 4 only

D. 1 and 4 only

73. Which pair of the following is correctly matched?

A. Societies Registration Act — 1850

B. Companies Act — 1976

C. Indian Trust Act — 1882

D. Foreign Contributions (Regulation) Act — 1956

74. Which pair of the following is not correctly matched?

A. Environmental Protection Act - 1986

B. National Rural Employment Guarantee Act - 2005

C. Consumer Protection Act - 1986

D. Special Marriage Act - 1964

75. Which of the following offences have been incorporated into the Indian Penal Code as per Criminal Law Ordinance of 2013?

1. Acid attack 2. Stalking
3. Voyeurism 4. Marital rape

Codes:

A. 1, 2 and 4 are true
B. 1, 2 and 3 are true
C. 1 and 4 are true
D. 1, 2, 3 and 4 are true

76. The Indecent Representation of Women (Prohibition) Act was passed in:

A. 1978 B. 1986
C. 1995 D. 2000

77. A wife is entitled to what part of the property of her husband after divorce:

A. One-Third B. Half
C. One-Fourth D. Nil

78. Who was the first Indian woman to become the President of the General Assembly of the United Nations?

A. Kamla Nehru B. Sarojini Naidu
C. Vijaya Laxmi Pandit D. Sucheta Kriplani

79. Find the correct sequence of the following Act:

A. PNDT; Dowry Prohibition Act, Sati Prevention Act; Sarda Act.
B. Sarda Act; Sati Prevention Act; Dowry Prohibition Act; PNDT.
C. Sati Prevention Act; Sarda Act; Dowry Prohibition Act; PNDT.
D. Dowry Prohibition Act; PNDT; Sarda Act; Sati Prevention Act.

80. Match the items in List-I and List-II:

List-I	***List-II***
(a) Durban Conference	(i) Population and Development
(b) Mexico Conference	(ii) Conference on Racism
(c) Cairo Conference	(iii) Human Rights Conference
(d) Vienna Conference	(iv) World Conference on Women

Codes:

	(a)	(b)	(c)	(d)
A.	(ii)	(iv)	(iii)	(i)
B.	(ii)	(iv)	(i)	(iii)
C.	(iv)	(iii)	(i)	(ii)
D.	(iii)	(iv)	(ii)	(i)

81. Match the following United Nations Conferences with the year when these were held:

(a) Fourth World Conference on Women	(i) 1980
(b) Conference on Environment and Development	(ii) 1993
(c) Vienna Conference on Human Rights	(iii) 1995
(d) Second World Conference on Women	(iv) 1992

Codes:

	(a)	(b)	(c)	(d)
A.	(iv)	(iii)	(ii)	(i)
B.	(iii)	(iv)	(ii)	(i)
C.	(iii)	(i)	(iv)	(ii)
D.	(ii)	(iii)	(i)	(iv)

82. Match the following Acts with their year of enactment:

(a) Dowry Prohibition Act	(i) 1955
(b) Equal Remuneration Act	(ii) 1961
(c) Family Courts Act	(iii) 1984
(d) Hindu Marriage Act	(iv) 1976

Codes:

	(a)	(b)	(c)	(d)
A.	(iv)	(ii)	(i)	(iii)
B.	(iii)	(iv)	(ii)	(i)
C.	(ii)	(iv)	(iii)	(i)
D.	(i)	(iii)	(ii)	(i)

83. Violence against women is a reflection of:

(i) Women's free mobility
(ii) Deep rooted 'gender ideology' of the society
(iii) Non-availability of legal provisions
(iv) Male control over material resources

Codes:

A. (i), (ii) and (iii) only true
B. (i) and (ii) only true
C. (ii) and (iv) only true
D. (ii), (iii) and (iv) only true

84. The convention on Elimination of All Forms of Discrimination Against Women (CEDAW) came into force in:

A. 1979 B. 1981
C. 1975 D. 1993

85. The UN Agency which works for women's issues only is:

A. UNDP
B. UNIFEM
C. UNFPA
D. UNICEF

86. Which of the following is not a "Gender based Violence"?

A. Female circumcision
B. Sati
C. Female infanticide
D. Female infant mortality

87. Under Muslim personal law the minimum age of bride must be:

A. 18 years B. 15 years
C. 17 years D. 12 years

88. Which of the following is not a Millennium Development Goal:

A. Promote Gender equality and empower women.
B. Improve maternal health.
C. Improve political participation of women.
D. Ensure environmental sustainability.

89. Match the political leaders and their political party:

(a) Sushma Swaraj (i) Congress
(b) Mayawati (ii) BSP
(c) Brinda Karat (iii) BJP
(d) Ambika Sony (iv) CPM

Codes:

	(a)	(b)	(c)	(d)
A.	(i)	(ii)	(iii)	(iv)
B.	(i)	(iii)	(iv)	(ii)
C.	(iii)	(ii)	(iv)	(i)
D.	(iii)	(iv)	(i)	(ii)

90. Arrange the following Acts in order in which they were passed:

1. Maternity Benefit Act
2. Commission of Sati (Prevention) Act
3. Minimum Wages Act
4. Equal Remuneration Act

Codes:

A. 3, 1, 4, 2
B. 3, 4, 2, 1
C. 4, 2, 1, 3
D. 4, 1, 2, 3

91. Match the following Articles and their provisions given in the Indian Constitution:

List-I	***List-II***
(a) Article-14	(i) Equal pay for equal work.
(b) Article-15	(ii) Equal rights and opportunities for men and women.
(c) Article-39	(iii) Prohibits discrimination against religion, caste, sex.
(d) Article-16	(iv) Equality of opportunities in public appointments.

Codes:

	(a)	(b)	(c)	(d)
A.	(ii)	(iv)	(iii)	(i)
B.	(i)	(ii)	(iii)	(iv)
C.	(ii)	(iii)	(i)	(iv)
D.	(iii)	(iv)	(i)	(ii)

92. Match the establishment of the following UN bodies from List-I with List-II:

List-I	***List-II***
(a) International Research and Training Institute for the Women	(i) 1946
(b) Commission on the Status of Women	(ii) 1979
(c) UNIFEM	(iii) 2010
(d) UN Women for Gender Equality and Empowerment of Women	(iv) 1976

Codes:

	(a)	(b)	(c)	(d)
A.	(iii)	(i)	(ii)	(iv)
B.	(iv)	(i)	(ii)	(iii)
C.	(iv)	(iii)	(i)	(ii)
D.	(ii)	(i)	(iv)	(iii)

93. Match the offences in List-I with Sections of IPC dealing with offences in List-II:

List-I	***List-II***
(a) Acid Attack	(i) Section 376 IPC
(b) Molestation	(ii) 498A IPC
(c) Cruelty	(iii) 326 IPC
(d) Custodial Rape	(iv) 354 IPC

Codes:

	(a)	(b)	(c)	(d)
A.	(iii)	(iv)	(ii)	(i)
B.	(iv)	(iii)	(i)	(ii)
C.	(ii)	(iv)	(iii)	(i)
D.	(i)	(iv)	(ii)	(iii)

94. Arrange chronologically the following:

(i) The UN Declaration on the Elimination of Violence against Women.
(ii) Convention on the Nationality of Married Women.
(iii) Optional Protocol to CEDAW.
(iv) SAARC Convention on Preventing and Combating Trafficking in Women and Children for Prostitution.

Codes:

A.	(ii)	(iv)	(i)	(iii)
B.	(iv)	(ii)	(iii)	(i)
C.	(iii)	(iv)	(ii)	(i)
D.	(ii)	(i)	(iii)	(iv)

95. Honour Killings are related to:
(i) Wife beating
(ii) Sex selective abortion
(iii) Inter caste marriage
(iv) Family violence in name of honour

Codes:
A. (i) and (iii) are true B. (ii) and (iv) are true
C. (iii) and (iv) are true D. (i) and (ii) are true

96. Arrange the following in a chronological sequence:
(i) Immoral Traffic Prevention Act
(ii) Maternity Benefit Act
(iii) Panchayat Vidhi Adhiniyam
(iv) Hindu Succession Amended Act

Codes:

A.	(i)	(iv)	(ii)	(iii)
B.	(ii)	(i)	(iii)	(iv)
C.	(iv)	(iii)	(ii)	(i)
D.	(iii)	(iv)	(i)	(ii)

97. Equal Remuneration Act provides that:
(i) Women and men will be paid equally for doing the same work.
(ii) There will be no discrimination against women at the time of recruitment.
(iii) The employer is bound to maintain a register of the workers.
(iv) There will be no discrimination against women workers in any condition of service like promotion, training or transfer.

Codes:
A. (i), (ii), (iii), (iv) B. (i) and (ii) only
C. (ii) and (iii only D. (i) and (iv) only

98. Match List-I with List-II as given below:

List-I	***List-II***
(a) Medical Termination of Pregnancy Act	(i) 1956
(b) Maternity Benefit Act	(ii) 1971
(c) Protection of Human Rights Act	(iii) 1961
(d) Immoral Traffic Prevention Act	(iv) 1993

Mark the correct answer from the codes given below:

Codes:

	(a)	(b)	(c)	(d)
A.	(ii)	(i)	(iv)	(iii)
B.	(i)	(ii)	(iv)	(iii)
C.	(iii)	(ii)	(i)	(iv)
D.	(ii)	(iii)	(iv)	(i)

99. Arrange the following International Conferences in Chronological sequence:

(a) UN Conference on Human Rights	(i) Vienna
(b) Environment and Development	(ii) Rio-de-Janeiro
(c) Population and Development	(iii) Cairo
(d) Fourth Conference on Women	(iv) Beijing

Codes:

	(a)	(b)	(c)	(d)
A.	(ii)	(i)	(iii)	(iv)
B.	(i)	(iii)	(ii)	(iv)
C.	(iii)	(ii)	(i)	(iv)
D.	(iii)	(i)	(ii)	(iv)

100. Choose the correct expansion of CEDAW:
A. Conference on the Eradication of All forms of Discrimination Against Women.
B. Convention on the Elimination of all forms of Discrimination Against Women.
C. Conference on the Eradication of all forms of Differences Among Women.
D. Controlling Elimination of all Forms of Discrimination Against Women.

101. Write the year of the UN Development Decade for women:
A. 1975-1985 B. 1985-1995
C. 1991-2000 D. 2001-2011

102. What was the slogan that was proposed at the International Women's Year Conference in Mexico City in 1975?
A. Equality, Development and Empowerment.
B. Equality, Development and Peace.
C. Equality, Education and Liberation.
D. Equality, Dignity and Freedom.

103. Which among the following is not covered under personal laws?
A. The Maternity Benefit Act
B. The Guardian and Wards Act
C. The Hindu Succession Act
D. The Special Marriage Act

104. What is correct about 'Personal laws'?
(i) Family laws are the personal laws.
(ii) These laws differ from person to person according to his/her religion.
(iii) These are related with the maternity benefits to the working women.
(iv) These are related with devolution and disposition of family property, maintenance and succession and inheritance

Codes:

A. (i), (ii), (iii), (iv) B. (i), (ii) and (iv) only
C. (i), (iii) and (iv) only D. (i), (ii) and (iii) only

105. The acronym 'UNESCO' stands for:

A. United Nations Educational Scientific and Cultural Organization
B. United Nations Employment, Social and Cultural Organization
C. United Nations Educational, Social and Coalition Organization
D. United Nations Educational, Social and Cultural Organization

106. Write the sequence of important Women's Bills in our country:

1. The Protection from Domestic Violence Act
2. The Sharda Act
3. The Uniform Civil Code
4. The Hindu Code Bill

Codes:

A. 4, 3, 2, 1 B. 3, 2, 4, 1
C. 1, 2, 3, 4 D. 2, 3, 4, 1

107. Which of the following laws provided for the share of a Hindu widow in her husband's family's property though she could not alienate or sell her share of the property?

A. Sharda Act (1829).
B. Hindu Widow Remarriage Act (1956).
C. Hindu Succession Act (1956).
D. Hindu Women's Right of Property Act (1937).

108. Match the Constitutional safeguards of List-I with Articles in List-II:

List-I	***List-II***
(a) Equality and equal protection for men and women	(i) Article 16(4)
(b) Prohibits discrimination under the grounds of religions/caste/sex	(ii) Article 16
(c) Prohibits discrimination at work place	(iii) Article 15
(d) Provisions for reservation in employment for any backward class citizens	(iv) Article 14

Codes:

	(a)	(b)	(c)	(d)
A.	(ii)	(iii)	(iv)	(i)
B.	(iv)	(i)	(ii)	(iii)
C.	(iv)	(iii)	(ii)	(i)
D.	(i)	(ii)	(iii)	(iv)

109. Arrange the following Acts chronologically:

1. Immoral Trafficking (Prevention) Act
2. Dowry Prohibition Act
3. Indecent Representation of Women Prohibition Act
4. National Commission for Protection of Child Rights

Codes:

A. 1, 2, 3, 4 B. 2, 3, 4, 1
C. 1, 3, 4, 2 D. 1, 2, 4, 3

110. Which of the following Bills provide measures to punish anyone who teases or molests women in public places?

A. Women and Girl Child Protection Bill 2012
B. Women and Girls Child Atrocities Bill 2012
C. Women and Girl Child (Prevention of Atrocities) Bill 2012
D. Women and Girl Child Bill 2012

111. Which section of the criminal law amendment provide death penalty to the repeat offenders of Gang Rape?

A. 374 E B. 376 E
C. 276 E D. 245 E

112. UN Decade of Women 1976-85 ended with the conference in:

A. Nairobi
B. Beijing
C. Bangkok
D Stony Point New York

113. Arrange the following conventions in the chronological order:

(i) Convention on the Elimination of All Forms of Discrimination against Women
(ii) Convention on the Rights of the Child
(iii) International Covenant on Economic Social and Cultural Rights
(iv) Convention against Torture

Codes:

A. (i), (iv), (ii) and (iii) B. (iii), (i), (iv) and (ii)
C. (iv), (i), (iii) and (ii) D. (ii), (iii), (i) and (iv)

114. According to the latest judgement of the Supreme Court, which category the Transgender belong to?

A. General Category B. SC Category
C. Backward Category D. OBC Category

115. Which fundamental right can't be suspended even during 'Emergency'?

A. Right to Equality
B. Right to Education
C. Right to Freedom
D. Right to Life and Personal Liberty

116. Match the following from List-I and List-II:

List-I (Crime)	***List-II (IPC Section)***
(a) Importation of girls from foreign country	(i) Section 373 IPC
(b) Procuration of minor girls	(ii) Section 366 B IPC
(c) Buying of girls for prostitution	(iii) Section 372 IPC
(d) Selling of girls for prostitution	(iv) Section 366 A IPC

Codes:

	(a)	(b)	(c)	(d)
A.	(iv)	(ii)	(iii)	(i)
B.	(iii)	(iv)	(ii)	(i)
C.	(iv)	(iii)	(i)	(ii)
D.	(ii)	(iv)	(i)	(iii)

117. Match the following from List-I and List-II:

List-I (General Recommendation of CEDAW)	***List-II (Issue)***
(a) General Recommendation 18	(i) Women and health
(b) General Recommendation 23	(ii) Violence against women
(c) General Recommendation 24	(iii) Disabled women
(d) General Recommendation 19	(iv) Women in political and public life

Codes:

	(a)	(b)	(c)	(d)
A.	(iii)	(ii)	(iv)	(i)
B.	(iii)	(iv)	(i)	(ii)
C.	(ii)	(iii)	(i)	(iv)
D.	(iv)	(ii)	(i)	(iii)

118. Who is the current Chief Executive Director of UN Women in 2019?

A. Lakshmi Puri
B. Michelle Bachelet
C. Phumzile Mlambo-Nyguka
D. Angela Merkel

119. The United Nation Commission on the status of women was established in:

A. 1950 B. 1995
C. 1946 D. 1947

120. Match the following from List-I and List-II:

List-I (Offence)	***List-II (Section IPC)***
(a) Insult to the modesty of women	(i) Section 354 D IPC
(b) Cruelty by husband and relatives	(ii) Section 354 IPC
(c) Assault on women with the intent to outrage her modesty	(iii) Section 498 A IPC
(d) Stalking	(iv) Section 509 IPC

Codes:

	(a)	(b)	(c)	(d)
A.	(i)	(iii)	(iv)	(ii)
B.	(iv)	(iii)	(ii)	(i)
C.	(ii)	(iii)	(iv)	(i)
D.	(iii)	(ii)	(i)	(iv)

121. Arrange the following Instruments of Law concerning women in chronological order:

I. Optional Protocol to the Convention on the Elimination of All forms of Discrimination against Women
II. Convention on the Political Rights of Women
III. Declaration on the Protection of Women and Children in Emergency and Armed Conflict
IV. Declaration on the Elimination of Violence against Women

Codes:

A. II, III, IV, I B. IV, II, I, III
C. II, IV, III, I D. III, II, I, IV

122. The 'aggrieved person' in the Protection of Women from Domestic Violence Act, 2005 means any women:

1. Who knows the respondent.
2. Who is or has been in a domestic relationship with the respondent.
3. Who alleges to have been subjected to any act of domestic violence by the respondent.
4. Who alleges harassment by the respondent.

Codes:

A. 1, 2, 3 and 4 B. 1 only
C. 2, 3 and 4 only D. 1, 2 and 3 only

123. Under the Hindu Successor (Amendment) Act 1956:

(a) A daughter is a coparcener at par with the son, and entitled to a share of the ancestral property owned by the coparcenary.
(b) The daughter of a coparcener shall by birth be a coparcener in her own right in the same manner as the son.
(c) The daughter of a coparcener shall be subjected to the same liabilities in respect of the said coparcenary property as that of the son.
(d) Daughter are entitled to a share in the property, and have the right to demand a partition in the dwelling house.

Codes:

A. (a), (b) and (c) only B. (b), (c) and (d) only
C. (a) and (d) only D. (a), (b) (c) and (d)

124. Under the Hindu Widow Remarriage Act, 1856:
(a) Marriage of Hindu widows legalised.
(b) Rights of widow in deceased husband's property cease on her remarriage.
(c) A child less widow cannot inherit any property.
(d) Ceremonies constituting valid marriage to have the same effect on widow's marriage.

Codes:

A. (a) and (c) only
B. (a), (b) and (c) only
C. (b), (c) and (d) only
D. (a), (b), (c) and (d) only

125. The term 'Scheduled Caste' was coined by:
A. B.R. Ambedkar B. Mahatma Gandhi
C. Kothari Commission D. Simon Commission

126. Mark the correct answer:
In the Indian Constitution, what does the Article 17 speak about?
A. Abolishing untouchability.
B. Social and economic backwardness.
C. Weaker section of the people in which scheduled castes and scheduled tribes are included.
D. Making provision for the state to investigate the condition of the backward classes.

127. Which Article of the Indian Constitution empowers the state to make special provision in favour of women and children?
A. Article 14 B. Article 15 (1)
C. Article 15 (2) D. Article 15 (3)

128. Under which of the following Articles of the Constitution, does the state provide for free and compulsory education to all the children in the age group of 6-14 years?
A. Article 21 B. Article 21A
C. Article 32 D. Article 14

129. Apparel Export Promotion Council vs. A.K. Chopra judgement relates with:
A. Women's representation
B. Sexual harassment of women at work place
C. Maternity benefits to women
D. Women's Rights to Property

130. Who initiated the 'One Billion Rising Movement', the campaign to end violence against women and promote justice and gender equality for women?
A. Eve Ensler B. Astrid Henry
C. Shira Tarrant D. Barbara Findlen

131. Which is the correct chronological sequence of enactments of the following Acts?
i) Muslim Women (Protection of Right on Divorce) Act
ii) Family Courts Act
iii) Protection of Children from Sexual Offences Act
iv) Hindu Adoption and Maintenance Act

Mark the correct sequence from the codes given below:

Codes:

A. (ii), (iv), (iii), (i) B. (iii), (i), (iv), (ii)
C. (i), (ii), (iii), (iv) D. (iv), (ii), (i), (iii)

132. Match List-I with List-II:

List-I **(Offence)**	***List-II*** **(Punishment)**
(a) Voluntarily causing grievous hurt by use of acid	(i) Imprisonment not less than 3 years may extend to 7 years and also liable to fine.
(b) Voyeurism	(ii) Punishment on first conviction, imprisonment which may extend to three years and also liable to fine.
(c) Stalking	(iii) Punishment on first conviction, imprisonment not less than one year, extend to three years and fine.
(d) Assault or use of criminal force to women with intent to disrobe her	(iv) Imprisonment not less than 10 years, may extend for life and with fine.

Codes:

	(a)	(b)	(c)	(d)
A.	(iv)	(ii)	(iii)	(i)
B.	(i)	(ii)	(iii)	(iv)
C.	(iv)	(iii)	(ii)	(i)
D.	(iii)	(iv)	(i)	(ii)

133. Arrange the following chronologically:
(i) Declaration on the Elimination of Violence against Women.
(ii) Convention on the Political Rights of Women.
(iii) Declaration on the Protection of Women and Children in Emergency Armed Conflict.
(iv) Optional Protocol to CEDAW

Codes:

A. (ii), (iii), (i), (iv) B. (ii), (i), (iv), (iii)
C. (iii), (i), (ii), (iv) D. (iv), (ii), (i), (iii)

134. Punishment for gang rape under Section 376 D of IPC is:

A. Death Sentence.
B. Rigorous imprisonment for a term not less than 20 years.
C. Rigorous imprisonment for a term not less than 20 years but which may extend to life, meaning the remainder of that person's natural life.
D. Rigorous imprisonment for a term not less than seven years.

135. Arrange the following chronologically:

(i) SAARC convention on Preventing and Combating Trafficking in Women and Children for Prostitution.
(ii) Convention on the Nationality of Married Women.
(iii) United Nations Convention on the Protection of the Rights of All Migrant Workers and Members of their Families.
(iv) Maternity Protection Convention.

Codes:

A. (i), (ii, (iii), (iv) B. (ii), (iv), (iii), (i)
C. (iii), (i), (ii), (iv) D. (i), (iii), (ii), (iv)

136. Mark the correct answer about the personal laws that govern women:

(i) The Hindu Succession Act
(ii) The Maternity Benefit Act
(iii) Custody and Guardianship Act
(iv) Equal Remuneration Act

Codes:

A. (i), (ii) and (iii) only
B. (i) and (iv) only
C. (i) and (iii) only
D. (ii) and (iii) only

137. The members of the Justice J.S. Verma Committee constituted by the Government of India were:

A. Justice J.S. Verma, Justice Sujata Manohar and Justice Leila Seth
B. Justice J.S. Verma, Justice Krishna Iyer and Justice Sujata Manohar
C. Justice Fatima Beevi, Justice Leila Seth and Justice J.S. Verma
D. Justice J.S. Verma, Justice Leila Seth and Gopal Subramanium

138. **Assertion (A):** The aim of All Women Police Station is to make enforcement machinery accessible to women.

Reason (R): Women police are empathic to women victims.

Codes:

A. (A) is true but (R) is false.
B. Both (A) and (R) are true, but (R) is not the true reason for (A).
C. (A) is false but (R) is true.
D. Both (A) and (R) are true.

139. **Assertion (A):** Violence against women such as rape, molestation, teasing and dowry deaths are prevailing in common.

Reason (R): Women are discriminated on the basis of gender, caste and class.

Codes:

A. Both (A) and (R) are true.
B. (A) is true and (R) is the cause for (A).
C. (A) is true and (R) is not the cause for (A).
D. Both (A) and (R) are false.

140. **Assertion (A):** Indian has been the signatory of convention on Elimination of All Forms of Violence Against Women (CEDAW).

Reason (R): Crimes against women in India is on the increase.

Codes:

A. Both (A) and (R) are true.
B. Both (A) and (R) are false.
C. (A) is true, (R) is false.
D. Both (A) and (R) are true, (R) is the correct explanation of (A).

141. **Assertion (A):** Laws do not automatically change social structure.

Reason (R): Laws are generally improperly enforced and are subject to the executive control of the State.

Codes:

A. Both (A) and (R) are true and (R) is the correct explanation for (A).
B. Both (A) and (R) are true, and (R) is not the correct explanation for (A).
C. Both (A) and (R) are false.
D. (A) is true, (R) is false.

142. **Assertion (A):** The Hindu Succession Act 1956 has failed to reduce social inequalities among women.

Reason (R): Religious traditions and customary practices came in conflict with the act.

Codes:

A. (A) is true but (R) is false.
B. Both (A) and (R) are true.
C. (A) is false, but (R) is true.
D. Both (A) and (R) are false.

143. Assertion (A): Under the Dowry Prohibition (Amendment) Act 1986, Cruelty by the Husband or his relatives leading to suicide or death of a woman is a cognizable offence.

Reason (R): The Dowry Prohibition (Amendment) Act 1986, bans dowry.

Codes:

A. (A) is true and (R) is false and (R) is not the correct explanation for (A).
B. Both (A) and (R) are true and (R) is not the correct explanation for (A).
C. (A) is false and (R) are true.
D. Both (A) and (R) are false.

144. Assertion (A): The persistence of discriminatory laws, policies, patriarchal customs and traditions in various countries are still blocking women from enjoying their land and property rights.

Reason (R): Most of the women are enjoying property and land rights in India.

Codes:

A. Both (A) and (R) are true.
B. Both (A) and (R) are false.
C. (A) is true and (R) is not the correct explanation for (A).
D. (A) is true and (R) is false.

145. Assertion (A): Violence against women cuts across caste, class, religion, age and even education.

Reason (R): Domestic violence is manifested in the form of foeticide, infanticide, dowry murder, marital cruelty, battering, child abuse etc.

Codes:

A. Both (A) and (R) are true and (R) is the correct explanation for (A).
B. (A) is false, but (R) is true.
C. (A) is true, but (R) is false.
D. Both (A) and (R) are true, but (R) is not the correct explanation of (A).

146. Assertion (A): Indian constitution states that women are a "weaker section" of the population, and therefore used assistance of function as equals.

Reason (R): Women in India have to struggle for basic rights as did women in the west.

Codes:

A. Both (A) and (R) are true.
B. Both (A) and (R) are false.
C. (A) is true (R) is false.
D. (A) is false (R) is true.

147. Assertion (A): Women's rights are human rights.

Reason (R): Violence against women receives protection from the Constitution of India and International Conventions.

Codes:

A. Both (A) and (R) are false.
B. Both (A) and (R) are true, and (R) is the correct explanation of (A).
C. Both (A) and (R) are true, and (R) is not the correct explanation of (A).
D. (R) is false.

148. Assertion (A): Men have continued to received Social and Institutional support for their violent abusive behaviour.

Reason (R): Statutory agencies such as criminal justice and social services have been slow to respond to violence against women.

Codes:

A. Both (A) and (R) are false.
B. Both (A) and (R) are true and (R) is not the correct explanation for (A).
C. Both (A) and (R) are true, (R) is the correct explanation for (A).
D. Both (A) and (R) are false and (R) is the correct explanation for (A).

149. Assertion (A): Women are subjected to rape, female circumstances and sex related crimes all over the world.

Reason (R): Family and society provide the mechanism for perpetuating male control over women's sexuality.

Codes:

A. Both (A) and (R) are true and (R) is the correct explanation for (A).
B. Both (A) and (R) are true and (R) is the not the correct explanation for (A).
C. (A) is true and (R) is false.
D. Both (A) and (R) are false.

150. Assertion (A): Violation of women's human rights are often linked to their sexuality and reproductive roles.

Reason (R): Women are frequently treated as commodities and are pushed into marriage, trafficking and sexual slavery.

Codes:

A. Both (A) and (R) are true and (R) is the correct explanation for (A).
B. Both (A) and (R) are true but (R) is not the correct explanation for (A).
C. (A) is true and (R) is false.
D. Both (A) and (R) are false.

Answers

1	2	3	4	5	6	7	8	9	10
D	A	A	D	D	B	C	A	B	C
11	**12**	**13**	**14**	**15**	**16**	**17**	**18**	**19**	**20**
A	B	D	A	B	D	C	B	D	B
21	**22**	**23**	**24**	**25**	**26**	**27**	**28**	**29**	**30**
A	C	C	B	A	A	A	D	C	B
31	**32**	**33**	**34**	**35**	**36**	**37**	**38**	**39**	**40**
B	A	D	D	A	A	A	B	B	C
41	**42**	**43**	**44**	**45**	**46**	**47**	**48**	**49**	**50**
C	C	B	B	C	C	D	C	D	D
51	**52**	**53**	**54**	**55**	**56**	**57**	**58**	**59**	**60**
C	C	A	B	C	A	C	A	C	B
61	**62**	**63**	**64**	**65**	**66**	**67**	**68**	**69**	**70**
B	A	D	C	B	B	C	C	B	A
71	**72**	**73**	**74**	**75**	**76**	**77**	**78**	**79**	**80**
A	C	C	D	B	B	B	C	B	B
81	**82**	**83**	**84**	**85**	**86**	**87**	**88**	**89**	**90**
B	C	C	B	B	D	B	C	C	A
91	**92**	**93**	**94**	**95**	**96**	**97**	**98**	**99**	**100**
C	D	A	D	C	B	A	D	A	B
101	**102**	**103**	**104**	**105**	**106**	**107**	**108**	**109**	**110**
A	B	A	B	A	D	D	C	A	C
111	**112**	**113**	**114**	**115**	**116**	**117**	**118**	**119**	**120**
B	A	B	D	D	D	B	C	C	B
121	**122**	**123**	**124**	**125**	**126**	**127**	**128**	**129**	**130**
A	C	D	D	D	A	D	B	B	A
131	**132**	**133**	**134**	**135**	**136**	**137**	**138**	**139**	**140**
D	C	A	C	B	C	D	B	B	A
141	**142**	**143**	**144**	**145**	**146**	**147**	**148**	**149**	**150**
A	B	B	D	D	C	B	C	A	A

❑❑❑

Gender and Media

- ➡ Discourse on Women and Media Studies–Mainstream Media, Feminist Media
- ➡ Coverage of Women's issues and Issues of Women in Mass Media and Media Organizations (Audio-Visual and Print Media)
- ➡ Digital Media and Legal Protection
- ➡ Alternative Media – Folk Art, Street Play and Theatre
- ➡ Indecent Representation of Women (Prohibition) Act, 1986, Impact of Media on Women

DISCOURSE ON WOMEN AND MEDIA STUDIES—MAINSTREAM MEDIA, FEMINIST MEDIA

- **Mass Media**: Any medium of communication that is used to reach out to society and masses.
- **Synchronous Media:** Any communication medium that requires both parties to be present at the same time; examples are radio, live news, TV shows, etc.
- **Asynchronous Media:** Involves communication of information with time-lag; e.g. newspapers, news websites, social media communications etc.
- Plays a vital role in the dissemination of information and contributes to mass culture. Hence, how women are represented by mass media directly influences how they are treated by society.
- But, the mass media remains another aspect of society that exploits and precipitates the gender oppression of women. It has reconstructed "femaleness" in the socio-cultural milieu.
- According to feminist discourse, society prescribes gender-related behavior and thinking to people which get internalized over time.
- Gender has become performative where women conform to and perform those behaviors categorized as female behaviors.
- Media contributes to this social construction and semantics of gender behavior.
- Media reflects the 'male gaze' by depicting women only as objects of desire, which constructs a negative identity of the female body. Women's body is used to sell products and media impose a standard of beauty for women by external sources.
- This commercial exploitation of women's image has affected women in multiple ways including food intake, self-image, and identity.
- By doing so, media prevents the positive identity of women and acts as an obstacle to the application and development of female agency.
- It also leads to women victimization due to the subversion created by media. Media's depiction and exploitation of women has created a body, image and identity crisis for women.
- Various feminist movements offer different analysis of media and its impact on gender in society.

- **Liberal Feminism** criticizes the mainstream media for depicting women only as wives, mothers, girlfriends and in traditionally female jobs like nurses, receptionists, etc. Media has perpetuated sex stereotypes and prescribes appropriate sex behaviors.
- **Radical Feminists** have played an important role in exposing issues of sexual violence, sex tourism and trafficking, pornography, etc. According to them, as long as the media is in the hands of male producers, the benefit of patriarchy will be the primary concern for the mainstream media.
- **The Socialist Feminist Media** agrees that at least in the early stages, media has contributed to the propagation of modernity and ideas of women's freedom and emancipation. But, the capitalization of media has led to a commercial view of modernity which has negatively impacted women with its consumerist culture. This capitalist controlled media not only exploits women for furthering its consumerist culture but also views women as objects for consumption.
- In Indian society, women's depiction in media has been one of dichotomy—it is either "*devi*" or "damned." Women are either extolled as the embodiment of virtues and godliness or castigated for defying traditionalism and patriarchy. The commercial media has both contributed to and accentuated this dichotomy.
- The depiction of women in advertisements, TV shows, soap operas and cinemas is usually as well-behaved submissive home-makers to the husband and the society. On the other hand, the urbane empowered women depictions involve objectification of their body and beauty.
- According to the New Delhi based feminist group, "Committee on Portrayal of Women in Media", not just the physical objectification, but the reinforcement of female stereotypes is very damaging to womanhood.
- In commercials, women are mostly used for selling kitchen products, household appliances, and cosmetics, etc.
- **Beijing Platform of Action** recommended self-regulatory mechanisms for media to eliminate gender-biased programming.
- The mainstream media is not giving space for women to voice their issues, ideas, and problems.
- According to Network for Women in Media (NWM), very limited space is given for female reporters. Only 32% of articles in print news are written by women. Women authored editorials make up only 24% of the total. NWM was founded in 2002 as a forum for women media professionals to come together.
- Women have to fight their way into working in mass media. They face obstacles in establishing their credibility and getting women-centric issues heard. There is a need to involve women in decision making.

COVERAGE OF WOMEN'S ISSUES AND ISSUES RELATED TO WOMEN IN MASS MEDIA AND MEDIA ORGANIZATIONS (AUDIO-VISUAL AND PRINT MEDIA)

- Issues related to women are not discussed in media widely. Only sensational news about women is given extensive coverage, while important discourses and discussions on women related issues never occur.
- According to a survey by MediaCloud, rape receives maximum media coverage. Other social issues related to women are largely ignored.
- Media does not offer any serious analysis of patriarchy and inter-relationships of social issues.
- Rape, dowry deaths and other serious violence against women are framed as criminal occurrences rather than the outcomes of patriarchy and inequality.
- Also, rape, child marriages, domestic violence are covered by the media if they are high-profile and involve statement from politicians.
- **Electronic and Print Media:** Television, radio, movies, the press, publications, advertisement photography, internet, animation, and paintings.
- Feature movies and television soap operas, still portray women in stereotypical roles as inferior, subordinate and submissive gender. It is justified by the producers as the demand of the masses. But, these depictions influence how women are perceived and treated in society.
- Women are also constantly given decorative roles or as domestic caregivers of family, reinforcing the gender dynamics in the family system.
- These electronic media, including news channels, can play a crucial role in the reconstruction of women's image, shaping gender norms, social-cultural values, and perceptions.

- But, mostly sensational news such as rape and violence against women are given the spotlight, while more severe women issues are not taken up.
- Sexual objectification and commodification of women are very common in movies and advertisements. Advertisements depict their own version of women perfection—slim, fair complexioned, glamorous—which sets a bad precedent among adolescent and young women.
- Advertisements, especially for home, kitchen, jewelry, sanitation, and hygiene products mirror the gendered view of society. Those ads depict women mostly as home-makers, concerned only with maintaining their houses, beauty and taking care of their families.
- Women's movements, led by feminists in India have been instrumental in highlighting the sexist attitude in advertisements. Though there have been some changes in the way corporates and product companies depict women, the tendency has always been towards reinforcing traditional regressive gender roles.
- Fashion and cosmetics industry also play a negative role in the gender discrimination of women. Its only women who are expected to maintain impossible standards of physical perfection and body shape. Objectification of women's body is subtly promoted by beauty pageants and the fashion industry that curtails women equality. Women are treated as trophies, celebrated for how they look, instead of intelligence, skill, character and their contribution. There have been feminist movements in the US and around the world against beauty pageants and the stereotypes they reinforce.
- Gendered media helps the maintenance of patriarchy in society. More women have to occupy managerial and higher positions in the field of print journalism, television, and publications.
- Women journalists, even now have to struggle to cover wars and conflicts. The chances of women reaching managerial positions are less.
- But, there have been women pioneers in journalism since before independence.
- **Vidhya Munshi** is considered to be the first Indian woman journalist who wrote for different papers and magazines.
- **Homai Vyarawalla** is the first Indian woman photojournalist who covered the Second World War on the Indian front. Most of her photos were published under the pseudonym "Dalda 13".
- Despite precedents and history, women journalists have become more vulnerable to attacks from conservative, anti-feministic sections of the society. Journalists who fight against social oppression, fundamentalism and patriarchy are threatened, attacked and even killed. Gauri Lankesh, the editor and publisher of *Lankesh Patrika*, was shot by members of a right-wing group in September 2016. She was killed for being an outspoken critic of religious extremism and social conservatism. The dangers to work safety and their lives are increasingly real.
- **Media Sports:** A branch of media dedicated to the sports domain, covering sports events, news, and updates. It includes sports magazines, e-magazines, sports pages in daily newspapers, dedicated sports channels, etc.
- Men have dominated sports due to our conservative social culture. But, lately, numerous sportswomen have shown the way in successful sport carrier for Indian women.
- But objectification of sportswomen by the sports-media remains an obstacle to Indian sportswomen and needs to be taken seriously. Some examples are articles such as "Sexiest female athletes in India." The sports-media concentrates on their fashion sense and style statements instead of their sports performance.
- Successes of sportswomen are attributed to a male authority figure in their life such as their father or coach, which never happens for sportsmen in India.
- **Comet Media Foundation:** Founded in 1985; a non-profit organization based in Mumbai; creates and distributes media that fosters education, social change, and sustainability; has produced several films and publications to further its agenda; provides an alternative medium for advocacy of gender equality and women's development.
- **Indian Journal of Gender Studies:** Started in 1994; published by Sage Publications for the Indian Council of Social Science Research; current editors-in-chief are Malavika Karlekar and Leela Kasturi; a triannual academic journal with a central focus in gender and society.
- **Chameli Devi Jain Award:** Outstanding award for women media persons in India, who have made a difference through their writing with depth, analytical skill, social concern, insights, and courage. It was instituted by the efforts of BG Varghese, one of the founders of Media Foundation. First awarded in 1981 to Ms Neeraja Chowdhuri.

PROMINENT INDIAN WOMEN WRITERS AND MEDIA PERSONS

Nidhi Razdan

- Journalist and anchor for NDTV news channel
- Has covered various issues such as the Tiber, POK, Iran, and Terrorism
- Received Ramnath Goenka award for her news coverage of Jammu and Kashmir and North-eastern states.

Sagarika Ghose

- Deputy Editor of CNN
- Has worked for Outlook, The Indian Express and Times of India
- First woman to have participated as an anchor in the BBC show Question time India.

Barkha Dutt

- Front-line war reporting during the Kargil war of 1999
- Hosted shows such as "We the people," "The buck stops here."
- Has won the Padma Shri, Commonwealth Broadcasting award, etc.

Urvashi Butalia

- Publisher and writer
- Along with Ritu Menon, founded 'Kali for Women', the first feminist publishing house in 1984
- Took initiatives to enhance and encourage female Indian writers
- Authored a number of books, including "The Other side of Silence: Voices from the Partition of India" with an emphasis on the violence faced by women during partition.

Ruth Vanita

- Activist and writer
- Co-founder of "Manushi: A Journal about Women and Society" along with Madhu Kishwar
- The magazine focuses on feminism, gender issues, and social activism
- Manushi is also a publishing house
- Her book "Dancing with the Nation," covers the journey of courtesans to Bombay cinema and simultaneously a study of sexism, gender, performing arts and culture in India.

Radha Kumar

- Indian feminist and author
- Her writings focus on conflict and peace processes with a feminist perspective.
- Her book "A History of Doing" provides a thematic elaboration of the feminist movement in India from the ninetieth century to the present day.

Deepa Mehta

- Indo-Canadian filmmaker
- Known for her Elements trilogy of movies: Fire, Earth, and Water
- Her film "Fire" was a study of conservative society and gender-defined roles in Indian culture.

Vandana Shiva

- Ecofeminist
- Authored "Ecofeminism" along with Maria Mies
- Member of International Organization for Participatory Society
- Received "Right Livelihood award" (alternative Nobel prize) in 1993
- She criticizes the **"Capitalist Reductionist Paradigm"** for its inability to perceive the interconnectedness among the environment, women's lives, and knowledge.
- Her book "Staying Alive" articulates how rural Indian women have perceived ecological destruction and their interconnectedness with regeneration of nature.
- She wrote the book "The Violence of the Green Revolution: Third World Agriculture, Ecology and Politics" in 1989. It examines the impact of the green revolution and biotechnology on traditional and organic agricultural systems.

Lalithambika Antharjanam

- Social reformer and writer
- Her work reflects sensitivity towards women's role and womanhood
- Her book, Agnisakshi (1976), won the Kendra Sahitya Akademi award
- The novel offered creative criticism of social structure and behavior and explored the ideas of choice, detachment.

Maha Shweta Devi

- Women social activist, journalist, writer, and a radical feminist
- Worked and wrote on tribal and Adivasi issues
- Has received various literary awards such as Sahitya Akademi Award, Jnanapith award, Ramon Magsaysay award, Padma Shri and Padma Vibhushan
- Raised her voice for the tribal people of India.

Dadasaheb Phalke Award

Dadasaheb Phalke award is the highest award of Indian Cinema given by the government of India. It was instituted in 1962 to honor outstanding contribution to the growth of Indian cinema. The first recipient of this award itself was a woman. Devika Rani was honored with this award in 1969.

Women Winners:

- 1969 – Devika Rani, Actress
- 1973 – Ruby Myers, Actress
- 1976 – Kanan Devi, Actress
- 1983 – Durga Khote, Actress
- 1989 – Lata Mangeshkar, Playback singer
- 2000 – Asha Bhosle, Playback singer

SOME IMPORTANT FEMINIST WORKS

Stri Purush Tulana (1882) by Tarabai Shinde – this article criticizes the dominance of patriarchal society over women and even questions the just rule of God when women are subjugated and deprived of any freedom and rights.

The Position of Women in Hindu Civilization (1938) by Anand Sadashiv Altekar – offers a critical survey of women's position in India from prehistoric times to the present day.

Being and Nothingness (1943) by Jean-Paul Sartre – an essay on phenomenological consciousness.

The Natural Superiority of Women (1954) by Ashley Montagu – argues against biological determinism and examines the relationship between man and woman.

The Hindu Women (1953) by Margaret Cormack – offers a comprehensive study of Indian women, their role and context in the new India.

Women's Role in Economic Development (1970) by Ester Boserup – investigates the process of socio-economic development in the developing world and the position of women in the contribution and benefit of growth.

Women on the Edge of Time (1976) by Marge Piercy – explores the themes of social transformation and feminism in a utopian setting.

Inside the Haveli (1977) by Rama Mehta won the Sahitya Akademi award; explores the condition of women in traditional-bound modern India through this fiction.

Reproduction of Mothering (1978) by Nancy Chodorow – a formulation of in-depth psycho and socio-analysis of female and male development.

Symbols of Power: Studies on the Political Status of Women in India (1979) by Vina Mazumdar- examines the role of women in national and state politics, the process of politicization of women in India.

Public Man, Private Woman: Women in Social and Political Thought (1981) by Jean Bethke Elshtain – explores the tendency of denigrating the private sphere occupied by women in favor of the public sphere by the western philosophical and contemporary feminists; offers a positive reconstruction of the public and private in feminist theory.

Can the Subaltern Speak? (1983) by Gayatri Spivak – an essay on how the subaltern (the third world) is divided by race, gender, religion and caste narratives. She also introduces the questions of gender and sexual difference and criticizes imposition of external knowledge as a method of colonialism.

A Daughter's Geography (1983) by Ntozake Shange – through this collection of poems, the poet explores the expanding horizons of the black imagination, women's struggle under social subjugation; she provides a lyrical description of her world, alternating between rejection and acceptance.

After the Second Sex (1983) by Alice Schwarzer – a biography of Simone de Beauvoir that clarifies and elaborates her position on politics, feminism, and condition of women.

The Handmaid's Tale (1985) by Margaret Atwood – explores the oppression and subjugation of women in a dystopian setting.

Demystification of Law for Women (1986) by Nandita Haksar- offers a simplified version of various legislations and statutes for women.

A Decade of Women's Movement in India (1988) by Neera Desai – a collection of essays on women-related issues and feminist thoughts presented at Research Center for Women's Studies, S.N.D.T. University, Bombay.

Socialization, Education and Women: Explorations in Gender identity (1988) by Karuna Chanana – explores how women are socialized into their gender roles and how it is internalized.

Recasting Women: Essays in Colonial History (1989) by Kumkum Sangari – explores the inter-relations of patriarchy religion, political-economy, culture, class and gender relations.

In Other Words: New Writing by Indian Women (1992) by Urvashi Butalia and Ritu Menon – a collection of literary works by Indian women writers.

Gender Planning and Development: Theory, Practice and Training (1993) by Caroline O. N. Moser – provides the essential introduction to issues of women subordination and better understanding needed for women's organization and collective action for women emancipation.

Women's Oppression in Public Gaze: An Analysis of Newspaper Coverage, State Action and Activist Response (1994) by Meera Kosambi – offers an elaborate and evidence-based coverage and case studies of women's status, press coverage of women's issues, crimes against women in India.

Dalits and the Democratic Revolution (1994) by Gail Omvedt – traces the history, ideology, and organization of Dalit movement in India.

Women's Empowerment in South Asia: Concepts and Practices (1994) by Srilatha Batliwala – offers a comparative analysis of education, status and other social conditions of women in various regions of South Asia and calls for a better understanding of power and empowerment and large-scale transformative action for women empowerment.

Kinship, Family and Socialization in South and South-East Asia (1994) by Leela Dube – explores the influence of kinship systems over material relations in South Asian societies and the ways in which gender operates within these structures.

A Field of One's Own (1994) by Bina Agarwal – offers an analysis of gender property relations; lack of land ownership rights for women of South Asia.

Reversed Realities: Gender Hierarchy in Development Thought (1994) by Naila Kabeer-undercovers the gender bias entrenched in mainstream development theory and pinpoints its role in the marginalized status of women in society.

Indian Women: Myth and Reality (1995) by Jasodhara Bagchi – explains how the myths about womanhood in India influences their current position and life in society.

Towards a Feminist Politics? The Indian Women's Movement in Historical Perspective (2000) by Samita Sen–an essay that explores the challenges faced by the women's movement in India through two important debates–the Uniform Civil Code and reservation for women in legislative bodies.

The Violence of Development: The Politics of Identity, Gender and Social Inequalities in India (2002) by Karin Kapadia – explores the inter-relationships between governance, gender and women's politicization, and their social experiences.

Narratives from the Women's Studies Family (2003) by Devaki Jain and Pam Rajput–highlight the evolution of women's studies, chief contributors to its development and its role in changing social development perspective. It collects together the personal accounts of 17 feminist scholars and activists who have played a pivotal role in the development of women's studies in India. The 17 narratives and their authors are:

- From Women's Education to Women's Studies ***–Neera Desai, Vina Mazumdar, and Kamalini Bhansali***
- Blazing a Quarter Century Trail ***–Maithreyi Krishnaraj***
- From Cycle Shed to Powerhouse ***–Pam Rajput***
- Integrating Activism and Academics ***–Chaya Datar***
- Catalysts and Deterrents ***–Susheela Kaushik***
- Being a Woman Is Not Enough ***–Surinder Jetley***
- A Challenging and Inspiring Journey ***–Jasodhara Bagchi***
- Towards Justice ***–Bharati Ray***
- Crossing Boundary Politics ***–Regina Papa***
- Taking Wings within a University: Many Struggles, a Few Successes ***–Amita Verma***
- From Presence to Identity ***–Rameshwari Varma***
- Building a Service Station Brick by Brick ***–Devaki Jain***
- Nurturing Links Between Scholarship and Activism ***–Anveshi Research Centre for Women's Studies***
- The Discourse Between Studies, Institutions and Critical Pedagogy ***–Kumud Sharma***
- My Journey into Women's Studies ***–V.S. Elizabeth***
- Full Circle ***–Leela Gulati***
- Oppositional Imaginations ***–Uma Chakravarti***

Make Me a Man!: Masculinity, Hinduism and Nationalism in India (2005) by Sikata Banerjee–examines the expression of nation and manliness in masculine Hinduism and how this constricts women's lives within its conservative norms and social structures.

Writing Caste, Writing Gender: Reading Dalit Women's Testimonies (2006) by Sharmila Rege–focuses on eight Dalit women's testimonies to counter the mainstream narrative of feminist movements.

Migrant Women and Work (2006) by Anuja Agarwal–analyses of patterns of migration among Asian women and the consequences affecting gender and social relations.

Gender, Generation and Poverty (2007) by Sylvia Chant–explores the feminization of poverty in the third-world countries and offers a gender perspective of poverty.

Translating Women: Indian Interventions (2009) by N. Kamala–explores the translations of women's language, writings, and views in the context of the Indian society.

Gender and Green Governance: The Political Economy of Women's Presence within and beyond Community Forestry (2010) by Bina Agarwal–a critical analysis of ignorance of gender in collective environmental action and green governance; makes a case for the involvement of women in forest governance.

Women's Movements in the Global Era: The Power of Local Feminisms (2010) by Amrita Basu – a study of the evolution of women's movement throughout the world; explores women's movement within the regions and their contribution to feminist thought.

Motherhood in India: Glorification without Empowerment? (2010) by Maithreyi Krishnaraj – provides an overview of varied motherhood experiences in India and how women do not have control over their reproductive agency.

Separated and Divorced Women in India (2013) by Kirti Singh – explains the economic entitlements, laws and supportive policies of separated and divorced women in India.

DIGITAL MEDIA AND LEGAL PROTECTION

- The advent of the internet and social media platforms such as Facebook, Instagram, SnapChat, Twitter, etc. has broadened the social space for women to raise their issues, reach out, network and collaborate for their common causes. Feminist blogging, NGO websites and women platforms have advanced the empowerment of women through technology.
- There is also a gender digital divide creating unequal spaces in digital media. Some of the reasons for this gender gap are lack of textual literacy, the wage gap, lack of context in local languages, gender division of labor causing time constraints for women etc.
- According to Women's Rights Online Network, women are 50% less likely to access the internet than men.
- At the same time, the same platforms reinforce gendered online behaviors and sex role stereotypes. Women who voice strong opinions on women's issues are exposed to verbal abuses and threats of violence. Social media also tend to create negative body image and low self-esteem by placing emphasis on obsessive celebrity culture, physical perfection, and beauty.
- According to the UN's Broadband Commission for Digital Development, 73% of women have already experienced cyber violence.
- Women receive rape, death threats and gendered abuses for expressing their opinions online.
- As per a survey by Feminism in India, 28% of women who faced online abuses, reduced their online presence and stopped posting on specific issues.
- These gendered online abuses effectively silence women's voices and discourses around women's issues.
- Cyber-crime against women is also on the rise. Stalking women online, sending unsolicited and persistent messages through WhatsApp and e-mails, developing pornographic content and morphed photos to target women are some of the ways in which women are harassed on social media. What's more, women do not know where to report such issues and how to deal with them. Women subjected to such cybercrimes and problems are vulnerable to mental health issues such as emotional stress, depression and hypertension further affecting their lives.
- Trolling on social media of women who defy the patriarchal conservatism and the mindset of the majority is another dangerous trend that has to be taken note of. Trolls are abusers who push defamatory, personally abusive content targeting individuals. Women, especially who voice non-mainstream and anti-conservative views are trolled extremely on social platforms.
- **Cyberstalking**: Using the Internet to stalk someone for online harassment and online abuses. A cyberstalker follows the victim's online activity to gather information and make threats in different forms of verbal intimidation.
- **Defamation**: It involves publishing defamatory information about the person on a website or circulating it among the social and friends circle to ruin a woman's reputation.
- **Morphing**: Editing the original picture to misuse it. Perpetrators download women's images from social media, WhatsApp or some other resources and upload morphed photos on other websites.
- **Cyber-pornography:** It includes publishing pornographic materials on pornography websites by using computers and the internet.

- **E-mail Spoofing**: Email that emerges from one source but has been sent from another source; can cause monetary damage.
- **Phishing:** Phishing is the attempt to gain sensitive information such as username and password and intent to obtain personal information.
- **Under the Information and Technology Act, 2000,** stalkers and cybercriminals can be booked under several sections for breaching of privacy. Some of the critical sections are:
  - **Section 67:** Deals with publishing or transmitting obscene material in electronic form. The earlier section in ITA was later widened as per ITAA 2008 in which child pornography and retention of records by intermediaries were all included.
  - **Section 66A:** Sending offensive messages through communication service, causing annoyance, etc., through electronic communication or email spoofing are all covered here. Punishment for these acts is imprisonment up to three years or fine.
  - **Section 66B:** Dishonestly receiving stolen computer resource or communication device with punishment up to three years.
  - **Section 66C:** Electronic signature or other identity theft like using others' password or electronic signature.
  - **Section 66D:** Cheating by a person on using computer resource or a communication device shall be punished with imprisonment of either description for a term which extends to three years and shall also be liable to fine which may extend to one lakh rupees.
  - **Section 66E:** Privacy violation–Publishing or transmitting private area of any person without his or her consent etc. Punishment is three years' imprisonment or two lakh rupees fine or both.
  - **Section 66F:** Cyber terrorism–Intent to threaten the unity, integrity, security or sovereignty of the nation.
  - **Section 72:** Punishment for breaching privacy and confidentiality.
  - **Section 72A:** Punishment for disclosing information during a lawful contract.
  - **Section 441 IPC:** This section deals with criminal trespassing.
  - **Section 354D:** Deals with stalking. It defines stalker as a man who follows a woman and tries to contact such woman and monitors every activity undertaken by the woman while using digital media.
- Despite laws and legislation, effective actions against perpetrators are not taken. As per National Crime Records Bureau data, around 12,000 cyber-crime incidents were reported in 2016, but the investigation is pending for the same amount of crimes that were reported the previous year.

ALTERNATIVE MEDIA–FOLK ART, STREET PLAY AND THEATRE

- Alternative media are those mediums of communication and information dissemination that reaches out to political and social minorities who are generally ignored by the mainstream media. They play an influential role in highlighting issues and perspectives of marginalized sections of society.
- **Folk Arts and Theatre** have been a part of human culture for millennia.
- Folk theatre involves a combination of music, dance, recitals, pantomimes, graphic arts, etc.
- In India, the theatre has been on the forefront in address-ing the gender division. Art is a widely used medium to highlight women's plight and issues in society.
- Rabindranath Tagore was the first person in India to execute an all-women play in 1888 when women from Tagore's house play-acted "Mayen Khela."
- The Calcutta theatre got most of its actresses from the red-light districts and daughters of prostitutes who were mostly looking for an alternative livelihood. In those days, elite and middle-class women faced restrictions to stage acting.
- Feminist theatre emerged in the 1970s as more women playwrights; performance artists began influencing the storytelling and gender perspectives.
- They centered on highlighting issues such as dowry system, domestic violence against women, female foeticide and the inherent gender oppression of women.
- Folk arts include street plays, an oral tradition of storytelling, dance dramas, masquerades and puppetry etc. that reaches out to rural and tribal people with modern messages.
- They play an important role in reshaping cultural outlooks conducive to women.
- In rural societies, power relations are deeply patriarchal. With folk theatres and traditional street plays, issues of domestic violence, gender crimes,

and patriarchal conservatism can be highlighted, and gender education among the rural and marginalized sections of the society can take place.

- Social theatres help to address unequal power relations, issues of domination, exploitation and stimulate women and the society on critical thought.
- These traditional alternative media incorporate women from tribal communities and rural areas. These women are trained in acting, providing them with economic as well as social empowerment.
- Women are more willing to join theatre groups when they have personally experienced or witnessed exploitation which drove them to act.
- The alternative media acts as a tool to challenge the patriarchal oppression and unequal gender relations as well as provide a cathartic experience by giving them an outlet to their emotions.
- The women involved in these theatres get greater space for their independence and mobility that other women from the same social section do not enjoy.
- Theatre also plays a huge role in breaking up the definition of stereotypical "bad" woman and creates the space for acceptance of women's right to expression, opinion, and activities.
- As more husbands, parents, in-laws, and neighbors understand how folk theatre and street plays work, it brings in a change in behavior and attitude in society towards the progress of these marginalized women actors.
- The various roles of alternative media in social empowerment include:
  - Testimony – enacting what has happened; testimonial performances serve as artistic documenting of stories of oppression, exploitation, and injustice.
  - Accusation – challenges systemic gender and social oppression by highlighting the mistakes, institutionalized subjugation of women.
  - Alleviation – provides collective catharsis and hope for a change in the system.
  - Action – mobilizes audience towards critical thought, social and gender awareness and changes in behavior.
- These performance arts stimulate community involvement by challenging apathy and motivating collective action.
- Alternative media thus has in-built social activism towards women emancipation.

INDECENT REPRESENTATION OF WOMEN (PROHIBITION) ACT (IRWA)

- The Indian Parliament passed the Indecent Representation of Women (Prohibition) Act in 1986 to prevent harmful depiction of women by the mass media.
- The Act prohibits indecent representation of women through advertisements, publications, writings, paintings, and figures or in any other manner.
- Distribution of pamphlets, photographs, sections of books that contain a vulgar portrayal of women in any form was made illegal.
- Punishment on first conviction is the maximum jail term of two years.
- On second and subsequent convictions, the offender can be jailed anywhere between six months to five years.
- The IRWA amendment bill was introduced in the Rajya Sabha on Dec. 13th, 2012 and passed on Dec. 13th, 2013.
- The bill widens the scope of the Act to cover new forms of communications such as the Internet, Satellite based communications, Cable TV, etc.
- In 2018, the Ministry of Women and Child Development has further proposed a draft bill to amend IRWA. The amendment include advertisement on digital or electronic form such as hordings, SMS, MMS, WhatsApp, Skype, Viber, Snapchat, Instagram etc. It requires constitution of a central body containing representation from National Commission for Women, Advertising Standards Council of India and Press Council of India to monitor violations of the provisions to IRWA and Ministry of infromation and broadcasting to strengthen the safeguards against women in mass media.

IMPACT OF MEDIA ON WOMEN

The portrayal of women in media has changed over time and has had both positive and negative impact on the image and position of women. Some mediums such as documentaries, radio, political and social content on TV, liberal print news, etc. have played an important role in ensuring a healthy public discourse on gender, dissemination of information, positive stories of women empowerment, reporting on achievements and progress of women in society. They inform and educate society on issues of gender and gender sensitization.

Ad content and portrayal of women in cinema are also changing by giving women lead roles, positive depiction of women and breaking gender stereotypes. Positive stereotypes help women to become assertive, independent and tackle gender abuse and discrimination. More brands and production houses utilize successful, career-oriented women roles and they are mostly shown as strong and independent persons, instead of being vilified. But, they have a long way to go.

Negative stereotypes of women in media such as submissive, timid and conservative women portrayals influence how women are perceived by society.

- It prevents women's abilities by limiting their choices and opportunities.
- It promotes and justifies overt and covert gender discrimination.
- It, directly and indirectly, causes an increase in gender and sexual violence.
- It perpetuates gender inequality and patriarchy in society.
- It promotes an unrealistic body image and beauty standards causing thin-ideal internalization and objectified body consciousness.
- It influences how men and women take up societal roles and behave in society.
- Gender abuse and violence against a woman in digital media and social media platforms cause depression, anxiety and self-esteem issues.
- Cyber-crimes against women cause psychological and emotional damage to women, and sometimes even physical harm.

Multiple Choice Questions

1. Match the following books with their authors:

(a) Susie Tharu	(i) The High Caste Hindu Women
(b) Pandita Ramabai Saraswati	(ii) Women in Modern India
(c) Tasleema Nasreen	(iii) Lajja
(d) Neera Desai	(iv) Women Writing in India

Codes:

	(a)	(b)	(c)	(d)
A.	(iv)	(i)	(iii)	(ii)
B.	(ii)	(iii)	(iv)	(i)
C.	(iii)	(i)	(ii)	(iv)
D.	(i)	(ii)	(iv)	(iii)

2. "The God of Small Things" is written by:

A. Veena Majumdar
B. Leela Dube
C. Iravati Karve
D. Arundhati Roy

3. Match the title of Books with Authors:

Title of Books	***Author***
(a) Women in India's Freedom Struggle	(i) Kamaladevi Chatopadhyaya
(b) The Hindu Women	(ii) Manmohan Kaur
(c) Indian Women's Battle for Freedom	(iii) Padmini Sen
(d) The Story of Women in India	(iv) Margaret Cormack

Codes:

	(a)	(b)	(c)	(d)
A.	(ii)	(iv)	(i)	(iii)
B.	(iv)	(i)	(iii)	(ii)
C.	(i)	(iii)	(ii)	(iv)
D.	(iii)	(ii)	(iv)	(i)

4. The first woman to appear in an Indian film was:

A. Nutan
B. Durga Bai Kamat
C. Nirupama Roy
D. Kaulabhi Ghokhle

5. Choose the correct expansion of FWPR:

A. Female Work Participation Rate.
B. Female Working in Production and Reproduction.
C. Field-based Work Participation Rate
D. Field-based Work in Production and Reproduction

6. Choose the correct expansion of GDI:

A. Gross Development Indicator
B. Gender Development Index
C. Gross Development Index
D. Gender Development Indicator

7. Who is the author of the book "Non-Sexiest Research Methods: A Practical Guide"?

A. Jessie Bernard
B. Margaret Eichler
C. Sylviea Strauss
D. Mary Warren

8. Match the items from List-I and List-II:

List-I	***List-II***
(a) Women in Modern India	(i) A.S. Altekar
(b) The position of women in Hindu Civilization	(ii) Devaki Jain and Pam Rajput
(c) Narratives from the Women's Studies family	(iii) Maithreyi Krishnaraj
(d) Introduction to Women's Studies	(iv) Neera Desai

Codes:

	(a)	(b)	(c)	(d)
A.	(iv)	(i)	(ii)	(iii)
B.	(iv)	(ii)	(iii)	(i)
C.	(iii)	(i)	(ii)	(iv)
D.	(i)	(ii)	(iii)	(iv)

9. Who is the author of the following book: Masculinity, Hinduism and Nationalism in India?

A. Nitya Rao B. Sikata Banerjee
C. Tanika Sarkar D. Paula Banerjee

10. 'Men have stolen the power of naming from women,' who must therefore fight against the deceptions of language and logic, the 'gang rape of minds and bodies'. Who said the above?

A. Cameron B. Tong
C. Eisenstein D. Daly

11. Match the Films from List-I with the Directors from List-II:

List-I	***List-II***
(a) Chokher Bali	(i) Revathi
(b) Firaaq	(ii) Sabiha Sumar
(c) Khamosh Pani	(iii) Nandita Das
(d) Mitr: My Friend	(iv) Ritu Parno Ghosh

Codes:

	(a)	(b)	(c)	(d)
A.	(iv)	(iii)	(ii)	(i)
B.	(iii)	(ii)	(i)	(iv)
C.	(ii)	(iv)	(iii)	(i)
D.	(i)	(ii)	(iii)	(iv)

12. Mahasweta Devi writes on issues of:

1. Archaeology 2. Adivasis
3. Women 4. Architecture

Codes:

A. 1 and 2 are correct
B. 2 and 3 are correct
C. 3 and 4 are correct
D. 1 and 4 are correct

13. "I do not wish women to have power over men, but over themselves." Who said this?

A. Margaret Mead B. Mary Wollstonecraft
C. Maithreyi Krishnaraj D. Devaki Jain

14. Match List-I (Authors) with List-II (Books):

List-I	***List-II***
(a) Juliet Mitchell	(i) The History of Doing
(b) Radha Kumar	(ii) The Second Sex
(c) Maithreyee Choudari	(iii) Women's Estate
(d) Simone de Beauvoir	(iv) Indian Women's Movement

Codes:

	(a)	(b)	(c)	(d)
A.	(iii)	(i)	(iv)	(ii)
B.	(iii)	(iv)	(i)	(ii)
C.	(iv)	(i)	(ii)	(iii)
D.	(ii)	(i)	(iii)	(iv)

15. Among the following which pair is not correctly matched?

A. Women in Modern India — Neera Desai
B. Manushi — Madhu Kishwar
C. Second Stage — Betty Friedan
D. Women and Society — Uma Charavarti

16. Manushi is a:

A. Newspaper B. Magazine
C. Film D. TV Programme

17. Match the items from List-I and II given below:

List-I	***List-II***
(a) Barkha Dutt	(i) Hindustan
(b) Mrinal Pandey	(ii) The Print
(c) Aruna Roy	(iii) UGC
(d) Armaity Desai	(iv) RTI Act

Codes:

	(a)	(b)	(c)	(d)
A.	(i)	(iii)	(iv)	(ii)
B.	(ii)	(i)	(iv)	(iii)
C.	(iv)	(ii)	(iii)	(i)
D.	(iii)	(i)	(ii)	(iv)

18. "If men would....Snap our chains.... They would find us more observant daughters, more faithful wives, ...in a word better citizens." Which of the following feminist thinkers made this statement?

A. Robert Owen
B. William Thompson
C. Harriet Taylor
D. Mary Wollstonecraft

19. Match the items in List-I with List-II:

List-I (Name of the Book)	***List-II (Author)***
(a) The Position of Women in Hindu Civilization	(i) Neera Desai
(b) Socialization, Education and Women Explorations in Gender Identity	(ii) Nita Kumar
(c) Women in Modern India	(iii) Karuna Chanana
(d) Lessons from Schools: The History of Education in Benaras	(iv) A.S. Altekar

Codes:

	(a)	(b)	(c)	(d)
A.	(i)	(iv)	(ii)	(iii)
B.	(iii)	(ii)	(i)	(iv)
C.	(iv)	(iii)	(i)	(ii)
D.	(ii)	(iii)	(iv)	(i)

20. Which of the following play major role in construction, presentation, representation and repression of women in modern society?

A. Religion
B. Culture
C. Media
D. Social System

21. Match List-I with List-II:

List-I (Authors)	***List-II (Books)***
(a) Vina Mazumdar	(i) Women and Science: Selected Essays
(b) Lotika Sarkar	(ii) Symbols of Power
(c) Maithreyi Krishnaraj	(iii) Law and Status of Women in India
(d) Neera Desai and Vibhuti Patel	(iv) Change and Challenge in the International Decade

Codes:

	(a)	(b)	(c)	(d)
A.	(i)	(ii)	(iii)	(iv)
B.	(ii)	(iii)	(i)	(iv)
C.	(ii)	(i)	(iii)	(iv)
D.	(iv)	(iii)	(ii)	(i)

22. Rural Women of India usually express their thoughts through traditional communication channel. Which among the following is not a traditional communication channel?

A Television
B. Folk Songs
C. Festivals
D. Puppetry

23. Match the following from List-I and List II:

List-I (Authors)	***List-II (Books)***
(a) Naila Kabeer	(i) Writing Caste, Writing Gender: Reading Dalit Women's Testimonies
(b) Vina Mazumdar	(ii) Reversed Realities
(c) Kirti Singh	(iii) Separated and Divorced Women in India
(d) Sharmila Rege	(iv) Memories of a Rolling Stone

Codes:

	(a)	(b)	(c)	(d)
A.	(iv)	(ii)	(i)	(iii)
B.	(ii)	(iv)	(iii)	(i)
C.	(iii)	(ii)	(i)	(iv)
D.	(iv)	(ii)	(iii)	(i)

24. Which one of the following is not a research based journal of Women's Studies?

A. Femina
B. Indian Journal of Gender Studies
C. Manushi
D. Journal of Women in Culture and Society

25. Match the following from List-I and List-II:

List-I (Authors)	***List-II (Books)***
(a) Arundhati Roy	(i) The Long Silence
(b) Shashi Deshpande	(ii) The Inheritance of Loss
(c) Anita Desai	(iii) The God of Small Things
(d) Kiran Desai	(iv) Fire on the Mountain

Codes:

	(a)	(b)	(c)	(d)
A.	(i)	(iii)	(ii)	(iv)
B.	(iii)	(i)	(iv)	(ii)
C.	(ii)	(iv)	(i)	(iii)
D.	(iv)	(ii)	(iii)	(i)

26. Pat Griffon in her book "Lesbians and Homophobia in Sports", notes that myths about lesbians have a number of consequences in sports. Which of the following is not one of these consequences?

A. A sense of loneliness among lesbians in sports.
B. Widespread beliefs that lesbians cannot play sports as well as heterosexuals.
C. Lesbians hiding their identity so that they are not harassed or cut from sports.
D. The extension of a "do not ask, do not tell atmosphere" in women's sports.

27. Who talks about the concept of "Capabilities failure"?

A. Syeda Hamid
B. Amartya Sen
C. Martha Nussabaum and Amartya Sen
D. Jayati Ghosh

28. Who of the following proclaimed?
"Woman is the companion of man, gifted with equal mental capacities. She has the right to participate in the minutest details of activities of men and she has the same right to freedom and liberty as he ..... By sheer force of vicious custom, even the most ignorant and worthless men have been enjoying a superiority over women."

A. Lakshmi Sahgal
B. Mahatma Gandhi
C. Dayanand Saraswati
D. Keshab Chandra Sen

29. Who is the author of the book, 'The Natural Superiority of Women'?

A. Ashley Montague　　B. Kamla Bhasin
C. Julliet Michell　　D. Sylvia Walby

30. Who wrote 'Stri Purush Tulna'?
A. Neera Desai　　B. Vina Mazumdar
C. Tarabai Shinde　　D. Leela Dube

31. Match the Items of List-I (Authors) and List-II (Books):

List-I (Authors)	***List-II (Books)***
(a) Bharati Mukherji	(i) In Search of Me
(b) Chhaya Dattar	(ii) Roots and Shadows
(c) Shashi Deshpande	(iii) The Tigers Daughter
(d) Shobha De	(iv) Second Thought

Codes:

	(a)	(b)	(c)	(d)
A.	(iii)	(i)	(ii)	(iv)
B.	(i)	(iii)	(ii)	(iv)
C.	(iii)	(i)	(iv)	(ii)
D.	(i)	(ii)	(iii)	(iv)

32. Match List-I (Books) and List-II (Authors):

List-I (Authors)	***List-II (Books)***
(a) The Violence of the Green Revolution: Third World Agriculture, Ecology and Politics	(i) Urvashi Butalia and Ritu Menon (Edited)
(b) In Other Words: New Writing by Indian Women	(ii) S.R. Bakshi
(c) Women's Rights and Modernization	(iii) Radha Kumar
(d) The History of Doing: An Illustrated Accounts of Movements	(iv) Vandana Shiva

Codes:

	(a)	(b)	(c)	(d)
A.	(iv)	(i)	(ii)	(iii)
B.	(i)	(ii)	(iii)	(iv)
C.	(ii)	(iii)	(iv)	(i)
D.	(iii)	(iv)	(i)	(ii)

33. The concept of 'Rights as trumps' that sets a limit on state action was propagated by:
A. Hohfeld　　B. John Rawls
C. Ronald Dworkin　　D. Laski

34. Who of the following is of the view?
"Wifing and Mothering" are two feminine roles that block women's freedom. Women could escape from these feminine roles only by assuming the role of a career.
A. Kate Millet　　B. Shulamith Firestone
C. Mary Daly　　D. Simone de Beauvoir

35. Who was the author of the book, 'A Decade of Women's Movement in India'?
A. Vandana Shiva　　B. Neera Desai
C. Vina Mazumdar　　D. Bina Agarwal

36. Pornography is:
1. Portrayal of sexual objectification of women and mainly targeted towards male audience.
2. Intentional act of depicting women for sexual advantage.
3. Sexual fantasies that men hope to achieve in real life.
4. Portrayal of choices that women make.

Codes:
A. 1 only　　B. 1 and 2 only
C. 1, 2 and 3 only　　D. 2 and 3 only

37. Which of the following pair is correctly matched?

	(Author)	***(Books)***
A.	Neera Desai	– History of Doing
B.	Radha Kumar	– Women and Politics Worldwide
C.	Barbara J. Nelson and Najma Chowdhary	– Women in Modern India
D.	Tara Ali Baig	– India's Women Power

38. Match the following from List-I (Authors) and List-II (Books):

List-I	***List-II***
(a) Pandita Rama Bai	(i) Recasting Women Essay in Colonial History.
(b) Neera Desai	(ii) High Caste Hindu Women.
(c) Sangari K.	(iii) Decade of Women's Movement in India.
(d) K. Jayawandana	(iv) Feminism and Nationalism in Third World.

Codes:

	(a)	(b)	(c)	(d)
A.	(ii)	(iii)	(i)	(iv)
B.	(i)	(iii)	(ii)	(iv)
C.	(iv)	(ii)	(i)	(iii)
D.	(iv)	(i)	(ii)	(iii)

39. In a social perspective, 'objectification' means:
1. To treat a woman as if she was a thing, or an object without regard to their emotion or dignity.
2. Treating someone as belonging to another person (usually belonging to a man).
3. Using as a tool for self fulfilment or needs.
4. Empowerment of women through visibility.

Codes:
A. 1 only　　B. 1 and 4 only
C. 1, 2 and 3 only　　D. 1, 3 and 4 only

40. Which of the following publishing houses are exclusively for/by women?

1. Zubaan, Delhi
2. The Feminist Press, New York
3. Modjaji Books, South Africa
4. Red Letter Press, Washington

Codes:

A. 1, 2 and 4 only
B. 1, 2, 3 and 4
C. 1, 2 and 3 only
D. 1 and 2 only

41. Which book was written "to persuade women to endeavor to acquire strength, both of mind and body, and to convince them that the soft phrases, susceptibility of heart, delicacy of sentiment and refinement of taste, are almost synonymous with epithets of weakness"?

A. Declaration of Sentiments by Elizabeth Cady Stanton and Lucretia Mott
B. The Bitch Rules by Elizabeth Wurtzel
C. A Vindication of the Rights of Women by Mary Wollstonecraft
D. The Female Eunuch by Germaine Greer

42. Who said "If women's work were accurately reflected in national statistics, it would shatter the myth that men are the bread winner of the world"?

A. Amartya Sen
B. Mahbub Ul-Haq
C. Mohammad Yunus
D. Robert Putnam

43. Match List-I and List-II:

List-I (Women Directors)	***List-II (Films Directed)***
(a) Deepa Mehta	(i) Salaam Bombay
(b) Kalpana Lajmi	(ii) Earth
(c) Gurinder Chadha	(iii) Rudali
(d) Mira Nair	(iv) Bend it like Beckham

Codes:

	(a)	(b)	(c)	(d)
A.	(iv)	(iii)	(ii)	(i)
B.	(i)	(ii)	(iii)	(iv)
C.	(ii)	(iii)	(iv)	(i)
D.	(iii)	(iv)	(i)	(ii)

44. Match the following Books with their authors:

(a) God of Small Things	(i) Vandana Shiva
(b) A Vindication of the Rights of Women	(ii) Kiran Bedi
(c) Staying Alive	(iii) Arundhati Roy
(d) Who Dares	(iv) Mary Wollstone Craft

Codes:

	(a)	(b)	(c)	(d)
A.	(i)	(ii)	(iii)	(iv)
B.	(ii)	(iv)	(i)	(iii)
C.	(iii)	(iv)	(i)	(ii)
D.	(iv)	(ii)	(iii)	(i)

45. Match the following authors with their books:

(a) Gyn-Ecology	(i) Betty Friedan
(b) Feminine Mystique	(ii) Mary Daly
(c) The Second Sex	(iii) Simone de Beavoir
(d) Sexual Politics	(iv) Katte Millet

Codes:

	(a)	(b)	(c)	(d)
A.	(i)	(ii)	(iii)	(iv)
B.	(ii)	(i)	(iii)	(iv)
C.	(iii)	(ii)	(i)	(iv)
D.	(iv)	(i)	(ii)	(iii)

46. Match the following women and their contribution:

List-I	***List-II***
(a) Agatha Christie	(i) Writer
(b) Annie Besant	(ii) Eco-Feminist
(c) Susan B. Anthony	(iii) Suffrage Movement
(d) Vandana Shiva	(iv) Theosophical Society

Codes:

	(a)	(b)	(c)	(d)
A.	(i)	(iv)	(iii)	(ii)
B.	(i)	(iii)	(ii)	(iv)
C.	(ii)	(iii)	(i)	(iv)
D.	(iii)	(ii)	(iv)	(i)

47. Which of the following pair is not correctly matched?

A. Kiran Desai — Inheritance of Law
B. Kate Millett — Sexual Politics
C. Irish Young — Gyn-Ecology
D. Simone de Beavoir — The Second Sex

48. Who is the Editor of "Manushi"?

A. Vandanra Shiva
B. Madhu Kishwar
C. Veena Majumdar
D. Maithreyi Krishnaraj

49. The feminist writer who got the Nobel Prize for Literature in 2007:

A. Margaret Drabble
B. Doris Lessing
C. Margaret Atwood
D. Shashi Deshpande

50. Who wrote "The Position of Women in Hindu Civilization"?

A. Radha Kumar
B. Susheela Kaushik
C. A.S. Altekar
D. Devaki Jain

51. The film FIRE was produced by:
A. Shabana Azmi B. Deepa Mehta
C. Aparna Sen D. Mira Nair

52. Who wrote 'The History of Doing'?
A. Matson Everett Jana
B. Kamla Bhasin
C. Neera Desai
D. Radha Kumar

53. Arrange the following books chronologically according to their year of publication:
(i) The Subjection of Women
(ii) The Second Sex
(iii) Feminine Mystique
(iv) A Vindication of the Rights of Women

Codes:
A. (iv), (iii), (i), (ii) B. (iv), (i), (ii), (iii)
C. (iv), (ii), (i), (iii) D. (ii), (i), (iv), (iii)

54. The Indecent Representation of Women (Prohibition) Act was enacted in:
A. 1987 B. 1986
C. 1992 D. 2003

55. Match the Books and Authors:
(a) Sexual Politics (i) Shulamith Firestone
(b) The Dialectic of Sex (ii) Kate Millett
(c) Sex, Gender and Society (iii) Juliet Mitchell
(d) Women's Estate (iv) Ann Oakley

Codes:

	(a)	(b)	(c)	(d)
A.	(ii)	(i)	(iv)	(iii)
B.	(i)	(ii)	(iv)	(iii)
C.	(iv)	(iii)	(ii)	(i)
D.	(iii)	(iv)	(i)	(ii)

56. The concept of alienation was important to?
A. Heal B. Barrett
C. Engles D. Marx

57. An understanding of how discourses of biological sex differences are mobilized, in a particular society at a particular moment, is the first stage in intervening in order to initiate change. Who affirms the above?
A. Lovibond B. Irigaray
C. Cixous D. Weedon

58. Match List-I (Authors) with List-II (Books):

List-I	***List-II***
(a) Karin Kapadia	(i) Women's Movements in the Global Era: The Power of Local Feminists
(b) Amrita Basu	(ii) The Violence of Development: The Politics of Identity, Gender and Social Inequalities in India
(c) Naila Kabeer	(iii) Migrant Women and Work
(d) Anuja Aggarwal	(iv) Reversed Realities

Codes:

	(a)	(b)	(c)	(d)
A.	(iii)	(iv)	(i)	(ii)
B.	(ii)	(i)	(iv)	(iii)
C.	(iv)	(ii)	(i)	(iii)
D.	(i)	(iii)	(iv)	(ii)

59. Arrange the chronological sequence of the Books with the Year of their publication:
(i) Money, Sex and Power: Towards a Feminist Historical Materialism
(ii) The Feminine Mystique
(iii) Recasting Women: Essays in Colonial History
(iv) Reproduction of Motherhood

Codes:

A.	(ii)	(iv)	(i)	(iii)
B.	(ii)	(i)	(iii)	(iv)
C.	(iv)	(iii)	(i)	(ii)
D.	(i)	(ii)	(iii)	(iv)

60. Who is the author of the following book? Gender and Green Governance: The Political Economy on Women's Presence within and beyond Community Forestry
A. Kalpana Kannabiran B. Zoya Hasan
C. Bina Aggarwal D. Rehana Ghadilly

61. Who is the author of the first autobiography by an Indian woman?
A. Sarladebi Caudhurani B. Haimabati Sen
C. Ras Sundari Debi D. Kadambini Basu

62. Who is the author of "Dalits and Democratic Revolution"?
A. Gayle Rubin B. Gail Omvedt
C. Sharmila Rege D. Ashwini Tambe

63. Who has edited the book on the "Narratives from the Women's Studies Family"?
A. Devki Jain and Pam Rajput
B. Neera Desai and Maithreyi Krishnaraj
C. Divya Pandey and Meera Sharma
D. Devki Jain and Neera Desai

64. The Indecent Representation of Women (Prohibition) Act, 1986 seeks to ban the depiction of women in any form which is:
1. Indecent for women

2. Denigrating to women
3. Corrupting or injure the public morality of women.
4. To deprive the women from certain set roles.

Codes:

A. 1, 2 and 3 only B. 1 and 2 only
C. 2 and 3 only D. 1, 2, 3 and 4

65. "Man is happy, self-accepting, healthy without guilt, only when s/he is fulfilling himself and becoming what s/he can be." Who said this?

A. Betty Friedan
B. Simone de Beauvoir
C. Julliet Mitchell
D. Sheila Rowbotham

66. What is Comet Media Foundation?

A. It is a media to conscientise women.
B. It advocates gender and development issues and also uses alternative media.
C. It is department of media.
D. It consistently monitors the media's representation.

67. Match the items from List-I and List-II:

List-I	*List-II*
(a) A Decade of Women's Movement in India	(i) Vina Mazumdar
(b) A Field of One's Own	(ii) Vandana Shiva
(c) Symbols of Power Studies on the Political Status of Women in India	(iii) Bina Agrawal
(d) Staying Alive	(iv) Neera Desai

Codes:

	(a)	(b)	(c)	(d)
A.	(iv)	(iii)	(i)	(ii)
B.	(i)	(iii)	(ii)	(iv)
C.	(i)	(iii)	(iv)	(ii)
D.	(iii)	(iv)	(ii)	(i)

68. Among the following who is a prominent 'Subaltern' Thinkers?

A. Arundhati Roy B. Bell Hook
C. Gayatri Spivak D. Anita Desai

69. 'The Demystification of Law for Women' has been a ground-breaking work of:

A. Flavia Agnes B. Nandita Haskar
C. Lotika Sarkar D. Esther Boserup

70. Which of the following group is not associated with queer theory?

A. Transgender B. Gay
C. Homophobic D. Heterophobic

71. "Women are much more likely to engage in practical rather than strategic actions". Who comments?

A. Molyneux B. Mclver
C. Talcot Parsons D. Anderson

72. Match the items from List-I and List-II:

List-I	*List-II*
(a) Rama Mehta	(i) Inside the Haveli
(b) Leela Dube	(ii) Women's Rule in Economic Development
(c) Ursula Sharma	(iii) Kinship, Family and Socialization in South and South-East Asia
(d) Ester Boserup	(iv) Women, Work and Property in North-East India

Codes:

	(a)	(b)	(c)	(d)
A.	(iii)	(iv)	(i)	(ii)
B.	(ii)	(iv)	(i)	(iii)
C.	(i)	(iii)	(iv)	(ii)
D.	(iv)	(iii)	(i)	(ii)

73. Who said: "The feminists had destroyed the old image of women, but they could not erase the hostility, the prejudice and the discrimination that still remained"?

A. Margaret Fuller B. Linda Phelps
C. Betty Friedan D. Sandra L. Barky

74. The concept of Socialization of 'Domestic Labour' was introduced by:

A. Margaret Benston B. Oakley
C. Firestone D. Nancy Chodorow

75. Which of the following is incorrect about "Queer Studies"?

A. Studies of non-normative and homosexuality.
B. It is new term for gays and lesbians.
C. These are post-modern studies.
D. These are studies with gender perspective.

76. Match List-I with List-II given below:

List-I (Authors)	*List-II (Books)*
(a) Neera Desai	(i) Recasting Women: An Introduction
(b) Kosambi Meera	(ii) Demystification of Law for Women
(c) Haksar Nandita	(iii) Women in Modern India
(d) Kumkum Sangari	(iv) Women's Oppression in the Public Gaze: An Analysis of Newspaper Coverage, State Action and Activist Response.

Codes:

	(a)	(b)	(c)	(d)
A.	(i)	(ii)	(iii)	(iv)
B.	(iii)	(iv)	(ii)	(i)
C.	(iv)	(ii)	(iii)	(i)
D.	(ii)	(iii)	(i)	(iv)

77. "The Mother is manifested as the mother of strength. She is pure Shakti." Who commented?

A. M.K. Gandhi
B. Aurobindo Ghosh
C. Bankim Chandra Chatterji
D. Vivekananda

78. "The property status of the household to which the women belong and women's participation in wage labour are deciding the status." Who does among the following believed in this?

A. Karl Marx
B. Alexanda Kollontai
C. Friedrich Engels
D. Mary Wollstone Craft

79. Who is of the view that men's relationship with nature was predatory from the beginning and in his lust for power, man established similar relationship with women?

A. Maithreyi Krishnaraj
B. Maria Mies
C. Simon de Beavoir
D. Bina Agarwal

80. Who wrote Humayun Nama?

A. Gulbadan Begum
B. Jahan Aara
C. Noor Jahan
D. Salima Begum

81. Match the Authors (List-I) with the title of Books (List-II):

List-I	*List-II*
(a) Simon de Beauvoir	(i) Sex and the Single Girl
(b) Kate Millet	(ii) The Dialectic of Sex: The Case for Feminist Revolution
(c) Julliet Mitchell	(iii) Sexual Politics: A Manifesto for Revolution
(d) Helen Brown	(iv) The Second Sex

Codes:

	(a)	(b)	(c)	(d)
A.	(iv)	(iii)	(ii)	(i)
B.	(iii)	(iv)	(i)	(ii)
C.	(ii)	(iii)	(iv)	(i)
D.	(i)	(ii)	(iii)	(iv)

82. Who said: "The relation of male to female is by nature a relation of superior to inferior and ruler to ruled"?

A. Yajnavalkya
B. Aristotle
C. Vasistha
D. Plato

83. Match the following from List-I (Authors) with List-II (Books):

List-I (Authors)	*List-II (Books)*
(a) Neera Desai	(i) Women and Politics World wide
(b) Tara Ali Baig	(ii) History of Doing
(c) Radha Kumar	(iii) India's Women Power
(d) Barbara J. Nelson and Najma Chowdhary	(iv) Women in Modern India

Codes:

	(a)	(b)	(c)	(d)
A.	(iv)	(iii)	(ii)	(i)
B.	(iii)	(ii)	(i)	(iv)
C.	(iv)	(ii)	(iii)	(i)
D.	(ii)	(iv)	(i)	(iii)

84. Match List-I (Authors) and List-II (Books):

List-I (Authors)	*List-II (Books)*
(a) Gayatri Spivak	(i) Public Man Private Woman
(b) Bell Hooks	(ii) Subaltern Speak
(c) Jean B. Elshtain	(iii) Woman on the Edge of Time
(d) Marge Piercy	(iv) Feminist Theory from Margin to Centre

Codes:

	(a)	(b)	(c)	(d)
A.	(iv)	(iii)	(i)	(ii)
B.	(iii)	(iv)	(i)	(ii)
C.	(ii)	(iv)	(i)	(iii)
D.	(i)	(ii)	(iii)	(iv)

85. Who said that: "The great question that has never been answered," and which I have not yet been able to answer, despite my thirty years of research into feminine soul, is what does a women want"?

A. Judith Butler
B. Sigmund Freud
C. J.S. Mill
D. Friedrich Engles

86. Match the following from List-I and List-II:

List-I (Books)	*List-II (Authors)*
(a) Indian Women: Myth and Reality	(i) Maithreyi Krishnaraj

(b) Empowerment of Women in South Asia: Concepts and Practices — (ii) N. Kamala
(c) Translating Women: Indian Interventions — (iii) Srilatha Batliwala
(d) Motherhood in India: Glorification without Empowerment — (iv) Josodhara Bagchi

Codes:

	(a)	(b)	(c)	(d)
A.	(ii)	(iv)	(i)	(iii)
B.	(ii)	(i)	(iv)	(iii)
C.	(iv)	(iii)	(ii)	(i)
D.	(iii)	(ii)	(i)	(iv)

87. The family is the place where we received our neuroses and phobias, where we grow up sexually well or mal-adjusted". Who said?

A. Patricia Hill Collins
B. Sigmund Freud
C. Robinson and Richardson
D. William J. Goode

88. Who has coined the term 'Capitalist Reductionist Paradigm'?

A. Evan Bondi
B. Vandana Shiva
C. Karl Marx
D. Clara Zetkin

89. Indian Journal of Gender Studies is published by:

A. Kali for Women
B. Zubaan Books
C. Women Press
D. Sage Publications

90. Match List-I with List-II:

List-I (Authors)	***List-II (Books)***
(a) Alice Schwarzer	(i) The Reproduction of Mothering
(b) Nancy Chodorow	(ii) After the Second Sex
(c) Jean Poul Sartre	(iii) The Handmaid's Tale
(d) Margaret Atwood	(iv) Being and Nothingness

Codes:

	(a)	(b)	(c)	(d)
A.	(i)	(ii)	(iii)	(iv)
B.	(ii)	(i)	(iii)	(iv)
C.	(ii)	(i)	(iv)	(iii)
D.	(iii)	(i)	(iv)	(ii)

91. Match List-I with List-II:

List-I (Books)	***List-II (Authors)***
(a) Gender, Generation and Poverty	(i) Amartya Sen
(b) Development as Freedom	(ii) Naila Kabeer
(c) Gender Planning and Development: Theory, Practice and Training	(iii) Sylvia Chant
(d) Reversed Realities: Gender Hierarchies in Development Thought	(iv) Caroline Moser

Codes:

	(a)	(b)	(c)	(d)
A.	(i)	(ii)	(iii)	(iv)
B.	(iii)	(i)	(iv)	(ii)
C.	(ii)	(iv)	(iii)	(i)
D.	(iv)	(iii)	(ii)	(i)

92. Who said that:

"Reared by women within a feminine world, the normal destiny of women is marriage, which still means practically subordination to man . . ."

A. Alfred Adler
B. Karen Horney
C. Simone de Beauvoir
D. Clara Thompson

93. Match the following List-I with List-II:

List-I (Authors)	***List-II (Books)***
(a) Amanda Root	(i) Empowerment of Women in South Asia Concepts and Practices
(b) Samita Sen	(ii) Woman to Woman: An Introduction to Feminism
(c) Radha Kumar	(iii) Towards a Feminist Politics-The Indian Women's Movement in Historical Perspective
(d) Srilatha Batliwala	(iv) The History of Doing: An Illustrated Account of Movements for Women's Rights and Feminism in India

Codes:

	(a)	(b)	(c)	(d)
A.	(ii)	(iii)	(iv)	(i)
B.	(iv)	(ii)	(iii)	(i)
C.	(i)	(iii)	(ii)	(iv)
D.	(iv)	(ii)	(i)	(iii)

94. Who said that women are producers first and are consumers next. Women as such "constitute a class which is responsible for the production of simple use values and whose activities are associated with home and family"?

A. Jane Flax
B. Margaret Benston
C. Heidi Hartmann
D. Juliet Mitchell

95. Match List-I with List-II:

List-I *(Academicians)*	**List-II** *(Narratives)*
(a) Maithreyi Krishnaraj	(i) From Cycleshed to Powerhouse
(b) Pam Rajput	(ii) Being a Woman is not Enough
(c) Regina Papa	(iii) Crossing Boundary Politics
(d) Surinder Jetley	(iv) Blazing a Quarter Century Trail

Codes:

	(a)	(b)	(c)	(d)
A.	(iii)	(i)	(ii)	(iv)
B.	(iv)	(i)	(iii)	(ii)
C.	(ii)	(iii)	(iv)	(i)
D.	(ii)	(i)	(iii)	(iv)

96. Match List-I with List-II:

List-I	**List-II**
(a) Lalithambika Antharjavam	(i) Editor of 'Streeswetcha', who launched an anti liquor movement and succeeded-in getting total prohibitions in a state in India in 1994.
(b) Savitribai Phule	(ii) Indian freedom fighter, lawyer and member Constituent Assembly of India and Planning Commission in India.
(c) Malladi Subbamma	(iii) Indian Author and social reformer whose book 'Agnisakshi' won the Kendra Sahitya Academy Award in 1976.
(d) Durgabai Deshmukh	(iv) Indian Social reformer and Poet who played a significant role in improving women's rights during British rule.

Codes:

	(a)	(b)	(c)	(d)
A.	(i)	(ii)	(iii)	(iv)
B.	(ii)	(iii)	(i)	(iv)
C.	(iii)	(iv)	(i)	(ii)
D.	(iv)	(i)	(ii)	(iii)

97. Match List-I with List-II:

List-I *(Film Directors)*	**List-II** *(Name of Films)*
(a) Mira Nair	(i) Monsoon Wedding
(b) Aparna Sen	(ii) Fire
(c) Shyam Bengal	(iii) The Japanese Wife
(d) Deepa Mehta	(iv) Ankur

Codes:

	(a)	(b)	(c)	(d)
A.	(i)	(ii)	(iii)	(iv)
B.	(ii)	(iii)	(iv)	(i)
C.	(i)	(iii)	(iv)	(ii)
D.	(iii)	(iv)	(i)	(ii)

98. Match List-I with List-II:

List-I *(Authors)*	**List-II** *(Books)*
(a) Paulo Freire	(i) 'Pedagogy of the Oppressed'
(b) Patli Lather	(ii) 'Getting Smart: Feminist Research and Pedagogy'
(c) Bell Hooks	(iii) 'Teaching to Trangress: Education as the Practice of Freedom'
(d) Henry Giroux	(iv) 'On Critical Pedagogy'

Codes:

	(a)	(b)	(c)	(d)
A.	(ii)	(iii)	(iv)	(i)
B.	(i)	(ii)	(iii)	(iv)
C.	(iv)	(i)	(ii)	(iii)
D.	(ii)	(iv)	(i)	(iii)

99. Match List-I with List-II:

List-I *(Authors)*	**List-II** *(Books)*
(a) Kate Millett	(i) The Female Eunuch
(b) Germaine Greer	(ii) Sexual Politics
(c) Simone De Beauvoir	(iii) The Second Sex
(d) Robin Morgan	(iv) Sisterhood is Powerful

Codes:

	(a)	(b)	(c)	(d)
A.	(ii)	(i)	(iii)	(iv)
B.	(iii)	(ii)	(i)	(iv)
C.	(iii)	(ii)	(iv)	(i)
D.	(i)	(ii)	(iii)	(iv)

100. Who is the author of the publication of the National Commission for Women: 'The Unfinished Agenda' – Towards Equality?

A. Devaki Jain
B. C.P. Sujaya
C. Nirmala Banerjee
D. Sarla Gopalan

101. Which status is a position in a social system that is beyond an individual's control?
A. Achieved status B. Ascribed status
C. Acquired status D. Social status

102. Match List-I with List-II:

List-I (Authors)	***List-II (Books)***
(a) Ester Boserup	(i) Patriarchy and Accumulation on a World Scale: Women in the International Division of Labour
(b) Padmini Swaminathan	(ii) Women's Role in Economic Development
(c) MariaMies	(iii) Women and Work
(d) Devaki Jain and Pam Rajput	(iv) Narratives from the Women's Studies Family: Recreating knowledge

Codes:

	(a)	(b)	(c)	(d)
A.	(ii)	(iii)	(i)	(iv)
B.	(i)	(ii)	(iii)	(iv)
C.	(iii)	(iv)	(ii)	(i)
D.	(iv)	(iii)	(ii)	(i)

103. Which of the following is not correctly matched?
A. KumKum Roy — Women in Early Indian Societies
B. Ruth Vanita — Marriage, Migration and Gender
C. KumKum Sangari — The Names of Violence
D. Vandana Shiva — Stolen Harvest: The Hijacking of the Global Food Supply

104. Who said this?
"Nature is to culture as female is to male".
A. Sherry Ortner B. Maria R. Ortner
C. Diane Elson D. Linda Mayoux

105. Who said this?
"Women are not powerless because they are feminine; rather they are feminine because they are powerless, because it is a way of dealing with the requirements of subordination".
A. Elson, D and N. Cagatay
B. Kathy E. Ferguson
C. Pearson R
D. Harding S

106. Sahitya Academy Award winner among the following women is:
A. Shobha De B. Amrita Patel
C. Amrita Pritam D. Kishwar Desai

107. India ranks in Human Development Index (2013) at:
A. 132 B. 136
C. 131 D. 128

108. The institutional manifestations of patriarchy can be seen in:
1. Media
2. Medical health practices and systems
3. Political process
4. Government and its various areas of control

Codes:
A. 2 and 3 are correct.
B. 3 and 4 are correct.
C. 1, 2, 3 and 4 are correct.
D. Only 2 is correct.

109. M.S. Rao distinguishes three levels of structural changes in a social movement:
A. Revolution, Reformation and Transformation
B. Transformation, Reformation and Revolution
C. Reformation, Transformation and Revolution
D. Revolution, Evolution and Transformation

110. Match the following from List-I and List-II:

List-I (Authors)	***List-II (Books)***
(a) Jean Bethke Elshtain	(i) Socialism, Feminism and Philosophy
(b) Toni Morrison	(ii) Public Man, Private Woman
(c) Susan Griffin	(iii) Pornography and Silence
(d) Sean Sayers	(iv) Beloved

Codes:

	(a)	(b)	(c)	(d)
A.	(iv)	(iii)	(i)	(ii)
B.	(iii)	(iv)	(ii)	(i)
C.	(ii)	(iv)	(iii)	(i)
D.	(i)	(iv)	(ii)	(iii)

111. Who is the author of the book 'The Economics of Discrimination'?
A. Becker, Gary S B. Boserup Ester
C. Baker Ross K D. Acker, Joan

112. The 'Demystification of Law for Women' is a ground breaking work of:
A. Flavia Agnes B. Nandita Haskar
C. Lotika Sarkar D. Ester Boserup

113. Who said: "I do not wish them (women) to have power over men, but over themselves"?
A. Simone de Beauvoir B. Mary Wollstonecraft
C. Rosemarie Tong D. Elshtain

114. Arrange the following books chronologically:
(i) The Vindication of the Rights of Women.
(ii) The Origin of the Family Private Property and The State.
(iii) The Feminine Mystique.
(iv) The Second Sex.

Codes:

	(a)	(b)	(c)	(d)
A.	(i)	(ii)	(iv)	(iii)
B.	(ii)	(i)	(iv)	(iii)
C.	(iv)	(i)	(iii)	(ii)
D.	(ii)	(iv)	(iii)	(i)

115. Which of the following book was written by Emmeline Pankhurst?
A. The Second Sex
B. Freedom of Death
C. The Feminine Mystique
D. The Dialectics of Sex

116. "The First Sex" was written by:
A. Umberto Eco
B. Juliet Mitchell
C. John Desrochers
D. Elizabeth Gould Davis

117. Which of the following is an example of cultural convergence?
A. The Sex and the City becomes wildly popular among female officer workers in Thailand.
B. Newsrooms place photographers, graphic artists, reporters and online writers in the same work space.
C. A Mexican soap opera gets high ratings among audiences in Russia.
D. All of the above

118. Synchronous media:
A. Do not require the audience to assemble at any given time.
B. Require using a personal computer to act as editor, publisher, and writer.
C. Require the audience to be assembled simultaneously with the broadcast, transmission or event.
D. All of the above.

119. The correlation function of mass communication is important because ________.
A. The media can help maintain social stability.
B. The media can keep audiences informed about issues, events and other developments in society.
C. The media help people learn society's rule and how to fit into society.
D. All of the above.

120. How gender identity stereotypes are mainly developed in young children?
A. Through interactions with a parent of the same sex.
B. Through interactions with a parent of the opposite sex.
C. Through interactions with a teacher of the same sex.
D. Through interactions with a teacher of the opposite sex.

121. How have media portrayals of women changed during the past two decades?
A. Women have been shown as having strong, individualized personalities.
B. Women have been shown in increasingly traditional roles.
C. Women have been shown largely as sexualized, stereotypical characters.
D. Women have been shown in a variety of body types that are representative of the general population.

122. Why do psychologists and experts on child behavior not recommend that children view genders as similar after the age of 10?
A. to prevent homosexual development.
B. to encourage dominant gender roles.
C. to limit peer group influences.
D. to support self-identity in children.

123. Why have media portrayals of women greatly changed in recent decades?
A. Male media portrayals have become increasingly stereotypical.
B. More women are taking high-ranking positions in the mass media.
C. Media usage by women has sharply decreased during this period.
D. Advertising is more focused on women than men during most programming.

124. Suggesting that new tools and machinery propel social change is ____________ determinism.
A. economic
B. media
C. cultural
D. technological

125. A concern of feminists regarding the media is ________.
A. images of men in control
B. ownership by men
C. objectification of women
D. All of above

126. Research on violence in the media concludes that exposure to violence leads to ____________ to real violence.

A. Devotion
B. Desensitization
C. Deference
D. Disinclination

127. Transvestism requires a change of:

A. sexual orientation
B. gender identity
C. clothes
D. anatomy

128. Indian Journal of Gender Studies is published by:

A. Kali for Women
B. Zubaan Books
C. Women Press
D. Sage Publications

129. Zaveri sisters as dancers are famous in the field of:

A. Kuchipudi
B. Manipuri dance
C. Odissi
D. Kathak

130. Which are the names of Journals on gender studies published by Sage?

I. Masculinities and Sexualities
II. Gender Studies
III. Feminist Theory
IV. Violence Against Women

Codes:

A. I, II, III, IV
B. II, III and IV only
C. II and III only
D. I, II and IV only

131. What is the title of the play translated into 48 languages and performed in over 140 countries written by American play-wright, performer and activist—Eve Enster?

A. A Daughter's Geography
B. Missexual Mystery
C. Vaginal Monologues
D. Dialectics of Sex

132. Which of the following is the correct number of women awardees of Dada Saheb Phalke Award till 2015?

A. Three
B. Four
C. Six
D. Eight

133. Who said the following?

"The language of a particular culture does not serve all its speakers equally, for not all speakers contribute in an equal fashion to its formulation. Women are not as free or as able as men are to say what they wish, because the words and the norms for their use have been formulated by the dominant group, men".

A. Edwin Ardener
B. Cheris Kramarae
C. Gerdrin
D. Catherine Mackinnon

134. The Chameli Devi Award is given to an outstanding woman who is a:

A. Vocalist
B. Lawyer
C. Journalist
D. Scientist

135. Which one of the following pairs is correctly matched?

List-I (Personalities)	***List-II (Fields)***
I. Meena Kandaswamy	1. Social Activist
II. Rehana Jhabvala	2. International Squash Player
III. Shubha Tole	3. Writer
IV. Dipika Pollikal	4. News Scientist

Codes:

	I	II	III	IV
A.	1	2	4	3
B.	4	1	2	3
C.	3	1	4	2
D.	3	4	1	2

136. Which of the following view considers communication as a source of power and oppression of individuals and social groups in the communication theory framework?

A. Psychological
B. Mechanistic
C. Critical
D. Systematic

137. What is communication in the context of the 'new view of development'?

A. The only catalyst of change.
B. An important catalyst for change.
C. An important cause of change.
D. Not important in bringing change.

138. Match List-I with List-II.

List-I (Indian Classical Dance form)	***List-II (Classical Dancer)***
(a) Kathak	(i) Sunanda Nair
(b) Bharatnatyam	(ii) Radha Reddy
(c) Kuchipudi	(iii) Padma Subramanyam
(d) Mohini Yattam	(iv) Kumudini Lakhiya

Codes:

	(a)	(b)	(c)	(d)
A.	(i)	(ii)	(iii)	(iv)
B.	(iv)	(iii)	(ii)	(i)
C.	(iv)	(i)	(ii)	(iii)
D.	(iii)	(i)	(iv)	(ii)

139. Which of the following is India's first Woman Photo-Journalist?

A. Shobhana Bhartia
B. Homai Vyarawalla
C. Arundhati Roy
D. Leela Menon

140. Who is the Director of the banned Documentary 'India's Daughter'?

A. Gurinder Chadda B. Meira Nayar
C. Leslee Udwin D. Kathrine Mayo

141. Which of the following indicates that The World of Advertising is highly gendered?

1. It reflects often stereotypical assumptions.
2. Being a woman and man is an important identity for people.
3. Objectification of women's body is the core at advertisement.
4. Advertisement re-inforces the social construction of gender.

Codes:

A. 1, 3 and 4 only B. 1, 2, 3 and 4
C. 1 and 4 only D. 2 and 4 only

142. As the definition of social media develops, what is one underlying element?

A. The intersection between technology, social interaction, and sharing information.
B. Microsoft is the primary developer.
C. Use of the various elements is free.
D. All of the above.

143. Social media audiences differ from those of traditional media because:

A. Traditional media audiences consume material created for them while social media audiences either dictate the type of product they want or bypass traditional producers to find products more suitable to their particular needs or desires.
B. Traditional media audiences tend to be within a certain age, gender and socio-economic group, while social media appeals to virtually every age, gender and economic status.
C. Social media audiences tend to be the millennial generation while traditional media are mainly Gen-Y.
D. None of the above.

144. Assertion (A): The worldwide trend towards consumerism has created a climate in which advertisements and commercial messages often portray women as consumers.

Reason (R): Gender sensitive training for media professionals encourage the creation and use of stereotyped images of women.

Codes:

A. Both (A) and (R) are true and (R) is the correct explanation for (A).
B. Both (A) and (R) are true and (R) is not the correct explanation for (A).
C. Both (A) and (R) are false.
D. (A) is true, (R) is false.

145. Assertion (A): Representations of gender in the media have reflected (and caused) the hegemonic reality of patriarchy.

Reason (R): Whilst the family is generally seen as primary agency of gender socialization, media plays a key role in teaching and reinforcing these cultural expectations.

Codes:

A. Both (A) and (R) are true.
B. Both (A) and (R) are not true.
C. Both (A) and (R) are true and (R) is the correct explanation of (A).
D. Both (A) and (R) are true and (R) is not the correct explanation of (A).

146. Assertion (A): The media is responsible for increase in sexism and violence against women.

Reason (R): Women are projected as sexual symbol in advertisements, films, books, and journals which leads to violence against women.

Codes:

A. (A) is false and (R) is true.
B. Both (A) and (R) are false.
C. Both (A) and (R) are true and (R) is the correct explanation of (A).
D. Both (A) and (R) are true but (R) is not the correct explanation of (A).

147. Assertion (A): The Post-modern Indian women is negating stereotypes and carving an Identity for herself that goes beyond the fact of her womanhood.

Reason (R): The post-modern Indian women is negotiating spaces that her many predecessors had been afraid to trespass.

Codes:

A. Both (A) and (R) are true but (R) is not the correct explanation for (A).
B. (A) is true and (R) is false.
C. (A) is false and (R) is true.
D. Both (A) and (R) are false.

148. Assertion (A): In a globalized world, media offers a lot of opportunities for employment for women.

Reason (R): Women have struggled a lot to become visible in the media today.

Codes:

A. Both (A) and (R) are true, and (R) is the correct explanation of (A).

B. Both (A) and (R) are true, and (R) is not the correct explanation of (A).
C. (A) is true but (R) is false and (R) is not the correct explanation of (A).
D. (A) is false but (R) is true.

149. Assertion (A): Women are made uncomfortable, anxious, or frightened by depictions of violence in the Media.
Reason (R): Scenes of violence against women in media may be especially painful for women who have been victims of sexual violence.
Codes:
A. Both (A) and (R) are true.
B. Both (A) and (R) are true and (R) is the correct explanation of (A).
C. Both (A) and (R) are false.
D. (R) is false, (A) is true.

150. Assertion (A): In many of the advertisements women's body, smile, curves are used only as commodities to sell other commodities.
Reason (R): No doubt a bare female body attracts but it is by no means creative advertising.
Codes:
A. (A) is false, (R) is true.
B. (A) is true, (R) is false.
C. Both (A) and (R) are true and (R) is not the correct explanation for (A).
D. Both (A) and (R) are false and (R) is the correct explanation for (A).

Answers

1	2	3	4	5	6	7	8	9	10
A	D	A	B	A	B	B	A	B	D
11	12	13	14	15	16	17	18	19	20
A	B	B	A	D	B	B	D	C	C
21	22	23	24	25	26	27	28	29	30
B	A	B	A	B	B	C	B	A	C
31	32	33	34	35	36	37	38	39	40
A	A	C	D	B	C	D	A	C	B
41	42	43	44	45	46	47	48	49	50
C	B	C	C	B	A	C	B	B	C
51	52	53	54	55	56	57	58	59	60
B	D	B	B	A	D	C	B	B	C
61	62	63	64	65	66	67	68	69	70
C	B	A	A	A	B	A	C	B	D
71	72	73	74	75	76	77	78	79	80
A	C	C	A	D	B	B	C	B	A
81	82	83	84	85	86	87	88	89	90
A	B	A	C	B	C	B	B	D	C
91	92	93	94	95	96	97	98	99	100
B	C	A	B	B	C	C	B	A	D
101	102	103	104	105	106	107	108	109	110
B	A	B	A	B	C	B	C	C	C
111	112	113	114	115	116	117	118	119	120
A	B	B	A	B	D	D	C	A	A
121	122	123	124	125	126	127	128	129	130
A	A	B	D	D	B	C	D	B	C
131	132	133	134	135	136	137	138	139	140
A	C	B	C	C	C	B	B	B	C
141	142	143	144	145	146	147	148	149	150
A	A	A	D	C	C	A	A	B	C

❑❑❑

Feminist Research Methodology

- ➠ Understanding Feminist Research – Concepts, Debates, and Limitations
- ➠ Feminist Epistemology, Feminist Standpoint, Sexist and Non-Sexist Research Methodology, Ethnography, Queer Theories
- ➠ Research Design and Methods – Exploratory, Diagnostic, Experimental, Action Research, Case Studies and Survey Research Method
- ➠ Quantitative versus Qualitative Research

UNDERSTANDING FEMINIST RESEARCH-CONCEPTS, DEBATES AND LIMITATIONS

- Feminist research – research done by, for and about women.
- Feminist research is interdisciplinary and begins with the standpoint of expression of women.
- Characterized by its double dimension – construction of new knowledge and the production of social change. It is informed by women's struggle against oppression and grounded in feminist values and beliefs.
- It involves;
    - ❑ Documenting women's experiences, concerns, and issues.
    - ❑ Illuminating gender stereotypes and biases in research.
    - ❑ Unearthing women's subjugated and muted knowledge.
    - ❑ Challenging the structures that oppress women and their knowledge.
- It actively seeks to remove power imbalances between research and the subject (women).

Limitations of the Scientific Research Method:

- ❑ Complexity and dynamic nature of social phenomenon
- ❑ Limited capacity of predictability
- ❑ Incapable of value judgments and moral decisions
- ❑ Cultural relativism

- Feminist scholars have developed
    - ❑ alternate paradigms of knowing
    - ❑ different conceptual frameworks to explain phenomena
    - ❑ different approaches to research
    - ❑ new data gathering techniques and innovative knowledge dissemination methods
- Nancy Kleiber and Linda Light developed the interactive method for research which incorporates all the three elements of feminist research namely by women, for women, and about women.
- Maria Mies suggests that the "truth" of research or theory is not dependent on the application of certain methodologies but in its orientation towards progressive emancipation.

- **Muted Group Theory**
  - Concerns certain groups of people who remain powerless in society.
  - It explains the causes of muteness in a section of population such as women.
  - Introduced by Edwin Ardener as he realized that voices of women and other suppressed people are unheard and ignored.
  - This theory can be applied to understand the problems of marginalized groups.
  - Muted group theory is based on three basic assumptions:
    - Men and women perceive the world differently because they have different perception shaping experiences–result of sexual division of labor within the family and society.
    - Men use their dominant position to appropriate and perpetuate more political power and obstruct the acceptance and main-streaming of women's ideas and experiences.
    - Women have to express their situated knowledge, experiences and ideas in male language in order to be heard.

FEMINIST EPISTEMOLOGY

- Epistemology is the study of the nature of knowledge. In many fields, it is concerned with sources and sufficient conditions of knowledge. Its emphasis is on how knowledge is acquired.
- Rationalism – knowledge is acquired through logic and reasoning.
- Empiricism – knowledge is acquired through experience and interaction with reality.
- Feminist epistemology is an outgrowth of feminist theorizing about gender and traditional epistemological concerns.
- It lays emphasis on epistemic salience of gender.
- Gender is used as an analytic category in criticism and reconstruction of epistemic practices, norms, and ideas.
- Feminist epistemology emerged from critical scrutiny of male biases in different disciplines. Forms of biases include:
  - Marginalizing women even on women's interests. Example: women's contribution is invisible in economic theory.
  - Embedded gendered metaphors and presupposition of cognitive styles.
  - Theories that reinforce and naturalize oppressive gender relations.
- This bias leads to bias in feminist research as well as gender bias in all fields of research.
- General epistemic norms are also biased this way. Traditional research assumes a value of objectivity, towards which all research processes aspire. But, feminist research rejects this on the argument that all procedures and measures of objectivity are male-biased and originates from the gendered thought process.
- This "bias paradox" provides the context in which core theories of feminist epistemology can be understood:
  - The ideological role of epistemic norms
  - The importance of situated knowledge
  - Nature of objectivity
- Non-feminist research treats women as "beneficiary" rather than acknowledging their agency, whereas feminist research doesn't view participants and audiences as separate entities.
- Sandra Harding, one of the important contributors to feminist epistemology argues for multiple standpoints and views.
- Lorraine Code calls for an epistemology that takes subjectivity into account.
- Naturalized epistemologists call for an empirical study of features of the epistemic agency that enables one to truth-track.
- Five basic epistemological principles in feminist methodology as identified by Judith Cook and Mary Margaret are as follows:
  - women and gender are the focus of analysis
  - importance of raising the consciousness
  - rejection of subject and object distinctions—knowledge of the participant is considered as expert knowledge, and objective research also reflects a specific local and historical standpoint.
  - a concern with ethics.
  - intention to empower women, change the power relations and inequality.

FEMINIST STANDPOINT

- Initially developed in social sciences.
- Has its origin in the works of Nancy Hartsock in political sciences and Dorothy Smith in sociology.
- Emphasizes the way in which marginalized groups are in a position of epistemic privilege with respect to social structure.

- The marginalized or "outsiders" have to learn how to get along in their own world as well as among the dominant group.
- This "outsider" status allows them to see things about social structure and their functions that the dominant groups cannot see.
- Knowledge is socially situated.
- Sandra Harding, another important contributor to feminist standpoint theory, says that the outsider standpoint can lead to the development of new perspectives, questions, and priorities due to the epistemic privilege.
- One doesn't have to be a marginalized person to start this thought process.
- Primary standpoint comes from the firsthand experience of domination and marginalization
- Secondary standpoint can be obtained by observing and embarking on critical theorizing of the "outsiders'" experience and knowledge.
- Feminist standpoint involves critical thoughts on their experiences and its relationships to larger political and social structures. The basis lies in the sexual division of labor, i.e., women's domestic labor and their role in childbearing and caring, the experience of female embodiment, relational self-conception, etc.
- Patricia Collins's Black feminist standpoint emphasizes experience, dialogue in assessing knowledge claims, black women's experience of multiple oppressions.
- Feminist standpoint rejects objectivity that discredits experiences and thought processes, that comes out of specific social locations.
- Criticism of feminist epistemology include:
    - ❑ Valorizing oppression
    - ❑ Presupposes an exclusionary conception of gender
    - ❑ Unable to explain which standpoints have epistemic privilege without circularity.

SEXIST AND NON-SEXIST RESEARCH METHODOLOGY

- Sexism–attitudes, and beliefs that one sex is inferior to other and discrimination based on gender.
- Feminist researchers have demonstrated that gender bias has led to false assumptions, faulty tools, inaccurate interpretations and a lack of representation of women and other gender in scientific research.
- Publications in academic and scientific journals assume sexual inequality and proceed from that point of view.
- Sex bias influences research studies in many ways such as by the researcher's choice of topics, the operationalization of variables, use of inappropriate gender comparisons, etc.
- **Gender Blindness** in research refers to treating all genders as the same regardless of the historical and biological differences, which results in gender-blind projects, policies, and theories that do not reflect reality and actual experiences.
- Gender bias in knowledge construction can be found in the following forms:
    - ❑ **Invisibility:** When a gender, male or female, is not included and completely ignored in work; Example: social studies textbooks, where the role of women is not included.
    - ❑ **Stereotyping:** When each gender is assigned a rigid set of characteristics and traditional roles.
    - ❑ **Imbalanced Selectivity:** Imbalance in a presentation by selective interpretation of event being reported; this distorts complex issues by omitting different perspectives.
    - ❑ **Unreality:** When the author chooses to ignore the controversial problems, and oversimplifies complex issues. The assumption of women involved in only non-productive activities, while in reality, they are directly and indirectly involved in productive activities. This leads to the construction of unreality.
    - ❑ **Linguistic Bias:** Researcher explores bias reflected in cross-sex and same-sex discourse behaviors; subordination is obvious in female discourse, behavior, authority and domination in male discourse; leads to the general use of masculine terms and pronouns.
- According to Margrit Eichler, sexism in the research process can manifest as:
    - ❑ Use of sexist language
    - ❑ Use of sexist concepts
    - ❑ Androcentric perspective
    - ❑ Use of sexist methodology
    - ❑ Sexist interpretation of results
- Margrit Eichler describes seven types of sexism in research.
- Four primary forms of sexism are androcentricity, overgeneralization, double standard, and gender insensitivity:

- **Androcentricity :**
  - The world is viewed from the male perspective only. We live in an androcentric social, political and intellectual environment.
  - Women are seen as passive objects rather than subjects.
  - It prevents us from understanding that both male and female are acted upon as well as actors.
  - Extreme forms are androcentricity are: gynopia–female invisibility in research and misogyny–hatred of women.
- **Overgeneralization:**
  - When a study deals with only one sex but taken to apply to both sexes.
  - Example: trial testing of new drugs for both sexes is done only on men and results are generalized.
- **Gender Insensitivity:** Ignoring sex as an important social variable in research.
- **Double Standard:** Research using different means of evaluating, treating and measuring identical behavior.
- There are three derived forms of bias: sex appropriateness, familism, and sexual dichotism.
- **Sex Appropriateness:**
  - An instance of the double standard
  - Dysphoria – the absence of appropriate gender identity
- **Familism:**
  - An instance of gender insensitivity
  - Treating family as the smallest unit of analysis in contexts where actually individuals are the smallest unit.
  - Assuming that all members of the family are uniformly affected by certain experiences and events.
- **Sexual Dichotism:**
  - A particular instance of the double standard.
  - Treating sexes as two entirely discrete social and biological groups, instead of as groups with overlapping standards.
  - Leads to exaggeration of sex differences.
- A non-sexist research methodology requires identifying structures that uphold the privileges of men and advancing non-exploitative research practices.
- Knowledge produced through non-sexist research will be instrumental in uplifting women and other marginalized groups.
- It should aim to reduce the power relations between the researcher and research participants.

ETHNOGRAPHY

- Ethnography is the study of people in their environment.
- It involves investigation through observation, interpretation, and representation and is central to investigations and classification of morality.
- It requires immersion in the social context to collect and interpret descriptive data about the people concerned.
- The method of data collection here is called participant observation—the researcher understands the group, its beliefs, and norms by participating in it.
- Main enlightening tool to generate classification and knowledge of others.
- Emphasis on experience and words, voices and lives of the participants.
- It is majorly used in the field of sociology, anthropology, education, and cultural studies.
- Feminist ethnography emerged from anthropology, with contributions from the women's movements of the 1960s and 1970s.
- Feminist ethnography is a theory about how research should proceed. The principal method is observational research over time.
- Feminist ethnography offers a critique of excluding women from field analyses that present them in reductive ways.
- Feminist advocate analyses that are detailed, flexible and subjective as that would better reveal women's patriarchal experiences.
- Initially, feminist ethnography was on-ground research by, about and for women to understand gendered constructions.
- Gradually, it has expanded to investigate men, masculinity and power relations in patriarchy.
- It draws attention to the distinction in approaches and outcomes based on gender of researchers, married and unmarried women researchers.
- It also analyses how power structures position participants as subordinate and primitive to the expert researcher.
- It discusses how variables such as ethnicity, color, sexuality, religion, etc. of the ethnographer influence experiences and observations.

- Postmodern critiques advocate innovative styles of writing, including poetry, photography, diary entries, and letters.
- Postmodern feminist ethnography deconstructs dominant discourses, revealing hidden assumptions.
- Participants and researcher can collaborate to produce multiple perspectives encountered.
- Feminist ethnographers recognize that choice and constraint are intertwined in women's lives. They incorporate the material and the symbolic realms and acknowledge accounts as partial, yet valuable in uncovering the complex ways in which women and men make sense of their gendered lives.

QUEER THEORIES

- **Queer Studies** – The study of issues related to sexual orientation and gender identity. It focuses on lesbian, gay, bisexual, transsexual people and cultures. It challenges the socially constructed categories of sexual identity and examines the issues of identity, history, and perception of queer people.
- **Queer Theory** – Studies of non-compliance of anything with the standards, norms and perceived ways of doing things. It is used as a tool to study the possibility of giving the LGBT community an identity. It focuses on the differences between sex, gender, and sexuality (desire).
- Established in the 1990s.
- The queer theory originated from multiple critical and cultural movements such as feminism, post-structuralist theory, radical anti-racism movements, gay and lesbian movements, AIDS activism and post-colonialism.
- It contests the set of ideas in many established fields and challenges the notion of defined and finite identity categories and norms that create a binary of good and bad sexualities.
- The term "Queer Theory" was first coined by Teresa de Lauretis in her 1991 work : "Queer theory : "Lesbian and Gay Sexualities."
- Three interrelated projects within the theory:
  - Refusing heterosexuality as a benchmark for sexual formations.
  - Challenging the belief that lesbian and gay studies are a single entity.
  - Focus on the multiple ways in which race shapes sexual bias.
- **Heteronormativity:** Institutions, structures of understanding and practical orientations that makes heterosexuality seem coherent and also privileged. Heteronormativity promotes heterosexuality as the normal and preferred sexual orientation. This is reinforced by the institutions of marriage, adoption rights, employment, etc.
- Heteronormativity as a form of power applies pressure to both heterosexual and queer people to conform via these institutional norms.
- Queer theory challenges this heteronormative worldview.
- Important contributors to queer theory: Michael Foucault, Gayle Rubin, Eve Kosofsky Sedgwick, Judith Butler
- **Michael Foucault:** Sexuality is rather a discursive production than an essential part of human; Power is acted in such a way that it makes sexuality look like a hidden truth that has to be dug out, but sexuality cannot be clearly defined. He focuses on expansive production of sexuality in the context of power and knowledge.
- **Gayle Rubin:** In his article "Thinking Sex" (1984), he explores the ways in which sexual identities and behaviors are hierarchically organized via sexual classifications. Certain sexual expressions are valued more than others, and those who do not possess them are oppressed. She rejects the belief that gender and sexuality are the same.
- **Eve Kosofsky Sedgwick:** In her book, "Epistemology of the Closet" (1990), she says that homo-hetero difference in sexual definition is disjointed. The Gender that one has and the gender of the persons one is attracted to define the sexuality of a person. Her definitions of sexual variations cannot be put into discrete locations.
- **Judith Butler:** In her book "Gender Trouble" (1990), she says that gender is not an essential truth derived from one's body, but it is a socially constructed reality. The assumption of "sex" as a truth creates a coherent binary of "feminine" and "masculine" and heterosexuality as the only proper outcome. Gender performativity such as drag, cross-dressing can be viewed as a resistance strategy against gender norms of society. In her book "Undoing Gender" (2004), she explains how gender performativity as a repetitive process that creates the subject as subject. These creations of gender contest the rigidity of existing hierarchical binaries.
- **Sexual Dimorphism**–The difference between male and female of the same species, beyond the differences in their sexual organs. Humans show a degree of sexual dimorphism in external appearances.

RESEARCH DESIGN AND METHODS

- Research is a systemic process undertaken to discover new facts and construct new knowledge.
- Steps involved in the research process are:
  - Selection of Research Problem
  - Extensive Literature Survey
  - Making Hypothesis
  - Preparing the Research Design
  - Sampling
  - Data collection
  - Data Analysis
  - Hypothesis Testing
  - Generalization and Interpretation
  - Preparation of Report
- Formulation of a research problem involves the following steps:
  - Identifying the broad research area of interest
  - Dissecting the broad area into sub-areas
  - Selecting one of the sub-areas
  - Raising research questions
  - Formulating research objectives
- A research hypothesis is a formal question that a researcher intends to solve. It can be defined as a set of prepositions or an objective conjecture to guide the research investigation.
- Hypothesis forms a major step in research. Hence it has to be clear, precise, capable of being tested, and state the relationship between the variables.
- Research approaches can be classified into inductive and deductive research:

  Inductive Research
  - concerned with the generation of theories from data analysis
  - uses research questions to explore new phenomena and perspectives
  - associated with qualitative research

  Deductive Research
  - Aimed at testing a theory
  - Begins with a hypothesis and focuses on causality and relationships
  - Mostly associated with quantitative research
- Data collected for research can be primary data or secondary data.
- Primary data is data collected at the source for that specific research purpose, such as via surveys, interviews, observations, and experiments.
- Secondary data refers to data collected by someone other than the user — already available data used for the research problem.
- **Sex-disaggregated Data**
  - Data is collected and tabulated separately for men and women
  - This allows for measuring differences between the sexes on various social and economic dimensions
  - Helps researchers integrate gender in their work
  - Helps to understand gender issues better and formulate well-aimed policies and strategies for women development
- Types of data collection techniques are:
  - **Interviews:**
    - Involve presenting verbal stimuli to obtain a verbal response
    - Types: telephone interviews, focused, struct-ured, unstructured interviews, clinical interviews, and non-directive interviews, formal or informal
    - Questions should be clear, focused and encourage open-ended responses
  - **Questionnaire:**
    - Set of questions are mailed to the respon-dents who read, understand and reply
    - Questions should be short, simple, easy to understand and the means of responses also have to be simplified
  - **Survey Scales**–Indexes that measure variables that cannot be directly observed. There are different ways in which response choices can be provided in a survey.

    Types of Survey Scales: Likert scale, Bogardus scale, Thurstone scale, Guttman scale
    - **Likert Scale:** Questions prompt respondents to select their level of agreement to a state-ment
    - **Guttman Scale:** Items are made in a single dimensional series so that the response for a certain item predicts the responses for other items in the series
    - **Bogardus Scale:** Measures the degree of closeness, prejudice in terms of warmth, intimacy, indifference or hostility between individuals and social groups
    - **Thurstone Scale:** A one-dimensional scale to track the respondent's attitude or feeling towards the subject. Each statement is assigned a numerical value to indicate respondent's agreement or disagreement.

- **Schedule:**
  - Like questionnaire, but responses filled by the enumerator
  - Requires field workers and training
- **Observations:**
  - Allows for the study of situation dynamics, behavior and provides additional information about the groups
  - Eliminates subjective bias
  - Observation can be structured or unstructured, participant, non-participant or disguised observation, controlled or uncontrolled exploratory observation
- **Focus Groups:**
  - A facilitated group of individuals with common variables is interviewed
  - Helps to obtain information about combined perspectives and opinions
- **Ethnography, Oral History, and Case Studies**
  - Involves studying a phenomenon and people in their natural setting
  - Uses a combination of observation, interviews, and surveys
- **Documents and Records**
  - Examining existing data in the form of a database, reports, logs, financial records, minutes, etc.

- Steps involve in data analysis, and processing are: Editing, Coding, Classification, Tabulation, Analysis and interpretation, documentation
- Other terms associated with the research process are:
  - **Construct:** The abstract data or subject matter that is being measured
  - **Coding:** Defining the data being analyzed
  - **Reliability of Research:** The extent to which the assessments are consistent
  - **Validity:** The extent to which assessments are correct/accurate
  - **Operational Definitions:**
    - A clear and concise definition of a measure
    - It provides a precise statement of how a conceptual variable is converted into a measured variable
    - They ensure that everyone involved has the same understanding of concepts, variables, and procedures
  - **Index:** a composite measure of variables or an accumulation of scores of individual items. Construction of index in research consists of the following steps:
    - Item Selection–Selecting the items to be included in the index
    - Examination of empirical relationships
    - Index Scoring–Assigning scores for all responses and making a composite variable out of several items
    - Index Validation–Making sure that the index measure what it intends to measure
  - **Observer Drift :** A gradual change in observations and documentation of observations made by the researcher. Usually happens in length research studies as observers become inconsistent in recording data and moves away from the established criteria for research.
- **Research Design :** Defining the research problem and preparing the design of the research project
- Provides a blueprint for collection, measurement, and analysis of data and a strategy for the investigation to obtain answers to the research questions.
- A research design consists of:
  - Statement of the research problem
  - Procedures and techniques for gathering data (strategy)
  - The population to be studied
  - Methods for processing and analyzing data
- The research design is split into the following parts:
  - **Sampling Design:** Methods of selecting items for observation
  - **Observational Design:** Conditions under which observations can be made
  - **Statistical Design:** How many items to be observed and how to analyze the data and information
- Research design can be categorized as follows:
  - Research design in case of exploratory studies
  - Research design in case of descriptive and diagnostic research studies
  - Research design in case of hypothesis-testing research studies

EXPLORATORY RESEARCH

- Also known as a formulative research study and does not require a hypothesis to start with, as it is intended towards the formulation of hypothesis.

- The focus is on discovering ideas and insights obtained from first-hand observation of the phenomenon or concept without considering the systems and theories.
- Involves developing a working hypothesis from an operational point of view or formulating problem to investigate accurately.
- Methods used in the context of exploratory research studies are: literature survey, expert survey, analysis of insight-stimulating examples, pilot surveys
- **Literature Survey:** Hypothesis by early workers and their usefulness are reviewed and critiqued. Also considers if a new hypothesis can be developed from existing ones.
- **Expert Survey:** Obtaining insight into the relationships between new ideas and variables by surveying people with practical experience on the phenomenon/issues concerned.
- **Analysis:** Intensive study of selected instances of the phenomenon. Involves examination of existing records, unstructured interviews, etc.
- **Pilot Study**
  - ❑ A scientific tool for soft research or to conduct a preliminary analysis before committing to the research process.
  - ❑ Conducted before the research design stage to test the feasibility, reliability, and validity of the proposed study design.
  - ❑ It involves a trail collection of data to check for errors in defined strategies.

DESCRIPTIVE AND DIAGNOSTIC RESEARCH

- **Descriptive Research :** Concerned with describing the characteristics and behavior of a particular individual or groups.
- **Diagnostic Research :** Concerned with determining the frequency with which some phenomenon occurs and its associations and causative symptoms.
- Diagnostic research involves finding out the relationship between express causes and suggesting solutions. It is mostly concerned with the hypothesis.
- Both of these studies require:
  - ❑ A precise definition of the objectives to ensure that relevant data is collected
  - ❑ Selecting the methods for data collection– mostly structured methods (observation, questionnaire, interviewing, examining records, etc.)

HYPOTHESIS TESTING RESEARCH STUDIES/EXPERIMENTAL RESEARCH

- Also called experimental studies. It is quantitative and deductive.
- The researcher tests the causal relationships between variables involved and determine cause and effect relationships.
- Systemic study based on observations under controlled conditions.
- Requires highly reliable procedures without any bias, from which inferences about causalities can be obtained.
- Experimental research involves problem identification, question formulation, research and hypothesis formulation.
- Uses test group and control group to study and compare the effects.
- Seven broad categories of experimental design are: After-only design, Before-only Design, Before-after with control group design, Four-group six-study design, After only with control group design, Ex-post facto design, Factorial design.

ACTION RESEARCH

- It is a qualitative research method that is considered responsive and a legitimate mode of knowing.
- Involves a continuous and systemic process of reflecting, evaluating and improving the quality of outcome.
- It is a participatory approach as it seeks to bridge the gap between the researcher and practitioner.
- It turns people involved into researchers, takes place in the real world and solves real-world problems.
- Pursues action and research at the same time.
- Stages in action research: identification of the issue, plan for action, implementation, evaluation, reflection and self-evaluation.
- Major types of action research:
  - ❑ **Traditional Action Research:** Encompasses the concepts of field theory, group dynamics, T-groups and clinical models.
  - ❑ **Contextual Action Research:** Entails reconstituting the structural relations in a social environment; participants acts as project designers and co-researcher
  - ❑ **Radical Action Research:** Strong focus on emancipation and overcoming of power relations;

strives for social transformation via an advocacy process that strengthens periphery groups.

- **Educational Action Research :** A strategy for the development of teacher into researchers.

CASE-STUDIES

- It is a qualitative and descriptive research design.
- Involves an empirical study of a phenomenon in its natural context or environment.
- The "case" can be an institution, organization, individual, group of people or event.
- Investigation of a single situation, process, and collection of a variety of information within a time period.
- Needs an investigator with skills of analytical thinking, creativity, and perseverance.
- It offers a comprehensive qualitative analysis of a phenomenon within a small group of participants.
- Types of Case studies research:
    - Case history
    - Case project
    - Illustrative case study
    - Exploratory case study
    - Critical incident case study
- The six-step process to conduct a case study:
    - Determining research questions
    - Selecting cases and determining data collection and analysis
    - Preparation for data collection
    - Data collection
    - Evaluation and analysis of data
    - Reporting

SURVEY RESEARCH METHOD

- A quantitative research involving the investigation of a sample of the entire population to infer theories, behaviors, and relationships.
- Surveys help identify important beliefs, attitudes, community interests, and individual opinions.
- Two key features of survey research are: questionnaires and sampling.
- **Questionnaires:** A predefined series of questions to collect information.
- **Sampling** is the process of selecting units from a population of interest for survey study and questioning.
- Sampling methods can be categorized into probability and non-probability sampling.

Probability Sampling Methods

- Every population element has a non-zero chance of being chosen.
- **Simple Random Sampling:** If the population consists of N objects and the sample "n" objects, then all possible samples of "n" are equally likely to occur.
- **Stratified Sampling:** The population is divided into groups(strata), and from each strata, a probability sampling is performed.
- **Cluster Sampling:** The population is divided into clusters. A sample of clusters is chosen by probability sampling, and then individuals within the sample clusters are surveyed.
- **Multistage Sampling:** Uses a combination of sampling methods for survey.
- **Systemic Random Sampling:** A list of every member of the population is created, and the first sample element is randomly selected from the first "k" elements.

Non-probability Sampling Methods

- Cannot be sure that each element has the probability of being chosen.
- **Voluntary Sampling:** People self-selected into the survey.
- **Convenience Sample:** Made of people who are easier to reach.
- **Purposive Sampling:** Samples are selected based on their relevance to the purpose of the study.
- **Snowball or Chain Sampling:** One respondent, identifies the other respondent for the study; used when it is very difficult to find sample population.

- Statistical Package for Social Sciences (SPSS)– a software research tool developed for complex statistical data analysis of social sciences data. It was launched in 1968, now owned by IBM since 2009.
- SPSS is used by health researchers, government entities, educational researchers for processing and analyzing survey data.
- SPSS can analyze and mine rich and deep survey data in text form.

Content Analysis

- A research technique that is used for objective, quantitative description of the content of the communication.

- It is used to quantify meanings, relationships, and behavior in the context.
- A study of recorded information, documents to infer knowledge.

QUANTITATIVE VERSUS QUALITATIVE RESEARCH

Research methods are mostly dichotomized as either qualitative or quantitative.

Quantitative Research

- Quantitative research methods are associated with positivism, scientific objectivity, statistics, and masculinity.
- They are often used to establish numbers, roles, and other characteristics.
- Primarily a deductive process that uses statistical tests for analysis.
- It involves using data sets—primary, secondary and macro data sets.
- The basic elements of quantitative research:
  - **Concepts and Constructs :** Used to explain abstract observations in a measurable form
  - **Variables :** Discrete and continuous variables
  - **Measurement of Variables :** 4 different levels –nominal, ordinal, interval, ratio
  - **Measures :** Scales and indices
- Quantitative research projects the researcher's point of view but is structured with concrete and reliable data.
- Important issues with respect to women such as unpaid work of women, violence against women, the emotional cost of structured oppression on women cannot be measured with consistency in quantitative research.
- Some important categories of quantitative research are:
  - **Inferential Approach :** Involves forming a database of information to infer character-istics and relationships. Example: survey research
  - **Experimental Research :** Variables in an environment are manipulated to observe the effects and changes.
  - **Simulation Research :** Construction of an artificial environment to study behavior and effects.

Qualitative Research

- Refers to research procedures that produce descriptive data—people's own spoken words and observable behavior
- Qualitative methods are associated with interpretivism, non-scientific, subjectivity and feminism.
- Primarily an inductive process that provides unstructured or semi-structured procedures.
- It mainly consists of ethnographic methods such as participant observation, in-depth interviews, group interview, and content analysis.
- It projects a participant's point of view and is unstructured with rich and deep data.
- Some feminist researchers reject and criticize quantitative approach as it is directly in conflict with the aims of feminist research.
- The second wave feminists in 1960s questioned how knowledge is produced, who produces it and how it is used.
- According to them, what is termed as "universal" knowledge is actually male knowledge derived from male scholarship.
- Social sciences have been historically androcentric, and there has been muting of women's voices.
- Men have established the norms and played a dominant role in research.
- Knowledge is usually measured by how objective it is. Scholars have to follow certain rules to discover "the truth" and ensure its reliability. According to feminist epistemology, this is problematic because it assumes objectivity is possible and should be desirable.
- But, several tools used during the research process such as highlighting, editing, cutting and transcribing are subjective acts. Subjective acts are incorporated into this supposedly pure objective analysis.
- This emphasis on objectivity downplays the importance of validity. As humans are subjective, research methods can never be completely objective. There is always some degree of subjective interpretation.
- Feminists describe the idea of objectivity in research as an excuse for maintaining power relationships. Hence the notion of complete objectivity has to be redefined and replaced by situational knowledge.
- This rejection of absolute standards of objectivity in favor of relativistic standards makes research participatory, reflective of actual experiences and offers realistic construction of knowledge.

- So, feminists suggest increased use of qualitative research to reflect the nature of human experience better.
- **Focus Group:**
  - The interview is conducted by a trained moderator on a small group of respondents.
  - Unstructured and in a natural setting.
- **In-Depth Interview:**
  - The unstructured, personal interview is conducted by a highly skilled interviewer.
  - May take an average of 1 hour.
  - Helps uncover motives, feelings, beliefs, and attitudes.
- Word association, completion techniques, and expressive techniques are some indirect, projective methods used for qualitative research studies.
- **Grounded Theory:**
  - Set of rigorous procedures leading to the emergence of conceptual categories from data.
  - It is a qualitative research method that enables the researcher to develop a theory that offers an explanation about concerns of the research area and provide solutions. This is obtained by discovering emerging patterns and theories from data.
  - It is developed inductively from a data corpus.
  - The basic approach is reading or analyzing a textual database and discovering concepts, categories, and interrelationships. Data is collected, coded, concepts are obtained, and categories are formed.
  - Methods used in grounded theory are:
    - ❖ Preparation
    - ❖ Data collection
    - ❖ Data analysis (coding)
    - ❖ Data analysis (constant comparative analysis)
    - ❖ Theoretical conception

Multiple Choice Questions

1. Match the List-I (Concept) with the List-II (Explanation):

List-I	*List-II*
(a) Validity	(i) The consistency in results of a test.
(b) Reliability	(ii) The abstract concepts used in social science theories.
(c) Coding	(iii) The act of giving the data numerical.
(d) Constructs	(iv) The accuracy of observations

Codes:

	(a)	(b)	(c)	(d)
A.	(iv)	(i)	(iii)	(ii)
B.	(i)	(iv)	(ii)	(iii)
C.	(ii)	(iv)	(iii)	(i)
D.	(iv)	(ii)	(i)	(iii)

2. Which of the following is not a secondary source of data collection?

A. Books
B. Literature Reviews
C. Interviews
D. Articles

3. Interactive Methodology demands the combined use of three elements of feminist research:

A. Research for men, by women and on women
B. Research on women, by women and for women
C. Research on women, by men and for women
D. Research of women, about women and on women

4. Experimental Analysis is called as a:

A. Journey that starts with training in survey research, continuing through participant observation.
B. Process that starts with training in research design, continuing through participant observation.
C. Mobility that starts with training in survey research, continuing through non-participant observation.
D. Transformation that starts with training in research plan, continuing through focused observation.

5. Feminist Research is:

A. Interdisciplinary
B. Multidisciplinary
C. Cross-disciplinary
D. All the above

6. Choose the appropriate methodology related to Women's Studies Research.

A. Descriptive, Exploratory and Experimental Designs.
B. Experimental Analysis, Oral Testimony and Interactive Methodology.
C. Observation, Interview and Interview Schedule.
D. Content Analysis, Historical and Comparative Methods.

7. Feminist perspective lays emphasis on the placing of:

A. Women's own experiences in the centre of process.
B. Men's shared experiences in the centre of process.
C. Women's shared experiences in the periphery of process.
D. Men's own experiences in the periphery of process.

8. ________ has an equal and independent chance of selection in the sample.

A. Random B. Quota
C. Stratified D. Cluster

9. Arrange the following steps of formulating a research problem in the correct order:

(i) Assess your Objective
(ii) Raise Research Questions
(iii) Formulate Objectives
(iv) Dissect the Broad Areas into Sub-Areas

Codes:

A. (ii), (i), (iii), (iv) B. (iv), (ii), (iii), (i)
C. (i), (ii), (iii), (iv) D. (i), (iv), (iii), (ii)

10. Research on gender stereotyping in the media suggests that femininity is routinely associated with:

A. Equality and Equity
B. Domesticity and Equality
C. Sexuality and Domesticity
D. Equity and Sexuality

11. Which of the following is correct about 'Multistage Sampling'?

A. Sample is selected at various stages and each sample is adequately studied before another sample is drawn for it.
B. Sample is selected in various stages but only the last sample of subject is studied.
C. Sample is selected from population which is divided into small units or sub-units.
D. Sample is selected from population which is divided into two or more mutually exclusive segments based on some categories of variables.

12. What is the significance of hypothesis?

1. It leads to reliability and validity.
2. It helps collecting useful facts.
3. It sets the direction of research.
4. It contributes to formation of theories.

Codes:

A. 2, 3 and 4 only
B. 1, 2, 3 and 4
C. 1, 2 and 3 only
D. 1, 2 and 4 only

13. Which is not the form of qualitative research?

A. Case study
B. Oral history
C. Survey
D. Focus group discussion

14. Feminist research aims to:

(i) Enquire into the origin and basis of the discriminatory practices against women.
(ii) Expose the patriarchal tools of socio-cultural and economic practices of family and society that lead to women's suppression.
(iii) Women are brought from visibility to invisibility.
(iv) Provide data on most of the sensitive problems of women's issue.

Codes:

A. (i) and (ii) only correct
B. (iii) only correct
C. (i) and (iii) only correct
D. (i), (ii) and (iv) only correct

15. The research which relies on first hand observation without due regard to systems and theory is termed as:

A. Experimental Research
B. Exploratory Research
C. Descriptive Research
D. Explanatory Research

16. Which of the following statement is correct?

A. Unstructured interviews lead to a waste amount of quantitative data.
B. The objectives of study and nature of subject matter jointly determine the method of data collection.
C. Social survey and interview method cannot be used simultaneously.
D. Content analysis is the best way to collect data on women issues.

17. Which is the correct chronological sequence of stages of development of feminist research?

(i) Research on gender as an organizing principle in all social systems.
(ii) Research on sex differences based on biological properties of individuals.
(iii) Research based on men's experiences.
(iv) Research on individual level sex roles and socialization.

Mark the correct sequence from the codes given below:

Codes:

A. (i), (ii), (iv), (iii) B. (iv), (iii), (i), (ii)
C. (iii), (iv), (ii), (i) D. (iii), (ii), (iv), (i)

18. Mark the correct sequence of "Data Collection Techniques" arranged in the descending order according to the size of the sample:
A. Mailed questionnaire, structures interview, observation, participant observation.
B. Observation, structured interview, mailed questionnaire, participant observation.
C. Participant observation, observation, structured interview, mail questionnaire.
D. Structured interview, mailed questionnaire, observation, participant observation.

19. Social survey does not aim at:
A. Collection of data related to the social aspects of a community.
B. Study of social problems regarding women.
C. Formulation of laws on the basis of collected data.
D. Utilization of knowledge acquired to teach the young researchers.

20. Which statement on hypothesis is wrong?
A. It states a logical relationship between facts.
B. It is a proposition.
C. It is a necessary link between theory and investigation.
D. It is an initial step in scientific research.

21. When the population is heterogeneous in terms of social class, age, income etc., which method of sampling is appropriately applicable?
A. Sampling
B. Cluster Sampling
C. Stratified Sampling
D. Systematic Sampling

22. What is correct about research design?
A. It provides insights into the problem to be investigated.
B. It gives relevance to the problem.
C. It helps in preparing hypothesis.
D. It is a plan of a piece of empirical research.

23. Nancy Kleiber and Linda Light's method of feminist research which combines the use of three elements of research i.e. research on women, by women and for women, is termed as:
A. Ethnomethodology
B. Action Research
C. Feminist Research
D. Interactive Methodology

24. Identify the correct set of data collection technique arranged in the ascending order according to the degree of personal involvement of the researcher:
A. Participant observation, mail questionnaires, unstructured interview, structured interview.
B. Mail questionnaires, unstructured interview, participant observation, structured interview.
C. Mail questionnaires, structured interview, unstructured interview, participant observation.
D. Unstructured interview, structured interview, participant observation, mail questionnaires.

25. Which of the following is not a characteristic of feminist research?
A. Researcher and subject are interdependent.
B. Observer and observed are not connected.
C. Subject and researcher are placed in the equal empirical level.
D. Science and nature are kept in harmony.

26. The Census data which is used and analyzed for some feminist research problem is known as:
A. Qualitative Data B. Random Data
C. Secondary Data D. Primary Data

27. Both conflict and feminist theories focus on:
A. Negotiated social orders
B. Manifest functions
C. Subjective meanings
D. Structured social inequality

28. What is 'population' in research method?
(i) It is a target group.
(ii) It is universe.
(iii) It is total number of people in a specific area.
(iv) It is a stratum.

Codes:
A. (ii) and (iii) only B. (ii), (iii) and (iv) only
C. (i) and (ii) only D. (i), (ii), (iii) and (iv)

29. What is correct about research methodology for feminist research?
A. Multi-stage sampling is always better than random sampling.
B. Qualitative methods are always used for feminist research by the feminists.
C. Feminist issues can be better understood by large samples.
D. Participatory research methodology is better than non-participatory for feminists' issues.

30. What is correct statement about sampling method?
A. It is widely used in social research, not in feminist research.
B. The widely used method in feminist research is random sample technique.
C. It is used for research only when census method becomes impracticable.
D. It is more reliable than census method.

31. Feminist Activism focuses on women's issues and has with time spread throughout many movements related to:
(i) Environment Rights
(ii) Feminist Art
(iii) Identity Rights
(iv) Homosexual Rights
Codes:
A. (i), (ii) and (iii) only
B. (i), (ii), (iii) and (iv)
C. (i) and (ii) only
D. (iv), (ii) and (i) only

32. Which method or methods can be useful for studying rural illiterate women?
(i) Interview method
(ii) Questionnaire method
(iii) Case study method
(iv) Participant observation method
Codes:
A. (i), (ii), (iii) and (iv) B. (i), (iii) and (iv)
C. (i), (ii) and (iv) D. (i) and (ii) only

33. Match List-I with List-II:

List-I (Theories)	***List-II (Explanation)***
(a) Biological Theory	(i) Gender is a social construction rather than a biological given.
(b) Cognitive Development Theory	(ii) Gender development and differentiation
(c) Gender Schema Theory	(iii) Gender identity is postulated as the basic organizer and regulator of children's gender learning.
(d) Sociological Theory	(iv) Emphasizes influence of genes and hormones

Codes:

	(a)	(b)	(c)	(d)
A.	(ii)	(i)	(iii)	(iv)
B.	(iv)	(iii)	(i)	(ii)
C.	(iii)	(iv)	(ii)	(i)
D.	(iv)	(iii)	(ii)	(i)

34. The research tool SPSS stands for:
A. Statistical Package for Social System
B. Systematic Package for Social Science
C. Special Package for Social System
D. Statistical Package for Social Science

35. Which of the following is not a primary source of data collection:
A. Questionnaire B. Interviews
C. Survey D. Books

36. Research Ethics do not include:
A. Honesty B. Subjectivity
C. Integrity D. Objectivity

37. Feminist research actively seeks to remove the power imbalance between:
A. Patriarchy and feminism
B. Researcher and subject
C. Social inclusion and power relationship
D. Power and politics

38. What is correct about feminist and participatory approaches of research?
1. Both agree that the voices of the marginal groups in traditional research were not taken care of.
2. Both believe in diversity in society as well as in the construction of social knowledge.
3. Both pose a challenge to the conventional disciplinary boundaries.
4. Both question the notion that traditional social research was value free.
Codes:
A. 1, 2, 3 and 4 B. 2 and 3 only
C. 1 and 4 only D. 2, 3 and 4 only

39. In which data collection technique, the researcher has the maximum degree of personal involvement with the respondents?
A. Unstructured interview
B. Structured interview
C. Participant observation
D. Mailed Questionnaire

40. Arrange in sequence the steps in the construction of Index in Research:
1. Selecting possible items
2. Scoring the index
3. Examining the empirical relationship
4. Index validation
Codes:
A. 1, 2, 3, 4 B. 1, 3, 4, 2
C. 1, 3, 2, 4 D. 2, 3, 4, 1

41. Which of the following statement is not an exposure of 'androcentric bias' in research?
A. Recording the experience of female only.
B. Assuming what applies to males as equally applicable to females.

C. Considering the experience of men as more important.
D. Considering the image of man for human beings.

42. This is correct about 'Values'?
1. Values exist at different levels of generality of abstraction.
2. Values tend to be hierarchically arranged.
3. Values are explicit and implicit in varying degrees.
4. Values often are in conflict with each other.

Codes:
A. 1, 2, 3 and 4
B. 2 and 3 only
C. 1, 2 and 3 only
D. 3 and 4 only

43. Which of the following statement is incorrect for Research Methods?
A. Social survey and interview method can be used simultaneously.
B. Unstructured interviews lead to a vast amount of quantitative data.
C. All methods of data collection have their own limitations.
D. Qualitative research methods can be used generally for micro-level studies.

44. Which of the following is correct about Grounded Theory in Research?
1. An Inductive Approach
2. Hypothesis Testing
3. Generate a Theory
4. Deductive Approach

Codes:
A. 1 and 3 only B. 1, 2 and 3 only
C. 2 and 3 only D. 1 and 4 only

45. Which of the following pair is not correctly matched?
A. Sexual dimorphism — The physical and psychological differentiation of girls and boys.
B. Sex stereotype — Differential expectations of girls and boys within a culture.
C. Gender sensitivity — The ability to acknowledge and highlight existing gender differentials and incorporate into strategies.
D. Gender-blind — Recognition of gender as an essential determinant of social outcomes impacting projects and policies.

46. Sequence the following process of research?
1. Thematizing 2. Designing
3. Transcribing 4. Interviewing

Codes:
A. 1, 2, 3 and 4 B. 1, 3, 4 and 2
C. 1, 2, 4 and 3 D. 2, 1, 4 and 3

47. In which form of scaling questionnaire, the use of response categories like strongly agree, agree, disagree and strongly disagree are made?
A. Thurstone Scale
B. Bogardus Scale
C. Gutman Scale
D. Likert Scale

48. Match the List-I with List-II:

List-I (Theories)	***List-II (Views)***
(a) Cognitive and behavioral	(i) To focus on psychology of individuals theories.
(b) Interactionist	(ii) Uncover the ways people actually understand their own experience.
(c) Interpretive	(iii) Views social life as a process of interaction.
(d) Critical	(iv) Concerned with the conflict of interests in society.

Codes:

	(a)	(b)	(c)	(d)
A.	(i)	(iii)	(ii)	(iv)
B.	(ii)	(iii)	(iv)	(i)
C.	(iii)	(iv)	(ii)	(i)
D.	(iv)	(iii)	(ii)	(i)

49. How the relationship between economic development and women's economic activity shown?
A. 'U' Shape B. 'Z' Shape
C. 'Y' Shape D. 'C' Shape

50. Feminist Research aims at:
A. Addressing women's issues with women's perspective
B. Promotion of women research scholars
C. To study women as an object
D. Study of women's education

51. Research design must contain:
(i) Statement of the problem
(ii) Objectives of the study
(iii) Report of the study
(iv) Population to be studied

Codes:
A. (i) and (ii) only
B. (i) and (iv) only
C. (i), (ii) and (iv) only
D. (i), (iii) and (iv) only

52. "We women will discover what we need for ourselves and get it for ourselves." Which of the following approaches is meant for the above?
A. Welfare B. Empowerment
C. Equity D. Participatory

53. Participatory Research is useful in understanding women's issues because it:
A. Provides alternative strategies.
B. Guarantees ideological and scientific purity.
C. Is a sophisticated technique to create knowledge.
D. Is based on quantitative research.

54. Gender disaggregated data are the basis for:
A. Analysis of women's work.
B. Gender sensitive policy formulation and programme planning.
C. Gender mainstreaming.
D. Gender sensitization.

55. Feminist Research aims to:
A. Research on women, by men and for women.
B. Research for women, by women and on women.
C. Research on women, about women, and of women.
D. Research of women by women and for women.

56. Which of the following research method is applied in discovering the underlying motives of human behavior?
A. Qualitative Research B. Action Research
C. Quantitative Research D. Policy Research

57. Mark the correct sequence of "Data Collection Techniques" arranged in the ascending order of the degree of personal involvement by the researcher:
A. Mailed questionnaire, unstructured interview, structured interview, participant observation.
B. Participant observation, structured interview, mailed questionnaire, unstructured interview.
C. Mailed questionnaire, structured interview, unstructured interview, participant observation.
D. Unstructured interview, structured interview, participant observation, mailed questionnaire.

58. In which type of sampling, every element of the population can have the chance to be selected?
A. Convenient sampling
B. Random sampling
C. Systematic sampling
D. Cluster sampling

59. Which of the following is not a characteristic of feminist research?
A. Researcher and subject are interdependent.
B. Observer and observed are not connected.
C. Subject and researcher are placed in the equal empirical level.
D. Science and nature are kept in harmony.

60. What is/are the weakness of survey method?
(i) Surveys demand a great deal of attention and honesty on the part of respondents.
(ii) Surveys can describe the characteristics of a large population.
(iii) Surveys make measurement more precise by enforcing uniform definitions upon the respondents.
(iv) Surveys are invariably context blind.

Codes:
A. (iv) only B. (iii) and (iv) only
C. (i) and (iv) only D. (i), (ii) and (iv)

61. What are Maria Mies' Methodological guidelines for feminist research?
(i) Conscious bias towards women's struggles for social change.
(ii) Value-free research.
(iii) Conscientization of the researcher about the issue.
(iv) Conscientization of the researched about the issue.

Codes:
A. (i), (ii), (iii), (iv) B. (i), (iii), (iv) only
C. (i) only D. (iii) and (iv) only

62. Which of the following is the funding agency for conducting research in social sciences?
A. ICAR B. ICSSR
C. CSIR D. ICMR

63. Which is correct about action research?
(i) It aims at dealing with real world problem at work and in organizations.
(ii) It is change oriented.
(iii) It is more of a theoretical nature.
(iv) It involves a feedback loop for the purpose of change.

Codes:
A. (i) and (iii) only
B. (i), (ii) and (iv) only
C. (ii), (iii) and (iv) only
D. (i), (ii), (iii) and (iv) only

64. While selecting sample, if every element has the chance to be selected, it is known as:
A. Cluster sample
B. Random sample
C. Systematic sample
D. Convenience sample

65. In which type of research design, hypothesis is not required?

A. Experimental
B. Descriptive
C. Diagnostic
D. Exploratory

66. Mark out the incorrect answer about survey method:

A. It is useful for the study of large population.
B. It can be conducted from remote locations.
C. It is relatively expensive.
D. It is invariably context blind.

67. Mark out the correct answer about Hypothesis:

(i) Hypothesis is a statement, which is yet to be tested.
(ii) Hypothesis are all positive.
(iii) Hypothesis can be null.
(iv) The sources of hypothesis can be the existing theories.

Codes:

A. (i), (iii) and (iv) only
B. (i), (ii), (iii) and (iv)
C. (ii), (iii) and (iv) only
D. (i), (ii) and (iii) only

68. Arrange the following steps in correct sequence for structuring the research in social science:

(i) Pilot Study
(ii) Selection of research techniques
(iii) Defining research problem
(iv) Review of literature

Codes:

A. (iii), (iv), (i), (ii)
B. (iv), (iii), (i), (ii)
C. (iv), (ii), (iii), (i)
D. (iii), (iv), (ii), (i)

69. Which of the following statements is incorrect?

A. There is no one best method of data collection for all the studies in social sciences.
B. Unstructured interviews rely upon unstandardized open ended questions.
C. Structured interviews are used for collecting vast amount of quantitative data.
D. Social survey and interview methods are mutually exclusive. Only one at a time can be used.

70. When the researcher assumes a role in the researched group and maintain a low profile as observer is known as:

A. Participant observation
B. Quasi-participant observation
C. Non-participant observation
D. Quasi-non participant observation

71. When sample is selected in various stages but only the last sample of subjects is studied, is known as:

A. Non-probability sampling
B. Multi-phase sampling
C. Multi-stage sampling
D. Cluster sampling

72. Who have coined the terminology 'Interactive Methodology' for feminist research?

A. Joan Huber and Killy
B. Nancy Kleiber and Linda Light
C. David Morgan and Keohane
D. Bernard Helen Roberts

73. Mark out the correct answer about culture:

(i) It is essentially an attribute of the individual rather than of the group.
(ii) It is learnt and includes both material and non-material aspects.
(iii) It is solely the product of civilized people.
(iv) It is the composite of values, norms, ethics, traditions, art etc.

Codes:

A. (i), (ii), (iv) only
B. (ii) and (iv) only
C. (ii), (iii) and (iv) only
D. (iii), (iv) only

74. Scientific Research Epistemology means:

A. Knowledge and Truth
B. Methodology
C. Question
D. Values

75. Which of the following is the correct statement about the characteristics of an empirical social science research?

(i) Collection of primary data about people
(ii) Research based on social context
(iii) Research based on secondary data
(iv) Use of a range of methods

Codes:

A. (i), (ii), (iii) are correct
B. (i) and (ii) are correct
C. (i), (ii) and (iv) are correct
D. (i), (ii), (iii) and (iv) are correct

76. Which state has started the programme 'Mana Bhavita' in the year 2015?

A. Jammu and Kashmir
B. Andhra Pradesh
C. Tamil Nadu
D. Kerala

77. The concept of 'Chilly Climate' in the class rooms means:

A. Males and females often treated differently in the classroom.
B. Non-response of students in the classroom.
C. Air conditioned classrooms.
D. Equal treatment of males and females in the classroom.

78. CSWI (1974) denotes as:
A. Council on the Status of Women in India
B. Committee on the Status of Women in India
C. Centre on the Status of Women in India
D. Commission on the Status of Women in India

79. Arrange the following steps in Research Process in a logical sequence?
(i) Data Collection
(ii) Setting of Objectives
(iii) Report Writing
(iv) Data Analysis

Codes:
A. (ii), (i), (iv), (iii) B. (i), (ii), (iii), (iv)
C. (iii), (iv), (i), (ii) D. (iv), (iii), (ii), (i)

80. What is CAPART?
A. It is a private funding agency
B. It is an NGO
C. It is a Government Funding Agency
D. It is an organ of State Advisory Welfare Board

81. Among the following statements which is correct about Inductive Research method?
A. Particular to General
B. General to Particular
C. Starts with Theory
D. Starts with Hypothesis

82. Which type of research is generally used for the development of hypothesis regarding potential problems?
A. Exploratory B. Experimental
C. Diagnostic D. Descriptive

83. What is incorrect about Action Research?
A. It emphasizes the notion of action as a legitimate mode of knowing.
B. It is actually a basic research.
C. It takes the realm of knowledge into the field of practice.
D. It is the basic for participatory action research.

84. Which one of the following pairs is correctly matched?
A. Those subjects exposed to the stimulus conditions under study — Static group
B. Those subjects to whom no experimental stimulus is administered — Control group
C. Those subjects who are selected for study — Experimental group
D. Those subjects who are to be studied — Interview group

85. "A research method usually applied to mass communication such as newspaper or television, for purposes of identifying specified characteristics of the material" is:
A. Contextual analysis
B. Statistical analysis
C. Content analysis
D. Secondary analysis

86. What are the limitations of the case study method?
(i) Study of the subjective aspects
(ii) Difficult to test reliability and validity of the data collected
(iii) Deep study of the problem
(iv) False generalizations

Codes:
A. (ii) and (iv) only
B. (i), (ii), (iii) and (iv)
C. (i), (ii) and (iv) only
D. (ii), (iii) and (iv) only

87. What is common in feminist and participatory approaches of research?
(i) Both question the notion that traditional social research was value free.
(ii) They pose a challenge to the conventional disciplinary boundaries.
(iii) They do not believe in diversity in society as well as in the construction of social knowledge.
(iv) Both agree that the voices of the marginal groups in traditional research were taken note of.

Codes:
A. (i), (iii) and (iv) only
B. (i) and (ii) only
C. (i) and (iv) only
D. (ii) and (iii) only

88. "A problem of reliability in systemic observation in which observers become less accurate in their observations over time" is:
A. Observer empathy
B. Observer subjectivity
C. Observer limitation
D. Observer drift

89. Which one of the following is a research tool:
A. Graph B. Illustration
C. Questionnaire D. Diagram

90. In the process of conducting research, "formulation of Hypothesis" is followed by:
A. Preparing the Research Design
B. Analysing Data
C. Hypothesis Testing
D. Collection of Data

91. Which is the main objective of research:
A. To review literature
B. To summarize already known
C. To get an academic degree
D. To discover new facts/refresh interpretation of known facts

92. Sampling error decreases with:
A. Decrease in Sample Size
B. Increase in Sample Size
C. Process of Randomization
D. Process of Analysis

93. India is regarded as a country with "Demographic Dividend". This is due to:
A. Its more population in the age group below 15 years.
B. Its more population in the age group of 15-64 years.
C. Its more population in the age group above 65 years.
D. Its more total population.

94. Which term/terms are used for state policy of Reservation in education, services and legislature etc.:
1. Affirmative action
2. Reverse discrimination
3. Compensatory discrimination
4. Protective discrimination

Codes:
A. 1, 2, 3 and 4 B. 4 only
C. 3 and 4 only D. 1 and 2 only

95. The Feminist Research:
1. begins with voices, visions and experiences of feminist activists, scholars and researches speaking across the ages.
2. is feminist consciousness that opens up intellectual and emotional spaces for all women to articulate their relations to one another.
3. provides a legacy of feminist research, praxis and activism.
4. leads to a transformation from personal to political.

Codes:
A. 1 and 2 only
B. 1, 2 and 3 only
C. 2 and 4 only
D. 1, 2, 3 and 4

96. Match the List-I with the List-II:

List-I	***List-II***
(a) Power-over	(i) Motivation
(b) Power-to	(ii) Domination
(c) Power-with	(iii) Enabling to solve
(d) Powerwithin	(iv) Organising for community work

Codes:

	(a)	(b)	(c)	(d)
A.	(i)	(ii)	(iii)	(iv)
B.	(ii)	(iii)	(iv)	(i)
C.	(iii)	(ii)	(i)	(iv)
D.	(iv)	(i)	(iii)	(ii)

97. Which of the following is hypothesis/hypotheses?
1. Girls should not misbehave with the in laws to be saved from the stigma of divorce.
2. The rate of divorces is rising because of the increase in the number of educated women.
3. Some feminists are very actively conducting research on the causes of rising divorce rate in India.
4. The rate of divorces is rising because more women are willing to break out of bad marriages rather than suffer a life in silence.

Codes:
A. 1 and 4 only B. 1, 2, 3 and 4
C. 2 and 4 only D. 1 and 3 only

98. Arrange in sequence the steps in data analysis stage of any empirical research:
1. Tabulation and analysis
2. Coding
3. Write up
4. Editing

Codes:
A. 2, 1, 3, 4 B. 2, 4, 3, 1
C. 1, 2, 3, 4 D. 4, 2, 1, 3

99. It is a method of instruction which encourages the transformation of students from passive recipients of knowledge to active knowers who see themselves as agents of social change.
A. Focused Group Discussions
B. Androgogy
C. Pedagogy
D. Participant Observation

100. What is correct about survey research?
1. It aims at collection of data related to social aspects of a community.
2. It can be census as well as sample based.
3. It is workable method of qualitative research.
4. It always collects information from each element in the population.

Codes:
A. 1, 2 and 4 only B. 1 and 2 only
C. 1 and 3 only D. 2 and 3 only

101. The Criteria for Feminist Research is that:

1. It understands that all research is essentially value driven and always results in some kind of new action or practice.
2. It is driven by the interests of the women whose problematic situation was the reason for raising the research question.
3. It questions the reproduction and perpetuation of power relationships that subordinate women.
4. It is research that is conducted by women.

Codes:

A. 1, 2, 3 are correct
B. 2, 3, 4 are correct
C. 1, 3, 4 are correct
D. 1, 2, 4 are correct

102. How is it argued that qualitative research can have "empiricist over tones"?

A. There is an emphasis on direct observation of people and social settings.
B. Semi-structured interview schedules are used to quantify behaviour.
C. Qualitative researchers prefer to conduct statistical analysis of their data.
D. It typically involves testing a clearly defined hypothesis.

103. The term Patriarchy implies:

1. Males holding primary power
2. Males Predominate in roles of Political Leadership
3. Subordination of men
4. In the domain of family fathers or father figures hold authority over women and children

Codes:

A. 1 and 2 B. 4 only
C. 1, 2 and 4 only D. 2 and 4 only

104. Which of the following statement is incorrect about hypothesis?

A. It is essential for every research design.
B. It is a statement which is yet to be tested.
C. It is derived from the existing theories of the concerned issue.
D. It can be null also.

105. When the researcher wants to know the impact of some variable on the target population, which research design can be appropriately applicable?

A. Exploratory B. Experimental
C. Diagnostic D. Descriptive

106. Find out the correct sequence concerning various steps to conduct research effectively:

(i) Developing hypothesis
(ii) Data analysis
(iii) Preparation of report
(iv) Formulating research problem

Codes:

A. (iii), (ii), (i), (iv)
B. (i), (ii), (iii), (iv)
C. (ii), (iv), (i), (iii)
D. (iv), (i), (ii), (iii)

107. Social Science Research aims at:

A. Social Equity
B. Social Harmony
C. National Integration
D. Integration

108. Match the List-I with List-II:

List-I	***List-II***
(a) Action Research	(i) Questionnaire
(b) Qualitative Data	(ii) Planning and Launching Programme
(c) Exploratory Research	(iii) Analysis of Insights
(d) Quantitative Data	(iv) Oral History

Codes:

	(a)	(b)	(c)	(d)
A.	(ii)	(iv)	(iii)	(i)
B.	(ii)	(iii)	(iv)	(i)
C.	(i)	(ii)	(iv)	(iii)
D.	(iii)	(iv)	(ii)	(i)

109. Which one of the following is not a bar diagram?

A. Broken Bars B. Histograms
C. Pie-Diagrams D. Deviation Bars

110. Which one of the following is a disadvantage of Cluster sampling?

A. Variation of cluster size may increase the bias.
B. It can cover large population and large areas.
C. Cost of this method is much less.
D. It does not take more time.

111. What is the correct expansion of ICRW?

A. International Committee on Research of Women
B. International Centre for the Research on Women
C. International Conference on Research of Women
D. International Committee for Research on Women

112. Random sample technique is more applicable if the target population is:

A. Homogeneous
B. Heterogeneous
C. Both Homogeneous and Heterogeneous
D. Heterogeneous across set and age only

113. The most essential step in making interview, a successful method of Data collection is:

A. Appropriate interview schedule
B. Arranging secondary information on the topic of research
C. Establishing rapport with the respondents
D. Having accurate research design

114. Match the List-I with List-II:

List-I	***List-II***
(a) Hypothesis	(i) Reasoning from particular to general
(b) Inductive	(ii) Reasoning from general to particular
(c) Observation	(iii) Tentative assumption
(d) Deductive	(iv) Empirical findings

Codes:

	(a)	(b)	(c)	(d)
A.	(i)	(ii)	(iii)	(iv)
B.	(iii)	(i)	(iv)	(ii)
C.	(ii)	(iii)	(i)	(iv)
D.	(iv)	(ii)	(iii)	(i)

115. A hypothesis must:

A. be amenable to testing within a timeframe
B. be an approximation of the final result
C. be unlimited in scope
D. none of the above

116. It is a method of instruction which encourages the transformation of students from passive recipients of knowledge to active knowers who see themselves as agents of social change.

A. Focussed Group Discussions
B. Androgogy
C. Pedagogy
D. Participant observation

117. What does the term "quasi-quantification" refer to?

A. The use of words like "many", "some" or "often" in qualitative research.
B. A poor attempt at statistical analysis.
C. The use of a survey instrument that has not been tested for intercoder reliability.
D. The way scientist talk about their data in numerical terms to enhance the credebility of their findings.

118. Which of the following is correct statement about qualitative research methods?

A. These are more suitable when research is carried out in a small setting.
B. These are useful when the researcher is looking for broad trends or patterns in a given population.
C. These are very useful when the researcher wants to know macro phenomena.
D. These can better study the extent and nature of poverty or disease of a given population.

119. Which of the following is correct statement about survey research?

A. It is said to be invariably context blind.
B. It is always conducted by specialists and professionals.
C. It is flexible and does not require a precise study design.
D. It provides enough scope for honesty and care for context.

120. Which of the following problems can be better studied by Quantitative method of data?

A. Attitude of men and women on contraceptive use.
B. Male and female wage rates in the informal sector.
C. Women's experiences of the constraints of working in the informal sector.
D. Men's and women's views on the causes and consequences of domestic violence.

121. In Social Research which type of following approaches does focus on the disadvantaged subjects to define their problems, define the remedies, designing the research that will help them to realize their aims?

A. Survey Research
B. Feminist Research
C. Participatory Action Research
D. Qualitative Research

122. Which of the following is correct about 'Grounded Theory in Research'?

A. It is an Inductive approach
B. It is a Deductive approach
C. It is a Hypothesis Testing approach
D. It is mostly used for Quantitative Research

123. Muted Group Theory rests on three assumptions. Which one of the following is incorrect?

A. Men and women perceive the world differently.
B. Men enact their power politically, perpetuating their power and suppressing women's ideas and meanings from gaining public acceptance.
C. Women must convert their ideas, experiences and meanings into male language in order to be heard.
D. Both men and women have unique knowledge.

124. Who said?

"Feminist research is expected to use theory not so much to test hypothesis but develop a better understanding through grounded concepts."

A. Maria Mies
B. Maithreyi Krishnaraj
C. Maitrayee Chaudhuri
D. Malavika Karlekar

125. Who said that 'Objectivity' in research is the term that men have given a name to their own 'Subjectivity' i.e. male subjectivity as research objectivity?

A. Adrienne Rich
B. Nancy Kleiber
C. Joan Huber
D. Noeleen Heyser

126. Which of the following are the characteristics of feminist research?

1. Challenging androcentric bias across the disciplines.
2. Accepting the plurality of women's lived experiences.
3. Promoting sexist research.
4. Exclusion of gender as a category of analysis in social research.

Codes:

A. 1, 2, 3 and 4 are correct.
B. 1 and 2 only correct.
C. 3 and 4 are correct.
D. 1, 3 and 4 are correct.

127. Which of the following settings are appropriate to use focus group discussion?

1. When gathering data is not sufficient and getting closer to people is required.
2. When quantitative data is not sufficient to draw conclusions and arrive at findings.
3. When the requirement is more statistical data to be used to understand the problem in hand.
4. When there is a gap between providers of the service and beneficiaries of the service.

Codes:

A. 1 and 2 only
B. 1, 2 and 3 only
C. 2 and 3 only
D. 1, 2 and 4 only

128. Margrit Eichler has made an arbitrary categorization of sexism as a problem in social researches. Which of the following are the sexist concepts covered under primary types as described by her?

1. Androcentricity
2. Overgeneralization
3. Gender Insensitivity
4. Double Standards

Codes:

A. 1 and 3 only
B. 1, 2 and 4 only
C. 1, 2, 3, 4
D. 1, 2 and 3 only

129. Which is correct about Interview guide method?

1. It is a person who guides how to conduct interview.
2. It contains the tentative questions related to the central research problem.
3. It makes use of largely only structured questions.
4. It requires a higher level of interviewing quality of research.

Codes:

A. 2 and 4 only
B. 1, 2, 3, 4
C. 1, 3 and 4 only
D. 2, 3 and 4 only

130. Match the List-I (Type of Research) and List-II (Explanation):

List-I	***List-II***
(a) Descriptive Research	(i) Methods developed for the specific purpose of testing causal relationship.
(b) Explanatory Research	(ii) An attempt to determine whether or not phenomenon exists.
(c) Experimental Research	(iii) Examining a phenomenon to characterize it more fully or to differentiate it from other phenomenon.
(d) Action Research	(iv) Research conducted to solve a social problem.

Codes:

	(a)	(b)	(c)	(d)
A.	(iii)	(ii)	(i)	(iv)
B.	(iii)	(i)	(ii)	(iv)
C.	(i)	(ii)	(iii)	(iv)
D.	(iv)	(i)	(ii)	(iii)

131. What is incorrect about pilot study?

A. It is conducted when the survey or research study is small.
B. It facilitates the framing of a workable schedule.
C. It may help to determine whether the schedule should be structured or open ended.
D. It helps to save time and money.

132. What is/are correct about close-ended schedule?

1. It ensures standardization and greater uniformity in presentation of results.
2. It may furnish a superficial understanding of a phenomenon.
3. It ensures that responses are pointedly directed towards the requirements of a research problem.
4. It is simple, quick to administer and is relatively inexpensive.

Codes:

A. 1, 2, 3 and 4
B. 1, 2 and 4 only
C. 2, 3 and 4 only
D. 3 only

133. What could be the considerations for selecting topic of research?

1. Structure and State of a discipline.
2. Preceived relevance of the topic.
3. The availability of grants for particular themes.
4. Cost involved in terms of time, money and personnel for the topic.

Codes:

A. 2 and 3 only B. 1, 2 and 3 only
C. 1, 3 and 4 only D. 1, 2, 3 and 4

134. What is true about hypothesis?

1. Some research studies are conducted merely to generate hypothesis.
2. All research studies begin and are carried out with the help of hypothesis.
3. Hypotheses help to the efficient organization of data.
4. Hypotheses are formulated in the form of tentative answers to research questions.

Codes:

A. 1, 2, 3 and 4 B. 1, 3 and 4
C. 2, 3 and 4 D. 2 and 3 only

135. Match the List-I (Sampling) and List-II (Explanation):

List-I (Sampling)	***List-II (Explanation)***
(a) Cluster Sampling	(i) Randomly selecting from a Sampling frame hierarchical group.
(b) Stratified Random Sampling	(ii) Random selection on separately for each sub group in a Sampling frame.
(c) Probability Sampling	(iii) Any technique that ensures a random Sample.
(d) Random Sampling	(iv) Any technique that provides each population element an equal probability of being included.

Codes:

	(a)	(b)	(c)	(d)
A.	(i)	(ii)	(iv)	(iii)
B.	(i)	(ii)	(iii)	(iv)
C.	(iv)	(iii)	(i)	(ii)
D.	(ii)	(iii)	(iv)	(i)

136. What is the common focus of most feminist therapies today?

A. Improving living conditions for women around the world.
B. Creating a gentler, loving, woman centered world.
C. Showing how society's view of treatment of non-dominant groups impacts mental health.
D. Seeking balance in the un-equal power relationships between women and men.

137. Which are the limitations of scientific research methods for women's studies?

1. Complexity of social phenomenon
2. Dynamic nature of social phenomenon
3. Limited capacity of predictability
4. Cultural relativism

Codes:

A. 1, 2 and 4 only
B. 1, 2, 3 and 4
C. 1, 2 and 3 only
D. 1, 3 and 4 only

138. Which of the following problems can be better studied by qualitative method of data?

1. Fertility rate in the country.
2. Views of men and women on strains in husband wife relations in joint families.
3. Children's experiences with the teachers in school.
4. Women's labour force participation in organized sectors.

Codes:

A. 1, 2, 3 and 4
B. 1, 2 and 3 only
C. 2, 3 and 4 only
D. 2 and 3 only

139. What is correct about tabulation?

1. Understanding of any table does not require any specialized knowledge.
2. Tabulation is used for economy of time and space.
3. Tabulation helps in understanding with clarity the objectives of study.
4. Tabulation can be used for any type of data.

Codes:

A. 1, 2 and 3 only B. 2 and 3 only
C. 1 and 4 only D. 2 and 4 only

140. What are the characteristics of hypothesis?

(a) Vastness
(b) Clarity
(c) Related with available techniques
(d) Related with majority of population

Codes:

A. (a) and (b) only
B. (a), (b), (c) and (d)
C. (a), (b) and (c) only
D. (b) and (c) only

141. By which of the following methods, can a feminist researcher study the impact of some new teaching method on the performance of girl students of a school in a village?

A. 'Before after' experimental design only.
B. By having an experimental group, control group-experimental design only.
C. By diagnostic design only.
D. By both 'before after' and by having an experimental group-control.

142. Which of the following are correct about descriptive and diagnostic research designs?

(a) Both the research designs are much more structured.
(b) Both differ little from exploratory research design.
(c) The research questions of these research designs are based on prior knowledge about the nature of research problem.
(d) Both the research designs are applicable to any type of research problem.

Codes:

A. (a), (b), (c) and (d)
B. (a), (b) and (c) only
C. (a) and (c) only
D. (c) and (d) only

143. Match List-I with List-II:

List-I (Type of Research)	***List-II (Explanation)***
(a) Action Research	(i) Oriented towards measuring organizational Performance.
(b) Evaluation Research	(ii) It seeks to implement policy through the research Itself.
(c) Experimental Research	(iii) Designed to test a hypothesis under controlled conditions.
(d) Case study Research	(iv) It is not designed to compare one individual or group to another.

Codes:

	(a)	(b)	(c)	(d)
A.	(i)	(ii)	(iii)	(iv)
B.	(i)	(ii)	(iv)	(iii)
C.	(ii)	(i)	(iii)	(iv)
D.	(iv)	(i)	(ii)	(iii)

144. What is correct about operational definitions?

1. Operational definitions bridge the conceptual theoretical level with the observational empirical level.
2. Operational definitions are devised for the convenience of the researcher.
3. Operational definitions create confusion in writing research report.
4. Operational definitions provide for their empirical application.

Codes:

A. 1 and 4 only
B. 2 and 3 only
C. 3 and 4 only
D. 2 and 4 only

145. Assertion (A): Gender based violence leads to devastating and long term mental and physical malfunctioning in women and can even lead to death.

Reason (R): Interventional and psychological therapies are needed to help women experiencing violence.

Codes:

A. Both (A) and (R) are true and (R) is the correct explanation for (A).
B. Both (A) and (R) are false.
C. Both (A) and (R) are true but (R) is not the correct explanation for (A).
D. (A) is correct but (R) is false.

146. Assertion (A): Feminist consciousness and knowledge have many challenges in society.

Reason (R): In the male dominated society women have more often considered as objects of knowledge then the producers of it.

Codes:

A. Both (A) and (R) are true, (R) is the correct explanation for (A).
B. (A) and (R) are false.
C. Both (A) and (R) are true.
D. (A) is correct and (R) is false.

147. Assertion (A): Quantitative methods are the best for data collection for Women's Studies Research.

Reason (R): They provide a vast amount of data and very useful insights into the issues of women.

Codes:

A. Both (A) and (R) are true and (R) is the correct explanation of (A).
B. (A) is correct, but (R) is false and (R) is the wrong explanation of (A).
C. Both (A) and (R) are false.
D. (A) is wrong, but (R) is true.

148. Assertion (A): Feminist enquiry have drawn attention to the oppression of women in many societies which in turn has shed light on oppression generally.

Reason (R): Feminist theory and research have focused on gender differences and how they relate to the rest of the social organization.

Codes:

A. Both (A) and (R) are true and (R) is the correct explanation for (A).

B. Both (A) and (R) are false.
C. (A) is correct and (R) is false.
D. (A) is wrong and (R) is true.

149. Assertion (A): Documentation of sex-disaggregated data is essential for women's development.

Reason (R): Collection and presentation of sex disaggregated data is not necessary to prepare suitable policies for women.

Codes:

A. Both (A) and (R) are true and (R) is the correct explanation for (A).
B. Both (A) and (R) are true and (R) is not the correct explanation of (A).
C. Both (A) and (R) are false.
D. (A) is true and (R) is false.

150. Assertion (A): Feminist Research insists that scientist and subject are interdependent rather than independent.

Reason (R): Feminist Research aims 'knowledge for its own sake'.

Codes:

A. Both (A) and (R) are true.
B. Both (A) and (R) are false.
C. (A) is wrong, (R) is true.
D. (A) is correct, (R) is false.

Answers

1 A	2 C	3 D	4 A	5 A	6 B	7 A	8 A	9 B	10 C
11 B	12 A	13 C	14 D	15 B	16 B	17 D	18 A	19 D	20 A
21 C	22 D	23 D	24 C	25 B	26 C	27 D	28 C	29 D	30 C
31 B	32 B	33 D	34 D	35 D	36 B	37 B	38 A	39 C	40 C
41 A	42 A	43 B	44 A	45 D	46 C	47 D	48 A	49 A	50 A
51 C	52 C	53 A	54 B	55 C	56 A	57 C	58 B	59 B	60 C
61 B	62 B	63 B	64 B	65 D	66 C	67 A	68 D	69 D	70 A
71 C	72 B	73 B	74 A	75 C	76 B	77 A	78 B	79 A	80 C
81 A	82 A	83 B	84 B	85 C	86 A	87 B	88 D	89 C	90 A
91 D	92 B	93 B	94 A	95 D	96 B	97 C	98 D	99 C	100 B
101 A	102 A	103 C	104 A	105 B	106 D	107 D	108 A	109 C	110 A
111 B	112 A	113 C	114 B	115 A	116 C	117 A	118 D	119 D	120 D
121 C	122 A	123 B	124 A	125 A	126 B	127 D	128 C	129 A	130 A
131 A	132 A	133 D	134 B	135 B	136 D	137 B	138 C	139 B	140 D
141 D	142 C	143 C	144 A	145 C	146 A	147 C	148 A	149 D	150 D

❑❑❑

11

Questions Based On Passage

Read the passages below and answer the questions that follow based on your understanding of the passage:

PASSAGE-1

The UN places access to information technology as the third most important issue facing women globally, after poverty and violence against women. Gender disparity is already entrenched in many sectors with women in a disadvantaged position particularly in developing countries like India. A series of factors, including literacy and education, language, time, cost, geographical location of facilities, social and cultural norms, and women's computer and information search and dissemination skills constrain women's access to information technology. As a result, few women are producers of information technology, whether as internet content providers, programmers, designers, inventors, or fixers of computers. Besides, women are also conspicuously absent from decision making structures in information technology in developing countries. From the gender perspective, therefore, inclusive democratic participation and governance entail issues of women empowerment and gender mainstreaming of public policies, including ICT Policies and Programmes. Many people dismiss the concern for gender and IT in developing countries on the basis that development should deal with basic needs first. However, IT can be an important tool in meeting women's basic needs and can provide access to resources to lead women out of poverty. While technology is not a panaceá for women's problems in developing countries yet it offers new possibilities for women in economic, social and political empowerment. In the context of the knowledge society and information economy, it is essential that the knowledge-sharing mechanism, recognizes the value of knowledge possessed by women and includes their knowledge as a valuable addition to the global knowledge pool. Because of their biological and social roles, women are likely to be more rooted than men in the environment and more aware than men of the social, economic and environmental needs of their own communities.

1. According to the UN, which of the following are significant issues that women all over the world are facing?

A. Gender disparity, Access to Information Technology, Poverty.

B. Access to Information Technology, Poverty, Violence against women.

C. Poverty, Violence against women, Inclusive democratic participation.

D. Gender disparity, Political empowerment, Poverty.

2. Assertion (A): Gender disparity is observed in many sectors with women in a disadvantaged position in India.

Reason (R): Social and Cultural norms in the country constrain women's access to Information Technology, education and vocational skills.

Codes:

A. (A) is false but (R) is True.

B. (A) is True but (R) is false.

C. Both (A) and (R) are True and (R) is the correct explanation for (A).

D. Both (A) and (R) are True and (R) is not the correct explanation for (A).

3. From which of the following areas, women largely remain absent in developing countries?

(a) Decision making structures in Information Technology.

(b) Production of Information Technology.

(c) Providing of Internet content.

(d) Programming, designing and fixing of computers.

Codes:

A. (a), (b), (c) and (d)   B. (a) only
C. (b) only   D. (b) and (c) only

4. From a Gender perspective, what is necessary to involve inclusive Participation and Governance?

(a) Gender mainstreaming of Public Policies.
(b) Gender budgeting of Public Policies and Programmes.
(c) Gender mainstreaming of ICT Policies and Programmes.
(d) Issues of Women Empowerment.

Codes:

A. (a), (b), (c) and (d)   B. (b), (c) and (d) only
C. (c) and d) only   D. (a), (c) and (d) only

5. Why do some people feel concerned about gender and IT in developing countries?

A. Technology is a panacea for women's problems in developing countries.
B. It can offer new possibilities for women in economic, social and political empowerment.
C. IT can level gender inequalities.
D. IT can bring independence and prosperity to women.

6. Assertion (A): Women are more aware that men of the social, economic and environmental needs of their own communities.

Reason (R): Women, being lesser educated than men have little concern for IT jobs and are more interested in the communities for fulfillment of their psychic gratification.

Codes:

A. (A) is True but (R) is False and (R) is not the correct explanation for (A).
B. Both (A) and (R) are True and (R) is the correct explanation for (A).
C. (A) is False but (R) is True.
D. Both (A) and (R) are False.

PASSAGE-2

In the context of feminism, concepts like 'autonomy,' 'freedom' and 'choice' can be read-only within the historical context of their utterance. It is important to recall that the language of self-reliance and non-alignment of a pre-liberalised era also, stemmed from a desire for freedom and dignity. Issues of class, caste, tribe, poverty, and social justice formed an intrinsic part of feminist struggles in India, both in colonial and independent India. Autonomous women's groups which emerged in the 1970s debated with women's organizations of the left about the centrality of class in the latter's formulation, a matter which tended in their view to obfuscate the specificity of the women's question. Both groups have moved a long way since then. While left groups have played a visible role in the women's movement, autonomous groups have increasingly taken up questions of economic deprivation and matters of class. The Dalit women's movement, in turn, has expressed dissatisfaction with upper-caste women activists in both the left and the autonomous women's movements. But the core concern with social justice and inequality however defined, has remained constant.

In contrast, the popular representation of feminism in the media reflects a retreat from questions of class, caste and social justice. Quite clearly, feminism is read here as a matter of the individual women's right to choose. The woman concerned is either the corporate woman or the high -powered consumer. A deliberate break is sought to be made with the women's movement, but the language used for the construction of her image is often appropriated from the women's movement. One notable example is the way International Women's day is marked in the media. It has been traditionally celebrated by women's organizations and other political forces that aligned themselves with democratic and progressive forces. We now have a riot of ads with the specific day's messages appearing on 8th March every year.

1. Which of the following is correct in terms of forming the base for self-reliance and non-alignment in the Pre-Liberalised era?

A. The centrality of the class issue
B. The desire for freedom and dignity
C. Self-interest
D. Autonomy and freedom

2. What is the core concern of women's organizations and autonomous women's movements which remained constant?

(a) Gender equality and development.
(b) Social justice and inequity.
(c) Freedom and autonomy.
(d) Freedom and choice.

Codes:

A. (a) only   B. (a) and (b)
C. (b) only   D. (a) and (c)

3. Which of the following questions were taken up by autonomous women's groups?

A. Class and Caste issues
B. Class struggle and Social justice
C. Self-reliance and Non-alignment
D. Economic deprivation and Matters of Class

4. Assertion (A): The popular representation of feminism in the media reflects a retreat from questions of class, caste, and social justice.

Reason (R): Media is concerned with issues of grass-root women and work for their justice.

Codes:

A. (A) and (R) are True.
B. (A) and (R) are False.
C. (A) and (R) are True but (R) is not the correct explanation for (A).
D. (A) is True and (R) is False and not the correct explanation for (A).

5. Which of the following formed an intrinsic part of Feminist Struggles in India?

(a) Women's equality for political participation.
(b) Gender and Poverty.
(c) Equal Remuneration for equal work.
(d) Class, caste, tribe, poverty and social justice.

Codes:

A. (a) only B. (d) only
C. (a) and (c) D. (b) and (d)

6. Which of the following is correct concerning Dalit Women's Movement?

A. Dalit women's movements were happy with autonomous women groups initiatives.
B. Dalit women movements were satisfied with the concerns of women's organizations.
C. Dalit women's movement worked together with the concern's of autonomous women's groups and left-oriented women's movement
D. Dalit women's movement has expressed dissatisfaction with upper-caste women activists in both the left and the autonomous women's movements.

PASSAGE-3

Gender inequality is both similar to and different from inequality based on other attributes such as race or ethnicity. Three differences are of particular relevance to the analysis of gender equality. First, the welfare of women and men living in the same household is difficult to measure separately, a problem that is compounded by the paucity of data on outcomes in the household. Second, preferences, needs, and constraints can differ systematically between men and women, reflecting both biological factors and "learned" social behaviours. Third, gender cuts across distinctions of income and class. These characteristics raise the question of whether gender equality should be measured as equality of outcomes or equality of opportunity. The economic and philosophical literature on this issue is divided. Those who defend framing gender equality as equality of opportunity argue that it allows one to distinguish between inequalities that arise from circumstances beyond the control of individuals and those that stem from differences in preferences and choices. A substantial body of research documents such as male-female differences in risk aversion, social preferences, and attitudes about competition. It follows that if men and women differ, on average, in attitudes, preferences, and choices, then not all observed differences in outcomes can be attributed to differences in opportunities. Those who argue for equality of outcomes argue that differences in preferences and attitude are largely "learned" and not 'inherent' i.e., they are the result of culture and environment that lead men and women to internalize social norms and expectations. Persistent differences in power and status between men and women can become internalized in aspirations, behaviours, and preferences that perpetuate the inequalities. So, it is challenging to define equality of opportunity without also considering how actual outcomes are distributed. Only by attempting to equalize outcomes can one break the vicious circle of low aspirations and low opportunity.

1. How are gender and race inequalities similar?

(a) Both are social
(b) Both are physical.
(c) In both, the people at the bottom of the social ladder suffer even in their own households.
(d) In both, the people at the lower rung of the social ladder suffer the atrocities in society.

Codes:

A. (a), (b), (c) and (d) B. (b) and (c) only
C. (a), (b) and (d) only D. (a) and (d) only

2. How can the vicious circle of low aspirations and the low opportunity be broken in society?

A. By creating more jobs for women.
B. By attempting to equalize outcomes both for men and women.
C. By providing protection to women.
D. By creating more educational facilities for women.

3. Assertion (A): It is challenging to define equality of opportunity without considering how actual outcomes are distributed.

Reason (R): Persistent differences in power and status between men and women can become internalized in aspirations, behaviours, and preferences that perpetuate the inequalities.

Codes:

A. Both (A) and (R) are True and (R) is the correct explanation for (A).

B. (A) is True but (R) is False.

C. Both (A) and (R) are True but (R) is not the correct explanation for (A).

D. (A) is False but (R) is True.

4. Why do some scholars argue that all observed differences in outcomes of men and women cannot be attributed to differences in opportunities?

(a) Some gender inequalities arise from circumstances beyond the control of individuals.

(b) Some gender inequalities arise due to social preferences.

(c) Some gender inequalities stem from risk aversion.

(d) Some gender inequalities are related to attitude.

Codes:

A. (b), (c) and (d) only B. (a) and (d) only

C. (b) and (c) only D. (a), (b), (c) and (d)

5. Why is it difficult to measure gender equality?

(a) Diversity among women and men across class.

(b) Less availability of data on outcomes for men and women separately in the same households.

(c) The difference in the preferences, needs, and constraints of men and women.

(d) Lack of adequate education among men and women of all the strata.

Codes:

A. (a), (b) and (c) only B. (a), (b), (c), (d)

C. (b) and (d) only D. (a) and (c) only

PASSAGE-4

Gender differences in access to economic opportunities are frequently debated in relation to gender differences in labour market participation. There is a need to look beyond such participation to focus on productivity and earnings—for two reasons. First, a focus exclusively on labour force participation provides only a partial picture of women's and men's experience in the labour market. Far from being a simple decision about whether or not to join the labour force, participation in market work involves reallocating time across a variety of activities—a process that can be difficult and costly, particularly for women. And a focus solely on participation masks gender differences in the nature and dynamics of work. Second, despite significant progress in female labour force participation over the past 30 years or so, pervasive and persistent gender differences remain in productivity and earnings across different sectors and jobs. Indeed, many women around the world appear to be caught in a productivity trap—one that imposes significant costs on women's welfare and economic empowerment today and serious disincentives to invest in the women of tomorrow.

Despite lower earnings and productivity, women are not worse farmers, entrepreneurs, and workers than men. The gender differences in labour productivity and earnings are primarily the result of differences in the economic activities of men and women—although gender differences in human capital and the returns to work and job characteristics also play a role.

Indeed, men's and women's jobs differ significantly, whether across sectors, industries, occupations, types of jobs or types of firms. While these differences evolve with economic development, the resulting changes in the structure of employment are not enough to eliminate employment segregation by gender. So women all over the world appear to be concentrated in low-productivity jobs. They are over-represented among unpaid family workers and in the informal sector. And they rarely rise to positions of power in the labour market. Gender differences in time use, gender differences in access to productive inputs and gender differences stemming from the market and institutional failures lead to gender segregation in access to economic opportunities.

It is precisely this interaction of segregation with the gender differences mentioned above (time use, access to inputs, and market and institutional failures) that traps women in low-paying jobs and low productivity business. Breaking out of this productivity trap requires interventions that lift time constraints, increase women's access to productive inputs, particularly land and credit and correct market and institutional failures.

1. Assertion (A): Gender segregation in access to economic opportunities traps women in low-paying jobs and low productivity business.

Reason (R): Women are lesser skilled and indulge in organizing interest groups. Which of the following is correct?

Codes:

A. Both (A) and (R) are True and (R) is the correct explanation of (A).

B. (A) is True, but (R) is False.

C. (A) is False and (R) is True.

D. Both (A) and (R) are False.

2. Assertion (A): Indeed, many women around the world appear to be caught in a productivity trap.

Reason (R): Despite lower earnings and productivity, women are not worse farmers, entrepreneurs, and workers than men.

Which of the following is True?

Codes:

A. (A) is True, but (R) is False and is not the correct explanation of (A).

B. Both (A) and (R) are False but (R) is not the correct explanation of (A).
C. (A) is False and (R) is True.
D. Both (A) and (R) are False.

3. Where do gender differences in labour productivity emanate from?
(a) Different economic activities for men and women.
(b) Gender differences in human capital.
(c) Increasing returns to all workers for different work.
(d) Differences evolving with economic development.

Codes:
A. (a), (b), (c), (d) B. (a), (c), (d)
C. (a), (b), (d) D. (b), (c), (d)

4. Which of the following is not the effect of productivity trap on women?
A. It imposes a cost on women's welfare.
B. It imposes cost on economic empowerment.
C. It discourages women from coming into the market.
D. It paves the way for disincentives to invest in the women of tomorrow.

5. What are the sources of gender differences?
(a) Flexy jobs.
(b) Failures of institutional arrangements.
(c) Privatization in the market.
(d) The gender gap in the accessibility to productive inputs.

Codes:
A. (a), (b), (c), (d) B. (b), (c), (d)
C. (b), (d) D. (a), (c)

6. Why should the analysis on the gender difference in access to economic opportunities focus on productivity and earnings rather than solely on labour market participation?
(a) Labour force participation mask gender differences in nature and dynamics of work.
(b) Progress in labour force participation has not undone existing gender differences in productivity and earnings in any sector or job.
(c) Lower earnings and productivity have not affected the quality of work of the women as farmers, entrepreneurs or workers.
(d) Labour force participation provides only a partial picture of women's and men's experience in the labour market.

Codes:
A. (a), (b), (d) B. (b), (c), (d)
C. (a), (c), (d) D. (a), (b), (c), (d)

PASSAGE-5

The most notable variant in income, labour market status, the division of labour is gender-based. On average, women participate less in the labour market than men, whereas they assume the lion's share of unpaid work in the household. Women also tend to be less well paid than men when they do work, and they occupy jobs with lower job security, fewer prospects of advancement and less responsibility. Often, these inequalities spill over into a gender gap in political preferences and voting behaviour. Following Becker's seminal work on the family, economists have traditionally explained the gender division of labour as an outcome of a coordination game where a more or less complete division of labour is the efficient solution due to increasing returns to human capital. Although the biological advantages of women specializing in household skills are rare in a modern economy, such specialization may be reinforced by childhood socialization in which parents rationally seek to impart values on their offspring that will maximize their chances of success later in life. Since gender roles are assigned before "correct" preferences are observable, the coordination game is solved by using inherently small, gender differences as the cue. But the efficiency model captures some key aspects of family as an institution, it is incapable of accounting for the stark difference in female labour force participation across economies at comparable levels of development, and it fails to explain why there is so much variance in the distribution of housework between the sexes after controlling for hours spent in paid work and earning.

1. Prominent Gender-based discrepancy includes:
(a) The difference in income.
(b) Better prospects for progress.
(c) Labour market status.
(d) Division of labour.

Codes:
A. (a) and (c) are True.
B. (a), (c) and (d) are True.
C. (a), (b) and (c) are True.
D. (a) and (d) are True.

2. An average increase in women's participation relative to men in the labour market will mean that women:
(a) Occupy secure jobs
(b) Have better prospects of progress
(c) Do unpaid work in the household
(d) Assume more responsibility

Which of the following is True?

Codes:
A. (a), (b) and (d) are True.
B. (a) and (b) are True.
C. (a), (b) and (c) are True.
D. (a) and (d) are True.

3. Recent political economy arguments do not link gender-based segregation to:
   A. Difference in income.
   B. Employment status.
   C. Gender-based division of labour.
   D. Women being better paid than men.

4. **Assertion (A):** On average, women participate less in the labour market than men, whereas they assume the lion's share of unpaid work in the household.
   Reason (R): Women also tend to be less well paid than men when they do work in the labour market.
   In the context of the two statements, which of the following is True?
   Codes:
   A. (A) is false, (R) is True.
   B. Both (A) and (R) are True, but (R) is not the correct explanation of (A).
   C. (A) is True (R) is False.
   D. Both (A) and (R) False.

5. Despite capturing the idea of family as an institution, the lacunae in the efficiency model is manifest in its:
   (a) Inability to account for the prominent discrepancy in female labour force participation across economics at comparable levels of development.
   (b) Comparison of incomparable economies.
   (c) Failure to explain the discrepancy between the sexes in the housework distribution.
   (d) Not accounting for hours spent on paid work and earnings.
   Codes:
   A. (a) and (c) are True B. (a) and (b) are True
   C. (a), (b), (c) are True D. (a) and (d) are True

PASSAGE-6

The writing of women's history has always been closely linked with contemporary feminist politics as well as with changes in the discipline of history itself. When women sought to question inequalities in their own lives, they turned to history to understand the roots of their oppression and to see what they could learn from challenges that had been made in the past.

Activists within the first organized women's movement of the late 19th and early 20th centuries found that women were largely absent from standard history texts and this inspired them to write their own histories. It was the Women's Feminist Movement, or 'Second wave feminism,' from the late 1960s that would have the greatest impact on the writing of women's history. Political activists again pointed to the lack of references to women in standard texts and sought to re-discover women's active role in the past. Sheila Rowbotham produced a pioneering study, Hidden Form History, that was followed by detailed investigations into varied aspects of women's lives, including employment, trade unionism, women's organizations, family life, and sexuality. A context was provided by developments in social history and the social sciences that sought to recover the history of less powerful groups—'history from below'—and challenged conventional wisdom about what should be seen as historically significant.

Women's history is now far more embedded in the curriculum in higher education than half a century ago, the number of professors in women's history has increased, and there are far more publishing outlets. On the other hand, women's studies courses both at undergraduate and at postgraduate level have declined over the same period, and many mainstream history texts still give little space to women and their specific experiences. Hence, it remains important to promote research into women's history both inside the academy and in the wider community. The close relationship between contemporary feminist policies and historical practice means that women's history is still able to excite enthusiasm and is constantly changing, developing new areas to research and new concepts and approaches with which to analyze them.

1. In which ways, Women Liberation Movement affected the writings of women's history?
   (a) Political Activists brought the lack of references to women in standard texts to the limelight.
   (b) The activists started the process of re-discovering women's activist role in the past.
   (c) This gave momentum to the research work on history.
   (d) It inspired the writing and publication of books on women issues.
   Which of the following is True?
   Codes:
   A. (a), (b), (c), (d) are True.
   B. (a) and (b) only are True
   C. (b) and (d) only are True.
   D. (a), (c) and (d) only are True.

2. Why does it remain important to promote research into women's history both inside the academy and in the wider community?
   A. Knowledge of women's history can be more useful than women's studies courses.
   B. Women's history is a more popular subject than women's studies courses.
   C. Women's studies courses are declining at a higher level of education, and history text still gives space to women and specific experiences.

D. Activists find that women's history is better science than women's studies.

3. **Assertion (A):** Women's history is now far more embedded in the curriculum in higher education than half a century ago.
Reason (R): Women's history is replacing Women's Studies Courses at undergraduate and postgraduate level in the country.
Which one of the following is True?
Codes:
A. Both (A) and (R) are True and (R) is the correct explanation for (A).
B. (A) is True, but (R) is False.
C. Both (A) and (R) are False.
D. (A) is False, but (R) is True.

4. **Assertion (A):** Women's Liberation Movement from the late 1960s has had the most significant impact on the writing of women's history.
Reason (R): The women activists wanted to promote the subject of history as it is very Exciting and they felt the need of developing new areas of research in the field.
Which one of the following is True?
Codes:
A. Both (A) and (R) are True and (R) is the correct explanation for (A).
B. (A) is False, (R) is True.
C. Both (A) and (R) are False.
D. (A) is True, (R) is False.

5. What was the impact of Sheila Rowbotham work 'Hidden From History' on research in History?
(a) It encouraged the conventional wisdom for defining the historically significant area.
(b) It inspired detailed investigations into varied aspects of women's lives.
(c) It gave impetus to the issues like employment of women, trade unionism, women's organizations, family life, and sexuality, etc. for research.
(d) It brought developments in social history and social sciences that led to recovering history from below.
Codes:
A. (a), (b), (c), (d)
B. (c) and (d) only are True.
C. (b), (c) and (d) only are True.
D. (a), (b) and (c) only are True.

PASSAGE-7

There are significant continuities in the link between caste and occupation. Agriculture although now open to all castes—still gives a distinct identity to a large number of castes of traditional cultivators. Equally, some other occupations remain the exclusive privilege of particular castes. A Brahman, for instance, still performs the functions of purohit (priest), for upper and middle-level castes. Among the artisan castes of goldsmiths, potters, and weavers, at least a few members of the group are imparted the necessary skills and make a living by the traditional craft. Finally, most ritually polluting occupations —the curing and tanning of hides, removal of dead animals, scavenging, and the activities of the barber, the washerman, and the midwife—retain their associations with specific castes.

In these castes—linked occupations, the work of women, carried out as members of households—the basic units of production and servicing is indispensable. It is difficult for weavers and potters to carry on their craft without the continuous help of women of the household. Women can also take on aspects of men's work: it is not unusual for the women in a Potter's family to go to the market to assist with selling goods. In horticulture, women often carry the major burden of work. In rural areas, it is common for women of households of petty traders to grind spices and prepare fries, fritters for sale in the family shop. Despite regional variations, these illustrations underscore the fact that occupational continuity depends upon a considerable measure on women.

1. Caste society provides women:
A. Socio-cultural setting
B. Economic security
C. Independence
D. Secured married life

2. In the caste-linked occupations, the work of women, carried as members of the household is:
(a) Supportive (b) Collaborative
(c) Peripheral (d) Extended
Codes:
A. (a) and (b) only B. (b) and (c) only
C. (c) and (d) only D. (a) and (d) only

3. Mark the correct statement:
A. All traditional occupations are still the exclusive privilege of specific castes.
B. Women independently can manage all aspects of traditional occupations.
C. Occupational continuity depends in large measure on women.
D. Men can carry the business of living without the help of women in traditional society.

4. **Assertion (A):** Caste determines the ways in which women are objectified and become instruments even as they provide continuity to the caste system.

Reason (R): Most ritually polluting occupations like the curing and tanning of hides, removal of dead animals, scavenging, etc. still retain their association with specific castes.

Codes:

A. (A) is False but (R) is True.
B. Both (A) and (R) are False.
C. Both (A) and (R) are False but (R) is not the correct explanation for (A).
D. (A) is True but (R) is False and not the correct explanation for (A).

5. **Assertion (A):** Social mobility for women in traditional society is quite high.

Reason (R): Women in traditional society, are trained enough in caste-linked occupations that they can have their own independent economic standing in society.

Codes:

A. Both (A) and (R) are True and (R) is the correct explanation for (A).
B. Both (A) and (R) are False.
C. (A) is True but (R) is False.
D. (A) is False but (R) is True and (R) is not the correct explanation for (A).

PASSAGE-8

In women's oral traditions in India, never mind where you are, you are all sisters in sorrow. Though the singers may wear different clothes, cook very different food, speak different languages, when they sing the story of Rama, they echo one another. Translated into English, the songs sound startlingly similar. I have used women's work songs and ritual songs from Marathi, Telugu, Maithili, and Bengali.

While weeding, sowing, husking or grinding, or preparing for a wedding, women all across the subcontinent sing these songs. These are connected with different moments of a woman's life, and here Sita is the name of one who grows up in neglect, attains puberty, gets married, gets pregnant, is abandoned and gives birth. They call it the Ramayana, but it is of Sita that they sing.

In women's retellings, the Rama myth is blasted automatically though probably unwittingly. Here Rama comes through as a harsh, uncaring and weak-willed husband, a far cry from the Maryada Purushottama, but Sita is no rebel; she is still the yielding suffering wife, though she speaks to her friends of her sufferings, of injustice, loneliness and sorrow. Even Chandrabati, who Chastises Rama under her own name let Sita remain the timid Hindu heroine.

The topics that interest men do not interest women. They leave out the details of war, Rama's glory, the details of brahminical rituals, etc. and sing of abandonment and injustice, and weddings, pregnancy, and childbirth. Naturally, the songs centre around Sita, rather than Rama. The Ramayana sung by the mainstream bards has little in common with the women's songs. Women sing privately for themselves; male birds sing for the public. Their approaches to the epic and the act of singing are totally different. The professional bard sings of Rama. The village woman sings of Sita.

1. Oral tradition by women reflect topics of interest only to women since:
(a) the songs tell stories of Rama.
(b) the songs narrate the abandonment and injustice towards women.
(c) the songs do not relate details of war.
(d) the songs could be sung by women while working.

Codes:

A. (a), (b) and (c) only
B. (b), (c) and (d) only
C. (b) and (d) only
D. (a), (c) and (d) only

2. The traditional songs by women are generally sung at/by:
A. Both men and women professional bards in public and private gatherings.
B. Women bards only in times of distress.
C. Women at any time and occasion.
D. Men at public gatherings only.

3. In the Ramayana rendered by women, Rama emerges as:
A. Maryada Purushottam
B. As a rebel and dominating husband
C. As a counterpoise to docile Sita
D. As a weak-willed and uncaring husband

4. Sita in the oral tradition emerges as:
(a) Happy, carefree and contented.
(b) Neglected, abandoned and lonely.
(c) Suffering, denied justice and yielding.
(d) Joyous, loved and cared for.

Codes:

A. (a), (c) and (d) only
B. (b) and (d) only
C. (b) and (c) only
D. (b), (c) and (d) only

5. **Assertion (A):** The traditional oral songs sung by women across India are generally songs of sorrow.

Reason (R): The women throughout the country suffer in their lives and therefore reflect their sorrow in their songs.

Codes:

A. Both (A) and (R) are True.
B. Both (A) and (R) are True and (R) is the correct explanation for (A).
C. Both (A) and (R) are True but (R) is not the correct explanation for (A).
D. Both (A) and (R) are False.

PASSAGE-9

Women's invisibility in the world of institutional politics is particularly striking in the contexts where women's political mobilization contributed to the demise of authoritarianism. The new wave of democratization has not, by any means, had a feminizing effect on the Parliament, Cabinets and Public Administrations of the new democracies. Deeply entrenched barriers exclude women from meaningful participation in political parties, where they are habitually relegated to "women's wings" performing "cheerleading" roles.

Globally, the figures for female representation in national and local politics have been remarkably consistent. The masculine construction of political authority makes it extremely difficult for women to be elected for different offices without some form of electoral engineerings-such as through quota systems or reserved seats to boost the election of women in the face of the "boys club's" prejudices of parties and electorates. The importance that is currently attached to the third remedy some have argued may reflect a sad but realistic assessment of how long it will take to alter the first two. It may also be a case of dealing with the symptoms rather than taking the underlying causes. Besides the issues of Political Equality and democratic justice, very often the argument for increasing women's representation in decision-making bodies also hinges on an implicit assumption that women can more effectively than men contribute to the formulation of "women-friendly" policies because they are somehow better able to represent women's interests.

Questions have been raised as to why the growing presence of women in politics is not translating into a substantive change in the content of policies that can impact positively on the lives of ordinary women. It has been argued that "a feminine presence in politics is not the same as a feminist one; getting more women into politics is a worthy project from the point of view of democratic justice," but it will not necessarily translate into gender equity in government policy and social outcomes.

1. Mark out the incorrect statement about women's participation in politics:

A. Women need some form of electoral engineering for their meaningful participation in politics.
B. A new wave of democratization has created a crisis for women in politics.
C. Reservation of seats for women can enhance the participation of women in politics.
D. The figures for female representation in national and local politics have been consistently low.

2. How can the anomaly between the new wave of democratization and the existing masculine structure of politics be checked?

(a) Removal of reservation and quota system for women.
(b) More equality between paid and unpaid work between men and women.
(c) Modifications in the working conditions of politicians.
(d) Providing cheer-leading roles to women.

Codes:

A. (a), (b) and (d) only B. (b), (c) and (d) only
C. (a), (b), (c) and (d) D. (b) and c) only

3. Which is/are the correct statements about Quotas or Reservation Policy for Women?

(a) It can boost the election of women.
(b) It will tackle the underlying causes of low participation of women in politics.
(c) It can remove the paradox between male-dominated politics and women's political mobilization.
(d) It cannot have a feminizing effect on the Parliament, Cabinets and Public Administrations.

Codes:

A. (a), (b) and (c) only B. (b) and (d) only
C. (a) and (d) only C. (a), (b), (c) and (d)

4. Why are the women invisible in the world of institutional politics?

(a) Quota system.
(b) Masculine construction of political authority.
(c) Equalization of paid work between men and women.
(d) Women perform "cheer-leading" roles.

Codes:

A. (b) and (d) only B. (a) and (b) only
C. (a), (b) and (d) only D. (a), (b), (c) and (d)

5. Assertion (A): The increasing number of women in politics is not leading to any structural change in the content of policies that can have a positive impact on the lives of common women.

Reason (R): "A feminine presence in politics is not the same as a feminist one" getting more women in politics hardly ensures gender equity in government policies.

A. (A) is False and (R) is True.
B. Both (A) and (R) are True and (R) is the correct explanation of (A).
C. (A) is True, but (R) is False.
D. (A) is True, but (R) is False and (R) is not the correct explanation of (A).

PASSAGE-10

Although feminists' primary commitment is to women and to ending women's oppression, their revolutionary goal nevertheless extends beyond women to men. For men and women are what history has made of them, and if women change, men, too, will change, albeit unwillingly. As Madeleine Gagnon rightly acknowledges, "I cannot liberate my sex without yours since we are inextricably linked by a history that has objectified our bodies."

This feminist revolution is not, however, always recognized as such by those impatient for social change, who identify revolution with the seizure of state power and evaluate political theory, organization, and strategy in terms of their effectiveness in achieving that goal. We do not believe that such revolutions hold out much hope for women. From our point of view, they can only be, at best, palace-revolutions, changes of government and not changes of power relations themselves. Such revolutions are incapable of generating the radical social transformations which women desire and required for their liberation because the men and women who make them will remain men and women created by, for, and within the social relations of patriarchy. We have internalized those oppressive relations, and we are constituted by them. Seizing state power will not change that. On the contrary, the kind of organizational structures and strategies required for such an assault —hierarchical, impersonal, disciplined, pragmatic, instrumental, authoritarian, self-sacrificing and inevitably blood-letting, demand the very same kind of human beings we are rebelling against men and women who will assume or submit to leadership, authority and bureaucratic control and to the fragmentation of their lives into the personal and the political, their actions into means and ends, themselves into rational and emotional, objective and subjective and so on. These characteristics will not disappear overnight once such a revolution has been won; indeed they cannot, for they are also required for the successful exercise of State power once it has been seized.

1. Assertion (A): Feminist revolutions are incapable of generating the radical social transformations which women desire and required for their liberation.
Reason (R): Men are controlling all the state power and authority in society.

Codes:
A. (A) is True and (R) is False and (R) is not the correct explanation of (A).
B. Both (A) and (R) are True and (R) is the correct explanation of (A).
C. (A) is False and (R) is False.
D. Both (A) and (R) are False.

2. What has been the major concern of the feminists' revolution?
(a) To liberate the sex.
(b) To end gender oppression.
(c) To seize political power.
(d) To end women's oppression.

Codes:
A. (a), (b), (c) and (d) B. (d) only
C. (a) and (b) only D. (a), (b) and (d) only

3. The outcome of the feminist revolution at best can be?
(a) Radical social transformation.
(b) Changes in government.
(c) Changes in power relations.
(d) Palace revolutions.

Codes:
A. (a), (b), (c), (d) B. (a) (c), (d) only
C. (a) and (b) only D. (b) and (d) only

4. What are the characteristics of existing organizational structures?
(a) Impersonal (b) Political
(c) Self-centered (d) Personal

Codes:
A. (a), (b) only B. (b), (c), (d) only
C. (a), (b), (d) only D. (a), (b), (c) only

5. Assertion (A): Feminists' primary commitment is to seizure the state power to change the social structure created by patriarchy.
Reason (R): Men and women are what history has made of them, and if women's position changes, men will also change.

Codes:
A. Both (A) and (R) are False.
B. (A) is False (R) is True but (R) is not the correct explanation of (A).
C. Both (A) and (R) are True and (R) is not the correct explanation of (A).
D. (A) is True and (R) is False.

PASSAGE-11

The most celebrated theoretical proposition that links women's labour force participation with economic development, the U-shaped feminization hypothesis, argues that when subsistence economic transform to developing economies, women withdraw from the labour force and thereafter beyond a minimum threshold the participation rates of women start rising. The U-shaped curve takes this form owing to the substitution and income effects on women's choice between unpaid domestic work and paid work. In subsistence economies women contribute labour towards subsistence agricultural production as unpaid family labour along with domestic activities, thus suffering from the double burden of work. With the rise of commercialized agriculture, structural transformation, enhancement in household income and gender-based wage differentials, the opportunity cost of domestic activities for women increases while that of paid labour of women decreases. Hence they tend to withdraw from the labour force, termed as the "income effect." With the rise of the service sector, white collar jobs, institutionalized caregiving, expansion of education among women and declining wage differentials, the opportunity cost of paid labour for women increases. Thereafter women "substitute" domestic activities for paid work. Yet this framework assumes away the fundamental gender relations that regulate women's participation in paid work. Socialist feminist construct of the development of capitalism exploits gender relations to explain de-feminization. With the development of the capitalist organization of production in a patriarchal social system, female labour progressively undergoes "female marginalization." The shift from attached labour in the feudal agricultural system to wage labour in capitalist farming realigns the households division of labour among worker households with sectoral diversification and technological change the emerging skill-biased domand for labour is gender-segregated due to gender-biased progress in education. Women are then obligated to either withdraw from the labour force or enter as secondary workers.

1. **Assertion (A):** When subsistence economies transform to developing economies, women withdraw from the labour force and thereafter beyond a minimum threshold, the participation rate of women starts rising.

   Reason (R): The substitution and income level hardly affect the women's choice between unpaid domestic work and paid work.

   Codes:

   A. (A) is True but (R) is False and (R) is not the correct explanation of (A).
   B. Both (A) and (R) are True, but (R) is not the correct explanation of (A).
   C. Both (A) and (R) are False.
   D. (A) is False, but (R) is True and (R) is the correct explanation of (A).

2. What are the reasons for 'female marginalization' in paid work?
   (a) Feudal system
   (b) Patriarchal social system
   (c) Capitalistic organization of production
   (d) Gender relations

   Codes:

   A. (a) and (b) only B. (b), (c) and (d) only
   C. (d) only D. (b) and (c) only

3. What leads the women to 'substitute' domestic activities for paid work?
   A. More jobs in the service sector.
   B. Incentives to the women for work.
   C. Institutionalized caregiving.
   D. Better wages to women.

4. Which of the following variables lead to an increase in the opportunity cost of domestic activities for women?
   (a) Structural transformation.
   (b) Household income.
   (c) Gender-based wage differential.
   (d) Commercialized agriculture.

   Codes:

   A. (a), (b), (c), (d) B. (c) and (d) only
   C. (b) and (c) only D. (a) and (c) only

PASSAGE-12

Development planning, whether national or international, has traditionally been gender neutral or even gender blind. This was partly because until recently we lacked information about women and their contribution to their regions and because aid organizations were administered with very little insight into gender roles. As a result, there was a tendency to marginalize women: development planners have often seen them as passive beneficiaries of social and health services. Women's active and productive roles in their society were not recognized and not included explicitly in development planning. Even today the target groups for development projects are often identified as genderless, such as "small farmers" or the "rural poor." In the minds of planners, these groups are men. In reality, many of them are women. It is an implicit assumption that the effects of development projects are potentially beneficial to both men and women. In reality, quite often the advantages go to the men in the form of increased earnings or labour-saving techniques, and the disadvantages go to the women in the form of an increased and un-remunerated workload. Should this be recognized, the proposed solution is often the initiation of special 'women's projects' which tend to marginalize women further as a "special group" within society.

Given below are multiple choice questions. Please select the correct answer.

1. Given neutral development:
   A. Takes care of women's needs.
   B. Takes care of both men and women's needs.
   C. Contributed to the marginalization of women.
   D. Contributed to the marginalization of men.
2. Gender blind development policies recognize:
   A. Women's productive roles.
   B. The disadvantages of the increased workload of women.
   C. The need to include women in development planning.
   D. Ignore women's active and productive roles.
3. Development policies in India seek the active involvement of:
   A. Women as well as men
   B. Women only
   C. Men only
   D. None of these
4. Target groups for development projects are:
   A. Gendered categories
   B. Genderless categories
   C. Labour saving categories
   D. Labour enhancing categories
5. Special women's projects:
   A. Further, marginalize women.
   B. Empower women.
   C. Bring women in mainstream development.
   D. Realize women's development goals.

PASSAGE-13

Gender discrimination is equally visible in several health and literacy indicators. Both gender inequality and educational backwardness are crucial causal antecedents of endemic undernutrition. Indeed, women's education has emerged in many empirical investigations as one of the most powerful determinants of child health. Maternal education results in increased knowledge about nutrition, hygiene, and health care and this is significant in the context of the remarkably uninformed and deficient nature of childcare practices in large parts of rural India. Basic education helps mothers to take advantage of public health-care services thereby reducing child mortality.

Given below are multiple-choice questions, please select the correct answer:

1. Indicators of gender discrimination are visibly seen in matters of:
   A. Health and Literacy
   B. Food and Nutrition
   C. Housing and Sanitation
   D. Hygiene and Health
2. Endemic undernutrition is caused by:
   A. Low Literacy and Gender Inequality.
   B. Gender Inequality and Educational Backwardness.
   C. Economic and Educational Backwardness.
   D. Social Backwardness and Poor Political Participation.
3. _______ is the most powerful determinant of child health:
   A. Adult Education
   B. Children's Education
   C. Women's Education
   D. Men's Education
4. What are the consequences of maternal education?
   A. Increased knowledge about reproductive health.
   B. Increased knowledge about health, hygiene, and sanitation.
   C Increased knowledge about the environment, pollution, and ill health.
   D Increased knowledge about nutrition, hygiene, and health care.
5. The childcare practices in large parts of rural India are:
   A. Sufficient B. Adequate
   C. Deficient D. Surplus

PASSAGE-14

Violence in its narrowest definition is physical assault or threat. But a broader understanding of violence includes:

A. All subtle forms of emotional and psychological control through intimidation, and misuse of personal or institutionalized power;
B. The socio-cultural and ideologically instituted discriminatory practices against a group.

Underlying all situations of ethnic and class tensions, it is a process of ideology formation through which the more powerless group is defined as the 'other,' stereotyped, subjugated and controlled. It denies them opportunities to earn a living and realize their potential as human beings. Politically motivated stereotypes of the 'Other' group is constructed to justify discriminatory practices. They are seen as "dangerous" to women of the dominant group. The aim of violence against women is to ensure their subordination and control in a patriarchal society and has existed in all patriarchal societies. They include subtle normative structures that justify the denial of personal autonomy and entitlements to food, education, health care and other opportunities of self-development in the family specifically in the Indian context, structural violence against women manifests itself through.

(a) Misuse of medical technology to abort female foetuses.
(b) Denial of food, nutrition, health care, education and opportunities to earn a livelihood.
(c) Normative ideals of subordination and compliance.
(d) The existence of prostitution, rape, dowry, sati, and witch-hunting in certain communities.

These normative values stereotype women as emotional, nurturing, sexually dangerous and foolish. Such construction of women's nature justifies discriminatory practices and denies women's access to economic and political decision making powers. It hampers the process by which the existing social structure could be altered into more egalitarian structures.

1. What are the broader implications of violence?
(a) Subtle forms of social and psychological control through intimidation.
(b) Socio-cultural and ideologically instituted discriminatory practices.
(c) Misuse of personal and institutionalized power.
(d) All of them.

Codes:
A. (a) and (b) B. (c), (b) and (d)
C. (b), (c) and (a) D. (a), (b), (c) and (d)

2. How is the power aspect involved in violence?
(a) The powerless group is defined as the 'other' stereotyped, subjugated and controlled.
(b) Powerful group dominates the powerless.
(c) Men and women are classified as powerful and powerless respectively.
(d) Men have power and women are treated as the 'other.'

Codes:
A. (a), (b), (c) and (d) B. (b), (d) and (a)
C. (c), (d) and (b) D. (d), (a) and (c)

3. What are the aims of violence against women?
(a) To justify discriminatory practices.
(b) To ensure women's subordination.
(c) To control women in Patriarchal society.
(d) To deny women's access to opportunities.

Codes:
A. (a) and (b) B. (b) and (c)
C. (c) and (d) D. (a) and (c)

4. How do normative structures justify violence against women?
A. By stereotyping women as emotional, nurturing, sexually dangerous and foolish.
B. By stereotyping women as loving, caring, sexually enjoyable and intelligent.
C. By stereotyping women as brave, courageous, dangerous and intelligent.
D. By stereotyping women as capable, potential, talented and skilled.

5. What are the various manifestations of structural violence against women in India?
(a) Misuse of medical technology.
(b) Refusal to basic livelihood.
(c) Idealizing subordination.
(d) Promoting the abuse of women.

Codes:
A. (a) and (b) B. (a), (b) and (c)
C. (c) and (d) D. (b) and (c)

PASSAGE-15

Men control women's productivity both within the household and outside, in paid work. Within the household, women provide all kinds of free services to their children, husbands and other members of the family, throughout their lives. In what Sylvia Walby calls the "Patriarchal mode of production," women's labour is expropriated by their husbands and others who live there. She says housewives are the producing class, while husbands are expropriating class, their backbreaking endless and repetitive labour is not considered work at all and housewives are seen to be dependent on their husbands.

Men also control women's labour outside the home in several ways. They force their women to sell their labour, or they may prevent them from working. They may appropriate what women earn; they may selectively allow them to work intermittently. Then women are excluded from better-paid jobs, they are forced to sell their labour at meager wages; or work within the home in what is called "home-based" production, a most exploitative system.

1. Men control:
A. Women's work
B. Women's productivity
C. Women's wages
D. Women's lives

2. In Patriarchal mode of production:
A. Women's labour is expropriated by their children.
B. Women's labour is expropriated by the state.
C. Women's labour is expropriated by their husbands.
D. Women's labour is expropriated by women.

3. Housewives are:
   A. Producing class   B. Working class
   C. Consumer class   D. Expropriating class

4. Men control women's labour by:
   (a) Forcing them to sell their labour.
   (b) Preventing them from working.
   (c) Appropriating what they earn.
   (d) Allowing them to decide.

   Codes:
   A. (a) and (b) are True
   B. (c) and (d) are True
   C. (a), (b) and (c) are True
   D. (a), (b), (c) and (d) are True

5. What is known as "home-based production"?
   A. Work within the factory
   B. Work within an industry
   C. Work within the institution
   D. Work within the home

PASSAGE-16

Patriarchy has been a fundamentally important concept in gender studies, leading to the development of a number of theories that aim to identify the bases of Women's subordination. Three of the most important theories in which patriarchy is a central concept are those commonly labeled as 'radical feminist,' 'Marxist feminist' and 'dual systems theory.' In 'radical feminist' analyses, patriarchy is regarded as the primary and fundamental social division in society. In some radical feminist analysis, the institution of the family is identified as a key means through which men's domination is achieved. In other radical feminist accounts of patriarchy, the control men have over women's bodies is regarded as important. For Firestone, inequalities between women and men are biologically based, with the different reproductive capacities of women and men being especially important. In other radical feminist analyses, it is masculine control over women's bodies through sexuality or male violence in the form of rape that is regarded as being of central importance. In a further grouping of feminist analyses, often labeled as 'Marxist feminism,' patriarchy is argued to arise from the workings of the capitalist economic system it requires, and benefits from, women's unpaid labour in the home. The subordination of women to men in society therefore tends, to be regarded as a by-product of capital's subordination of labour. Class inequality is argued to be the central feature of society and is seen to determine gender inequality. The third grouping of feminist perspectives gives theoretical priority to two systems—capitalism and patriarchy in the explanation of patriarchy often referred to as 'dual systems theory,' this perspective in many ways represents a synthesis of Marxist and radical feminist accounts of gender relations.

1. What patriarchy does not mean?
   A. Domination by the male.
   B. Approach to gender theorizing.
   C. The rule by the female.
   D. System of social structure.

2. Radical feminists identify the key means of patriarchy:
   (a) Institution of family.
   (b) Women's bodies.
   (c) Different reproductive capacities of women and men.
   (d) Capital's subordination of labour.

   Codes:
   A. (a) and (c) only   B. (a) and (b) only
   C. (a), (b) and (c) only   D. (c) only

3. 'Dual systems theory' refers to:
   A. Class inequality
   B. Biologically based domination
   C. Capitalism and Patriarchy
   D. Universalism

4. **Assertion (A):** Feminist writers have used the concept of patriarchy to analyze the social system of masculine domination over women.

   Reason (R): Patriarchy has been the fundamental concept to identify the bases of Women's oppression in society.

   Codes:
   A. (A) is True, (R) is False.
   B. Both (A) and (R) is False.
   C. Both (A) and (R) are True.
   D. (A) is False, (R) is True.

5. What are the bases of inequalities between women and men according to Firestone?
   A. Women are physically week.
   B. Different reproductive capacities.
   C. Women's unpaid labour.
   D. Masculine control over women's bodies.

PASSAGE-17

Whether education is vie.wed as an asset in raising earning capacity, as a gateway to knowledge and information, or as a spur to inculcate values of concern for social transformation and establishment of gender justice for women education is a primary necessity. Elementary education empowers women by providing information and confidence, while higher education emboldens them so that they are confident about entering any field or profession not previously open to women. However, access to education does not depend upon will but on the availability of educational institutions, familial support, and quality of education. The future trend seems to be that while there will be a growing demand for girls education, the high cost of living will force families to turn their daughters towards short-term courses or correspondence courses which in the long run may deprive the girl of vital interaction available in educational institutions. It seems that the strategy of lowering the cost of a girl's education will have to be given serious thought so that girls may not be the victims of gender discrimination. It is indeed a sad situation when a mother would like her daughter to go to school/college but is unable to send her because the child must help in the housework. In the 19th century, we pleaded for the education of women to make her a better partner for her husband, in the last century, education was for her empowerment, and today we are pleading for her right to education as a citizen.

1. Elementary Education empowers women by:
A. Increasing their learning ability.
B. Enhancing their literacy skills.
C. Empowering them in decision-making.
D. Providing information and confidence.

2. Assertion (A): Mother would like to send her daughter to school/college but unable to send.
Reason (R): The child must help in housework.
Codes:
A. Both (A) and (R) are true and (R) is the correct explanation of (A).
B. (A) is true, (R) is not true.
C. (A) is false and (R) is true.
D. (A) and (R) are true, but (R) is not the correct explanation of (A).

3. Families send their daughters to short-term and correspondence courses because:
A. The girls will look after housework.
B. The girls will be employed.
C. The high cost of living.
D. Girls are a substitute for mothers.

4. 21st century, the demand for girls education has a goal of:
A. Empowerment
B. Right to Education
C. Better partner to her husband
D. Better decision maker

5. Factors affecting access to education are:
(a) Availability of Educational Institutions.
(b) Family support.
(c) Quality of education.
(d) Income.
Codes:
A. (a), (b) and (d) B. (b) and (c)
C. (d) and (b) D. (a), (b) and (c)

PASSAGE-18

The increasing participation of women in the waged labour force has brought into focus a number of gender-related issues, including inequality and sexual harassment at the workplace. However, what constitutes sexual harassment, especially in the less severe form is still being debated (Wise and Stanley, 1987, Ramaznoglu, (1987). The term sexual harassment came first into use in 1974 during a Cornell University course on "Women and Work" in which women were encouraged to talk about their experiences in the workforce (Farley, 1978: xi). Unlike rape, sexual harassment had occurred for centuries without being named, as such (Bulsarnik, 1978, Backhouse and Cohen, 1978, Farley 1978), this has important implications. In Mc Kinnon's words lacking a teem to express it, sexual harassment was literally unspeakable which made a generalized shared and social definition of it inaccessible. The unnamed could not be mistaken for the non-existent.

The sexual harassment could be prevalent and yet nameless is a paradox. This may be understandable in the context of the private/public split, the "desexualization" of organizations, and "male sexual prerogative."

The private/public division is featured prominently in much feminist literature. There it is viewed as crucial in understanding gender relation and power allocation between men and women and between adult and children (Elishtain, 1981. Stacey and Price 1981. Hamilton, 1978). Until this century men have dominated the public realm; women have been identified with the private realm, unpaid labour biological functions, and nature (Sydie, 1988). This is not to say that men have not also been dominant in the private domain. The private/public split is crucial in understanding how sexuality view as Hearn and Parkin comment. "Sexuality is often considered primarily biological and socially part of the private domain. Both these assumptions have been disputed." Until very recently organizations have been viewed as "desexualized" apparently inhabited, the words of Hearn and Parkin by "bread of strange, a sexual eunuch figure." This portrayal, it is argued is partly related to the way organizational theories have neglected the more general issue of gender. This avoidance has been described as "bizarre." In addition, the process of the asexual portrayal of organization and their desexualization have involved a number of developments. These include: Privatizing sexuality, rationality, and control over the body and time.

1. According to Elishtain the use of private and public division in feminist literature is useful in:
   (a) Understanding gender relations between men and women.
   (b) Understanding power allocation between men and women.
   (c) Understanding the relations in the private realm.
   (d) Understanding the relations in the public realm.

   Codes:
   A. (c) and (d) only True
   B. (b) and (c) only True
   C. (a) and (b) only True
   D. (a), (b) and (c) only True

2. **Assertion (A):** Sexuality is often considered primarily biological and socially the part of the private domain.
   Reason (R): Men dominate over women in sexual relations.

   Codes:
   A. (A) is true, (R) is false.
   B. (R) is true, (A) is false.
   C. (A) and (R) both are false.
   D. (A) and (R) both are true.

3. The term 'Bizarre' is associated with:
   A. Inclusion of sexual harassment issues at the workplace.
   B. Exclusion of sexual harassment issues at the workplace.
   C. Desexualization of the workplace.
   D. Advocacy against sexual harassment at workplace.

4. Sexual harassment at workplace prevalent and yet nameless because:
   (a) Of biological division of labour.
   (b) Of male sexual prerogative.
   (c) Of male dominance at the workplace.
   (d) Women do not accept sexual harassment as normal behaviour of men.

   Codes:
   A. (a) and (b) are True
   B. (a) and (c) are True
   C. (c) and (d) are True
   D. (a), (b), and (c) are True

5. What is the need for the term 'sexual harassment'?
   (a) Sexual harassment remained unspeakable for centuries.
   (b) Sexual harassment being prevalent but nameless.
   (c) Increased workforce participation of women in wage labour.
   (d) Sexual harassment reduces women's workforce participation.

   Codes:
   A. (a) and (b) only True
   B. (a), (b) and (c) only True
   C. (c) and (d) only True
   D. (d) only True

PASSAGE-19

A closer analysis carried out by feminists in recent years has revealed that the dominant social relations are also part and parcel of the technology itself. We can no longer argue whether reproductive technology or genetic technology as such are good or bad; the very basic principles of this technology have to be criticized no less than its methods. These are based on exploitation and subordination alike of nature, women and other peoples (colonies). In this context lies the inherent sexist, racist and ultimately fascist bias of the new reproductive technologies.

Reproductive technology and genetic engineering are based on the same principles as physics and other sciences. Like other sciences, they involve the dissection of living organisms into ever smaller particles, molecules, cells, nuclei, genes, DNA and their various recombinations according to the plan of the (male) engineering. In these processes to select desirable elements and eliminate undesirable ones is crucial. In fact, without the principle of selection and elimination, the whole technology of reproduction and genetics would make no sense. What purpose would a study of genetics serve if not to promote the propagation of what are considered to be desirable attributes and the elimination of those seen as undesirable? This applies as much to human genetics as to plant and animal genetics and applies equally to reproductive technology, which is based on the selection of fertile elements (Sperm, Ova) and their combination outside the female body. This selection and elimination would not be possible if those living organisms were left intact and free to regulate their reproduction in accordance with their own desires, love, and lust.

Carolyn Merchant finds a parallel to the dissection and invasion of nature in the torture of women in witch pogroms and shows that both types of violence are intrinsic to the method of modern science and technology. Francis Bacon, the founding father of the modern scientific method, perceived nature as a witch whose secrets has to be extracted by force. Force and violence constitute the invisible foundation upon which modern science was built. Hence violence against women in the witch pogroms, and violence against nature which was perceived as a woman.

1. What kind of analysis carried out by feminists in recent years?

A. Dominant social relations are part and parcel of the technology itself.

B. Social constraints are not leading to gender discrimination.

C. Exploitation and oppression are in the roots of technology.

D. All the above

2. The basic principles of reproductive technology or genetic technology is:

A. Exploitation and subordination alike of nature, women and other people.

B. Superiority over inferiority.

C. Hierarchy and valuation.

D. Women's reproductive role.

3. What applies equally to reproductive technology?

A. The selection of fertile elements.

B. The elimination of undesirable.

C. To select desirable elements.

D. To regulate their reproduction.

4. Assertion (A): Francis Bacon perceived nature as a witch whose secrets has to be extracted by force.

Reason (R): Force and violence constitute the invisible foundation. Hence violence against women in the witch pogroms and violence against nature which was perceived as a woman.

Codes:

A. (A) is false (R) is true.

B. Both (A) and (R) are true.

C. Both (A) and (R) are false.

D. (A) is true (R) is false.

PASSAGE-20

Actually, there is no historical evidence of the existence of matriarchy anywhere. Sometimes people confuse matrilineal or matrilocal systems with matriarchy. What existed amongst the Nairs of Kerala was matrilineality and matrilocality. It is important to distinguish between these terms. In a matrilineal society, the lineage is traced through the mother, i.e., the property passes from mothers to daughters. Such communities may also be matrilocal, i.e., the husband comes to live with the wife who continues to live in her own home. Although the position of women is much better in matrilineal and matrilocal societies, they are still not matriarchal. In a matriarchal society, women would be in a dominant position, in control of state power, religious institutions, economic production, trade, etc. Even in matriarchal societies, real control is in the hands of brothers and uncles, but there is no denying the fact that the status of women in such systems is far higher than it would be otherwise. The matrilineal, matrilocal system which existed among the Nairs of Kerala and in the North - East of India has been weakening and disappearing under the pressure of patriarchal ideology, legal systems which have displaced customary and community diversity and the pervasiveness of "modernity" which demands uniformity. Their existence, however, proves that there can be and have been different ways of organizing families, inheritance, residence, labour, etc. and that there is nothing fixed or immutable about a particular order. It is, after all, man made not preordained.

Given below are multiple choice questions. Please select the correct answer.

1. Matriarchy implies:

A. Rule of the father

B. Rule of the mother

C. Rule of the Grandmother

D. Rule of the son

2. In a matrilineal society, the property passes from:

A. Mothers to daughters

B. Fathers to daughters

C. Mothers to sons

D. Fathers to sons

3. Society in India is:

A. Matriarchal B. Patriarchal

C. Matrilineal D. Matrilocal

4. Matrilineal Societies exist in:

A. Punjab B. Madhya Pradesh

C. Rajasthan D. Kerala

5. In a patriarchal Society, women are:

A. Subordinated B. Empowered

C. Dominant D. In control

PASSAGE-21

Gender is a term that has psychological and cultural rather than biological connotations if the proper terms of sex are 'male' and 'female' the corresponding terms for gender are masculine and feminine, the latter may be quite independent of sex. Gender denotes the degree of masculinity or feminity found is a person, and obviously, while there is a mix of both in many humans, the normal male has a preponderance of masculinity and the normal female a preponderance of masculinity, and we believe that attitudes, behaviours, traits are socially prescribed, taught and learned. We imbibe them through socialization and gendering which take place within the family, in schools, religious institutions, etc. Because socialization and gendering begin as soon as we are born (sometimes even earlier), it seems as though feminine and masculine qualities are inborn and natural. If that was so, then no man would be gentle and caring, and no woman aggressive and dominators. Yet such men and women exist. If gender traits were natural and in-born why would societies and cultures spend so much time, energy and resources teaching children their gender roles?

1. The normal male has the qualities of:
A. Masculinity
B. Feminity
C. Sensitivity
D. Both Masculinity and Femininity

2. Attitudinal and behavioural traits are:
A. Taught through religion
B. In-born
C. Imbibed through socialization
D. Natural

3. Gender roles are created by:
A. Society B. Culture
C. Religious Institution D. All the above

4. Assertion (A): Feminine and Masculine qualities are in born and natural.
Reason (R): No men are gentle and caring.
Codes:
A. Both (A) and (R) are true.
B. Both (A) and (R) are false.
C. (A) is false, (R) is true.
D. (A) is true, (R) is false

5. Gender is:
A. Biologically determined.
B. Biologically and psychologically determined.
C. Politically determined.
D. Socially and culturally determined.

PASSAGE-22

Patriarchy is an apt term to express the entire gamut of ideas that support and rationalize the principle of male dominance. It is an important term used in women's studies to describe the existing social structures and arrangements within which women are oppressed. Historically, it refers to an ideology which grew out of men's power to exchange women between kinship groups; it is now used in feminism to represent the symbolic male principle, expressed as the power of the father. In its essence, patriarchy represents men's control over women's sexuality, fertility, and production. Patriarchy's chief institution is the family, headed by the father; and this principle of male dominance in the family is reproduced in the wider social realm. The principles of organization of a patriarchal family go beyond tracing descent through the male line to justify male authority and control over the resources of the family. When this system is replayed in society, the social inequalities between the sexes get reinforced. Anthropologists agree that the development of the patrilineal family system is a relatively late phenomenon in the history of humankind. According to the Marxist view, this may be directly linked to the growth of private property and the state. Patriarchy has enabled men to legitimize their control over socio-political and economic systems in society. It is a system created through male inter-dependence and solidarity. This is not to imply that there are no differences between men. Men are also divided and are in a competitive relationship with each other, but the central point of all male group formations is that they seek to control women. In almost all patriarchal societies, the work done by men is accorded a higher prestige or rank, when compared to the work done by women.

1. Marxist believed that patriarchy is linked with:
A. Private property and the state.
B. Sex segregation.
C. Control over the socio-political system.
D. The system created by male-interdependence.

2. The central point of all male group formation is to:
A. Complete each other.
B. Control women.
C. Interdependence to each other.
D. Divide each other.

3. Patriarchy represents:
(a) Men's control over women's sexuality.
(b) Symbolic male principle.
(c) Power of the father.
(d) Ideology of dominance.
Codes:
A. (a), (b), (c) and (d) are True
B. (a), (b), and (d) are True
C. (a) and (b) are True
D. (b) and (d) are True

4. The social inequalities between the sexes get reinforced by:
A. Male control over the resources.
B. Male inter-dependence and solidarity.
C. Female control over the resources.
D. Male group formation.

5. Assertion (A): Women are oppressed in all the patriarchal societies.
Reason (R): Patriarchy enabled men to control the social and economic system.

Codes:

A. Both (A) and (R) are false.
B. (A) is true, (R) is false.
C. Both (A) and (R) are true, (R) is the correct explanation for (A).
D. (R) is true, (A) is false.

PASSAGE-23

Income is one of those areas of equality where one might imagine it would be possible to develop agreed measures. Equal pay for equal work has undoubtedly been an underpinning feature of equity campaigns. None the less, the pay gap between women and men continues unabated.

Thus Reskin and Padavic Comment. 'In every country in the world, men outearn women.' The reason that economists have given for this range from differences between the sexes in their investment in human capital to differences in the productive capabilities of women and men. Feminists have critiqued these arguments and have pointed out the horizontal, and vertical segregated labour markets operate to women's disadvantage as they are mainly employed in sectors that are devalued as "women's work" and are also positioned at the bottom levels of organizational hierarchies. Feminist research has, therefore, illustrated how sex segregation in the labour market combines with a devaluation of women's work. This creates comparable-worth discrimination where employers underpay workers who are doing jobs that are different from predominantly male jobs but are of equal value.

1. What has been the underpinning feature of equity campaigns?
A. High pay in the job market
B. Pay gap among women
C. Equal jobs in the job market
D. Equal pay for equal work

2. Women are employed in the sectors that are devalued as:
A. Men's work
B. People's work
C. Women's work
D. Children's work

3. Which is the comparable worth discrimination in the passage?
A. Workers underpay employers.
B. Employers underpay workers.
C. Employers underpay employers.
D. Workers underpay workers.

4. What labour did the author mean to operate to women's disadvantage?
A. Horizontal and vertical segregated labour market.
B. Sex-segregated labour market.
C. Male dominated labour market.
D. Organized and unorganized market.

5. Assertion (A): In every country in the world men out-earn women.
Reason (R): Feminists critiqued that labour markets one not to women's disadvantage.

Codes:

A. (A) is true, (R) is false.
B. Both (A) and (R) are true.
C. Both (A) and (R) are false.
D. (A) is false, (R) is true.

PASSAGE-24

The family is the basic unit of society; this is because everyone is born into a family and nurtured through it. Nevertheless, in a large and culturally diverse society like India, there is no one kind of a family. They vary according to their class, regional, geographical and cultural locations. Despite considerable variation in forms of the family as well as the norms mediating family relationships such as rules of residence after marriage, lineage, divorce, widow remarriage, the inheritance of property, monogamous versus polygamous and consanguineous marriages, families in India have largely ascribed to patriarchal ideologies. In the Indian context, the family is largely located within the caste and kinship systems. These institutions, therefore, become important principles of social organization and analysis. So pervasive is the caste ideology that even the more egalitarian religious of Christianity and Islam have not been able to make an indent into it. The continued hold of caste is significant because of the absence of alternate social security systems; caste and kin networks provide individuals with support to meet life's crisis and to celebrate marriages, births, and deaths. Women's sexual purity becomes a matter of paramount concern and a mechanism by which the group maintains its boundaries. Such controls of women's sexuality are exerted through the family and kinship. The socialization process seeks to discipline the girl consistently. She is given low self-esteem, denied knowledge of her body and made incapable of thinking of an independent future, apart from the family.

1. Indian families are characterized by:
(a) Patriarchal ideologies.
(b) Caste and kinship systems.
(c) Egalitarian ideologies.
(d) Culturally diverse.

Codes:

A. (a) and (b) are True.
B. (a), (b) and (d) are True.

C. (b) and (c) are True.
D. (a) only True.

2. In India, there is 'no one kind of family,' because:
A. India is culturally diverse.
B. Indian Society is patriarchal.
C. Indian families are traditional.
D. Indian families are value oriented.

3. **Assertion (A):** Women's sexuality is exerted through the family and kinship.
Reason (R): Women are socialized to have a low level of self-esteem.
Codes:
A. Both (A) and (R) are true.
B. Both (A) and (R) are false.
C. (A) is true, (R) is false.
D. (R) is true, (A) is false.

4. In India caste has a prominent hold because:
(a) Absence of alternate social security.
(b) Caste and kin networks provide individual support.
(c) Caste control women's sexuality.
(d) Caste support to celebrated marriage, births, and deaths.
Codes:
A. (c) and (d) are True.
B. (a) and (c) are True.
C. (a), (b) and (c) are True.
D. (a), (b), (c) and (d) are True.

5. Women are incapable of thinking of an independent future, because:
A. Women have low self-esteem.
B. Denied knowledge of her body.
C. Socialization process consistently disciplined the girls.
D. Caste ideologies dominate in society ideologies.

PASSAGE-25

Gender equity is defined as "the socially constructed expectations for male and female behaviour that is found in every known human society." Mason observes, "Studies explicitly concerned with gender system and their impact on demographic change are relatively new." She subdivides the gender system into gender stratification between male and female members of society and gender roles. Gender equity derives from both these elements of the gender system. This can be evaluated from the perspective of rights—social, political and reproductive. Levels of equity in such an evaluation of rights determined the level of gender equity. Thus, it is a value-laden concept that begs the question of whose values should be applied. Gender inequity in contemporary societies is a problem. It can be measured through social as well as psychological scales.

Women require autonomy to have better gender equity. Autonomy is defined as the ability to obtain information and to use it as the basis of making decisions about one's private concerns and those of one's intimates and the degree of women's access to material resources within the family, in the community and the society at large but we don't necessarily enhance women's autonomy. Autonomy is shaped by traditional factors. Hindu women had more autonomy than Muslim women. Education and employment don't necessarily enhance women's autonomy, and the traditional factors conferring status on women remain strong and need to be expanded beyond education and employment and delayed marriage. More comprehensive, direct and content specific strategies to increase women's autonomy must be sought simultaneously.

1. The author is primarily concerned with:
A. Discussing the need for autonomy.
B. Explaining the elements of the gender system.
C. Presenting the history of gender inequity.
D. Describing the dynamics of power relations.

2. According to the passage, which of the following encourages gender equity?
(a) Access to material resources.
(b) Access to information.
(c) Lack of agency and autonomy.
Codes:
A. (a) only B. (b) only
C. (a) and (c) only D. (a) and (b) only

3. The author mentions levels of equity to evaluate the level of gender inequity in contemporary societies through:
A. Psychological scales.
B. Social measures.
C. Challenging traditional norms.
D. Both Social and Psychological measures.

4. Which of the following pairs of terms seem synonymous in the passage?
A. Gender equity and gender behaviour.
B. Gender equity and gender system.
C. Gender equity and gender autonomy.
D. Gender consciousness and gender autonomy.

5. The material in the passage could be used as an argument for:
A. Raising women's consciousness.
B. Enabling women to access and mobilize community resources and public services.
C. Providing support for challenging traditional norms underlining gender inequalities.
D. All the above.

PASSAGE-26

Feminists with varying intellectual frames of reference have put forth diverse positions about privileging the category of gender over women. The shift from women to gender has been viewed by some as a replacement of the study of sexual inequality with the study of the differences between the sexes (Evans 1990). They make a case for the continuing usefulness of the term 'woman' for analysis as against the category of gender. The category 'gender' is seen as diverting the focus from specific issues concerning women both in the political and academic sphere. However, feminists, especially the third world, black and Dalit feminists, have underlined the dangers of presuming a set of common meanings for the category women. They have argued that the category women universalizes and homogenizes the experience of white, middle-class and upper-caste women.

On the other hand, the use of the category gender allows for the analysis of differences of race, class, caste, nation and sexual orientation between women. The use of the category woman assumes commonality between all women and can at best allow the analysis of the differences among women in an additive or add-on manner. In the analysis of a caste-based society, for instance, such an assumption of commonality amounts to a reiteration of the normative status of the upper-caste women. Often the commonality between women is assumed on the basis of their experiences of victimhood as 'women' in a patriarchal society. Such an assumption not only universalizes the concept of patriarchy but also argues as if the oppression of caste and class is located in some 'non-woman' part of Dalit women. The use of the category of gender allows for an analysis of the interlocking structures of oppression and goes beyond the analysis of the differences among women by underlining the gendered nature of caste and class oppression.

1. Mark out the correct answer:
   A. The category gender universalizes and homogenizes the experience of race, class and upper caste women.
   B. The category women allow for the analysis of differences of race, class and sexual orientation between women.
   C. The category of women assumes commonality between all women.
   D. All are True.

2. The category of gender is useful for:
   A. An analysis of the interlocking structures of oppression.
   B. The analysis of the differences among women.
   C. The analysis of the nature of the oppression of low caste women.
   D. The analysis of the nature of oppression of both caste and class women.

3. What is the danger perceived by the feminists in using category gender over women?
   A. It will break the commonality between women.
   B. It diverts the focus from specific issues concerning women in the political and academic sphere.
   C. It will analyze the experiences of victimhood as women.
   D. It will not help in universalizing the concept of patriarchy.

4. The shift from women to gender for some feminist implies:
   A. The study of differences between the sexes.
   B. The study of sexual inequality.
   C. Both the study of sexual inequality and the differences between the sexes.
   D. The study with the focus of women issues.

5. **Assertion (A):** The shift from women to gender for some feminists is a replacement of the study of the differences between the sexes.
   Reason (R): There is the continuing usefulness of the term "woman" for analysis as against the category of gender.
   Codes:
   A. Both (A) and (R) are True and (R) is the correct explanation of (A).
   B. Both (A) and (R) are True and (R) is not the correct explanation for (A).
   C. (A) is True and (R) is False.
   D. Both (A) and (R) are False.

PASSAGE-27

In proving women's inferiority, the anti-feminists began to draw not only upon religion, philosophy, and theology, as before, but also upon science-biology, experimental psychology, etc. At most, they were willing to grant 'equality indifference' to the other sex. That profitable formula is most significant; it is precisely like the 'equal but separative' formula of the Jim Crow laws aimed at the North American Negroes. As is well known, this so-called equalitarian segregation has resulted only in the most extreme discrimination. The similarity just noted is in no way due to chance, for whether it is a race, a caste, a class, or a sex that is reduced to a position of inferiority, the methods of justification are the same. The 'eternal feminine' corresponds to 'the black soul' and to 'the Jewish character.' Correct, the Jewish problem is on the whole very different from the other two-to the anti-Semite the Hew is not so much an inferior as he is an enemy for whom there is to be granted no place on earth, for whom annihilation is the fate desired. But there are deep similarities between the situation of women and that of the Negro. Both are being emancipated today from a like paternalism, and the former master class wishes to keep them in the place—that is, the place chosen for them. In both cases, the former masters lavish more or less sincere eulogies, either on the virtues of 'the good Negro' with his dormant, childish, merry soul—the submissive Negro or on the merits of the woman who is 'truly feminine'—that is, frivolous, infantile, irresponsible—the submissive woman. In both cases, the dominant class bases its argument on a state of affairs that it has itself created. As George Bernard Shaw puts it, in substance, 'The American white relegates the black to the rank of shoeshine boy; and he concludes from this that the black is good for nothing but shining shoes.' This vicious circle is met with in all analogous circumstances; when an individual (or a group of individuals) is kept in a situation of inferiority, the fact is that he is inferior. But the significance of the verb to be must be rightly understood here; it is in bad faith to give it a static value when it really has the dynamic Hegelian sense of to have become. Yes, women, on the whole, are today inferior to men; that is, their situation affords them fewer possibilities.

1. Anti-feminists argued for women's inferiority on the basis of:
(a) Philosophy
(b) Caste
(c) Biology
(d) Experimental Psychology
Codes:
A. (a), (b), (c), (d)   B. (b), (c) and (d) only
C. (a), (c) and (d) only   D. (c) and (d) only

2. Mark out the correct answer:
The formula of 'equality in difference' is profitable for?
A. Emancipating all relegated to the position of inferiority.
B. Maintaining the status-quo or even enhancing discrimination against women.
C. Solving the issues of Negroes and Jews.
D. Minimizing discrimination against women.

3. Assertion (A): 'The eternal feminine' corresponds to 'the black soul' and to 'the Jewish Character.'
Reason (R): There are profound similarities among the situation of the Jews, the situation of woman and that of the Negro.
Codes:
A. Both (A) and (R) are True.
B. (A) is True, but (R) is False and (R) is not the correct explanation of (A).
C. (A) is False and (R) is True and (R) is the correct explanation of (A).
D. Both (A) and (R) are False.

4. How are the situation of women and that of the Negro is similar?
(a) Both are biologically inferior.
(b) Both have been liberated from alike paternalism
(c) Both have been a slave to their masters for their submissiveness.
(d) Both are responsible for their state of affairs
Codes:
A. (b), (c) and (d) only   B. (a) and (d) only
C. (a), (b), (c) and (d)   D. (b) and (c) only

5. Assertion (A): Women, on the whole, are today inferior to men and their situation will continue.
Reason (R): The vicious circle of inferiority is static and not dynamic.
Codes:
A. (A) is True and (R) is False.
B. (A) is False and (R) is True.
C. Both (A) and (R) are False.
D. Both (A) and (R) are True and (R) is the correct explanation of (A).

PASSAGE-28

Industrialization, rapid social change and a public discussion on individual's rights set the stage for the emergence of the first wave of feminism in the 1800s The country was expanding, industrialization was changing how Americans thought about work and the family, and social reforms were interested in helping the 'unfortunate' in society. Many women were drawn to issues of social reform and, despite a lack of public roles, rights, and responsibilities, were instrumental in organizing and participating in the abolition movement to end slavery. In 1837, women organized the first Anti slavery convention of American Women without the assistance of men. Although women such as Sarah and Angelina Grimke were active participants in the movement, they were largely denied the right to speak on the issues at conventions and were often attacked in public when they attempted to address the wrong of slavery. This unequal treatment and silencing helped women connect their lack of individual rights to the issue of slavery and led to the organizing of the first women's rights convention. Organized by the abolitionist Lucretia Mott and Elizabeth Cady Stanton, the Seneca Falls Women's Rights Convention held on 14 July 1848 focused on multiple issues including education rights property reforms and women's restricted roles within th family. The convention resulted in a declaration of sentiments and a series of resolutions. The resolutions included the rights of women to determine their own lives, seek employment, enjoy equality within marriage and find freedom from oppressive legal and religious dictates. After much deliberations, the attendees also decided to address the controversial issues of women's suffrage. It is a misconception that the first wave of U.S. feminism was concerned only with obtaining women's right to vote. Early feminists addressed a variety of women's concerns including fair custody arrangements, the right to own property as an individual after marriage, and freedom from the restricted dress. The campaign to change women's dress was called the Bloomer Movement after Amelia Bloomer who advocated a more rational dress in her women's rights journal of the 1850s.

1. Bloomer movement was about:

A. Campaign to change religious rights.

B. Campaign to change Women's dress codes.

C. Campaign for voting rights.

D. Campaign for property rights.

2. Assertion (A): The first wave of U.S. feminism was concerned only with obtaining women's right to vote.

Reason (R): Early feminists addressed only the controversial issues of women's suffrage in public meetings.

Codes:

A. Both (A) and (R) are true, (R) is the correct explanation for (A).

B. Both (A) and (R) are true and (R) is not the correct explanation for (A).

C. Both (A) and (R) are false.

D. (A) is true, (R) is false.

3. The emergence of the first wave of feminism is mainly due to:

(a) Industrialization.

(b) Discussion on Individual rights.

(c) Lack of women's private roles.

(d) Lack of women's public roles.

Codes:

A. (a) and (b) only B. (a) and (d) only

C. (a), (b) and (d) only D. (b), (c) and (d) only

4. Why did women of America organize the first convention of women without the Assistance of men?

A. Women were given opportunities to speak in public places.

B. Women were denied the rights of property.

C. Women were largely denied the rights to talk about the issues of women.

D. Women were denied voting rights.

PASSAGE-29

Even though the early Vedic family was of the patriarchal type, women had some control over the entire household. The Rig Veda reveals a stage where women enjoyed equal status with men. ". . . . A Rig Vedic hymn describes how a maiden could take a soma twig and offer herself as a sacrifice to Indra, Vedic sacrifices were performed jointly by husband and wife" ....Society never denied women their rights and privileges. From the 4th century B.C. to 3rd Century B.C. girls were given education. But this was confined to the well-to-do families. There existed the initiation ceremony or upanayana, for both girls and boys. According to A.S. Altekar ". . . . . education was regarded as very essential to secure a suitable marriage."

In Rig Vedic society ". . . . .the practice of child marriage did not exist." So women got an opportunity to acquire education. If they wanted to pursue knowledge without getting married, they were allowed to do so, without any constraints. The educators wisely divided women into two groups, namely Brahmavadinis and Sadyodvahas. "The former was life-long students of theology and philosophy; the latter used to prosecute their studies till their marriage at the age of 15 or 16". Many educated women became teachers or Upadhyayinis. No wonder, the age witnessed many sagacious and capable women "like Visvavara, Apala, and Ghosha even composed mantras and rose to the rank of rishis." Lopmudra, one of the female preachers, is said to have preached as many as 179 hymns of the first book of the Rig Veda along with sage Agasthya. There were many women poets and philosophers during this period. This confirms the fact that if given equal opportunities, women can definitely prove that they are as capable and as intelligent as men. Mazumdar points out that the Aryans never neglected or showed prejudice towards women as far as their education was concerned. Maybe they were not conscious of the gender power-politics and conflicts at that time, as society was not so complex and was at a developing stage. Thus during the period of the Vedas, the Aryans, we can say we're concerned about the rightness of the social order in which they lived.

1. Identify the correct statements about gender equality during the Vedic period:

(a) There existed a practice of initiation ceremony for all the boys and girls.

(b) Education was a privilege given to all the girls of well-to-do families.

(c) Early Vedic society was not aware of gender power politics.

(d) Women like men could become lifelong students of theology and philosophy.

Codes:

A. (c) and (d) only.
B. (a), (b) and (c) only.
C. (b), (c) and (d) only.
D. (a), (b), (c) and (d).

2. What was common between Lopamudra and Agasthya?
(a) They contributed to the writing of the Vedas.
(b) They were preachers.
(c) They were female philosophers.
(d) They were conscious of gender prejudices.

Codes:

A. (a), (b), and (c) only B. (a) and (b) only
C. (a), (b), (c) and (d) D. (a), (b) and (d) only

3. Identify the correct statement about the Vedic Society:
A. Gender power politics prevailed in the Vedic period.
B. Majority of the women were Brahmavadinis during the Vedic Period.
C. All the girls were free to enjoy all the ceremonies like men.
D. The Vedic period witnessed many sagacious women.

4. What were the characteristics of the Vedic Society?
(a) The Vedic Society was simple.
(b) It was conscious of gender power politics.
(c) Aryans had a concern for the rightness of the social order.
(d) Aryans showed prejudice toward women.

Codes:

A. (a), (b), (c) and (d) B. (a), (b) and (d)
C. (c) only D. (a) and (c) only

5. Assertion (A): From the 4th century BC to 3rd century B.C, all girls were given education irrespective of caste, class or creed.
Reason (R): Education was regarded as very essential to secure a suitable marriage.

Codes:

A. (A) is True (R) is False.
B. Both (A) and (R) are True.
C. (A) is False (R) is True.
D. Both (A) and (R) are False.

PASSAGE-30

The politics of language has played an important role in promoting and strengthening the subordination of women, especially in highly stratified societies. In India, the virtual invisibility of women in Social Science literature, agricultural Sciences/Economics, as well as national planning and the educational process, could certainly be traced to the gradual disappearance (from non-use?) of a feminine form in the word for peasants in different Indian languages—when such forms continued for all the traditional artisanal or service sector occupations (barber, weaver, etc.) The loss of this vocabulary is symptomatic of the processes unleashed in colonial India. It is well known that agricultural surplus was the primary source of 'revenue' earning in colonial India. The marginalization of women in the "official" records of the Department of Revenue and Agriculture highlights the "erasure" of women from the most visible domain of economic activity and the patriarchal bias that went into the casting of the Indian peasant as male. Contradictorily, the Indian Census recorded decade after decade that the largest numbers of women workers were in agriculture, sometimes outnumbering men in the category of landless agricultural labourers. Terms like gender-gap/ disparities, gender-mainstreaming reflect a lack of understanding that subordination of women has been an advancing process historically: a dynamic that is by no means over for all. To suggest that all that is required is for women to catch up with men is to ignore or underplay the transformative role of the ideology and agenda of the "Gender Revolution" of the twentieth century. In other regions, such criticisms came from women's organizations, occasionally from under-resourced and ill-equipped State agencies (for example Commissions)—who complained of their status as unwanted children by the mainstream of governance.

1. The marginalization of women in the 'official' records of the Department of Revenue and Agriculture is due to:
A. Patriarchal bias in the existing vocabulary.
B. Gender disparities.
C. Gender bias in women's organizations.
D. Status of women as unwanted children.

2. The invisibility of women in national planning is due to:
A. Largely women indulge in unpaid work.
B. Women are landless labourers.
C. Women only do supportive work for men.
D. The lack of feminine vocabulary for women's occupations.

3. "The subordination of women has been an advancing process historically."
Cannot be understood by the terms like:
(a) Gender Gap (b) Gender Disparities
(c) Gender Mainstreaming (d) Gender Revolution

Codes:

A. (c) & (d) only B. (a), (b), (c) & (d)
C. (a) & (b) only D. (b), (c) only

4. **Assertion (A):** The politics of language has promoted and strengthened the subordination of women in stratified societies.

   Reason (R): A large number of women workers have been in the category of landless agricultural labourers.

   Codes:

   A. Both (A) and (R) are True and (R) is the correct explanation of (A).
   B. (A) is True but (R) is False and (R) is not the correct explanation of (A).
   C. Both (A) and (R) are True and (R) is not the correct explanation of (A).
   D. Both (A) and (R) are False and (R) is the correct explanation of (A).

PASSAGE-31

The family is not a closed community: its isolation is qualified by communications set up with other social units; they have not merely an 'interior' within which the couple is shut away; it is also the expression of that couple's standard of life, its financial status, its taste, and thus the home must need be on view to other people. It is essentially the woman's part to direct this social life. The man is joined to the community, as producer and citizen, by bonds of an organic solidarity based upon the division of labour; the couple is a social unit, defined by the family, the class, the circle, and the race to which it belongs, attached by bonds of a mechanical solidarity to groups of corresponding social situation; the wife can embody this relation most purely, for the husbands professional associations are often out of tune with his social standing, whereas the wife, with no occupational demands, can confine herself to the society of her equals. Furthermore, she has the leisure to keep up, by 'paying calls' and having 'at-homes', those relations which are of no practical use and which, of course, are important only in classes whose members are intent upon holding their rank in the social scale— that is to say, who consider themselves superior to certain others. She delights in the display of her 'interior,' even of her own appearance, which her husband and children do not notice because they are familiar with them. Her social duty, which is to 'make a good show,' combines with her pleasure in letting herself be seen. She must 'make a good show' where she is herself concerned; in the house, attending to her work, she is merely clothed; to go out, to received, she 'dresses up.' Formal attire has a double function: it indicates the social standing of the woman (her standard of living, wealth and the social circle), it is also feminine narcissism in concrete form; it is uniform and an adornment; by means of it's the woman who is deprived of doing anything feels that she expresses what she is. To care for her beauty, to dress up is a kind of work that enables her to take possession of her person as she takes possession of her home through housework; her ego then seems chosen and recreated by herself. Social custom furthers this tendency to identify herself with her appearance.

1. A family is a social unit marked by the bonds of:
   A. Organic solidarity
   B. Mechanical solidarity
   C. Both organic and mechanical solidarity
   D. Financial solidarity

2. The solidarity based on the division of labour in the community is termed as:
   A. Mechanical solidarity
   B. Professional solidarity
   C. Organic solidarity
   D. All of the above

3. Why does the woman dress up, when she goes out?
   (a) To show her social standing
   (b) Feminine narcissism
   (c) Social duty
   (d) To take possession of her husband

   Codes:

   A. (a) only (c) B. (b) and (d)
   C. (a), (c) and (d) D. (a), (b), (c) and (d)

4. **Assertion (A):** The role of the wife of 'paying calls' and having 'at homes' the relationships are significant for those classes whose members intend to hold some rank in the social scale.

   Reason (R): It helps the wives (with no occupational demands) having occupational benefit for themselves.

   Codes:

   A. Both (A) and (R) are true and (R) is the correct explanation of (A).
   B. (A) is true but (R) is false and (R) is not the correct explanation of (A).
   C. (A) is true but (R) is false and (R) is the correct explanation of (A).
   D. Both (A) and (R) are false.

5. **Assertion (A):** The family is not a closed community.

   Reason (R): From other social units, its isolation is approved and qualified, and the members of a family live independently.

   Codes:

   A. (A) is true, (R) is false and (R) is not the correct explanation of (A).
   B. Both (A) and (R) are true and (R) is the correct explanation of (A).
   C. Both (A) and (R) are true and (R) is not the correct explanation of (A).
   D. Both (A) and (R) are false.

Answers

PASSAGE-1

1	2	3	4	5	6
B	C	A	D	B	A

PASSAGE-2

1	2	3	4	5	6
B	C	D	D	B	D

PASSAGE-3

1	2	3	4	5
C	B	A	D	A

PASSAGE-4

1	2	3	4	5	6
B	B	C	C	C	A

PASSAGE-5

1	2	3	4	5
B	A	D	B	A

PASSAGE-6

1	2	3	4	5
A	C	B	D	C

PASSAGE-7

1	2	3	4	5
A	A	C	C	A

PASSAGE-8

1	2	3	4	5
B	C	D	C	B

PASSAGE-9

1	2	3	4	5
D	A	D	A	B

PASSAGE-10

1	2	3	4	5
A	B	D	B	B

PASSAGE-11

1	2	3	4
A	B	C	A

PASSAGE-12

1	2	3	4	5
C	D	A	A	C

PASSAGE-13

1	2	3	4	5
A	A	C	D	C

PASSAGE-14

1	2	3	4	5
A	A	B	A	A

PASSAGE-15

1	2	3	4	5
B	C	A	C	D

PASSAGE-16

1	2	3	4	5
C	A	C	C	B

PASSAGE-17

1	2	3	4	5
D	B	C	B	D

PASSAGE-18

1	2	3	4	5
C	D	C	D	B

PASSAGE-19

1	2	3	4
A	A	A	D

PASSAGE-20

1	2	3	4	5
B	A	B	D	A

PASSAGE-21

1	2	3	4	5
D	C	D	B	D

PASSAGE-22

1	2	3	4	5
A	B	A	A	C

PASSAGE-23

1	2	3	4	5
D	C	B	A	B

PASSAGE-24

1	2	3	4	5
B	A	A	D	C

PASSAGE-25

1	2	3	4	5
A	D	D	C	D

PASSAGE-26

1	2	3	4	5
C	A	B	A	B

PASSAGE-27

1	2	3	4	5
C	B	B	A	C

PASSAGE-28

1	2	3	4
B	C	C	C

PASSAGE-29

1	2	3	4	5
D	B	D	D	C

PASSAGE-30

1	2	3	4
A	D	B	C

PASSAGE-31

1	2	3	4	5
B	C	D	B	A

❑ ❑ ❑

Suggested Readings

- Adams C. Eco-feminism and the Sacred. Continuum. New York. 1993.
- Adiseshiah S. Malcom. Economics of Environment. Lancer International. New Delhi. 1987.
- Agarwal Anurag. Female Foeticide Myth and Reality. Sterling Publishers. 2003.
- Agarwal Bina. (ed.). Structures of Patriarchy, State, Community and Household in Modernising Asia. Kali for Women. New Delhi.1988.
- Agarwal Bina. Patriarchy and the Modernizing State : An Introduction. Kali for Women. New Delhi. 1988
- Agarwal S.P and Agarwal J.C. Women's Education in India : Historical Review, Present Status perspective plan with statistical Indicators. Gyan publishing House. New Delhi. 1993.
- Agarwal S.P. Women's Education in India. Concept Publishing Company. New Delhi.2003.
- Agarwal Sushila. Status of Women. Printwell Publishers. Jaipur. 1988.
- Agnes Flavia. Women and Law in India. New Delhi. 2004.
- Ahlawat Neeraja. Women Organizations and Social Networks. Rawat. Jaipur. 1995.
- Ahmed Imtiaz. Women in Politics. In Devaki Jain (ed.). Indian Women. Publication Division. New Delhi. 1975.
- Ahooja Patel Krishna. Women and Development. Ashish Publication House. New Delhi. 1995.
- Ahuja Ram. Crime Against Women. Rawat. New Delhi. 1987.
- Altekar A.S. The Position of Women in Hindu Civilization. Motilal Banarasidass. Delhi. 1983.
- Asthana Pratima. Women's Movement in India. Rawat. Delhi. 1974.
- Attray I.P. Crimes Against Women. Vikas Publishing House. New Delhi. 1988.
- Babbie Earl. The practice for social Research. Himalaya Publishing House. Bombay. 1979.
- Bagchi Jasodhara., Jaba Guha and Piyali Sen Gupta. Loved and Unloved : The Girl Child in The Family. Stree. Calcutta. 1999.
- Bajwa G.S. Human Rights in India : Implementation and Violations. Anmol Publications Pvt. Ltd.. New Delhi. 1995.
- Baker Mary Anne. Women Today : A Multidisciplinary Approach to Women's Studies. Brooks/Cole Publishing Company. Monterey, California. 1980.
- Bakshi S.R. Gandhi and Status of Women. Criterion Publication. New Delhi. 1987.
- Bassnett Susan. Feminist Experiences : The Women's Movement in Four Cultures. London. Allen and Unwin. 1986.
- Basu Aparna. The Role of Women in the Indian Struggle for Freedom. Vikas Publishers. New Delhi. 1990.
- Bathila Sonia. Women, Democracy and The Media : Cultural and Political Representations in The Indian Press. Sage. India. 1998.
- Beauvoir De Simone. The Second Sex. Trans. H.M. Parshley. Vintage. New York. 1974.

- Beauvoir Simone. The Coming of Age : Great Britain. André Deutsch Ltd and George Weidenfeld and Nicolson Ltd. 1972.
- Berbert C. and Deshbandhu. Environmental Education for Conservation and Development. Nataraj. Dehradun. 1985.
- Beteille Andre. Caste, Class & Power. University of California Press, 1969.
- Bhasin Kamala and Nigate Said Khan. Feminism and its Relevance in South Asia. Kali for Women. New Delhi. 1986
- Bhasin Kamala. What is Patriarchy? Kali for Women. New Delhi. 1993.
- Bhatt Ela. Shramshakti : Report of the National Commission on Self Employed Women and Women in the Informal Sector. 1988.
- Blalock M. Hubert. Conceptualization and Measurement in the Social Sciences. Sage Publication. New Delhi. 1982.
- Bose Ashish. India's Population Policy—Changing Paradigm. B.R. Publishing Corporation. Delhi. 1996
- Boserup Ester. Women's Role in Economic Development. St. Martin's Press. New York. 1970.
- Bowles and Duelli Kleim (ed.). Theories of Women's Studies. London. Routledge & Kegan Paul. 1988.
- Breton M.J. Women Pioneers for the Environment. Northeastern University Press. Boston. 1998.
- Budhwar Pawan, Debi S., Saini S. and Jyotsna Bhatnagar. Women in Management In The New Economic Environment. The Case of India Asia Pacific Business Review. 2005.
- Caeden Maren L. The New Feminist Movement. New York. 1974.
- Cahanana Karuna. (Ed.) Socialisation, Education and Women : Explorations in Gender Identity. Orient Longman Ltd.. New Delhi. 1988.
- Calman Leslie. Towards Empowerment : Women and Movement Politics in India. Boulder Co and Oxford. UK. West view.1992.
- Caplan Patricia. Class and Gender in India : Women and Their Organizations in a South Indian City. London. 1985.
- Caroline O.N. Moser. Gender Planning in the Third World : Meeting Practical and Strategic Gender Needs. In World Development. 1989.
- Caroline Ramazanocglu and J Holland. Feminist Methodology : Challenges and choices. Sage publications. New Delhi. 2003.
- Caroline Ramazanocglu, Holland. Feminist Methodology. Sage Publications. London. 2002.
- Chandler E.M. Educating Adolescent Girls. George Allen and Unwin. London. 1980.
- Chatterji Jyotsna. Religions and the status of women. Uppal Publishing House. New Delhi. 1990
- Chaudhry Prem. The Veiled Women. Oxford University Press. Bombay. 1994
- Chauhare Indira. Purdha to Profession. B.R. Delhi. 1982.
- Chen Martha, Alter. Widows in India : Social Neglect and Public Action. Sage. New Delhi. 1998.
- Connell R.W. Masculinities. University of California Press. Berkeley. 1995.
- Coombs Philips H. The Works Crisis in Education. Oxford University Press. New York. 1985.
- Crites L. Lavra el. Women. The Court and Equality. Sage. New Delhi. 1987
- Dalal K. Ajit and Ray Subha. Social Dimensions of Health. Rawat Publications. Jaipur. 2005.
- Das Gupta Monica and Krishnan T.N. Women and Health. Oxford. New Delhi. 1998.
- Das Man Singh. Woman and Her Environment. M.D. Publications Pvt. Ltd. New Delhi. 1995
- Das Sandhya Rani. Empowerment of Women : A Holistic Approach. Third Concept. 2002.
- Datta V.N. Sati : A Historical, Social and Philosophical Enquiry into the Hindu Rite of Widow Burning. New Delhi. 1988.
- David Ater. The Politics of Modernization. The University of Chicago Press. Chicago. 1965.
- Davis Martin Brett. Doing a Successful Research Project : Using Qualitative or Quantitative Methods. Palgrave. Hampshire. 2007.
- Deckard Barbara Sinclaire. The Women's Movement. Harper & Row Publishers. New York. 1983.
- Desai A.R. Women's Liberation and Politics of Religious Personal Laws in India. C.G. Shah Memorial Trust. Bombay. 1986.
- Desai Neera. A Decade of Women's Movement in India. Himalaya Publishing House. Bombay. 1988.
- Desai Neera and Krishnaraj Maithreyi. Women and Society in India. Ajantha Publications. New Delhi. 1987.
- Desai Neera and Thakar Usha. Women in Indian Society. National Book Trust of India. New Delhi. 2001.

- Desai Neera and Patel Vibhuti. Critical Review of Researches in Women's Studies. Research Centre for Women's Studies. S.N.D.T. University. Bombay. 1989.
- Desai Neera and Patel Vibhuti. Indian Women : Change & Challenge in the International decade 1975-85. Popular Prakashan Pvt. Ltd. Bombay. 1985.
- Deutach H. Psychology of women. Vol. I and II. Crune and Stratton. N.Y. 1945.
- Devasia Leelamma & Devasia V.V. Girl Child in India. Ashish Publishing House. New Delhi. 1991
- Devgan Aadesh. Crime Against Women and Children : An Emerging Social Problem. Cyber Tech. New Delhi. 2008.
- Dhanda Amita and Parashar Archana. (eds.). Engendering law : Essays in honour of Lotika Sarkar. Eastern Book. Lucknow. 2007
- Dhruvarajan Vanaja. Hindu Women and The Power of Ideology. Vistaar. Delhi. 1989.
- Dietrich Gabriele. Reflections on the Women's Movements in India. Horizon India Books. 1992.
- Dines Gain and Jean M. Humez. Gender, Race and Class in Media. Sage. 1994.
- Diwan Paras. Dowry and Protection to Married Women. Deep and Deep Publication. New Delhi. 1987
- Diwan Paras. Family Law. (Law of Marriage and Divorce in India). Sterling Publishers Pvt. Ltd. New Delhi. 1983.
- Dominic Salvatore. Micro Economic Theory. Tata Mc Graw Hill. New Delhi. 1992.
- Dreze Jean and Amartya Sen. India : Development and Participation. Oxford University Press. 2005.
- Eichler M. Non-Sexist Research Methods : A Practical Guideline. Routledge Chapman & Hall. 1991.
- Elacody E. and Jackin W.C. The psychology of sex differences. Standard Uni. Standard. 1974.
- Engineer Asghar Ali. The Rights of Women in Islam. Delhi. Sterling. 1982.
- Escobar Arturo. Encountering Development : The Making and Unmaking of the Third World. Princeton University Press. Princeton. 1995.
- Farooqui Vimla. A Short History of Women's Movement in India. Communist Party Publication. New Delhi. July. 1996.
- Fernades Menon Geeta & Viegas. Water, Forests, Environment and Tribal Economy. Indian Social Institute. New Delhi. 1988.
- Firestone Shulamith. The Dialectics of Sex. Trans. H.M. Parshely. Bantam. New York. 1970.
- Forbes Geraldine. Women in Modern India. New Delhi. CUP. 1998.
- Friedan Betty. The Feminine Mystique. London. 1963.
- Gaard G. Ecological Politics, Eco-feminists and the Greens. Philadelphia. Temple University Press. 1998.
- Gandhi Nandita and Shah Nandita. The Issues at Stake : Theory and Practice in the Contemporary Women's Movement in India. Kali. New Delhi. 1992.
- Ghadially R. Women in Indian Society–A Reader. Sage Publications. New Delhi. 1988
- Gill Kulwant. Hindu Women's Right to Property in India. Deep & Deep. New Delhi. 1986.
- Gloria Bowles. Theories of Women's Studies London. Renate Duelliklein (Eds.). Routledge and Kegan
- Glover David, Cora Kaplan. Genders. Routledge. London. 2007.
- Goffman Erving. Gender and Advertisement. Harpet and Row. New York. 1976.
- Goode and Hatt. Methods in Social Research. Mc Graw Hill. Bombay. 1952.
- Goode William J. and Hatt Paul K. Methods in Social Research. Mc Graw Hill Book Company. USA. 2006.
- Goonesekere Savitri (ed.). Violence, Law and Women's Rights in South Asia. Sage. New Delhi. 2004.
- Gornick V. and Moren B.K. Women in sexist society. Basic Books N.Y. 1971.
- Goswami Sambodh. Female Infanticide and Child Marriage. Rawat. Jaipur. 2007.
- Government of India. Census Report. 2011
- Govt. of India. Blue Print of Action Points and National Plan of Action for Women, Development of Social Welfare. New Delhi. 1976.
- Gready Paul and Jonathan Ensor. Reinventing Development? Translating Rights-based approaches from theory to practice. Jed Books. London. 2005.
- Gupta Jyotsna, Agnihotri. New Reproductive Technologies : Women's Health and Autonomy. Sage Publications. New Delhi. 2000.
- Gupta Krishna. Women, Law and Public opinion. Rawat. Jaipur. 2001.
- Gutmann Amy. Liberal Equality. Cambridge University Press. New York. 1978.

- Handbook of Policy and Related Documents on Women in India. National Institute of Public Cooperation and Child Development. New Delhi. 1988
- Hanson M. Review of Eco-feminism as Politics. Green Politics Newsletter. March 12. 1998.
- Harding Sandra. Feminism & Methodology. Indiana. Indiana University Press. 1987.
- Harris and Liebert. The Child. Development from Birth through Adolescence. New Jersey. Prentice-Hall. 1984.
- Higginbotham Elizabeth, Mary Romeo. Women and Work : Exploring Race, Ethnicity and Class. New Delhi. Sage. 1997.
- Hofrichter R. (ed.). Toxic Struggle : The Theory and Practice of Environmental Justice. Philadelphia. New Society Publishers. 1993.
- IAWS. Feminist Approaches to Economic Theories. A Report. IAWS. New Delhi. 1995.
- Irene Tinker. (Ed.) Persistent Inequalities : Women and World Development. Oxford University Press. 1990.
- Iyer Padma. Women in Developing Countries. Jaipur. Aavishkar. 2006.
- Jain Devaki. Women, Development and the UN—A Sixty-year quest for Equality and Justice. Orient Longman. Hyderabad. 2005.
- Jain Devaki and Rajput Pam (Ed). Narratives from the Women's Studies Family : Recreating Knowledge. Sage Publications. 2003.
- Jain Jasbir. (Ed). Women in Patriarchy, Cross Cultural. Rawat Publications. Jaipur. 2005.
- Jain Jasbir. (ed.). Women's Writing-Text and Context. Jaipur. Rawat. 1997.
- Jain L.C. Grass without Roots : Rural Development under Government Auspices. New Delhi. 1985.
- Jaising Indira. Through the looking glass—Indira in wonderland. From the Lawyers Collective. 22(5). p.8-13. June 2007.
- Jaisingh Indira(ed) Justice for Women : Personal Laws, Women's Rights and Law Reforms. The Other India Press. Mapuse. Goa. 1996.
- Jane Pilcher and Imelda Wheelan. 50 Key Concepts in Gender Studies. London. Sage Publications. 2004.
- Jayawardena Kumari. Feminism and Nationalism in the Third World. Zed. London. 1986.
- Jessy K. Outraging the modesty of a woman. Legal News and Views. 22(4). April 2008. p.7-8.
- Jha Ashok Kumar. (ed.). Women in Panchayati Raj Institutions. Anmol Publications Pvt. Ltd. New Delhi. 2004.
- Joanna Liddle and Joshi Rama. Daughters of Indepen-dence : Gender, Caste and Class in India. Kali for Women. New Delhi. 1986.
- Kabeer Naila. Reserved Realities–Gender Hierarchies In Development Thought. London. 1994.
- Kant Anjani. Women and Law. A.P.H. Publishing Corporation. 2003.
- Kapadia K.M. Marriage and Family in India. Oxford University. New Delhi. 1980.
- Kaplan Patricia (ed.). The Cultural Construction of Sexuality. London. Tavituck. 1987.
- Kapur Promilla. (ed). Empowering Indian Women. Publication Division. Government of India. New Delhi. 2000.
- Kapur Ratna (ed.) Feminist Terrains in Legal Domain : Interdisciplinary Essays on Women and Law in India. Kali for Women. New Delhi. 1996
- Kapur Ratna. Knowing Ours Rights. Zubaan Publications. New Delhi. 2003.
- Kapur Ratna. Subversive sites : Feminist engagements with law in India/by Ratna Kapur and Brenda Cossman. New Delhi. Sage. 1996.352p. 346.0134 KAP.S 7069.
- Karl Marilee. Women and Empowerment : Participation and Decision-Making. London and New Jersey. Zed. 1995.
- Kaushik Susheela. Women's Participation in Politics. Vikas Publishing House Pvt. Ltd. New Delhi. 1993.
- Kerlinger F. N. Foundation of Behavioural Research. Half Ronehartand Winston. New York. 1973.
- Khanna B.S. Panchayati Raj in India. Deep & Deep Publications. New Delhi. 1994.
- Khullar Mala. (ed.). Writings in Women's Studies. A Reader. Zubaan Publications. New Delhi. 2005.
- Kishwar Madhu. Off the beaten track : Re-thinking gender justice for Indian women. New Delhi. Oxford University.1999.
- Kohli Atul. The State and Poverty in India, The Politics of Reform. New York. 1987.
- Kosambi D.D. The Culture and Civilization of Ancient India in Historical Outline. Routledge Pub. London. 1965.
- Kosambi M. At the Intersection of Gender : Reform, Religion, Belief. Mumbai. SNDT. 1993.

✦ Kosambi M. Women's Oppression in The Public Gaze. RCWS. Mumbai. 1994.

✦ Kothari C.R. Research Methodology : Methods and Techniques. Wiley Eastern Ltd.. New Delhi. 1985

✦ Krishanaraj Maithreyi (ed.). Evolving New Methodologies in Research on Women's Studies. SNDT Women's University. Bombay. 1985.

✦ Krishnaraj Maithreyi. Women and Development : The Indian Experience. Subdhada Saraswati Publications. Bombay. 1988.

✦ Krishnaraj Maithreyi. Contributions to Women's Studies. SNDT Bombay. 1991

✦ Krishna Murthy. Women in Colonial India. Oxford University Press. New Delhi. 1989

✦ Krishna Sumi. Livelihood and Gender Equity in Community Resource Management. Sage. New Delhi. 2004.

✦ Krishnaraj Maithreyi (ed). Gender, population and deve-lopment. Oxford. New Delhi. 1999.

✦ Krishnaraj Maithreyi. Women Studies in India : Some Perspectives. Popular Prakashan. Bombay. 1986.

✦ Kumar Ajay. Marriage Laws in Indian Society. Manak Publications Pvt. Ltd. New Delhi 2005.

✦ Kumar Hajira, Jaimon Varghese. Women's Empowerment. Regency Publications. New Delhi. 2005.

✦ Kumar Mala. Writing the Women's movement. Zubaan. 2005

✦ Kumar R. Environmental Pollutions and Health Hazards in India. New Delhi. Ashish. 1985.

✦ Kumar Radha. The history of Doing. Zubaan. New Delhi. 1993.

✦ Kumar Vijay. Ed. Ghosh G.K. Environment and Women Development : Lessons from Third World. Ashish Publishing House. New Delhi. 1995.

✦ Kumba M. Bahati. Gender and Social Movements. Rawat Publications. New Delhi. 2003.

✦ Sangari Kumkum and Vaid Sudesh. Recasting Women: Essays in Colonial History. 1989.

✦ Kuriakose Tina. Womens rights movement—International dimensions and national experiences. Women's Link. 11(2). April-June 2005. p.10-15

✦ Lancaster R.N. and Leonardo M. (eds.). The Gender /Sexuality Reader : Culture, History Political Economy. New York. Routledge. 1997.

✦ Laureties De Teresa. (ed.). Feminist Studies/Critical Studies. The Macmillan Press Ltd. London 1986

✦ Lenin. Women and Mental Health. press N.V. 1985.

✦ Lerner Gerda. The Creation of Patriarchy. Oxford University Press. New Delhi. 1986.

✦ Lewin Ellen, Olesen Virginia. Women–Health & Healing : Toward A New Perspective. Tavistorck Publications. New York. 1985.

✦ Philip M. and Bagchi K.S.. The Endangered Half. Upalabhadi Pub. New Delhi. 1995.

✦ Macdonald Myra. Representing Women. London. Arnold. 1995.

✦ Mackinnon Katherine. 'Sexuality' in Linda J. Nicholson (ed.). The Second Wave : A Reader in Feminist Theory. Routledge. 1997. pp-158-180.

✦ Maddala G.S. Miller Helen. Micro Economics : Theory and Applications. New Delhi. Tata Mc Graw Hill. 1989.

✦ Maggie Human. Feminist Criticisms. Harvest Press. 1986.

✦ Maharani of Baroda and Mitra S.M. The position of women in Indian Life. Neeraj Publications. 1984.

✦ Chaudhri Maitrayee. Indian Women's movement : Reform and Revival. Radiant Publishers. 1993

✦ Majumdar Veena. Report on the committee on the Status of Women: Towards Equality. Journal of Women Studies. 1974.

✦ Manfred & Maxneef. Human Scale Development. The Apex Press. N. 1991.

✦ Mazumdar Vina. Symbols of Power : Studies on The Political Status of Women in India. New Delhi. 1979.

✦ Mehta Rama. Divorced Hindu Woman. Vikas Publishing House (Pvt.) Ltd. New Delhi. 1975.

✦ Mehta Sushila. Revolution and the Status of Women in India. Metropolitan Book Co. (P) Ltd. New Delhi. 1982.

✦ Mellor M. Feminism and Ecology. Cambridge. Polity. 1997.

✦ Menon Latika. Women Empowerment and Challenge of Change. New Delhi. Kanishka. 1998.

✦ Mies M. and Shiva. V. Eco-feminism. London. Zed Books. 1993.

✦ Mies Maria. Indian Women and Patriarchy. Concept Publishing Company. New Delhi. 1980.

✦ Miglani Deepak & Dinesh. Are women still abla? Legislative and judicial approach towards empowerment of women. Women's Link. 14(3). July-September 2008.

✦ Miglani Deepak. Role of legislation in women empowerment. Mahila Vidhi Bharati. No. 48. July-Deptember. 2006.

✦ Miglani Deepak. Some legal provisions to facilitate women's empowerment in India. Legal News and Views. 20(11). 2006. November.

- Mikkilsen B. Methods of Development Work & Research. London. Zed.1993.
- Mills Mary Beth. Gender and Inequality in the global labour force. Annual Review of Anthropology. 2003.
- Mishra Anupam and Tripathi Satyendra. Chipko Movement : Uttarakhand Women's Bid to Save Forest Wealth. Radhakrishna for People's Action. New Delhi. 1978.
- Mitchell Juliet and Ann Oakley. What is Feminism? Blackwell. UP. 1989.
- Mitter Swasti. Technological Changes and the Search for a New Paradigm for Women's Work—Gender, Technology and Development. United Nations. 1999.
- Mocormark C and Strathern M. Nature, Culture and Gender. CUP. 1980.
- Mody Perveez. The intimate state, love marriage and the law in Delhi. New Delhi. Routledge. 2008.
- Mohan I. Environmental Awareness and Urban Development. Ashish. New Delhi. 1988.
- Mohanty CT. Feminism Without Borders : Decolonising Theory Practising Solidarity. Duke Univ. 2003.
- Molyneux Maxine and Martha Nussbaum. eds. Gender Justice : Development and Rights. OUP. New Delhi. 2002.
- Mukherjee Roma. Women, Law and Free Legal Aid. Deep and Deep. New Delhi. 1999.
- Mukhopadhyay Swapna. In the Name of Justice : Women and Law in Society. Manohar. New Delhi. 1998.
- Mulvey Laura. Visual Pleasure and Narrative Cinema. Screen 16.3 Autumn 1975.
- Murthy Laxmi and Dasgupta Rajashri. Our pictures and our worlds. Oxford India Paperbacks. New Delhi. 2005.
- Myers K.A., Anderson C.D and Risman. Feminist Foundations London and United Kingdom. Sage. 1998.
- Naess A. Ecology, Community and Lifestyle. Trans. D. Rothernberg. Cambridge University Press. Cambridge. 1989.
- Nagla Bhupendra Kumar. Women, Crime and Law. Rawat. New Delhi. 1991.
- Nanda GL. Plans and Prospects of Social Welfare in India (1951-61). Planning Commission. Publication Division. Delhi. 1963.
- Nanda B.R. Indian Women (F ›m Purdah to Modernity). Radiant Publishers. New Delhi. 1990.
- Nandan R.(Ed). Indian Women : From Purdah to Modernity. Nehru Memorial Museum and Library and Vikas. Radiant Pub. New Delhi. 1990.
- Narrain Arvind. Rethinking citizenship : A queer journey. Indian Journal of Gender Studies. 14(1). January-April 2007.
- National Family Health Survey Reports.
- National Perspective Plan for Women. 1988-2000. Department of Women and Child Development. Ministry of HRD. New Delhi. 1988
- National Policy on Education 1986. Govt. of India. Ministry of Human Resources Development. Dept. of Education. New Delhi
- O'Connell Helen. Dedicated Lives : Women Organizing for A Fairer World. Oxford. U.K. Oxfam UK and Ireland. 1993.
- O'Leary V. Towards understanding Women. Books and Cole. Pub. Chicago. 1977.
- Oakely An. Sex, Gender and Society. Harper and Row. New York. 1972.
- Oakley An and Mitchell Juliet. What is Feminism? Basil Blckwell. UK. 1986.
- Omvedt Gail. Violence against Women : New Movements and New Theories in India. New Delhi. 1990.
- Pandey D. Empowerment of Women : Participatory Action Research Approach. RCWS. 1995.
- Parikh Indira J. and Kollan Bharti. Women Managers: From Myth to Reality. IIMA Research and Publication Department. 2004.
- Park J.R. and Park K. Text Book of Preventive and Social Medicines. Habalpure. M. S. Banarside. 1983.
- Parsons T. Family Socialisation and Interaction Process. Free press. 1955.
- Patel Surabhi P. Equality of Educational Opportunity in India : A Myth or Reality? National. Delhi. 1983.
- Patel Tulsi. Sex-Selective Abortion in India : Gender, Society and New Reproductive Technologies. Sage. New Delhi. 2007.
- Patel Tulsi. (Ed.). Sex selective Abortion in India : Gender, Society and New Reproductive Technologies. Sage. New Delhi. 2007.
- Pati R.N. Ed. Health, Environment and Development. Ashish Publishing House. New Delhi. 1992
- Penttinen Elina. Globalization, Prostitution and Sex-trafficking—Corporeal Politics. Routledge. 2008.
- Pereira Faustina. The fractured scales : The search for a Uniform Personal Code. Stree. Calcutta. 2002.
- Petchesky Rosalind Pollack. Gendering Health and Human Rights. Jed Book. London. 2003.

- Pillai J. K and Rajeswari. Readings in Women's Education. Mother Teresa Women's University. Chennai. 1988.
- Poonacha Veena. Understanding Violence. SNDT. Mumbai. 1990.
- Prasad Madhusudan. Anita Desai the Novelist. New Horizon. Allahabad. 1981.
- Raha Manish Kumar. Matriliny to Patriliny : A Study of the Rabha Society. Gyan Publishing House. New Delhi. 1989.
- Rajawat Mamta. Dalit Women–Issues and Perspectives. Anmol Pub. New Delhi. 2005.
- Rajeshwari Sunder Rajan. The scandal of the state : women, law and citizenship in postcolonial India. Permanent Black. Delhi. 2003.
- Rao Mohan. (Ed). The Unheard Scream : Reproductive Health and Women's Rights in India. Zubaan. New Delhi. 2004.
- Rao MSA. Social Movements in India. Manohar. New Delhi. 1979.
- Rege Sharmila. (Ed.). Sociology of Gender : The Challenge of Feminist Sociological Knowledge. Sage. New Delhi. 2003.
- Rendall Jane. The Origins of Modern Feminism, Women in Britain, France and the U.S.A. 1780-1860. The Women's Press. London. 1982.
- Report of the Committee on the Panchayati Raj Institutions. Ministry of Agriculture and Irrigation. Govt. of India. New Delhi. 1978.
- Rice D.G. Dual career : marriages-conflict and treatment. Free Press. N.Y. 1971.
- Rich Andrienne. Of Women Born—Motherhood as Experience and Institution. New York. 1976.
- Roberts Helen. (ed.). Feminist Research. Routledge & Kegan Paul. London. 1988.
- Roberts Herbert. (ed.). Doing Feminist Research. Rutledge and Kegan Paul. London. 1984.
- Rocheleau D. Thomas-Slayter B. and Wangari E. Feminsit Political Ecology : Global Issues and Local Experiences. Routledge. New York. 1996.
- Rohde Jon, Chatterjee Meera and Morley David Ed. Reaching Health for All. Oxford University Press. Bombay. 1993.
- Ruth Sheila. Issues in Feminism : An Introduction to Women's Studies. Mayfield Publishing Company. California. 1990.
- Saksena K.P. Human Rights : Perspective and Challenges. Lancers Books. New Delhi. 1994.
- Salleh A. Ecofeminism as Polity : Nature, Marx and the Postmodern. Zed Books. London.1997.
- Sarkar Lotika, Sivaramayya. B.(Ed.). Women and Law : Contemporary Problems. Vikas Publishing House Pvt. Ltd. New Delhi. 1994.
- Saxena Shobha. Crime against Women and Protective Laws. Deep and Deep. New Delhi. 1999.
- Sehgal B.P. Singh. Population Policy and the Law. Deep and Deep Publications. New Delhi. 1998.
- Sen Amartya. The Argumentative India : Writings on Indian History. Culture and Identity. Penguin. London. 2005.
- Sen Gita. Subordination and sexual control : A comparative view of the control of women. In Nalini Visvanathan. Lynn Duggan. Laurie Nisonoff (ed). Gender and Development Reader. Zubaan. 2005.
- Seth Leila. Uniform Civil Code: Towards gender justice. Vikasini. The Journal of Women's Empowerment. 20(1). January-March 2005.
- Seth Mira. Women and Development : The Indian Experience. Sage Publications Pvt. Ltd. New Delhi. 2001.
- Sahai Shailly. Social Legislation and Status of Hindu Women. Jaipur. Rawat. 1986.
- Sharabi H. Neopatriarchy : A theory of Distorted change in Arab Society. New York. OUP. 1988.
- Sharma and Patrick C. Mckenny. Divorce. Sage Publications. Delhi. 1988.
- Sharma B.N. Women and Education–Global Education Series. Commonwealth publishers. New Delhi. 1994.
- Sharma K.S. Social Stratification in India, Sage Publication. New Delhi. 1997.
- Sharma M.R. Perspectives on Feminism. Ritu. Jaipur. 2008.
- Sharma Ram S. Education of Women and Empowerment. Gyan Publishing House. New Delhi. 1996.
- Sharma Usha & Sharma B.M. Women's Education in Ancient and Medieval India. Inter India Publications. New Delhi. 1992.
- Sharma Usha. & B.M. Sharma. Women's Education in Modern India. Commonwealth Publishers. New Delhi. 1995.
- Shiva V. Staying Alive : Women, Ecology and Development. Zed Books. London. 1989.
- Shiva Vandana. Ecology and the Politics of Survival. Sage Publications. New Delhi. 1991.

- Shukla P.K. Nutritional Problems of India. Prentice Hall of India. New Delhi. 1982.
- Siddiqui M.H. Women and Education. Ashish publishing house. New Delhi.1992.
- Singh Alka. Women in Muslim Personal Law. Rawat. Jaipur. 1991.
- Singh Andrea, Menefee Kellers, Vittanen Anita (Eds.). Invisible Hands : Women in Home-Based. Rawat. New Delhi. 1985.
- Singh Jasbir and Vohra Anupama. Citizenship rights of women in Jammu and Kashmir : an uncertain future. Indian Journal of Gender Studies. 14(1). January-April 2007.
- Sood Sushma. Violence Against Women. Arihant Publishers. Jaipur. 1990.
- Souza De Alfred. (ed.). Women in Contemporary India. Manohar. Delhi. 1975.
- Spender Dale. (Ed). Feminist Theories : Three centuries of women's intellectual traditions. Pantheon Books. 1983.
- Sreen Poonam Smith. Accountability in Development Organizations. Sage Publications. New Delhi. 1995.
- Srinivas M.N. Village, Caste, Gender and Method : Essays in Indian Social Anthropology. OUP. Delhi. 1998.
- Stein R. New Perspective on Environmental Justice, Gender, Sexuality and Activism. Rutgers University Press. New Jersey. 2004.
- Steingraber S. Living Downstream : A Scientist's Personal Investigation of Cancer and the Environment. Vintage. New York. 1998.
- Stiver Lie. Suzanne and Virginia 0'Leary. (ed.). Storming the Tower : Women in The Academic World. New York.1999.
- Subha K. Women in Local Governance. RBSA Publishers. Jaipur. 1994
- Subrahmaniyan Lalitha. Women Scientists in the Third World : The Indian Experience. Sage. New Delhi. 1998.
- Swaminathan M. Principles of Nutrition and dietetics. Bangalore printing and publishing. Bangalore. 1986.
- Swarup Hemlata and Rajput Pam. Gender Dimensions of Environmental and Development Debate : The Indian Experience. in Stuart S. Nagel. (ed.). India's Development and Public Policy. Ashgate. Burlington. 2000.
- Tang Rose, Marie. Feminist Thought. Routledge. London. 1992.
- Thakur B.S., Binod C. Agarwal. Media Utilisation for the Development of Women and Children. Concept. New Delhi. 2004.
- Tharu Susie and Lalitha K. (ed). Women's Writing in India Vol. I and II. The Femisnit Press. New York. 1991.
- Tikoo P.N. Indian Women : A brief socio-cultural survey B.R. Publishing Corporation. Delhi. 1985.
- Towards Equality. Report of the Committee on Status of Women in India. Government of India. 1975.
- United Nations. Human Development Report.
- Upadhyay H.C. Status of Women in India. Anmol Pub. 1991.
- Usha V.T. Gender, Value and Signification. KRPLLD. CDS. 2003.
- Varghese Sheela. Employment of Women in the unorganized manufacturing sector. University Book House Private limited. Jaipur. 2003.
- Venkateshwara Sandhya. Environment, Development and the Gender Gap. Sage Publications. India Pvt. Ltd.. New Delhi. 1995.
- Walby Sylvia. Theorising Patriarchy. Sociology. 1989
- Wallace Tina and Candida March (ed.). Changing Perceptions : Writings on Gender and Development. Oxford. 1991.
- Warren Karen J. (ed.). Eco-feminism : Women, Culture and Nature. Bloomington. Indiana University Press. 1997.
- Warren K. Ecological Feminism. Routledge. New York. 1994.
- Wharton S. Amy. The Sociology of Gender : An Introduction to Theory and Research. (KeyThemes in Sociology) Blackwell Publishing. UK. Indian Reprint. Kilaso Books. New Delhi. 2005.
- Whyte R.O and Whyte P. The Women of Rural Asia. Westview. Colardo. 1982.
- Wignaraja Ponna. Women. Poverty and Resources. Sage Publications. New Delhi. 1990.
- Zollinger Janat, Giele. Women and the Futures : The changing role in America. Macmillan. London. 1979.
- Zoonen Van Lisbet. Feminist Media Studies. Sage. New Delhi. 1994.

❑❑❑

MODEL TEST PAPERS

UGC—WOMEN'S STUDIES

Model Test Paper-1

1. What concept refers to the ways in which society conveys to the individual its norms or expectations for his/her behaviour?
   A. Socialization
   B. Gender schema
   C. Gender scripts
   D. Gender stereotypes

2. Research by Oliver and Hyde (1993) suggests that one of the most significant gender differences in the area of sexuality is in:
   A. Incidence of premarital intercourse.
   B. Attitudes about casual sex.
   C. Acceptance of premarital intercourse.
   D. Experience of sexual dysfunction.

3. What is the normative gender?
   A. Whatever is considered normal for each gender.
   B. That which is normed to the population at large.
   C. Males in a male-dominated society
   D. An idealistic term that does not exist in the real world.

4. The structural functionalist perspective sees gender roles as a product of:
   A. The definitions we make of gender differences.
   B. The gravitation toward power between the "haves" and the "have nots."
   C. Social institutions.
   D. All of the above.

5. Which one of the following prenatal conditions causes an individual to think they are female when they are male?
   A. Congenital adrenal hyperplasia (CAH)
   B. Androgen-insensitive syndrome (AIS)
   C. Turner syndrome
   D. The mega male

6. A hierarchical system in which cultural, political, and economic structures are dominated by males is a(n) _______________.
   A. elite model
   B. patriarchy
   C. pluralist model
   D. the gendered division of labour

7. Gender roles refer to:
   A. Chromosomal and hormonal differences that cause inevitable differences in the behaviour of men and women.
   B. The rights, responsibilities, expectations, and relationships of women and men.
   C. The subordination of women based on the assumption of the superiority of men.
   D. None of the above.

8. Which of the following term refers to individuals' beliefs and actions that are rooted in anti-female prejudice and stereotypic beliefs?
   A. Gender socialization
   B. Institutionalized sexism
   C. Individual sexism
   D. Gender segregation

9. Linguistic sexism is a problem studied primarily by analysts using a(n) ___________ perspective.
   A. conflict
   B. feminist
   C. interactionist
   D. functionalist

10. The _______ perspective combines the exploitation of women by capitalism with patriarchy in home in its analysis of gender inequality:
    A. socialist feminist
    B. liberal feminist
    C. radical feminist
    D. democratic feminist

11. Contemporary ideologies have arisen to challenge traditional ones mainly because:
    A. Traditional ideologies bear no relevance to contemporary circumstances.
    B. Traditional ideologies were too optimistic in their assumptions about human nature.
    C. Traditional ideologies are vulnerable to the criticism that they rested on far-reaching. 'narratives' which over-simplify our complex world.
    D. People are no longer as interested in politics as they used to be

12. Postmodernists typically argue that:
A. 'Universalist' narratives which attempt to explain the world are invariably false.
B. The world is socially constructed in a variety of ways.
C. Differences of viewpoint should be celebrated not deplored.
D. All of the above.

13. All liberal feminists advocate:
A. The banning of sexually-explicit imagery.
B. Abortion on demand.
C. Equal treatment in the public sphere.
D. The strict segregation of the sexes.

14. The idea that feminist goals cannot be realized without the destruction of economic inequalities is associated with:
A. Liberal feminism B. Socialist feminism
C. Radical feminism D. Postmodernism

15. Why is postmodernism attractive to some feminists?
A. Both positions tend to be supported with a large quantity of pretentious jargon.
B. Postmodernists provide a vision for a more equal world.
C. Postmodernists are useful allies in campaigns of civil disobedience.
D. Postmodernism emphasizes difference and variety, as well as highlighting the importance of the private and the personal.

16. Why should environmentalism be distinguished from ecologism?
A. The latter has a more realistic view of the challenges facing the world.
B. The first argues for piecemeal change, while the second urges radical change.
C. Environmentalists are full-hearted supporters of economic growth, regardless of the cost.
D. Ecologists prefer plants to human beings.

17. Environmental reformism is based on:
A. An anthropocentric view of the world.
B. An apoplectic view of the world.
C. The view that the non-human parts of nature are of primary importance.
D. The view that claims about climate change have been seriously exaggerated.

18. Samuel Huntington is associated with:
A. 'The Clash of Civilisations'
B. 'The End of History'
C. 'The End of Ideology'
D. 'The New World Order'

19. One phase of feminist counseling vigorously communicates the goals and tenets of feminism- which includes (a) encouraging financial independence, (b) viewing women's problems as being influenced by external factors, and (c) suggesting that the client become involved in social action. That phase is which ONE of the following?
A. Radical B. Liberal
C. Moderate D. Fundamental

20. Which One of the following feminist theorist(s) said, regarding human growth and development, "Women organize their sense of identity, find existential meaning, achieve a sense of coherence and continuity, and are motivated in the context of a relationship."
A. Nancy Chodorow
B. Carol Gilligan
C. Jean Baker Miller
D. J.V. Jordan and J.L. Surrey

21. Which of the following best describes the concept of hegemonic masculinity?
A. The inherent promotion of feminine characteristics in society.
B. The social dominance of men over women that results from the designation of 'masculine' characteristics as more valued than 'feminine' characteristics.
C. The acknowledgment that gender identity exists in many forms and is not binary.
D. A universal norm that is non-changeable.

22. In which type of unemployment do the marginal productivity of the workers is zero?
A. Disguised Unemployment
B. Involuntary Unemployment
C. Seasonal Unemployment
D. Structural Unemployment

23. What type of unemployment is found in the agriculture sector of India?
A. Disguised Unemployment
B. Voluntary Unemployment
C. Frictional Unemployment
D. None of the above

24. Who developed the concept of disguised unemployment?
A. John Keynes
B. Amartya Sen
C. John Robinson
D. Alfred Marshall

25. Who are counted in the labour force of a country?
    A. The population of 18 to 60 years of age.
    B. The population of 15 to 65 years of age.
    C. The population of 18 to 65 years of age.
    D. The population of 21 to 62 years of age.

26. Women-owned businesses may be smaller than those owned by men because they:
    A. Cannot find good quality training programs.
    B. Have a more difficult time finding employees.
    C. Do not have equal access to capital.
    D. Do not have as much management experience as men.

27. Madam C.J. Walker was:
    A. The first black female millionaire.
    B. The first successful Hispanic entrepreneur.
    C. The first successful Asian-American entrepreneur.
    D. None of the above.

28. __________ implies that women entrepreneurs are now economically independent and take decisions independently.
    A. Better utilization of resources
    B. Improved quality life
    C. Economic development
    D. Employment generation

29. There is increasing concern about the importance of adequate nutrition in the pre-conception period to support a successful pregnancy. This is because:
    A. In the embryonic period, the foetus is vulnerable to external factors in its environment.
    B. The embryonic period often occurs before a woman knows she is pregnant.
    C. Interventions in late pregnancy may be too late to be effective.
    D. All of the options given are correct.

30. How many calories should a woman should eat each day during pregnancy?
    A. Less than 200 kCal
    B. An additional 200 kCal in the third trimester only
    C. An additional 200 kCal throughout pregnancy
    D. No change from pre-pregnant levels

31. How can smoking affect breastfeeding?
    A. Suppresses milk production.
    B. Alters the composition of breast milk.
    C. Increases the risk of early cessation of breast-feeding.
    D. All of the options given are correct.

32. Infants born to vegan mothers may be at increased risk of deficiency of which nutrient?
    A. Vitamin C B. Folate
    C. Vitamin B12 D. Calcium

33. Which of the following would be considered components of Public Health Nutrition?
    A. Dietary guidelines.
    B. Nutritional Epidemiology.
    C. Fortification of foods with vitamins and minerals
    D. All of the options listed are correct

34. In what ways can governments promote proper nutrition?
    A. Surveys to monitor nutrition.
    B. Publishing dietary guidelines.
    C. Legislating against false claims.
    D. All of the options listed are correct.

35. Which of the following are highly prevalent global nutrition problems?
    A. Vitamin A deficiency.
    B. Undernutrition.
    C. Obesity.
    D. All of the options listed are correct.

36. In which of the following regions of the world have both the number and prevalence of undernourishment declined over the last quarter century?
    A. Asia B. Africa
    C. Oceania D. All of the above

37. Which group of the global population is most affected by anemia?
    A. Preschool children B. Pregnant women
    C. Nonpregnant women D. Men

38. What is the global prevalence of obesity in adult men and women?
    A. 11% of men; 15% of women.
    B. 6% of men; 20% of women.
    C. 27% of men; 34% of women.
    D. 45% of men; 36% of women.

39. Indirect or nutrition sensitive interventions include:
    A. Vitamin D supplements.
    B. Increasing crop yields.
    C. Improving weaning foods.
    D. All of the above.

40. Causes of malnutrition can be classified as immediate, underlying and root causes. Which of the following would be in the underlying cause?
    A. Low wages.
    B. Unclean drinking water.
    C. Sedentary lifestyle.
    D. All of the options listed are correct.

41. What is eLENA?
A. A North American learning and education system.
B. An online slimming method.
C. A WHO database.
D. A method for reducing fat in commercial products.

42. After which incident have family planning programs been initiated in most countries?
A. After the industrial revolution.
B. After World War 2.
C. After British invasion to India.
D. After the United States independence.

43. Which one of the following is the main target of family welfare programs?
A. Couples in the fertile age.
B. Children below 12 years.
C. Women after fertile age.
D. Male after fertile age.

44. Which organization works as an administrative unit for implementation of Family Welfare Programme in all districts of the State and functioning at State Headquarter?
A. The District Family Welfare Bureau.
B. The National Family Welfare Bureau.
C. The State Family Welfare Bureau.
D. The International Family Welfare Bureau.

45. Which one of the following is the activity of the Family Welfare Programme?
A. Malnutrition programme
B. Child marriage.
C. IUD programme.
D. One child one nation policy

46. What is the main aim of Janani Suraksha Yojana which is the programme by the Family Welfare programme?
A. To provide pensions to widows.
B. To provide shelters to poor people.
C. To encourage people to use safe sexual methods.
D. Reducing maternal and neonatal mortality.

47. When did Janani Suraksha Yojana launch?
A. 2000 B. 2005
C. 2010 D. 2015

48. Which is the first country to initiate a Family Planning program in the world?
A. Brazil B. Pakistan
C. India D. France

49. When was the Family Planning Insurance Scheme introduced?
A. 2003 B. 2005
C. 2007 D. 2009

50. Which is the first State in India to recognize the basic relevance of family planning to nation planning?
A. Kerala B. Goa
C. Karnataka D. Tamil Nadu

51. Why is family planning important?
A. For birth control issues.
B. For having unwanted pregnancies.
C. For having a child every year.
D. To get pregnant before the age of twenty.

52. In a Hormonal method of family planning, maximum how many hormones are included?
A. One B. Two
C. Three D. Four

53. In analytic induction, what happens if the researcher finds a deviant case?
A. They ignore it and carry on.
B. They must either redefine or reformulate the hypothesis.
C. They conduct a parametric statistical test.
D. They give up and decide to be quantitative researchers instead.

54. Which of the following is not a tool of grounded theory?
A. Theoretical sampling
B. Coding
C. External validity
D. Constant comparison

55. What do Strauss & Corbin mean by "open coding"?
A. Breaking data down and examining it to identify themes and concepts.
B. Coding without the intention of building a theory.
C. Drawing open brackets alongside keywords and phrases.
D. Telling everybody about the way you have coded the data.

56. What is a "substantive theory" in Strauss & Corbin's view?
A. One that operates at the highest level of abstraction.
B. One that is highly controversial and provokes a critical response.
C. One that relates to an empirical instance or substantive topic area.
D. One that is amenable to statistical analysis.

57. What are memos?

A. Notes that researchers write to themselves.

B. Reminders of what is meant by key terms or phrases

C. Building blocks for theorizing

D. All of the above

58. Why should you start coding your data as soon as possible?

A. To sharpen your focus and help with theoretical sampling.

B. Because researchers always run out of time at the end of a project.

C. Because it is the easiest task to do.

D. To make sure that your initial theoretical ideas are imposed on the data.

59. Why are Coffey & Atkinson critical of the way coding fragments qualitative data?

A. Because this is incompatible with the principles of feminist research.

B. Because it results in a loss of context and narrative flow.

C. Because they think it should fragment quantitative data instead.

D. Because they invented the life history interview and want to promote it.

60. What do advocates of narrative analysis prefer to study?

A. The extent to which analytic induction can be value-free.

B. The iterative process of grounded.

C. The ethical implications of conducting a secondary analysis of qualitative data.

D. The ways in which people use stories to make sense of events in their lives.

61. What is a narrative analysis?

A. A literary approach to documents.

B. An approach that is sensitive to questions that concern how people choose to sequence and represent people and events.

C. A form of thematic analysis.

D. A method of improving the quality of interview material.

62. What is one of the main ethical problem associated with conducting a secondary analysis of qualitative data?

A. The participants may not have given informed consent to the reuse of their data.

B. It involves deceiving respondents about the nature of the research.

C. The secondary analyst must adopt a covert role and is at risk of "going native."

D. Respondents are likely to experience physical harm as a result of the process

63. What are Scott's four criteria for assessing the quality of documents?

A. Objectivity, subjectivity, authenticity, and value.

B. Comprehensiveness, accuracy, value, and rigor.

C. Authenticity, credibility, representativeness, and meaning.

D. Credibility, reliability, accuracy, and meaning.

64. What is the chief strength of semiotics?

A. It lets the researcher see beyond everyday situations.

B. It is an impressive research tool which demonstrates your research skill to an external examiner.

C. It is a novel approach to research.

D. It is a different approach which researchers are usually unsure of.

65. Why might a collection of personal letters from the early twentieth century be low in representativeness?

A. Because it would be difficult to read old-fashioned styles of handwriting.

B. Because it can be hard for a modern day researcher to understand such materials.

C. Because they are protected under the Right-to-Privacy legislation.

D. Because they were preserved by a small number of powerful companies only.

66. Why might business researchers be interested in analyzing photographs as a form of visual data?

A. They are interesting to look at.

B. To study the way photographs were taken by the photographer.

C. To help them to see what has not been photographed and why.

D. All of the above.

67. Which of the following is not an example of an official document?

A. A report of a public inquiry into government finances.

B. A Ph.D. student's collection of interview transcripts.

C. Documentation from a pharmaceutical company about a new drug.

D. A leaked memo from one member of parliament to another.

68. Which of the following can be studied as a documentary source from the mass media?

A. The minutes of a company's board meeting.
B. Correspondence between an employee and an employer.
C. Newspaper articles about a particular issue or event.
D. The staff newsletter produced by a private company.

69. Why can it be challenging to establish the authenticity of virtual data?
A. Because we do not know who wrote the material on a web site.
B. Because virtual data are not as good as proper data.
C. Because it may require specialist "inside knowledge" to understand the text.
D. Because it is usually written using 'webspeak.'

70. Why is it important to study the way audiences "read" cultural documents?
A. To demonstrate how audiences passively accept whatever they are told.
B. Because their interpretation of it may differ from that intended by the author.
C. Because sociologists are running out of new things to research.
D. Because there is a lot of funding available for focus group studies.

71. How does qualitative content analysis differ from the quantitative content analysis?
A. It is always preceded by ethnographic research.
B. It involves counting the number of times certain words appear in a text.
C. It is less rigid, as researchers are constantly revising their concepts.
D. It is less likely to be used by feminist researchers.

72. What is semiotics?
A. The study of semi-detached houses.
B. A half-baked attempt at social research.
C. The method of semi-structured interviewing.
D. The science of signs.

73. The concept of a "media iceberg" regarding digitization of media refers to?
A. The slow speed of change seen in major media organizations.
B. The way that traditional media organizations are heading toward a figurative "iceberg" that will eventually sink them.
C. The so-called media "ice age" that was experienced in the era of mass communication during most of the twentieth century.
D. The changes seen in the production of content from largely analog to largely digital production and distribution.

74. Critical theory can be defined as:
A. A theoretical approach broadly influenced by Marxist notions of ideology, exploitation, and the economy in understanding and eventually transforming society.
B. A theoretical approach taken by researchers who do not believe that traditional scientific methods hold any value for media studies.
C. A theoretical approach in which the researcher looks for any weaknesses in proposed theories and attempts to debunk them.
D. A research method that breaks down the components of communication in a minute and exacting scientific detail.

75. The core model of communication has been criticized for its:
A. Negligence of people in the process, and potential for media corruption.
B. Oversimplification and potential for information deviance.
C. Oversimplification, and potential for media corruption.
D. Negligence of media in the process, and potential for information deviance.

76. Opinion leaders and opinion formers are an integral part of which model of communication:
A. Influencer
B. Interactional
C. Relational
D. Linear

77. Messengers perceived to be physically attractive lead to two main outcomes. These Ads:
A. Promote strong engagement and improved responses.
B. Stimulate involvement and increased recall.
C. Are more easily recognized and promote positive associations.
D. Attract more attention and are evaluated more positively.

78. There are two particular influences on the communication process. These are:
A. Culture and technology.
B. Systems and people.
C. Media and people.
D. Media and technology.

79. Littlejohn (1992) identifies four main contexts within which communication occurs. These are:
A. interpersonal, group, organizational and linear communication.
B. interpersonal, group, organizational and relational communication.
C. interpersonal, group, organizational and interactional communication.
D. interpersonal, group, organizational and mass communication

80. In studying how media's influence is affected by people's intelligence and education, individual differences theory is an example of the era of:
A. Limited effects.
B. Mass society theory.
C. Cultural theory.
D. None of these.

81. Klapper's reinforcement theory argues that:
A. Only selected, especially well-crafted, media messages can influence a reinforcement.
B. Media have little power, but what influence they do have is in the form of reinforcement.
C. Media are quite powerful, especially in the realm of reinforcement.
D. None of these.

82. A paradigm is
A. An idea that explains or predicts only limited aspects of the mass communication process.
B. Another name for grand social theory.
C. A theory that summarizes and is consistent with all known facts.
D. None of these.

83. The leading case on the abolition of triple talaq is:
A. Shayara Bano v. Union of India and Others.
B. Mohd. Ahmed Khan v. Shah Bano Begum
C. Danial Latifi and anothers v. U.O.I
D. Shamim Ara v. the State of U.P.

84. If the women entitled to maternity benefit or any other amount dies before receiving such amount and maternity benefit, the amount will be paid to.
A. Her father
B. Her mother
C. The person nominated by the women in the notice under section 6
D. The person nominated by the women in the notice under section 6 and in case there is no such nominee to her legal representative.

85. Under which article of Indian constitution equal pay for equal work is given?
A. Article 39 (a) B. Article 39(c)
C. Article 39(e) D. Article 39(d)

86. The Scheduled Tribes and Other Traditional Forest Dwellers (Recognition of Forest Rights) Act was passed in the year:
A. 2006 B. 2007
C. 2008 D. 2009

87. Under the Scheduled Tribes and Other Traditional Forest Dwellers (Recognition of Forest Rights) Act, 2006, who shall be the authority to initiate the process for determining the nature and extent of individual or community forest rights or both?
A. State Forest Department.
B. District Collector/Deputy Commissioner.
C. Tahsildar/Block Development Officer /Mandal Revenue Officer.
D. Gram Sabha.

88. When was the sexual harassment of women at workplace (prevention, prohibition & redressal) act 2013 came into force?
A. 9th December 2013
B. 19th December 2013
C. 19th November 2013
D. 19th January 2013

89. Who will get the benefit of maternity benefit act, 1961 if the woman dies during delivery?
A. Legal heirs B. Mother
C. Husband D. Children

90. Who has written 'A Vindication of the Rights of Women'?
A. Harriet Taylor B. Sojourner Truth
C. Mary Wollstonecraft D. Mary Shelly

91. Who founded the Self Employed Women's Association (SEWA)?
A. Ela Bhatt B. Medha Patkar
C. Sucheta Kriplani D. Vina Mazumdar

92. Rukma Bai is famous for:
A. Age of Consent Bill
B. Child Marriage Act
C. Hindu Code Bill
D. Sharda Act

93. 'That Long Silence' is written by:
A. Shashi Deshpande B. Anita Desai
C. Salman Rushdie D. Fatima Bhutto

94. The Indecent Representation of Women (Prohibition) Act,1986 enacted to prohibit:
A. Indecent representation of women through the only advertisement.

B. Indecent representation of women through publications, writings, paintings, figures or in any other manner.
C. Indecent representation of women through advertisement or in publications, writings, paintings, figures or in any other manner.
D. None of the above.

95. When did India ratify the CEDAW convention?
A. 1993 B. 1992
C. 1994 D. 1995

96. Child Marriage Restraint Act 1929 was replaced by:
A. The Prohibition of Child Marriage Act 2006
B. The Prohibition of Child Marriage Act 1978
C. The Child Marriage Restraint Act 1974
D. None

97. The Universal Declaration of Human Rights was adopted by the United Nations on:
A. 10 December 1947
B. 10 December 1948
C. 1 August 1950
D. 15 September 1945

98. When was the Hindu Succession Act amended?
A. 9th September 2005.
B. 9th August 2005.
C. 19th August 2005.
D. 9th August 1956.

99. Centre for Women's Development Studies is located in:
A. Mumbai B. Delhi
C. Kolkata D. Hyderabad

100. Founder of Bombay Talkies is:
A. Devika Rani B. Satyajeet Ray
C. Prithvi Raj Kapoor D. Guru Dutt

ANSWERS

1	2	3	4	5	6	7	8	9	10
A	B	C	C	B	B	B	C	C	A
11	**12**	**13**	**14**	**15**	**16**	**17**	**18**	**19**	**20**
C	D	C	B	D	B	A	A	A	D
21	**22**	**23**	**24**	**25**	**26**	**27**	**28**	**29**	**30**
B	A	A	C	B	C	A	B	D	B
31	**32**	**33**	**34**	**35**	**36**	**37**	**38**	**39**	**40**
D	C	D	D	D	A	A	A	B	D
41	**42**	**43**	**44**	**45**	**46**	**47**	**48**	**49**	**50**
C	B	A	B	C	D	B	C	B	D
51	**52**	**53**	**54**	**55**	**56**	**57**	**58**	**59**	**60**
A	B	B	C	A	C	D	A	B	D
61	**62**	**63**	**64**	**65**	**66**	**67**	**68**	**69**	**70**
B	A	C	A	D	D	B	C	A	B
71	**72**	**73**	**74**	**75**	**76**	**77**	**78**	**79**	**80**
C	D	D	A	A	A	D	C	D	A
81	**82**	**83**	**84**	**85**	**86**	**87**	**88**	**89**	**90**
B	C	A	D	D	A	D	A	A	C
91	**92**	**93**	**94**	**95**	**96**	**97**	**98**	**99**	**100**
A	A	A	C	A	A	B	A	B	A

❑❑❑

Model Test Paper-2

1. First woman Managing Director and Chief Executive Officer of India's leading stock exchange National Stock Exchange was:

A. Kiran Mazumdar Shaw
B. Arundhati Bhattacharya
C. Chitra Ramakrishna
D. Chanda Kochhar

2. Citizens enjoy equal rights in ________?

A. Autocratic country
B. Communist country
C. Republic country
D. None

3. The entire month of March is celebrated as 'Women's History Month' in which country?

A. Russia B. Britain
C. China D. United States

4. In which year did the women's movement start in the USA?

A. 1848 B. 1989
C. 1891 D. 1988

5. Which of the following under ICDS are delivered through Public Health Infrastructure under the Ministry of Health & Family Welfare?

1. Immunization
2. Supplementary nutrition
3. Health check-up
4. Sanitation

Codes:

A. 1 & 3 are correct
B. 1 & 2 are correct
C. 2 & 3 are correct
D. All the above are correct

6. Who was the first Woman Doctor of India?

A. Subha Lakhsmi B. Aruna Asif Ali
C. Anandi Bai Gopal D. Raziya Sultan

7. The Safe motherhood intervention under the National Rural Health Mission (NRHM) launched in 2005 is popularly known as:

A. Matritva Vikas Yojna
B. Janani Suraksha Yojana
C. Balika Samriddhi Yojna
D. Women's Helpline

8. The Government of India enacted the Commission of Sati (Prevention) Act in the year:

A. 1987 B. 1829
C. 1940 D. 1941

9. Shobhana Bharatia is associated with which organization?

A. Hindustan Times Group
B. ICICI Bank
C. Axis Bank
D. HSBC

10. Which Amendment to the US Constitution granted the right to vote to women?

A. The Nineteenth Amendment
B. The Sixteenth Amendment
C. The Fifteenth Amendment
D. The Thirty-first Amendment

11. An inclusive worldwide movement to end sexism and sexist oppression by empowering women is termed as:

A. Male bashing B. Anti Sexism
C. Gynocentrism D. Feminism

12. What was the title of the report of the committee on the status of women commissioned by the government of India?

A. Towards Equality
B. Inequality Revisited
C. Equal Opportunities Commission
D. Equal Rights

13. First Woman Prime Minister in the World:

A. Indira Gandhi
B. Sirimavo Bandaranaike
C. Isabel Perin
D. Ellen Johnson Sirleaf

14. Every year Women's day is celebrated on:
A. 8th March B. 10th December
C. 26th January D. 14th February

15. Changes to the natural greenhouse effect are a result of which of the following human-made emissions of Green House Gases?
A. Nitrous Oxide (N_2O)
B. Hydro & Perfluorocarbons
C. Sulphur Hexafluoride (SF_6)
D. All of the above

16. Patriarchy is central to which of the following kinds of feminism?
A. Black feminism
B. Marxist Feminism
C. First wave feminism
D. Radical Feminism

17. First Indian woman to win the title of International Grand Master of Chess:
A. Punita Arora
B. P.V. Sindhu
C. Bhagya Shree Thipse
D. Bachendri Pal

18. Who is the author of 'A Room of One's Own'?
A. Virginia Woolf B. M. Devi
C. Mary Wollstone Craft D. Kiran Bedi

19. National Human Right Commission was established in which year:
A. 1991 B. 1992
C. 1993 D. 1994

20. The Male-Female sex ratio in India as per 2011 census is:
A. 940 females per 1000 males
B. 900 females per 1000 males
C. 930 females per 1000 males
D. 980 females per 1000 males

21. The report of the National Commission on Self Employed Women and Women in the Informal Sector (1988) is called as
A. Towards Equality Report
B. Verma Committee Report
C. Sacchar Committee Report
D. Shramshakti Report

22. Who became the first woman to head the State Bank of India?
A. Arundhati Bhattacharya
B. Chanda Kochhar
C. Indra Nooyi
D. Naina Lal Kidwai

23. Who was appointed Chairperson of the commission appointed in the aftermath of the gang rape in Delhi, tasked with reforming and invigorating anti-rape law?
A. Jagdish Sharan Verma
B. Urvashi Bhutalia
C. C. Lakshmana
D. Ushaben Mehta

24. Who is the author of 'The Accidental Prime Minister'?
A. Sanjaya Barua B. Manmohan Singh
C. Shashi Tharur D. Jitendra Bhargawa

25. Which article is known as Soul of Indian Constitution?
A. Article 32 B. Article 19
C. Article 29 D. Article 15

26. Which of the following statements is/are correct about Integrated Child Development Services (ICDS)?
1. ICDS is aimed at children under five years of age.
2. It also includes their mothers.
3. The scheme was launched in 1981.
4. Under the scheme, the mid-day meal is provided to children in schools.

Codes:
A. Only 1 is correct
B. Only 2 is correct
C. Both are correct
D. None is correct

27. In which year was the report Towards Equality released?
A. 1993 B. 1974
C. 1919 D. 1995

28. NCERT stands for:
A. National Committee for Educational Research and Training
B. National Committee for Educational Research and Teaching
C. National Council of Educational Research and Teaching
D. National Council of Educational Research and Training

29. Which among the following book is written by the famous activist, Aung San Suu Kyi?
A. Freedom in Exile
B. The Algebra of Infinite Justice
C. Freedom from Fear
D. Untouchable

30. Which of the following cases triggered off the movement against rape in the 1980s?
A. Mathura Case B. Ruchika Case
C. Shah Bano Case D. Bhavari Devi Case

31. In which of the following years the famous National Policy on Education (NPE) was formulated:
A. 1996 B. 1986
C. 1982 D. 1992

32. Who is the executive head and famously known as the first citizen of India:
A. The Prime Minister
B. The President
C. The Governor
D. The Chief Justice of India

33. In which year did the mid-decade UN Conference on women take place?
A. 1995 B. 1975
C. 1945 D. 1980

34. Given below are the places where the four UN World Conference on women took place. Rank them in chronological order:
(i) Mexico (ii) Beijing
(iii) Nairobi (iv) Copenhagen
Codes:
A. (i), (iv), (iii), (ii) B. (i), (ii) (iii), (iv)
C. (iv), (iii), (ii), (i) D. (iii), (ii), (i), (iv)

35. Which among the following is known as the 'academic arm of women's movement':
A. Women's Biographies
B. Feminist Epistemology
C. Women's Studies
D. Feminist Postmodernism

36. Which of the following articles of the constitution stands for a Uniform Civil Code?
A. Article 44 B. Article 38
C. Article 14 D. Article 46

37. In order to reinforce the patriarchal ideologies, the state adopts a policy of non-interference in:
A. Familial Sphere B. Economic Sphere
C. Political Sphere D. Social Sphere

38. The study of old people which aims to create a social consciousness is known as:
A. Objectivity B. Gerontology
C. Subjectivity D. Alienation

39. Who proclaimed "Truth is God"?
A. BR Ambedkar
B. Mahatma Gandhi
C. Jawarlal Nehru
D. Sir Syed Ahmed Khan

40. Roop Kanwar was famous because:
A. She was a Dalit woman and was raped in police custody.
B. She retaliated against her in-laws against the atrocities for dowry and lodged a case against them.
C. Khap panchayats punished her for being involved in love with a lower-caste boy.
D. She was forced to commit Sati to prove her chastity.

41. The first elected woman president of Congress party in independent India was:
A. Sarojini Naidu B. Vijaya Lakshmi Pandit
C. Indira Gandhi D. Sonia Gandhi

42. Who said that 'Women are Passive Citizens?'
A. Rosseau B. Kiran Desai
C. Hobbes D. Emmanuel Kant

43. The National Federation of Indian Women was formed in:
A. 1952 B. 1954
C. 1956 D. 1958

44. Article 42 of the Constitution deals with which of the following areas
A. Maternity
B. Equality
C. Child Labour
D. Right against exploitation

45. Who was the chairperson of the Committee for the Status of Women in India, constituted in 1971:
A. Veena Mazumdar
B. Lotika Sarkar
C. Hansa Mehta
D. Phulrenu Guha

46. Cairo Conference held in 1994 is famous for raising the issue of:
A. Feminization of the employment market.
B. Women and Political Development.
C. Property rights for women.
D. Reproductive rights for women.

47. New Education Policy in India was passed in the year:
A. 1956 B. 1966
C. 1976 D. 1986

48. Which Section of Indian Penal Code deals with the issue of rape:
A. Section 375 B. Section 393
C. Section 220 D. Section 498

49. Which of the following women's organizations was founded in pre-Independence India?
A. AIWC B. AIDWA
C. SEWA D. NCW

50. Eco-feminist means:
A. Feminist who is very vocal for women's rights.
B. Feminist who believes that the destruction of nature is a patriarchal agenda.
C. A woman economist.
D. Economist of female work.

51. Misogyny is:
A. A woman who hates men.
B. A man who hates women.
C. A person having mistaken gender identity.
D. A person who hates the third gender.

52. A surrogate mother is a woman:
A. Whose children are adopted by other's mother.
B. A woman who nurtured the child of her relative.
C. A woman who is hired for the care of an infant.
D. A woman who carry in their womb ovum of another person

53. The first World Summit to end sexual violence against women took place in:
A. London B. Paris
C. Lisbon D. New York

54. When was India's First woman Bank 'Bhartiya Mahila Bank' founded?
A. 2013 B. 1975
C. 1995 D. 2010

55. Which of the following cases was pertaining to sexual harassment at the workplace?
A. Apparel Export Promotion Council V A.K. Chopra
B. Nargesh Mirza vs. AIR India
C. Madhu Kishwar vs. the State of Bihar
D. Gaurav Jain V Union of India

56. What year did the United Nations adopt CEDAW?
A. 1975 B. 1978
C. 1979 D. 1993

57. Muslims of India primarily follow the Sunni Law of inheritance, which is based upon:
A. Hanafi doctrine B. Maliki doctrine
C. Deeni doctrine D. Imani doctrine

58. National Credit Fund for women is also called:
A. Nari Mukti Kosh
B. Rashtriya Nari Sewa Kosh
C. Rashtriya Bachat Kosh
D. Rashtriya Mahila Kosh

59. Which of the following sections of the Indian Penal Code deals with sexual harassment?
A. Section 154 B. Section 234 b
C. Section 354 a D. Section 276 b

60. Who authored 'The Second Sex'?
A. Mary Astell B. Rebecca Walker
C. Simone de Beauvoir D. Margret Fuller

61. First Indian woman scientist to head a Missile Project in India 'Missile Woman of India'?
A. Tessy Thomas B. Radhika Balakrishna
C. Janaki Ammal D. Sunita Willams

62. In which year the Hindu Succession Act was amended:
A. 2000 B. 2005
C. 2006 D. 2007

63. For Hindu law of succession, there are two famous doctrines prevail in the country?
A. Dayabhaga and Mitakshara school of law
B. Veda and Purana school of law
C. Smriti and Gita school of law
D. Ramayana and Mahabharata school of law

64. A branch of political science which deals with the study and scientific analysis of elections?
A. Psephology B. Psychology
C. Zoology D. Anthropology

65. Sexism is not prevalent in societies which are:
A. Patriarchal B. Ethnocentric
C. Egalitarian D. Matriarchal

66. Who authored the book 'Female Eunuch'?
A. Jhumpa Lahiri B. Shobhna Narayana
C. Virginia Woolf D. Germaine Greer

67. What is the Shah Bano Judgement famous for?
A. Post Divorce Maintenance
B. Domestic Violence
C. Changes in rape laws
D. Dowry laws

68. Who is the founder of the political party All India Trinamool Congress?
A. Vijaya Raje Scindhia B. Mamta Banerjee
C. Janaki Patel D. Nira Ben Patel

69. P.V Sindhu is associated with which sport?
A. Badminton B. Boxing
C. Tennis D. Cricket

70. In the Name of Honour: A Memoir is written by
A. Mukhtar Mai B. Tehmima Durrani
C. Kiran Desai D. Ayesha Jalal

71. A woman dacoit who became a member of the Parliament was:
A. Phulan Devi B. Putli Bai
C. Jagat Mai D. None of these

72. Which constitutional amendment provided reservation of seats for women in panchayats and local bodies?
A. 71st Amendment B. 73rd Amendment
C. 75th Amendment D. 91st Amendment

73. The first woman judge of the SC of India was?
A. Leela Seth B. Fathima Bibi
C. Indira Jaising D. Justice Verma

74. The 'primary authority' in the family under Patriarchy, rests with:

A. Father B. Mother
C. Maternal Uncle D. Village Headman

75. Humayunama is authored by:

A. Noorjahan B. Razia Sultan
C. Gulbadan Begum D. Salima Begum

76. This lady is the founder of one of the first biotech company of India and rated as the richest woman in India?

A. Kiran Mazumdar Shaw
B. Lalita D. Gupta
C. Prabhavati Shule
D. Nirmal Godrej

77. Which one of the following is a Black Feminist?

A. Bell Hooks B. Rosemary Tong
C. Simon de Beauvoir D. Mary Astle

78. AITUC is acronym of:

A. All India Trade Union Council
B. All India Trade Union Conference
C. All India Trade Union Congress
D. All India Trade Union Convention

79. Who is the founding editor of Manushi?

A. Rajeshwari Sunder Rajan
B. Madhu Kishwar
C. Flavia Agnes
D. Indira Jaising

80. Shri Mahila Griha Udyog Lijjat Papad, a model attempt to make women economically self-reliant was begun in:

A. 1955 B. 1957
C. 1959 D. 1961

81. Uma Soren, the first woman M.P from the Santhal community, is a member of:

A. Jharkhand Mukti Morcha
B. Trinamool Congress
C. BJP
D. Biju Janata Dal

82. Who coined the term 'third wave feminism'?

A. Mary Dally B. Germaine Greer
C. Rebecca Walker D. Lucy Stone

83. First Dada Saheb Phalke award was won by?

A. Jatin Lalit B. Dada Saheb Phalke
C. Dileep Kumar D. Devika Rani

84. 'The state of martial rule: the origins of Pakistan's political economy of defense' is authored by:

A. Ayesha Jalal B. Tasleema Nasreen
C. Tehmima Durrani D. Saadat Hasan Manto

85. Which of the following sections of the IPC deals with cruelty on wife:

A. Section 498a B. Section 304b
C. Section 376 D. Section 789

86. Which of the following sections of the Indian Penal Code deals with sexual harassment

A. Section 154 B. Section 234 b
C. Section 354 a D. Section 276 b

87. Which of the following constitutional provisions deals with equality before the law?

A. Article 14 B. Article 21
C. Article 19 D. Article 17

88. Janaki Ammal was:

A. Indian Botanist B. Feminist Philosopher
C. Sportsperson D. Politician

89. Which among the following is not a correct statement regarding Jyotiba Phule?

A. He used Dalit word for the first time in the nineteenth century.
B. He was the staunch supporter of Mahatma Gandhi's Harijan Sevak Sangh.
C. He is known as the author of Gulamgiri.
D. He formed Satyashodhak Samaj in 1873.

90. Nawab Sultan Jahan Begum, First chancellor of AMU and one of the leading figure in the field of promoting female education among the Muslims, was the Begum of:

A. Pahasu (Aligarh) B. Hyderabad
C. Sardhana (Meerut) D. Bhopal

91. Name the author of 'My Feudal Lord'?

A. Tehmima Durrani B. Ayesha Jalal
C. Bapsi Sidwa D. Madhu Kishwar

92. Anjolie Ela Menon is a famous woman of India having excellence in the field of:

A. Sports B. Media
C. Acting D. Painting

93. Who was Khadija?

A. The first wife of the prophet Muhammad.
B. The first Abbasid caliph.
C. A twentieth-century reformer.
D. A modern Egyptian woman who took off her headscarf.

94. Who was the founder of the American Liberal Feminist magazine 'Ms.'?

A. Gloria Steinem B. Susan B Antony
C. Alison Jaggar D. Jane Freedman

95. The first woman Prime Minister of England:

A. Margaret Thatcher B. Theresa May
C. Nicky Morgan D. Justine Greening

96. The Hindu Succession Act 2005 grants daughters:
A. Equal share in coparcenary property.
B. Half share in coparcenary property.
C. 1/3 share in coparcenary property.
D. No share in coparcenary property.

97. The first woman to climb Mount Everest was:
A. Malavath Purna B. Junko Tabei
C. Tamae Watanabe D. Arunima Sinha

98. Honor killing has been explained as a brutal and barbaric death met out to a woman on bringing dishonor to the family, class or community by :
(a) Marrying against the wishes of the parents.
(b) Having extra-marital and pre-marital relations
(c) Entering into wedlock within the same gotra or outside one's caste or community
(d) Violating the social codes laid down by the caste panchayats

Codes:
A. (a), (b), (c) and (d) B. (b), (c) and (d) only
C. (a) and (c) only D. (b) and (d) only

99. Who said that :
"Reared by women within a feminine world, the normal destiny of women is marriage, which still means practically subordination to man ..."
A. Alfred Adler B. Karen Horney
C. Simone de Beauvoir D. Clara Thompson

100. **Assertion (A):** Widows from high-class background tend to face more economic exploitation whereas the lower class widows are more prone to sexual harassment.
Reason (R): The ill-treatment by the society is more oppressive in case of young widows as compared to the elderly or the middle-aged, in that order.

Codes :
A. (A) is wrong, but (R) is correct.
B. Both (A) and (R) are correct, but (R) is not the correct explanation of (A).
C. Both (A) and (R) are wrong.
D. (A) is correct, but (R) is wrong and (R) is not the correct explanation of (A).

ANSWERS

1	2	3	4	5	6	7	8	9	10
C	C	D	A	A	C	B	A	A	A
11	**12**	**13**	**14**	**15**	**16**	**17**	**18**	**19**	**20**
D	A	B	A	A	D	C	A	C	A
21	**22**	**23**	**24**	**25**	**26**	**27**	**28**	**29**	**30**
D	A	A	A	A	B	B	D	C	A
31	**32**	**33**	**34**	**35**	**36**	**37**	**38**	**39**	**40**
B	B	D	A	C	A	A	B	B	D
41	**42**	**43**	**44**	**45**	**46**	**47**	**48**	**49**	**50**
C	D	B	A	D	D	D	A	A	B
51	**52**	**53**	**54**	**55**	**56**	**57**	**58**	**59**	**60**
B	D	A	A	A	C	A	D	C	C
61	**62**	**63**	**64**	**65**	**66**	**67**	**68**	**69**	**70**
A	B	A	A	C	D	A	B	A	A
71	**72**	**73**	**74**	**75**	**76**	**77**	**78**	**79**	**80**
A	B	B	A	C	A	A	C	B	C
81	**82**	**83**	**84**	**85**	**86**	**87**	**88**	**89**	**90**
B	C	D	A	A	C	A	A	B	D
91	**92**	**93**	**94**	**95**	**96**	**97**	**98**	**99**	**100**
A	D	A	A	A	A	B	A	C	B

❑❑❑